T0344308

Handbook of Research on Computer Vision and Image Processing in the Deep Learning Era

A. Srinivasan
SASTRA University (Deemed), India

A volume in the Advances in Computational
Intelligence and Robotics (ACIR) Book Series

Published in the United States of America by
IGI Global
Engineering Science Reference (an imprint of IGI Global)
701 E. Chocolate Avenue
Hershey PA, USA 17033
Tel: 717-533-8845
Fax: 717-533-8661
E-mail: cust@igi-global.com
Web site: http://www.igi-global.com

Library of Congress Cataloging-in-Publication Data

Names: Srinivasan, A., 1978- editor.
Title: Handbook of research on computer vision and image processing in the deep
  learning era / A. Srinivasan, editor.
Description: Hershey, PA : Engineering Science Reference, an imprint of IGI
  Global, [2022] | Includes bibliographical references and index. |
  Summary: "This book explores traditional and new areas of the computer
  vision, machine and deep learning combined to solve a range of problems
  with the objective to integrate the knowledge of the growing
  international community of researchers working on the application of
  Machine Learning and Deep Learning Methods in Vision and Robotics"--
  Provided by publisher.
Identifiers: LCCN 2022013966 (print) | LCCN 2022013967 (ebook) | ISBN
  9781799888925 (h/c) | ISBN 9781799888949 (e-book)
Subjects: LCSH: Computer vision. | Deep learning (Machine learning) |
  Diagnostic imaging.
Classification: LCC TA1634 .C648924 2022 (print) | LCC TA1634 (ebook) |
  DDC 006.3/7--dc23/eng/20220523
LC record available at https://lccn.loc.gov/2022013966
LC ebook record available at https://lccn.loc.gov/2022013967

This book is published in the IGI Global book series Advances in Computational Intelligence and Robotics (ACIR) (ISSN: 2327-0411; eISSN: 2327-042X)

British Cataloguing in Publication Data
A Cataloguing in Publication record for this book is available from the British Library.

For electronic access to this publication, please contact: eresources@igi-global.com.

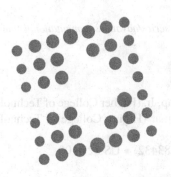

Advances in Computational Intelligence and Robotics (ACIR) Book Series

Ivan Giannoccaro
University of Salento, Italy

ISSN:2327-0411
EISSN:2327-042X

MISSION

While intelligence is traditionally a term applied to humans and human cognition, technology has progressed in such a way to allow for the development of intelligent systems able to simulate many human traits. With this new era of simulated and artificial intelligence, much research is needed in order to continue to advance the field and also to evaluate the ethical and societal concerns of the existence of artificial life and machine learning.

The **Advances in Computational Intelligence and Robotics (ACIR) Book Series** encourages scholarly discourse on all topics pertaining to evolutionary computing, artificial life, computational intelligence, machine learning, and robotics. ACIR presents the latest research being conducted on diverse topics in intelligence technologies with the goal of advancing knowledge and applications in this rapidly evolving field.

COVERAGE

- Cyborgs
- Fuzzy Systems
- Computational Logic
- Synthetic Emotions
- Cognitive Informatics
- Agent technologies
- Robotics
- Heuristics
- Algorithmic Learning
- Artificial Intelligence

IGI Global is currently accepting manuscripts for publication within this series. To submit a proposal for a volume in this series, please contact our Acquisition Editors at Acquisitions@igi-global.com or visit: http://www.igi-global.com/publish/.

Titles in this Series

For a list of additional titles in this series, please visit: www.igi-global.com/book-series/advances-computational-intelligence-robotics/73674

Controlling Epidemics With Mathematical and Machine Learning Models
Abraham Varghese (Higher College of Technology, Oman) Eduardo M. Lacap, Jr. (Higher College of Technology, Oman) Ibrahim Sajath (Higher College of Technology, Oman) Kamal Kumar (Higher College of Technology, Oman) and Shajidmon Kolamban (Higher College of Technology, Oman)
Engineering Science Reference • © 2023 • 300pp • H/C (ISBN: 9781799883432) • US $270.00

Multidisciplinary Applications of Deep Learning-Based Artificial Emotional Intelligence
Chiranji Lal Chowdhary (Vellore Institute of Technology, India)
Engineering Science Reference • © 2023 • 296pp • H/C (ISBN: 9781668456736) • US $270.00

Principles and Applications of Socio-Cognitive and Affective Computing
S. Geetha (VIT University, Chennai, India) Karthika Renuka (PSG College of Technology, India) Asnath Victy Phamila (VIT University, Chennai, India) and Karthikeyan N. (Syed Ammal Engineering College, India)
Engineering Science Reference • © 2023 • 330pp • H/C (ISBN: 9781668438435) • US $270.00

Revolutionizing Industrial Automation Through the Convergence of Artificial Intelligence and the Internet of Things
Divya Upadhyay Mishra (ABES Engineering College, Ghaziabad, India) and Shanu Sharma (ABES Engineering College, Ghaziabad, India)
Engineering Science Reference • © 2023 • 279pp • H/C (ISBN: 9781668449912) • US $270.00

Convergence of Big Data Technologies and Computational Intelligent Techniques
Govind P. Gupta (National Institute of Technology, Raipur, India)
Engineering Science Reference • © 2023 • 335pp • H/C (ISBN: 9781668452646) • US $270.00

Design and Control Advances in Robotics
Mohamed Arezk Mellal (M'Hamed Bougara University, Algeria)
Engineering Science Reference • © 2023 • 320pp • H/C (ISBN: 9781668453810) • US $305.00

Handbook of Research on Applied Artificial Intelligence and Robotics for Government Processes
David Valle-Cruz (Universidad Autónoma del Estado de México, Mexico) Nely Plata-Cesar (Universidad Autónoma del Estado de México, Mexico) and Jacobo Leonardo González-Ruíz (Universidad Autónoma del Estado de México, Mexico)
Information Science Reference • © 2023 • 434pp • H/C (ISBN: 9781668456248) • US $315.00

IGI Global
PUBLISHER of TIMELY KNOWLEDGE

701 East Chocolate Avenue, Hershey, PA 17033, USA
Tel: 717-533-8845 x100 • Fax: 717-533-8661
E-Mail: cust@igi-global.com • www.igi-global.com

List of Contributors

Table of Contents

Detailed Table of Contents

Chapter 1
    Aswathy Ravikumar, Vellore Institute of Technology, India
    Harini Sriraman, Vellore Institute of Technology, India

Image processing combined with computer vision is creating a vast breakthrough in many research, industry-related, and social applications. The growth of big data has led to the large quantity of high-resolution images that can be used in complex applications and processing. There is a need for rapid image processing methods to find accurate and faster results for the time-crucial applications. In such cases, there is a need to accelerate the algorithms and models using the HPC systems. The acceleration of these algorithms can be obtained using hardware accelerators like GPU, TPU, FPGA, etc. The GPU and TPU are mainly used for the parallel implementation of the algorithms and processing them parallelly. The acceleration method and hardware selection are challenging since numerous accelerators are available, requiring deep knowledge and understanding of the algorithms. This chapter explains the deployment of HPC accelerators for CNN and how acceleration is achieved. The leading cloud platforms used in computer vision for acceleration are also listed.

Chapter 2
    Ezhilarasie R., SASTRA University (Deemed), India
    Aishwarya N., SASTRA University (Deemed), India
    Subramani V., SASTRA University (Deemed), India
    Umamakeswari A., SASTRA University (Deemed), India

Cameras used for surveillance have grown in popularity since the technology boom and are now part of our everyday life. It appears to be laborious and time-consuming to monitor the surveillance cameras manually. Computer vision is reshaping the security and surveillance industry. Despite their revolutionary nature, modern CCTV cameras are insufficient because they are passive units that assist investigations but do not give preventative measures. They need to be replaced with active systems. Recreational issues in public security necessitate computer vision, artificial intelligence, and machine learning (ML). Due to the advancements in deep surveillance, we should expect a massive boost in inefficiency. The outstanding performance in image identification and the capacity to absorb temporal information that convolutional and recurrent neural networks offer intelligent surveillance systems bodes well for their future growth in this area. The goal of this chapter is to examine the challenges in surveillance systems, the usage of deep learning techniques, and various new applications.

Chapter 3

Sangeetha J., SASTRA University (Deemed), India

According to the reports from the World Health Organization (WHO), one of the primary causes that led to death in the world was road accidents. Every year, numerous road accidents are caused by drivers due to their drowsiness. It can be minimized by alerting the driver, and it has been done by identifying and recognizing the initial stages of drowsiness. Several models have been proposed to detect drivers' drowsiness and alert them before a road accident occurs. However, the most prominent one is VGG16 with a transfer learning mechanism that is utilized to view the status of the respective regions of interest. By utilizing these models, the drivers are monitored, and alarms are generated to alert the drivers as well as the passengers. This experimental analysis was carried out on the Kaggle Yawn-Eye-Dataset (KYED), and the results showed the low computational intricacy and high precision of the eye closure estimation and the ability of the proposed system for drowsiness detection.

Chapter 4

Manivannan Doraipandian, SASTRA University (Deemed), India
Sriram J., SASTRA University (Deemed), India
Yathishan D., SASTRA University (Deemed), India
Palanivel S., SASTRA University (Deemed), India

Under vision research, processes, and criteria for robotic vision based on multiple stages were set based on prerequisites for robot vision success, need for vision in industries, and advancements in image processing techniques. AI helps robotics by allowing a collaborative robot to accomplish new jobs based on data trends. Deep learning-based artificial vision is used to replicate human vision. Deep learning uses general-purpose learning techniques and convolution neural networks to learn data-driven representations. Deep learning helps vision robots remove overlaps, distortions, and misalignments. Vision control using a recognition algorithm based on vision schemes is highlighted. In this chapter, existing forms of mobile, data acquisition and control, manipulating, and vision-based robotic systems are introduced. Robotics' key focus areas, such as posture estimation, path planning, and mobility based on picture memory and deep learning, enable qualitative topological navigation, localization, and mapping of the environment.

Chapter 5

T. Kavitha, New Horizon College of Engineering (Autonomous), Visvesvaraya Technological University, India
Malini S., AMC Engineering College, India
Senbagavalli G., AMC Engineering College, India

Deep learning is a type of machine learning that trains a computer to recognizing speech, identifying images or making predictions. Computer vision allows machines to visualize and sense the visual world from digital images or videos. Computer vision can be used for face detection, recognition, and emotion detection. There is a growing demand for emotion analysis in the computer vision market. Expressions play an important role in the recognition of emotions for medical sentiment analysis that can be detected by a deep learning model with the help of trained classes. This chapter focuses on emotion recognition and discusses the different algorithms/architecture developed for emotion recognition using deep learning with the data set. Current research and applications based on emotion recognition are also discussed. This chapter can guide beginners in the field of emotion recognition and provide a general understanding of the latest state of art models, as well as guide the researchers looking for directions for future work.

Chapter 6
Smart Surveillance System Using Deep Learning Approaches...92

Uma K. V., Thiagarajar College of Engineering, India

Aakash V., Thiagarajar College of Engineering, India

Deisy C., Thiagarajar College of Engineering, India

In modern days, CCTVs are being used for monitoring, and most shops have surveillance cameras up and running during the night times, but still, robberies are happening since the surveillance footage is being checked only after a robbery on the next day. To overcome the problems of having manual security and cost wastage along with automating the monitoring of the surveillance during the night times once the shops are closed, the authors propose the smart surveillance system. Deep learning algorithms and computer vision techniques are used to detect the presence of humans/intruders in a given video. The smart surveillance system along with the reduction in the cost of manual securities also provides robust nighttime monitoring, and it provides immediate notification to the authority as soon as it spots the intruder in the specified monitoring time, thereby reducing the robberies and the business impact caused.

Chapter 7
Role of Deep Learning in Image and Video Processing..115

Alageswaran Ramaiah, SASTRA University (Deemed), India

Arun K. S., Accenture, Australia

Yathishan D., SASTRA University (Deemed), India

Sriram J., SASTRA University (Deemed), India

Palanivel S., SASTRA University (Deemed), India

Image and video processing research is becoming an important area in the field of computer vision. There are challenges such as low-resolution images, poor quality of videos, etc. in image and video data processing. Deep learning is a machine learning technique used in the creation of AI systems. It is designed to analyse complex data by passing it through many layers of neurons. Deep learning techniques have the potential to produce cutting-edge results in difficult computer vision problems such as object identification and face recognition. In this chapter, the use of deep learning to target specific functionality in the field of computer vision such as image recovery, video classification, etc. The deep learning algorithms, such as convolutional neural networks, deep neural network, and recurrent neural networks, used in the image and video processing domain are also explored.

Chapter 8
Gesture and Posture Recognition by Using Deep Learning...132

Alageswaran Ramaiah, SASTRA University (Deemed), India

Subramani V., SASTRA University (Deemed), India

Aishwarya N., SASTRA University (Deemed), India

Ezhilarasie R., SASTRA University (Deemed), India

Sign language facilitates communication in the community with speaking and hearing problems. Those people communicate with one another using hand gestures and body movements. These techniques of human-computer interaction range from primary keyboard inputs to complex vision-based gesture detection systems. One of the fascinating HCI technologies is hand gesture recognition. The goal of gesture recognition is to construct a system to use as a communication medium in various applications. The application of gesture recognition has become popular in healthcare, robotics, etc. Posture recognition is deployed in several sectors, including medicine. Deep learning-based models are used to understand gesture and posture recognition results better. This chapter covers the challenges of gesture and posture recognition and how deep learning techniques are used to assist machines in overcoming these challenges more effectively. In addition, this chapter also discusses the applications in which gesture and posture recognition can be employed in detail.

Chapter 9

Biometrics is a method based on the recognition of the biological characteristics of an individual like fingerprint, vocal, and facial features. Biometric features hold a unique place when it comes to recognition, authentication, and security applications as they cannot be easily duplicated. Deep learning-based models have been very successful in achieving better efficiency in biometric recognition. They are more beneficial because deep learning-based models provide an end-to-end learning framework.

Chapter 10

Plant leaf recognition has been carried out widely using low-level features. Scale invariant feature transform technique has been used to extract the low-level features. Leaves that match based on low-level features but do not do so in semantic perspective cannot be recognized. To address this, global features are extracted and used. Similarly, convolutional neural networks, deep learning networks, and transfer learning-based neural networks have been used for leaf image recognition. Even then there are issues like leaf images in various illuminations, rotations, taken in different angle, and so on. To address such issues, the closeness among low-level features and global features are computed using multiple distance measures, and a leaf recognition framework has been proposed. Two deep network models, namely Densenet and Xception, are used in the experiments. The matched patches are evaluated both quantitatively and qualitatively. Experimental results obtained are promising for the closeness-based leaf recognition framework as well as the Densenet-based leaf recognition.

Image denoising is a class of image processing algorithms that aim to enhance the visual quality of the acquired images by removing noise inherent in them and is an active area of research under image enhancement and reconstruction techniques. Traditional model-driven methods are motivated by statistical assumptions on data corruption and prior knowledge of the data to recover while the machine learning (ML) approaches require a massive amount of training data. However, the manual tuning of hyperparameters in model-driven approaches and susceptibility to overfitting under learning-based techniques are their major flaws. Recent years have witnessed the amalgamation of both model and ML-based approaches. Infusing model-driven Bayesian estimator in an ML-based approach, supported by robust mathematical arguments, has been shown to achieve optimal denoising solutions in real time with less effect of over-fitting. In this chapter, the evolution of image denoising techniques is covered from a mathematical perspective along with detailed experimental analysis for each class of approach.

    Ramya S., SASTRA University (Deemed), India
    Madhubala P., SASTRA University (Deemed), India
    Sushmitha E. C., SASTRA University (Deemed), India
    D. Manivannan, SASTRA University (Deemed), India
    A. Al Firthous, CYRYX College, Maldives

Industry 4.0 reshapes the industrial landscape through new technologies such as robotics, data networking, machine learning (ML), and computer vision (CV). ML is a critical innovation in technology that enables enterprises and factory floors to embrace Industry 4.0. Systems and algorithms can learn from their failures using machine learning, a form of artificial intelligence (AI). A vision system becomes an essential component of sophisticated industrial systems for the quality control throughout the manufacturing process, and it allows robotic assembly to be provided with the necessary knowledge to create products from simple components. Predictive maintenance (PdM) is a form of digital transformation that services repairs as immediately as an issue emerges. The criterion above leads to a manufacturing environment that is intelligent and autonomous on recent breakthrough information and communication technologies. This chapter explores the challenges in Industry 4.0 with technologies such as cyber-physical systems (CPS), image processing, internet of things (IoT), computer vision, etc.

    Sreedevi B., SASTRA University (Deemed), India
    Durga Karthik, SASTRA University (Deemed), India

The World Health Organization (WHO) has conducted a survey on road accidents around the world. According to the survey, 13.5 lakh die each year due to road casualties and more concerning is that India accounts around 1.5 lakh road deaths every year. Major factors to blame on road accidents are driver carelessness, drowsiness, traffic discipline, vehicle faults, or even animal crossing. Different sensors, stability control systems, anti-breaking systems, navigation are added in the vehicles to make driving easier. Still, road accidents happen due to human mistakes. Drinking and driving and tiredness may cause a driver to go for torpidity. A machine learning system is developed to monitor the eye movements to detect if the driver is sleepy or not. If found, an alarm is issued to warn the driver to wake up or else to stop the vehicle and have a nap. In addition, if neither response is made, water sprinkling is automated on the driver's face.

    Umamaheswari P., SASTRA University (Deemed), India
    Abiramasundari S., SASTRA University (Deemed), India
    Kamaladevi M., SASTRA University (Deemed), India
    Dinesh P., Anjalai Ammal Mahalingam Engineering College, India

Bitcoin is a type of digital currency or computerized money that is utilised for speculation around the world. Bitcoins are files that are saved in a digital wallet programme on a mobile phone or a PC. Every transaction and its timestamp data are recorded in a common list known as blockchain. In this research, the cost of bitcoin is estimated utilising data mining techniques and machine learning algorithms. The dataset is preprocessed with the use of data mining algorithms, which reduces data noise. Bitcoin's price fluctuates, and it is estimated using long short-term memory (LSTM), a type of neural networking, to extract acceptable patterns for modelling and prediction. Discovering recurring patterns in the bitcoin market is a necessary endeavour in order to achieve optimal bitcoin price functionality. The dataset consists of numerous regularly reported bitcoin price features every year. Linear regression (LR) technique is used to estimate the future cost of bitcoin. Daily price shift with the best possible precision by using the available data is also estimated.

    Bala Krishnan Raghupathy, SASTRA University (Deemed), India
    Rajesh Kumar N., SASTRA University (Deemed), India
    Priya Govindarajan, SASTRA University (Deemed), India
    Manikandan G., SASTRA University (Deemed), India
    Senthilraj Swaminathan, University of Technology and Applied Sciences, Oman

Secured data transmission between the communication channels would be a challenging. Attainment of secured key transmission of cryptographic algorithms between communication channel partners is one of the most difficult tasks in data communication. Various cryptography and steganographic principles have been presented for this purpose. This chapter presents a new steganographic approach in which the 56-bit key of data encryption standard (DES) algorithm is safely conveyed between communicators by embedding it in a color digital image. The popular chess game-based 8 Queens placement scheme is used to identify pixel positions for the key embedding process. From observational consequences, it is accomplished that the nominated scheme would lead to achieving assured content contagion over the network.

    Pratibha Verma, Dr. C.V. Raman University, India
    Sanat Kumar Sahu, Govt. Kaktiya P.G. College Jagdalpur, India
    Vineet Kumar Awasthi, Dr. C.V. Raman University, India

Coronary artery disease (CAD) is of significant concern among the population worldwide. The deep neural network (DNN) methods co-operate and play a crucial role in identifying diseases in CAD. The classification techniques like deep neural network (DNN) and enhanced deep neural network (EDNN) model are best suited for problem solving. A model is robust with the integration of feature selection technique (FST) like genetic algorithm (GA) and particle swarm optimization (PSO). This research proposes an integrated model of GA, PSO, and DNN for classification of CAD. The E-DNN model with a subset feature of CAD datasets gives enhanced results as compared to the DNN model. The E-DNN model gives a more correct and precise classification performance.

Chapter 17

Diabetic retinopathy (DR) affects blood vessels in the retina and arises due to complications of diabetes. Diabetes is a serious health issue that must be considered and taken care of at the right time. Modern lifestyle, stress at workplaces, and unhealthy food habits affect the health conditions of our body. So the detection of lesions and treatment at an early stage is required. The detection and classification of early signs of diabetic retinopathy can be done by three different approaches. In Approach 1, an image processing algorithm is proposed. In Approach 2, convolutional neural network (CNN-VGG Net 16) is proposed for the classification of fundus images into normal and DR images. In Approach 3, a signal processing method is used for the detection of diabetic retinopathy using electro retinogram signal (ERG). Finally, the performance measures are calculated for all three approaches, and it is found that detection using CNN improves the accuracy.

Chapter 18

The use of digital image in a variety of disciplines has skyrocketed, particularly in multimedia, medicine, and social media. The integrity and confidentiality of digital images communicated over the internet can be jeopardized by a variety of security threats. As a result, the content of these digital images must be preserved at all costs for a variety of domain-specific applications. Visual cryptography scheme (VCs) is an image-based approach to encrypt the secret image in such a way, and human visual system (HVS) can be used to decrypt the image. The core concepts of visual cryptography and applications of several visual cryptography schemes are covered in this chapter. The authors describe a unique reversible data hiding method for protecting secret shares using a covering subset and recovering the secret image using an overlaying technique. This chapter also covers a comparative analysis of 2-out-of-n and 3-out-of-n visual cryptography schemes.

Chapter 19

Mukesh Kumar Chandrakar, Bhilai Institute of Technology, Durg, India
Anup Mishra, Bhilai Institute of Technology, Durg, India
Arun Kumar, Bhilai Institute of Technology, Durg, India

Brain tumor segmentation is a new automated medical image diagnosis application. A robust strategy to brain tumor segmentation and detection is an ongoing research problem, and the performance metrics of present tumor detection systems are little understood. Deep neural networks employing convolution neural networks (CNN) are being investigated in this regard; however, no generic architecture that can be employed as a robust technique for brain tumor diagnosis has been discovered. The authors have suggested a multipath CNN architecture for brain tumor segmentation and identification that outperforms existing approaches. The proposed work has been tested for datasets BRATS2013, BRTAS2015, and BRATS2017 with significant improvement in dice index and timing values by utilizing the capability of multipath CNN architecture, which combines both local and global paths. It was the objective to provide a simple and reliable method to determine segmentation and detection of brain tumor using brain tumor interface techniques (BCI).

Chapter 20

Hazique Aetesam, Indian Institute of Technology, Patna, India
Suman Kumar Maji, Indian Institute of Technology, Patna, India
Jerome Boulanger, MRC Laboratory of Molecular Biology, Cambridge, UK

Remote sensing technologies such as hyperspectral imaging (HSI) and medical imaging techniques such as magnetic resonance imaging (MRI) form the pillars of human advancement. However, external factors like noise pose limitations on the accurate functioning of these imaging systems. Image enhancement techniques like denoising therefore form a crucial part in the proper functioning of these technologies. Noise in HSI and MRI are primarily a mixture of Gaussian and impulse noise. Image denoising techniques designed to handle mixed Gaussian-impulse (G-I) noise are thus an area of core research under the field of image restoration and enhancement. Therefore, this chapter discusses the mathematical preliminaries of G-I noise followed by an elaborate literature survey that covers the evolution of image denoising techniques for G-I noise from filtering-based to learning-based. An experimental analysis section is also provided that illustrates the performance of several denoising approaches under HSI and MRI, followed by a conclusion.

Chapter 21

Priya Govindarajan, SASTRA University (Deemed), India
Balakrishnan R., SASTRA University (Deemed), India
Rajesh Kumar N., SASTRA University (Deemed), India

Mining has gained its momentum in almost every arena of research. The mining can be either spatial or non-spatial based on the search query. For classifying or for grouping the spatial data, algorithms with extended perspectives are projected in this chapter. Besides framing algorithms, one can also provide mass points based on the required attributes as well as indexing techniques. The extended algorithms can also be manipulated for efficient and robust solution with respect to different parameters.

S. Meganathan, SASTRA University (Deemed), India
A. Sumathi, SASTRA University (Deemed), India
Ahamed Lebbe Hanees, South Eastern University of Sri Lanka, Sri Lanka

Feature selection has become revenue to many research regions that manage machine learning and data mining since it allows the classifiers to be cost-efficient, time-saving, and more precise. In this chapter, the feature selection strategy is consolidating by utilizing the combined feature selection technique, specifically recursive feature elimination, chi-square, info-gain, and principal component analysis. Machine learning algorithms like logistic regression, random support vector machine, and decision trees are applied in three different datasets that are pre-processed with combined feature selection technique. Then these algorithms are ensembled using voting classifier. The improvement in accuracy of the classifiers is observed by the impact of the combined feature selection.

Hemalatha J., Department of Computer Science and Engineering, AAA College of
        Engineering and Technology, India
Vivek V., AAA College of Engineering and Technology, India
Kavitha Devi M. K., Thiagarajar College of Engineering, India
Sekar Mohan, AAA College of Engineering and Technology, India

Biometric identification systems are highly used for verification and identification like fingerprint recognition, voice recognition, face recognition, etc. The very famous biometric technique is fingerprint recognition. A fingerprint is the pattern of ridges and valleys on the surface of a fingertip. The endpoints and crossing points of ridges are called minutiae. The basic assumption is that the minutiae pattern of every finger is unique and does not change during one's life. In the present era, fingerprint-based biometric authentication system gets popularized, but still, this biometric system is vulnerable to various attacks, particularly presentation attacks. This chapter explains how the knowledge-driven neural networks work on fingerprint anomaly detection. In addition, the various features available to detect the anomaly in biometric are also discussed.

Simi M. S., Adi Shankara Institute of Engineering and Technology, India
Manish T. I., SCMS School of Engineering and Technology, India

With the accessibility of healthcare data for a significant proportion of patients in hospitals, using predictive analytics to detect diseases earlier has become more feasible. Identifying and recording key variables that contribute to a specific medical condition is one of the most difficult challenges for early detection and timely treatment of diseases. Conditions such as infertility that are difficult to detect or diagnose can now be diagnosed with greater accuracy with the help of predictive modeling. Infertility detection, particularly in females, has recently gained attention. In this work, the researchers proposed an intelligent prediction for female infertility (PreFI). The researchers use 26 variables for the early diagnosis and determine a subset of these 26 variables as biomarkers. These biomarkers contribute significantly to a better prediction of the problem. The researchers designed PreFI using ensemble methods with biomarkers and improved the performance of the predictive system.

Preface

Image processing is one of the rapidly developing technologies that is spawning important research fields in Engineering discipline. Image Processing refers to the application of algorithms to images meant to improve the quality of the image or to alter it for a different visual effect. It plays a very important role to prepare images for Computer Vision models, such as applying segmentation or labelling known objects. Computer vision and image processing are inseparably linked. A computer vision system receives an image as input and produces task-specific data, such as item labels and coordinates. Computer vision systems rarely use unprocessed image data obtained directly from hardware such as cameras or sensors. Instead, they employ photos that have undergone various forms of image processing.

Today, Computer Vision applications have achieved tremendous success which includes applications like image classification, Defect inspection, autonomous driving, Robotics, Text classification, facial recognition etc., However, for these models to work, the images need to first be labelled, segmented, or to have gone through other pre-processing steps taken with the help of image processing algorithms.

Deep learning plays a prominent role in a variety of computer vision problems, such as object detection motion tracking action recognition human pose estimation and semantic segmentation etc., The reason behind it is that Deep learning is a rich family of methods, encompassing neural networks, hierarchical probabilistic models, and a variety of unsupervised and supervised feature learning algorithms. The recent surge of interest in deep learning methods is due to the fact that they have been shown to outperform previous state-of-the-art techniques in several tasks like visual, aural, medical, social, and sensorial ability. Thus, the chapters of the book focusses on role of deep learning technologies in variety of application with higher emphasis/priority for image processing and computer vision problems as the world is running behind smarter and autonomous environment.

Image processing, computer vision, pattern recognition, and their related applications are topics of general interest to researchers. They have been researching 3D face reconstruction, object tracking, structure from motion, and medical image processing and will continue to do so. Object detection and processing in photos and videos has received a lot of attention in the computer vision and pattern recognition communities in recent years. To replicate even a small portion of the average person's ability to identify objects, one would need to combine several distinct algorithms to create a combined system that runs in real time, which is extremely difficult with the hardware available today. In the field of computer vision, deep learning neural network techniques are replacing statistical methods and are producing cutting-edge results on some specific issues by overcoming the difficulties prevailing with traditional problem-solving method.

Computer vision technologies will be used in conjunction with other technologies or branches of AI to develop more engaging applications. Natural language generation (NLG), for example, can be linked with image captioning apps to assist the visually impaired in understanding the objects around them. Computer vision can help the development of artificial general intelligence (AGI) and artificial super intelligence (ASI) by allowing them to analyse information on par with or better than the human visual system. As a growing market, computer vision technology is closely related to virtual and augmented reality (VR and AR). The combination of VR and AR has piqued the interest of the most recent market participants. And this focus is growing rapidly.

Faculty and students of higher education, Business leaders, Scientists, Researchers and Engineers working in industries would find this book very engaging and useful.

The chapter "Acceleration of Image Processing and Computer Vision Algorithms" discusses the need for rapid image processing methods to find accurate and faster results for the time crucial applications. In such cases, there is a need to accelerate the algorithms and models using the HPC systems. The acceleration of these algorithms can be obtained using hardware accelerators like GPU, TPU, FPGA, etc. The GPU and TPU are mainly used for the parallel implementation of the algorithms and processing them parallelly. The acceleration method and hardware selection are challenging since numerous accelerators are available, requiring deep knowledge and understanding of the algorithms. This chapter explains the deployment of HPC accelerators for CNN and how acceleration is achieved. The leading Cloud platforms used in computer vision for acceleration are also listed.

The aim of the chapter "Acceleration of Computer Vision and Deep Learning: Surveillance Systems" is to reshape the security and surveillance industry which in spite of modern CCTV cameras and other advanced equipment ,prove to be highly insufficient because they are passive units that assist investigations but do not give preventative measures. It appears to be laborious and time-consuming to monitor the surveillance cameras manually. With the emerging deep learning technologies, surveillance systems can be smarter. Thus, the goal of this chapter is to examine the challenges in surveillance systems and role of deep learning in computer vision applications for creating smarter environments.

The objective of the chapter "Deep Learning Architecture for Real-Time Driver Safety Drowsiness Detection System" is to identify and recognize the initial stages of driver drowsiness so as to alert the driver in time. If the model notices the driver's drowsiness, it would start to alert the user. By utilizing VGG16 model, driver is monitored and alarms are generated to alert the driver as well as the passengers.

The chapter "Deep Learning-Based Computer Vision for Robotics" equips vision robots with complex search and corrective movement abilities, such as removing overlaps, distortions, or misalignments. It has enabled a paradigm change in pattern recognition using general-purpose learning processes and Convolution neural network for learning data-driven representations. In this chapter how vision enhance the pose estimation, path planning, mobility based on image memory using deep learning provides qualitative topological navigation, localization and mapping of the environment with Simultaneous Localization and Mapping algorithms were explored.

The chapter titled "Deep Learning for Emotion Recognition" is one of the important topics of research that enable many applications. Since next-generation artificial intelligence is expected to interact with people more frequently, the capacity to perceive and express human emotions will be a key component. With deep learning's astounding success, several architectures of this technology are being used to identify user emotions and improve performance through computer vision. For a better computer prediction, researchers in this field created a variety of approaches to read, code, and extract the information. Human emotions can be detected using parameters like facial expressions, body language gestures, Text, speech and physiological signals, or a combination of more than one parameter. This chapter highlights recent advances in emotion recognition techniques and datasets, as well as problems and difficulties in the field.

The author proposes in the chapter "Smart Surveillance System Using Deep Learning Approaches" that smart surveillance is used in most of the shops. In modern days CCTVs are being used for monitoring and most shops have surveillance cameras up and running during the night times but still, robberies are happening since the surveillance footage is being checked only after a robbery on the next day. To overcome the problems of having manual securities and cost wastage along with automating the monitoring of the surveillance during the night times once the shops are being closed, we are proposing the Smart Surveillance System. Deep learning algorithms and computer vision techniques are being used to detect the presence of humans/intruders in a given video. The Smart Surveillance system along with the reduction in the cost of manual securities also provides robust nighttime monitoring and it provides immediate notification to the authority as soon as it spots the intruder in the specified monitoring time thereby reducing the robberies and the business impact caused by it.

In the chapter "Role of Deep learning in Image and Video Processing", the author explores to produce a lot of photo and video data from gadgets like webcam security cameras, which are monitored by the military, hospitals and other organisations. Due to the complexity of real-world settings, it is still challenging to achieve acceptable performance in target detection & recognition, video tracking, picture categorization, and other domains e.g., noise, deformation, etc. Deep learning techniques have the potential to produce ground-breaking results in difficult computer vision tasks including face recognition, object detection and classification. Thus the chapter aims to examine the necessity of Deep Learning in Image and video processing

The work entitled "Gesture and Posture Recognition by Using Deep Learning" can help People, hard-of-hearing, communicate with the outside world using a recognition process. Posture recognition is extensively used in various sectors, including senior health care, environmental awareness, Human-Computer Interaction, surveillance, and physical training. Thus, with the help of deep learning, it can be strengthened. Therefore, this chapter aims to examine the challenges and needs of posture and gesture recognition and the role of deep learning for the same.

The chapter "Evolution of Deep Learning for Biometric Identification and Recognition" explains biometric recognition is an information system that allows the identification of a person based on some of their main physiological and behavioral characteristics. Deep learning-based models have been very successful in achieving state-of-the-art results in many of the computer vision, speech recognition, and natural language processing tasks in the last few years. Deep learning-based methods automate the process of learning the best feature representation irrespective of biometric trait and hence can be more widely and robustly applied. Deep learning models have been successfully applied in face recognition, iris recognition, fingerprint recognition, voice recognition.

In the chapter "Hand-Crafted Feature Extraction and Deep Learning Models for Leaf Image Recognition," the author has carried out plant leaf recognition widely using low level features. Scale invariant feature transform technique has been used to extract the low level features. Leaves that match based on low level features but does not do so in semantic perspective cannot be recognized. To address this global features are extracted and used. Similarly, convolutional neural networks, deep learning networks, transfer learning based neural networks have been used for leaf image recognition. Even then there are issues like leaf images in various illuminations, rotations, taken in different angle and so on. To address such issues, the closeness among low level features and global features are computed using multiple distance measures and a leaf recognition framework has been proposed. Two deep network models namely, Densenet and Xception are used in the experiments. The matched patches are evaluated both quantitatively and qualitatively. Experimental results obtained are promising for the closeness based leaf recognition framework as well as the Densenet based leaf recognition.

The chapter "The Evolution of Image Denoising From Model-Driven to Machine Learning: A Mathematical Perspective" begins with the mathematical intuition of image-related inverse problems in general, and the use of probabilistic distributions to model various types of noise in particular. The following two sections create background by highlighting recent developments in optimization-based and learning-motivated schemes. The maximum a posteriori estimator is used as the central theme in optimization-based techniques to introduce the concept of data fidelity/regularization term/s and optimization techniques. Back-propagation, convolutional/recurrent neural networks, normalization, neural network optimization techniques, and discriminative/generative modelling, on the other hand, are introduced as basic building blocks in deep learning-based approaches. The final section experiments on synthetically corrupted data using three types of noise-removal methods: model-driven, data-driven learning-based, and a combination of the previous two.

The chapter "Machine Learning and Image Processing Based Computer Vision in Industry 4.0" integrates several new technologies. Industry 4.0 is driving the industrial environment. The most often used techniques include robots, data networking, Machine Learning, Computer Vision, and Predictive Maintenance. A manufacturing environment that is fundamentally real-time, intelligent, and autonomous on cutting-edge information and communication technologies will be produced as a result of the criteria mentioned. This chapter explores the challenges in industry 4.0 with the emerging technologies such as really Cyber-Physical Systems, Image Processing, Internet of Things, Computer Vision, etc.

The chapter "Real-Time Torpidity Detection for Drivers in Machine Learning Environment" describes road accidents that happen due to human mistakes. Drunk and drive, tiredness may cause a driver to go for torpidity. A machine learning system is developed to monitor the eye movements to detect the driver is sleepy or not. If found, an alarm is issued to warn the driver to wake up else to stop the vehicle and have a nap. In addition, if neither response is made, water sprinkling is automated on drivers face.

The author proposes in the chapter "Potential Market-Predictive Features-Based Bitcoin Price Prediction Using Machine Learning Algorithm" that a bitcoin is digital or virtual money designed to be used for trade. It is pretty similar to real-world cash, except that it has no physical existence and operates through encryption. The transaction cost for crypto currencies is minimal to none, unlike the price for moving money from a digital wallet to a bank account. People may conduct transactions at any time of day or night, and there are no purchase or withdrawal limitations. In addition, unlike opening a bank account, which needs verification and other procedures, anybody may use bitcoin. This study uses potential market predictive features to forecast bitcoin using a machine learning algorithm. This proposed methodology has been implemented using three layer LSTM model.

In the chapter "An Intelligent 8-Queen Placement Approach of Chess Game for Hiding 56-Bit Key of DES Algorithm Over Digital Color Images," a lossless color image based Steganography approach is described. The suggested study, uses a chess game d 8-Queen placement principle based pixel locating process for LSB replacement. Our proposed method, along with accompanying probe remarks, demonstrates that the formed principle provides a meliorated scheme for executing secret content hiding on all levels of color images with dimensions 120 * 120. The model also provides no discernible trainings on the freshly created stego image, hence improving the scheme's quality via the metrics Mean Squared Error and Peak Signal Noise Ratio values. The proposed hidden content embedding strategy has been compared to certain democratic current principles, and the model's competency has been demonstrated through experimental results. To summarize, the proposed principle is very effective and ideal for information concealment applications.

The chapter "Deep Neural Network with Feature Optimization Technique for Classification of Coronary Artery Disease" describes the seriousness in unequivocal terms over a disease of great concern among the population worldwide. The Deep Neural Network methods co-operate and play a crucial role in identifying diseases in CAD. The classification techniques like Deep Neural Network and Enhance Deep Neural Network Model are best suited for problem solving. A model is robust with the integration of feature selection technique like Genetic Algorithm and Particle Swarm Optimization. This research proposes an integrated model of GA, PSO and DNN for classification of CAD. The E-DNN Model with a subset feature of CAD datasets gives enhanced results as compared to DNN model. The E-DNN model gives a more correct and precise classification performance.

The aim of the chapter "Detection and Classification of Diabetic Retinopathy Using Image Processing Algorithms, Convolutional Neural Network, and Signal Processing Techniques" explains the diabetes causes leakage of blood and excretion of biochemical materials in the retinal blood vessels. It will affect the vision and lead to eye disease, Diabetic Retinopathy (DR). The detection of lesions and treatment at an early stage is required. Three different approaches can detect and classify early signs of diabetic retinopathy. In approach 1, an Image processing algorithm is proposed. In approach 2, Convolutional Neural Network is proposed to classify fundus images into normal and DR images. In approach 3, a signal processing method is used to detect diabetic retinopathy using an Electroretinogram signal. Finally, the performance measures are calculated for all three approaches, and it is found that detection using CNN improves the accuracy.

The chapter "Image Security Using Visual Cryptography" presents an efficient construction of VSI using the skill of linear programming. This scheme minimizes the pixel expansion subject to the constraints satisfying the region incrementing requirements. Unit matrices are introduced as the building blocks and the numbers of the unit matrices chosen to form the basis matrices of VSI are set as the decision variables. A solution to these decision variables by our linear program delivers a feasible set of basis matrices of the required VSI with the minimum pixel expansion. The pixel expansions and contrasts derived from our VSI are better than the previous results. Since no construction method has ever been reported in the literature survey, a minimum pixel expansion method based on linear programming approach is a better approach in this context. VSI is novel and innovative from both the theoretical and practical point of view. The experimental results show that the proposed scheme achieves high level contrast on different secret regions of secret image. It enhances the adaptability and flexibility of our VSI in practical applications.

The work "Multipath Convolutional Neural Network for Brain Tumor Detection" describes a new automated medical image diagnosis application in brain tumor segmentation . A robust strategy to brain tumor segmentation and detection is an ongoing research problem, and the performance metrics of present tumor detection systems are little understood. Deep neural networks employing convolution neural networks are being investigated in this regard, however no generic architecture that can be employed as a robust technique for brain tumor diagnosis has been discovered. We have suggested a multipath CNN architecture for brain tumor segmentation and identification that outperforms existing approaches. The proposed work has been tested for datasets BRATS2013, BRTAS2015 and BRATS2017 with significant improvement in dice index and timing values by utilizing the capability of multipath CNN architecture which combines both local and global paths. It was our objective to provide a simple and reliable method to determine segmentation and detection of brain tumor using brain tumor interface techniques.

The chapter "Image Enhancement under Gaussian Impulse Noise for Satellite and Medical Applications" discusses the removal of mixed Gaussian-impulse (G-I) noise from images. Two representative application domains are selected as the potential candidates suffering from a mixture of these noise sources: remotely sensed hyperspectral images (HSI) and magnetic resonance imaging (MRI). The image acquisition process in these domains is discussed, as well as the factors responsible for Gaussian and impulse noise therein. The later section discusses recent advances in noise removal techniques when the underlying corruption is a combination of Gaussian and impulse noise. Four different categories are introduced: filtering-based, optimization-based, filtering+ optimization based and learning-based techniques. A set of experiments are carried out on the two representative domains: HSI and MRI, in which synthetic images corresponding to both application domains are corrupted by G-I impulse. A set of competing methods specific to each domain are used for the experimentation purpose. Real-world data from the domains are also used to assess the efficacy of these methods. The final section contains concluding remarks.

The chapter "Algorithmic Approach for Spatial Entity and Mining" projects algorithms for mining spatial data, with regard to classifying or grouping the same. The algorithm is also implemented with different parameters for obtaining efficient and robust outcome.

The work "A Combined Feature Selection Technique for Improving Classification Accuracy" observes the impact of feature selection on four classifiers Logistic regression, Random Forest, Decision Tree and Support Vector Machine. A consolidated component determination is employed to select the rule credits. The segment affirmation method like Chi-square, RFE, Info-gain and PCA are joined to perform out the undertaking. These frameworks task differently on the dataset. Classification accuracy is improved in Post-usable dataset for all the classifiers. The Classifiers are then combined using an ensemble Voting Classifier. The CFS with ensemble classifier are employed with three different datasets, which provides the best accuracy when compared with the other classifiers.

The objective of the chapter "Generalization and Efficiency on Fingerprint Presentation Attack Anomaly Detection" is to explain the biometric technology which is used to recognize the individuals involved in the act based on their unique biological or behavioral traits. Biometric Identification Systems are highly used for verification and identification. The very famous biometric technique is Face recognition. The activity of recognizing or verifying a person's identification using their face is known as facial recognition. This chapter explains how the knowledge driven neural networks working on face recognition anomaly detection. In addition the various features available to detect the anomaly in biometric is also discussed.

The chapter "Predictive Analytics on Female Infertility Using Ensemble Methods" discusses the infertility statistics. It is a global health issue that affects millions of people of reproductive age worldwide. As per available data, infertility affects 48 million couples and 186 million individuals worldwide. Women's infertility can be caused by a number of factors, all of which have a significant impact on infertility statistics. The society needs to be able to predict the possibility of infertility in advance using available features and data, and to provide corrective measures prior to the occurrence. In this chapter, the researchers proposed an intelligent prediction for female infertility in this study (PreFI). They employ 26 variables for early detection and identify a subset of these variables as biomarkers. The researchers created PreFI by combining ensemble methods with biomarkers and improved the performance of the predictive system with 98.4% of accuracy.

The goal of computer vision is to develop techniques that will help computers recognize and understand the information contained in digital images like pictures and movies. It has been a subject of extensive inquiry, accumulating attention for many years. There are many things to think about regarding how computer vision will change how people view and live their lives as its influence on the human world grows. The capabilities of computer vision will expand in the future with further study and development of the technology. In addition to being simpler to train, the technology will be able to extract more information from the images than what is possible currently.

Keeping these facts in mind, this book focusses on major topics that are relevant to day-to-day technical advancements in Bio metric identification, robot vision, cyber physical systems, industry 4.o etc., It is important to get to know about how these technologies rapidly change the world. This book helps in understanding the emerging concepts like DNN, CNN, Image processing with Machine learning, robotics, cryptography etc. These technologies have become a part and parcel of life, and are being used knowingly or unknowingly. Also, this book provides an excellent opportunity for budding technologists to learn new concepts and serves as a window for experienced professionals to upskill their domain knowledge.

A. Srinivasan
SASTRA University (Deemed), India

Chapter 1
Acceleration of Image Processing and Computer Vision Algorithms

Aswathy Ravikumar

iD https://orcid.org/0000-0003-0897-6991

Vellore Institute of Technology, India

Harini Sriraman

Vellore Institute of Technology, India

ABSTRACT

Image processing combined with computer vision is creating a vast breakthrough in many research, industry-related, and social applications. The growth of big data has led to the large quantity of high-resolution images that can be used in complex applications and processing. There is a need for rapid image processing methods to find accurate and faster results for the time-crucial applications. In such cases, there is a need to accelerate the algorithms and models using the HPC systems. The acceleration of these algorithms can be obtained using hardware accelerators like GPU, TPU, FPGA, etc. The GPU and TPU are mainly used for the parallel implementation of the algorithms and processing them parallelly. The acceleration method and hardware selection are challenging since numerous accelerators are available, requiring deep knowledge and understanding of the algorithms. This chapter explains the deployment of HPC accelerators for CNN and how acceleration is achieved. The leading cloud platforms used in computer vision for acceleration are also listed.

INTRODUCTION

Image Processing combined with computer vision is creating a massive breakthrough in many research, industry-related and social applications. The image processing algorithms involve many complex processing steps like wavelet, Fourier, convolutions, vector multiplications, solving linear and quadratic equations, dimensionality reductions, graphical, sorting, and searching algorithms, etc. All these operations are

DOI: 10.4018/978-1-7998-8892-5.ch001

computationally demanding, and they can be effectively parallelized. Image processing is a fast-growing discipline that combines mathematical and computer programming principles. It is intrinsically linked to and impacted by image capture. The user community is diverse and includes not only regular consumers with digital photography but also astronomers who analyze the data from observatories and satellites, professionals in MRI scans, and biologists who utilize ocular microscopes. Users' expectations for picture quality are constantly increasing in high definition, sensor ratio, and dynamic range.

Consequently, pictures collecting equipment and image processing techniques continue evolving to meet user requirements. On the other hand, complicated image processing algorithms may be very time-intensive to calculate, even with modern computer technology. As a result, optimization is a vital aspect of the field, allowing complicated algorithms to be executed in an acceptable amount of time. The growth of big data has led to the enormous large quantity of high-resolution images that can be used in complex applications and processing. There is a need for rapid image processing methods to find accurate and faster results for the time crucial applications in the field of medicine, communication, autonomous driving cars, etc. In such cases, there is a need to accelerate the algorithms and models using high-performance computing systems. The traditional CPU systems are insufficient to attain the required speed, reduce processing time, and perform better. The acceleration of these algorithms can be obtained using hardware accelerators like GPU, TPU, and FPGA. The GPU and TPU are mainly used for the parallel implementation of the algorithms and processing them parallelly. These processors can be made energy efficient by adding high precision arithmetic units and more programmable units. Vision-based applications' processing speed is a major determining factor for the suitable selection of acceleration methods. The choice of the acceleration method and hardware is challenging since several accelerators are available, requiring deep knowledge and understanding of the algorithms. The GPU architectures are highly suitable for image processing algorithms. The use of GPU in computer vision is now increasing due to the ease of programming and its architecture. GPU faces many challenges like high power consumption, which is mainly effective for large datasets and the slow data transfer between GPU and CPU. For effective utilization of GPU and TPU, a clear idea of working the computer vision algorithms in them is needed. Similarly, the memory management of the HPC has become a significant concern. This chapter explains a detailed explanation of the computer vision algorithms on HPC systems and how acceleration can be achieved.

IMAGE PROCESSING AND COMPUTER VISION

Image processing research has resulted in developing several sophisticated operators that provide visually arresting results. In the recent decade, techniques have been developed that may drastically improve detail in a picture by adopting the style of a master photographer (Aubry et al., 2014), smooth the image for the goal of simplification (Xu et al., 2012; Zhang et al., 2014) and reduce the effects of scattering. Existing operators have a wide range of computing requirements and run times. Certain operators, such as filtering methods, have benefited from almost a decade of focused effort to accelerate their growth. One well-known technique for speeding up a wide variety of image analysis operators is to down sample the picture, run the operator at a low resolution, and then up a sample (J. Chen et al., 2016). This strategy has two significant downsides. The original operators must be assessed on a lower-resolution version of the picture. This may be a considerable disadvantage since certain operators are sluggish, and present implementations are incapable of running at interactive rates, even at different resolutions.

Numerous approaches for speeding image processing operators have been devised. Particularly the bilateral filter has benefited from infrastructure investments in its improvement(Barron & Poole, 2016; Gastal & Oliveira, 2012; Paris & Durand, n.d.). Another class of dedicated acceleration algorithms is concerned with the median filter and its derivatives (Zhang et al., n.d.). Additional research has been done on the speed of variational methods (Y. Chen et al., 2015; Pock et al., n.d.), gradient-domain approaches(Krishnan et al., 2013), convolutions with high spatial support (Farbman et al., 2011), and local Laplacian filters (J. Chen et al., 2016). Although most of these strategies effectively accelerate the operators in their targeted families, they lack the universality we desire. A basic technique for increasing the speed of image analysis operators is to subsample the picture, assess the operator at a low resolution, and then up the sample (He & Sun, 2015). It is mostly operator-independent but needs the operator to avoid spatial transformations to utilize the source picture to guide the upsampling. With a capable cloud back and a bandwidth-constrained network connection, it can offload high-resolution computation to the cloud (Gharbi et al., 2015). Arrange image processing pipelines using domain-specific languages to use existing hardware resources (Hegarty et al., 2016).

Scale-invariant feature transform (SIFT) (Lowe, 2004) was the most prominent method for feature extraction for content-based image retrieval (CBIR) during the last two decades. Technically, SIFT is inherently resistant to geometric alterations and performs well for near-identical picture retrieval. Despite significant efforts, it remains challenging to completely overcome the semantic gap between image features and human comprehension of an image using SIFT-based features alone.

Computer vision has evolved into a major field spanning from capturing original data through visual pattern recognition and retrieval (Patel et al., 2012). It combines ideas, methods, and principles from image analysis, pattern matching, machine learning, and computer graphics. Most tasks within computer vision pertain to the ability to extract facts or characteristics from source images and identify features. Computer vision combines image processing with pattern recognition. Customizing the human eye's information-gathering capacity supports this discipline's development. Computer Vision is primarily concerned with creating models, data extraction, and information from pictures. In contrast, Image Processing is concerned mainly with performing computational changes for images, such as brightness, contrast, and others. One cannot assume computer vision to imitate the human eye exactly. It is because the machine vision system lacks the performance and functionality of the human eye. Although several researchers have developed a wide range of computer vision algorithms to simulate the human eye, the performance of computer vision systems is often constrained. The parameters' responsiveness, the algorithm's power, and the findings' precision represent one of the critical obstacles posed by the approach. Generally, performance assessment entails evaluating some of the fundamental behaviors of an algorithm to achieve precision, robustness, or extensibility to regulate and manage system performance. Computer vision was already extended into the branch of machine learning and emulated human visualization, in contrast to traditional time-consuming approaches that need complex laboratory investigation. In considerable detail, the phases of image analysis are as follows: image formation, image preprocessing, image segmentation, image measurement and interpretation. Several computer vision issues, such as object identification, motion tracking, human posture estimate, and semantic segmentation, have significantly progressed due to deep learning. This summary will examine the most significant advancements in neural network architectures and methods for computer vision tasks.

CONVOLUTIONAL NEURAL NETWORK

Deep learning enables computer models with several processing elements to understand and describe data with various degrees of abstraction, simulating how well the brain receives and comprehends multimodal information, so indirectly capturing the complicated patterns of widescale data. Deep learning encompasses neural networks, probabilistic hierarchies, and several unsupervised and supervised learning techniques for feature extraction. The current spike in interest in deep learning is owing to the fact that they've been proved to outperform earlier approaches in several applications, as well as the amount of complex data from various sources.

Convolutional Networks were inspired by the structure of the visual cortex and, more specifically, by the model of the visual system described in (Hubel & Wiesel, 1962). The first computational models were based on such local interconnections among neurons, and hierarchically structured image transformations are found in Neocognitron (Fukushima, 1980). Yann LeCun and his coworkers eventually developed Convolutional Neural Networks using the error gradient and achieving excellent performance in various pattern recognition applications(Huo et al., 2018).

A CNN consists of three primary kinds of neural layers: convolution layer, pooling layers, and fully connected layers. Each sort of layer has a distinct purpose. Every layer of a CNN translates the input volume into an output volume of neuron activity, leading to a translation of the data input to a 1-dimensional vector. CNN's have proved wildly effective in computer vision tasks, including computer vision, object identification, robotic vision, and self-driving automobiles.

Convolutional Neural Networks are gaining popularity in image processing because they integrate filtering and neural networks in a fashion biologically motivated by the working of the human brain. Over two decades have passed since the inception of fully convolutional network (CNN) designs. Compared to other neural network models such as the multiple hidden layers perceptron, CNN is intended to accept multiple arrays as input and process them using convolution operations. As a result, it excels at addressing computer vision challenges such as picture categorization, identification, and comprehension. CNN architecture grows deeper and more sophisticated to achieve high prediction performance and more demanding objectives. The basic structure of a CNN is shown in Figure 1.

Due to the high computational cost of CNN training and inference, its implementation becomes constrained owing to its high training time. Although speeding and refinement for CNN have been investigated since the technology was introduced, there seems to be a renewed interest in recent years due to the technology's positive industrial effect. Google's 2nd Tensor Processing Unit (TPU) is optimized for the TensorFlow framework and has a peak performance of 92 TFLOPS and on-chip memory of 28 MiB. It is more potent in computational intelligence training since it handles numerical and floating-point computations. NVIDIA introduces the NVIDIA Machine - learning Accelerator (NVDLA), an open-source initiative with a ready-to-use open license for anybody interested in data-intensive computations.

Deep CNNs, is computationally costly, requiring several floating-point multiplications over multiple layers of neurons. Researchers first shifted from standard CPUs to GPUs to minimize training time, using both CNNs and GPUs' inherent parallelism. A few industries came up with ASIC-based systems that embed converters in a pool of RAM to obtain maximal performance in terms of implementation versatility, but at a high financial cost(Abadi et al., n.d.). Accelerating CNNs may be performed by concentrating on the individual techniques or the platform used to implement them. When deciding the adequate hardware architecture, several factors must be considered, including flexibility in design, the

Figure 1. CNN structure

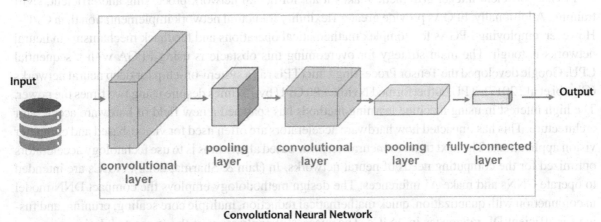

target platform's computational efficiency, the availability of fast memory, performance, energy consumption, and the system's financial cost.

Due to the exponential expansion of data and model sizes, it is necessary to spread models over several nodes. Distributed computing increases the model's flexibility, training duration, and cost efficiency. However, in the event of stale nodes, the distribution may result in higher calculation times. Numerous variables impact the computing time of remote nodes, including communication delay, network connection, sharing resources, and processing capacity. In deep learning, increasing the quantity of training data often improves model performance.

Nonetheless, as data amount and model complexity rise, the training process of the deep learning algorithm is computationally costly and time-consuming. Using several processors, such as GPUs and Google TPUs, distributed training is gaining popularity to expedite the training process. Multiple processors cooperating to train a single job might theoretically lower the total time for training, but the communication overhead between processors often limits the system's scalability. The primary issue with distribution is staleness across worker nodes. Stragglers are caused mainly by problems in storage, discs, uneven workloads, and resource sharing. Stragglers may increase computation time and degrade the model's performance (Ravikumar & Sriraman, 2021). Mitigation of Stale gradient and stragglers are essential for proper distribution of the model (Ravikumar, 2021).

ACCELERATION OF COMPUTER VISION ALGORITHM

Machine learning and deep learning approaches are widely used for computer vision applications. GPUs are well suited to developing neural networks due to the mathematical foundations of neural nets and the image manipulation activities performed by GPUs. GPUs are particularly well-suited for training deep neural networks since they involve several matrix multiplications. Due to their inherent benefits, GPUs were the most often used hardware implementation. ImageNet, one of the most well-known deep learning-based image categorization algorithms, was trained using dual GTX 580 3GB GPUs (Krizhevsky et al., 2012). In another instance, a deep learning-based picture enhancement technique was constructed on a Titan X GPU (Gharbi et al., 2017).

FPGAs' efficient integer arithmetic makes it apt for neural network processing and efficient, swift training. Additionally, FPGAs provide greater flexibility for neural network implementation than GPUs. However, employing FPGAs for complex mathematical operations and feedback mechanisms in neural networks is tough. The main strategy for overcoming this obstacle is using FPGA with a sequential CPU. Google developed the Tensor Processing Unit (TPU) as a system-on-chip for deep neural networks (Gharbi et al., 2017). TPU outperformed Nvidia k80 GPU by 15 times despite using two times the power. The high interest in using machine learning methods has spawned a new field of hardware accelerator architecture. This has impacted how hardware accelerators are often used for vision-based and computer vision applications. The next trend for neural network-based algorithms is to use technology accelerators optimized for the computing needs of neural networks. In (Jain & Sharma, 2022), ASICs are intended to operate CNNs and make AI inferences. The design methodology employs the compact DNN model in conjunction with quantization, quick mathematical reduction, multiple core scaling, pruning, and fusing for efficient DL inferences in ASICs. The successful application of the suggested design may give companies with a competitive edge in terms of its quality, price, and improved efficiency throughout the production process. A framework (Huynh, 2022)for effectively co-designing hardware and software for deep learning techniques on the PYNQ-Z2 chip.

HIGH-PERFORMANCE COMPUTING ACCELERATORS

For specific applications, real-time execution is critical, but for others, merely increasing the processing speed may be enough. The selection of an appropriate hardware accelerator is very application- and algorithm-dependent. A single FPGA or GPU does not always reflect the capacity of that particular equipment accelerator in general. The hardware specifications are often exclusive to a single piece of hardware and are thus useless for comparing various hardware accelerators. For specific applications, heterogeneous computing (the mixture of CPUs and TPU, FPGAs, or GPUs) is used. One of the primary difficulties in comparing various hardware accelerators is providing a fair comparison. In deep learning, the most significant breakthrough in image recognition and object detection language processing was made by Convolutional Neural Network (CNN). With the rapid growth in data and neural networks, the DNN algorithms' performance depends on the devices' computation power and storage capacity (Ravikumar et al., 2022). Unfortunately, hardware accelerators are much too intricate to compare performance based on processing speed, which could also convey any information about the relative merits of one equipment accelerator over the other, mainly when they are not members of the same family.

Additionally, an algorithm's processing speed is reliant not just on the hardware accelerators but also on the coder's expertise. This chapter introduces and discusses the essential aspects of FPGAs, TPU, and GPUs for image processing, deep learning and computer vision algorithms. The main ways of acceleration of image processing are shown in Figure 2.

FPGA

Arrays of programmable logic gates comprise the FPGA chip. In contrast to CPUs and graphics processing units, FPGA frameworks lack a predefined device design and central processing unit. Before coding reconfigurable FPGAs, the developer must create a hardware design per their requirement utilizing

Figure 2. Acceleration of Image Processing

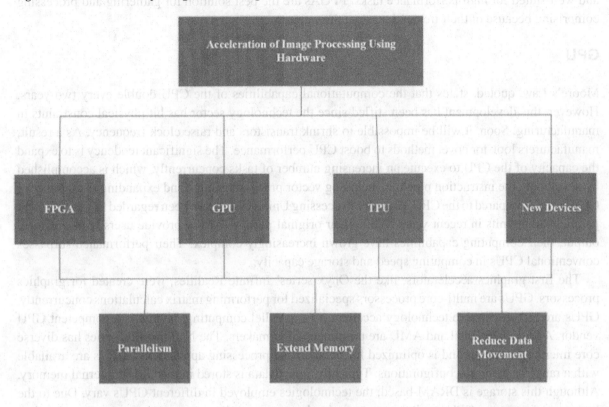

the logic gates included inside the FPGA hardware. FPGA programming methods differ from those of CPUs, TPUs, and GPUs.

Developing practical algorithms on FPGAs, in general, needs a thorough grasp of hardware intricacies. Block RAMs store or buffer data and are critical for storing data within the FPGA. When selecting an acceptable choice, the storage requirements for the algorithms should be considered, as well as the accessible block RAMs in an FPGA.

Significant benefits of employing FPGAs for image processing and computer vision algorithms: FPGAs process data faster than other types of hardware accelerators. No additional hardware accelerator has been able to match these speeds. FPGAs offer a high data flow, making them ideal for data acquisition cards. The parallelism and reconfigurability of FPGAs are advantageous features since they enable the hardware to be built and customized for high-end applications. By modifying the FPGA hardware tuned for the algorithm, programmers may construct efficient and flexible algorithms in FPGAs. Significant drawbacks of employing FPGAs for image processing techniques include the following: FPGAs have a lengthy development period, making efficient building code challenging. Even though software inventions for FPGAs have simplified and accelerated this process, the developer still needs appropriate technical expertise to produce robust code in FPGAs. FPGAs are the most versatile hardware accelerators for developing unique object recognition and image processing techniques. As a result, getting acceptable performance on FPGAs requires modifying and optimizing the method for parallel processing.

FPGAs are the appropriate solution for procedures requiring a more excellent standard of computation in a portable, PC-independent machine. FPGAs are energy efficient, compatible with embedded systems, and well-suited for high-performance tasks. FPGAs are the best solution for gathering and processing comprising because of their tremendous data throughput.

GPU

Moore's Law, quoted, states that the computational capabilities of the CPU double every two years. However, this development has been stifled since the technology sector has hit physical constraints in manufacturing. Soon, it will be impossible to shrink transistors and raise clock frequency. As a result, manufacturers look for novel methods to boost CPU performance. The significant tendency is to expand the capacity of the CPU to execute an increasing number of tasks concurrently, which is accomplished by developing the instruction pipeline, including vector processing units, and expanding the number of CPU cores. Compared to the CPU, Graphics Processing Units (GPU) have been regarded as very efficient parallelization units in recent years. While their original purpose was to provide users with graphical output, their computing capabilities have grown increasingly complex. Their performance surpasses conventional CPUs in computing speed and storage capacity.

The first graphics accelerators, like the Onyx series' Infinite Realities, were created for graphics processors. GPUs are multi-core processors specialized for performing matrix calculations concurrently. GPUs are a cost-effective technology accelerator for parallel computing. Nvidia is a competent GPU vendor. Additionally, Intel and AMD are prominent GPU makers. The NVidia GPU series has diverse core microarchitectures and is optimized for many image processing applications. GPUs are available with a range of memory configurations. Typically, image data is stored in the GPU's internal memory. Although this storage is DRAM-based, the technologies employed in different GPUs vary. Due to the high cost of memory, GPUs with the same version but more excellent storage are more expensive than ones with less memory.

Consequently, while choosing an appropriate GPU, the algorithm's memory needs should be considered. Developing parallel processing methods for computer vision applications on GPUs with many CUDA cores is feasible. All contemporary GPUs communicate with PCs using the PCIe interface. On the other hand, the maximum data transfer rate is governed by the PCIe connection and the count of information bus available to the GPU.

The following are just a few of the many advantages of GPUs compared to other hardware accelerators: GPUs are developed on a vast scale. They are consequently more inexpensive than FPGAs, and it has the highest computational power-to-price ratio of any specialized device. GPUs are specialized graphics rendering units (GPUs) designed for video processing. Designing and evaluating code in Graphical is far faster and more straightforward than developing and debugging code in an FPGA. Nvidia GPUs are well suited for instrumentation applications because they can be controlled using National Instruments LabView software. GPU technologies are constantly developing, and despite their increased capabilities, newer technologies are typically not much more expensive.

Drawbacks of GPU: GPUs use more energy than FPGAs in the same capability class, often making them unsuitable for energy systems that include advanced image processing algorithms. The fundamental performance restriction when GPUs are used in CPC-based systems is the data transfer time between the host CPC and the GPU. The data transfer between GPU and CPU is shown in Figure 3. It is conceivable that unoptimized GPU code will not contribute to increased processing speed. As a result, minimizing the GPU's access to data on the host CPC is vital.

Figure 3. Data Transfer between CPU and GPU

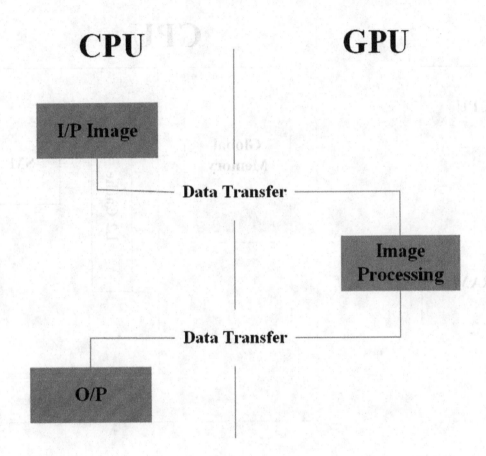

The GPU architecture is more pre-structured than FPGAs and provides less flexibility. Most published articles do not compare FPGAs with GPUs at equivalent technological levels, with GPUs often belonging to the latest era than FPGAs. This might be a result of GPUs' lower cost than FPGAs or their greater simplicity of programming. However, comparing many implementations of the same method on FPGAs and GPUs might assist engineers in obtaining an approximation of performance. The GPU architecture is shown in Figure 4.

Typically, an NVIDIA device's memory is organized hierarchically into six distinct memory levels: registers, shared memory/L1 cache, memory unit, static memory/texture, memory L2 cache, and global memory. Global memory is accessible to all threads on a grid. Specific threads can be started for work while others wait for data. Nevertheless, the line utilized to complete a job depends on the issue's magnitude. Persistent memory and texture storage is unique to GPUs in that they may significantly boost performance due to their read-only nature. At the same time, threads have exclusive access to local memory. Registers are the quickest memory tiers, although they are restricted in quantity. Generally, shared memory on a GPU is utilized to optimize performance.

Figure 4. GPU Architecture

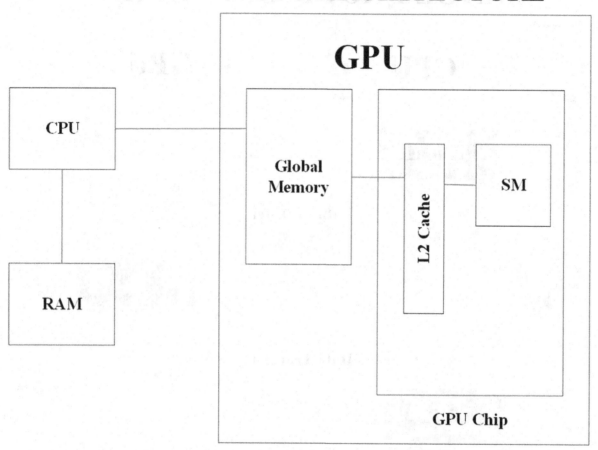

A high number of ALU units facilitates quicker data analysis while GPU caches facilitate data reuse. The GPU can combine multiple data access requests via controllers and supports parallel and multi-threaded processing. This helps to obtain higher speed and throughput for DL applications than CPU. The primary objective of GPU design is high instruction throughput, not instruction-specific delay reduction. GPU processors are more than CPU cores, and several threads operate concurrently in the CPU. CNN executes the convolutional, filtering, flattening, and classifying layers in GPU before passing the final result to the CPU. Using the computational transformation function for CNN, GPUs boost the throughput. The execution of each CNN layer in GPU is seen in detail in Figure 5.

TPU

Google's Tensor Processing Unit (TPU) is a domain-specific technology designed to accelerate the processing of deep learning models. TPUs outperform CPU/GPU-based acceleration for two main reasons: quantization and systolic array. Quantization is the initial stage of optimization, in which 8-bit integers are used to mimic 16- or 32-bit floating-point quantities. This may result in a reduction in the amount

Figure 5 Execution of a CNN model in CPU with GPU Acceleration

CNN Execution in CPU with GPU Acceleration

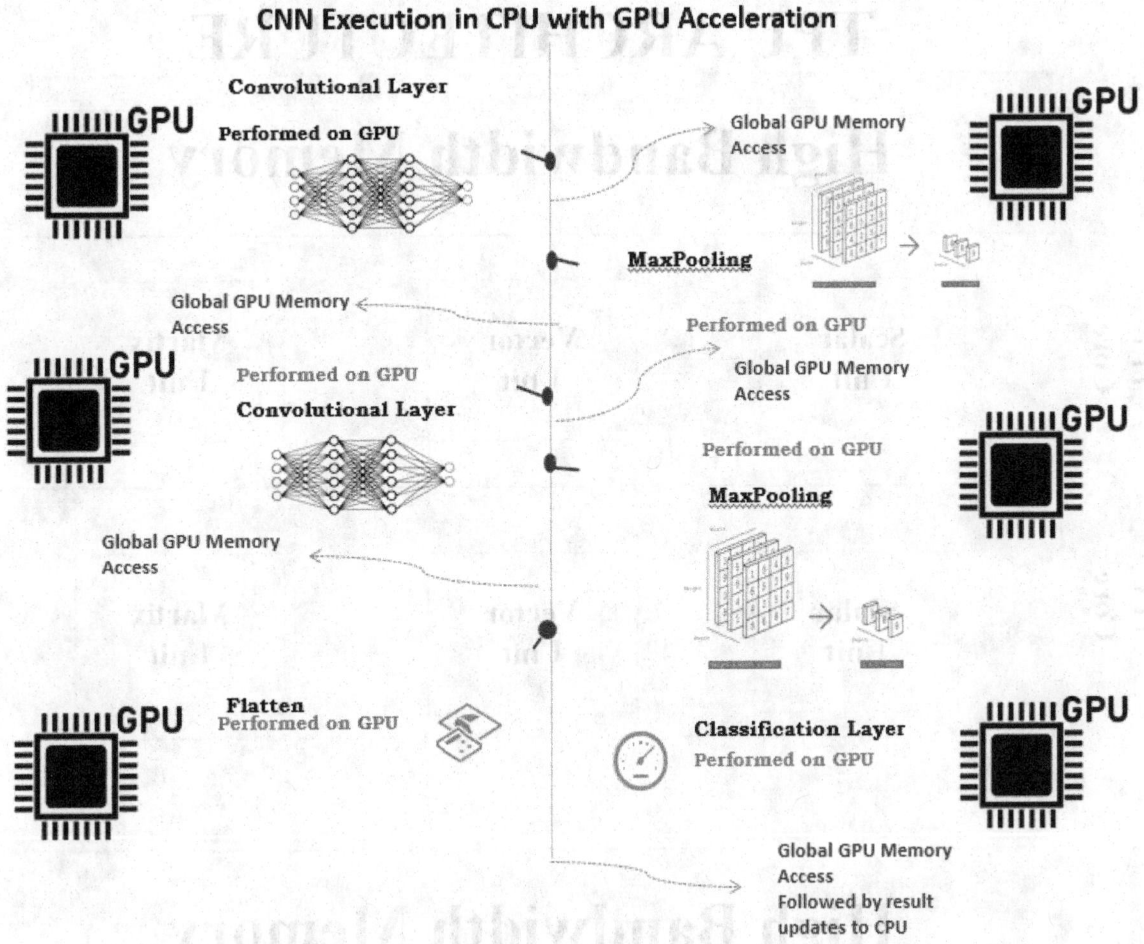

of memory and processing resources needed. Systolic arrays significantly contribute to TPU efficiency because they are naturally compatible with matrix manipulation and because computation in neural nets can be expressed as matrix operations. The Matrix Multiply Unit, which would be a 256x256 systolic array made of numerous compute cells, is the TPU's central processing unit, as shown in Figure 6. At the moment, each cell gets a weight parameter and an input signal and accumulates its products. After all weights and input signals have been transmitted top to bottom and left to right, it begins the next iteration cycle. The whole matrix multiplication is performed by participating all calculation cells in this calculation technique. The MXU's systolic array has 256 x256 = 65,536 ALUs, implying that the TPU can do 65,536 8-bit arithmetic multiplication operations and adds each cycle. Because of the systolic design, it is possible to reuse input data numerous times. As a result, it may increase throughput while using less memory bandwidth.

TPU, unlike GPU, eliminates characteristics not utilized by the neural net, hence conserving energy. CNN implementations on TPU will simultaneously use the TPU and CPU to execute linear and non-linear CNN components. Since CNN is a GEMM operation, the convolutional and classification layers

Figure 6. Tensor Processing Unit Architecture

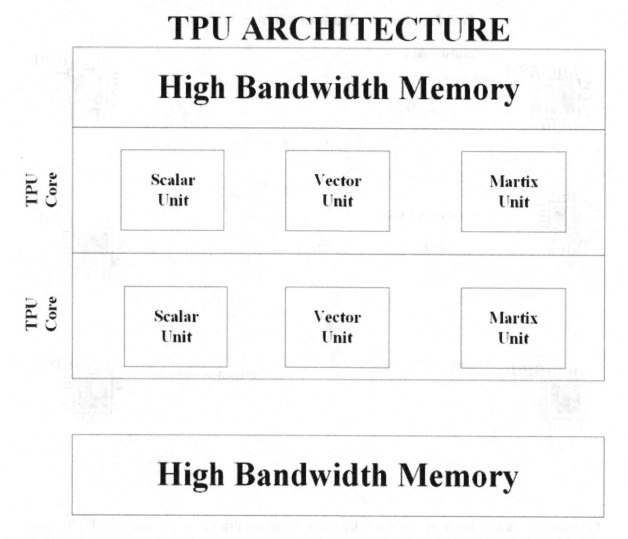

are conducted on the TPU, while the Pooling and Flatten layers are executed on the CPU. The execution of each CNN layer in TPU is shown in Figure 7.

A novel CNN model was studied with layer-wise implementation in GPU and TPU (Ravikumar et al., 2022). The CNN implementations on the GPU and TPU were evaluated layer by layer, and the bottleneck locations on the TPU and GPU were determined. The convolutional network should be constructed, with each job being an MISD task to obtain maximum utilization of TPU. While designing a network, it is necessary to prioritize the neural network jobs. GPUs excel in small-batch processing and provide more flexibility and ease of programming. GPUs are better suited to small data sets and batch sizes owing to their processing pattern in wraps and fast on-stream multiprocessor scheduling. GPUs excel at massive datasets and network models because of their memory reuse optimization. Weight reuse is limited in fully-connected networks, which results in increased memory traffic as the size grows. The memory bandwidth of the GPU enables it to be used for experience applications. Due to the increased parallelism, large neural networks perform better on GPUs than on CPUs. While GPU outperforms CPU for

Figure 7. Execution of a CNN model in CPU with TPU Acceleration

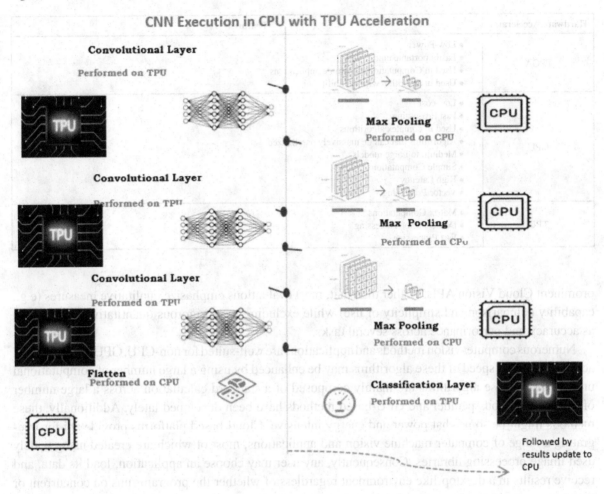

fully-connected networks, TPU outperforms GPU for big batch sizes. Using a systolic array structure, TPU works well on CNNs with big batches, resulting in a high throughput throughout training time. Large quantities of data are required to fully use the matrices and multiply units of the TPU's systolic array. In CNN, the performance improvement is proportional to the batch size. TPU is the optimal choice for large batch sizes and complicated CNNs because of the spatial reuse properties of CNNs. However, since weight reuse is low in fully linked networks, TPU is not preferable.

COMPUTER VISION IN CLOUD PLATFORMS

With the proliferation of machine-learning applications, many images have been uploaded to the cloud containing such digital image processing algorithms, which are often implemented as deep learning models. Major cloud providers Google, Microsoft, and Amazon, provide Web APIs enabling computer vision activities execution. This dramatically reduces the entry barriers for firms that lack the means or infrastructure necessary to maintain their platforms. Currently, there is no systematic comparison of the

Table 1. Hardware Accelerators

Hardware Accelerator	Features
FPGA	• Low-Power • Easily portable unit • Used in Computationally simple applications • Used in algorithm with flexibility
GPU	• Low cost • Fast Processing • Used in complex algorithms • Algorithms that can be massively parallelized • Medium to Large models • Simple Computations • High Latency • Vector Processing
TPU	• Matrix Computations • Dense Vector Processing • Fast Processing

prominent Cloud Vision APIs. Rather than that, most evaluations emphasize qualitative measures (e.g., capability comparison and simplicity of use) while excluding more rigorous quantitative studies such as accuracy and performance across several tasks.

Numerous computer vision methods and applications are well-suited for non-CPU, GPU, or multi-GPU acceleration. The speed of these algorithms may be enhanced by using a large number of computational units because these algorithms are mainly composed of a standard calculation across a large number of pixels. Numerous parallel and GPU-based methods have been developed lately. Additionally, these methods might be somewhat power and energy intensive. Cloud-based platforms provide api for integrating a range of computer machine vision and applications, most of which are created using widely used image processing libraries. Consequently, any user may choose an application, load its data, and receive results in a desktop-like environment regardless of whether the program runs on concurrent or heterogeneous platforms.

Computer Vision In GCP

Cloud Vision API enables development teams to incorporate vision detection capabilities into their applications, such as picture labelling, face and landmark identification, optical character recognition (OCR), and explicit content tagging. Cloud Based Vision is an image processing tool that enables us to analyze an image's information and extract its key elements remotely. Developers may use this technology in their apps using a specific API named Google Cloud Vision API. By encapsulating a strong machine learning algorithm in an easy-to-use API, the Google Cloud Vision API allows developers to comprehend the information of a picture. It categorizes photos fast into hundreds of categories, recognizes particular objects and faces inside images, and locates and reads written text included within images. Through sentiment analysis, you may add information to your image database, control objectionable material, and allow new marketing scenarios. The Vision API continues to improve over time as different ideas and accuracy are added. Vision API can analyze the emotional facial characteristics of individuals in your photographs, such as joy, grief, and rage. Object recognition and item logo detection can determine how people see your logo. Optical Character Recognition (OCR) permits the detection of text inside photographs and the automated identification of languages. The Vision API is available in a wide variety of languages.

Computer Vision In AWS

Amazon Machine Learning is a service that helps designers of all skill levels use machine learning algorithms. Amazon Machine Learning includes visualizations and wizards that assist you through the process of developing neural network models without requiring you to be an expert in machine learning techniques and technology. Once your models are complete, Amazon Machine Learning makes it simple to receive predictions for your application through simple APIs without needing proprietary prediction generating code or infrastructure management. Amazon Machine Learning is built on the same time-tested, highly scalable machine learning technology that Amazon's internal information scientist community has used for years. The service creates Machine Understandable models by identifying trends in your current data. Then, using these models, Amazon Machine Learning processes new data and generates recommendations for your application. Amazon Machine Learning is highly scalable, producing billions of predictions daily and serving them in real-time and at high throughput. There is no initial hardware and software investment required with Amazon Machine Learning, and you pay as you go, allowing you to start small and expand as your application develops.

Computer vision in Microsoft Azure

Azure Machine Learning Studio is pre-loaded with hundreds of packages and supports custom code. It was created for applied machine learning. Utilize best-in-class analytics and a simple drag-and-drop interface to go from concept to implementation quickly. You can quickly deploy your model to reality as a web service that can be accessed from any device, anywhere, and with any data source. Microsoft Cognitive Services delivers an Enterprise Cloud Environment that enables applications with robust algorithms to be developed using only a few programming languages in a matter of minutes. They operate on various devices and platforms, including iOS, Android, and Windows, which are constantly developing and are simple to set up.

CONCLUSION

When used with the CPU, GPU, TPU computing is a potent tool for accelerating computer vision tasks. Distributed processing parallelizes algorithm processing and maximizes performance for various applications. The technique works much quicker when GPU processing is used. The GPU will process the heavier code sections, while the central processor unit will handle the remainder. The hybrid approach of running the CPU in conjunction with the GPU is a potent combo. Combining GPU and CPU while developing computer vision applications improves task performance due to the GPU's hundreds of parallel processing cores. GPU computing has progressed to the point where many computer vision jobs use it to improve task efficiency and optimization. Optimizing the computation time of image processing algorithms is a critical challenge. Due to its massively parallel design, the GPU is regarded as one of the most acceptable alternatives for computationally intensive applications. With its vast number of ALUs,

GPUs are useful for DNN; however, the high memory access required by the single data multiple data architecture creates a challenge.

The GPU is insufficient for complicated Deep Neural Networks with significant DRAM access and a massive number of floating-point operations. Tensor computations are performed using specialized computer vision ASIC accelerators for vector computations. Using the systolic array structure, TPU performs well on CNNs with big batches, resulting in a high throughput throughout training time. TPU is the optimal choice for big batch sizes and complicated CNNs because of the spatial reuse properties of CNNs. However, since weight reuse is low in fully linked networks, TPU is not preferable. CNN structures may be classified into convolutional, pooling, and fully connected. Each component has distinct computational needs, and the paper explains how they are implemented in GPU and TPU. The leading cloud platforms and their computer vision functionalities are listed.

REFERENCE

Abadi, M., Barham, P., Chen, J., Chen, Z., Davis, A., Dean, J., Devin, M., Ghemawat, S., Irving, G., Isard, M., Kudlur, M., Levenberg, J., Monga, R., Moore, S., Murray, D. G., Steiner, B., Tucker, P., Vasudevan, V., Warden, P., … Zheng, X. (n.d.). *TensorFlow: A system for large-scale machine learning*. Academic Press.

Adek, R. T., & Ula, M. (2020). A Survey on The Accuracy of Machine Learning Techniques for Intrusion and Anomaly Detection on Public Data Sets. *2020 International Conference on Data Science, Artificial Intelligence, and Business Analytics (DATABIA)*. 10.1109/DATABIA50434.2020.9190436

Aubry, M., Paris, S., Hasinoff, S. W., Kautz, J., & Durand, F. (2014). Fast Local Laplacian Filters: Theory and Applications. *ACM Transactions on Graphics, 33*(5), 167:1-167:14. doi:10.1145/2629645

Barron, J. T., & Poole, B. (2016). *The Fast Bilateral Solver*. doi:10.1007/978-3-319-46487-9_38

Chen, J., Adams, A., Wadhwa, N., & Hasinoff, S. W. (2016). Bilateral guided upsampling. *ACM Transactions on Graphics, 35*(6), 203:1-203:8. doi:10.1145/2980179.2982423

Chen, Y., Yu, W., & Pock, T. (2015). *On learning optimized reaction diffusion processes for effective image restoration*. doi:10.1109/CVPR.2015.7299163

Farbman, Z., Fattal, R., & Lischinski, D. (2011). Convolution Pyramids. *ACM Transactions on Graphics, 30*(6), 175. doi:10.1145/2070781.2024209

Fukushima, K. (1980). Neocognitron: A self-organizing neural network model for a mechanism of pattern recognition unaffected by shift in position. *Biological Cybernetics, 36*(4), 193–202. doi:10.1007/BF00344251 PMID:7370364

Gastal, E. S. L., & Oliveira, M. M. (2012). Adaptive manifolds for real-time high-dimensional filtering. *ACM Transactions on Graphics, 31*(4), 1–13. doi:10.1145/2185520.2185529

Gharbi, M., Chen, J., Barron, J. T., Hasinoff, S. W., & Durand, F. (2017). Deep bilateral learning for real-time image enhancement. *ACM Transactions on Graphics, 36*(4), 1–12. doi:10.1145/3072959.3073592

Gharbi, M., Shih, Y., Chaurasia, G., Ragan-Kelley, J., Paris, S., & Durand, F. (2015). Transform recipes for efficient cloud photo enhancement. *ACM Transactions on Graphics, 34*(6), 228:1-228:12. doi:10.1145/2816795.2818127

He, K., & Sun, J. (2015). *Fast Guided Filter.* https://arxiv.org/abs/1505.00996

Hegarty, J., Daly, R., DeVito, Z., Ragan-Kelley, J., Horowitz, M., & Hanrahan, P. (2016). Rigel: Flexible multi-rate image processing hardware. *ACM Transactions on Graphics, 35*(4), 1–11. doi:10.1145/2897824.2925892

Hubel, D. H., & Wiesel, T. N. (1962). Receptive fields, binocular interaction and functional architecture in the cat's visual cortex. *The Journal of Physiology, 160*(1), 106-154.2.

Huo, Z., Gu, B., Yang, Q., & Huang, H. (2018). *Decoupled Parallel Backpropagation with Convergence Guarantee.* https://arxiv.org/abs/1804.10574

Huynh, T. V. (2022). FPGA-based Acceleration for ConvolutionalNeural Networks on PYNQ-Z2. *International Journal of Computing and Digital Systems, 11*(1), 441–449. doi:10.12785/ijcds/110136

Jain, A., & Sharma, N. (2022). Accelerated AI Inference at CNN-Based Machine Vision in ASICs: A Design Approach. *ECS Transactions, 107*(1), 5165–5174. doi:10.1149/10701.5165ecst

Krishnan, D., Fattal, R., & Szeliski, R. (2013). Efficient preconditioning of laplacian matrices for computer graphics. *ACM Transactions on Graphics, 32*(4), 142:1-142:15. doi:10.1145/2461912.2461992

Krizhevsky, A., Sutskever, I., & Hinton, G. E. (2012). ImageNet Classification with Deep Convolutional Neural Networks. *Advances in Neural Information Processing Systems, 25.* https://papers.nips.cc/paper/2012/hash/c399862d3b9d6b76c8436e924a68c45b-Abstract.html

Lowe, D. G. (2004). Distinctive Image Features from Scale-Invariant Keypoints. *International Journal of Computer Vision, 60*(2), 91–110. doi:10.1023/B:VISI.0000029664.99615.94

Paris, S., & Durand, F. (n.d.). *A Fast Approximation of the Bilateral Filter using a Signal Processing Approach.* Academic Press.

Patel, K. K., Kar, A., Jha, S. N., & Khan, M. A. (2012). Machine vision system: A tool for quality inspection of food and agricultural products. *Journal of Food Science and Technology, 49*(2), 123–141. doi:10.100713197-011-0321-4 PMID:23572836

Pock, T., Unger, M., Cremers, D., & Bischof, H. (n.d.). 2008. Fast and Exact Solution of Total Variation Models on the GPU. *CVPR Workshop on Visual Computer Vision on GPUs. Cited On*, 101–124.

Ravikumar, A. (2021). Non-relational multi-level caching for mitigation of staleness & stragglers in distributed deep learning. *Proceedings of the 22nd International Middleware Conference: Doctoral Symposium*, 15–16. 10.1145/3491087.3493678

Ravikumar, A., & Sriraman, H. (2021). Staleness and Stagglers in Distibuted Deep Image Analytics. *2021 International Conference on Artificial Intelligence and Smart Systems (ICAIS)*, 848–852. 10.1109/ICAIS50930.2021.9395782

Ravikumar, A., Sriraman, H., Sai Saketh, P. M., Lokesh, S., & Karanam, A. (2022). Effect of neural network structure in accelerating performance and accuracy of a convolutional neural network with GPU/TPU for image analytics. *PeerJ. Computer Science, 8*, e909. doi:10.7717/peerj-cs.909 PMID:35494877

Xu, L., Yan, Q., Xia, Y., & Jia, J. (2012). Structure extraction from texture via relative total variation. *ACM Transactions on Graphics, 31*(6), 139:1-139:10. doi:10.1145/2366145.2366158

Zhang, Q., Shen, X., Xu, L., & Jia, J. (2014). Rolling Guidance Filter. In D. Fleet, T. Pajdla, B. Schiele, & T. Tuytelaars (Eds.), Computer Vision – ECCV 2014 (pp. 815–830). Springer International Publishing. doi:10.1007/978-3-319-10578-9_53

Chapter 2
Acceleration of Computer Vision and Deep Learning:
Surveillance Systems

Ezhilarasie R.
SASTRA University (Deemed), India

Aishwarya N.
SASTRA University (Deemed), India

Subramani V.
SASTRA University (Deemed), India

Umamakeswari A.
SASTRA University (Deemed), India

ABSTRACT

Cameras used for surveillance have grown in popularity since the technology boom and are now part of our everyday life. It appears to be laborious and time-consuming to monitor the surveillance cameras manually. Computer vision is reshaping the security and surveillance industry. Despite their revolutionary nature, modern CCTV cameras are insufficient because they are passive units that assist investigations but do not give preventative measures. They need to be replaced with active systems. Recreational issues in public security necessitate computer vision, artificial intelligence, and machine learning (ML). Due to the advancements in deep surveillance, we should expect a massive boost in inefficiency. The outstanding performance in image identification and the capacity to absorb temporal information that convolutional and recurrent neural networks offer intelligent surveillance systems bodes well for their future growth in this area. The goal of this chapter is to examine the challenges in surveillance systems, the usage of deep learning techniques, and various new applications.

DOI: 10.4018/978-1-7998-8892-5.ch002

INTRODUCTION

In the recent past, the world has been moving towards development in economic sectors, due to which the lifestyle has become complex in different views, including the people's safety and security. Thus, we are in dire need and necessity of monitoring and being secure, (Elharrouss.O, 2021). A solution for this problem that has been discovered is Surveillance cameras, which are deployed in public and private places to assure the safety of the individuals.

Surveillance is a developing section which focuses on obtaining information from various images or sequences of images. Surveillance cameras (CCTV) have become an indispensable part of our lives, (Wang. X, 2013). They have been gaining attention since the technology boom and can be called as third eye of society. Through the camera's crimes, vandalism and property theft can be prevented. The surveillance cameras can be used as a material of evidence in a court of law. It transmits the video coverage only to authorized users and used in retail outlets, banks, restaurants and homes (Shana.L, 2019). They are motion-activated; hence, they detect motion and send alerts when they sense any abnormal behaviour. The advent of technology has enabled surveillance at every juncture of human existence, ensuring crime prevention. The presence of surveillance curbs trespassers of any kind by acting as a deterrent force to reckon with (Iqbal.M.J, 2021). Surveillance of production lines has enabled quality control at industrial units and serves as an ever-seeing eye for management.

In common, human beings are dedicated to observing the cameras every day, which makes the task of monitoring not only tedious and laborious for the workers but also excessive. This necessitates the automation of monitoring studies at different locations by using surveillance cameras. This process of industrialization is feasible and acts as a support for the human operator to perform the monitoring tasks. The tasks could be varied based on applications such as traffic control, crime prevention, crowd analysis etc. Other applications may include indoor and outdoor scenes like parking spaces, airport lounges, and railway platforms. The video surveillance system's analysis is described in detail, with this system's tendencies and future possibilities taken into consideration. An up-gradation to these features can be implemented to enhance monitoring efficiency and rule out possible human parallax errors.

CHALLENGES IN REAL-TIME FACE DETECTION

When it comes to surveillance systems, cameras are typically positioned in places where people can't get their hands on them. When a camera is placed at a height, the angle at which the face is seen changes. It is also important to note that because of the camera-face orientation (upside down, 45 degrees, frontal or profile), face photographs may vary and some facial characteristics may be completely or partially blocked. Other objects can sometimes conceal the faces due to geometric distortion. In photographs of a gathering of people, some faces may partially cover others. When reading something in the mirror, you may notice that the image is orientated from left to right instead of from top to bottom, or vice versa. Face images also change directly for various rotations around the optical axis of the camera. A person's face can have a wide range of dimensions and Faces closer to the camera appear larger than faces further away.

DEEP LEARNING IN COMPUTER VISION

Deep learning algorithms for deep surveillance have advanced over the last decade. These advancements have demonstrated an important trend in deep surveillance and promise a significant increase in efficiency. Deep surveillance is commonly used to identify theft, detect violence, and predict the likelihood of an explosion. The need of deep learning in surveillance includes:

- Automated Feature Extraction's Promise. There are many ways in which image data can be used to learn and extract features automatically.
- Enabling Models that Cover the Whole Lifecycle. Instead of a network of specialised models, one single end-to-end model can be used.
- Potential of Model Reuse. You can employ the same skills you've developed for a different challenge.
- The Guarantee of Outstanding Results. When it comes to difficult jobs, techniques outperform classical methods.
- General Method's Promise. Convolutional neural networks, for example, can be applied to a wide range of activities

The steps in working with Computer vision go hand in hand with Deep Learning, as shown in Figure 1. The real-time images are sent for processing; the images are processed for feature extraction. The deep learning models are incorporated into the extracted data, and the output is predicted for the classification of images.

Figure 1. Working Strategy of Computer Vision with Deep Learning

OBJECT DETECTION

Object detection is the process of identifying the instance of the class to which the object belongs and predicting the object's location by displaying the bounding box around the object. Single class object identification is the process of identifying a single instance of a class from a picture, while multi class object detection is the process of identifying the classes of all the objects in the image. It is now possible to construct more complex and accurate computer vision applications using deep learning approaches, which are becoming increasingly advantageous. Object detection can be broadly classified into two categories, namely dedicated object detection and generic object detection. Under Dedicated object detection we have face detection, traffic detection, Pedestrian detection etc.

ALTERNATIVES TO OBJECT DETECTION

Semantic Segmentation

While object detection is based on a set of general pixels, semantic segmentation uses the individual pixels associated with a given object. This eliminates the use of bounding boxes and allows for a more exact characterization of image objects. Semantic segmentation typically makes use of fully convolutional networks (FCNs) or unsupervised neural networks (U-Nets).

The training of autonomous vehicles is one notable use for semantic segmentation. Using this method, researchers can use photos of streets or throughways with clearly defined object boundaries.

Pose Estimation

When photographing a person or an object, a pose estimate is used to determine where the joints are and what their posture means. It works with both 2D and 3D images. Most typically used for pose estimation is the Pose Net architecture, which is a CNN-based design.

Predicting where a person's body will appear in an image using gesture prediction might help animators generate more lifelike poses and gestures. For example, augmented reality, robotic movement mirroring, and motion analysis all use this feature.

DEEP LEARNING ALGORITHMS

The industrial revolution has recently made use of computer vision for their work. Deep learning is widely used in the automation, robotics, medical, and surveillance industries. Deep learning has become the most talked-about technology because of the results it achieves in applications such as language processing, object detection, and image classification. The most important components of object detection are image classification and detection. The following section provides a comprehensive summary of the algorithms used for the object detection.

Yolo

You Only Look Once (YOLO) only needs to process an image once in order to detect. Bounding boxes and class probabilities are predicted by a single neural network.

The basic YOLO architecture is shown in Figure 2. Based on performance detection, it is possible to optimise it from the beginning to the end. On a PC with a GPU card, execution is more efficient. An image-based method can be used to safeguard surveillance camera data.

AlexNet

The AlexNet includes eight levels, each with its own set of parameters that may be learned. The model comprises five layers, each of which uses Relu activation, except the output layer, which uses a combination of max pooling and three fully connected layers. Employing the Relu as an activation function increases the training process' speed by nearly six times. To prevent over fitting, dropout layers can be used.

Figure 2. YOLO Architecture Diagram

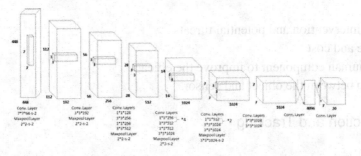

FCN

Fully Convolutional Network is a network that lacks "Dense" layers (as in typical CNNs) and instead uses 1x1 convolutions to serve the function of fully connected layers (Dense layers). Although the lack of dense layers allows variable inputs to be fed in, a few approaches will enable us to use thick layers while still preserving variable input dimensions, (Yu.C, 2018).

APPLICATIONS OF COMPUTER VISION

Monitor International Border Security

The management of a country's international borders is its most difficult challenge. Crossing international borders can lead to conflict between countries. Protection from infiltration, terrorist attacks, and other threats is the fundamental goal of land defence. As a result, keeping a close eye on the country's borders is a must. We can prevent illegal immigrants from entering the country by deploying surveillance cameras at the international borders. It's difficult for humans to keep track of such a wide variety of borders over such a long period of time in any season, which is why computer vision is preferable. We can use a self-driving car with a facial recognition algorithm-based monitoring system. The technology will raise a warning to the central hub if the face of the person does not match that of an existing stored soldier. The central control system must receive a constant stream of video from the site. Face-recognition algorithms and video streaming must be improved in order to reduce the amount of time spent transmitting and receiving data (Ahmed.H.M, 2021).

A robotic system based on a Raspberry Pi can be used to automatically identify and notify the control centre of an intrusion (Brunetti.A, 2018). Open CV image processing technology is used to detect the presence of humans and provide alerts via SMS or e-mail. Facial recognition algorithms or a camera can be used as sensors to avoid obstacles and see human face contours. When the sensor's camera is active, the system is triggered. However, they are unable to quickly distinguish between an unfamiliar and a well-known individual. Image processing techniques are employed in the building of a robotic system that can identify a known individual in a crowd. The system will notify the user if a suspicious event occurs within the surveillance region. People can be identified by their voice, eyes, hand or face using biometrics, which encodes their bodily characteristics into a single ID. To get the most out of biometric apps, users will need personal identification that is both secure and automatic.

The main goal of the surveillance system is to do the following:

- Limit Human intervention and potential threats
- Minimize time and cost
- Utilizing the human component to improve the efficacy
- Lessen the gap between the object and sensor.

Pedestrian Detection and Tracking

The persistent curiosity among the people about automated cars has resulted in heavy investments by automotive and IT giants, and the communications made possible for the interaction of humans with machines and applications, are playing a vital role in the emerging techniques for video-based pedestrian tracking. Intelligent machines being able to behave in an unconstrained environment pose a threat to any human in contact with them. The statistical data informs that pedestrians were at higher risk of death than the pillion rider during an accident on the roads. Recently, the ends have been reduced due to the inventions of driving supports like Auto braking systems. Due to this anomaly in automated travel, people detection and tracking is becoming the talk of the computer vision research community in the recent past. The areas of research vary from human detection to pedestrian tracking using 3D and 2D vision systems. Commonly, vision-based pedestrian detection constitutes three basic steps: (i) Image Acquisition (ii) Feature Extraction (iii) Classification.

The system apprehends human motion and uses subsystems to sense and process data. The intricacy of the subsystems is interrelated, and the complexity of the present step depends on the next. The next step will be more uncomplicated than the previous steps if the last step is simpler. The subtle distinction between the complexities connects with active and passive sensing (Sreenu.G, 2019).

Crowd Dynamics and Crowd Analysis

Even in the most mundane of areas, such as theme parks and entertainment venues, people are constantly confronted with crowds or large gatherings. The subjects range from the social and cultural to the spiritual in nature of the shows. When it comes to public safety, high pedestrian flow throughput, preventing stampedes, and delivering superior emergency services in the event of a crowd-related incident or congestion, having an intelligent Crowd Monitoring System (CMS) is vital (Manikandan V.P, 2022). The different steps in crowd monitoring is given in Figure 3.

For the most part, the possible applications for crowd control, monitoring, and analytics are quite broad. Swarm-based applications are few and far between in terms of safety, emergency response services, traffic flow, and administration in both private and public spaces. Group analysis, estimation and summarising, density and prediction, flow analysis and specific behaviour prediction and mass monitoring are all examples of applications that require study and development in crowd management and analysis. There are a variety of applications where group detection and density estimates can be useful, as well as the accompanying cognitive analytics procedures. There are three types of individual counting: object-based counting, clustered counting, and regression-based counting.

In the last decade, CMS has garnered a lot of attention. Crowd management systems can be useful in many image analysis tasks. Another issue is that, despite some modest success in the last 10-15 years, crowd control is still a problem, especially for recordings shot in unrestricted environments. Due of the

Figure 3. Steps in Crowd Monitoring

preceding two factors, crowd control is still a difficult problem to solve, and academics are constantly presenting new state-of-the-art (SOA) solutions. It's tough for organisers to keep a lid on a crowd if it gets out of hand. In these kinds of circumstances, issues like abnormal behaviour or even stampedes may arise.

Real-time crowd surveillance is now possible because to unmanned aerial vehicles (UAVs) and closed-circuit television cameras. Unmanned aerial vehicles (UAVs) can capture images in high definition and in real time while CCTV cameras have a much smaller field of view. The use of a UAV with facial recognition to monitor a crowd was tested. As a result, the work of analysing visual input was outsourced. Colour segmentation was used to identify pedestrians in a practical application. The device was able to precisely detect the mass of people in the area. A single or a few classes that are primarily black and white make up the majority of the feature classes. This made the system's task of identifying more straightforward.

Using the Internet of Things, researchers created a crowd counting method based on a deep convolutional neural network (CNN) IoT (Tuia.D, 2022). Due to the program's custom design, it could properly count people in both sparsely populated areas and densely populated ones.

Wildlife Protection

Conservation efforts are increasingly relying on camera trap imaging (automatic photography of wild animal species). Precision monitoring of large areas has never been possible before thanks to this technology. However, the sheer volume of data created by these devices makes it difficult for people to interpret. Now that machine learning and computer vision have made significant strides, the biodiversity community may take advantage of the knowledge created by systems activated by a mix of heat and motion.

Cropped images of gorilla faces were recovered from surveillance images using the YOLO object detection method. The CNN model has a 90% accuracy rate when it was stripped of its aesthetics. It was investigated how deep learning could be used in ecological research, specifically in biological species identification, spatiotemporal coverage, and socio-ecological insight. A subset of photo categorization is wildlife identification, in which various cats have a great deal of visual resemblance. This sort of classification is known as fine-grained classification. A classification based on similar visual qualities, for example, is what face recognition can be considered (Gomez-Donoso.F, 2021).

Figure 4. Samples present in the wildlife dataset

Face pre-processing, on the other hand, is common in modern procedures because of the inherent geometric similarities between faces. Photos of biological species have their own idiosyncrasies, such as the appearance of individuals from the same species depending on their gender and age, as well as how they seem in various conditions. Using low-quality photographs, this study attempts to identify 20 different species of wild animals using a method for animal recognition. When it comes to building an effective solution, one of the most major hurdles is a lack of balanced data. Data augmentation and network topologies like Efficient Net are also taken into account. As a result, although using ensemble learning and acknowledging significant gains, these systems do not go into great detail as only a handful of experts can select the correct class for each category. As a result, the number of photographs is frequently restricted due to the added complexity of include thorough expert annotations. However, this strategy will include a data transfer learning approach. The problem is that this technique requires retraining models with enormous datasets that do not perform well in comparison to the amount of time it takes to run the computations. Each class's frequency drops as the similarity scale is dipped further down. There must be the creation of automated systems that are able to distinguish between an immense number of potentially identical categories, even if only a few samples are available for some categories (Liu.Y, 2020).

Architectures were tested and validated using the dataset. The specimens in this collection are arranged in a taxonomic hierarchy depending on the taxonomic rank of the biological units. There is a category for each level of the taxonomic tree from the first to the last. The dataset includes 1010 images of plants, insects, birds, and reptiles and the samples are shown in Figure 4 (Gomez-Donoso.F, 2021).

Despite having high-quality and resolution photos and many samples, the dataset includes significant flaws that may impair the effectiveness of algorithms trained with it.

Anomaly Detection

Unusual events such as people fighting or fires are the focus of the video's abnormal event detection segment. The task is crucial in computer vision, both in academia and industry. "Automatic detection of rare or exceptional events and behaviours in surveillance footage is becoming increasingly necessary as the number of cameras increases. The definition ambiguity and limitations of the data-generating mechanism make it difficult to create a generic detection framework for anomalous events, which has prompted a number of computer vision-based studies (Schmidhuber.J, 1997).

Deep learning technologies have been used to detect anomalous events utilising unsupervised and weakly supervised methods. One of the more recent developments in deep learning video processing is the use of two-stream networks, which have been successfully employed for video-based action identification, often with state-of-the art results. Deep learning models present a black-box conundrum that none of these solutions consider, despite their excellent performance. A model's interpretability is critical for a method's ability to produce dependable findings in the real world.

Combining Convolutional Long Short-Term Memory (Conv-LSTM), (Chen.C, 2018) with the Auto encoder model, which outputs the reconstructed sequence input at the present and last time, can help you learn the video's appearance and action information. Spatiotemporal structure of video anomaly detection, including crowd scenes, is ideal for this method. We use multiple instance learning (MIL) to automatically develop a deep anomaly ranking model that predicts high anomaly scores for anomalous video segments by treating normal and anomalous films as bags and video segments as instances. In addition, we apply sparsity and temporal smoothness requirements in the ranking loss function to improve anomaly localization during training.

CONCLUSION

In industry and research, big data applications are taking up the majority of the space. Video streams from CCTV cameras play an equal part in big data as other sources such as social media data, sensor data, farm data, medical data, and data derived from space research. Surveillance videos contribute significantly to unstructured big data. Pre-processing is required prior to analysis and predictions because of the vast volume of picture and video data generated by computer monitoring systems as a result of the development of new technologies. This chapter focuses on the application of deep learning to solve problems with image and video processing. FCN, AlexNet, YOLO, and other deep learning models have improved elements such as processing power, accuracy and input parameters as well as reducing computation time through advances.

REFERENCES

Ahmed, H. M., & Essa, H. S. (2021). Survey of intelligent surveillance system for monitoring international border security. *Materials Today: Proceedings.*

Brunetti, A., Buongiorno, D., Trotta, G. F., & Bevilacqua, V. (2018). Computer vision and deep learning techniques for pedestrian detection and tracking: A survey. *Neurocomputing, 300,* 17–33. doi:10.1016/j.neucom.2018.01.092

Chen, C., & Shah, M. (2018). Real-World Anomaly Detection in Surveillance Videos. IEEE.

Elharrouss, O., Almaadeed, N., & Al-Maadeed, S. (2021). A review of video surveillance systems. *Journal of Visual Communication and Image Representation, 77,* 103116. doi:10.1016/j.jvcir.2021.103116

Gomez-Donoso, F., Escalona, F., Pérez-Esteve, F., & Cazorla, M. (2021). Accurate multilevel classification for wildlife images. *Computational Intelligence and Neuroscience.* PMID:33868399

Iqbal, M. J., Iqbal, M. M., Ahmad, I., Alassafi, M. O., Alfakeeh, A. S., & Alhomoud, A. (2021). Real-Time Surveillance Using Deep Learning. *Security and Communication Networks.*

Liu, Y., Yu, H., Gong, C., & Chen, Y. (2020). A real time expert system for anomaly detection of aerators based on computer vision and surveillance cameras. *Journal of Visual Communication and Image Representation*, *68*, 102767. doi:10.1016/j.jvcir.2020.102767

Manikandan, V. P., & Rahamathunnisa, U. (2022). A neural network aided attuned scheme for gun detection in video surveillance images. *Image and Vision Computing*, *120*, 104406. doi:10.1016/j.imavis.2022.104406

Schmidhuber, J., & Hochreiter, S. (1997). Long short-term memory. *Neural Computation*, *9*(8), 1735–1780. doi:10.1162/neco.1997.9.8.1735 PMID:9377276

Shana, L., & Christopher, C. S. (2019, March). Video Surveillance using Deep Learning-A Review. In *2019 International Conference on Recent Advances in Energy-efficient Computing and Communication (ICRAECC)* (pp. 1-5). IEEE.

Sreenu, G., & Durai, S. (2019). Intelligent video surveillance: A review through deep learning techniques for crowd analysis. *Journal of Big Data*, *6*(1), 1–27. doi:10.118640537-019-0212-5

Tuia, D., Kellenberger, B., Beery, S., Costelloe, B. R., Zuffi, S., Risse, B., Mathis, A., Mathis, M. W., van Langevelde, F., Burghardt, T., Kays, R., Klinck, H., Wikelski, M., Couzin, I. D., van Horn, G., Crofoot, M. C., Stewart, C. V., & Berger-Wolf, T. (2022). Perspectives in machine learning for wildlife conservation. *Nature Communications*, *13*(1), 1–15. doi:10.103841467-022-27980-y PMID:35140206

Wang, X. (2013). Intelligent multi-camera video surveillance: A review. *Pattern Recognition Letters*, *34*(1), 3–19. doi:10.1016/j.patrec.2012.07.005

Yu, C., Wang, J., Peng, C., Gao, C., Yu, G., & Sang, N. (2018). Bisenet: Bilateral segmentation network for real-time semantic segmentation. In *Proceedings of the European conference on computer vision (ECCV)* (pp. 325-341). 10.1007/978-3-030-01261-8_20

Chapter 3

Deep Learning Architecture for a Real-Time Driver Safety Drowsiness Detection System

Sangeetha J.

SASTRA University (Deemed), India

ABSTRACT

According to the reports from the World Health Organization (WHO), one of the primary causes that led to death in the world was road accidents. Every year, numerous road accidents are caused by drivers due to their drowsiness. It can be minimized by alerting the driver, and it has been done by identifying and recognizing the initial stages of drowsiness. Several models have been proposed to detect drivers' drowsiness and alert them before a road accident occurs. However, the most prominent one is VGG16 with a transfer learning mechanism that is utilized to view the status of the respective regions of interest. By utilizing these models, the drivers are monitored, and alarms are generated to alert the drivers as well as the passengers. This experimental analysis was carried out on the Kaggle Yawn-Eye-Dataset (KYED), and the results showed the low computational intricacy and high precision of the eye closure estimation and the ability of the proposed system for drowsiness detection.

INTRODUCTION

Drowsiness is considered to be a prime factor in causing road accidents. It is a central point behind injuries and fatalities happening in high-risk workplaces and road traffic. It is expressed by a diminished degree of concentration and vigilance that can produce health consequences, impaired performance, cognition, workplace accidents, and motor conveyance crashes (Gangadharan, S.et al., 2022). Consistently, drowsy driving records for around 71,000 injuries, 1,550 fatalities, and 100,000 crashes, as indicated by the National Safety Council (NSC). The principal impacts of drowsy driving are nodding off, inability to focus, inability to judge distance and speeds, poor judgment, and delayed reaction times.

The main objective of the drowsiness detection system is to prevent accidents involving commercial vehicles. Three networks are considered to be potential networks for eye status classification, one of

DOI: 10.4018/978-1-7998-8892-5.ch003

which is a Convolutional Neural Network (CNN). By utilizing this network based on the VGG16 model, it can be used to detect the drowsy state depending on the eye aspect ratio. This system will detect the early symptoms of drowsiness before the drivers have completely lost all attention and it will caution the drivers that they are presently not equipped to operate the vehicle securely.

RELATED WORK

A system was implemented by using the Convolution Neural Network (CNN) and the Bidirectional Long-Term Dependencies (BiLSTM) approach (Rajamohana, S. P et al., 2021) to detect the driver's drowsiness. This system works in three phases. In the first phase, a web camera was used to observe the driver's face image. In the second phase, the eye image features were extracted using the Euclidean algorithm. In the final phase, the eye blinks were continually monitored. When drowsiness was detected, the system warns the driver with an alarm message. A new deep learning algorithm (Guarda, L.et al., 2022) known as a capsule neural network for detecting drowsiness was developed by Guarda *et al.,* This algorithm was used to maintain the data's hierarchical relationships, which was an essential role in working with biomedical signals. It has been used concatenated spectrogram images of Electroencephalogram (EEG) signal channels for detection purposes. By using this CapsNet model, the average accuracy has been obtained by 86.44% and 87.57% of sensitivity.

A wireless consumer-grade electroencephalogram to detect symptoms of driver drowsiness based on EEG signal was proposed (Gangadharan, S.et al., 2022). Data accumulation was done by utilizing a muse headband with concurrent heart rate measurement and performed feature selection to find optimal features for detection. EEG data was used to segregate the drowsy states and alerts, and it has been done with a precision of 78%.

A deep-rhythm-based method has been proposed (Turkoglu, M.et al., 2021) to detect drowsiness efficiently. The Short-time Fourier transform (STFT) has been used to convert EEG signals into EEG images and also, based on frequency intervals, by partitioning EEG images, the rhythm images were then extracted from them. There are five kinds of rhythm, Delta, Theta, Alpha, Beta, and Gamma. Based on pre-trained CNN with ResNet (Residual Network), the deep features were extracted for each rhythm image. The obtained features were fed into the long short-term memory (LSTM) layer to recognize the class labels of input signals. The average accuracy has been achieved at 97.92%.

The Genetic Algorithm-based Support Vector Machine (GA-SVM) for detecting drowsiness was implemented (Wang, H.et al., 2021). In this experiment, by dividing the initial signals into several epochs, a disintegration process has been carried out on the signals of every epoch by utilizing the Haar wavelet transform and db10. For detection purposes, two methods have been widely used for selecting a definite rhythm and evaluating its performance. They are GA-SVM and LOSO-CV (Leave-One-Subject-Out Cross-Validation), respectively, with an accuracy rate of 89.52%.

Based on the Convolutional Neural Network, the drowsiness state has been identified by using deep learning algorithms (Allam, J. P.et al., 2022). From the raw EEG signal, different features have been extracted automatically by using this algorithm, and the most important one is that the signal should be a single channel. By using the deep learning classifier, the detection of the drowsiness state was done with an accuracy of 98.20%. To discover shared EEG features across different subjects for driver drowsiness detection was done (Cui, J.et al., 2022) using CNN. Incorporating a Global Average Pooling (GAP) layer into this model structure, the input signal regions were localized using the CAM (Class

Activation Map) method in these models, and they contributed the most to classification. The average precision has been achieved at 73.22%.

Signals from multiple frequency sub bands have been decomposed by using the Flexible Analytic Wavelet Transform (FAWT) method (Sharma, S.et al., 2021), and also multiple features have been extracted from them. Using statistical analysis to select an optimal feature and various classification techniques have been employed to classify alert signals and drowsy states. The average accuracy rate has been obtained by 95.6%.

A new model approach has been designed (Zhang, X.et al., 2020) in this model by combining the differences in individuality with the time cumulative effect (TCE) of drowsiness to detect the drowsiness level. Through a driving simulator, the data was accumulated, and based on their state of drowsiness, the drivers' perceptions were recorded by using the Karolinska Sleepiness Scale (KSS). A model called Mixed-effect Ordered Logit (MOL) was established when the degree of drowsiness was shown to be increasing at that time. By using the MOL-TCE model, the detection accuracy was achieved by 62.84%.

Based on EEG signals, a multi-dimensional feature classification system and Multi-Source Signal alignment (MSSA) were implemented (Shen, M.et al., 2021) for detection. Signals from multiple sources were precisely aligned with the target using one-versus-one minimization of signal matrices and multi-dimensional features were extracted and separated by using a tensor network (TN). MSSA-TN has improved classification accuracy by at least 3.71%.

A system has been approached for extracting the drowsy features to accurately detect the drowsiness state. For this implementation, two extraction techniques (Vijayan, V.et al., 2020) have been used, known as Root SIFT (an enhanced SIFT) and SIFT (Scale Invariant Future Transform). By utilizing these methods, the feature extractions have been done individually, and some comparisons have been made between them to find accuracy. This experiment has shown that the Root SIFT algorithms work better than the SIFT ones in terms of speed, latency, performance, and run time. The detection precision rate has been obtained at 93.55%. However, it has been done successfully only by extracting the relevant and valid features.

There are various algorithms and methods that I have been referred to, and those are given in the following Table 1.

VGG16 ARCHITECTURE

The most prominent substructure of this ground-shattering object concession model is the VGG architecture. When compared to ImageNet, VGGNet outperforms in a wide range of datasets and tasks. In addition, it is currently quite possibly the most famous image recognition architecture. The VGG model, or VGGNet, that upholds 16 layers is additionally alluded to as VGG16 (Al-Masawabe, M. M.et al., 2022), which is a convolutional network model.

For any inputs with RGB channels, the network configuration is always considered to be a fine-tuned 224 x 224 image. During the preprocessing method, the RGB values for every pixel should be normalized. This process has been successfully done only by reducing the mean value of every pixel.

The image was given as an input to the first main stack that contains two convolution layers with a minute size of 3x3, followed by Rectified Linear Unit (Salman, F. M.et al., 2022). There are a total of 64 filters for each of these two layers. The padding is 1 pixel and the convolutional stride is fixed at 1

Table 1. Literature Review

S.NO	Year	Author	Methods	Advantages	Disadvantages
1	Mar 2021	Siwar Chabene, Bassem, *et al.,* [12]	EEG Signal Detection, Signal Annotation	High Accuracy and Data Augmentation to overcome overfitting.	EEG Classification Expensive ad can't be implemented practically.
2	2021	Abedelmalik moujahid, Fadi Dornaika, JorgeReta *et al.,* [13]	Face monitoring system to extract the effective features from the face image	The performance is superior to several approaches that are based on deep neural networks.	It is a static approach, and the drowsy gestures are simulated and could be far from natural symptoms.
3	Jan 2020	Rateb Jabbar, Mohammed Shinoy, Mohammed Karbeche *et al.,* [14]	Signal Collection using a wearable Emotiv EPOC+ headset to record 14 channels of EEG.	Model Size, storage, and complexity had a great markdown in complexity	Obstruction of Facial Features by wearing sunglasses and bad lighting conditions.
S.NO	Year	Author	Methods	Advantages	Disadvantages
4	2020	Haider Kaseem, Ahmed al-sudani, *et al.,* [16]	Used RESNET-50 to classify the state	Using RESNET-50 allowed them to classify the states as early fatigue/Extremely fatigued.	Video Capturing of Space-Temporal Elements can have drawbacks in case of low levels of illumination.
5	Nov 2020	Zuopeng Zhao, Nana Zhao, Lan Zhang, Hualin Yan *et al.,* [17]	MTCNN Architecture for facial bounding box and PERCLOS and POM to evaluate the state of Mouth	MTCNN Architecture constructs a perfect facial bounding box.	Detection was profoundly dependent on the road environment and the individual driving characteristics.

pixel. The size of the resultant activation map and the spatial resolution was protected by this design, which is equivalent to the input image dimensions.

These maps are then generated through max pooling with a 2-pixel stride. It truncates the range of the activation map by half. Thus, the first stack yields the activation map, whose range is 112 x 112 x 64. These activations are then passed through the second stack. Unlike the first one, it contains 128 channels for each convolutional layer.

Consequently, the size of the activation map is reduced to 56 x 56 x 128 and it can be given as an input to the third stack. This stack contains the maximum pool layer and 3 convolutional layers.

Unlike the second stack layer, it contains 256 filters for each layer, which makes the resulting intensity of the stack 28 x 28 x 256.

This diminished map was given as an input to the following two stacks of three convolutional layers, where each layer contains 512 filters. At the end of both of these stacks, the range of the activation map will be 7 x 7 x 512.

These layers are then trailed by three completely associated layers (Salman, F. M.et al., 2022), each containing some flattening layer in between them. The first two associated layers contain 4096 neurons each, and the last contains 1000 neurons, which gives the resultant layer. These neurons are related to the ImageNet dataset, which contains over 1000 potential classes. Then, the resulting layer is trailed by a softmax activation layer (Salman, F. M.et al., 2022), which is utilized for absolute grouping.

PROPOSED WORK

Driver drowsiness is one of the primary reasons for road accidents every year. Identifying and recognizing the initial stages of driver drowsiness can alert the driver. If the model notices the driver's drowsiness, it would start to alert the user. With a transfer learning mechanism, VGG16 is used as a potential network for classifying eye and mouth status.

To detect extreme cases of drowsiness, the state of the eyes was looked at while the drivers were driving. They looked to see if the eye was closed or open for successive frames, and if it was closed for more than 12 frames, an alarm was sent to alert the driver. Figures 2 and 3 shows the pre-processing Unit for the eye status feature

The images are initially sent via pre-processing unit shown in Figures 2 and 3, which removes the frame's background information, leaving us with the ROI of a person's head, from which the ROI (Eye) is retrieved, transformed to greyscale, and reshaped to fit the input of the VGG Model. The image from the preprocessing input is fed into the model shown in Figure 4 and 5, which predicts the driver's state.

The proposed methodology has been adjusted to include a new feature that allows us to keep track of the user's mouth. To predict the subtle indications of drowsiness, a similar VGG-16 model can be utilized, which is trained with images of two classes of mouth representing open and closed which is shown in Figures 6 and 7.

The following Figure 8 shows the proposed methodology for detecting soft indicators of tiredness in the user.

Figure 1. Architecture of VGG16

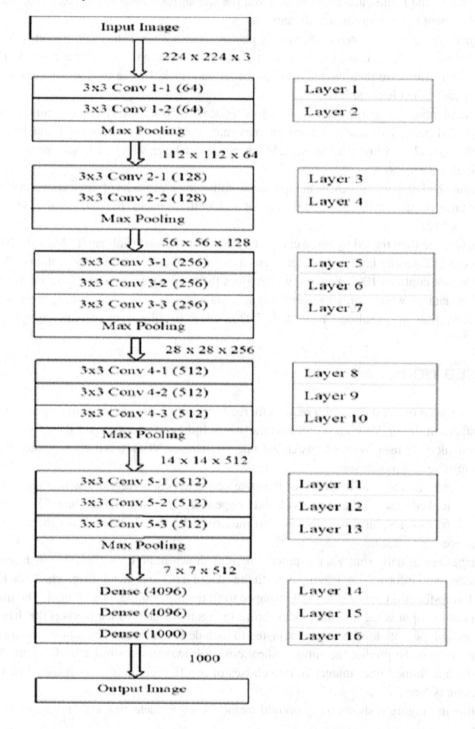

Figure 2. Pre-processing unit for Feature Extraction

```
                          ┌─────────────────────┐
              ┌──────────▶│  Video Feed Input   │◀──────────┐
              │           └─────────────────────┘           │
              │                      │                       │
              │                      ▽                       │
              │               ◇───────────◇                  │
         No   │              ╱             ╲                 │
    ◀─────────┘            ◇  Face Detected?  ◇              │
                            ╲             ╱                   │
                             ◇───────────◇                   │
                                   │ Yes                     │
                                   ▼                         │
                          ┌─────────────────────┐            │
                          │   Extract ROI       │            │
                          │   Head              │            │
                          └─────────────────────┘            │
                                   │                         │
                                   ▼                         │
                          ┌─────────────────────┐            │
                          │   Extract ROI Eye   │            │
                          └─────────────────────┘            │
                                   │                         │
                                   ▼                         │
                          ┌─────────────────────┐            │
                          │ Transform Image to  │            │
                          │ Grayscale           │            │
                          └─────────────────────┘            │
                                   │                         │
                                   ▼                         │
                          ┌─────────────────────┐            │
                          │ Reshape image to fit│────────────┘
                          │ VGG Model           │
                          └─────────────────────┘
```

Figure 3. Sample pre-processing unit for Feature Extraction

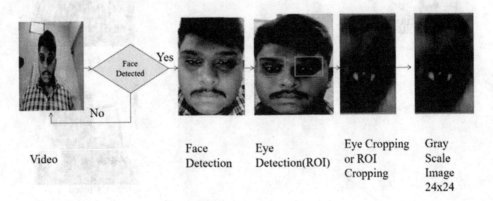

| Video | Face Detection | Eye Detection(ROI) | Eye Cropping or ROI Cropping | Gray Scale Image 24x24 |

Figure 4. Flowchart for detecting drowsiness using eye status

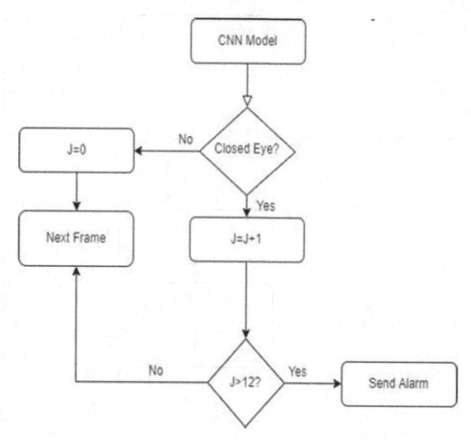

Figure 5. Flowchart for drowsiness using eye status

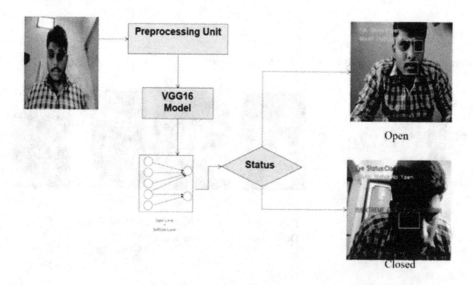

Figure 6. Flowchart for detecting drowsiness using mouth status

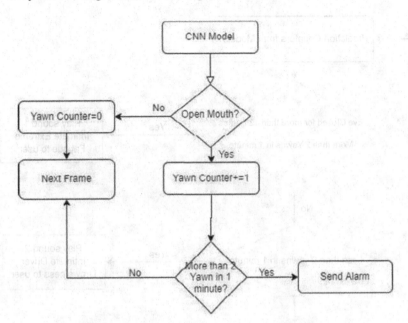

EXPERIMENTAL RESULTS

The VGG-16 Model is used with the transfer learning mechanism, which allows for the prediction of accurate changes in the condition of the eyes and mouth by only training a few layers and leaving the rest untrained. The purpose of the transfer learning mechanism is to take the features learned during training and apply them to an entirely new dataset. To do so, convolution and max pooling layers are unchanged while modifying the dense layers to create a transfer learning Model. So even if most of the layers are being retained as non-trainable there are only 14.7 million non-trainable parameters being produced

Figure 7. Sample drowsiness detection using mouth status

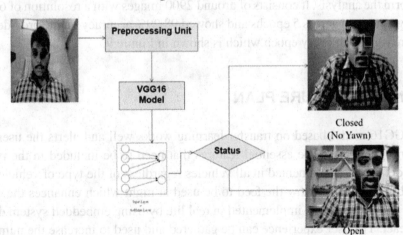

Figure 8. Flowchart for Final drowsiness detection system using Eye status and mouth state features

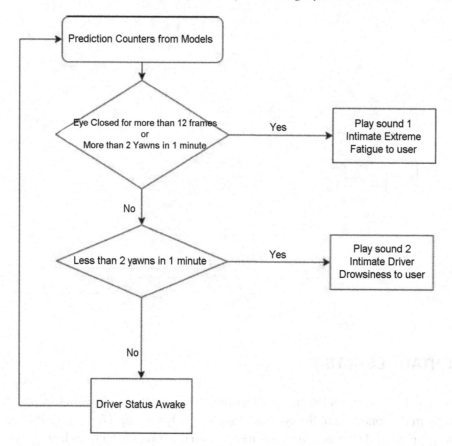

from the model training, the reason being that most of the trainable parameters are being changed as a part of transfer learning. Since most of the parameters are being changed in the dense layer constitute roughly 86% of the trainable parameters near 134 million trainable parameters are a part of the model which helps us in giving good accuracy and precision. In this work, Kaggle Yawn-Eye-Dataset (KYED) was used to perform the analysis. It consists of around 2900 images with a resolution of 640x480 Pixels. The final model was trained across 5 epochs and showed 98.29% accuracy on the provided dataset, with the accuracy increasing with every epoch which is shown in Figure 9.

CONCLUSIONS AND FUTURE PLAN

The proposed VGG16 model based on transfer learning works well and alerts the users to encounter potential disasters. There are some essential features that need to be included in the project to make sure that this model can be implemented in all vehicles regardless of the type of vehicle. For example, IR imaging can be included to allow the feed to be used at night which enhances the driving experience of the user. This work can be implemented in real life by using embedded system design and how drivers usually react. The user experience can be gathered and used to increase the number of features that might help to extract signs of drowsiness and correct them. By increasing the number of features,

Figure 9. Graph for change in Accuracy and Loss in VGG-16 Model

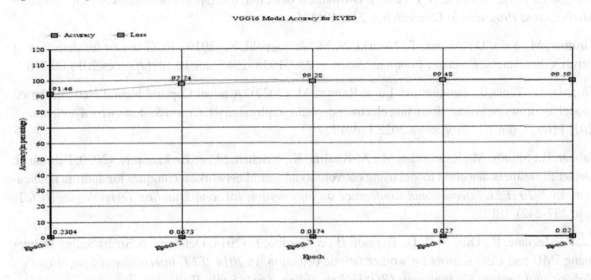

self-braking/self-decelerating features can also be added to slow down cars. A sequence of steps can be implemented to allow the model to identify drowsiness, pull over to the service part of the road and put up hazard warning symbols, to warn the other drivers. By leveraging the utilities provided safer driving can be ensured.

REFERENCES

Al-Masawabe, M. M., Samhan, L. F., Alfarra, A. H., Aslem, Y. E., & Abu-Naser, S. S. (2022). Papaya maturity Classification Using Deep Convolutional. *Neural Networks*.

Al-sudani, A. R. (2020). Yawn based driver fatigue level prediction. *Proceedings of 35th International Confer, 69*, 372-382.

Allam, J. P., Samantray, S., Behara, C., Kurkute, K. K., & Sinha, V. K. (2022). A customized deep learning algorithm for drowsiness detection using single-channel EEG signal. In *Artificial Intelligence-Based Brain-Computer Interface* (pp. 189–201). Academic Press.

Barua, S., Ahmed, M. U., Ahlström, C., & Begum, S. (2019). Automatic driver sleepiness detection using EEG, EOG and contextual information. *Expert Systems with Applications, 115*, 121–135. doi:10.1016/j.eswa.2018.07.054

Chaabene, S., Bouaziz, B., Boudaya, A., Hökelmann, A., Ammar, A., & Chaari, L. (2021). Convolutional neural network for drowsiness detection using EEG signals. *Sensors (Basel), 21*(5), 1734. doi:10.339021051734 PMID:33802357

Cui, J., Lan, Z., Liu, Y., Li, R., Li, F., Sourina, O., & Müller-Wittig, W. (2022). A compact and interpretable convolutional neural network for cross-subject driver drowsiness detection from single-channel EEG. *Methods (San Diego, Calif.), 202*, 173–184. doi:10.1016/j.ymeth.2021.04.017 PMID:33901644

Gangadharan, S., & Vinod, A. P. (2022). Drowsiness detection using portable wireless EEG. *Computer Methods and Programs in Biomedicine, 214*, 106535.

Gromer, M., Salb, D., Walzer, T., Madrid, N. M., & Seepold, R. (2019). ECG sensor for detection of driver's drowsiness. *Procedia Computer Science, 159*, 1938–1946. doi:10.1016/j.procs.2019.09.366

Guarda, L., Tapia, J., Droguett, E. L., & Ramos, M. (2022). A novel Capsule Neural Network based model for drowsiness detection using electroencephalography signals. *Expert Systems with Applications, 201*, 116977. doi:10.1016/j.eswa.2022.116977

Jabbar, R., Shinoy, M., Kharbeche, M., Al-Khalifa, K., Krichen, M., & Barkaoui, K. (2020, February). Driver drowsiness detection model using convolutional neural networks techniques for android application. In *2020 IEEE International Conference on Informatics, IoT, and Enabling Technologies (ICIoT)* (pp. 237-242). IEEE.

Li, P., Meziane, R., Otis, M. J. D., Ezzaidi, H., & Cardou, P. (2014, October). A Smart Safety Helmet using IMU and EEG sensors for worker fatigue detection. In *2014 IEEE International Symposium on Robotic and Sensors Environments (ROSE) Proceedings* (pp. 55-60). IEEE.

Mohana, B., & Rani, S. (2019). CM Drowsiness Detection Based on Eye Closure and Yawning Detection. *Int. J. Recent Technol. Eng, 8*, 1–13.

Moujahid, A., Dornaika, F., Arganda-Carreras, I., & Reta, J. (2021). Efficient and compact face descriptor for driver drowsiness detection. *Expert Systems with Applications, 168*, 114334. doi:10.1016/j.eswa.2020.114334

Nojiri, N., Kong, X., Meng, L., & Shimakawa, H. (2019). Discussion on machine learning and deep learning based makeup considered eye status recognition for driver drowsiness. *Procedia Computer Science, 147*, 264–270. doi:10.1016/j.procs.2019.01.252

Poursadeghiyan, M., Mazloumi, A., Saraji, G. N., Baneshi, M. M., Khammar, A., & Ebrahimi, M. H. (2018). Using image processing in the proposed drowsiness detection system design. *Iranian Journal of Public Health, 47*(9), 1371. PMID:30320012

Rajamohana, S. P., Radhika, E. G., Priya, S., & Sangeetha, S. (2021). Driver drowsiness detection system usina g hybrid approach of convolutional neural network and bidirectional long short term memory (CNN_BILSTM). *Materials Today: Proceedings, 45*, 2897–2901. doi:10.1016/j.matpr.2020.11.898

Salman, F. M., & Abu-Naser, S. S. (2022). Classification of Real and Fake Human Faces Using Deep Learning. *International Journal of Academic Engineering Research, 6*(3).

Schwarz, C., Gaspar, J., Miller, T., & Yousefian, R. (2019). The detection of drowsiness using a driver monitoring system. *Traffic Injury Prevention, 20*(sup1), S157-S161.

Sharma, S., Khare, S. K., Bajaj, V., & Ansari, I. A. (2021). Improving the separability of drowsiness and alert EEG signals using analytic form of wavelet transform. *Applied Acoustics, 181*, 108164.

Shen, M., Zou, B., Li, X., Zheng, Y., Li, L., & Zhang, L. (2021). Multi-source signal alignment and efficient multi-dimensional feature classification in the application of EEG-based subject-independent drowsiness detection. *Biomedical Signal Processing and Control, 70*, 103023.

Turkoglu, M., Alcin, O. F., Aslan, M., Al-Zebari, A., & Sengur, A. (2021). Deep rhythm and long short term memory-based drowsiness detection. *Biomedical Signal Processing and Control*, *65*, 102364. doi:10.1016/j.bspc.2020.102364

Vijayan, V., & Pushpalatha, K. P. (2020). A comparative analysis of RootSIFT and SIFT methods for drowsy features extraction. *Procedia Computer Science*, *171*, 436–445. doi:10.1016/j.procs.2020.04.046

Wang, H., Zhang, L., & Yao, L. (2021). Application of genetic algorithm based support vector machine in selection of new EEG rhythms for drowsiness detection. *Expert Systems with Applications*, *171*, 114634.

Zhang, X., Wang, X., Yang, X., Xu, C., Zhu, X., & Wei, J. (2020). Driver drowsiness detection using mixed-effect ordered logit model considering time cumulative effect. *Analytic Methods in Accident Research*, *26*, 100114. doi:10.1016/j.amar.2020.100114

Zhao, Z., Zhou, N., Zhang, L., Yan, H., Xu, Y., & Zhang, Z. (2020). Driver fatigue detection based on convolutional neural networks using EM-CNN. *Computational Intelligence and Neuroscience*.

Chapter 4
Deep Learning–Based Computer Vision for Robotics

Manivannan Doraipandian
SASTRA University (Deemed), India

Sriram J.
SASTRA University (Deemed), India

Yathishan D.
SASTRA University (Deemed), India

Palanivel S.
SASTRA University (Deemed), India

ABSTRACT

Under vision research, processes, and criteria for robotic vision based on multiple stages were set based on prerequisites for robot vision success, need for vision in industries, and advancements in image processing techniques. AI helps robotics by allowing a collaborative robot to accomplish new jobs based on data trends. Deep learning-based artificial vision is used to replicate human vision. Deep learning uses general-purpose learning techniques and convolution neural networks to learn data-driven representations. Deep learning helps vision robots remove overlaps, distortions, and misalignments. Vision control using a recognition algorithm based on vision schemes is highlighted. In this chapter, existing forms of mobile, data acquisition and control, manipulating, and vision-based robotic systems are introduced. Robotics' key focus areas, such as posture estimation, path planning, and mobility based on picture memory and deep learning, enable qualitative topological navigation, localization, and mapping of the environment.

INTRODUCTION

"Robotic vision" is one of the most recent advancements in robotics and automation. In essence, robot vision is a sophisticated technology that aids a robot, usually an automated robot, in better-recognizing things, navigating, finding objects, inspecting, and handling parts or bits before performing an application.

DOI: 10.4018/978-1-7998-8892-5.ch004

Robot vision typically employs a variety of complicated algorithms, calibration, and temperature sensing sensors, all of which have variable degrees of complexity and application. Robotic vision is continually developing and going in smoother directions, just as technology is rapidly advancing in sophistication.

The method of processing, characterizing, and decoding data from photos leads to vision-based robot arm guiding, dynamic inspection, and increased identification and component position capabilities. One of the most recent developments in robotics and automation is robotic vision. In essence, robotic vision is a sophisticated technology that helps a robot, usually an autonomous robot, recognize items, navigate, identify objects, inspect, and handle parts or pieces before completing an application.

Importance of Vision in Robotics

Vision has received the greatest research attention, maybe even more than the senses of touch and hearing. Visual inspection software and artificial intelligence tools for scene analysis are frequently used interchangeably when discussing robot vision Sethuramasamyraja, B et al(2003). The apparent discrepancy between image processing technology and robot vision requirements simply cannot be resolved. Prerequisites for successful robot vision include the following:

- Dependable operation
- Cheap cost
- Fundamental simplicity
- Quick image processing
- Scene illumination simplicity

These requests contradict research organisations' conclusions. High-resolution greyscale image processing can provide amazing results, but it costs processor architecture and time. Dedicated image processing systems solve the problem of processing speed spectacularly, however many academics prefer to find a technological challenge in image processing for their own study rather than simplify the imaging difficulties.

ROBOT VISION

Theorem

"The manipulation of a point in space, x_1, by either a robot manipulator which moves it to another point, x_2, or through a camera system which images the point onto a camera sensor at x_2, is described by the same matrix transformation which is of the form: $x_2 = T x_1$. The transformation matrix, T, can describe the first order effects of translation, rotation, scaling, projective and perspective projections."

The detection of a collection of points on an object is connected in some way, according to this theorem. The question is how to make a smart robot system out of this interaction. It can continue by deducing or inducing, two logical techniques that have previously served science well.

Procedure for Robot Vision

The Internet of Things, Industry 4.0, and the increased usage of artificial intelligence, machine learning, and other technologies confront users and developers of vision systems with significant obstacles in selecting the best solution for their application. On the other hand, machine vision is not limited to highly automated operations; it may also be used in areas where a lot of manual labour is required. Machine vision engagement can be divided into four stages.

Stage 1: Aiding manual assembly
Stage 2: Integrating a manual assembly process
Stage 3: Automated inspection
Stage 4: Process control using vision

Aiding Manual Assembly

Many goods are manually constructed in the manufacturing industry, relying on the operator's competence to 'get it right.' As part of the QC process, another staff member frequently visually inspects these products. Installing a vision system to take over inspection reduces the likelihood of a defective product reaching a customer, which is good for reputation but does little to lower rework costs. Each completed step can be validated and recorded, providing data for assembly work analysis and traceability.

Integrating a Manual Assembly Process

A more sophisticated vision system will assist with manual assembly, providing a broader range of measurement and inspection tools while highlighting any assembly errors on the display monitor. As needed, assembly instructions and manufacturing data could be downloaded to the system from a central database. This approach would also allow for the introduction of various safeguards; the availability of these advanced vision tools also enables the system to accommodate new requirements as new products enter the market.

Automated Inspection

Products or components are inspected, often at high speed, and either accepted or rejected based on measurements. Vision systems can range from a single-point self-contained smart camera, where all processing and measurement are done in the camera and a pass/fail result is sent back to the reject mechanism, to PC-based systems with multiple cameras and inspection stations.

Process Control using Vision

Using automated vision as a QC tool significantly reduces the possibility of an 'out of spec' product reaching an end-user. When combined with statistical process control and feedback methods, it can check critical measurements and analyze trends in these measurements and make process changes. In this manner, interventions can be made to adjust the process before producing any out-of-tolerance product.

Figure 1. Robotic vision system

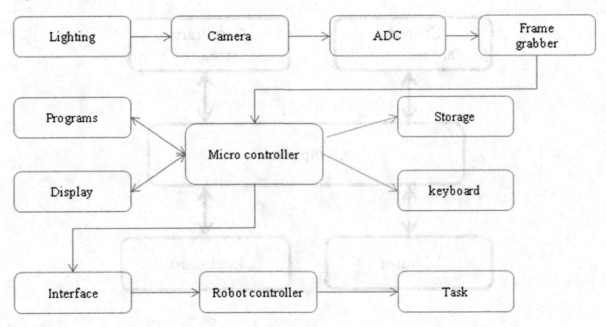

Robotic Vision System

Sensing and Digitizing Image Data

A camera is used for sensing and digitizing pictures. It will use specialized lighting to boost visual contrast. The frame of vision data is the digital representation of these pictures. A-frame grabber takes digitized images at 30 frames per second. Rather than a scene projection, each frame is a matrix. This technique converts each pixel's intensity into a digital value recorded in the com memory. These include structured light, front/backlighting, beam splitters, and retro reflectors.

Image Processing and Analysis

The image interpretation and data reduction processes are carried out in this function. For data reduction, the threshold of an image frame is created as a binary image. The components of robotic vision system are shown in figure 1. Data reduction will aid in converting the frame from raw image data to feature value data. Computer programming can be used to calculate the feature value data. This is accomplished by comparing image descriptors such as size and appearance to previously stored data on the computer. The complete interface is how in figure 2.

Regularly training the machine vision system will improve the image processing and analysis function. Several data types are collected during the training process, including perimeter length, outer and inner diameters, area, etc.

Image processing is forming an image for later analysis and use. It identifies, simplifies, modifies, or enhances an image using techniques such as image analysis and histograms.

Figure 2. Interfacing components

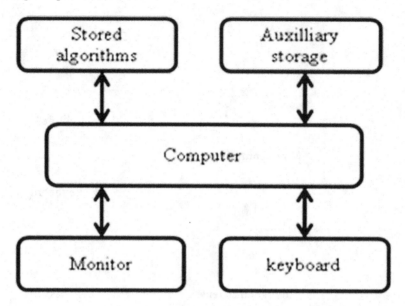

Threshold is a method that identifies each image and then compares it to the database of pixels that have been categorised by the threshold. To create a picture, the pixels are aligned to various levels after being compared. Pixels that share a colour and texture region can be connected to each other through a "**connectivity route.**"

Types of Robotic System

Industrial robots with many-degrees-of-freedom manipulators and specialised actuators have reduced manual labour. A high-degree-of-freedom manipulator is like a human hand in movement and function. A manipulator's control system is application-specific. Industrial robots with several manipulators are prevalent. Robotic systems are classified into three applications.

- Mobile robotic system
- Manipulation robotic system
- Data acquisition and control robotic system

Manipulation Robotic System

In the industrial sector, the manipulation robot system is the most extensively used. Robot arms with 4-6 axes of motion and degrees of freedom are used in these systems. They can be used for a variety of purposes, including welding, material removal, and material handling, among others.

Mobile Robotic System

Moving things from one location to another is a frequent function of mobile robotic systems. With a pre-programmed destination from which the device may load or unload itself, autonomous mobility is also conceivable. Moving tools and replacement parts is its principal function in the manufacturing business. Mobile robotic systems can also be used on farms to pull ploughs or convey agricultural goods.

Data Acquisition and Control Robotic System

For the purpose of generating signals, the data acquisition and control robotic system collects, processes and transfers data. The signals generated by a robotic control system can be utilized to operate additional robots. Robotic systems for data collecting and control are used in CAD systems for engineering and business. Data acquisition and control robotic systems aboard autonomous ships used for seabed research capture and deliver signals back to shore.

AI AND ITS SUBSETS IN ROBOTICS

AI and machine learning influence four areas of robotic operations to make present applications more efficient and lucrative. The scope of AI in robotics covers the following:

Vision- AI assists robots in detecting stuff they have never seen before and recognizing objects in greater detail.

Gripping - Robots are grasping objects they've never seen before, with AI and machine learning assisting them in determining the ideal posture and orientation to grasp an object.

Motion Control - Machine learning assists robots in maintaining productivity through dynamic interaction and obstacle avoidance.

Data - AI and machine learning both assist robots in understanding physical and logistical data trends in order for them to be proactive and behave appropriately.

Need for Deep Learning in Robotics

Deep Learning Teaches the Robot's Purpose

Deep learning improves processing capability and the necessary datasets, which are ultimately the strongest assets of machine learning. Engineers and scientists must decide how AI learns in order to teach robots machine learning.

Planning and Learning are Fed to Robots

Planning is a physical method of training robots that assumes the robots must move every joint at a specific rate to perform a job. Learning takes many inputs and reacts to the data provided in a dynamic context. Physical demonstrations in which motions are learned, stimulation of 3D artificial environments, and feeding video and data of a person or another robot executing the action it hopes to perfect for itself are all part of the learning process.

Educating and Training Using Up-To-Date Information

Inaccurate or faulty data will result in nothing but unrest. Inadequate training data will prevent the robot from reaching its maximum performance potential.

Getting the Most out of Physical Assistance

These robots have recently been employed in many areas for various purposes. Aerial robots are taking over building sites. It helps other sectors besides construction. It is used in medicine to detect tumours using computer vision models in MRI and CT images.

A Fuzzy Based Mobile Robot Navigation

When a vision is employed for distance measurements and obstacle detection, a lower-level software framework is necessary. This upper-level system intelligence used a fuzzy decision mechanism.

A neuro-fuzzy system is shown in figure 3. It combines stereo vision and AI technologies handles information exchange and mobile behaviours in navigation maps for mobile intelligence's top layer. At this layer, it's a knowledge-based system Al-Mutib, K et al (2015). PCA-ANN learning reduces the problem's size and scale because to the vast amount of visual sensory and environmental data. SLAM data was used to create maps.

COMPUTER VISION

Computer Vision in Robotics

Robots that lack visual perception are analogous to blind machines designed for repetitive tasks in a single location. Robots are becoming more intelligent due to computer vision, allowing them to see their surroundings and move accordingly to perform various tasks. With the right inputs, computer vision in robotics plays a critical role in making them more intelligent. Robots became robotics when a large amount of training data was used to train such machines and make them more competent even to perform essential tasks in various fields.

Vision Based Control in Harvesting Robot

The natural objects that are managed by harvesting robots are those that have different variations in fruit shape, colour, texture, size and hardness owing to environmental and genetic changes. These variations may be seen in the fruit. Second, the working environment is chaotic and has a disorganised structure, with substantial shifts in illumination and occlusion from various objects. Third, because the locations of the target fruits are chosen at random, choosing them requires following a path that is three-dimensional and always shifting Šuligoj, F et al (2014).

Figure 3. Fuzzy based mobile robot navigation

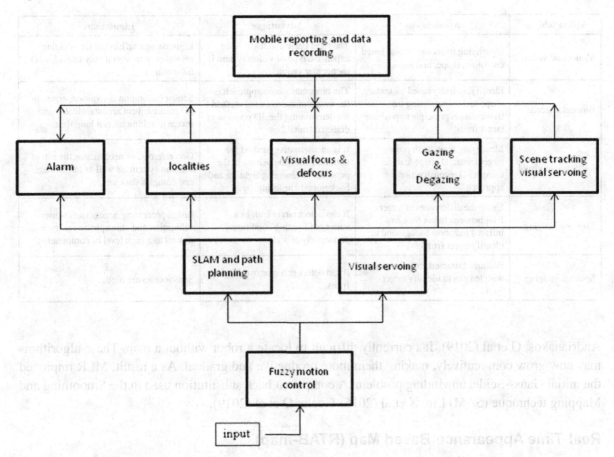

Vision Schemes

Edge detection, color-based analysis, and clustering are among the techniques reviewed in this table.

OBJECT DETECTION AND AUTONOMOUS NAVIGATION

Object detection and convolution neural networks are used in deep learning to identify obstacles in the environment (CNN).Visual SLAM was utilised to help the vehicle determine its position.Object avoidance was made possible through the integration of selfposition and object detection data.Accuracy in selfpose estimate was improved by the addition of a landmark with a known location.

Simultaneous Localization and Mapping (SLAM)

SLAM methods used to construct a map of the environment while concurrently localizing the robot inside it. In practice, these two issues cannot be separated because the robot must first understand how these impressions generated before identifying what nature surrounds it that matches those perceptions

Table 1. Vision schemes and its applications

Vision scheme	Applications	Advantages	Limitations
Monocular vision	Identifying fruits monocular based on colour, shape, and texture	The most basic and least expensive type of vision system is monocular vision.	Light change influences the imaging results even though it only provides 2D information.
Binocular stereo	Identifying fruits based on texture, shape and colour; using the triangulation principle to position target fruits	The binocular stereo approach is the most commonly used method for determining the 3D position of detected fruit.	Sensor calibration is required, errors in 3D measurement are unavoidable and image matching takes a long time.
Laser active visual	Identifying fruits with posing target fruits;3D shape features using a 3D reconstruction approach	It is an alternative method for obtaining the 3D position in the presence of changing lighting and background clustering.	Geo-referencing necessitates the use of a vision system, as well as large image and complex data sets.
Thermal imaging	Using the differences in target fruit between target fruit and infrared radiation background to identify target fruits	It can detect target fruit in a variety of lighting conditions, particularly at night.	Image processing necessitates sensor calibration and atmospheric correction, as well as a high level of computation.
Spectral imaging	Features extracted from invisible wavelengths to identify target fruits	It can detect green or overlapping fruits.	Sensor costs are high.

Andrianakos, G et al (2019). It's currently difficult to locate a robot without a map. These algorithms may now grow consecutively, making them more productive and gradual. As a result, MLR improved the initial Gauss-Seidel unwinding problem. A competent back substitution used in the Smoothing and Mapping technique (SAM) Liu, X et al (2016)-Guclu, O et al (2019).

Real-Time Appearance-Based Map (RTAB-map)

RGB-D, stereo and LIDAR SLAM loop closure detection is provided by the RTAB-Map toolkit. To determine if a new picture is old or new, the loop closure detector makes use of a vocabulary bag. A new restriction is introduced by the graph optimizer. Due to the need for real-time constraints in large-scale applications, loop closure detection and graph optimization sites are restricted. It is possible to map six degrees of freedom using RTAB-Map and a portable Kinect, stereo camera, or 3D LIDAR Liu, X et al (2016)-Guclu, O et al (2019).

Self-Position Estimation

Self-positioning was estimated using RTAB-map, a Visual SLAM framework that uses real-time appearance-based mapping (RTAB-map). To compute the amount of movement between frames, Visual SLAM considers feature points from successive shots and matches the feature points of the images.

You Only Look Once (YOLO V3) Algorithm

YOLO v3 was used to identify barriers and landmarks. YOLO v3 divides an image into grids and guesses each grid's bounding box. Internet images of trees were carefully annotated. Using the depth image and sensed position, the robot's location is established. Direction estimated using the centre pixel coordinates and camera parameter.

There was less of a drift in the anticipated position when a landmark was identified by CNN. According to the monument, the robot's status had been established. Adding information on the estimated location to the necessary SLAM node and changing the frame of reference helped fix the self-position.

OBJECT TRACKING AND ROBOT MANIPULATION

When using a robot to manipulate items, the location of the TCP is critical. Stereo vision cameras and a steering mechanism are built into the robot's two arms Remazeilles, A et al (2007). The final robot is equipped with a waypoint to help it get there. Images are processed, markers are detected, 3-D coordinates are extracted, and coordinate systems are transformed using TCP/IP protocols.

Image Processing with Open CV

Open CV was used to detect 2-D picture markers. First, image circles are detected using the feature extraction method (Hough circle algorithm). Second, two planar templates are used to obtain characteristics using the Speeded Up Robust Features algorithm (SURF)

Hough Circles Algorithm

The Hough circles algorithm looks for circles and stores their two-dimensional coordinates. The picture is filtered by hue, saturation, and value to reduce false readings and add illumination. First, RGB is transformed to HSV (hue, saturation, value). Range filters eliminate all colours except red.

Speeded Up Robust Features Algorithm (SURF)

This method provides 4-corner 2-D scene coordinates. These methods use 2-D image feature extraction; the marker is tilted away from the capture plane. Surf's planar template markers are approximated mathematically.

After calculating object and arm coordinates, a new user frame may be produced. All robot movement happens in an object utilising a user frame, which is beneficial for object handling, camera tracking, and tooling.

NAVIGATION FROM IMAGE MEMORY

The path is defined by a sequence of images or picture paths that have been selected from the database. This image path is designed to give the robots the information they need to do their tasks effectively. In order to get the robot to its final destination, the closed-loop control algorithm uses this visual path. This control does not necessitate a global 3D reconstruction or a time-based planning step.

Figure 4. Image memory based navigation

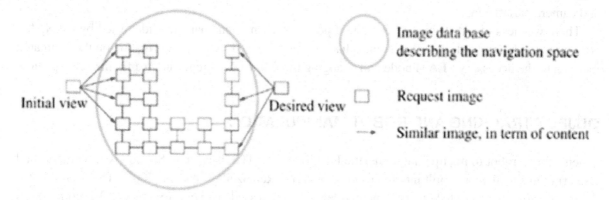

Appearance Based Approach

Appearance-based (or topological) technique doesn't require 3D environment model. It allows direct sensor work. Topological graphs show the surroundings. A connection between two nodes illustrates the robot's autonomous navigation capacity. Vision sensor descriptions pertain to the camera's learning pictures Inoue, K et al (2019). The camera's view and database photos are used to localise.

After linking original and planned photographs to database views, reduce the database to robot movement area images. The robot needs an image path. The proposed approach is unusual because the robotic system is not needed to converge towards each intermediate site associated with route photos, allowing for additional navigational flexibility. Navigation uses visual servoing.

Qualitative Visual Servoing

General Control Loop

- **Point Tracking:** prior view features are monitored to determine their present position.
- **Point Projection Update:** previously unseen features appear. It alerts the system if new objects enter the camera's view.
- **Update Visible Points:** for each set of correspondences in the image path, the current visible points are stored.
- **Interest Set Selection:** Most noticeable interest set is picked. It sets the camera's view.
- **Control Law Update:** The robot's motion is calculated using the interest set. This action allows the robot to go towards a location where the full set is more visible.

ROBOT VISION IN AUTOMATION

In recent years, hybrid systems combining industrial robots and operators have been examined as part of ongoing industrial productivity research. They combine the precision, speed, and repeatability of a

Figure 5. Control loop for visual servoing

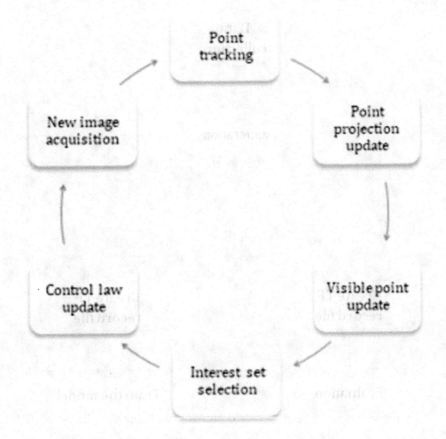

robot with the skill of a person to execute delicate jobs. Sensing systems protect operators, whereas basic workflow monitoring systems, depending on operator feedback, improve the system's dynamic behaviour.

Methodology for Monitoring Human-Based Assembly

Object identification is a challenging topic in computer vision, greatly aided by recent advances in hardware (GPUs) and deep learning techniques Pugh, A. (1983). Object detection is becoming a standard strategy for AI, with algorithms like face detectors being utilized in numerous applications. Object detection is a technique for locating an object in a photograph.

Single Shot Detection Algorithm

SSD (Single Shot Detection) offers a quicker, more accurate way of recognizing items of several categories than region proposal approaches. SSD uses a feed-forward convolution network to recognize objects, which provides a fixed-size collection of boundary boxes and scores. Use a single network without region recommendations. Steps for creating an object detector is shown in figure 6

Instead, modest convolution filters applied to feature maps provide boundary boxes and scores. Predictions from various size feature maps separated by aspect ratio to improve detection accuracy. A

Figure 6. Steps for creating an object detector

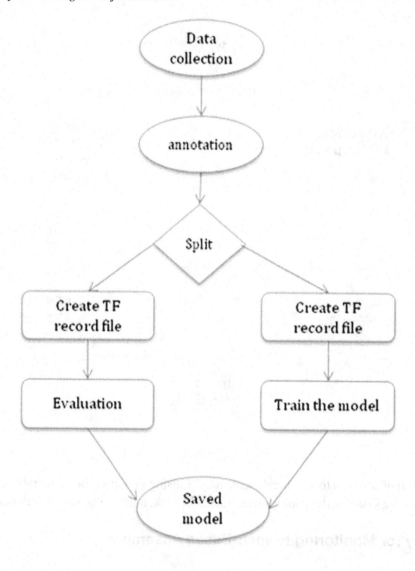

conventional convolution is divided into depth-separable convolutions. By adding this method, it ensures that overlapping occurs when both objects are stable.

CONCLUSION

In this chapter, a study under the advancement in industrial robotics with vision is provided with various vision schemes with different types of robotic systems. Automated navigation with SLAM, RTAB mapping techniques with real time environment is mapped. Object detection with algorithm like SURF provided with fuzzy based decision system provides more accuracy in detecting objects. Implementation of machine vision in automated inspection with qualitative visual servoing is explained in detail.

REFERENCES

Al-Mutib, K., Mattar, E., & Alsulaiman, M. (2015). Implementation of fuzzy decision based mobile robot navigation using stereo vision. *Procedia Computer Science*, *62*, 143–150. doi:10.1016/j.procs.2015.08.427

Andrianakos, G., Dimitropoulos, N., Michalos, G., & Makris, S. (2019). An approach for monitoring the execution of human based assembly operations using machine learning. *Procedia CIRP*, *86*, 198–203. doi:10.1016/j.procir.2020.01.040

Guclu, O., & Can, A. B. (2019). k-SLAM: A fast RGB-D SLAM approach for large indoor environments. *Computer Vision and Image Understanding*, *184*, 31–44. doi:10.1016/j.cviu.2019.04.005

Hall, E. L. (1993, August). Fundamental principles of robot vision. In Intelligent Robots and Computer Vision XII: Active Vision and 3D Methods (Vol. 2056, pp. 321-333). SPIE.

Inoue, K., Kaizu, Y., Igarashi, S., & Imou, K. (2019). The development of autonomous navigation and obstacle avoidance for a robotic mower using machine vision technique. *IFAC-PapersOnLine*, *52*(30), 173–177. doi:10.1016/j.ifacol.2019.12.517

Kim, J. H., Matson, E. T., Myung, H., Xu, P., & Karray, F. (Eds.). (2014). *Robot Intelligence Technology and Applications 2*. Springer. doi:10.1007/978-3-319-05582-4

Liu, X., Guo, B., & Meng, C. (2016, November). A method of simultaneous location and mapping based on RGB-D cameras. In *2016 14th International Conference on Control, Automation, Robotics and Vision (ICARCV)* (pp. 1-5). IEEE. 10.1109/ICARCV.2016.7838786

Prakash, A., & Walambe, R. (2018). *Military surveillance robot implementation using robot operating system. In 2018 IEEE Punecon*. IEEE.

Pugh, A. (1983). Second generation robotics. In *Robot Vision* (pp. 3–10). Springer. doi:10.1007/978-3-662-09771-7_1

Remazeilles, A., & Chaumette, F. (2007). Image-based robot navigation from an image memory. *Robotics and Autonomous Systems*, *55*(4), 345–356. doi:10.1016/j.robot.2006.10.002

Sayed, A. S., Ammar, H. H., & Shalaby, R. (2020, October). Centralized multi-agent mobile robots SLAM and navigation for COVID-19 field hospitals. In *2020 2nd Novel Intelligent and Leading Emerging Sciences Conference (NILES)* (pp. 444-449). IEEE. 10.1109/NILES50944.2020.9257919

Sethuramasamyraja, B., Ghaffari, M., & Hall, E. L. (2003, September). Automatic calibration and neural networks for robot guidance. In Intelligent Robots and Computer Vision XXI: Algorithms, Techniques, and Active Vision (Vol. 5267, pp. 137-144). SPIE. doi:10.1117/12.515036

Šuligoj, F., Šekoranja, B., Švaco, M., & Jerbić, B. (2014). Object tracking with a multiagent robot system and a stereo vision camera. *Procedia Engineering*, *69*, 968–973. doi:10.1016/j.proeng.2014.03.077

Zhao, Y., Gong, L., Huang, Y., & Liu, C. (2016). A review of key techniques of vision-based control for harvesting robot. *Computers and Electronics in Agriculture*, *127*, 311–323. doi:10.1016/j.compag.2016.06.022

Chapter 5
Deep Learning for Emotion Recognition

T. Kavitha

New Horizon College of Engineering (Autonomous), Visvesvaraya Technological University, India

Malini S.

AMC Engineering College, India

Senbagavalli G.

AMC Engineering College, India

ABSTRACT

Deep learning is a type of machine learning that trains a computer to recognizing speech, identifying images or making predictions. Computer vision allows machines to visualize and sense the visual world from digital images or videos. Computer vision can be used for face detection, recognition, and emotion detection. There is a growing demand for emotion analysis in the computer vision market. Expressions play an important role in the recognition of emotions for medical sentiment analysis that can be detected by a deep learning model with the help of trained classes. This chapter focuses on emotion recognition and discusses the different algorithms/architecture developed for emotion recognition using deep learning with the data set. Current research and applications based on emotion recognition are also discussed. This chapter can guide beginners in the field of emotion recognition and provide a general understanding of the latest state of art models, as well as guide the researchers looking for directions for future work.

INTRODUCTION

Facial expressions are a simple way for humans to tell how another person is feeling, but machines find it incredibly difficult to do the same. Partial occlusion and fake emotion expression are some of the challenging issues in emotion recognition. Effective Deep Learning (DL) algorithms in deeper network architectures can mitigate these issues by training, self-adapting and learning the emotional features to recognize the feelings accurately with respect to applications. One can make use of deep learning

DOI: 10.4018/978-1-7998-8892-5.ch005

algorithms to train the computer to understand human emotions. DL is a sort of machine learning that teaches a computer to execute activities similar to those performed by humans. DL is considered as an important topic within the area of machine learning, due to its learning capabilities from the given data. DL has given a great way to crack a variety of computer-vision problems such as image recognition, tracking of an object, human action recognition, emotion recognition, identifying images, and prediction of results. This chapter will examine the main advancements in deep learning algorithms and architecture for emotion detection using sentimental analysis. Emotion recognition allows the machine to understand human feelings through multimedia contents such as images, videos, texts, speech, gestures, and physiological signals.

In this context, DL models like Convolutional Neural Networks(CNNs), Deep Belief Networks(DBNs), Deep Boltzmann Machines(DBMs), and stacked(denoising) autoencoders, Long Short-Term Memory(LSTM), in the category of Recurrent Neural Networks(RNN), is applied in emotion analysis in combination or as stand-alone based on the domain area of application. The advantage of using DL is that it requires less amount of human effort and field knowledge compared to predecessors. Feature extraction is an important topic in emotion analysis. For feature extraction, several layers of nonlinear processing are used by DL algorithms. While lower layers learn basic features from the data input and higher layers derive more advanced features from lower-layers.

Humans will express his emotions through face, gesture, speech, and text that will impact the physiological signals in the human body. Computers now have the ability to understand human emotions and act in accordance with those feelings, which has made the research of Face Emotion Recognition (FER) particularly intriguing. Human-computer interaction, entertainment, and the field of medicine can all benefit from physiological pattern identification of emotion. Stress, rage, and other emotions that have an impact on health can be recognised by physiological pattern recognition. Textual Emotion recognition has become a trend in recent years. Nowadays, everyone started using Twitter for posting their opinions regarding a topic about a movie, product, and politics etc. So it is very important to understand the emotions of a text message on any social media. As human-machine interaction is going to be on its next level with the help of deep learning, machines need to understand what emotion people have conveyed through their speech. Since emotions improve our ability to understand one another, it makes sense to apply this understanding to machines as well. Speech recognition is already a part of daily life; for example, smart mobile devices may accept voice instructions and respond to them with synthesised speech. Robots and human-computer interaction (Abeer et al., 2022) could both benefit from the usage of speech emotion recognition (SER), which would allow computers to recognise human emotions (Schuller, 2018). (Huahu et. al., 2010).

With the development of technologies, there has been an increase in demand for sentiment analysis in a variety of applications, from opinion mining (getting an idea about opinions, and attitudes of humans regarding a topic), medical field, online classes, tourism-based feedback, monitoring of social media, product review, service review. Emotion recognition is critical for human interactions (Cowie et. al., 2001), entertainment (Cosentino et. al.,2018), education, safe driving, and multimedia integration, as well as sentiment analysis, social media monitoring and forecasting, smarter decision aid, dynamic quality adaption to game players, depression recognition (Yang et. al.,2019), and medical rehabilitation for children with autism spectrum disorders.

Emotion Model in DL: Fatemeh et. al., (2021) classified emotion model into three types as follows: In categorical model,emotions are grouped into a collection of discrete classes, such as happiness, sorrow, fear, rage, disgust, and surprise (Figure 1a). In dimensional models, emotions are grouped into

Figure 1. Three categories of emotion models. (a) Categorical (b) dimensional (c) componential model
Fatemeh et. al. (2021)

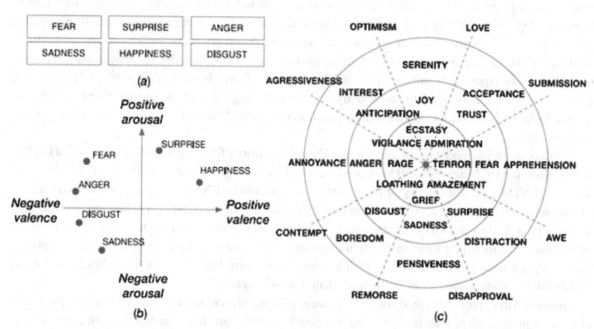

positive and negative quadrants of the 2D space, as indicated in Figure 1b, and are characterized as valence, arousal, and control. Emotions are grouped in a hierarchical order in componential models as illustrated in Figure 1c.

FACIAL EMOTION RECOGNITION

Overview

Facial Expression Categories: Barrett et. al., (2019) discussed the challenges in identifying the emotions from human face movements and in specific it is directed toward the utmost famous emotion consisting of anger, disgust, fear, happiness, sadness, and surprise (ADFHSS). scowling of the face corresponds to anger, a nose-wrinkled face is disgust, a gasping face is fear, a smiling face is happiness, a frowning face is sadness, and a startled face is surprise. But, based on the cultures, situations, and individual expression of ADFHSS varies substantially.

Computers' perception of the face: Human faces in images are recognized by computers decades ago, but now artificial intelligence in computer systems is rivalling humans' ability to classify faces or objects in photos and videos. Techniques developed to detect the face are detecting the facial features and measuring the facial dimensions which are represented as numbers and compared with the data extracted from other reference images. Closer the values, the better the prediction. So, the result depends on the collection of reference images called a dataset. Such techniques require greater computing power and data set with larger size. (Jonathan et. al., 2018).

Figure 2. Conventional FER approach
Ko (2018)

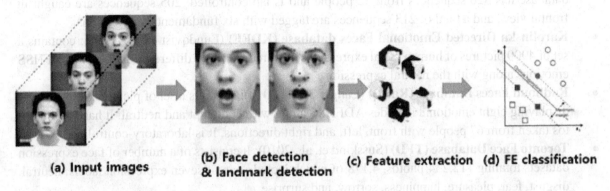

(a) Input images   (b) Face detection & landmark detection   (c) Feature extraction   (d) FE classification

Conventional FER: There are three main steps followed as mentioned in Figure 2: (i) From the input image, a face is recognised, and landmarks like the eyes, nose, mouth, etc. are identified, (ii) In feature extraction, temporal and spatial features extracted and (iii) pre-trained classifier (SVM, AdaBoost, random forest) are used to classify the expressions.

The Deep Learning technique, which yields numerous computer vision algorithms, is the state-of-the-art way to recognize facial expressions in contrast to the conventional approach. The benefit of the deep learning approach is that it relies less on face physical characteristics-based models and preprocessing methods. **(Ko 2018).**

FER Database

Different databases employed 2D static images or 2D video sequences in FER. But addressing significant position variations and facial behaviours is challenging when using 2D picture or 2D video. In the case of 3D facial emotions, it makes it easier to examine the subtle structural alterations seen in unprompted expressions. As a result, this subsection briefly describes a few well-known databases that contain still photographs and 2D and 3D video sequences. Ko (2018), Daniel, António and, Neves(2019), Li and Deng, (2020).

- **Extended Cohn–Kanade database (CK+)** (Lucey et.al., 2010): contains 593 image sequences labelled with eight emotions: It includes ADFHSS along with contempt and neutral.
- **Japanese Female Facial Expression database (JAFFE)** (Lyons et. al., 1998): It is the collection of 213 images of ADFHSS emotions.
- **Binghamton University 3D Facial Expression database (BU-3DFE)** (Yin et. al., 2006): consists of 606 3D facial expression sequences of ADFHSS emotions, plus the neutral expression.
- **Facial Expression Recognition 2013 database (FER-2013)** (Goodfellow et. al., 2013) : 35,887 grayscale images with a 48 × 48 resolution, mapped into the ADFHSS emotions, plus the neutral expression.
- **Emotion Recognition in the Wild database (EmotiW)** (Benitez-Quiroz et. al., 2016) : It has Acted Facial Expression in the Wild (AFEW) and the Static Facial Expression in the Wild (SFEW) with the ADFHSS emotions, plus the neutral expression, and the image size is 128 × 128.

- **MMI database** (Michel et. al., 2010): This database was built on ADFHSS emotions. The MMI database has 326 sequences from 32 people and is lab-controlled. 205 sequences are caught in frontal view, and a total of 213 sequences are tagged with six fundamental expressions.
- **Karolinska Directed Emotional Faces database (KDEF)** (Lundqvist et. al., 1998): contains a set of 4900 pictures of human facial expressions captured from five different angles with ADFHSS emotions along with the neutral expression.
- **Radboud Faces Database (RaFD)** (Langer et. al., 2010): contains a set of pictures of 67 models displaying eight emotional includes ADFHSS along with contempt and neutral. It has 1,608 photos taken from 67 people with front, left, and right directions. It is laboratory-controlled.
- **Toronto Face Database (TFD)** (Susskind et. al., 2010): It consists of a number of face expression datasets totaling 112,234 photos, 4,178 of which include one of seven expression labels: neutral, disgust, fear, pleasure, happiness, sorrow, and surprise.
- **Acted Facial Expressions in the Wild (AFEW)** (Dhall et. al., 2012): 2000 samples roughly divided into 3 sets. ADFHSS and neutral are the seven expressions assigned to Train (773 samples), Val (383 samples), and Test (653 samples).
- **The Static Facial Expressions in the Wild (SFEW)** (Dhall et. al., 2011): Three sets of SFEW 2.0 have been created: Train (958 samples), Val (436 samples), and Test (372 samples).
- **Multi-PIE** (Gross et. al., 2010): The CMU Multi-PIE database contains 755,370 images. . Each facial image is assigned one of the expressions (disgust, neutral, scream, smile, squint, and surprise)that are generally used for multiview facial expression analysis.
- **IRDatabase** (Kopaczka et. al., 2018): It is developed by RWTH Aachen University. The facial expressions present in the dataset includes ADFHSS along with contempt and neutral with a total of 1782. High-resolution thermal infrared camera Infratec HD820 was used to capture the photos for this database.

FER Using Deep Learning

Autoencoders for FER: Muhammad and Junaid (2018), proposed a FER system that consists of face detection using image processing, feature extraction using the HOG algorithm, Stacking stacked autoencoders from high dimensional HOD features to low dimensional features, and lower-dimensional features are used to organize the facial expressions. Input data with a length of "m" is encoded to a lower-dimensional feature vector "a" with a length of "n" and reconstructed as "y" architecture of the auto encoder, is shown in Figure 3. ('n' < 'm'). The performance of auto encoders with encoded features of lengths 5 to 100 is investigated. Authors concluded that as the hidden layers increasing, the enhanced capability of the network which provides optimal features for FER is also increasing.

Infrared thermal images FER using DL: Due to the thermal distribution feature recorded in the infrared spectrum, the thermal images produced by infrared thermal imaging (IRTI) cameras have become more significant. For FER, this is very useful due to the cognitive responses from facial expressions. Bhattacharyya et. al., (2021) proposed a model using CNN called Human InfraRed Facial Expression Network that is designed for infrared images. The deep CNN architecture recognizes different facial expressions more accurately which is useful for facial feature extraction from the input images. It has the Residual unit and the Transformation unit, to extract key elements relevant to the expressions from the input images. The traits that were extracted make it possible to precisely identify the participants under

Figure 3. Architecture of an autoencoder network.

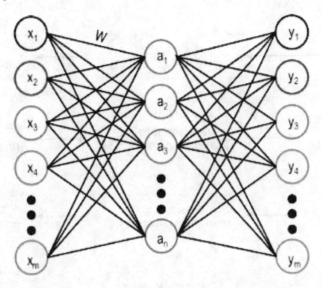

study's emotions. To boost overall performance without raising computational overheads, the Snapshot ensemble approach is used with a Cosine annealing learning rate scheduler.

Figure 4 shows the IRFacExNet model used for HFER, that has been evaluated with facial expression ADFHSS along with contempt and neutral. In the absence of visible light, this model offers a solid framework for the detection of precise expression.

Attentional convolutional network: A convolutional network with less than 10 layers and attention can produce promising results because there aren't many classes in facial expression identification. Based on this fact, Minaee et al. (2021) proposed an end-to-end deep learning framework based on an attentional convolutional network that focuses exclusively on particular regions to gain a sense of the underlying emotion with the aid of an attention mechanism, through a spatial transformer network, in light of this fact.

Figure 5 shows the attentional convolutional model, which has the spatial transformer (the localization network) and Feature extraction part. An affine transformation is utilised in the spatial transformer module, which essentially seeks to concentrate on the most important areas of the image. By estimating a sample over the area of interest, these pertinent portions of the image are created.

Deep Convolutional Neural Networks with Rectified Adam Optimizer: Melinte and Vladareanu (2020) presented the Pipeline technique, which uses two optimised CNNs, one for face recognition (FR) and another for facial expression recognition (FER), to achieve real-time inference speed for the entire procedure.

Two different face recognition architectures methods are considered:

1. Inception for Single Shot Detector (SSD) architecture and ResNet.
2. Inception for Faster Region Proposal Network-based CNN (Faster RPN-CNN)

Face localization is achieved with the help of SSD or RPN architecture, hence only some bottleneck layers are trained. (Transfer learning and Fine Tuning). For emotion recognition, here three CNN models,

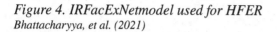

Figure 4. IRFacExNetmodel used for HFER
Bhattacharyya, et al. (2021)

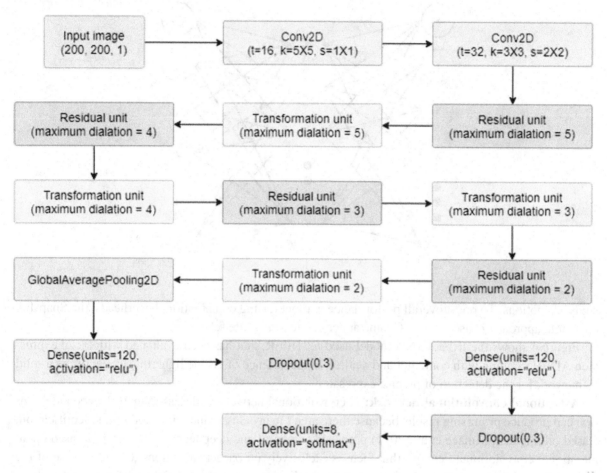

Figure 5. Attentional Convolutional Model
Minaee et. al. (2021)

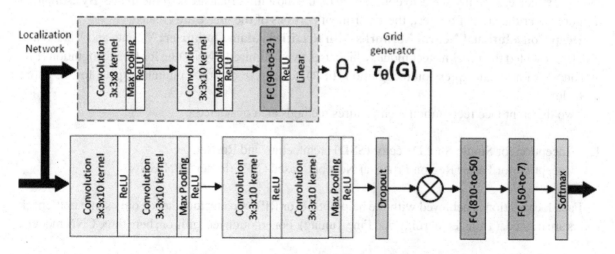

Figure 6. FER Architecture: (a) VGG; (b) ResNet50; and (c) Inception V3
Melinte and Vladareanu (2020)

Figure 6. FER Architecture: (a) VGG; (b) ResNet50; and (c) Inception V3
Melinte and Vladareanu (2020)

(a)   (b)   (c)

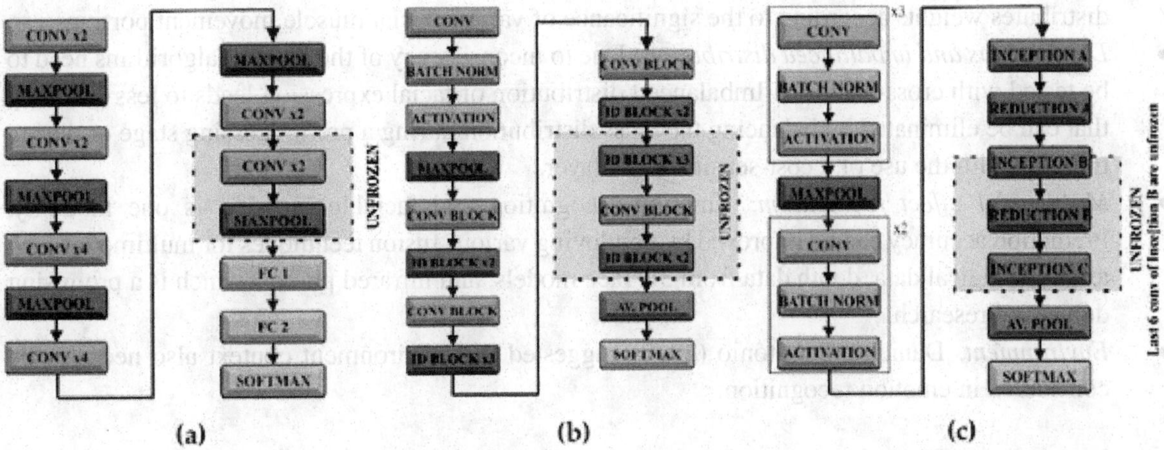

VGG, Inception V3 and ResNet have been used that are shown in Figure 6. The three FER CNN models were trained using a more modern optimization technique termed corrected Adam, which improved generalisation. For face detection, the SSD and Faster R-CNN offer the same accuracy and total loss. ResNet results with the best overall performance for FER detection.

Issues, Challenges and Opportunities in FER

Issuesin FER (Li and Deng 2020):

- *Occlusion and non-frontal head pose:*It alters the face expression's initial visual appearance.
- *RGB or Gray data:* It is vulnerable to ambient lighting conditions. But infrared data are not sensitive to illumination variations.
- *2D FER:* Illumination changes and pose variations are not predicted by the 2D FER. 3D face data are alternative that has depth information with facial deformations which are not affected by the pose and lighting variations.
- *Large Dataset:* Large data set with realistic facial expressions is tedious. Data augmentation will be replaced by facial expression synthesis in order to avoid manually gathering and labelling enormous datasets.
- *Face regions for FER:* Activations of some filters have a strong correlation with the face regions corresponding to the Automatic action Unit. (AU). So, there is a need for visualization techniques to identify the part of the face which produces the utmost discriminatory information that is used for appearance-based learning of FER.
- *Other Issues:* Emotion recognition for Dominant Vs Complementary; Real vs Fake; Unfelt emotions; Depressions recognition also need to be addressed in depth.

Challenges and Opportunitiesin FER (Li and Deng 2020):

- *Dataset:* There is no significant face expression, occlusion, or head-pose annotations.
- *Incorporating other affective models:* Deep neural network filters require a new architecture that distributes weights according to the significance of various facial muscle movement portions.
- *Dataset bias and imbalanced distribution:* Due to inconsistency of the dataset, algorithms need to be tested with cross-database. Imbalanced distribution of facial expression leads to less accuracy that can be eliminated by balancing the class distribution during a pre-processing stage or during training, with the use of a cost-sensitive loss layer.
- *Multimodal affect recognition:* Emotion recognition and facial expression is one modality. Prediction accuracy can be improved by employing various fusion techniques for multimodal such as physiological data, depth data from 3D face models, and infrared photos, which is a promising domain of research.
- *Environment:* Daniel and António (2018) suggested that environment context also needs to be considered in emotion recognition.

GESTURES-BASED EMOTION RECOGNITION(GER)

Overview

According to research done by Ray Birdwhistell on emotion identification using body language (Jolly. 2000), nonverbal communication affects stated information by 65 percent. Body movements, both intrinsic and extrinsic, are nonverbal expressions of sentiments and emotions. Fatemeh et. al., (2021) outline the typical bodily movements connected with emotions. For emotion identification via gestures, deep learning approaches are used. The steps of the emotional body gesture recognition system are as follows: Figure 7 depicts i) Human detection ii) Body pose estimation iii) Feature extraction iv) Emotion identification or recognition.

Human Detection: Humans are recognized in images, and human body models are constructed using machine learning algorithms to map to a specific abstraction of emotion. Models of the Human Body based on 1. Part based 2.Grammer Models 3.Kinematic Models.

As shown in Figure 8a, a **Part based model** comprises pictorial structures with 2D assembly of parts. The human body is represented as a composition of face, limbs, and trunk in **grammar models** using compositional principles. As illustrated in figure 8b, the **kinematic Model** contains a collection of linked joints created by reducing the human mechanics and its skeleton using cyclical tree graphs.

For multi-person pose estimation, deep learning approaches such as three dimensional pose estimation, shape reconstruction, correspondence and shape completion using a collection of connected 3D meshes can be employed. By integrating categorization with area localization, fast regional based convolutional neural networks (RCNNs) have become the industry standard in human detection. Faster-RCNN and its adaptation to human detection resulted in the creation of a region proposal network (RPN), which shares full-image convolution characteristics with good performance in deep architectures such as ResNet.

Body Pose Estimation: Through 3D pose estimation, deep learning approaches are utilized to estimate human posture from visuals in imagery. A cascade of component identification and deep regression networks regressing all parts' locations, as well as confidence map regression training (Bulat and Tzimiropoulos 2016). To estimate the posture of numerous people, a body-part connection network and feed-forward convolutional architecture are utilised. (Insafutdinov et. al., 2017)

Figure 7. General Emotional Body Gesture Recognition System
Fatemeh et. al. (2021)

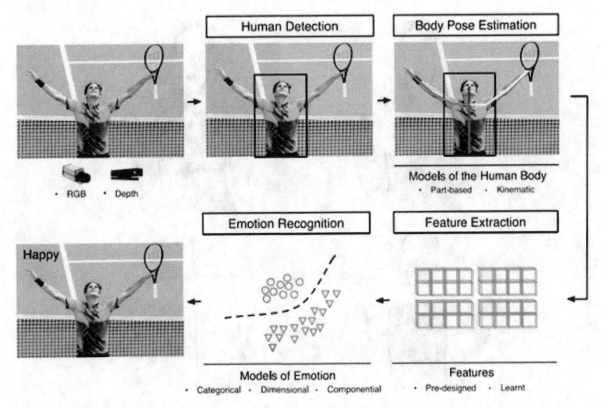

Feature extraction: Part-based models and skeleton models are used to extract static and dynamic aspects of body motions, such as hand and palm position, motion cues, and so on. The descriptors quantity of motion (QoM), silhouette motion images (SMI), contraction index (CI), and angular metrics for shape similarity (AMSS) are used to extract features in multichannel CNN and pulse-coded neural networks for learning a deep representation from the top half of the body.

Emotion Recognition: Emotions are recognized based on the model **classified by** Fatemeh et. al., (2021).

GER Database

Major Datasets with recordings of expressions are listed below. Yan et. al.,(2022), Fatemeh et. al., (2021)

- **Geneva Multi-modal Emotion Portrayals (GEMEP): 7,000 audio-video portrayals of 18 emotions**
- **HUMAINE:** six male and four female participants with eight emotions
- **THEATRE:** play "Death of a Salesman", namely, DS-1 and DS-2 with 8 emotions.
- **LIRIS-ACCEDE:** 32 males and 32 females, with six basic emotions
- **GEMEP-FERA:** short videos of the upper body of the actors.
- **emoFBVP:** multi-modal (face, gesture, physiological and voice signals) recordings of actors.

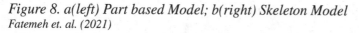

Figure 8. a(left) Part based Model; b(right) Skeleton Model
Fatemeh et. al. (2021)

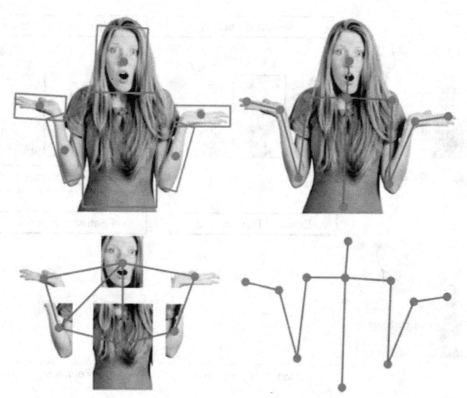

Deep Learning Algorithms in GER

To analyze body movement characteristics, deep learning techniques such as multilayer perceptron, restricted boltzmann machines (RBMs), and stacked RBMs outperformed classifiers. Convolutional neural network (CNN) can be trained to assess a person and detect their emotional state using two low-rank filters.

Three Dimensional Convolutional Neural Network(3DCNN) GBER: In the convolution phases of CNNs, 3D convolutions are utilized to calculate features in both the spatial and temporal dimensions. Convoluting a 3D kernel to the cube generated by stacking numerous contiguous frames together yields 3D convolution. To capture motion information, the 128 feature maps in the convolution layer are coupled to numerous continuous frames in the preceding layer.

Seven 60x40 input frames with gestures were transformed into a 128D feature vector, which captured the visual features in the frames. Figure 9 shows a 3D CNN architecture with one hardwired layer, three convolution layers, two sub-sampling levels, and one full connection layer.

SIFT descriptors are used to compute auxiliary features from motion edge history images (MEHI). During training, these features are linked to the last hidden layer of CNN to learn a feature vector that is similar to this feature using the online error back-propagation technique, as illustrated in Figure 10.

Convolutional Long Short Term Memory (ConvLSTM) GBER: CNN extracts video frames and converts them into feature maps. To obtain the keyframes, the CNN extracted features are binarized

Figure 9. A 3D CNN architecture for gesture based emotion recognition.
Ji et. al. (2013)

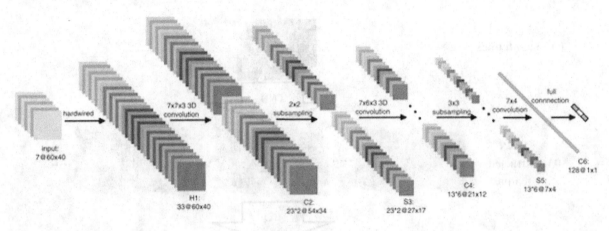

using Iterative Quantization and the Hamming distance between successive frames is determined. To detect the emotion, normalized keyframes are input into a CNN + convolutional lSTM (ConvLSTM) network. By retaining the spatio-temporal smoothness between local pixels, the Convolutional long short term memory (ConvLSTM) may be utilised to record better spatio-temporal correlations. Because ConvLSTM uses a convolution layer with low coverage connections, it uses less memory. The network parameters are therefore lowered in comparison to a fully dense connection in LSTM. Figure 11 depicts the structure of the ConvLSTM network.

Figure 10. The regularized 3D CNN architecture
Ji et. al. (2013)

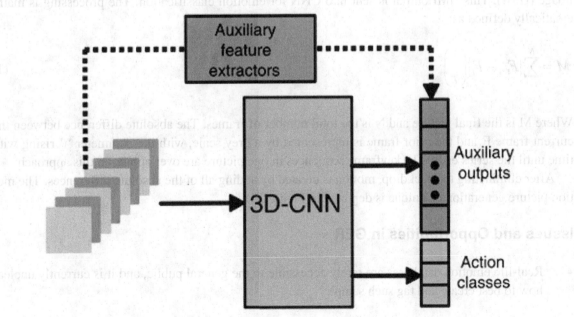

Figure 11. Keyframe selection procedure.
Son et. al. (2018)

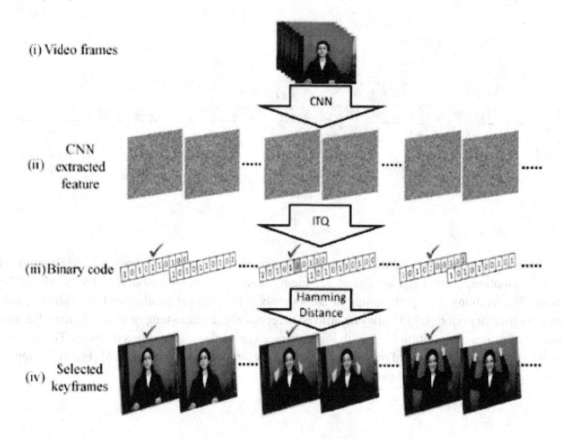

A parallel channel with all motions in grey scale and piled in a single image creates a motion history image (HMI). This HMI output is sent into CNN for emotion classification. The processing is mathematically defined as:

$$M = \sum_{i=1}^{N} |F_{i-1} - F_i| \left(\frac{i}{t} \right) \tag{1}$$

Where M is the final picture and N is the total number of frames. The absolute difference between the current frame F_i and the prior frame is represented by a grey scale, with the parameter 't' rising with time until the series ends. The keyframe sequences in one picture are overlapping in this approach.

After eliminating the backdrop, motion is created by adding all of the absolute differences. The motion picture generation technique is depicted in Figure 13.

Issues and Opportunities in GER

- Real-life emotion databases are rarely accessible to the general public, and it is currently unclear how to best create and tag such samples.

- In sentiment analysis, the visual is more successful than audio due to audio's susceptibility to noise.

Figure 12. Structure of CNN + ConvLSTM network.
Son et. al. (2018)

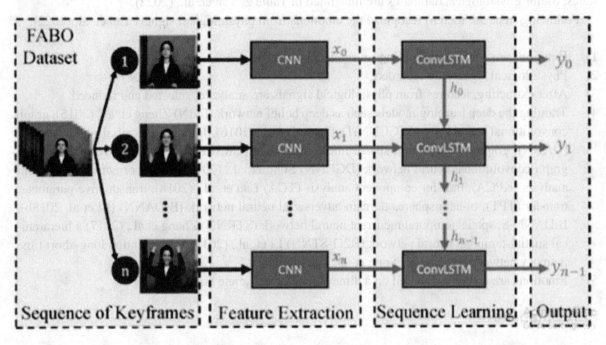

Figure 13. Example for motion image generating process.
Son et. al. (2018)

PHYSIOLOGICAL BASED EMOTION RECOGNITION (PER)

Overview

Electrocardiogram, skin conductance, electroencephalogram, heart rate and respiration rate data directly reflect changes in human sentiments, which can aid people in identifying and deciphering emotional states. Major Physiological databases are illustrated in Table 2. Yan et. al., (2022).

Following steps are used to recognize the emotions from physiological signals Yan et. al.,(2022).

1) Emotions are stimulated by using music, videos and images.
2) Physiological signals are recorded.
3) After extracting, features from physiological signals are analyzed, selected and reduced.
4) Training the deep learning models such as deep belief network (DBN) Zheng et. al., (2015), graph convolutional neural network (GCNN) Defferrard et. al., (2016), domain adversarial neural network (DANN), graph regularization sparse linear regression (GRSLR) (Li et. al., 2018c), dynamical graph convolutional neural network (DGCNN) Song et. al., (2018), kernel principal component analysis (KPCA), transfer component analysis (TCA) Lan et. al., (2018), transductive parameter transfer (TPT), bi-hemispheres domain adversarial neural network (BiDANN) (Li et al. 2018b), BiDANN-S, spatial temporal recurrent neural network (STRNN) Zhang et.al., (2017) a hierarchical spatial-temporal neural network (R2G-STNN) Li et. al., (2019), and attention long-short time memory networks (A-LSTM) Song et. al., (2019) etc.
5) Emotions are recognized based on a dimensional or a discrete emotion model.

PER Database

DEAP (Koelstra et al.,2012): From 32 subjects, a 4-channel EOG, 32-channel EEG, plethysmograph, body temperature, a 4-channel EMG, RESP, and Galvanic Skin Response (GSR) signals.

SEED (Zheng et al.,2015): EEG-15 subjects.

DSdRD(Healey et al.,2005): From 24 volunteers, EMG,GSR,ECG signals with a rest after their driving tasks.

AMIGOS (Miranda Correa et al.,2018): From 40 participants, EEG, GSR,ECG emotional signals from 16 short videos.

WESAD (Schmidt et al.,2018): EMG, RESP,ECG.

DL Algorithms for EEG emotion Recognition

Instance-AdaptiveGraph: Self-adaptive graphs are generated with input EEG data. With the generated graphs, the multilevel and multi-graph convolutional operation and graph coarsening, region dependency modeling, full connection layer (FC) and softmax layer are applied to extract more discriminative features for classification.

Variational Pathway Reasoning (VPR): EEG signals are recorded using electrodes that are spatially closed. Random walk is used to produce candidate paths, which are then coded. The Pseudo salient route is chosen using Sparse Variation Scaling. Then, as seen in figure 15, scaled PSPs are linked to a fully connected layer to detect the emotion.

Figure 14. The framework of the IAG.
Song et. al. (2020)

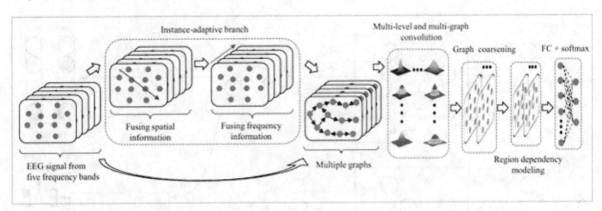

Regularized Graph Neural Networks (RGNN): Each EEG channel is represented in the graph as a node. For training samples, the degree matrix, normalised adjacency matrix, and Kullback-Leibler divergence loss (KL) are calculated. Figure 16 shows a gradient reversal layer (GRL) that was generated for domain classification.

A Channel-fused Dense Convolutional Network: As input, a convolution 1F layer is used, and feature maps for each electrode are produced. The transition block is used to reduce the size of feature maps. The dense block is used to reuse features. For emotion recognition, average pooling and the Softmax classifier are used. (Gao et. al., 2020).

Regional-Asymmetric Convolutional Neural Network (RACNN): To learn the temporal characteristics of each EEG channel, RACNN uses temporal feature, regional feature, asymmetric feature extractors, and a classifier, as illustrated in figure 18.

Figure 15. Structure of VPR
Zhang et al. (2020)

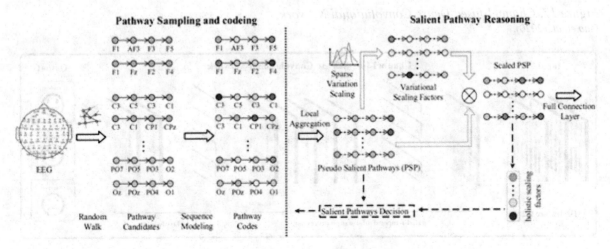

Figure 16. The overall architecture of our RGNN model
Zhong et. al. (2020).

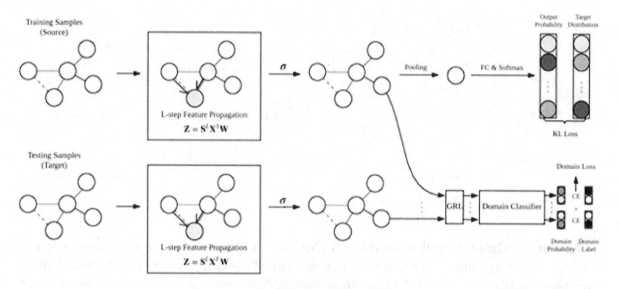

DL Algorithm for ECG emotion Recognition

Multi-task CNN: To identify signal modifications, a multi-task CNN is trained using automatically generated labels. The weights are then transmitted to the emotion identification network, which is trained to categorize emotions using fully connected layers.

Issues and Opportunities in PER

- It is more challenging to gather physiological signals from wearable sensors than it is to obtain physical signals.

Figure 17. Channel-fused Dense Convolutional Network
Gao et. al. (2020).

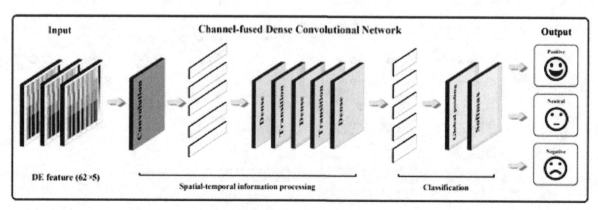

Figure 18. Regional-Asymmetric Convolutional Neural Network
Cui et. al. (2020).

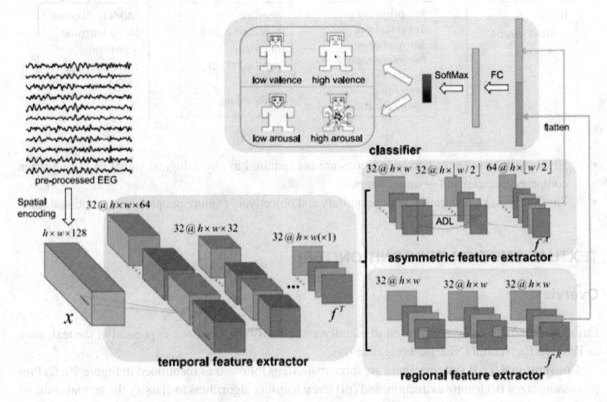

Figure 19. Self-supervised architecture
Sarkar and Etemad (2020)

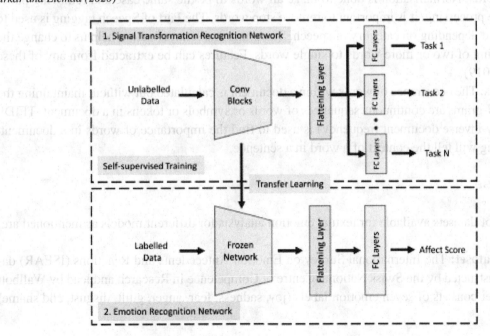

Figure 20. Overview of emotion recognition from text

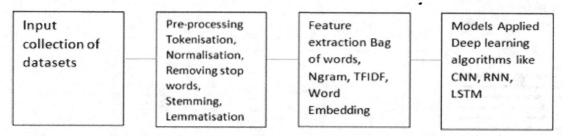

- High-quality images in good conditions are not required in physiological signal capturing when compared to facial and gesture images.
- Physiological signals could more accurately and objectively capture people's true emotional state.

TEXTUAL EMOTION RECOGNITION(TER)

Overview

Emotion classification is mainly used to identify and classify the emotions expressed in the text, such as Positive(P), Neutral (NEU)and Negative (N).

Conventional TER system: There are three main steps followed as mentioned in Figure 20: (i) Pre-processing stage (ii) feature extraction, and (iii) Deep learning algorithms to classify the textual emotion

People convey their feelings through different expressions and informal ways. So, it is very important to pre-process the data before actual processing through algorithms. We can reduce the noise and size of data to be processed. There are a lot of pre-processing steps like tokenisation where sentences are converted to words. Normalisation is done to make all words to be the same case and removing punctuations. Before processing, it is important to remove stop words. The Part of Speech tagging is used to classify the word depending on category of speech. Stemming and lemmatization help us to change the tense and merging of two or more words to single words. Features can be extracted from any of these (Ahuja et. al., 2019)

Bag of words: The occurrence of words within a document is calculated but without maintaining the order. Ngram-N-grams are continuous sequences of words or symbols or tokens in a document. TFIDF (term frequency-inverse document frequency) is used to find the importance of words in a document. Word embedding will tell the context of a word in a sentence.

TER Database

There are a lot of datasets available for textual emotion analysis for different models as mentioned are

- **ISEAR Dataset:** The International Survey on Emotion Antecedents and Reactions (ISEAR) database constructed by the Swiss National Centre of Competence in Research and lead by Wallbott and Scherer consists of seven emotion labels (joy, sadness, fear, anger, guilt, disgust, and shame)

obtained as a result of gathering series of data from cross-cultural questionnaire studies in 37 countries.

- **SemEval:** The Semantic Evaluations (SemEval) is a database consisting of Arabic and English news headlines extracted from news websites such as BBC, CNN, Google News, and other major newspapers. The dataset contains 1250 data in total. The data in this database are rich in emotional content for emotion extraction and it is labeled using the 6 emotional categories (ie, joy, sadness, fear, surprise, anger, and disgust) presented by Ekman.
- **WASSA-2017 Emotion Intensities (EmoInt) Data:** The Workshop on Computational Approaches to Subjectivity, Sentiment, and Social Media Analysis (WASSA-2017) data was constructed to detect emotion intensities in tweets. It is annotated for four discrete emotions, including joy, anger, fear, and sadness.
- **International Survey of Emotional Antecedents and Reactions (ISEAR):** It is annotated for emotions guilt, joy, shame, fear, sadness, disgust
- **NRC Emotion Intensity Lexicon:** 6k entries, mapped into 4 emotions
- **Depeche Mode:** 188k tokens 186k lemmas, 285k lemma, mapped into 8 emotions

TER using Deep Learning

Deep learning has a tremendous growth in recent years. Its effect has been used in textual emotion recognition also. There are multiple deep learning algorithms. Among them, CNN (Convolutional Neural Network), RNN (Recurrent Neural network), LSTM (Long short-term memory), are widely used in text emotion recognition and emotions can be identified.

Deep Belief Network: Ravi and Basavaraj (2021), proposed a method, where the customer feedback for the review of the product will be collected. The data after pre-processing, the dataset feature extraction word2vec is applied with the combination of both the BOW (Bag of words) and TF-ID (Term Frequency/Inverse Document Frequency) algorithms. The output vector is sent as input to DBN (Deep belief Network). Restricted Boltzmann Machine (RBM) is used in a loop manner to get the final result in the output layer. The complete process is achieved through the Deep Belief Network algorithm, as illustrated in Figure 21.

Recurrent Neural network and LSTM: A Recurrent Neural Network (RNN) is one of the type of neural network. It makes use of feed forward network, mentioned in Figure 22. Both current and previous information are the input for RNN. The main disadvantage of RNN is vanishing and exploding gradient problems. To remove these problems, LSTM was introduced. As the name indicates it studies long term dependencies on data.

Shilpa et. al., (2021) used a method in which the classifier is used twice, in the first case classifier is used to identify positive and negative emotions. Once these emotions are identified, it goes through sub emotion identification like positive emotions can be further classified like surprise, love, relief etc. Likewise, negative emotions are further classified into sadness, worry etc. In this paper, around 14 sub emotions are identified. For doing this classification, recurrent Neural Networks and Long short-term memory were used in this method as illustrated in Figure 23.

Convolutional Neural Network and LSTM: A Convolutional Neural Network is also a feed forward network. it has multiple layers. Input layer, Convolution layer, pooling layer and an output layers are the name of the layers used in convolutional neural Network. The output from input layer is given to the convolution layer. Once extracted words are taken from convolution layer, these extracted words

Figure 21. System architecture used in Deep belief network model
Ravi and Basavaraj (2021)

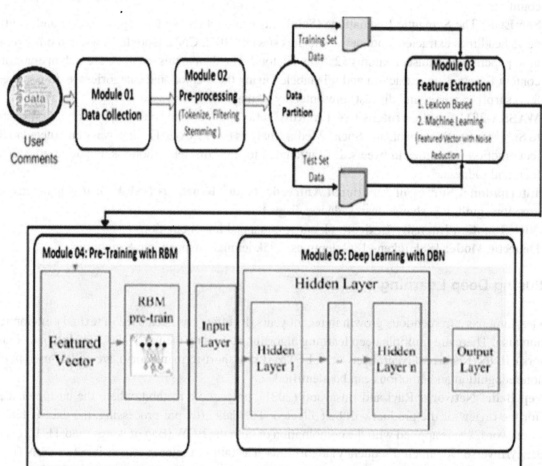

Figure 22. Recurrent Neural Network architecture

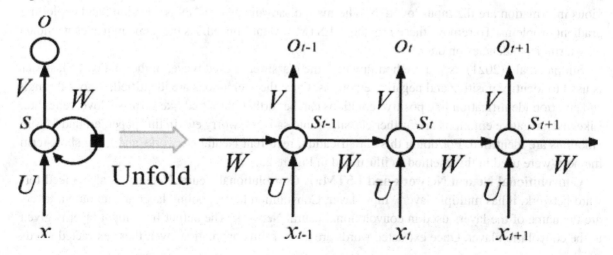

Figure 23. System architecture used in LSTM AND RNN
Shilpa et al. (2021)

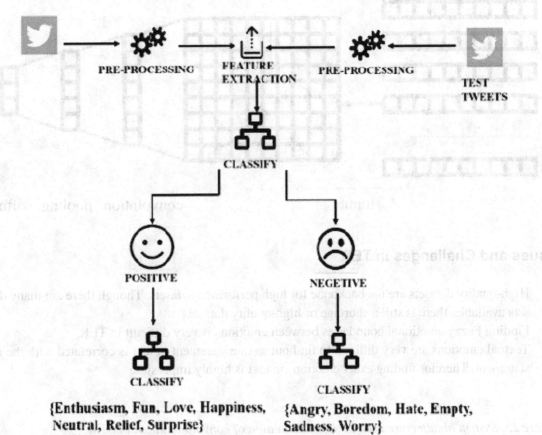

PRE-PROCESSING   FEATURE EXTRACTION   PRE-PROCESSING   TEST TWEETS

CLASSIFY

POSITIVE   NEGETIVE

CLASSIFY   CLASSIFY

{Enthusiasm, Fun, Love, Happiness, Neutral, Relief, Surprise}   **{Angry, Boredom, Hate, Empty, Sadness, Worry}**

go through pooling layer. The output from pooling layer is given to output layer to get the result. Result obtained is shown in, Figure 24.

Cach et.al, (2021), proposed four hybrid deep learning models .The CNN and LSTM were used in deep learning layers and CNN and SVM were used in the classifier layers. As hybrid model was used, the advantages of above said models outperformed all other models where single type model was used. As SVM was used in classifier model, it gave better result rather than using SVM alone. Since a combination of models were used time consumption to get the result was more. But the computational time is much longer for the ones with SVM alone as illustrated in Figure 25

Combination of Convolutional and Recursive Neural Network: Hossein et. al., (2019) proposed a method which combines Convolutional and Recursive Neural Networks. A hybrid model of both combination of recursive method with addition of convolutional network yielded a better rather than using these methods alone. In this method recursive method acted as a pooling layer. By using this method, the data loss can be reduced as illustrated in Figure 26.

BiLSTM: A Bidirectional LSTM (BiLSTM) makes two LSTMs, one takes the input in a forward direction and the other in a backward direction. Additionally, the attention mechanism is applied to the output of LSTM-BiLSTM to emphasize different words. The model is as illustrated in Figure 27

Figure 24. CNN Architecture

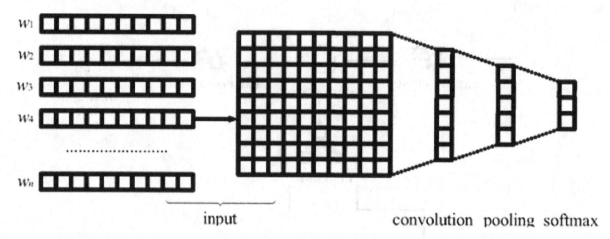

Issues and Challenges in TER

- High-quality datasets are the backbone for high performed datasets. Though there are many datasets available, there is still a shortage of high-quality datasets
- Finding Fuzzy emotional boundaries between emotions is very difficult in TER.
- Textual emotions are very difficult to find out as one statement in text is correlated with the next statement. Therefor finding exact emotions in text is highly impossible

Figure 25. System architecture used in the combination of convolutional and LSTM
Cach et.al. (2021)

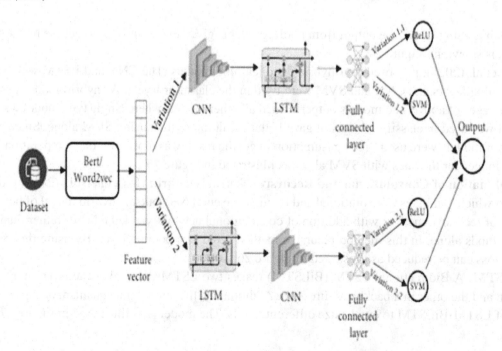

Figure 26. *System architecture used in the combination of convolutional and recursive Neural network* Hossein et.al. (2019)

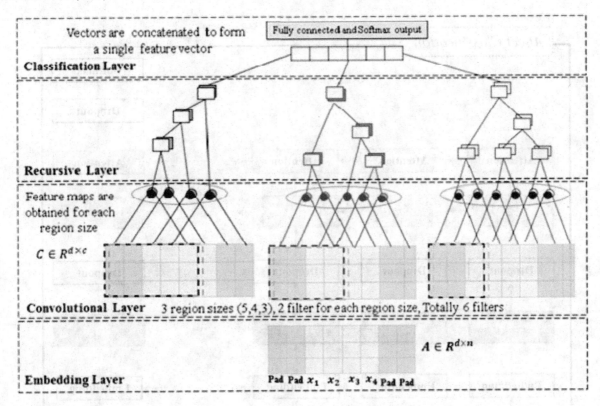

Nowadays people are interested in tweets more. This can be used in some applications where we can identify emotions while they have typed these tweets. We can effectively use these emotions to find the depression level of patients or threatening messages used by the victims

SPEECH EMOTION RECOGNITION(SER)

Overview

Emotions can be detected using different forms of inputs, such as speech, short phrases, facial expression, video, long text, short messages, and emoticons. There are three main steps followed in SER (i) Pre-processing stage (ii) feature extraction, and (iii)Deep learning algorithms to classify the emotion. Speech pre-processing is highly recommended before applying any deep learning algorithm as the input speech signal is often affected by the noise. The important features of speech are extracted from the pre-processed speech like mean, standard deviation, pitch, intensity etc. Feature can be extracted from MFCC (Mel Frequency Cepstral Coefficients) which is used in almost every speech processing. The features in MFCC are derived from mel-frequency cepstrum where the frequency bands are non-linearly spaced based on mel-scale. Harmonic to Noise ratio describes the distribution of the acoustic energy between the harmonic part and the in harmonic part of the radiated vocal spectrum. Zero cross rate is

Figure 27. System architecture using bilstm
Hanane and El-Habib (2021)

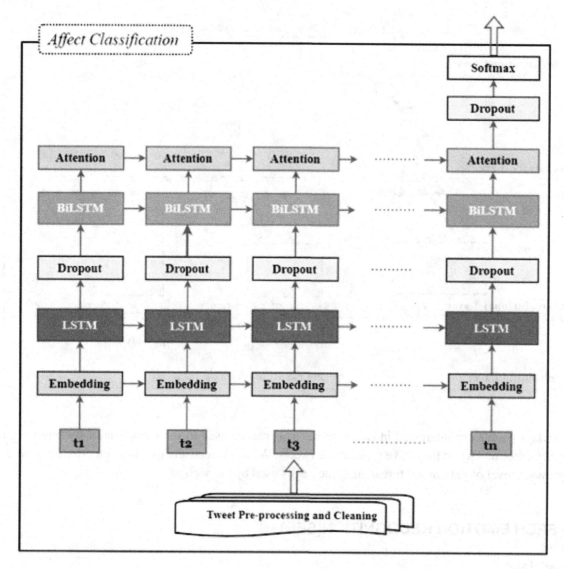

a discrete time signal's rate of having positive or negative consequent samples. Various classifiers like Bayes classifier, PCA (Principal component analysis) classifier, SVM (support vector machine) classifier can be used for speech recognition. Emotions can be identified with the help of databases available for speech processing. The various deep learning algorithms such as DBMs, DBNs, CNNs, RNNs, RvNNs, and AEs are discussed.

SER Database

Following are the data base that are used in speech emotion recognition. The data we collect should be precise and clear as input data are very important for any analysis. Any mistake in input can lead to incorrect predictions. Hence data we collect should be correct

- **Berlin Emotional Database (EmoDB):** It deals with 7 emotions like happiness, anger, boredom, neutral, fear, disgust and sadness. This is done in German language.
- **Chinese Emotional Speech Corpus (CASIA):** It deals with 7 emotions like happiness, anger, surprise, neutral, fear and sadness. This is done in Mandarin language.
- **The Interactive Emotional Dyadic Motion Capture Database (IEMOCAP):** It deals with 7 emotions like happiness, anger, frustration, neutral and sadness. This is done in English language.
- **Emotion (SAVEE) (Surrey audio-visual expressed emotion database):** It deals with emotions like happiness, anger, surprise, neutral, fear and sadness. This is done in English language.
- **Toronto Emotional Speech Database(TESS) (Toronto emotional speech database):** It is of English language and it deals emotions like happiness, neutral, fear, Sadness anger, disgust, pleasant, and surprise.
- **Beihang University Database of Emotional Speech (BUDES):** It is of English language and deals with emotions like Anger, happiness, fear, disgust, and surprise
- **Ryerson Audio-Visual Database of Emotional Speech and Song (RAVDESS):** It deals with emotions like happy, surprise, calm, sad, angry, fearful, disgust moods.

SER using Deep Learning

Melissa et. al., (2017), proposed a methodology that tested on the Berlin Emotional Speech (EMO-DB) data, employed frequently in the evaluation of SER systems. The EMO-DB database contained speech samples representing 7 categorical emotions (anger, happiness, sadness, fear, disgust, boredom, and neutral speech) spoken by 10 professional actors (5 female and 5 male) fluent in German. Each speaker was expected to simulate all 7 emotions while pronouncing 10 different utterances (5 short and 5 long) with linguistically neutral contents. In total, the database included 43371 speech samples, each with time duration of 2-3 seconds.

Margaret et. al., (2020), proposed a method in which labelled speech samples were buffered into short time blocks. For each block, a spectral amplitude spectrogram array was calculated, converted into an RGB image format, and passed as an input to the pre-trained CNN

Hadhami et. al., (2021) proposed a work in which an emotion recognition system using the parameters 39 MFCC (Mel Frequency Cepstral Coefficients), HNR(Harmonic to Noise Ratio), ZCR (Zero Crossing Rate), TEO(Teager Energy Operator) using the Support Vectors Machines firstly and secondly Auto-Encoder (AE) used to extract the relevant parameters from the previously extracted parameters and classified them with SVM

Yeşim and Asaf (2020), proposed a method in which the 1BTPDN model, the combination of 1DLBP (1-dimensional local binary pattern) and 1D-LTP (1-dimensional local ternary pattern). Dongdong et. al., (2021), proposed a method in which Bilstm with DSA(directional self-attention mechanism) the speech signal features are decoded by bi-directional LSTM forward and backward respectively, then encode them with DSA.

Figure 28. System architecture using CNN
Margret et.al (2020)

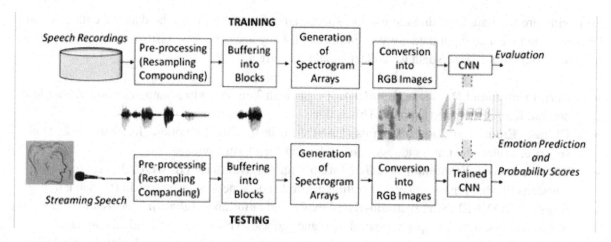

Apeksha et. al., (2022), proposed a method in which 2 approaches are made in one approach, that makes use of MFCC, Spectrogram, centroid, and roll-off before Principal component analysis is done. In approach II, Mel-spectrogram images are extracted from audio files, and the 2D images are given as input to the pre-trained VGG-16 model

Issues and Challenges in TER

- Selecting the best features in SER is challenging as it is very difficult to distinguish between different emotions.
- The presence of various languages, accents, sentences, speaking styles, and speakers also add another difficulty because these characteristics directly change most of the extracted features including pitch, and energy.

Figure 29. System architecture using support vector machine
Hadhami et. al. (2021)

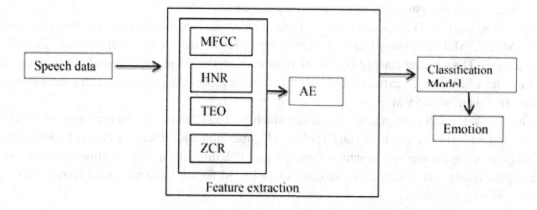

Figure 30. System architecture using Bilstm and DSA
Dongdong et. al. (2021)

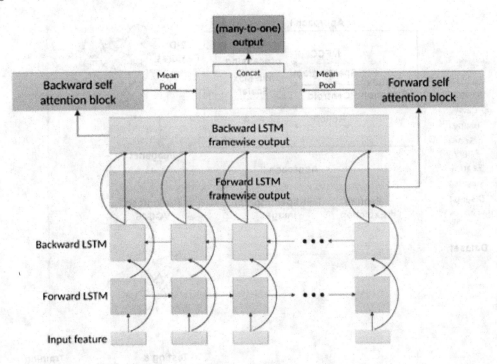

- It is possible to have more than one specific emotion in the same speech signal, each emotion correlates with a different part of speech signals.

MULTIMODAL EMOTION RECOGNITION(MER)

Overview

Emotions are recognized in unimodal and multimodal approaches. Unimodal approaches can utilize any one of the single modes of expression such as the face, gestures, and physiological signals. Emotion analysis will change gradually by integrating different media, forms, scales, and domains of emotional information. Multimodal approaches can utilize the multimode of expressions by combining the two or more single mode expressions. While traditional emotion analysis focuses on single forms of media, multi-modal information (e.g., audio, video, and image) can often express emotional effects in a better way. With the rapid development of social networks, a large amount of user interaction data has been generated that influences society.

MER Database

The recordings of this database contain all the modalities of emotional expressions namely - facial, body, physiological and vocal signals. *(Ranganathan et. al., 2016)*

Figure 31. System architecture using Deep neural network
Apeksha et.al. (2022)

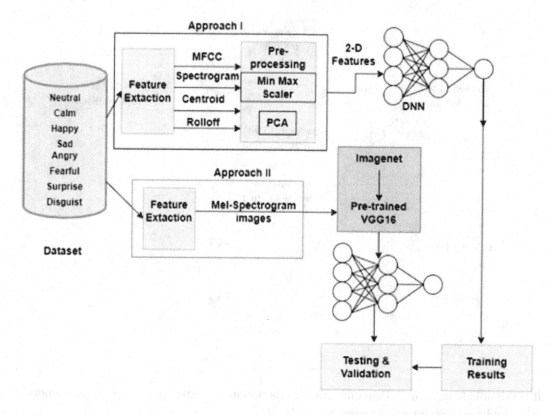

- **emoFBVP:** Ten participants were involved in data capture, and every participant displayed 23 different emotions. Recordings of each emotion were done six times: three in a standing position and three in a seated position when the body gestures and facial expressions were tracked and recorded along with vocal expressions, physiological data and activity respectively. Therefore, the database provides six examples of each of the 23 emotions in varying intensities of expression. Interactive Emotional Dyadic

- **Motion Capture (IEMOCAP):** Hypothetical scenarios designed from 10 actors to elicit 5 specific types of emotions during recording.

- **CreativeIT:** From 16 actors, visual-audio, text and full-body motion data collected, during their dyadic interactions from 2 to 10 minutes each.

- **Harvesting Opinions from the Web database (HOW):** YouTube videos with 22 neutral, 12 negative and 13 positive emotions.

- **Institute for Creative Technologies Multimodal Movie Opinion database (ICT-MMMO):** From ExpoTV, 78 movie review videos and 308 YouTube videos.

- **Multimodal Opinion Sentiment and Emotion Intensity (CMU-MOSEI):** From online YouTube speakers, 3,228 videos and 23,453 sentences.

Figure 32. Multimodal DemoDBN models: (a) DemoFBVP, (b) f+DemoFBVP, (c) DemoFBVP+f, (d)3DemoFBVP (Ranganathan et. al., 2016)

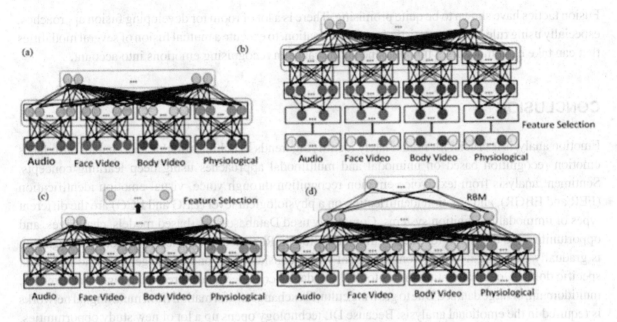

MER using Deep Learning

Convolutional deep belief network (CDBN): Unsupervised stacked restricted boltzmann machines (RBMs) are used to construct deep belief networks (DBNs). Training Layers are i) First Layer: Gaussian RBMs ii) Deeper Layer: Bernoulli-Bernoulli RBMs. Convolutional RBMs with probabilistic max-pooling are used in CDBNs. Two layers in CDBNs are: i) V-a Visible layer ii) H -a hidden layer. (Ranganathan et. al., 2016). CDBNs are used to recognize emotions from audio, face, body gesture and physiological signals.

The first deep layer learns how to recognise edges and fundamental forms, the second layer learns how to recognise more intricate shapes and objects (such as eyes, noses, and mouths), and the third layer discovers which shapes and items may be utilised to create a face expression. When performing multi-modal emotion recognition, prosodic and spectral features such as pitch, energy, and mel-frequency filter banks from voice data are used, as well as the mean, variance, lower and upper quantiles, and quantile range of audio features, facial tracking features from facial expressions, and skeletal tracking features from body gestures and physiological signals. All of these characteristics have been standardised to prevent individual reliance. A total of 1380 features were retrieved, including 180 features from speech expressions, 540 features from face expressions, 540 features from body motions, and 120 features from physiological signal data. For comparison and validation of the outcomes of deep learning techniques, baseline models are required. Cross-validation techniques that leave one individual out are used to optimise the baseline models.

Issues and Challenges in MER

Fusion tactics have shown to be quite promising. There is a lot of room for developing fusion approaches, especially using rule-based or statistic-based information, to execute a mutual fusion of several modalities that can take each modality's function and significance in recognising emotions into account.

CONCLUSION

Emotion analysis is crucial for immediately identifying trends in public attitude. This chapter introduces emotion recognition based on unimodal and multimodal approaches using deep learning concepts. Sentiment analysis from text, voice emotion recognition through voice, visual emotion identification (FER and EBGR), and emotion identification on a physiological level (EEG and ECG) are the different types of unimodal recognition systems. Commonly used Databases, DL-based models, challenges, and opportunities are discussed for each unimodal approach. Research in the field of emotion recognition is gradually changing its focus from unimodal which considers any one language, one kind of media, specific domain, or small data samples to Multimodal by considering different languages, multimodal, multidomain, or large data set. Due to growing cultural exchanges, information from multilingual networks is required in the emotional analysis. Because DL technology opens up a lot of new study opportunities, this chapter will serve as the foundation for additional study in the area of emotion analysis.

REFERENCES

Abeer, A. A., Mohammed, Z., Prashant, K. S., Aseel, A., Wesam, A. H., Hussam, T., Sureshbabu, R., Rajnish, R., (2022). Human-Computer Interaction for Recognizing Speech Emotions Using Multilayer Perceptron Classifier. *Journal of Healthcare Engineering.* doi:10.1155/2022/600544

Ahuja, R., Chug, A., Kohli, S., Gupta, S., & Ahuja, P. (2019). The impact of features extraction on sentiment analysis. *Procedia Computer Science, 152,* 341–348. doi:10.1016/j.procs.2019.05.008

Apeksha, A., Akshat, S., Ajay, A., Nidhi, C., Dilbag, S., Abeer, A. A., Aseel, A., & Heung-No, L.,(2022). *Two-Way Feature Extraction for Speech Emotion Recognition Using Deep Learning.* doi:10.3390/s22062378

Barrett, L. F., Adolphs, R., Marsella, S., Martinez, A. M., & Pollak, S. D. (2019). Emotional Expressions Reconsidered: Challenges to Inferring Emotion From Human Facial Movements. *Psychological Science in the Public Interest, 20*(1), 1–68. doi:10.1177/1529100619832930 PMID:31313636

Benitez-Quiroz, C. F., Srinivasan, R., & Martinez, A. M. (2016). Emotionet: An accurate, real-time algorithm for the automatic annotation of a million facial expressions in the wild. *Proceedings of IEEE International Conference on Computer Vision & Pattern Recognition (CVPR).* 10.1109/CVPR.2016.600

Bhattacharyya, A., Chatterjee, S., Sen, S., Sinitca, A., Kaplun, D., & Sarkar, R. (2021). A deep learning model for classifying human facial expressions from infrared thermal images. *Scientific Reports, 11*(1), 20696. doi:10.103841598-021-99998-z PMID:34667253

Bulat & Tzimiropoulos, G. (2016). Human pose estimation via convolutional part heatmap regression. *Proc. Eur. Conf. Comput. Vis.*, 717–732.

Cach, N. (2021). *Hybrid Deep Learning Models for Sentiment Analysis.* doi:10.1155/2021/9986920

Cosentino, S., Randria, E. I. S., Lin, J., Pellegrini, T., Sessa, S., & Takanishi, A., (2018). Group emotion recognition strategies for entertainment robots. *2018 IEEE/RSJ International Conference on Intelligent Robots and Systems (IROS)*, 813-818. 10.1109/IROS.2018.8593503

Cowie, R., Douglas-Cowie, E., Tsapatsoulis, N., Votsis, G., Kollias, S., Fellenz, W., & Taylor, J. G. (2001). Emotion recognition in human-computer interaction. *IEEE Signal Processing Magazine*, *18*(1), 32–80. doi:10.1109/79.911197

Cui, H., Liu, A., Zhang, X., Chen, X., Wang, K., & Chen, X. (2020). EEG-based emotion recognition using an end-to-end regional-asymmetric convolutional neural network. *Knowledge-Based Systems*, *205*, 106243. doi:10.1016/j.knosys.2020.106243

Daniel, C., & António, J. R. (2019). Facial Expression Recognition Using Computer Vision: *A Systematic Review. Applied Sciences (Basel, Switzerland)*, *9*(21), 4678. doi:10.3390/app9214678

Defferrard, M., & Bresson, X. V. P. (2016). Convolutional neural networks on graphs with fast localized spectral filtering. Advances in Neural Information Processing Systems, 3844–3852.

Dhall, A., Goecke, R., Lucey, S., & Gedeon, T. (2011). Static facial expression analysis in tough conditions: Data, evaluation protocol and benchmark. *IEEE International Conference on Computer Vision Workshops (ICCV Workshops)*, 2106-2112. 10.1109/ICCVW.2011.6130508

Dhall, A., Goecke, R., Lucey, S., & Gedeon, T. (2012). Collecting large, richly annotated facial-expression databases from movies. *IEEE MultiMedia*, *19*(3), 34–41. doi:10.1109/MMUL.2012.26

Fatemeh, N., Ciprian, A. C., Dorota, K., Tomasz, S., Sergio, E., & Gholamreza, A. (2021). Survey on Emotional Body Gesture Recognition. IEEE Transactions on Affective Computing, 12(2).

Gao, Z., Wang, X., Yang, Y., Li, Y., Ma, K., & Chen, G. (2020). A Channel-fused Dense Convolutional Network for EEG-based Emotion Recognition. *IEEE Transactions on Cognitive and Developmental Systems*, 1–1. doi:10.1109/TCDS.2020.2976112

Goodfellow, I. J., Erhan, D., Carrier, P. L., Courville, A., Mirza, M., Hamner, B., Cukierski, W., Tang, Y., Thaler, D., & Lee, D. H. (2013). Challenges in representation learning: A report on three machine learning contests. *International Conference on Neural Information Processing*, 117–124. 10.1007/978-3-642-42051-1_16

Gross, R., Matthews, I., Cohn, J., Kanade, T., & Baker, S. (2010). Multi-pie. *Image and Vision Computing*, *28*(5), 807–813. doi:10.1016/j.imavis.2009.08.002 PMID:20490373

Hadhami, A., & Yassine, B. A. (2021). *Speech Emotion Recognition with deep learning.* . doi:10.1016/j.procs.2020.08.027

Hanane, E., El-Habib, N., (2021). *Combining Context-Aware Embeddings and an Attentional Deep Learning Model for Arabic Affect Analysis on Twitter.* . doi:10.1109/ACCESS.2021.3102087

Healey, J. A., & Picard, R. W. (2005). Detecting stress during real-world driving tasks using physiological sensors. *IEEE Transactions on Intelligent Transportation Systems, 6*(2), 156–166. doi:10.1109/TITS.2005.848368

Hossein, S., Mir, M. P., & Mohammad, T., (2019). *A Robust Sentiment Analysis Method Based on Sequential Combination of Convolutional and Recursive Neural Networks.* . doi:10.1007/s11063-019-10049-1

Huahu, X., Jue, G., & Jian, Y. (2010). Application of speech emotion recognition in intelligent household robot. *International Conference on Artificial Intelligence and Computational Intelligence, 1*, 537-541. 10.1109/AICI.2010.118

Insafutdinov, E., Andriluka, M., Pishchulin, L., Tang, S., Levinkov, E., Andres, B., & Schiele, B. (2017). ArtTrack: Articulated multi-person tracking in the wild. *Proc. IEEE Conf. Comput. Vis. Pattern Recognit., 1293–1301.*

Ji, S., Xu, W., Yang, M., & Yu, K. (2013). 3D Convolutional Neural Networks for Human Action Recognition. *IEEE TPAMI, 35*(1), 221–231. doi:10.1109/TPAMI.2012.59 PMID:22392705

Jolly, S. (2000). Understanding body language: Birdwhistell's theory of kinesics. *Corporate Communications, 5*(3), 133–139. doi:10.1108/13563280010377518

Jonathan, A. P., Paoline, G. P. K., & Amalia, Z. (2018). Facial Emotion Recognition Using Computer Vision. *IEEE The 1st 2018 INAPR International Conference.*10.1109/INAPR.2018.8626999

Ko, B. (2018, January 30). A Brief Review of Facial Emotion Recognition Based on Visual Information. *Sensors (Basel), 18*(2), 401. doi:10.339018020401 PMID:29385749

Koelstra, S., Muhl, C., Soleymani, M., Lee, J.-S., Yazdani, A., Ebrahimi, T., Pun, T., Nijholt, A., & Patras, I. (2012). DEAP: A Database for Emotion Analysis;Using Physiological Signals. *IEEE Transactions on Affective Computing, 3*(1), 18–31. doi:10.1109/T-AFFC.2011.15

Kopaczka, M., Kolk, R., & Merhof, D. (2018). A fully annotated thermal face database and its application for thermal facial expression recognition. *IEEE International Instrumentation and Measurement Technology Conference (I2MTC), 1–6.* 10.1109/I2MTC.2018.8409768

Lan, Z., Sourina, O., Wang, L., Scherer, R., & Muller-Putz, G. R. (2018). Domain adaptation techniques for EEG-based emotion recognition: A comparative study on two public datasets. *IEEE Transactions on Cognitive and Developmental Systems, 11*(1), 85–94. doi:10.1109/TCDS.2018.2826840

Langner, O., Dotsch, R., Bijlstra, G., Wigboldus, D. H., Hawk, S. T., & van Knippenberg, A. (2010). Presentation and validation of the radboud faces database. *Cognition and Emotion, 24*(8), 1377–1388. doi:10.1080/02699930903485076

Li, S., & Deng, W. (2020). Deep Facial Expression Recognition: A Survey. IEEE Transactions on Affective Computing. doi:10.1109/TAFFC.2020.2981446

Li, Y., Zheng, W., Cui, Z., Zong, Y., & Ge, S. (2018c). EEG emotion recognition based on graph regularized sparse linear regression. *Neural Processing Letters*, 1–17. doi:10.100711063-017-9609-3

Li, Y., Zheng, W., Wang, L., Zong, Y., & Cui, Z. (2019). From regional to global brain: A novel hierarchical spatial- temporal neural network model for EEG emotion recognition. *IEEE Transactions on Affective Computing*.

Li, Y., Zheng, W., Zong, Y., Cui, Z., Zhang, T., & Zhou, X. (2018b). A bi-hemisphere domain adversarial neural network model for EEG emotion recognition. *IEEE Transactions on Affective Computing*.

Li, Liu, Yang, Sun, & Wang. (2021). *Speech emotion recognition using recurrent neural networks with directional self-attention*. . doi:10.1016/j.eswa.2021.114683

Lucey, P., Cohn, J. F., Kanade, T., Saragih, J., Ambadar, Z., & Matthews, I. (2010). The Extended Cohn-Kanade Dataset (CK+): A complete dataset for action unit and emotion-specified expression. *IEEE Computer Society Conference on Computer Vision and Pattern Recognition - Workshops*, 94-101. 10.1109/CVPRW.2010.5543262

Lundqvist, D., Flykt, A., & Ohman, A. (1998). *The Karolinska Directed Emotional Faces – KDEF, CD ROM from Department of Clinical Neuroscience, Psychology section, Karolinska Institutet*. KDEF. Available online https://www.emotionlab.se/resources/kdef

Lyons, M. J., Akamatsu, S., Kamachi, M., & Gyoba, J. (1998). Coding facial expressions with Gabor wave. *Proceedings of the IEEE International Conference on Automatic Face and Gesture Recognition*, 200–205. 10.1109/AFGR.1998.670949

Maragret, L. M., Christopher, B., & Robert, B. (2020). Real-Time Speech Emotion Recognition Using a Pre-trained Image Classification Network. *Effects of Bandwidth Reduction and Companding, 2020*, 14. Advance online publication. doi:10.3389/fcomp.2020.00014

Melinte, D. O., & Vladareanu, L. (2020, April 23). Facial Expressions Recognition for Human-Robot Interaction Using Deep Convolutional Neural Networks with Rectified Adam Optimizer. *Sensors (Basel)*, *20*(8), 2393. doi:10.339020082393 PMID:32340140

Melissa, N., Stolar, M. L., Robert, S. B., & Michael, S., (2017). *Real Time Speech Emotion Recognition Using RGB Image Classification and Transfer Learning*. doi:10.1109/ICSPCS.2017.8270472

Michel, F., & Valstar, M. P. (2010). Induced Disgust, Happiness and Surprise: an Addition to the MMI Facial Expression Database. In *Proceedings of IREC*. MMI. Available online: https://mmifacedb.eu/

Minaee, S., Mehdi, M., & Amirali, A. (2021). Deep-Emotion: Facial Expression Recognition Using Attentional Convolutional Network. *Sensors, 21*(9). . doi:10.3390/s21093046

Miranda Correa, J. A., Abadi, M. K., Sebe, N., & Patras, I. (2018). AMIGOS: A Dataset for Affect, Personality and Mood Research on Individuals and Groups. *IEEE Transactions on Affective Computing*, 1–1. doi:10.1109/TAFFC.2018.2884461

Muhammad, U. S. L., & Junaid, Q. (2018). *Using Deep Autoencoders for Facial Expression Recognition*. arXiv:1801.08329v1

Ranganathan, H., Chakraborty, S., & Panchanathan, S. (2016). Multimodal Emotion Recognition using Deep Learning Architectures. *IEEE Winter Conference on Applications of Computer Vision*. 10.1109/WACV.2016.7477679

Ravi, C., & Basavaraj, V. (2021). Sentiment Analysis using Deep Belief Network for User Rating Classification. *International Journal of Innovative Technology and Exploring Engineering, 10*(8).

Sarkar, P., & Etemad, A. (2020). Self-Supervised Learning for ECG-Based Emotion Recognition. *ICASSP 2020 - 2020 IEEE Int. Conf. Acoust. Speech Signal Process,* 3217–3221. 10.1109/ICASSP40776.2020.9053985

Schmidt, P., Reiss, A., Duerichen, R., Marberger, C., & Van Laerhoven, K. (2018). Introducing WESAD, a Multimodal Dataset for Wearable Stress and Affect Detection. *Proc. 20th ACM Int. Conf. Multimodal Interact.,* 400–408. 10.1145/3242969.3242985

Schuller, B. W. (2018). Speech emotion recognition: Two decades in a nutshell, benchmarks, and ongoing trends. *Communications of the ACM, 61*(5), 90–99. doi:10.1145/3129340

Shilpa, P. C., Rissa, S., Susmi, J., Vinod, P., (2021). *Sentiment Analysis Using Deep Learning.* doi:10.1109/ICICV50876.2021.9388382

Son, T. L., Guee-Sang, L., Soo-Hyung, K., & Hyung-Jeong, Y. (2018). Emotion Recognition via Body Gesture:Deep Learning Model Coupled with Keyframe Selection. MLMI. doi:10.1145/3278312.3278313

Song, T., Liu, S., Zheng, W., Zong, Y., & Cui, Z. (2020). Instance-Adaptive Graph for EEG Emotion Recognition. *Proc. AAAI Conf. Artif. Intell., 34,* 2701–2708. 10.1609/aaai.v34i03.5656

Song, T., Zheng, W., Lu, C., Zong, Y., Zhang, X., & Cui, Z. (2019). MPED: A multi-modal physiological emotion database for discrete emotion recognition. *IEEE Access: Practical Innovations, Open Solutions, 7,* 12177–12191. doi:10.1109/ACCESS.2019.2891579

Song, T., Zheng, W., Song, P., & Cui, Z. (2018). EEG emotion recognition using dynamical graph convolutional neural networks. *IEEE Transactions on Affective Computing.*

Susskind, J. M., Anderson, A. K., & Hinton, G. E. (2010). *The Toronto face database. Department of Computer Science, University of Toronto* Tech. Rep.

Yan, W., Wei, S., Wei, T., Antonio, L., Dawei, Y., Xinlei, L., Shuyong, G., Yixuan, S., Weifeng, G., Wei, Z., & Wenqiang, Z. (2022). *A Systematic Review on Affective Computing: Emotion Models.* Databases, and Recent Advances.

Yang, C., Lai, X., Hu, Z., Liu, Y., & Shen, P. (2019). Depression tendency screening use text based emotional analysis technique. *J. Phys. Conf., 1237*(3), 1–10. doi:10.1088/1742-6596/1237/3/032035

Yeşim, Ü. S., & Asaf, V. (2020). *A Speech Emotion Recognition Model Based on Multi-Level Local Binary and Local Ternary Patterns.* doi:10.1109/ACCESS.2020.3031763

Yin, L., Wei, X., Sun, Y., Wang, J., & Rosato, M. J. A. (2006). 3D facial Expression database for facial behavior research. *Proceedings of the International Conference on Automatic Face and Gesture Recognition,* 211–216.

Zhang, T., Cui, Z., Xu, C., Zheng, W. J., & Yang. (2020). Variational Pathway Reasoning for EEG Emotion Recognition. *Proc. AAAI Conf. Artif. Intell., 34,* 2709–2716. . doi:10.1609/aaai.v34i03.5657

Zhang, T., Zheng, W., Cui, Z., Zong, Y., & Li, Y. (2017). Spatial-temporal recurrent neural network for emotion recognition. *IEEE Transactions on Cybernetics PP*, (99), 1–9.

Zheng, W. L., & Lu, B. L. (2015). Investigating critical frequency bands and channels for EEG-based emotion recognition with deep neural networks. *IEEE Transactions on Autonomous Mental Development, 7*(3), 162–175. doi:10.1109/TAMD.2015.2431497

Zhong, P., Wang, D., & Miao, C. (2020). EEG-Based Emotion Recognition Using Regularized Graph Neural Networks. *IEEE Transactions on Affective Computing*, 1–1. doi:10.1109/TAFFC.2020.2994159

Chapter 6
Smart Surveillance System Using Deep Learning Approaches

Uma K. V.
Thiagarajar College of Engineering, India

Aakash V.
Thiagarajar College of Engineering, India

Deisy C.
Thiagarajar College of Engineering, India

ABSTRACT

In modern days, CCTVs are being used for monitoring, and most shops have surveillance cameras up and running during the night times, but still, robberies are happening since the surveillance footage is being checked only after a robbery on the next day. To overcome the problems of having manual security and cost wastage along with automating the monitoring of the surveillance during the night times once the shops are closed, the authors propose the smart surveillance system. Deep learning algorithms and computer vision techniques are used to detect the presence of humans/intruders in a given video. The smart surveillance system along with the reduction in the cost of manual securities also provides robust nighttime monitoring, and it provides immediate notification to the authority as soon as it spots the intruder in the specified monitoring time, thereby reducing the robberies and the business impact caused.

INTRODUCTION

Video analytics and pedestrian detection is a vastly growing domain that has multiple application in various domains like self-driving cars, behavioral analysis, crowd management as well as surveillance purpose. The absence of real time monitoring of surveillance footage is the main cause of the robberies that are taking place during the night times in the shop.

Below were real time robbery images where the robbery took place in-spite of surveillance camera. Figure 1 show the real time robberies that happens despite of having CCTVs.

DOI: 10.4018/978-1-7998-8892-5.ch006

Figure 1. Showing the real time robberies despite the presence of CCTV camera.

We still need to monitor the CCTV by humans to make some kind of decision. In this project we propose the end-to-end automated surveillance monitoring system during the night times to prevent the robberies and to reduce the cost of human securities using the convolutional neural networks and computer vision techniques. The convolution neural networks are being used as the start-of-art image classification algorithm and for image processing in the modern days. The problem of intruder detection comes under the task of human detection binary classification. A binary classification CNN model can be trained with images of two classes (image with humans and image without humans). Using computer vision techniques, the CCTV footage video can be processed in frames and can be converted into RGB matrices. These processed RGB frames of the surveillance footage can be passed onto the trained CNN model to detect intruders. A properly trained CNN model can able to detect intruders even if they wear mask on their face. This system alerts and notifies the using a python notification and calling library as soon as it detects the intruders thereby preventing the loss incurred due to the robbery.

Video analytics represent a middle thing of many wi-fi offerings that require processing of voluminous information streams emanating from hand-held devices. MultiAccess Edge Computing (MEC) is a promising answer for helping such resourcehungry offerings, however there's a plethora of configuration parameters affecting their overall performance in an unknown and probably timevarying fashion. To triumph over this obstacle, we recommend an Automated Machine Learning (AutoML) framework for at the same time configuring the provider and wi-fi community parameters, in the direction of maximizing the analytics` accuracy problem to minimal body charge constraints. Our experiments with a bespoke prototype screen the risky and system/data dependent overall performance of the provider, and encourage the improvement of a Bayesian online mastering set of rules which optimizes on the fly the provider overall performance. We show that our answer is assured to discover a nearoptimal configuration the use of secure exploration, i.e., without ever violating the set body charge thresholds. Use the testbed to in addition examine this AutoML framework in numerous eventualities with real-international datasets (Galanopoulos, 2021).

New video analysis tasks based on deep learning require computationally intensive neural networks and powerful computing resources in the cloud to achieve high accuracy. Due to latency requirements and limited network bandwidth, edge cloud systems adaptively compress data to find a balance between overall analytical accuracy and bandwidth consumption. However, when the data deteriorates, another problem arises: the tail becomes less accurate. This means that some semantic classes and video frames are extremely inaccurate. Autonomous robot applications place particular emphasis on tail accuracy performance, but there are problems with using older Edgecloud systems. Introducing Runespoor, an Edgecloud video analysis system that manages tail accuracy and enables new robotics applications. Train and implement super-resolution models tailored to the tail accuracy of analytical tasks on the server to significantly improve the performance of hard-to-find classes and demanding frames. Online operations further improve tail performance by using an adaptive data rate controller to instantly adapt the data rate policy to the video content. According to our assessment, Runespoor improves tail accuracy per class by up to 300%, tail accuracy per frame by up to 22% / 54%, and significantly improves overall bandwidth accuracy. trade off (Wang, 2022).

Human Behavior Recognition (HAR) is an essential but rewarding task for observing human movements. This problem involves observing changes in the discrimination between human movements and activities through machine learning algorithms. This article addresses the challenges of activity detection through intelligent segmentation, feature reduction, and implementation and testing of the selection framework. A new approach for merging segmented frames is introduced to extract the multi-level features of interest. A feature reduction technique based on entropy skewness is implemented, and the reduced features are converted into a codebook by series-based fusion. A custom genetic algorithm is implemented in the generated trait codebook to select powerful and well-known traits. These features are leveraged by multiclass SVMs for action identification. Comprehensive experimental results are created with four action datasets: Weizmann, KTH, Muhavi, and WVU Multiview. We achieved recognition rates of 96.80%, 100%, 100%, and 100%, respectively. Analysis shows that the proposed behavior detection approach is more efficient and highly accurate than existing approaches (Chengyi,2021).Bottom of Form

LITERATURE SURVEY

Existing solutions were available for human detection as well human classification tasks on which each model had been trained and evaluated with images especially with daylight images, pedestrians on roads and other similar scenarios. For Example, Yeonghun Lee in (1) Development of Specific Area Intrusion Detection System using YOLO has used YOLOv2 (You only look once) algorithm for detection of intrusion and has obtained over 80% of Intersection over union (IOU is intersection between the predicted human region and the human region in the actual image). ImageNet Classification used with Deep Convolutional Neural Networks has used deep CNN to classify 1.3 million high resolution images (Krizhevsky,2012). Convolutional Neural Network-Based Human Detection in Nighttime Images Using Visible Light Camera Sensors has used CNN after normalization and histogram equalization of images on different databases such as CVC-14, DNHD-DB1, KAIST and obtained an overall average F1-score of 97.29% (Kim,2017). Human Detection and Tracking on Surveillance Video Footage Using Convolutional Neural Networks has used CNN and obtained accuracy of 76.4% (Dinama,2019). A Study on CNN Transfer Learning for Image Classification has analyzed the performance of transfer learning model namely INCEPTION V3 which has the pretrained weights, on the popular datasets with human, cars and animals and obtained accuracy of 93, 87 and 73 respectively on the individual classes by train (Hussain,2018). EfficientNet: Rethinking Model Scaling for Convolutional Neural Networks has explored the working of the transfer learning model Efficientnet which has 8 variants from b0 to b8 with the popular imagenet dataset and has shown a considerably good performance with the same dataset when compared to other popular transfer learning models with a very small number of parameters and in size. Detailed scores about the EfficientNet model performance and comparison was discussed (Tan,2020).

Automated video surveillance addresses human beings' real-time commentary to explain their behaviours and interactions. This paper offers a singular multi-man or woman monitoring device for crowd counting and normal/ unusual occasions detection at indoor/outside surveillance environments. The proposed device includes 4 modules: human beings' detection, head-torso template extraction, monitoring and crowd cluster evaluation. Firstly, the device extracts human silhouettes the use of inverse rework in addition to median clear out lowering the value of computing and dealing with numerous complicated tracking situations. Secondly, human beings are detected through their head torso because of much less numerous and rarely occluded. Thirdly, every person is tracked via consecutive frames the use of the Kalman clear out strategies with Jaccard similarity and normalized cross-correlation. Finally, the template marking is used for crowd counting having cues localization and clustered through Gaussian mapping for normal/unusual occasions detection. The experimental consequences on tough datasets of video surveillance which includes PETS2009 and UMN crowd evaluation datasets display that the proposed device gives 88.7% and 95.5% in phrases of counting accuracy and detection rate (Shehzed,2019).

Surveillance systems are an important part of industry, factories, organizations, and homes. They can store information and actually provide additional support for the work of the guards. In addition, it provides excellent support for various automated processes in the chemical industry that require continuous monitoring of specific chemical reactions. To control theft and avoid catastrophic behavior, you need to install such a system at a fraction of the cost of time. In this article, we have proposed the hardware and software implementation of an intelligent monitoring system using Espressif's latest ESP32 microcontroller. The proposed implementation captures a continuous video, sends it using the microcontroller's built-in WiFi feature described above, and displays it in a SPITFT module connected to the receiver (Rai,2019). This article proposes an integrated framework based on a deep convolution framework for detecting anomalous human behavior from standard RGB images. The Deep Convolutional Framework, in contrast to previous object detection algorithms, is a (1) human subject detection and identification module, (2) space, proposed to solve the problem of object entity isolation. The results show that the proposed method provides satisfactory performance for detecting anomalous behavior in real-world scenarios.[9] Sustainable smart city initiatives around the world have recently had a major impact on the lives and social changes of our citizens. More specifically, data-driven intelligent applications that efficiently manage scarce resources provide a futuristic vision for smart, efficient and secure city operations. However, the ongoing COVID 19 pandemic has revealed the limits of existing smart city deployments. As a result; the development of systems and architectures that can provide fast and effective mechanisms to limit the further spread of the virus is paramount. An active surveillance system capable of monitoring and implementing social distances between people can effectively delay the spread of this deadly virus. This paper proposes a data-driven deep learning-based framework for the sustainable development of smart cities that provides a timely response to counter the COVID 19 pandemic through massive video surveillance. To implement social distance monitoring, we used three deep learning-based real-time object detection models to detect people in a video captured by a monocular camera. For effective deployment, we validated the system performance against a real video surveillance dataset (Shorfuzzaman,2021).

Managing distributed intelligent surveillance systems is recognized as a major challenge for the extensive aggregation and analysis of video information in the cloud. In smart healthcare applications, remote monitoring of patients and the elderly requires robust responses and alerts from monitoring systems within the available bandwidth. Creating a robust video surveillance system requires fast response and fast data analysis between connected devices located in a real-time cloud environment. Therefore, the proposed research work will introduce a cloud-based object tracking and behavior identification system & # 40; COTBIS & # 41;. You can integrate the Edge Computing Functional Framework into the gateway layer. This is a new Internet of Things (IoT) research area that can bring robustness and intelligence to distributed video surveillance systems by minimizing network bandwidth and response time between wireless cameras and cloud servers. is. Further improvements are made by integrating background subtraction and deep convolution neural network algorithms into moving objects and using rank queries to detect and classify monitored anomalous fall activity. Therefore, the IoT-based intelligent video surveillance system proposed for healthcare with edge computing significantly reduces network bandwidth and response time, and overturns when compared to existing cloud-based video surveillance systems. Maximize the accuracy of your predictions (Rajavel,2022).

Most of the models in the above review are trained with images taken on daylight with high resolution cameras and it works fairly with the nighttime CCTV images. So, the datasets in the above papers are not completely sufficient for our case. Since YOLO outperforms the other existing solutions, it is chosen to be the base model and even YOLO is hard to bring into production due to its size as well as the huge dependencies of it.

DATASET DESCRIPTION

Data Collection

Preparing right data is the most important thing to train a robust CNN model. Neural networks also take large amount of data to train than the traditional ML algorithms to recognize the pattern in the data. So huge amount of data has been prepared from multiple sources. Several important aspects are considered while preparing the data to prevent the overfitting of the model. Data has been collected from different possible sources such as Kaggle, Stanford computer vision database, UCI ML repository with various lighting, position and mostly images taken at night. Some manual photos collected from robbery incidents have also been added so that the model only focuses on learning the key pattern of humans. An overall 10,000 images have been collected from various sources such as Kaggle, Stanford computer vision database, CIFAR dataset, PASCAL object detection dataset. Out of 10000 images 4200 images have human in it and 5800 images don't have human it and by the way binary classification dataset is prepared. Figure 2 shows the distribution of Class variables of human and non-human from the training dataset.

Data Samples Visualization

Figure 3 shows the sample images considered for training the data with the class label as Humans and considered as Class 1 (with Humans)

Figure 4 shows the sample images considered for training the data with the class label as Humans and considered as Class 2 (without Humans)

Figure 2. showing the class distribution

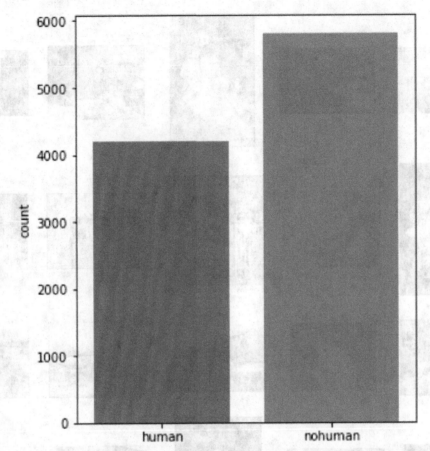

Data Augmentation

Several augments such as random crop, flip, brightness, contrast have been applied to the original data of 10000 images with the help of image processing techniques so the model learns the pattern of human properly as well as to increase the size of training dataset. The overall performance of maximum ML fashions, and deep mastering fashions in particular, relies upon at the quality, amount and relevancy of education records. However, inadequate records is one of the maximum not unusual place demanding situations in imposing device mastering withinside the enterprise. This is due to the fact gathering such records may be highly priced and time-ingesting in lots of cases. Data augmentation is a fixed of strategies to artificially boom the quantity of records through producing new records factors from present records. This consists of making small modifications to records or the use of deep mastering fashions to generate new records factors. Machine mastering packages specially withinside the deep mastering area maintain to diversify and boom rapidly. Data augmentation strategies can be an excellent device towards demanding situations which the synthetic intelligence global faces. Data augmentation is beneficial to enhance overall performance and results of device mastering fashions through forming new and extraordinary examples to educate datasets. If the dataset in a device mastering version is wealthy and sufficient, the version plays higher and greater accurately. For device mastering fashions, gathering

Figure 3. Showing the examples of images with humans

and labeling of records may be onerous and highly-priced processes. Transformations in datasets through the use of records augmentation strategies permit groups to lessen those operational costs. One of the stairs right into a records version is cleansing records that's important for excessive accuracy fashions.

Figure 4. Showing the examples of images without humans

However, if cleansing reduces the representability of records, then the version cannot offer appropriate predictions for actual global inputs. Data augmentation strategies permit device mastering fashions to be greater strong through growing versions that the version might also additionally see withinside the actual global. The benefits of data expansion are: improved model prediction accuracy, add training data to the model, avoiding data shortages for better models, reduces data overfitting (that is, statistical errors, that is, the function is very closely associated with a limited set of data points) and creates data variability, increase the generalization ability of the model, help solve the problem of class imbalance in classification, reduce data collection and labeling costs, allows prediction of rare events, prevent privacy issues.

PROPOSED METHODOLOGY

Approach Overview

A CNN based Deep learning model (Binary classification model) is trained with the prepared dataset along with its augmentations to detect whether there is a human in an Image. A properly trained model can detect humans even if they wear any mask/helmet. Now once the model's training and validation is complete and model is finally deployed. Now on the test time CCTV footage is accessed and video is converted into frames and then frames into RGB values using computer vision techniques and then preprocessing steps are applied and is passed on to the model deployed on python to detect is there a human in the image. If model detects any humans, then it means someone has trespassed the shops in the restricted time and now alarms in the shops can be activated. An alert notification and call also be sent to the authority immediately.

Architectural Design

The overall architecture for the complete smart surveillance system is initially designed which involves reading the video from CCTV, processing it into frames, passing it into the model for prediction and an alarm notification section. Detailed view of the architecture is given below in figure 5.

Deep learning models are used for the binary classification task of detecting the humans in the image. The binary output is used to make the decision of alarm and notification ringing. Computer vision techniques are used for the image capturing from the video preprocessing into RGB values, several data augmentation techniques such as contrast, saturation, flip, rotate which increases the dataset size. Machine Learning is basically giving computers the power of decision-making without being explicitly programmed for the specific task. Instead, the data related to the task are collected and rich attributes based on which the output is determined are extracted. Now the extracted attributes are fed to the learning algorithms along the appropriate label to each sample. Figure 6 shows the steps involved in the working of ML algorithm.

The learning algorithms tries to optimize the error it makes using the derivative based gradient descent algorithms thereby increasing the accuracy of the prediction. The parameters associated with the learning algorithms are randomly initialized and is changed at each step based on the derivative of the error function which is calculated as the difference between the actual labels and the predicted labels. The training of the model stops at the point when the algorithm reaches the global or local minima for the cost function where the error cannot be reduced further. There are two types of machine learning algorithms namely supervised and unsupervised learning. Supervised learning algorithm is a technique where the extracted features and the corresponding label related to the data are feed to the model and the model tries to minimize the error it makes. If the algorithm makes a prediction from a discrete set of values, then it comes under classification. Whereas if the model tries to predict a value from a continuous range, then it comes under Regression. Each algorithm differs from one another on the basis of parameters, how it tries to optimize and other things. Unsupervised learning is basically trying to finding the pattern from the raw unlabeled data. The tasks such as dimensionality reduction as well as clustering can be performed with such algorithms.

The major drawback of the Machine learning algorithms is that it needs rich extracted features and cannot able to very complex functions. It can't able to process and find the pattern in very high dimensional

Figure 5. Overall architectural design of the system

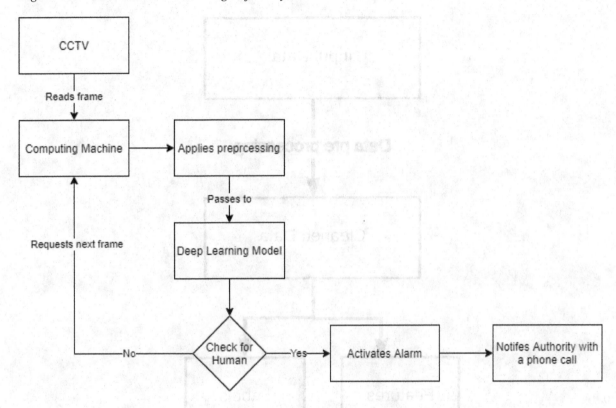

data and thereby it cannot be used to for image classification tasks since a simple 30 x 30 RGB image will creates 900 x 3 = 2700 features. Not only it has performance issues it will also end up in memory issues since ml algorithms are not incrementally trainable and all data has to be loaded before training.

To overcome the issues with ML algorithms, neural networks and deep learning is being used. Neural networks are kind of supervised algorithms which are capable of learning the complex patterns in the data. It consists of an input layer, hidden layers followed by an output layer which is also known as the classification layer based on classification and regression task and it comes with the cost of high computation cost. Neural networks take very high learning time due to the computational complexity it has and also it needs very large amount of data for the large number of parameters to get optimized. Unlike machine learning these algorithms are incrementally trainable so data can be loaded and processed in forms of chunks. Figure 7 showing the performance of traditional ML algorithms and deep learning algorithms when the data size increases

Even though neural networks can deal with high dimensional data it is not sufficient enough to deal with the huge dimension of images and also not sufficient to find the pattern in the images. This is the place convolution neural networks are introduced to learn the patterns in the data. Convolutional Neural Networks (CNN) is a specialized form of neural network model specially designed to work with the image data and has a primary usage on the modern computer vision applications. It differs from the ordinary neural network from the aspects of parameter sharing, sparsity of connections, and the number of parameters learned. In ordinary deep neural there will be a input layer, hidden layer and a output layer and also weight matrices as connection between each neuron. In Convolution neural network model fil-

Figure 6. Showing the working of the ML algorithm

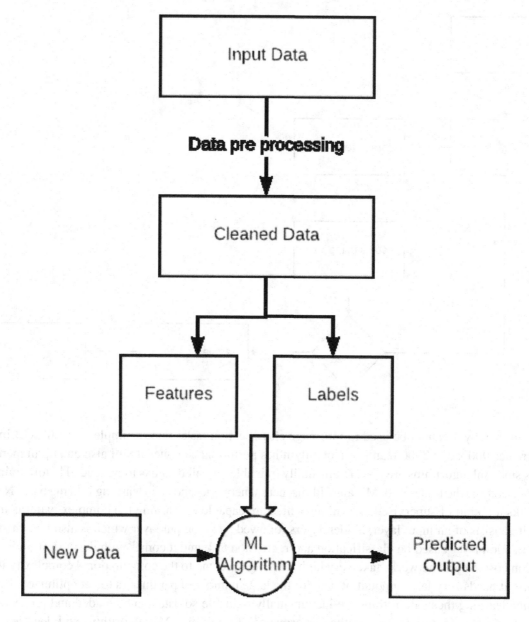

ters/convolution operations are used with pooling layer for dimensionality reduction and a final softmax layer for classification. The important benefit of having a sparse connection is that it improves greatly in reducing the training time and also it reduces the data requirement and memory management. It is widely used for the image classification task and the Convolution operations has the tendency to capture the pattern in the image data to a much better extend than the ordinary neural networks or traditional machine learning algorithms. Figure 8 showing the overall architectural design of the CNN model

Several convolutions and pooling layers are used in the process of feature extraction. In the convolution layer, the number of filters of specified size is used which is applied as a mask to the image, and dot product is generated. Based on the value of stride, the filter mask is moved and the process is repeated,

Figure 7. Showing the performance of traditional ML algorithms and deep learning algorithms when the data size increases

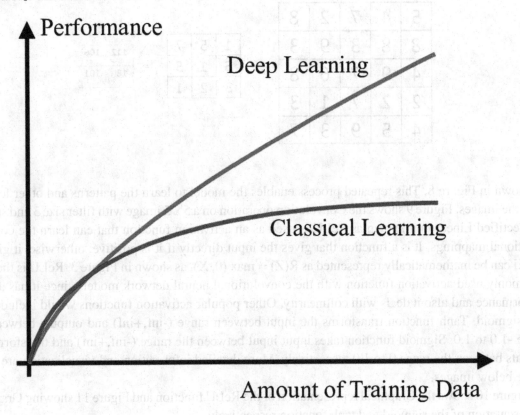

Figure 8. Showing the overall architectural design of the CNN model

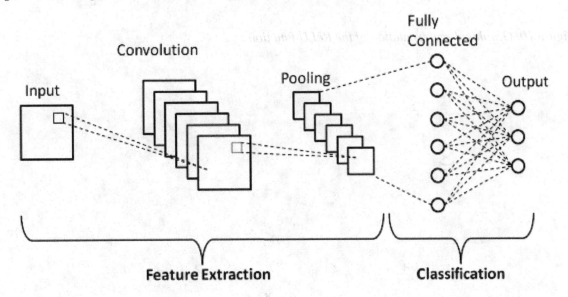

Figure 9. Convolution operation on a 5 x 5 image with filter size 3 and stride 2

5	4	7	2	8
8	8	3	9	3
4	9	7	6	8
2	2	7	1	3
4	5	9	3	7

X

1	5	7
6	1	5
3	2	1

=

112	106
18	101

as shown in Figure 8. This repeated process enables the model to learn the patterns and other features with the images. Figure 9 shows the Convolution operation on a 5 x 5 image with filter size 3 and stride 2

Rectified Linear unit known as ReLU is used as an activation function that can learn the complex functional mappings. It is a function that gives the input directly if it is positive; otherwise, it gives 0. ReLU can be mathematically represented as $R(Z) = max(0, X)$, as shown in Figure 3. ReLU is the most commonly used activation function with the convolutional neural network models since it has a good performance and also it deals with collinearity. Other popular activation functions would include tanh and sigmoid. Tanh function transforms the input between range (-inf,+inf) and outputs between the range -1.0 to 1.0. Sigmoid function takes input input between the range (-inf,+inf) and transforms the outputs between the range 0 to 1.0 respectively. More detailed information and visualization are given in the below images.

Figure 10 shows the Graphical representation of the ReLU function and Figure 11 showing Graphical representation of the sigmoid and tanh function respectively.

Pooling layer is then used to minimize the spatial size of the convolved features. It can overcome the overfitting issue. Max-pooling is commonly used, it considers the maximum of the region from the feature map obtained from the convolution operator, as shown in Figure 12.

Figure 10. Graphical representation of the ReLU function

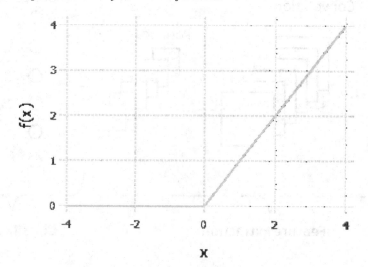

Figure 11. Showing Graphical representation of the sigmoid and tanh function respectively

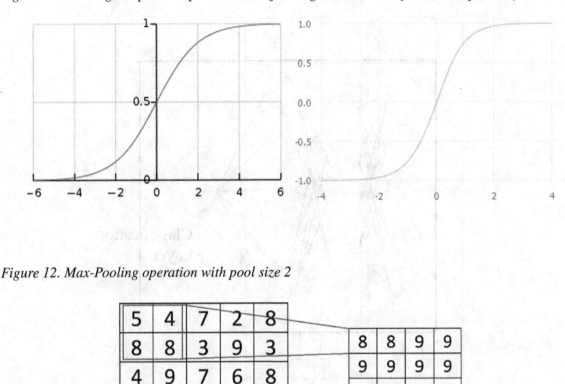

Figure 12. Max-Pooling operation with pool size 2

The learned features are then unrolled. The fully connected dense layer utilizes the flattened features and a single neuron in the last layer acts as a classifier. Sigmoid activation is used to make a prediction. It generates probability value between 0 and 1where the values greater than 0.5 are classified as class positive others are negative. Figure 13 Fully connected layer for classification

Transfer learning is a another biomimic from the human knowledge. Humans have the ability to use the knowledge gained for one task and reuse the knowledge for another task without starting from scratch. For example, a tennis player will feel more comfortable to learn badminton than a guy who never been in sports. In traditional machine learning each algorithm has a primary goal of minimizing the error it makes from a random assignment of weights. In deep learning this random assignment of weights can be kickstarted with the weights that are trained for some other similar tasks. So, Transfer learning is the process using the models which are already pre-trained for a certain task as a starting point to another similar task so the model generalizes more quickly since most of the parameters are already modified in accordance to the new task. Transfer learning has a wide usage and application particularly in the fields of Computer Vision. Figure 14 showing the working of the transfer learning algorithm and Natural Language Processing as creating an extensive set of annotated data is a time-consuming process. The main motivation for the transfer learning is that pre-trained models already has updated weights so the model can train with considerably small amount of data. Also, the training time associated with the

Figure 13. Fully connected layer for classification

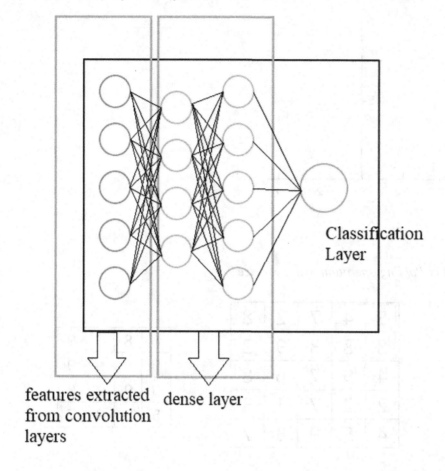

model can also be reduced by reducing the number of epochs. Each transfer learning model is designed for appropriate use case with a heavy modification in the architecture and size. The below image gives the detailed overview about the popular transfer learning models such as EfficientNet, Inception, Resnet, Densenet, Nasnet with their performance on the Imagenet dataset and their associated size.

IMPLEMENTATION

Algorithmic Overview

Based on Figure 6 Efficient net is found to outperform the popular the deep learning models with a good margin considerably with very less parameters. So as a good to start Efficient net B3 model architecture is chosen for training and modelling for the Human detection binary classification task. The architecture is reused along with the weights file which are pre-trained already with the ImageNet dataset. The model chosen is trained with the annotated image dataset of 10k images for 50 epochs with early stopping and learning rate scheduler functions.

Figure 14. Showing the working of the transfer learning algorithm

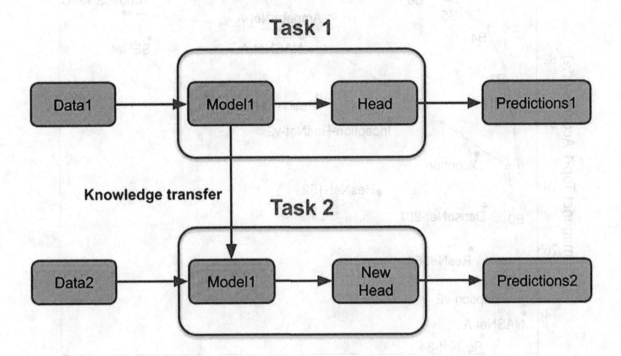

Early stopping function automatically stops further training when the validation scores are continuously decreasing for n rounds. This ensures that the model is not overfitted to the training dataset. Similarly learning rate scheduler reduces the learning rate exponentially after each epoch and it ensures that the global/local maxima is not skipped and the model generalizes properly. Precision and Recall were used as the evaluation metrics and the performance details are provided on section 8. The F1 score is a common metric for assessing the performance of a classification model. For the multiclass classification, apply the averaging technique to calculate the F1 score and create different average scores (macro, weighted, micro) in the classification report.

Use precision for general model performance reports with balanced datasets. Use specificity / recall / sensitivity when all the instances of what you are looking for are not to be missed. Examples include healthcare testing, fraud detection, and security issues. It catches some false positives, but it's not that bad if you avoid the actual illness / scam / danger. Use precision if you want to make sure that what your model is pinging is correct. You'll miss some of what you're looking for, but if your model pings something, rest assured that it's actually what it says. Think about screening applicants. Some viable applicants escape, but if the model pings a viable applicant, you can trust it. Use the F1 score as the average of recall and fit, especially when working with unbalanced datasets. If either the recall or the fit rate is 0, the F1 score reflects that it is also 0. For example, categorize tweets by emotion, positive, negative, or neutral, but the dataset was unbalanced with a much more neutral rating than positive or

Figure 15 showing the performance comparison of the transfer learning algorithms.

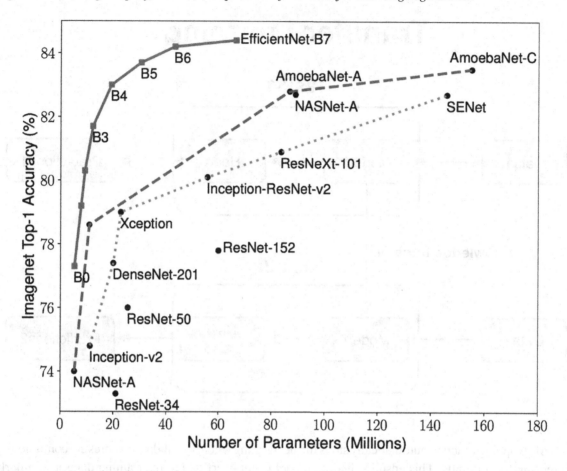

negative. Only the macro F1 score properly described the overall performance of the model (all three classes are taken into account equally).

The trained Efficientnet-B3 model is saved for validation and deployment purpose. Google AI introduced EfficientNet and, as the name implies, tried to suggest a more efficient method while improving the results so far. Models are typically created with too wide, too deep, or very high resolutions. Increasing these properties will help the model at first, but it will soon saturate and the model created will have more parameters and will be inefficient. With EfficientNet, they are scaled more primarily. H. Gradually everything will increase. The entire dataset of 10000 images is split using 70/30 strategy (70% data for training and 30% data for validation). Now the trained CNN model is validated using the 30% validation data and an overall f1-score of 95% as well as accuracy of 95% is obtained on the unseen data. More detailed performance metrics are shown on the table 1.

Comparison With Existing Models

The chosen YOLOv3 which is currently the best state-of-art human detection model as per literature survey is used for the comparing the results with the proposed model. YOLOv3 (You Only Look Once, Version three) is a real-time item detection set of rules that identifies particular items in videos, stay

Table 1 displaying the validation results of the efficientnet-b3 model

Classes	Precision	Recall	F1 - Score	Support
0	0.95	0.98	0.96	1731
1	0.97	0.93	0.95	1257
Accuracy			**0.95**	2988
Macro Avg	0.96	0.95	0.95	2988
Weighted Avg	0.96	0.95	0.95	2988

feeds, or images. YOLO makes use of functions discovered with the aid of using a deep convolutional neural community to stumble on an item. Versions 1-three of YOLO had been created with the aid of using Joseph Redmon and Ali Farhadi.

The object classification system is used by artificial intelligence (AI) programs to recognize specific objects in a class as areas of interest. The system classifies the objects in the image into groups. Objects with similar properties are placed together in the group, and other objects are ignored unless specifically programmed. As is common with object detectors, the features learned from the convolution layer are passed to the classifier, which makes the detection predictions. At YOLO, predictions are based on convolutional layers using 1x1 convolutions.

YOLO means "see only once" because it uses 1x1 times in prediction. The size of the prediction map is exactly the same as the size of the previous feature map.

The first model of YOLO become created in 2016, and model three, that is mentioned considerably on this article, become made years later in 2018. YOLOv3 is an progressed model of YOLO and YOLOv2. YOLO is carried out the usage of the Keras or OpenCV deep mastering libraries. Now with the same validation dataset used on the proposed model YOLO obtained **91%** overall accuracy and the proposed efficientnet model outperforms the existing solution. More detailed performance metrics for the YOLO are shown in the table 2.

Table 2. Displaying the validation results of the YOLOv3 model

Classes	Precision	Recall	F1 - Score	Support
0	0.87	0.99	0.93	1731
1	0.99	0.79	0.88	1257
Accuracy			**0.91**	2988
Macro Avg	0.93	0.89	0.90	2988
Weighted Avg	0.92	0.91	0.91	2988

Clearly the proposed model outperforms the YOLO with a margin of 4% and the below figure shows the scores in graphical format. Figure 16 showing the scores comparison between the two models.

The YOLOv3 model is around 249 MB in size. Whereas the proposed Efficientnet b3 model is around 131 MB in size. Figure 17 showing the comparison of sizes of the two models.

Figure 16. Showing the scores comparison between the two models

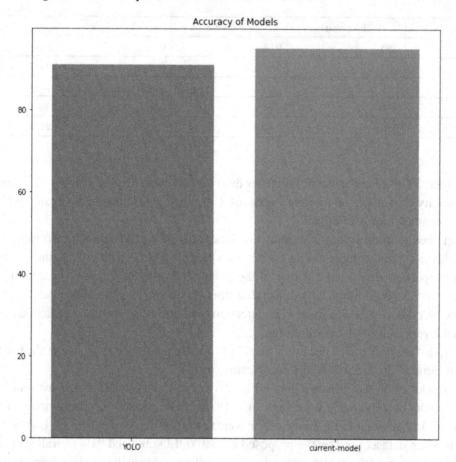

SAMPLE DEMONSTRATION

The tested model is then deployed in the python environment for the real time testing. A real robbery footage is used to check the working simulation and the performance of the model. The model was successfully able to detect the intruders immediately upon their entry and an alert call is send successfully to the respective authority. Figure 18 showing the robbery footage frames

In the above video footage frame the robber approximately enters the shop around 53rd second and around the same second our model correctly detects intruder detection. Figure 19 showing the alarm start as well as the alert call made to the authority

The main aim and the goal of this project is to make the cities and human settlements safe, secure and sustainable. For our safety, security and welfare, we need an intelligent monitoring system that creates affordable environment. Our application promotes security and welfare of the Shop owners. Not only it promotes safety, also it decreases loss that occurs in economy due to robbery.

Figure 17. Showing the comparison of sizes of the two models.

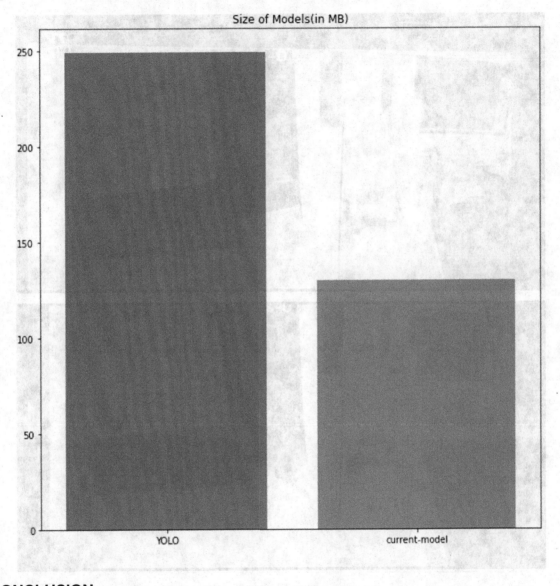

CONCLUSION

The aim of the project was to create an end-to-end fully automated surveillance monitoring system to overcome the existing issues. The study within a short span of time addressed an AI powered solution with Deep learning and computer vision techniques.

We could be able to find a good architecture and with a reliable performance over the test data the model has succeeded the aim and also the proposed model has also clearly outperformed YOLO which the existing solution for human detection in terms of both performance as well as space. Transfer learning model EfficientNet-B3 is used which has a robust performance had greatly helped to save the time in architectural design and fine tuning of parameters of hyperparameters of various layers in the CNN model. It also reduced the data preparation work to some extent since the pretrained model can be trained with a short amount data.

Figure 18. Showing the robbery footage frames

The developed model should be very useful for the business sectors to monitor the workspace in the absence of the authority along with the robbery prevention in the shops. The main constraint for the project deployment is the requirement of a CCTV camera in the shops.

In future, activity recognition methodologies (which is presently an active research topic) can be incorporated which involves learning the patterns from image using CNN and passing it on to the Recurrent Neural Networks (RNN) models in hybrid mode to analyze and track the individual movement of humans so based on their suspicious behavior and actions even daytime robbery at the stores can also be prevented.

Figure 19. Showing the alarm start as well as the alert call made to the authority

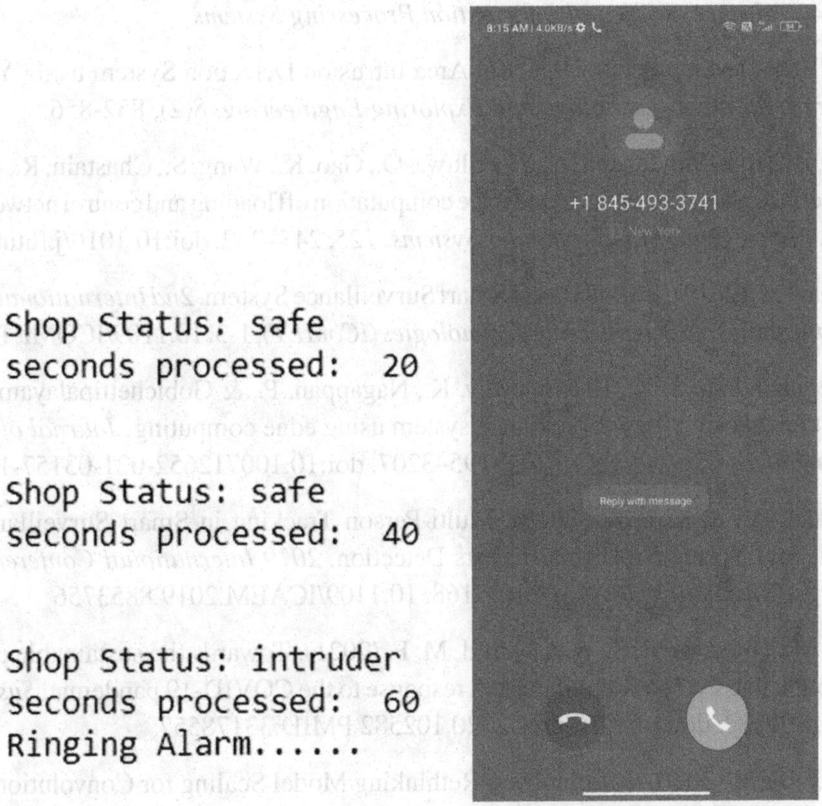
+1 845-493-3741
New York
Shop Status: safe
seconds processed: 20
Shop Status: safe
seconds processed: 40
Reply with message
Shop Status: intruder
seconds processed: 60
Ringing Alarm......

REFERENCES

Dinama, D. M., A'yun, Q., Syahroni, A. D., Sulistijono, I. A., & Risnumawan, A. (2019). Human Detection and Tracking on Surveillance Video Footage Using Convolutional Neural Networks. *International Electronics Symposium (IES)*, 534-538. 10.1109/ELECSYM.2019.8901603

Galanopoulos, A., Ayala-Romero, J. A., Leith, D. J., & Iosifidis, G. (2021). AutoML for Video Analytics with Edge Computing. *IEEE INFOCOM 2021 - IEEE Conference on Computer Communications*, 1-10. 10.1109/INFOCOM42981.2021.9488704

Hussain, M., Bird, J. J., & Faria, D. R. (2018). A Study on CNN Transfer Learning for Image Classification. *UK Workshop on computational Intelligence*, 191-202.

Kim, J. H., Hong, H. G., & Park, K. R. (2017). Convolutional Neural Network-Based Human Detection in Nighttime Images Using Visible Light Camera Sensors. *Sensors (Basel)*, *5*(5), 1065. doi:10.339017051065 PMID:28481301

Ko, K.-E., & Sim, K.-B. (2018). Deep convolutional framework for abnormal behavior detection in a smart surveillance system. *Engineering Applications of Artificial Intelligence*, *67*, 226–234. doi:10.1016/j.engappai.2017.10.001

Krizhevsky, A., Sutskever, I., & Hinton, G. E. (2012). ImageNet Classification with Deep Convolutional Neural Networks. *Advances in Neural Information Processing Systems*.

Lee & Kim. (2019). Development of Specific Area Intrusion Detection System using YOLO. *International Journal of Innovative Technology and Exploring Engineering, 8*(2), 852-856.

Qu, C., Calyam, P., Yu, J., Vandanapu, A., Opeoluwa, O., Gao, K., Wang, S., Chastain, R., & Palaniappan, K. (2021). DroneCOCoNet: Learning-based edge computation offloading and control networking for drone video analytics. *Future Generation Computer Systems, 125*, 247–262. doi:10.1016/j.future.2021.06.040

Rai, P., & Rehman, M. (2019). ESP32 Based Smart Surveillance System. *2nd International Conference on Computing, Mathematics and Engineering Technologies (iCoMET)*, 1-3. 10.1109/ICOMET.2019.8673463

Rajavel, R., Ravichandran, S. K., Harimoorthy, K., Nagappan, P., & Gobichettipalayam, K. R. (2022). IoT-based smart healthcare video surveillance system using edge computing. *Journal of Ambient Intelligence and Humanized Computing, 13*(6), 3195–3207. doi:10.100712652-021-03157-1

Shehzed, A., Jalal, A., & Kim, K. (2019). Multi-Person Tracking in Smart Surveillance System for Crowd Counting and Normal/Abnormal Events Detection. *2019 International Conference on Applied and Engineering Mathematics (ICAEM)*, 163-168. 10.1109/ICAEM.2019.8853756

Shorfuzzaman, M., Hossain, M. S., & Alhamid, M. F. (2021). Towards the sustainable development of smart cities through mass video surveillance: A response to the COVID-19 pandemic. *Sustainable Cities and Society, 64*, 102582. doi:10.1016/j.scs.2020.102582 PMID:33178557

Tan, M., & Le Quoc, V. (2020). EfficientNet: Rethinking Model Scaling for Convolutional Neural Networks. *International conference on machine learning*, 6105-6114.

Wang, Y., Wang, W., Liu, D., Jin, X., Jiang, J., & Chen, K. (2022). Enabling Edge-Cloud Video Analytics for Robotics Applications. IEEE Transactions on Cloud Computing. doi:10.1109/TCC.2022.3142066

Chapter 7
Role of Deep Learning in Image and Video Processing

Alageswaran Ramaiah
SASTRA University (Deemed), India

Arun K. S.
Accenture, Australia

Yathishan D.
SASTRA University (Deemed), India

Sriram J.
SASTRA University (Deemed), India

Palanivel S.
SASTRA University (Deemed), India

ABSTRACT

Image and video processing research is becoming an important area in the field of computer vision. There are challenges such as low-resolution images, poor quality of videos, etc. in image and video data processing. Deep learning is a machine learning technique used in the creation of AI systems. It is designed to analyse complex data by passing it through many layers of neurons. Deep learning techniques have the potential to produce cutting-edge results in difficult computer vision problems such as object identification and face recognition. In this chapter, the use of deep learning to target specific functionality in the field of computer vision such as image recovery, video classification, etc. The deep learning algorithms, such as convolutional neural networks, deep neural network, and recurrent neural networks, used in the image and video processing domain are also explored.

DOI: 10.4018/978-1-7998-8892-5.ch007

INTRODUCTION

The mechanism used to construct or deconstruct visual images and videos for Deep learning applications are new area of machine learning that can be quite difficult to meet the challenges like low resolution images, recovery of data from old images, human and object detection through computer vision in real time etc. Video processing works with detection and classification, whereas image processing deals with picture enhancement and image analysis. In order to tackle obstacles, image data is examined and analysed using picture filtering, morphological processes, and segmentation. Deep learning necessitates the ability to learn features automatically from data, which is often only achievable when a large amount of training data is available, particularly for issues with high-dimensional input samples, such as photographs.

Image Processing

The process of transferring a picture to a digital format and processing it to extract useful information is known as image processing. When using specific signal processing approaches, the image processing system normally interprets all pictures as 2D signals. Visualization, Pattern recognition, Retrieval, Recognition, Sharpening and Restoration are five types of image processing techniques Image filtering, morphological procedures, and segmentation are used to evaluate and analyse image data to address these difficulties. It needs masses of training data, particularly for issues with high-dimensional input samples, like photos, to learn features automatically.

Deep learning is a concept that aims to mimic how the human brain analyses information to make decisions, predictions, and recognition. In deep learning, computers learn from a given data set to discover patterns and traits. Deep learning uses training data to construct a model that can categorise data. In deep learning, data is input into a deep neural network to learn and forms a model to generate the intended output. Figure 1 shows the work flow of data (SRC: https://nanonets.com/blog).

Deep learning is a promising topic in picture and video analysis. Deep learning methods aid in automated imaging segmentations with emphasis on different attributes collected from the picture or video datasets. It gives a novel technique of identifying anomalies and improved diagnosis. The software is led to describe a model able to anticipate the proper result using training datasets. The prediction model is evaluated against a known dataset apart from the training set.

Applications of Image Processing

The modern day is emerging with new technology, and the digital revolution is in full swing. Image processing can be done in various domains like health, non-destructive evaluation, forensic studies (for handling evidences), material science, film industry (For editing, visualising), document processing, graphical arts, and printing industry are all examples of image processing applications.

Some use cases of Image Processing are as follows.

- Defence Services: Vehicle navigation, Target tracking and detection, automatic target recognition and missile guidance.
- Medical Imaging / Visualization: Assist medical practitioners in interpreting medical imaging and diagnosing abnormalities more quickly.
- Aid in surveillance and biometric authentication for law enforcement and security.

Figure 1. Data work flow

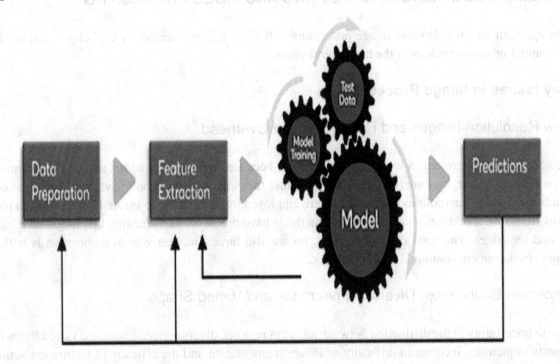

- Self-Driving Technology: Assists in the detection of objects as well as the imitation of human visual cues and interactions.
- Image Restoration & Sharpening: Enhance the quality of photographs by using common filters, for example.

Applications of Video Processing

The programme generates video captions automatically. These video captions identify objects in the video sequence. Video processing is particularly useful for helping policymakers understand and react to current events (Sharma.V et al., 2021).

Some of the use cases of Video Processing are as follows:

- Hospitals: Video surveillance is used by healthcare organisations to monitor their facilities for fire-prone zones/thermal temperature, Asset Tracking Solutions, and workplace safety.
- Military Services: The objects within the footage would have been labelled to know the objects, such as a travelling car, a weapon, or a person.
- Smart cities: Traffic management, transportation, flame and smoke detection, safety, and security.
- Crowd management is a popular application of video analysis and assists in the real-time or periodic counting of persons at exit and access points within a facility.

CHALLENGES IN IMAGE PROCESSING AND VIDEO PROCESSING

The applications on video and image processing still faces a great number of challenges despite the substantial progress made over the last several years.

Key Issues in Image Processing

Low Resolution Images and Reconstruction Overhead

Researchers are interested in low-resolution images because they are easy to get and don't cost much to process. However, they are hard to classify because they are noisy and don't have much information. Traditional linear interpolation techniques were employed by researchers to create high-resolution pictures from low-resolution photos, but these methods have problems like aliasing, blurring, and a halo around the edges. The costs of building back up are also high. The best way to reconstruct is with a super-resolution convolutional neural network.

Uncertain Boundaries, Diverse Appearance and Varied Shape

Due to uncertainty in the distinction between adjacent regions, diverse appearance, and varied forms of objects in pictures, increase in difficulty of image segmentation and the efficacy of feature extraction decreases.

Low-Resolution Photos are hard to make High-Resolution

A high-resolution picture cannot be generated from a low-resolution image because of aliasing, blurred continuous scenes created by the low-resolution sensor's physical dimensions, blurring caused by sensor motion that changes from image to image, and noise induced by the acquisition process. The high-resolution images may help fix these issues.

Insufficient Size and Labelling of Picture Collections

Deep learning needs a vast amount of well-labelled training data. Manually annotating all of the images in a collection requires a significant amount of time and skill. Over-labelling with excessive information prevents clinical flow and wastes time, which is a problem for researchers who urge for standardised, methodical, and easy labelling.

Low Lighting Image

Images acquired in low-light circumstances are prone to low visibility, which can decrease the performance of most computational photography and computer vision systems. High-level activities like object tracking, identification, and detection are hampered by pictures of poor aesthetic quality and insufficient information transfer (Pandey.B et al., 2021), (Ganesh.B et al., 2018).

Key Issues in Video Processing

Videos of Poor Quality

Long-distance live camera footage causes significant occlusions in video surveillance applications. There are a lot of occlusions at religious festivals, airport arrival and departure terminals, and other places with a lot of people. Surveillance cameras with low traffic can't take high-quality videos like the ones that already exist, where the target person is clear and obvious. The subject is small because the camera is far away, which makes the operation harder.

Racking and Locating of Multisubject

Tracking even a single moving object from many is a challenge in real time. Because the tracker lacks a precise dynamic model, the major issue of tracking is the target motion uncertainty. There is no guarantee that the transition function will work between time series will be calculated correctly.

Dynamic Backgrounds

The surveillance camera is used in most real-world applications to record complicated and changing backdrops. As a result, these videos are shot against a variety of dynamic backgrounds. In addition, real-time video sequences almost always feature varying lighting, occlusions, and changing views, complex and dynamic situations complicate video processing.

Lack of Well-Formed Dataset

The evaluation of Deep Learning techniques necessitates the use of large video processing datasets. Action identification on Joint-annotated Human Motion Data Base (JHMDB) proved difficult due to its data annotation technique. In research, it's performed poorly. Proper annotation in video datasets is very important. For video processing, the lack of a well-formed dataset is a barrier. Videos from a variety of fields are also sought for. According to studies, video data availability is a problem.

Lack of Computation Power

The current success of video processing is owing to developments in hardware, in addition to technique innovations and large amounts of accessible training data. Researchers were confronted with a number of problems, including a lack of sufficient computational resources for massive amount of video data processing. Deep learning techniques require specialised processing hardware known as Graphics Processing Unit (GPU), which is responsible for handling memory accesses and memory manipulations in order to create pictures faster and send them to a display device, (Sharma.V et al., 2021).

NEURAL NETWORKS IN IMAGE AND VIDEO PROCESSING DOMAIN

Neural Networks are used to classify images, sounds, and language. For example, to predict sequences, Recurrent Neural Networks (LSTM) is utilised, and to classify images Convolution Neural Networks and Deep Neural Networks are used. It is the layer to feed model data. This layer's neurons are the number of features in the data (number of pixels in the case of an image).

The information is then obtained by the hidden layer from the input layer. There might be several hidden layers depending on the model and the amount of the data. The number of neurons in each hidden layer might vary, although it is often more than the number of features. The output of each layer is calculated by multiplying the output of the layer before it by the weights of that layer, which can be learned, and then adding biases that can also be learned, followed by an activation function that makes the network nonlinear.

Convolution Neural Network

Convolution Neural Network (CNN) is a mesh-based feed-forward neural network for data processing. This neural network detects and classifies items in images. Figure 2 shows CNN Architecture.

Figure 2. CNN Architecture

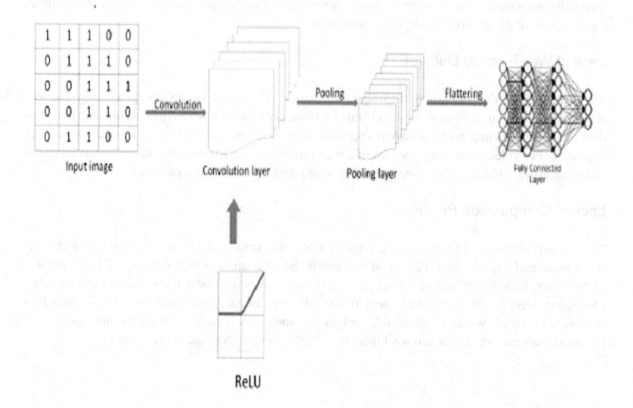

Layers in CNN

The various hidden layers of CNN aid in the extraction of data from images. The CNN's four important layers are as follows

- Convolutional layer
- Activation layer
- Pooling layer
- Fully connected layer

Convolutional Layer

The convolution layer consists of many filters that execute the convolution process, which extracts important characteristics or features from a picture. Every image is considered as a matrix of pixel values. It also detects edges in the images. The result of the Convolutional layer is called the "Feature map," and it shows details like the corners and edges of the picture. Afterward, this feature map is fed to other layers to learn more about the original picture.

Consider 5*5 image, where each pixel has value either 0 or 1. There is also a filter matrix with 3*3 cells is shown in Figure 3. The convolved feature matrix, is obtained from the dot product of matrix of input image and filter.

Figure 3. Pixel values of Input Image and Filter

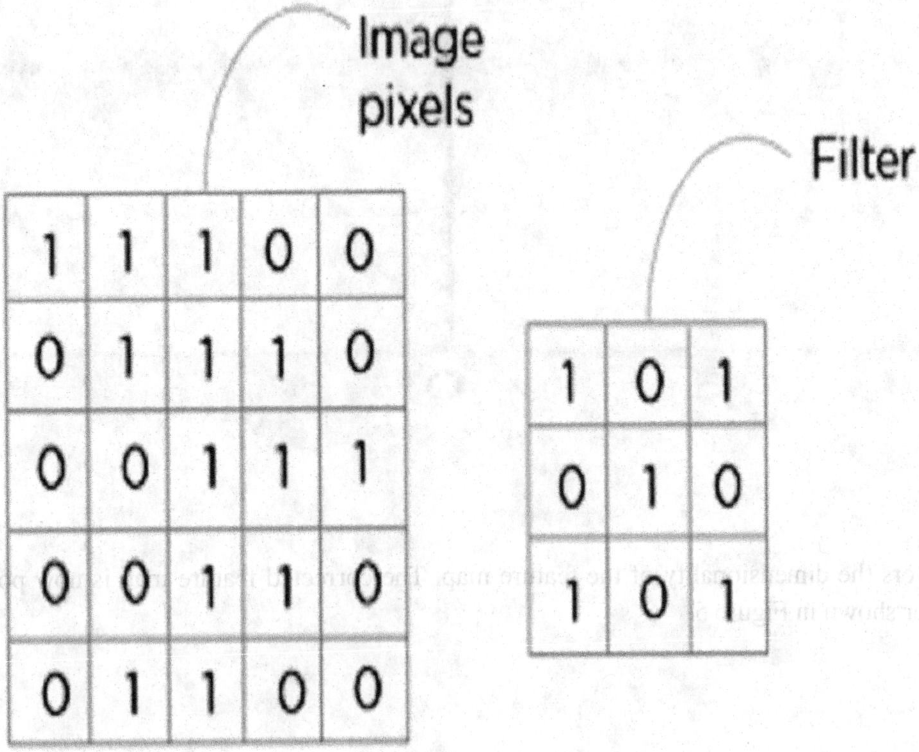

Activation Layer

On adding bias to a weighted sum, the activation function figures out whether a neuron should be turned on or not. The activation function of a neuron is designed to make the output of the neuron non-linear, which is the primary goal of the function. The ReLU, Softmax, tanH, and Sigmoid functions are among the most often utilised activation functions. They all serve a distinct purpose. Here, Activation Function ReLU is discussed below.

After extracting the feature maps, place them to a Rectified linear unit layer, which operates element-by-element, converting all negative pixels to 0. It adds nonlinearity to the network and produces a corrected feature map is shown in Figure 4. R(Z)=max (0, Z), It gives an output Z if Z is positive and 0 otherwise.

Figure 4. ReLU

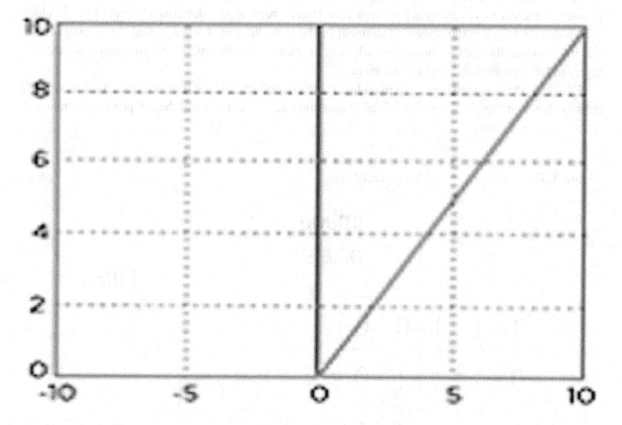

Pooling

Pooling lowers the dimensionality of the feature map. The corrected feature map is now pooled by a pooling layer shown in Figure 5.

Figure 5. Maximum Pooling layer

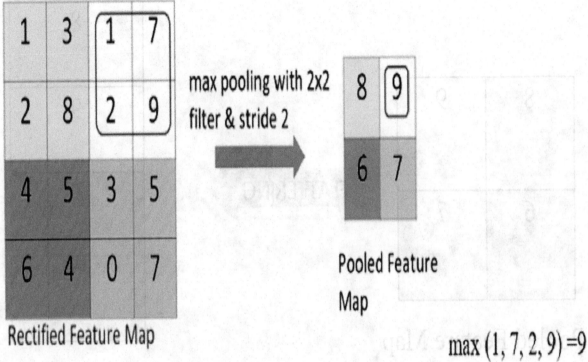

Fully Connected Layer

Fully Connected Layer are feed forward networks. The output of the final Pooling or Convolutional Layer is sent into the fully linked layer after being flattened. The next phase is flattening. Flattening turns all 2-D arrays from pooled feature maps into single linear vector is shown in Figure 6 (Avijeeth Biswal, 2022).

Recurrent Neural Networks

Recurrent Neural Network (RNN) operates based on the notion of storing the output of a certain layer and sending it back as the input. Hidden state in RNN, which remembers certain information about a sequence is the most essential characteristic of RNN. Architecture diagram of RNN is shown in Figure 7.

y denotes the output layer, x denotes the input layer and h denotes the hidden layer. The network parameters A, B, C used to improve the output of the model. The input layer x processes the input and sends it to the middle layer. h is the middle layer which contains many numbers of hidden layers. By delivering the identical biases and weights for every layer, raising parameters in RNNs are reduced in complexity by passing each previous output onto the next hidden layer, making it easier for the RNN to retain what it has learned before.

The RNN will standardise the activation functions, weights, and biases across hidden layers. A single hidden layer is created and looped as many times as needed.

Figure 6. Data after Flattening

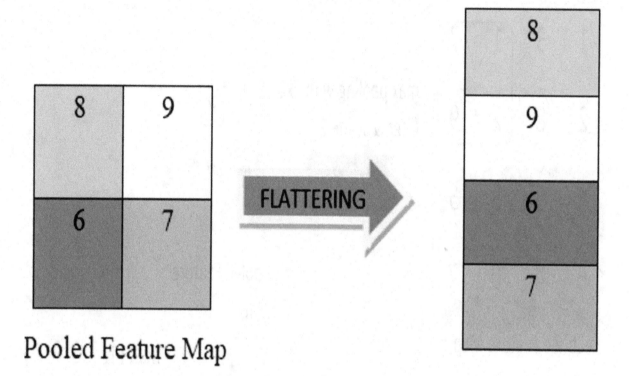

Figure 7. RNN Architecture

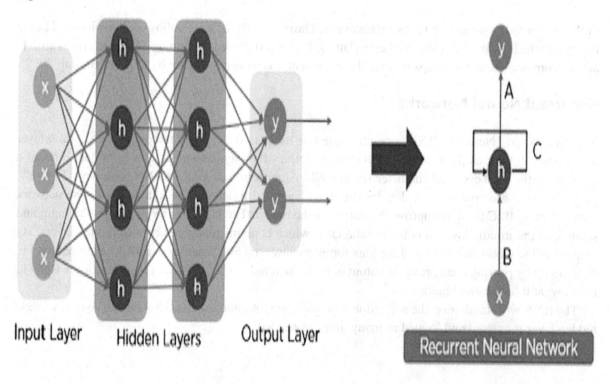

Using RNNs, a picture may be captioned based on the actions that are taking place in the image e.g., if the image as shown in Figure 8 is given as input. It analyses activities and results "A bird is flying in the sky" (Avijeeth Biswal, 2022).

Figure 8. Sample Input for RNN

ROLE OF DEEP LEARNING IN IMAGE PROCESSING

The act of processing a picture to extract information or improve it is known as image processing. medical imaging, image segmentation, Picture restoration, etc. are all examples of digital image processing applications. Methods for each step vary. The image processing techniques for deep learning are as follows:

1. Image Recovery
2. Linear Filtering
3. Independent Component Analysis
4. Pixelation
5. Template Matching

Image Recovery

There are several reasons why an image may get damaged or worse, for instance, an ancient photograph shot with the earliest camera technology may lose its original shape or become fuzzy. This may occur if the picture is subjected to physical stress, or if it is stored digitally, it may degrade due to motion blur or additive noise. Degradation model, which can remove the degradation effects on the input picture, may be used to address the problem which is shown in Figure 9. The deterioration model is based on a linear shift-invariant convolution. So, take the True Image before deterioration and the Observed Image after deterioration, and estimate the True Image using the degradation filter. Image recovery using inpainting is shown in Figure 10. Image inpainting (or "paint loss compensation"). This approach is often used to eliminate undesirable elements from images and repair damaged areas (Gopal Singh Panwar, 2022).

Figure 9. Image Recovery

Linear Filtering

Linear filtering is a method in which the value of the output pixel is a linear combination of the adjacent input pixel values. Convolution is the method used to accomplish this operation which is shown in Figure 11. Convolution is the process of adding each picture component to its nearby neighbours, weighted by the size of the kernel (Gopal Singh Panwar, 2022).

Figure 10. Image Inpainting

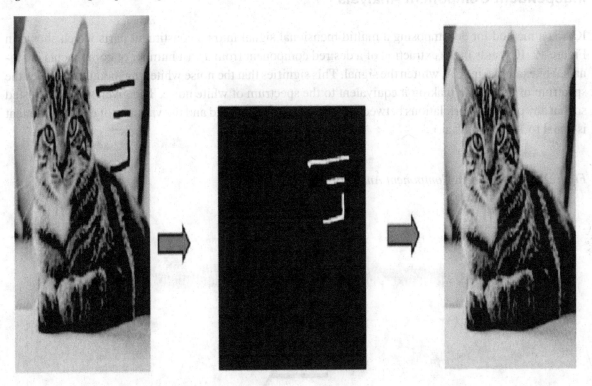

Figure 11. Linear Filtering

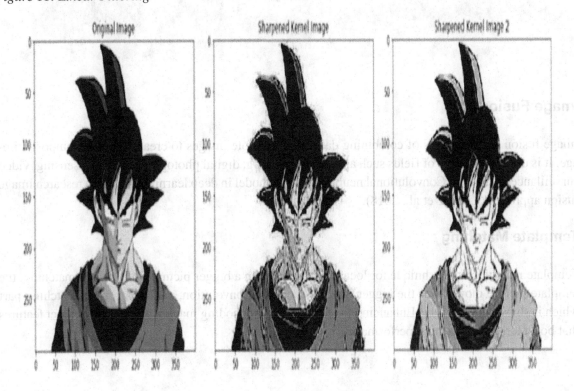

Independent Component Analysis

ICA is a method for decomposing a multidimensional signal into its constituent parts which shown in Figure 12. ICA aids in the extraction of a desired component from a vast number of components or signals. For example, in ICA, whiten the signal. This signifies that the noise whitening module equalises the spectrum of the signal, making it equivalent to the spectrum of white noise. The given will be adjusted so that any potential correlations between its components are erased and the variance of each component is equal to 1 (Neputune.ai.).

Figure 12. Independent Component Analysis

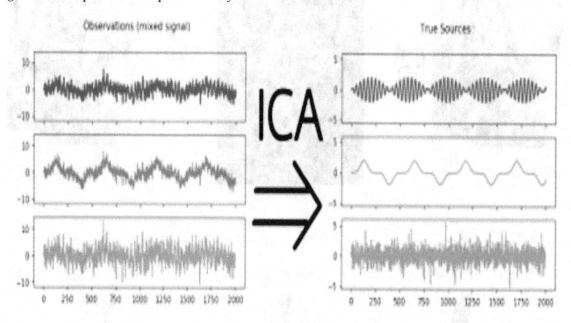

Image Fusion

Image fusion is the process of combining data from multiple images to create a single composite image. It is used in a variety of fields such as medical imaging, digital photography, remote sensing, video surveillance, and so on. Convolutional neural networks model in deep learning is used to research image fusion approach (Chou.Y et al., 2018).

Template Matching

Template matching is a technique for locating a template in a bigger picture. In template matching, the template picture moves over the bigger image, much like convolution, and look for the matching part which is shown in Figure 13. Enhancing the CNN's shape encoding may result in more distinct features that boost template matching performance.

Figure 13. Template Matching

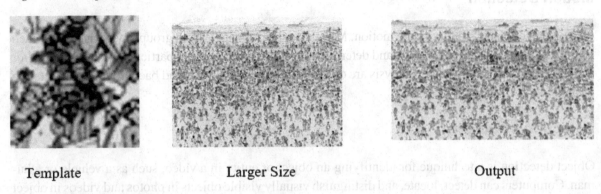

| Template | Larger Size | Output |

Low Light Image Enhancement

Images taken in outdoor scenes can be severely degraded due to poor lighting conditions. These images can have low dynamic range with high levels of noise affecting the overall performance of computer vision algorithms. To make computer vision algorithms robust in low light, use LightenNet, which takes an input low light image and outputs its light map, which is then used to acquire the image. Enhanced image based on Retinex model. Both in terms of quality and the quantitative test results show that our method produces accurate light maps and achieves more natural and detailed results than existing methods (Li.C et al., 2021), (Li.C et al., 2018).

ROLE OF DEEP LEARNING IN VIDEO PROCESSING

In video processing, security camera feeds are encoded or encrypted. Analysis of human behaviour and crowd anomalies are important research areas in video processing. By employing RNN, DNN, and CNN and other deep learning techniques such as AlexNet, ResNet, and LSTM substantially improves the video processing. For machine learning, video processing approaches include the following:

1. Recognition of Human Action
2. Motion Detection
3. Object Detection
4. Video Classification
5. Background Subtraction

Recognition of Human Action (HAR)

HAR monitors walking, bending, falling, climbing, and sitting for activity analysis. HAR identifies one or more people's behaviours in a circumstance and provides relevant information. HAR systems are used to monitor human behaviour, including injury detection in sports, behaviour analysis recognition, surveillance. ageing and child care. Deep learning architectures for sequential data, such as RNNs and LSTMs, may be better for HAR issues than CNN (Liu.Y et al., 2018).

Motion Detection

Motion detection determines scene motion. Motion analysis identifies and groups motions inside video frames, Object tracking in real time and determines motion direction. Two particular methodologies for deducting motion or movement analysis are differential equation models and background segmentation (San.P.P et al., 2018).

Detection of Object

Object detection is a technique for identifying an object or entity in a video, such as a vehicle or a human. Computers can detect, locate, and distinguish visually visible objects in photos and videos in object detection tasks. Detecting moving objects in video footage offers a variety of real-world applications. Furthermore, object recognition in video data is very useful in real life. LSL-Net to perform high-precision detection of low-altitude flying objects in real time to provide information. Both You Need Only One (YOLO and Single Shot Detector (SSD) are end-to-end learning detection methods, which fundamentally solve the problem of speed detection (Gong.M et al., 2020).

Video Classification

Video classification aims to classify movies automatically based on their content and frame composition. It's similar to photo classification, in which photographs are categorised based on their content and the features of a certain class. In the case of video categorization job, video frame division (image) each second, followed by a comparable picture categorization task performs. In terms of precision and independence extraction functions, the RNN, CNN and combination approach performs better than the CNN dependent method.

Background Subtraction

In a video clip, the important part is sometimes not the background, but the items in the foreground. These fascinating items might be animals, humans, automobiles, and so on. Background subtraction is the detection and processing of a foreground item from a video. Background removal techniques are also a typical way for search-space reduction and focus of attention modelling in video analysis. Eventually, it is simple to identify foreground objects. background subtraction methods based on DNNs and Generative Adversarial Network (GANs) architecture, (Tao.Y et al., 2021), (Bouwmans.T et al., 2019).

CONCLUSION

As there are large amount of picture and video data created by developing technologies in computer monitoring systems, the data must be pre-processed. Analysing and making prediction on those data is not simple and hence deep learning algorithms are used to solve this issue and the same is explored in this chapter. Advancements in deep learning models like CNN, RNN and approaches improve aspects such as computing power, accuracy, and the amount of input parameters, while also reducing computation time. The role of deep learning in image and video processing and its challenges are dealt in detail.

REFERENCES

Biswal. (2022). *Top 10 Deep Learning Algorithms You Should Know in 2022*. https://www.simplilearn.com/tutorials/deep-learning-tutorial/deep-learning-algorithm

Bouwmans, T., Javed, S., Sultana, M., & Jung, S. K. (2019). Deep neural network concepts for background subtraction: A systematic review and comparative evaluation. *Neural Networks*, *117*, 8–66. doi:10.1016/j.neunet.2019.04.024 PMID:31129491

Chou, Y., Roy, S., Chang, C., Butman, J. A., & Pham, D. L. (2018, April). Deep learning of resting state networks from independent component analysis. In *2018 IEEE 15th International Symposium on Biomedical Imaging (ISBI 2018)* (pp. 747-751). IEEE. 10.1109/ISBI.2018.8363681

Ganesh, B., & Kumar, C. (2018). Deep learning Techniques in Image processing. *National Conference On Emerging Trends in Computing Technologies (NCETCT-18)*.

Gong, M., & Shu, Y. (2020). Real-time detection and motion recognition of human moving objects based on deep learning and multi-scale feature fusion in video. *IEEE Access: Practical Innovations, Open Solutions*, *8*, 25811–25822. doi:10.1109/ACCESS.2020.2971283

Gopal, S. P. N. (2021). *Image Processing Techniques That You Can Use in Machine Learning Projects*. neptune.ai/blog/image-processing-techniques-you-can-use-in-machine-learning

Li, C., Guo, C., Han, L. H., Jiang, J., Cheng, M. M., Gu, J., & Loy, C. C. (2021). Low-light image and video enhancement using deep learning: A survey. *IEEE Transactions on Pattern Analysis and Machine Intelligence*, (01), 1–1. doi:10.1109/TPAMI.2007.250595 PMID:34752382

Li, C., Guo, J., Porikli, F., & Pang, Y. (2018). LightenNet: A convolutional neural network for weakly illuminated image enhancement. *Pattern Recognition Letters*, *104*, 15–22. doi:10.1016/j.patrec.2018.01.010

Liu, Y., Chen, X., Wang, Z., Wang, Z. J., Ward, R. K., & Wang, X. (2018). Deep learning for pixel-level image fusion: Recent advances and future prospects. *Information Fusion*, *42*, 158–173. doi:10.1016/j.inffus.2017.10.007

Pandey, B., Pandey, D. K., Mishra, B. P., & Rhmann, W. (2021). A comprehensive survey of deep learning in the field of medical imaging and medical natural language processing: Challenges and research directions. *Journal of King Saud University-Computer and Information Sciences*.

San, P. P., Kakar, P., Li, X. L., Krishnaswamy, S., Yang, J. B., & Nguyen, M. N. (2017). Deep learning for human activity recognition. In *Big data analytics for sensor-network collected intelligence* (pp. 186–204). Academic Press. doi:10.1016/B978-0-12-809393-1.00009-X

Sharma, V., Gupta, M., Kumar, A., & Mishra, D. (2021). Video Processing Using Deep Learning Techniques: A Systematic Literature Review. *IEEE Access: Practical Innovations, Open Solutions*, *9*, 139489–139507. doi:10.1109/ACCESS.2021.3118541

Tao, Y., Zongyang, Z., Jun, Z., Xinghua, C., & Fuqiang, Z. (2021). Low-altitude small-sized object detection using lightweight feature-enhanced convolutional neural network. *Journal of Systems Engineering and Electronics*, *32*(4), 841–853. doi:10.23919/JSEE.2021.000073

Chapter 8
Gesture and Posture Recognition by Using Deep Learning

Alageswaran Ramaiah
SASTRA University (Deemed), India

Subramani V.
SASTRA University (Deemed), India

Aishwarya N.
SASTRA University (Deemed), India

Ezhilarasie R.
SASTRA University (Deemed), India

ABSTRACT

Sign language facilitates communication in the community with speaking and hearing problems. Those people communicate with one another using hand gestures and body movements. These techniques of human-computer interaction range from primary keyboard inputs to complex vision-based gesture detection systems. One of the fascinating HCI technologies is hand gesture recognition. The goal of gesture recognition is to construct a system to use as a communication medium in various applications. The application of gesture recognition has become popular in healthcare, robotics, etc. Posture recognition is deployed in several sectors, including medicine. Deep learning-based models are used to understand gesture and posture recognition results better. This chapter covers the challenges of gesture and posture recognition and how deep learning techniques are used to assist machines in overcoming these challenges more effectively. In addition, this chapter also discusses the applications in which gesture and posture recognition can be employed in detail.

DOI: 10.4018/978-1-7998-8892-5.ch008

INTRODUCTION

Gesture Recognition

A gesture is an example of nonverbal communication. When speaking, a gesture is a motion of the hand, arms, or other body part that is used to communicate or accentuate something. In other words, gestures are motions of the body that convey something (Alnaim, 2020). A wave of the hand, for example, is a typical gesture used to greet someone. Hands and face are the most prevalent. Some advancement in glove-based systems finally enabled the realisation of computer vision-based recognition without needing any sensors mounted to the glove (Praveen & Shreya, 2015).

The purpose of gesture recognition is to identify distinct human gestures, for which domestic & global research experts have sought to use deep neural networks. To capture data, early gesture recognition systems relied mostly on wired machinery and devices in direct contact with the hand, such as data gloves, accelerometers, and multi-touch displays (Abhishek et al., 2020). These sensors can detect the angle and position of fingers, joints, and arms, among other things.

Facial gesture recognition is another method for efficiently developing non-contact interfaces between humans and robots. Despite the many physical differences between users, the major goal of facial gesture recognition for robots is to capture emotions and communication indicators among people.

Posture Recognition

Posture refers to how human body is positioned when sitting, standing, or laying down. Posture is good when train the body on how to sit, stand, walk, and lay in such a way that muscles and ligaments are not overworked when moving or doing weight-bearing tasks.

Posture recognition is extensively used in a variety of sectors, including geriatric health care, environmental awareness, HCI (Human-Computer Interaction), surveillance, and physical training.

The posture recognition system is divided into two parts.

- The stage of training and assessment.
- The stage of deployment.

Posture Analysis

A good posture recognition result may be used to analyse and anticipate people's movement, which can be useful in the smart home, gaming entertainment, and motion analysis fields. People's lives will be made easier by incorporating posture detection into smart devices and services. Figure 1 shows hand gesture of human (SRC: Coldewey, 2019). In the future, posture recognition capabilities might be extended to a variety of smart gadgets, broadening the range of products and services available. The postures made by human are shown in Figure 2 (SRC: Ding, W et al., 2020).

Figure 1. Hand Gesture

Figure 2. Human Posture

TYPES AND WORKING OF GESTURE RECOGNITION AND POSTURE RECOGNITION

Types in Gestures and Postures

Gesture: Adaptors, emblems, and illustrators are the three primary types of gestures.

- **Adaptors:** An adapter is a physical movement that humans use to adapt or adjust to a communication process. Tapping foot before starting a test is an example.
- **Emblems:** Gestures have highly specific symbolism within a particular ethnic, cultural, or subcultural group. Waving to say hello is an example.
- **Speech Illustrators:** Speech illustrators are gestures are used to enhance human speech. A good example is saying no while waving finger.

Posture: The way to hold the body is called posture. There are two kinds of them: When walking, running, or bending over to pick something up is called dynamic posture (Islam M. Z. at el., 2019). It is called static posture when not moving, such as sitting, standing, or sleeping.

Working of Recognition and Analysis System

Gesture

Images from a webcam are necessary for the model to train and validate. The input photos are believed to include essentially one hand, with gestures done with the hand, the palm facing the webcam, and the hand nearly in vertical. If the surrounding is simple and the contrast on the hand is great, the identification process will be less complicated and more efficient. As a result, it's thought that the photos' backgrounds are simpler and more consistent. The photographs' backgrounds were eliminated using the background subtraction technique. Background subtraction is primarily based on the K-gaussian, which determines the proper Gaussian distribution and allows for improved adaptation to change sceneries due to variations in light. Only the picture of the hand remains after the background has been removed. The photos were then turned to grayscale. Because grayscale pictures only have one colour channel, Convolutional neural network (CNN) will have a simpler time in learning them.

Gesture recognition can be handled using models based on mathematical hidden Markov chains or soft computing approaches. The capacity to recognise a range of data for gesture recognition is a crucial benefit of employing the hidden Markov model. The automated detection of gestures necessitates their temporal segmentation, often identifying the gesture's start and finish locations in terms of mobility frames in both time and space. The process of recognition is shown in Figure 3. Furthermore, the prior context has an impact on gestures as well as other motions.

Figure 3. Progression of recognition-based control

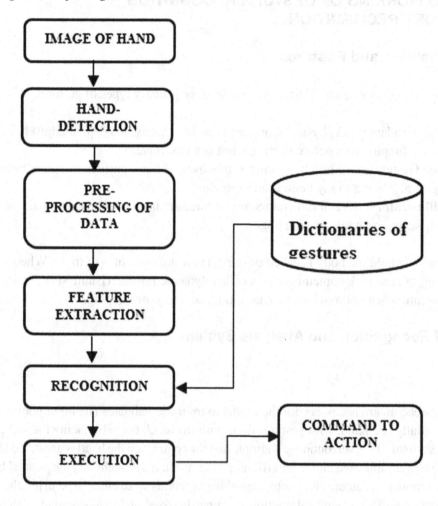

POSTURE RECOGNITON AND ANALYSIS

Based on CNN Algorithm

Visual Geometry Group Network (VGGNet), Residual Network (ResNet), Densely Connected Convolutional Networks (DenseNet), Inception Residual Network (InceptionResNet), and Extreme-Inception (Xception) are just a few pre-trained deep models based on CNN (Nikitha.J at el., 2022). Figure 4 shows ensemble of all above model to recognise posture.

VGG-Net

With up to 19 layers, VGG is an object-recognition model. Beyond the ImageNet, VGG, created as a deep Network, surpasses baselines on a range of tasks and datasets. The VGG-Net accepts images with a size of 224×224. VGG is currently one of the most extensively used image-recognition models. Rectified Linear Unit used in the VGG hidden layers.

Dense-Net

A dense net is a convolutional network that is densely linked. All previous output is input for a subsequent layer in Dense-Net. Dense-Net was created to increase accuracy in elevated neural networks due to the diminishing gradient. This becomes unstable as it advances deeper into the network; for example, when going from the third layer to the fourth layer, the fourth layer receives input from not only the third layer but all previous levels.

XCEPTION

In Extreme Inception, 1x1 convolutions are used to compress the original input, and model applied different filters to each depth space based on the input spaces (Chollet.F, 2017).

Resnet

The Res-Net network employs a VGG-19-inspired 34-layer plain network design, after which the skip connection is added. Res-Net's skip connections alleviate the problem of gradients that are vanishing in deep neural networks by enabling the gradient to flow on an additional shortcut path.

Inception-ResNet v2

Inception and residual connections are combined in the Inception-ResNet architecture. A 299-by-299 image is fed into the network, which returns a list of predicted probability. In the Inception-Resnet block, multiple-sized convolution filters are combined with residual connections. Adding residual blocks not only overcomes the issue of deep structural deterioration but also decreases training time in half.

CHALLENGES IN GESTURE AND POSTURE RECOGNITION AND ANALYSIS

Gesture Recognition System

- Gesture recognition is based on an image of a hand performing a single gesture against a clean white backdrop under well-lit conditions. However, such is rarely the case in reality.
- Human does not always have the opportunity of exhibiting gestures on solid, clean backgrounds.
- The gesture recognition system must be built to remove the time lag between executing and recognising a gesture.
- The way human conduct certain gestures varies greatly. While human has a high error tolerance, this variance may make gesture recognition more challenging.

Posture Recognition

- Due to the massive number of possible cases, human posture recognition is a challenging task.

- The number of possible postures determines by the degree of freedom available to the human body.
- The morphology of the individual does affect how the posture is recognized. Furthermore, clothing can create various appearances for the same posture.
- Human limbs are many, flexible, and complicated. It isn't easy to detect when there is a rapid interchange of comparable bodily motions.
- A variety of identical movements are challenging to distinguish.

Figure 4. Ensemble of deep models using CNN models.

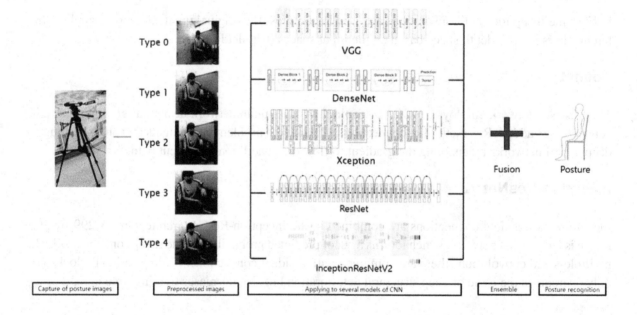

DEEP LEARNING

Deep learning is a branch of machine learning that concentrates on methods inspired by the brain's structure and function. Artificial neural networks are the name given to these algorithms. Deep learning eliminates a few of the input pre-processing that machine learning requires. These algorithms can absorb and interpret unstructured data, including text and images, and automate feature extraction, eliminating the need for human experience. For instance, suppose having a collection of images depicting various gestures that wanted to classify. The deep learning system then changes and fits itself for accuracy via gradient descent and backpropagation, enabling it to generate more precise predictions about a new image of a gesture.

However, deep learning algorithms are pretty complex, and various neural networks have been developed to address particular issues or datasets. For example, CNNs, commonly used in computer vision applications and image classification, can recognise characteristics and patterns within a picture, allowing activities like object detection and recognition.

Hardware for Deep Learning

Deep learning needs a massive amount of computing power. With high performance, Graphical Processing Units (GPUs) are suitable as they can handle an enormous volume of computations in multiple cores with enough memory. On the other hand, managing multiple GPUs on-premises may significantly demand internal resources and be very expensive to scale.

Need for Deep Learning

- Deep learning handles challenging issues that need discovering hidden patterns in data and a thorough grasp of the complex interactions between a large number of interdependent values.
- One of deep learning's most compelling features is its ability to work with unstructured data. This feature is vital for the business context, given that most company data is unstructured. Businesses usually use text, images, and voice as data formats. Since traditional machine learning algorithms are limited in their capacity to analyse unstructured data, this wealth of knowledge often remains untapped. And this is where deep learning has the most significant potential for impact.

THE NEED FOR DEEP LEARNING IN GESTURE RECOGNITION

a) Non-Standard Backgrounds

Gesture recognition should operate well irrespective of the environment: it should recognise well in a vehicle, at home, or while down in the street. Deep learning enables the machine to differentiate the hand from the background consistently.

b) Movement

By definition, the gesture is a movement rather than a static image. Thus, gesture recognition should be capable of identifying patterns; for example, rather than recognising a picture of an open palm, human may recognise a waving action and interpret it as an order to exit the currently used application.

c) Combination of Movements

Additionally, since gestures may consist of multiple movements, human must offer context and recognise that patterns such as moving fingers clockwise and displaying a thumb may be used to indicate a limited number of files or a limited region.

d) Diversity of Gestures

Humans perform specific gestures in a wide variety of ways. While humans have a great tolerance for inaccuracy, this inconsistency may make it more difficult for robots to recognise and classify movements. This diversity is another area where deep learning may be beneficial.

e) Fighting the Lag

The gesture detection system must be designed so that there is no latency between performing and classifying a gesture. Adoption of hand gestures can only be facilitated by displaying their consistency and instantaneity. There is no other incentive to begin using gestures if that cannot improve the speed and convenience of human interaction. In an ideal world, we'd want to attain a negative latency (classification even before the gesture is completed) to instantly provide user feedback.

THE NEED FOR DEEP LEARNING IN POSTURE RECOGNITION

- The traditionally used methods for human posture recognition divides into two categories: computer vision and acceleration sensor data processing. While acceleration sensor-based methods have the drawback of requiring extensive data processing, their violation of privacy is well tolerable. Computer vision-based posture recognition systems are mature and accurate in recognising individual postures.
- Accelerometer-based methods may achieve excellent recognition accurate in motion states. As acceleration sensors could not capture static data, they have difficulty recognising positions, structures, etc. As a result, the demand for deep learning is expanding faster than the need for sensor-based recognition.

APPLICATIONS OF GESTURE AND POSTURE RECOGNITION SYSTEM

The gesture is a non-verbal communication by which using a recognition process that can not only help hard of hearing people communicate with the outside world. Gesture recognition can help in a variety of areas, including:

- **Public health:** Businesses and organisations might assist prevent the transmission of germs by eliminating the need for touchscreen devices on self-service kiosks. This is particularly useful in preventing the spread of viral infections like Covid-19.
- **Health diagnostics:** Doctors may identify patients with ailments or fall risks by analysing their movements, which can help them improve their overall attitude. Aside from gait patterns, gesture analyses and deep learning may be used to detect minor movements like tics and spasms, which can assist in recognition of probable diagnoses.
- **Security:** Programs that identify hand movements and transmit response alarms can be set up. In contrast, home security protocols may be programmed to distinguish the appearance of hands carrying firearms and provide a warning as a response. Or, in the case of a heist, an organisation may set up and teach personnel around a particular hand movement so that when cameras pick up the motion, that can immediately inform law enforcement.

Because of its potential uses, human posture detection is an appealing and demanding problem in computer vision. Several areas can benefit from posture recognition such as:

- Personal health care
- Environmental awareness
- Surveillance systems
- Sports

The following applications of gesture recognition are available:

- Hand Gesture Recognition,
- Gesture identification for the sign language interpretation
- Aid to physically challenged.

Hand Gesture Recognition

The identification of gestures is the most significant and widely accepted technological advancement. This technology has evolved in both commercial and non-commercial products. Gesture recognition incorporates a range of gestures, including greeting and nodding. Computers and other information technology devices are primarily based on the detection process, tracking the item and eventually recognising it. Hand gestures may be an excellent approach to convey emotions and convey a message. It includes many applications, such as sign languages, that are utilised for various reasons. There are two sorts of gesture modes: offline and online gestures. Online Gestures are primarily aimed at the rotation of tangible objects. At the same time, Offline gestures are gestures that get involved and processed with an object due to the user's interaction, for example, menu activation.

The hand Recognition system involves different types of four phases.

- Data acquisition
- Pre-processing and Hand segmentation
- Feature extraction
- Recognition

Transfer learning is used to train the classifier for hand pattern identification. Only the hand pattern is needed to recognise a static gesture. The computer is given the command once the trained classifier has categorised the hand pattern as a static gesture. Dynamic gestures, unlike static gestures, involve both the shape and motion of the hand. Uni - directional and multi-directional is two types of dynamic hand shapes. For commanding, unidirectional hand signals necessitate the form and direction of movement of the hand, but multi-directional gestures necessitate the location of the hand as well as its shape.

Gesture Identification for the Sign Language Interpretation

Since the beginning of time, gestures have been an essential part of effectiveness. Sign language, a visual communication method, is built on hand gestures (Sharma.S & Singh.S, 2021).

There are two types of hand motions in sign language: static and dynamic. Static gestures are described as the positioning of fingers and hands in space with no movement regarding time. In contrast, dynamic gestures are described as continuous hand movement with time. The hand gesture recognition method for sign language translation may be done in two ways: vision-based recognition and contact-based recognition.

Challenges in Contact-Based Recognition

The signer must wear electronic equipment, such as data gloves, accelerometers and other similar devices, in the contact-based procedure. These components detect movement changes and send the information to a computer for further evaluation. This method has produced strong identification results, but it is costly and cumbersome for everyday HCI interface users.

Solution by using Deep Learning

A vision-based method uses to improve the convenience of hand recognition. The vision-based technique is more user-friendly since the signer's data is captured using a camera. This technology, based on image processing techniques to analyse the obtained data, lowers users' reliance on sensory equipment. The sign language translation system might use a vision-based approach for recognising static hand motions. A unique and resilient approach based on a CNN can present a solution to this problem.

Aid to Physically Challenged

Gesture recognition is the process of identifying distinct bodily motions and human behaviours. Analysing information embedded in the gesture not expressed by speech or text is the actual efficacy of gesture recognition. Movements resulting from muscle and joint problems, such as Lumbar spondylosis, Tennis elbow, and others, are used as inputs to the system. The Kinect sensor creates a 3D depiction of the body gestures utilising twenty joint body coordinates. The symptoms of seniors suffering from muscular and joint problems are the medical disorders considered for this suggested effort (Saha.S at el., 2013). These diseases develop due to accident, exhaustion, or ageing and exacerbate by the disabled people's lifestyle. As a result, this algorithm may be used in home monitoring systems for the elderly.

When an elder conducts their whole day's activities, the Kinect sensor records their skeleton and compares each frame of the footage to the database in a real-time identification scenario. Using a neural network creates the best-matched body gesture. If the user has discomfort in any region of their body, the system suggests doing specific exercises. If the pain persists, it recommends that patient to seek medical advice.

The following applications of Posture recognition are available:

- Classroom student posture recognition
- Elderly health care
- Sports
- Bird posture recognition

Classroom Student Posture Recognition

Pose detection and recognition technologies have been developed in recent years to address the rising demands of numerous businesses, thanks to the rise of monitoring systems for public and private use.

For example, university students may engage in various deviant behaviours in the classroom, such as napping, using cell phones, and conversing, all of which can substantially impact students' academic performance in the long run. As a result, in the context of an intelligent university classroom, the problem of detecting and recognising student poses using computer vision technology has important academic implications and high practical value. Recognising students' postures in a classroom pose four significant obstacles (Zhang.Y at el., 2021).

- Because certain human joints are invisible to webcams owing to occlusions, the calculation of human body key points has a high false-positive rate and poor accuracy rate; as a consequence, there are only a few unreliable characteristics for calculating human body key points.
- Due to the slow computation rates of most top-down pose estimate algorithms, the final findings cannot avail in real-time. If the model uses object detection to recognise postures, detecting a single gesture with limited scalability may only be possible.

Presentation of a posture identification approach used in a classroom that integrates the pose estimation method with the object detection algorithm to address these issues. You Only Look Once Version-3 (YOLOv3) chose as the detection network for recognising hunch postures because of its efficiency.

Activity and Posture Analysis for Patients

Detecting the patient's posture and bodily motions is critical to restoring or improving their functional abilities.

A person's posture defines the position our bodies maintain, whether standing, sitting, or laying down. This definition is decided by the spinal cord and the muscles surrounding it, such as the hamstrings and most back muscles, and is critical for the rest of our body to function normally (Agarwal. D, 2020).

A proper posture may help relieve muscle and ligament tension and prevent backaches and chronic diseases such as arthritis, joint discomfort, and muscle wear and tear. The angles between various joints on various body parts, most notably the shoulder and knees, may determine a person's posture. The device may obtain input via pre-recorded visuals of the user or through the webcam to record the user's movements. The algorithm may train the model according to the patient's requirements, such as height and weight. The angle between the key points is calculated in the XY plane concerning the X-axis to estimate the patient's postures. As previously stated, if the angle is less than 70 degrees, the posture is considered Hunchback. The angle greater than degrees of 110, the posture is reclined. Finally, if the angle is between 70 and 110 degrees, the posture is considered Straight, and the suggested posture to follow.

Sports Field

Athletes' body data, particularly gymnasts', are essential in sporting competitions. Due to the unique structure of human limbs, there is no continuity in the movement process, and the athletes' movement changes rapidly, which cannot be accurately recognized by human eyes alone, resulting in an inability of fitness gymnasts to recognize their posture during competition. With the rise of technology, various posture tracking recognition systems were increasingly used in fitness gymnastics competitions and positively impacted. The existing system is speedy and effective in athlete limb monitoring. Still, there are numerous scores due to countless factors in the process of athletes in competition and fitness gymnastics in general. When the athlete's posture is detected, the regions with high pixel values in the image will respond, resulting in recognition errors in tracking the athlete. The accuracy of athlete tracking recognition is low. Implementing a deep learning-based gymnast position monitoring and recognition system to solve the mentioned problems is beneficial.

Bird Posture Recognition

Bird behaviour is based on posture recognition and reflects the health and habitat conditions of the bird. Bird movement analysis is critical for bird research because birds' feeding, nesting, and migratory habits are all linked to environmental changes and bird illnesses (Lin C.W at el., 2022). Recognising bird postures is a requirement for researching bird behaviour and can serve as a vital decision-making basis for bird behavioural science. Birds' anomalous posture detection now relies on the manual system of monitoring, which has considerable limitations, such as the fact that birds live in a range of environments, and frequently occupy high areas, making it challenging to precisely identify their posture. Professionals must understand the birds' posture and activity completely to recognise unusual postures; the procedure is time-consuming and complicated, and the monitoring expenses are considerable. As a result, computer vision algorithms are ideal tools for bypassing these constraints. Deep learning approaches in computer vision automate feature extraction, offer discriminative features, and significantly advance in various research fields. As a result, researchers have developed different CNNs. They are the Region based CNN (R-CNN), Pose Normalized CNN, and Deep CNN (D-CNN); the above may use that to perform datasets for bird identification.

CONCLUSION

Gestures are the most expressive kind of nonverbal communication that a speaker may use. One of the obvious methods to create adaptable interaction between devices and people is to employ hand gestures. The significance of recognising human postures, particularly to recognise or avoid human falls. The various challenges in gestures and posture recognition are explored. The meaning of gestures and postures explained in this chapter, paired with certain combinations of deep learning algorithms that are ensembled to recognize the data of gestures and postures. This makes the system work in more complex applications to solve complex problems that a human can't understand. Important deep learning models that are used to recognise postures are discussed. The applications in which gesture and posture recognition can be employed are discussed in detail.

REFERENCES

Abhishek, B., Krishi, K., Meghana, M., Daaniyaal, M., & Anupama, H. S. (2020). Hand gesture recognition using machine learning algorithms. *Computer Science and Information Technology*, *1*(3), 116–120.

Agarwal, D. D. (2020). Posture and activity analysis for patients in rehabilitation. *IJARIIT*, *6*, 148–153.

Alnaim, N. (2020). *Hand gesture recognition using deep learning neural networks* [Doctoral dissertation]. Brunel University London.

Arowolo, O. F., Arogunjo, E. O., Owolabi, D. G., & Markus, E. D. (2021). Development of a Human Posture Recognition System for Surveillance Application. *International Journal of Computing and Digital Systems, 10.*

Byeon, Y. H., Lee, J. Y., Kim, D. H., & Kwak, K. C. (2020). Posture recognition using ensemble deep models under various home environments. *Applied Sciences (Basel, Switzerland), 10*(4), 1287. doi:10.3390/app10041287

Chollet, F. (2017). Xception: deep learning with depthwise separable convolutions. *The IEEE Conference on Computer Vision and Pattern Recognition (CVPR).* 10.1109/CVPR.2017.195

Coldewey. (2019). *This hand-tracking algorithm could lead to sign language recognition, techcrunch.* https://techcrunch.com/2019/08/19/this-hand-tracking-algorithm-could-lead-to-sign-language-recognition/

Deepa, R., & Sandhya, M. K. (2019, June). An efficient hand gesture recognition system using deep learning. In *International Conference on Intelligent Computing, Information and Control Systems* (pp. 514-521). Springer.

Ding, W., Hu, B., Liu, H., Wang, X., & Huang, X. (2020). Human posture recognition based on multiple features and rule learning. *International Journal of Machine Learning and Cybernetics, 11*(11), 2529–2540. doi:10.100713042-020-01138-y

Gupta, S. (2021). Deep learning based human activity recognition (HAR) using wearable sensor data. *International Journal of Information Management Data Insights, 1*(2), 100046. doi:10.1016/j.jjimei.2021.100046

Islam, M. Z., Hossain, M. S., ul Islam, R., & Andersson, K. (2019, May). Static hand gesture recognition using convolutional neural network with data augmentation. In *2019 Joint 8th International Conference on Informatics, Electronics & Vision (ICIEV) and 2019 3rd International Conference on Imaging, Vision & Pattern Recognition (icIVPR)* (pp. 324-329). IEEE.

Lin, C. W., Hong, S., Lin, M., Huang, X., & Liu, J. (2022). Bird posture recognition based on target keypoints estimation in dual-task convolutional neural networks. *Ecological Indicators, 135*, 108506. doi:10.1016/j.ecolind.2021.108506

Murugeswari, M., & Veluchamy, S. (2014, May). Hand gesture recognition system for real-time application. In *2014 IEEE International Conference on Advanced Communications, Control and Computing Technologies* (pp. 1220-1225). IEEE. 10.1109/ICACCCT.2014.7019293

Nikitha, J., Keerthana, S., Balakrishnan, S., & Sathya, S. P. (2022, April). Comparative Analysis on Datasets for Sign Language Detection System. In *2022 International Conference on Sustainable Computing and Data Communication Systems (ICSCDS)* (pp. 1652-1657). IEEE. 10.1109/ICSCDS53736.2022.9761026

Praveen, K. S., & Shreya, S. (2015). Evolution of hand gesture recognition: A review. *International Journal of Engineering and Computer Science, 4*, 9962–9965.

Saha, S., Pal, M., Konar, A., & Janarthanan, R. (2013, December). Neural network based gesture recognition for elderly health care using kinect sensor. In *International Conference on Swarm, Evolutionary, and Memetic Computing* (pp. 376-386). Springer. 10.1007/978-3-319-03756-1_34

Sharma, S., & Singh, S. (2021). Vision-based hand gesture recognition using deep learning for the interpretation of sign language. *Expert Systems with Applications, 182*, 115657. doi:10.1016/j.eswa.2021.115657

Wang, S., Wang, A., Ran, M., Liu, L., Peng, Y., Liu, M., Su, G., Alhudhaif, A., Alenezi, F., & Alnaim, N. (2022). Hand Gesture Recognition Framework Using a Lie Group Based Spatio-Temporal Recurrent Network with Multiple Hand-Worn Motion Sensors. *Information Sciences, 606*, 722–741. doi:10.1016/j.ins.2022.05.085

Zhang, Y., Zhu, T., Ning, H., & Liu, Z. (2021). Classroom student posture recognition based on an improved high-resolution network. *EURASIP Journal on Wireless Communications and Networking, 2021*(1), 1–15. doi:10.118613638-021-02015-0

Chapter 9
Evolution of Deep Learning for Biometric Identification and Recognition

S. Miruna Joe Amali
K.L.N. College of Engineering, India

Manjula Devi C.
Velammal College of Engineering and Technology, India

Rajeswari G.
K.L.N. College of Engineering, India

ABSTRACT

Biometrics is a method based on the recognition of the biological characteristics of an individual like fingerprint, vocal, and facial features. Biometric features hold a unique place when it comes to recognition, authentication, and security applications as they cannot be easily duplicated. Deep learning-based models have been very successful in achieving better efficiency in biometric recognition. They are more beneficial because deep learning-based models provide an end-to-end learning framework.

INTRODUCTION

In this digital era, improvements in technology have led to the emergence of advanced security and authentication systems, including biometrics, a method based on the recognition of fingerprints, vocal and facial features. Biometric features hold a unique place when it comes to recognition, authentication, and security applications as they cannot be easily duplicated. Biometric recognition is an information system that allows the identification of a person based on some of their main physiological and behavioral characteristics. The functioning of the biometric recognition systems varies according to their two main objectives namely, verification or identification of a person. Deep learning-based models have been very successful in achieving state-of-the-art results in many of the computer vision, speech recog-

DOI: 10.4018/978-1-7998-8892-5.ch009

nition, and natural language processing tasks in the last few years. In recent past deep learning-based models have been used widely to improve the accuracy of different biometric recognition systems. This is achieved through a multi-layer neural network, also known as Deep Neural Networks (DNNs). Deep learning-based methods automate the process of learning the best feature representation irrespective of biometric trait and hence can be more widely and robustly applied. Usage of deep learning for different biometric applications involves specific characteristics for information acquisition, feature extraction and segmentation and classification. Although deep learning research in biometrics has given promising results, there is still scope for research in different directions, such as creating larger and more challenging datasets, model interpretation, integrating multiple biometrics features, security and privacy issues etc. In this chapter an overview of different biometric applications, different datasets for implementing deep learning and their implementations modules are presented.

DEEP LEARNING MODELS

Deep learning models in general are prepared based on an objective function, yet the way in which the objective function is planned uncovers a ton about the reason for the model.

Deep Learning in Computer Vision

Computer vision is the technological advancement which exemplifies interpretation capability of machines with respect to images and videos. Computer vision algorithms extract specific features and criteria in images and videos for analysis purpose. They then use the extracted features for interpretations, predictions or for decision making. In recent years deep learning techniques have gained prominence in the application of computer vision. In particular, Convolutional Neural Networks (CNNs) architecture is prominently used. CNN is a multi-layered architecture that enables a neural network to focus on the most relevant features in the image. CNNs have been successfully applied to various fields relating to computer vision like object recognition, face recognition, scene identification etc.

Deep Learning in Speech Recognition

Speech recognition is the technique of understanding the spoken words. Automatic speech recognition (ASR) refers to the recognition of human speech and translating it into text. In recent years, neural networks have been widely used in speech recognition task with improved efficiency (Ye & Yang, 2021). The various techniques used are recurrent neural networks (RNNs), Convolution Neural Networks (CNNs), and Transformer networks for achieving better performance.

Deep Learning in Natural Language Processing

Natural language processing (NLP) is the process of developing computational algorithms to automatically analyze human language (Khdier et al., 2020). NLP-based systems have been widely applied in a range of applications like the search engine provided by Google and the voice assistant called Alexa by Amazon. Complex applications like machine translation, human interaction systems, dialogue generation etc. apply NLP as their major technology.

Deep Learning in Biometric Recognition

Biometric recognition is a technology that employs unique individual human features for authentication. With the success of deep learning-based models in various fields like computer vision, natural language processing, speech recognition and similar applications in the last few years, they have also been applied to biometric systems. These models tend to be the perfect choice for taking care of the ever expanding biometric recognition problems. Biometric systems are effectively utilized in a wide range of applications from trivial systems like authentication in mobile phone to security clearance in airport. Due to the success in various domains Deep learning techniques likes CNNs have been increasingly utilized to improve the accuracy of various biometric recognition systems in recent years.

BIOMETRIC RECOGNITION

Biometric characteristics of an individual can be divided into physical or behavioral features. Physical feature based on personal being, and behavioral features based on how they act. Biometrics characteristics are of two categories:

Physiological biometrics: This includes the features that can be used to uniquely describe an individual through the five senses namely, sight – looks of a person like hair and eye color, teeth, or facial features, sound – the pitch of voice of a person, smell – the odor of a person, taste – the DNA composition of a person and touch – the fingerprints or handprints of a person. Physiological biometrics include fingerprint, finger pattern, palm print, entire hand topography, and geometry, hand veins, shape of ear and lips etc.

Behavioral biometrics: This includes an individual's features like body language, handwriting, walking style, etc. these characteristics requires continued identification for implementation. They must also be reliable, unique, collectable, convenient, long term, universal, and acceptable for real time applications. Behavioral characteristics include voice modulation, retina pattern, signature rhythm, iris contour, keystroke pattern, and signature etc. The categories of biometric characteristics are given in Figure 1.

Types of Biometric Devices

Iris cameras: They perform recognition of an individual using random pattern that is visible in the iris of an eye by mathematical analysis. They provide high resolution images with quick responsiveness and adapt to different light conditions.

Iris recognition: The iris is unchanged over a long period of time and a onetime registration can last a lifetime. They are also not easily affected by the presence of contact lenses or glasses and the scanning distance can be from 10 cm to a few meters.

Hand scanner and finger reader recognition systems: They measure various features associated with a hand like, the overall structure shape including all metric like length and width and thickness of the hand, joints, fingers, and also other characteristics of the skin surface such as creases and ridges for analysis purpose.

Facial recognition device: They capture an image or video of a person for comparison to an existing database. It is performed by comparing the features of the face such as structure, shape, distance between the eyes, nose, mouth, upper outlines of the eye sockets, cheek bones. The important facial features recognition systems are feature analysis, neural network, and automatic face processing.

Figure 1. Categories of biometric characteristics

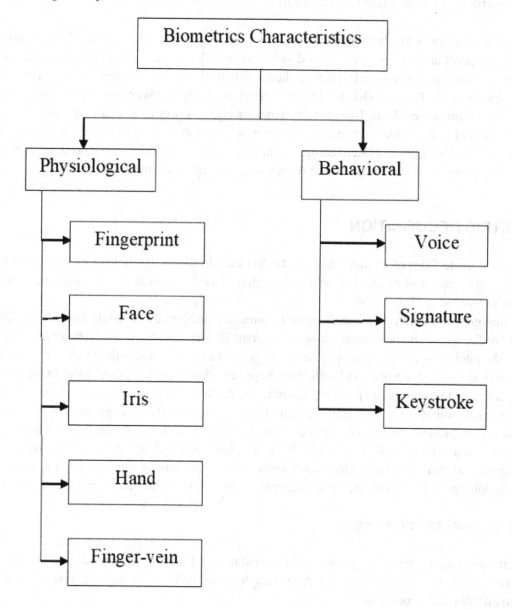

Voice recognition spectrogram: This is a graph that shows the frequency of sound variation with time. Different temper of speech creates different graph regions. In order to represent the acoustical qualities of sound spectrograms use color or shades of gray.

Digital biometrics signature: They are similar to traditional *handwritten* signature, but it is more difficult to forge than the traditional type. Digital signature uses *cryptographic techniques* for improved effectiveness. Digital signatures can be used for e-mail, contracts, or any electronic document.

Vein recognition: Vein recognition is a type of biometrics similar to fingerprint. It is used to identify individuals based on the vein patterns in the human finger.

ROLE OF DEEP LEARNING IN BIOMETRIC RECOGNITION

In recent years, deep learning-based models have achieved state-of-the-art results in a variety of computer vision, speech recognition, and natural language processing applications. From mobile phone authentication to airport security systems, these models appear to be a perfect match for dealing with the ever-increasing scope of biometric recognition difficulties. In recent years, deep learning-based models have been widely used to increase the accuracy of various biometric recognition systems. Many factors can be used to achieve biometric recognition. The three main features are discussed here.

1. Face recognition
2. Iris recognition
3. Finger vein recognition

Face Recognition

Facial recognition is a method of identifying or authenticating an individual's identity by observing their face. People can be identified in pictures, films, or in real time using facial recognition technology (Hui & Yu-jie, 2018). It is a biometric security category. Face recognition technology is well-known to many people thanks to FaceID, which is used to unlock mobile phones (however, this is only one application of face recognition). Facial recognition, in addition to unlocking phones, works by comparing people's faces to a database of numerous faces. Images might originate from anywhere, including social media accounts. The following is how facial recognition systems work:

Step 1: Face detection

The camera recognizes and tracks the picture of a face, whether it is alone or in a crowd. The individual in the photograph might be staring straight ahead or in profile.

Step 2: Face analysis

After that, a picture of the face is taken and examined. Because it is easier to match a 2D image with public photos or those in a database, most facial recognition technology uses 2D images rather than 3D images. The geometry of the face is read by the program. The distance between the eyes, the depth of the eye sockets, the distance between the forehead and chin, the curve of the cheekbones, and the contour of the lips, ears, and chin are all important considerations. The goal is to determine the facial landmarks that are essential for differentiating the face.

Step 3: Converting the image to data

Based on a person's facial traits, the face capture method converts analogue information, i.e. a face into a wide range of digital information which is the data. The examination of the face is essentially reduced to a mathematical formula. A face print is created for the individual under consideration and it is called the numerical code. Each person has their own facial print, just like thumbprints are unique.

Figure 2. Face recognition models in DeepFace library

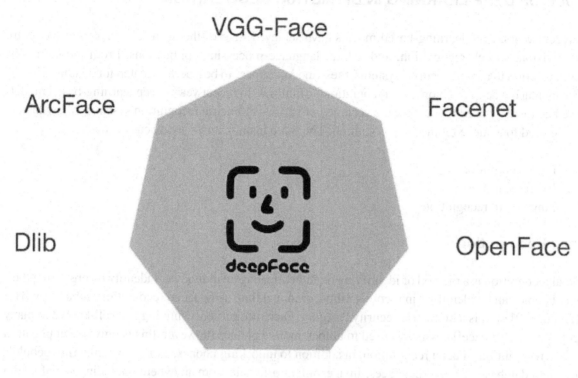

Step 4: Finding a match

After that, the face print is compared to a database of other people's faces. Any photo tagged with a person's name on Facebook, for example, becomes part of Facebook's database, which may be used for face recognition. A judgment is made if the face print matches an image in a facial recognition database. Despite the fact that facial recognition has been widely explored, there are still obstacles to solve issues such as Misalignment, Variation in Pose, Variation in Illumination, and Variation in Expression. To increase the accuracy and precision of face recognition, a variety of methodologies must be evaluated. A wide range of information from photos can be extracted using Convolutional Neural Networks. DeepFace has grown in popularity and is now utilized in a variety of facial recognition applications.

DeepFace

DeepFace is a Python package for face identification and facial attribute analysis. The open-source DeepFace library comprises all cutting-edge AI face recognition models and conducts all facial recognition operations in the background. The DeepFace library supports 7 state-of-the-art face recognition models as given in Figure 2.

The DeepFace library may be used with the following deep learning face recognition algorithms.

VGG-Face

The Visual Geometry Group (VGG) is an organization dedicated to the study of visual geometry. A VGG neural network (VGGNet) is a deep convolutional neural network-based image recognition model that is widely utilized. The VGG architecture became well-known for its amazing results in the ImageNet challenge. Researchers from the University of Oxford created the model. The VGG-Face has the same structure as the conventional VGG model, but it has been tweaked with facial photos. On the widely used Labeled Faces in the Wild (LFW) dataset, the VGG face recognition model obtains 97.78 percent accuracy.

Google FaceNet

This model was developed by Google researchers. FaceNet is a deep learning model for face detection and identification that is regarded to be state-of-the-art. FaceNet is a facial recognition, verification, and grouping algorithm. Face clustering is used to cluster photos of people with the same identity. FaceNet's key advantage is its excellent efficiency and performance; according to reports, it achieves 99.63 percent accuracy on the LFW dataset and 95.12 percent on the Youtube Faces DB while utilizing just 128 bytes per face.

OpenFace

Researchers from Carnegie Mellon University developed this facial recognition model. As a result, Open-Face is largely influenced by the FaceNet project, however it is lighter and has a more flexible licensing type. On the LFW dataset, OpenFace achieves a precision of 93.80%. OpenFace is also easy to use.

Facebook DeepFace

Researchers at Facebook created this facial recognition model. The Facebook DeepFace algorithm was trained using a labelled dataset of four million faces belonging to over 4000 people, which at the time of its release was the biggest facial dataset available. The method is based on a nine-layer deep neural network. On the LFW dataset benchmark, the Facebook model obtains an accuracy of 97.35 percent (+/- 0.25 percent). On the same dataset, the researchers predict that the DeepFace Facebook algorithm would close the gap to human-level performance (97.53 percent). This suggests that when it comes to facial identification, DeepFace is sometimes more successful than humans.

DeepID

The DeepID face verification technique uses deep learning to accomplish face recognition. It was one of the first models to achieve better-than-human performance on face recognition tests using convolutional neural networks. Deep-ID was developed by Chinese University of Hong Kong academics. DeepID facial recognition-based systems were among the first to outperform humans on the challenge.

Figure 3. Structure of an eye

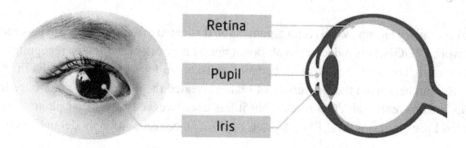

Dlib

The Dlib face recognition model claims to be the world's easiest facial recognition API for python. Faces are recognized and manipulated using a machine learning model that can be run from the command line or Python. Despite the fact that the dlib library was initially designed in C++, it contains Python bindings that are simple to use. The Dlib model, however, was not created by a research group. Davis E. King, the principal creator of the Dlib image processing library, introduced it. Dlib's face recognition program converts a human face image into a 128-dimensional vector space, where photos of the same person are close together and images of other persons are separated. As a result, dlib recognises faces by mapping them to the 128d space and then testing them.

ArcFace

This model is the most recent addition to the model repertoire. Imperial College London and Insight-Face researchers collaborated on the project. On the LFW dataset, the ArcFace model achieves 99.40 percent accuracy.

Iris Recognition

Iris recognition, also known as iris scanning, is the technique of taking a high-contrast snapshot of a person's iris using visible and near-infrared light. The iris is the colorful, donut-shaped part of the eye that surrounds the pupil and is located beneath the cornea as given in Figure 3. The iris pattern is unique to each individual and does not alter throughout their lives. The iris is also highly protected from harm since it is covered by the cornea, making it an ideal body component for biometric identification (Azam & Rana, 2020).

The position of the pupil is identified first, followed by the iris and the eyelids. Unnecessary components (noise), such as eyelids and eyelashes, are removed, leaving just the iris, which is then separated into blocks and turned into feature values to quantify the picture.

For the iris recognition system, the CNN tends to offer resilience and effective structure (Proenc & Neves, 2018). The picture must first go through the following stages: improving image quality, determining the iris and pupil center and radius for iris segmentation, and transforming the image from Cartesian to polar coordinates to minimize processing time. The workflow for iris recognition is given in Figure 4.

Iris Recognition operates as follows:

Figure 4. Workflow for iris recognition

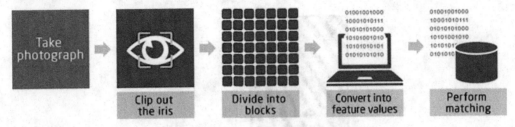

1. Image Acquisition
2. Iris Segmentation
3. Normalization
4. Feature Extraction

Image Acquisition

The initial phase in iris recognition is picture acquisition, which involves employing cameras and sensors to capture a series of high-quality iris photos from the subject. These photos should clearly display the complete eye, particularly the iris and pupil, and then some preprocessing may be used to improve the image quality.

Iris Segmentation

Iris segmentation is the next stage in iris recognition, and it is a method that isolates the real iris region in a digitized eye picture. Two circles can be used to approximate the iris region: one for the iris/sclera border and another for the iris/pupil boundary. The circular iris area is found using the Hough Transformation.

Normalization

The circular iris area is turned into a fixed size rectangular block after successfully segmenting the iris region from an eye picture. During the normalization phase, the iris areas with the same constant dimensions are created.

Feature Extraction

Feature extraction is the most critical phase in iris recognition. The method of extracting the most discriminating information from an iris pattern is known as feature extraction. The feature extraction approach has a big impact on the recognition rate and run duration of matching two iris templates. A CNN is made up of layers of locally linked convolutional layers that alternate. The number of filters on each layer is the same. The fully linked layers and the down-sampling layers function as a classifier. Every neuron in the previous layer takes information from a small piece of the local receptive field. It also has the same convolution filter size. Convolutional and down-sampling layers employ local receptive fields. The convolutional layer is subjected to weight sharing in order to regulate capacity and reduce

Figure 5. A typical fingerprint image

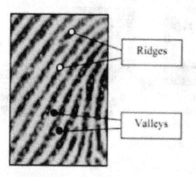

model complexity. Finally, nonlinear down-sampling is utilized in the down-sampling layers to reduce the image's spatial dimension as well as the number of free parameters in the model.

Finger Vein Recognition

Fingerprint is a unique feature for an individual. The recognition of fingerprint to identify a person is performed through the analysis and comparison of his or her finger dermal ridges. Fingerprint identification is one of the first methods for automatically recognizing people, and it remains one of the most common and successful biometric approaches today (Alam et al., 2021). Different ways to matching fingerprint pictures can be utilized, such as transform-based algorithms, correlation-based algorithms, minutiae algorithms, and so on. Local elements of a fingerprint picture are extracted solely by minutiae-based techniques. Minutiae are the properties of finger ridges such as ridge bifurcation or ridge termination.

In a typical fingerprint picture as given in Figure 5, ridges are represented by black lines, while valleys are represented by white lines. The core point of a fingerprint picture is the center region, whereas minutiae points appear as little lines. The rises in usage of fingerprint authentication systems have commercially increased detection of fingerprint spoofing in mobile devices. Using a convolutional neural network (CNN), a fingerprint liveness-detection approach extracts characteristics from fingerprint patches (Preetha & Sheela, 2010). The preprocessing step improves the input fingerprint image, and the recognition phase compares the improved fingerprint to database templates. The workflow for finger vein recognition using CNN is given in Figure 6.

The CNN technique satisfies both the preprocessing and recognition phases, boosting the system's total performance (Abrishambaf et al., 2008). Normalization reduces noise and increases the quality of the fingerprint image's features. The fingerprint picture is separated from the backdrop using a segmentation approach. Binarization is applied based on the threshold value, and the image is enhanced. Filtering with a Gabor or a similar sort of filter is performed. On the ridges, the next thinning technique is used. Finally, the placements and types of minutiae are established. To identify fingerprint photos, the directions of the full ridges are evaluated. To achieve recognition and preprocessing stages, CNN methods are applied. A skeletonization procedure is used to thin the ridgeline. Extracted lines of higher quality are further processed, improving the overall system performance.

Figure 6. CNN workflow for finger vein recognition

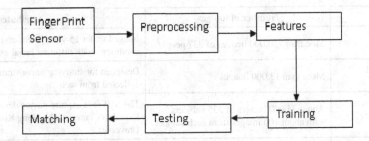

RESEARCH IN BIOMETRIC SYSTEMS

Creating Larger and More Challenging Datasets

The main challenge in the advancement of biometric research is the development of large datasets. The biometric and forensic research community needs access to large public datasets. The next important issue is the security and usage of the collected datasets. Identifying data gaps and data updates should also be ensured. Biometric researchers should ensure that the datasets organized ensures Representation to real-world operational data, data with heterogenous representation, availability of metadata namely, data pertaining to sex, age, nationality or race, data acquisition method, resolution, illumination or positioning etc. Data diversity should also be ensured for fair analysis. There should be provision for dynamic updates of data from time to time, so that data acquired should emerging technology can also be easily integrated such as contactless scanners. The ground truth namely the attribution of source should be established for the data collection. Uniform research policies should be maintained for any alteration in the data or metadata to maintain unambiguity. The datasets currently available and widely used are listed in Table 1.

Integrating Multiple Biometric Features

Multi-biometric system is a technique that integrates the uniqueness of different anatomical and behavioral characteristics of individuals. Due the availability of multiple features it offers improved matching accuracy, reliability and security against attacks (Lin, 2020). They also aid to noise in sensed data, non-universality and large data variations. It is difficult to circumvent a multi-biometic system compared to a single feature biometric system as many intricate aspects of a single person should be collected. In order to capture and process different biometric feature, various integration techniques are used as given below.

Multi-Sensor Systems

In this technique multiple sensors are used to capture a particular biometric trait. Fusion methodology is used to integrate the sensor data. For a fingerprint recognition system an optical and capacitive sensor can be used to sample biometric data, and then consolidate it using sensor level fusion methodology.

Table 1. Datasets available for biometric recognition analysis

Dataset	Number of images	Attributes
CMU Multi-PIE	Moe than 750,000 images of 337 people	Imaged under 15 view points and 19 illumination conditions with different facial expressions
Labeled Face in The Wild (LFW)	More than 13,000 images	Designed for studying unconstrained face recognition collected from web
PolyU NIR Face Database	About 34,000 images of 335 subjects with about 100 images from each subject	The NIR face capture device developed by Biometric Research Centre at The Hong Kong Polytechnic University
VGGFace2	3.31 million images of 9131 subjects	Downloaded from Google Image Search and have a large variation in pose, age, illumination, ethnicity and profession
CASIA-WebFace	453 images over 10,575 subjects	One of the largest publicly available face datasets
MS-Celeb	10 million face images extracted from the Internet from nearly 100,000 individuals	Face attributes dataset with more than 200K celebrity images
PolyU High-resolution Fingerprint Database	1480 images of 148 fingers	Provided by the Hong Kong Polytechnic University
CASIA Fingerprint Dataset	20,000 fingerprint images of 500 subjects	Each subject contributed 40 finger print images with 5 images per finger.
NIST Fingerprint Dataset	258 latent fingerprints	Availability of corresponding reference finger prints
CASIA-Iris-1000 Database	20,000 iris images from 1,000 subjects	IKEMB-100 camera for data collection
IIT Delhi Iris Dataset	2240 iris images captured from 224 subjects	The resolution of these images is 320x240 pixels with different color distribution and iris sizes.
MICHE Dataset	3,732 images acquired from 92 subjects	Images acquired under unconstrained conditions using smart phones.

Multi-Modal Systems

In this technique more than one biometric feature is used. In order to authenticate a subject both fingerprints as well as iris scan can be used for personal identification on a multi-biometric system. It combines data sensed from both the biometric identifiers. They are expensive to initially set up in any organization due to implementation of more than one biometric sub-system, but they provide the advantage of improved matching performance, security and wide range of applicability.

Multi-Instance Systems

In this technique multiple instances of a single biometric feature is captured. A multi-instance system uses multiple fingerprints or iris capture of both left and right eye to authenticate a subject. These systems can be cost effective compared to multi-modal systems as they use a single sensor.

Multi-Algorithm Systems

This technique applies different algorithms of feature extraction and matching on a single biometric feature. These systems are also inexpensive compared to multi-modal systems as they use single sensor. As they use different algorithms for extraction and matching, they are more complex than other biometric systems.

Hybrid Systems

An amalgamation of more than one technique is called a hybrid system. A biometric system that uses multiple sensors to capture a biometric feature and integrates it with multiple algorithms to process the extracted data is an example of a hybrid system (Chao et al., 2013).

Security and Privacy Issues

Biometric systems offer many advantages for authentication and person verification. But the major issue is the security and privacy of data acquired. Artificially manipulated human features can be created and used to counter a biometric sensor. This is commonly known as spoofing. Generally, biometric systems contain techniques to counter such spoofing attacks by using liveness detection to identify a person from a 2D or 3D image. As biometric characteristics cannot be altered easily for a person, it becomes a grave problem if the biometric feature is compromised. The privacy of the biometric features collected from an individual should also be adequately maintained. Hackers can steal sensitive biometric data and create more hazards to privacy. Thus, the security requirements of confidentiality, integrity, authenticity, non-repudiation, and availability are essential in biometrics data also.

CONCLUSION

The biometric technology uses an individual's unique features pertaining to physiology or behavior as input and uses them to identify the individual for authentication or verification purpose. The uniqueness of each individual in terms of face feature, fingerprint, iris, palm print, voice etc. are leveraged for identifying a person. They have many benefits compared to traditional security systems. They are mainly used in fraud and theft reduction. Face recognition is a non-touching method that is convenient for information gathering using a camera. There are wide ranges of face datasets for implementing deep learning algorithms. Fingerprint recognition is a more accurate method compared to other methods and it is easier for information gathering. It uses a special device of information gathering. Voice recognition is a non-contact method which allows the machine to identify people without physically in touch. But the environmental condition largely affects the accuracy of information collection. Iris images contain a rich set of features embedded in their texture and patterns which do not change over time. In spite of their wide applicability, there is lot of research domains in biometric systems to make them more efficient and robust to attacks. Many research and development techniques are constantly being carried out to improve the security and privacy of biometric authentication.

REFERENCES

Abrishambaf, R., Demirel, H., & Kale, I. (2008). A Fully CNN Based Fingerprint Recognition System. *IEEE International Workshop on Cellular Neural Networks and Their Applications*. 10.1109/CNNA.2008.4588667

Chao, W.-L., Liu, J.-Z., & Ding, J.-J. (2013). Facial age estimation based on label-sensitive learning and age-oriented regression. *Pattern Recognition*, *46*(3), 628–641. doi:10.1016/j.patcog.2012.09.011

Hugo Proenc, A. (2018). Deep-Prwis: Periocular Recognition without The Iris And Sclera Using Deep Learning Frameworks. *IEEE Transactions on Information Forensics and Security*, *13*(4), 888–896. doi:10.1109/TIFS.2017.2771230

Hui, L., & Song, Y. (2018). Research on face recognition algorithm based on improved convolution neural network, *IEEE Conference on Industrial Electronics and Applications (ICIEA)*. 10.1109/ICIEA.2018.8398186

Khdier, Jasim, & Aliesawi, (2020). Deep Learning Algorithms Based Voiceprint Recognition System In Noisy Environment, *Journal of Physics, International Conference of Modern Applications on Information and Communication Technology*, 1804.

Lin. (2000). An Introduction to Face Recognition Technology. *Informing Science Special Issue on Multimedia Informing Technologies Part 2*, *3*(1).

Nur-A-Alam, A.M., Based, M.A., Haider, J., & Kowalski, M. (2021). An intelligent system for automatic fingerprint identification using feature fusion by Gabor filter and deep learning. *Computers & Electrical Engineering*, *95*(107387).

Preetha, S., & Sheela, S. V. (2010). *Analysis of Fingerprint Biometric Authentication Using CNN, Social Science Research Network*. Elsevier.

Shafiul Azam, M. (2020). Iris Recognition Using Convolutional Neural Network. *International Journal of Computers and Applications*, *175*(12), 24–28. doi:10.5120/ijca2020920602

Ye, F., & Yang, J. (2021). A Deep Neural Network Model for Speaker Identification. *Applied Sciences (Basel, Switzerland)*, *11*(3603), 1–18. doi:10.3390/app11083603

Chapter 10
Hand–Crafted Feature Extraction and Deep Learning Models for Leaf Image Recognition

Angelin Gladston
Anna University, India

Sucithra B.
Anna University, India

ABSTRACT

Plant leaf recognition has been carried out widely using low-level features. Scale invariant feature transform technique has been used to extract the low-level features. Leaves that match based on low-level features but do not do so in semantic perspective cannot be recognized. To address this, global features are extracted and used. Similarly, convolutional neural networks, deep learning networks, and transfer learning-based neural networks have been used for leaf image recognition. Even then there are issues like leaf images in various illuminations, rotations, taken in different angle, and so on. To address such issues, the closeness among low-level features and global features are computed using multiple distance measures, and a leaf recognition framework has been proposed. Two deep network models, namely Densenet and Xception, are used in the experiments. The matched patches are evaluated both quantitatively and qualitatively. Experimental results obtained are promising for the closeness-based leaf recognition framework as well as the Densenet-based leaf recognition.

INTRODUCTION

Since creation, there have been numerous plant species available globally. To categorize the large varieties of plants, development of an efficient plant recognition method is of utmost importance. As trees and plants are very important to ecology, accurate recognition and classification becomes necessary.

DOI: 10.4018/978-1-7998-8892-5.ch010

Classification procedure is carried out through number of sub procedures. An identification or classification issue is managed by mapping an input data with one of the unique classes. In this procedure, at first, database of a leaf images is created, that comprises of images of test leaf with their equivalent plant information. Essential features are extracted using image processing techniques. The features have to be stable in order to make the identification system robust. Subsequently the plant/leaf is recognized using machine learning techniques (Pankaja et. al., 2017).

Early works in automatic leaf disease recognition followed the general workflow (Lawrence et al., 2021). Image capture involves collection of photographic information using a suitable camera. Image pre-processing is carried out on the captured images in order to improve image quality. Examples of procedures carried at this stage are image resizing, filtering, color space conversion and histogram equalization. In plant disease recognition applications, segmentation is twofold. Segmentation is first done to isolate the leaf, fruit or flower from the background. A second segmentation is then done to isolate healthy tissue from diseased tissue. Feature extraction involves mining of information from the segmented image which could facilitate accurate classification of the anomaly. Features that could be extracted are texture features namely, energy, contrast, homogeneity, and correlation, along with shape, size and color.

Textural features can be extracted using statistical measures such as Local Binary Patterns (LBP), Grey Level Co-occurrence Matrix (GLCM), Color Co-occurrence Matrix (CCM) and Spatial Grey Level Dependence Matrix (SGLDM). Physical characteristics called morphological features are prominently used for identification. The shape of a leaf is an important feature, and it often varies from species to species (Amala et al., 2017). Textural features can also be extracted using model-based methods such as Auto-Regressive (AR) and Markov Random Field (MRF) models. Machine learning algorithms are supplied with feature vectors and trained to categorize features associated with each disease to be recognized. The trained algorithm can then be used to recognize features from new images captured from the field. Classification deals with matching a given input feature vector with one of the distinct classes learned during training. The designer may use more than one learning algorithm for training and classification and fuse the results from the algorithms.

There are a wide variety of plant species, many of them are useful to humans as food or as medicine (Chithra & Janes, 2018), some are close to extinction and few others are harmful to man. Apart from this, plants are vital in their role they are not only essential for human beings; they are also the base of all food chains, being the producers of food. To protect such plants and sustain biodiversity, we need to acquire in-depth knowledge on how to use and protect these plant species (Guoqing et al., 2019), in spite of the existing challenges (Erick & Jose, 2018) in studying and classifying these plants correctly. First and foremost is identifying the unknown plants which mainly depends on the expertise gained by an expert botanist (Guoqing et al., 2019). Traditionally, the successful method to identify plants easily, is by using the manual-based method based on their morphological characteristics. The success behind using this method for classifying the plant species is mainly rooted on the acquired knowledge and human skills. Plant components such as flowers, fruits, stem, seeds, root and leaves are used in plant identification and classification (Jibi et al., 2018). Predominantly leaf has been used for plant recognition, since leaves stay on the plants for more months. The leaves look completely different from one another exhibiting various characteristics (Neha et al., 2018) such as color, size, kind like maple, and oak, number of points, as well as arrangement of veins. Different plant species contains different leaf characteristics.

Botanists use their knowledge on leaves to identify the plant species and classify them as dangerous species, species having medicinal purposes as well as plant species that are edible. However, this process of manual-based leaf recognition had been often laborious and also consumes more time for leaf recognition. Hence, researchers have conducted studies to support the automatic classification of plants based on their physical characteristics such as the color, shape (Feng & Bin, 2018) and size (Cao et al., 2017). Many leaf recognition systems were developed following the sequence of processing steps, namely preparing the leaf dataset, pre-processing to extract their specific features, classification of the leaves, populating the database, training for recognition and finally evaluating the results. Such automatic leaf classification of plants uses various machine learning algorithms (Affix et al., 2018) & (Zhou et al., 2016). Leaf features can be categorized into low level and high level features. Low level leaf features are the boundary, color, illumination, as well as scaling features of the leaf and high level leaf features are the shape descriptors, texture features, length, leaf tips, color representations, venation structure, and morphology namely, the form and structure of the leaf.

In recent years, CNNs have demonstrated outstanding performance as feature extractors and classifiers in image recognition tasks such as the ImageNet challenge. This idea has been extended to agricultural applications in order to accomplish tasks such as disease recognition, pest recognition, weed detection, fruit and flower counting as well as fruit sorting and grading. In particular, since 2015 most research in leaf disease recognition using IPTs has leveraged deep learning (Lawrence et al., 2021). Deep learning is defined as a representation learning method whereby the algorithm finds the best way to represent data through a series of optimizations instead of semantic features. With this learning procedure, there is no need to do feature engineering since features are automatically extracted.

Deep learning will enable advances in the agricultural industry in the fields of disease diagnosis, pest detection, quality management, marketing, automation, robotics and big data. Large datasets comprising thousands of images are required for the training of CNNs. Unfortunately, in the field of plant disease recognition, such large and diverse datasets have not yet been assembled and availed for use by researchers. At the present time, transfer learning is the most effective way to train robust CNN classifiers for plant disease recognition. Transfer learning enables the adaptation of pre-trained CNNs by retraining them with smaller datasets whose distribution is different from the larger dataset previously used to train the network from scratch. Indeed, studies show that using CNN models pre-trained on the ImageNet dataset and then retraining them for leaf disease recognition gives better results.

Deep learning models developed for leaf disease detection and recognition such as those presented in this survey have mostly relied on well-known CNN architectures such as AlexNet, GoogLeNet, Inception and ResNet (Lawrence et. al., 2021). These architectures were developed and optimized for the ImageNet dataset which currently has over 14 million images in more than 20,000 categories. For this reason, these CNN architectures had to be very deep and have millions of learnable parameters in order to categorize images in the ImageNet dataset. In the field of plant disease recognition, however, datasets do not have as much diversity as the ImageNet dataset and as such a much leaner CNN model should suffice. Study showed that up to 75% of the network parameters can be discarded without a degradation in the model's performance. In that study, an Inceptionv3 CNN was trained from scratch using images from the PlantVillage dataset.

Four broad techniques namely, Hidden Layer Output visualization, Feature visualization, Semantic Dictionary and Attention Map were considered for visualizing feature maps at hidden layers within the CNN. It was discovered that Attention Map techniques Grad-CAM and Explanation Map offered the most descriptive layer-wise attention maps. Using these visualizations, the authors were able to determine that the feature extraction layers of their Inceptionv3 model could be truncated at the Mixed5 layer yet maintain the same level of performance with 97.15% accuracy and 0.097 loss as the original network.

The resulting model had 75% fewer parameters compared to the original Inceptionv3 model as discussed by Lawrence et al., (2021). Subsequently, issues like overfitting, overtraining, undersized example sets, test sets with low representativeness and predisposition are to be taken into consideration (Amrita, 2019). Further, compared with traditional models, transfer learning models have faster convergence speed and lower model loss after convergence (Han et al., 2020).

Although the leaves are most commonly used for the plant identification systems, the stem, flowers, petals, seeds and sometimes, even the whole plant can be used in an automated plant identification process. Hence, the automated leaf recognition system developed can be used by the non-botanists to quickly identify plant species effortlessly. In this chapter, a leaf recognition framework has been proposed which comprises of the following components: SIFT based leaf recognition, CNN based leaf recognition and closeness based leaf recognition. If a leaf image is taken at a different angle or illumination, it makes the leaf recognition difficult and considers it as a non-relevant image (Zhang et al., 2012). Hence, the combination of these low level and high level features can be used for the leaf recognition system, more accurately even for a tilted leaf image or illuminated leaf image. The proposed leaf recognition system utilizes the combination of the low level and high level features for more accurate results so that a leaf image taken, even in a different angle or illumination can be recognized.

The contributions discussed in this chapter are a) a new leaf recognition framework, b) a combined approach utilizing SIFT and CNN for leaf recognition, c) utilization of both low level and high level features for characterizing the leaf varieties, d) application of distance measures into the closeness based leaf recognition along with the experimentation of more than one distance measure for leaf recognition,e) adoption of deep convolutional neural network for leaf recognition f) Xception, a deep Learning with depth wise separable convolutions for leaf recognition and g) illustration of suitability of DenseNet201 for leaf disease recognition.

The remainder of this chapter is organized as follows: Section 2 presents discussion on various leaf recognition related recent works using prominent strategies. Section 3 presents the design details of the leaf recognition system experimented in detail. Section 4 provides the experimental details, description of the dataset used in the experiments, experimental results obtained and the compilation of inferences drawn along with discussion on results. Conclusions drawn from the experiments are presented in Section 5.

LITERATURE SURVEY

There has been significant progress in the development of plant leaf classification and retrieval, and numerous approaches have been used so far in the literatures. Machine learning approaches (Vasudevan et. al., 2022) can easily recognize these diseases compared to physical method. So, the machine learning techniques in addition to image processing is used to identify diseased leaf. These methods will help in recognizing plant diseases thus increasing the yield of plants. It describes the various plant disease types, image processing methods and also various techniques of plant disease systems are analyzed with accuracy.

Classical machine learning methods have been used to classify leaves using handcrafted features from the morphology of plant leaves which has given promising results. However, Yagan et. al., (2022) focused on using non-handcrafted features of plant leaves for classification, utilized a deep learning approach for feature extraction and classification of features. Recently Deep Convolution Neural Networks have shown remarkable results in image classification and object detection-based problems. With the help of the transfer learning approach, explored and compared a set of pre-trained networks and defined the best classifier. That set consists of eleven different pre-trained networks loaded with ImageNet weights: AlexNet, EfficientNet B0 to B7, ResNet50, and Xception. These models are trained on the plant leaf image data set, consisting of leaf images from eleven different unique plant species. It was found that EfficientNet-B5 performed better in classifying leaf images compared to other pre-trained models.

Yafeng et. al., (2022) used DoubleGAN (a double generative adversarial network) to generate images of unhealthy plant leaves to balance such datasets. DoubleGAN is divided into two stages. In stage 1, we used healthy leaves and unhealthy leaves as inputs. First, the healthy leaf images were used as inputs for the WGAN (Wasserstein generative adversarial network) to obtain the pretrained model. Then, unhealthy leaves were used for the pretrained model to generate 64*64 pixel images of unhealthy leaves. In stage 2, a super resolution generative adversarial network (SRGAN) was used to obtain corresponding 256 256 pixel images to expand the unbalanced dataset. The dataset expanded with DoubleGAN, the generated images are clearer than DCGAN, and the accuracy of plant species and disease recognition reached 99.80 and 99.53 percent, respectively.

Various hybrid leaf condition recognition techniques using both hand-crafted feature extraction and deep learning are discussed by Lawrence et al., (2021). While recognizing the superiority of deep CNNs over hand-crafted feature extraction methods, have nonetheless sought to improve classifier performance by combining both feature extraction methods. They showed that obtaining the feature vector result from the CNN at the fully connected layer, combining it with a hand-crafted feature vector led to more accurate classifier performance. Further a technique for detecting Olive Quick Decline Syndrome (OQDS) using deep learning with data fusion has been used. The authors modified the CNN such that additional hand-crafted order statistics, texture, shape and geometric relation feature vectors were concatenated with the CNN's fully connected layers. It enabled the network to generalize better and hasten convergence of the model even when the dataset was small. The performance of the deep learning model was compared to hand-crafted techniques used in conjunction with Radial Basis Function SVM (RBF-SVM) classifiers. The CNN showed superior recognition performance compared to the hand-crafted approaches for all scenarios where the CNN was trained for 200 epochs or more.

Mahmudul et al., (2021) used a deep convolutional neural network (CNN) based model for the identification of plant species using plant leaf images. The main intuition of using CNN is learning the leaf features directly from the input images/data. Furthermore, it is observed that CNN-based techniques significantly increase the performances in case of different plant species having identical shape and sizes of leaves. The proposed model is compared with other existing techniques in the same domain. It is found that our model improves the recognition accuracy significantly. Truong et al., (2020) used two methods for the problem of plant species identification from leaf patterns. Firstly, they used a traditional recognition shallow architecture with extracted features histogram of oriented gradients (HOG) vector, then those features are used to classifying by SVM algorithm. Secondly, they applied a deep convolutional neural network (CNN) for recognition purpose. Experiments are conducted on leaves data set in the Flavia leaf data set and the Swedish leaf data set.

Yan Guo et al., (2020) used a mathematical model of plant disease detection and recognition based on deep learning, which improved accuracy, generality, and training efficiency. First, the region proposal network (RPN) is utilized to recognize and localize the leaves in complex surroundings. Then, images are segmented based on the results of RPN algorithm contain the feature of symptoms through Chan–Vese (CV) algorithm. Finally, the segmented leaves are given as input to the transfer learning model and trained by the dataset of diseased leaves under simple background. Furthermore, the model is examined with black rot, bacterial plaque, and rust diseases. The results showed that the accuracy of the method is 83.57%, which is better than the traditional method, thus reducing the influence of disease on agricultural production and being favorable to sustainable development of agriculture. Therefore, the deep learning algorithm introduced is of great significance in intelligent agriculture, ecological protection, and agricultural production.

Jiang, (2020) extracted plant leaf features and identified plant species based on image analysis. Firstly, plant leaf images are segmented by various methods, and then feature extraction algorithm is used to extract leaf shape and texture features from leaf sample images. Then the comprehensive characteristic information of plant leaves is formed according to the comprehensive characteristic information. In this work, 50 plant leaf databases are tested and compared with KNN-based neighborhood classification, Kohonen network based on self-organizing feature mapping algorithm and SVM-based support vector machine. At the same time, the leaves of 7 different plants were compared and it was found that ginkgo leaves were easier to identify. For leaf images under complex background, good recognition effect has been achieved. Image samples of the test set are input into the learning model to obtain reconstruction errors. The class label of the test set can be obtained by reconstructing the deep learning model with the smallest error set. The results showed that this method has the shortest recognition time and the highest correct recognition rate.

Guoqinget. al. (2019) in their unified multi-scale method captured leaf geometric information for fast plant leaf classification and image retrieval. The unified multi-scale method used a simple yet effective three-step strategy to capture geometric information of leaf contours through extracting angle, area, and arch-height features. There is no scale parameter to be adjusted, and these features are very simple to compute. For a leaf contour point, pairs of neighbor points are located using a simple yet effective three-step strategy. Then, the method is used to extract geometric information of leaf shape including angular, arch height, and triangle-area descriptors. These geometric information are based on the unequalarc-length partitions of leaf contour and can describe the leaf contour from coarse to fine by different scales. Fast Fourier transform is applied on the extracted geometric information of leaves for fast leaf classification and retrieval. Leaf classification and retrieval experiments are conducted the effectiveness of the proposed method was demonstrated.

Feng et. al (2018) focused on extracting discriminative shape features for accurate classification and retrieval of leaf images. They used a novel shape description, Integral Contour Angle. It has the inherent invariance to the translation, rotation and scaling and has the desirable property of capturing the discriminative shape features at various scales. For a contour point, two bunches of vectors emanate from it and ends at its left neighbor contour points and its right neighbor ones respectively. Their average vectors form an angle having inherent invariance to translation, rotation and scaling of leaf shape. Changing the size of the neighborhood of the contour point naturally yields a set of descriptors at different scales. They are grouped to form a multi-scale descriptor for the contour point. The dissimilarity between two leaf shapes is measured by calculating the enhanced Hausdorff distance between the sets. Their experimental results indicated the effectiveness oftheir method.

Jibiet. al. (2018) extracted the leaf vein patterns with improved Canny edge detection algorithm. Problem with Canny edge detection is that it misses important edges with high threshold and create false edges by low threshold. Smoothing process using Gaussian mask reduced the noise. Nehaet. al. (2018) presented a comprehensive study about plant species identification methods based on various feature extraction methods, and classification techniques, namely support vector machine and probabilistic neural network on Flavia dataset.

A query image and the candidate images are given as input to the Content Based Image Retrieval (CBIR) framework which is a traditional method, and it detects the local interested patches for each image using Bag of Words. A query image is an image from the dataset that is given as input to test the trained model. The matched pairs are detected from the local interested patches. All the matched pairs determine whether the Euclidean distances between two interested patches are less than a fixed threshold. The similarity score is calculated between each of the query image and candidate image pairs, which are considered as the quantitative measure of the matched components and then the candidate images are ranked accordingly (Tolias & Chum, 2017).

Numerous image retrieval techniques based on the local descriptors have been evaluated (Zhou et al., 2016) Image retrieval methods comprise of four components, namely feature extraction, quantization, indexing, and ranking (Mairal et al., 2014; Babenko & Lempitsky, 2015; Mohedano et al., 2016; Gordo et al., 2016), which mostly concentrates on the feature extraction improvement and the indexing scheme. A local descriptor allocates its closest k visual words then the compatible term frequency with its image label is stored in the entry.

The hierarchical construction of the visual vocabulary tree facilitates storing a large amount of visual words and efficient search. However, detailed information of local features is not retained since choosing k is a compromise between efficiency and the quality of the descriptors. Tolias et al. (2013) aggregated local descriptor, which is allocated to the identical visual word into one vector, and binarizes it using the hamming embedding. Here, aggregation shows that all the local descriptors allotted to the identical visual word are averaged. Experimental results show that aggregation is difficult in image retrieval as it effectively encodes the local descriptors and removes noise (Xiaohan et al., 2015). Both texture and color have been considered for image retrieval (Cao et al., 2017).

In conclusion, compared to the works discussed, this chapter describes a leaf recognition framework investigate the application of various distance measures into the closeness based leaf recognition. This chapter details the adoption of deep convolutional neural network for leaf recognition. In specific, training Xception, a deep Learning model with depth wise separable convolutions and further the illustration of suitability of DenseNet201 for leaf disease recognition.

MATERIALS AND METHODS

In this section, design details of leaf recognition systems namely, SIFT based leaf recognition, CNN based leaf recognition, closeness based leaf recognition, Densenet based leaf recognition as well as Xception based leaf recognition are presented. The closeness based leaf recognition system utilizes both low level and high level features for better recognition of leaves. In this system, the query image called input image and candidate images that are images in the dataset are given as input to two methods: Bag of Words (BOW) and Convolutional Neural Network (CNN). In the first method, Bag of Words uses Scale Invariant Feature Transform (SIFT) to extract the SIFT Features from the image. In the second method, AlexNet is used to extract the semantic features from the image utilizing deep techniques. Low features recognize leaf images even with illuminations, rotation in the image or even if the same leaf image is taken at a different angle. Global features provide preference in allowing more local matches for relevant leaf images, while rejecting most matches for irrelevant ones (Jufeng et al., 2018). Hence the combination of these low and high features has been used for more accurate results in the leaf recognition system.

Manhattan distance and Semantic distance, namely Euclidean distance, are calculated from the SIFT features and semantic features respectively. Then, closeness based leaf recognition is used where we compare the distances between the query image and candidate image. The leaf images that are closer with the given query image are displayed. The leaf recognition systems namely, SIFT based leaf recognition and CNN based leaf recognition are utilized in closeness based leaf recognition. The leaf recognition systems are implemented in MATLAB R2017a. The detailed description of the leaf recognition systems are explained in the following subsections.

SIFT Based Leaf Recognition

The SIFT based leaf recognition method is implemented and for the experimentation two datasets namely Flavia (Neha et al., 2018) and Folio (Pornntiwa et al., 2017) datasets are used. These datasets are split into training and validation images. Each leaf image from the training images is pre-processed to get its corresponding gray scale images. The point locations can be extracted from the preprocessed image by three steps. First, the interested regions in the leaf images are observed by detecting the number of patches using the grid method in BOW technique (Junfeng et al., 2016). Second, The SIFT features called local features are extracted from the interested regions using the SIFT Descriptor (Chi-Man & Moon-Chuen, 2003; Sathya et al., 2011) and third, from these key point locations a feature vector is computed. The SIFT Descriptor utilizes four phases which includes Scale-Space Extrema Detection, Keypoint Localization, Orientation Assignment and Keypoint Descriptor.

Scale-space extrema detection attempts to identify locations and scales that are identifiable from multiple views of the same leaf. This is achieved using a "scale space" function; it is based on the Gaussian function. The scale space is defined by the function:

$$L(x,y,\sigma) = G(x,y,\sigma) \times I(x,y) \tag{1}$$

where $\times$ is the convolution operator, $G(x, y, \sigma)$ is a variable-scale Gaussian and $I(x, y)$ is the input leaf image. Various techniques can then be used to detect stable keypoint locations in the scale-space. The keypoint localization attempts to eliminate more points from the list of keypoints by finding those that have low contrast or are poorly localized on an edge. This is achieved by calculating the Laplacian, value for each key point found in previous stage. The location of extremum, z, is given by:

$$\mathbf{z} = -\frac{\partial^2 D^{-1}}{\partial X^2}\frac{\partial D}{\partial X} \tag{2}$$

If the function value at $\mathbf{z}$ is below a threshold value then this point is excluded. This removes extrema with low contrast. To eliminate extrema based on poor localization it is noted that in these cases there is a large principle curvature across the edge but a small curvature in the perpendicular direction in the difference of Gaussian function. If this difference is below the ratio of largest to smallest eigenvector, from the 2x2 Hessian matrix at the location and scale of the keypoint, the keypoint is rejected. The orientation assignment aims to assign a consistent orientation to the keypoints based on local image properties. To find an orientation the keypoints scale are used to select the Gaussian smoothed image L. Gradient magnitude, m can be computed using equation 3 and orientation using 4.

$$M(x,y)=\sqrt{\left(\left(L\left(x+1,y\right)-L\left(x-1,y\right)\right)^2+\left(L\left(x,y+1\right)-L\left(x,y-1\right)\right)^2\right)} \tag{3}$$

$$\theta(x,y) = \tan^{-1}\left(L\left(x,y+1\right)-L\left(x,y-1\right)\right)/\left(L\left(x+1,y\right)-L\left(x-1,y\right)\right) \tag{4}$$

An orientation histogram from gradient orientations of sample points is formed and the highest peak in the histogram is located. This peak and any other local peak within 80% of the height of this peak are used to create a keypoint with that orientation. These features are collected as key point locations. The SIFT features extracted from the interested local regions for rosa leaf is shown in figure 1. From these key point locations a feature vector is computed. These feature vectors indicate the strength of each feature. From this SIFT Descriptor, we can recognize leaf images even with illuminations, rotation in the image or even if the same leaf image is taken at a different angle. Further, these feature vectors, signatures are generated for each region using vector quantization technique. Vector quantization is said to be a technique which allows the modeling of probability density function by distributing prototype feature vectors. It can be used for data compression. Finally, the similarity score for each image is calculated using hamming distance. The images related to the query image are obtained with these similarity scores and are displayed.

Figure 1. Extracted SIFT features from a Rosa leaf

CNN Based Leaf Recognition

CNN based leaf recognition technique (Zheng et al., 2018) is implemented using AlexNet. AlexNet is employed to extract high level features and contains eight layers. First five are convolutional layers and next three are fully connected layers. Features are extracted from the fully-connected layer without aggregation or additional transformations. Normalization is applied on deep features as empirically it performs well for image recognition. Each convolutional layer is defined with several parameters including the input size, kernel size, depth of the map stack, zero-padding and stride. Among the eight layers five are convolutional layers and three are fully connected layers. It uses non-saturatingReLU activation function, which shows better training performance over tanh and sigmoid activation functions. ReLU activation function is given by:

$$f(x) = \max(0, x) \tag{5}$$

Experiments are conducted on datasets namely Flavia and Folio dataset. These datasets are split into training and validation images. The training images are resized to 227*227*3 since AlexNet processes 227*227*3 sized images. The semantic features are extracted using the activation function used in 7th fully connected layer represented as fc7. Then, the labels for the training and testing images are extracted. The training images are classified using the SVM classifier. Then, the semantic distance is calculated from the features by using normalization method. The utilization of high level feature extraction is for leaf recognition is illustrated in figure 2.

Figure 2. Predicted Leaf Images using High Level Features

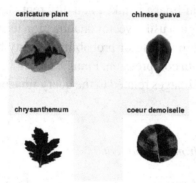

Closeness Based Leaf Recognition

The closeness based leaf recognition makes use of closeness measures computed using distance metrics, namely Euclidean distance and Manhattan distance. These distance measures are computed for each query image and candidate image pair. The distance between the query image and candidate image are computed using equations (6) and (7).

$$\text{Euclidean distance} = \sqrt{\sum_{i=1}^{m} (x_i - y_i)^2} \tag{6}$$

$$\text{Manhattan distance} = \sum_{i=1}^{m} |x_i - y_i| \tag{7}$$

The distances are calculated based on their intensity values with the help of the imhist function in MATLAB R2017a. By finding the image with lowest distance, the related image to the query image can be displayed. The predictions of chocolate leaf image using both the distance measures are shown in figure 3. There are situations, when the query image is predicted wrongly with another image while using the distance. The mismatched prediction of correct caricature leaf image using Euclidean distance is shown in figure 4.

Figure 3. Prediction of Chocolate Tree Leaf Image

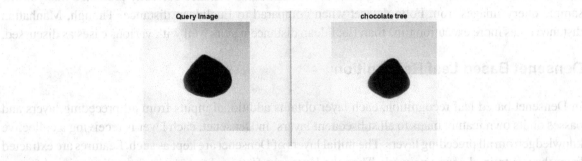

Figure 4. Mismatched Prediction of Caricature Leaf Image

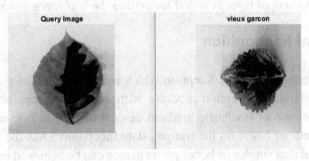

The calculation of the closeness of the leaf images combining Euclidean and Manhattan distances can be a solution to the wrong predictions. This can be used to find the related images for the given query image with a major difference in the recognition rate. The Euclidean distance and Manhattan distance are calculated based on the intensity values of the images. Further, the two distances are compared using the closeness based leaf recognition system and the related images of the given query image are displayed. Table 1 shows whether the query image is correctly predicted or not using Euclidean distance

Table 1. Closeness based Leaf Recognition for the given subset of Leaf Images

S. No	Leaf Name	Closeness based leaf recognition using	
		Euclidean	Manhattan
1	Beamier du peron	No	Yes
2	Barbados cherry	Yes	No
3	Betel	Yes	Yes
4	Caricature plant	Yes	No
5	Chinese guava	Yes	No
6	Chocolate tree	Yes	Yes
7	Chrysanthemam	Yes	No
8	Ashanti blood	Yes	Yes
9	Bitter Orange	Yes	Yes
10	Hibiscus	Yes	No

and Manhattan distance. By analyzing table 1, the Manhattan distance correctly predicted many of the sample query images from Folio dataset when compared to Euclidean distance. Though, Manhattan distance takes more execution time than Euclidean distance it suits well with various cases as discussed.

Densenet Based Leaf Recognition

In Densenet based leaf recognition, each layer obtains additional inputs from all preceding layers and passes on its own feature maps to all subsequent layers. In Densenet, each layer is receiving a collective knowledgefrom all preceding layers. The initial layers of Densenet are kept as such. Features are extracted from the pre-trained neural network. Then the layers are flattened to convert the n dimensional feature vector into a single dimensional feature vector. To the pruned Densenet the fully connected layers or dense layers are added. An output layer is added for getting the leaf recognition results.

Xception Based Leaf Recognition

In Xception based leaf recognition uses Xception which is an extension of the Inception architecture wherein it replaces the standard Inception modules with depth wise separable convolutions. Adam optimizer an advanced version of stochastic gradient descent algorithm is used to update the network weights in an iterative manner based on the training data.Inceptionv3 has the least training time. The studies have demonstrated that similar or better performance can be achieved by modified Inceptionv3, thus Xception has been used.

RESULTS AND DISCUSSION

This section presents the results obtained with the leaf recognition system implemented and the discussion on result analysis. The leaf recognition system implemented was evaluated experimentally. For the experiments, the leaf images which are obtained from Folio dataset (Pornntiwa et al., 2017) and Flavia dataset (Neha et al., 2018) are used. The leaf recognition system takes a leaf image as input and returns the label of the leaf image by recognizing the leaf image using its local and global features extracted by means of SIFT descriptor and CNN technique respectively. The dataset used, the local features and the deep features in the proposed leaf recognition system are described as follows:

Dataset

The leaf datasets used in the experiments are Folio dataset and Flavia dataset. Folio dataset contains 637 images of 32 different leaves such as betel, chocolate tree, eggplant, guava, hibiscus, as well as jack fruit and Flavia dataset contains 1867 images of 32 other different leaves such as Anhui barberry, Castor aralia, Deodar, Ford wood Lotus, Japanese cheesewood, as well as Southern magnolia. Extensive experiments on these datasets are carried out and the generality of the proposed method was validated. The leaf images of the dataset are divided into testing and training images.

30% of the Folio dataset are considered as the validation images, which means 191 images out of 637 images and the remaining 70% of the dataset are considered as the training images, implying 446 images from the 637 images in Folio dataset. Similarly, 30% of the Flavia dataset are considered as the validation images, which means 560 images out of 1867 images and the remaining 70% of the dataset are considered as the training images, implying 1307 images from the 1867 images in Flavia dataset. Features are extracted from the training images. Feature vectors are computed from the extracted features and the proposed leaf recognition system is implemented utilizing BOW and CNN techniques. Query images, which are leaf images from the validation images are given as input, to get the proposed leaf recognition system tested and validated.

Local features describe the image patches which are the key points in the image object (Liu et.al., 2015). They are low level features which include translation, scaling, color intensity, rotation, contour detection line called bounding feature, and illumination. For example, the boundary, color, illumination, scaling are the features of a leaf image. These low level features are also known as the local descriptors. SIFT, SURF, LBP and FREAK (Muhammad et al., 2016) are some examples of local descriptors. Local descriptors are used for higher level applications such as object recognition and object identification.

Deep features called global features describe the image as a whole generalizing the entire object. Global features are the high level features which include shape descriptors, texture features, length, leaf tips, color representations, venation structures; morphology features namely the form and structure of the leaf and so on considering the image as a whole. Global features are also known as the global descriptors. Invariant Moments (Hu, Zerinke), Histogram Oriented Gradients (HOG) and Co-HOG (Sujith & Jyothiprakash, 2014) are some examples of global descriptors. Global descriptors are generally used for low level applications such as image retrieval, object detection and classification (Jufeng et al., 2018).

The results obtained are evaluated using the evaluation metrics, namely accuracy, precision, recall and F-score using equations given in eq. (8), (9), (10) and (11). The metric values of the measures namely, accuracy, precision, recall and F-score are calculated from the confusion matrix generated by both SIFT and CNN techniques using true positive (TP), true negative (TN), false positive (FP) and false negative (FN).

$$\text{Accuracy} = \frac{TP + TN}{TP + TN + FP + FN} \tag{8}$$

$$\text{Precision} = \frac{TP}{TP + FP} \tag{9}$$

$$\text{Recall} = \frac{TP}{TP + FN} \tag{10}$$

$$\text{F-score} = \frac{2 * Precision * Recall}{Precision + Recall} \tag{11}$$

The evaluation metrics are obtained by constructing confusion matrices in both SIFT based leaf recognition and CNN based leaf recognition. The measures namely, accuracy, recall, precision and f-score for the Flavia Dataset using SIFT descriptor and CNN technique are shown in figure 5. From figure 5, we can infer that the accuracy for recognizing a leaf image using SIFT based leaf recognition as well as

CNN based leaf recognition is more than 90%. Higher the accuracy, the better the leaf recognition model recognizes leaves from the dataset. The evaluation metrics for the Folio Dataset using SIFT descriptor and CNN technique are shown in figure 6. From figure 6, we can infer that the accuracy for recognizing a leaf image using SIFT based leaf recognition as well as CNN based leaf recognition is more than 90%. High accuracy indicates that the model recognizes well, the leaves from the Folio dataset. From figure 5 and figure 6, by comparing SIFT based leaf recognition and CNN based leaf recognition; we can infer that the CNN based leaf recognition is better than SIFT based leaf recognition on both datasets.

Figure 5. Evaluation metrics for the Flavia dataset using SIFT descriptor and CNN

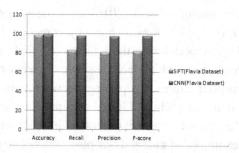

Figure 6. Evaluation metrics for the Folio dataset using SIFT descriptor and CNN

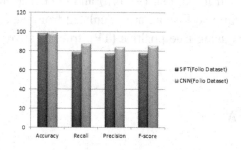

Figure 7. Graph representing the closeness for the Beamier du peron leaf from Folio dataset

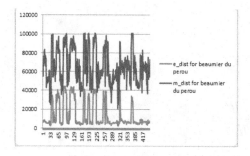

Comparing the recognition performance across the datasets, CNN based leaf recognition works better on the Flavia dataset than on the Folio dataset. Figure 7 shows the graph representing the distances for the Beamier du perou leaf from Folio dataset. The graph shows that both distances have same depressions and peaks indicating the similarity in their evaluating methodology but may differ in execution time. In table 1, the test cases executed using the Closeness based leaf recognition for ten sample leaf images with illuminations, rotation in the image, and same leaf image taken at different angle are given. Leaf recognition system using the Euclidean distance predicted most of the query images correctly when compared to the Manhattan distance. By analyzing the test cases in table 1, we could observe that the Manhattan distance based leaf recognition recognized half of the cases from the set; whereas Euclidean distance based leaf recognition arrived at 90% accuracy for the same set of leaf test cases. Thus, closeness based leaf recognition addresses illumination and rotation uses which can be further enhanced by careful selection of features.

Two deep learning models namely, Densenet and Xception are used in the experimentation. Densenet and Xception are trained using folio and flavia dataset images. Experimental results are analyzed in terms of Precision, Recall, F1 score and Accuracy. Theevaluation metrics show that there is a significant improvement in the recognition accuracy of Densenet model for both datasets compared to Xception model.

Among the larger CNN models, it would appear that DenseNet is suitable for implementing a leaf disease recognition system based on deep learning. DenseNet holds the advantage of having the best performance and least storage requirements but with the disadvantage of having the longest training time among the three architectures. On the other hand, Inceptionv3 has the least training time. The studies have demonstrated that similar or better performance can be achieved by modified Inceptionv3, thus Xception has been used. Therefore, careful consideration should begiven when choosing among these networks since each offers some advantages and suffers some limitations.

CONCLUSION

In conclusion, this chapter discusses in detail the issues in leaf recognition, the closeness based leaf recognition framework which leverages both the local and the global features obtained using SIFT based leaf recognition and CNN based leaf recognition respectively as well as the deep network models for leaf recognition. The closeness based leaf recognition framework calculates the similarity relationship between query and candidate leaf images for plant leaf recognition. The evaluation measures obtained for the SIFT based leaf recognition, CNN based leaf recognition and closeness based leaf recognition illustrate benefit of addressing the low level and global features for addressing illuminations and rotations. The experimental results show that the proposed closeness based leaf recognition performs better compared to the SIFT based and CNN based techniques discussed in the literature on the two datasets, Folio and Flavia. Accuracy for recognizing a leaf image using SIFT based leaf recognition as well as CNN based leaf recognition is more than 90%. The performance of the closeness based leaf recognition with respect to the distance measure employed is also discussed for the leaf images. The proposed closeness based leaf recognition method presented remarkable leaf recognition performance. Euclidean distance based leaf recognition arrived at 90% accuracy. The main reason behind this is that the closeness based leaf recognition can be implemented easily and recognize leaf images even with illuminations, rotation in the image or even if the same leaf image is taken at a different angle very well. In the future, this can be extended with more features and experimented with various datasets. Further, leaf recognition using deep networks has performed well because of the learning that has happened. Densenet as well as Xception recognizes leaf well.

REFERENCES

Affix, M., Indah, S., & Oyas, W. (2018). Herbal Leaf Classification Using Images in Natural Background. *International Conference on Information and Communications Technology (ICOIACT)*, 612-616.

Arun & Viknesh. (2022). Leaf Classification for Plant Recognition Using EfficientNet Architecture. In *2022 IEEE Fourth International Conference on Advances in Electronics, Computers and Communications (ICAECC)*. IEEE.

Babenko, A., & Lempitsky, V. (2015). Aggregating deep convolutional features for image retrieval. *Proc. IEEE International Conference on Computer Vision*, 1269–1277.

Bao, Kiet, Dinh, & Hie. (2020). Plant species identification from leaf patterns using histogram of oriented gradients feature space and convolution neural networks. *Journal of Information and Telecommunication, 4*(2), 140-150.

Cao, Y., Long, M., Wang, J., & Liu, S. (2017). Collective deep quantization for efficient cross-modal retrieval. *Proc. Thirty-First AAAI Conference on Artificial Intelligence*, 3974–3980. 10.1609/aaai.v31i1.11218

Chi-Man, P., & Moon-Chuen, L. (2003). Log-Polar Wavelet Energy Signatures for Rotation and Scale Invariant Texture Classification. *IEEE Trans. on Pattern Analysis and Machine Intelligence, 25*(5), 590-603.

Chithra, P. L., & Janes, P. S. (2018). A Survey on Various Leaf Identification Techniques for Medicinal Plants. *Proc. International Conference on Advancements in Computing Technologies*, 38-42.

Erick, M., & Jose, C. (2016). Automated Plant Species Identification: Challenges and Opportunities. *Proc. ICT for Promoting Human Development and Protecting the Environment*, 26-36.

Feng, N., & Bin, W. (2018). Integral Contour Angle: An Invariant Shape Descriptor for Classification and Retrieval of Leaf Images. *25th IEEE International Conference on Image Processing (ICIP)*, 1223-1227.

Gordo, A., Almaz'an, J., Revaud, J., & Larlus, D. (2016). Deep image retrieval: Learning global representations for image search. *Proc. European Conference on Computer Vision*, 241–257. 10.1007/978-3-319-46466-4_15

Guo, Y., Zhang, J., Yin, C., Hu, X., Zou, Y., Xue, Z., & Wang, W. (2020). Plant Disease Identification Based on Deep Learning Algorithm in Smart Farming. *Discrete Dynamics in Nature and Society*, 1–11. doi:10.1155/2020/2479172

Guoqing, X., Chen, L., & Qi, W. (2019). Unified multi-scale method for fast leaf classification and retrieval using geometric information. *IET Image Processing, 13*(12), 2328–2334. doi:10.1049/iet-ipr.2018.6551

Jiang, H. (2020). The Analysis of Plants Image Recognition Based on Deep Learning and Artificial Neural Network. *IEEE Access. Special Section on Data Mining For Internet of Things*, (8), 68828–68841.

Jibi, G. T., Ashwani, K. D., & Thomas, M. T. (2018). Advanced Plant Leaf Classification Through Image Enhancement and Canny Edge Detection. *7th International Conference on Reliability, Infocom Technologies and Optimization (ICRITO)*, 518-522.

Jufeng, Y., Jie, L., Hui, S., Kai, W., Paul, L. R., & Ming-Hsuan, Y. (2018). Dynamic Match Kernel with Deep Convolutional Features for Image Retrieval. *IEEE Transactions on Image Processing*, (99), 1–15. PMID:29994213

Junfeng, W., & Yitong, W. (2016). A novel image retrieval approach with Bag-of-Word model and Gabor feature. *Proc. IEEE TrustComBigData SEISPA*, 1706-1711.

Kapil & Nitin. (2018). Plant Species Identification using Leaf Image Retrieval: A Study. *International Conference on Computing, Power and Communication Technologies (GUCON)*, 405-411.

Liu, Z., Li, H., Zhou, W., Hong, R., & Tian, Q. (2015). Uniting keypoints: Local visual information fusion for large-scale image search. *IEEE Transactions on Multimedia*, *17*(4), 538–548. doi:10.1109/TMM.2015.2399851

Mahmudul Hassan, S. K., & Kumar Maji, A. (2021). Identification of Plant Species using Deep Learning. In *Proceedings of International Conference on Frontiers in Computing and Systems. Advances in Intelligent Systems and Computing*, (1255), 115-125. 10.1007/978-981-15-7834-2_11

Mairal, J., Koniusz, P., Harchaoui, Z., & Schmid, C. (2014). Convolutional kernel networks. Proc. Advances in Neural Information Processing Systems, 2627–2635.

Mohedano, E., McGuinness, K., O'Connor, N. E., Salvador, A., & Marqu'es, F. (2016). Bags of local convolutional features for scalable instance search. *Proc. International Conference on Multimedia Retrieval*, 327–331.

Muhammad, K. N., Thomas, M. D., Daniel, H., & Stephan, J. (2016). Feature description with SIFT, SURF, BRIEF, BRISK, or FREAK? A general question answered for bone age assessment. *Computers in Biology and Medicine*, 68, 67–75. doi:10.1016/j.compbiomed.2015.11.006 PMID:26623943

Ngugi, Abelwahab, & Abo-Zahhad. (2021). Recent advances in image processing techniques for automated leaf pest and disease recognition – A review. *Information Processing in Agriculture, 8*(1), 27-51.

Pankaja, K., & Thippeswamy, G. (2017). Survey on Leaf Recognization and Classification. *International Conference on Innovative Mechanisms for Industry Applications*, 442-450. 10.1109/ICIMIA.2017.7975654

Pornntiwa, P., Emmanuel, O., Lambert, S., & Marco, W. (2017). Data Augmentation for Plant Classiδcation. *Proc. International Conference, ACIVS*, 615-626.

Ryfial, A., Desmin, T., & Dasrit, K. (2015). Image Classification Using SIFT Feature Extraction, Bag of Features and Support Vector Machine. *Procedia Computer Science*, 72, 24–30. doi:10.1016/j.procs.2015.12.101

Sathya, B. S., Mohana, V. S., Raju, S., & Abhai, K. V. (2011). Content based leaf image retrieval (CBLIR) using shape, color and texture features. *Indian Journal of Computer Science and Engineering*, 2(2), 202–211.

Sujith, B. (2014). Jyothiprakash. Pedestrian Detection-A Comparative Study Using HOG and COHOG. *IJIRCCE*, 2(5), 358–364.

Tolias, G., Avrithis, Y., & J'egou, H. (2013). To aggregate or not to aggregate: Selective match kernels for image search. *Proc. IEEE International Conference on Computer Vision*, 1401–1408. 10.1109/ICCV.2013.177

Tolias, G., & Chum, O. (2017). Asymmetric feature maps with application to sketch based retrieval. *Proc. IEEE conference on computer vision and pattern recognition*, 6185–6193. 10.1109/CVPR.2017.655

Vasudevan, N., & Karthick, T. (2022). Analysis of Plant Leaf Diseases Recognition using Image Processing with Machine Learning Techniques. *2022 International Conference on Advances in Computing, Communication and Applied Informatics (ACCAI)*. 10.1109/ACCAI53970.2022.9752577

Xiaohan, Y., Shengwu, X., & Yongsheng, G. (2015). Leaf Image Retrieval Using Combined Feature of Vein and Contour. *Proc. International conference image and vision computing New Zealand (IVCNZ)*, 1-6.

Zhang, L., Wang, L., & Lin, W. (2012). Generalized biased discriminant analysis for content-based image retrieval. { *Cybernetics*, 42(1), 282–290. PMID:21968743

Zhao, Y., Chen, Z., Gao, X., Song, W., Xiong, Q., Hu, J., & Zhang, Z. (2022). Plant Disease Detection Using Generated Leaves Based on DoubleGAN. IEEE/ACM Transactions on Computational Biology and Bioinformatics, 19(3).

Zheng, L., Yang, Y., & Tian, Q. (2018). SIFT meets CNN: A decade survey of instance retrieval. *IEEE Trans. Pattern Anal.*, 40(5), 1224–1244. doi:10.1109/TPAMI.2017.2709749 PMID:29610107

Zhou, W., Yang, M., Wang, X., Li, H., Lin, Y., & Tian, Q. (2016). Scalable feature matching by dual cascaded scalar quantization for image retrieval. *Proc. IEEE conference on computer vision and pattern recognition*, 38(1), 159–171. 10.1109/TPAMI.2015.2430329

Chapter 11
The Evolution of Image Denoising From Model–Driven to Machine Learning:
A Mathematical Perspective

Hazique Aetesam
Indian Institute of Technology, Patna, India

Suman Kumar Maji
Indian Institute of Technology, Patna, India

Jerome Boulanger
MRC Lab of Molecular Biology, Cambridge, UK

ABSTRACT

Image denoising is a class of image processing algorithms that aim to enhance the visual quality of the acquired images by removing noise inherent in them and is an active area of research under image enhancement and reconstruction techniques. Traditional model-driven methods are motivated by statistical assumptions on data corruption and prior knowledge of the data to recover while the machine learning (ML) approaches require a massive amount of training data. However, the manual tuning of hyperparameters in model-driven approaches and susceptibility to overfitting under learning-based techniques are their major flaws. Recent years have witnessed the amalgamation of both model and ML-based approaches. Infusing model-driven Bayesian estimator in an ML-based approach, supported by robust mathematical arguments, has been shown to achieve optimal denoising solutions in real time with less effect of over-fitting. In this chapter, the evolution of image denoising techniques is covered from a mathematical perspective along with detailed experimental analysis for each class of approach.

DOI: 10.4018/978-1-7998-8892-5.ch011

INTRODUCTION: IMAGE DENOISING AS AN INVERSE PROBLEM

Given the parameters m, the computation of data (observations) is given by forward model in Figure 1 (left). On the other hand, in order to compute the parameters from data (observations), it is given by inverting the forward model. Here, a model acts as a bridge between data and parameters (see Figure 1 (right)). In other words, finding the effect from the cause is the forward model and finding the causal factors given the effect is the inverse modelling or simply an inverse problem. From the imaging restoration point of view, given a noisy image y, estimating the clean image x falls under the domain of inverse transformation; as shown in Figure 2.

Figure 1. Forward and inverse model

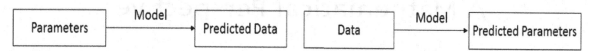

Figure 2. Forward and inverse modelling in image denoising problem.

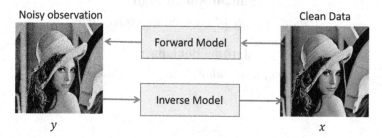

Mathematically speaking, considering an image corrupted by forward observation operator H and noise term η, image degradation model is given by:

$$y = Hx \odot \eta \tag{1}$$

However, under the denoising scenario (as the scope of this chapter is noise removal), the term $H=I$ where I is the identity matrix having the same dimension as H. In other words, Equation (1) can be seen as a generalization of different inverse problems under image restoration where H can take different forms depending on whether the given problem is a denoising, deconvolution, super-resolution or image inpainting problem. $\odot$ is an operator whose exact form depends on whether the noise term η is additive or multiplicative. More about it is discussed in the section: *Noise modelling and probabilistic assumptions.*

There is another way in which an inverse problem can be defined, using a terminology known as *well-posed problem*. According to the definition provided by Jacques Hadamard, a problem is said to be well-posed if:

- the solution exists
- the solution is unique and
- the solution is stable

A problem is said to be ill-posed if it is not well-posed. So, estimation problems like image denoising are most often posed as an inverse problem. If the problem is well-posed, then it can be solved uniquely using a stable algorithm. Even if a problem is well-posed, it may be ill-conditioned. Under such cases, it needs to be reformulated to be effectively modelled numerically. Generically, this idea is formulated using functional analysis. Inverse problem has got wide applications in the field of signal processing, remote sensing, optics, radar, geophysics, acoustics, communication theory, medical imaging, computer vision, oceanography, astronomy, machine learning, natural language processing, non-destructive testing, and many other fields.

From Equation (1), it can be easily noticed that no observation is free from error and hence the term η gets appended to the expression. Further, if any of the conditions of the well-posed problem is not satisfied, the problem is ill-posed. One way of estimating the error introduced in Equation (1) and ensuring the *existence* of the solution is to calculate the least square of the error term. *Least Square* is a standard approach in regression analysis and is most often used in the context of linear regression. Historically, Adrian-Marie Legendre is credited with the development of this approach for estimating the shape of the earth. Later, Carl Friedrich Gauss in the year 1809 went one step ahead in providing the relationship between statistics and the methods of least squares while estimating the movement of celestial bodies. Mathematically, least square is defined as minimizing the sum of squared error in the observation, called residuals; given as:

$$y = Hx \odot \eta \tag{2}$$

$\|y - x\|_2^2$ is also called the data fidelity term since it measures the distance between ground truth and the estimation. However, we are interested in the best estimation. Therefore, the estimation problem here is posed as an optimization problem with respect to the original data x that is to be estimated such that estimation $\hat{x}$ is as close as possible to the original data $\hat{x} \simeq x$. It is further considered that the data is lexicographically arranged in the form of a vector.

Finding the least square estimate guarantees existence of the solution but the uniqueness of the solution cannot be guaranteed because there can be multiple equally good estimations of the same corrupted image. Hence, it is an ill-posed problem. Solution to this is to regularize the optimization problem (Equation (3)) as:

$$\hat{x} = \arg \min_{x} \|y - x\|_2^2 + \lambda \|Mx\| \tag{3}$$

where M is a matrix operator that can take different forms. More about these operators is discussed in sub-section *Regularization Schemes*. λ is a constant; called regularization hyper-parameter adjusting the relative contribution of data fidelity and regularization terms.

Noise Modelling and Probabilistic Assumptions

Noise is an error introduced in the image during the acquisition and transmission phases. There are three different characteristics of noise:

- **Noise is random:** According to the probabilistic definition of a random variable, it is a function that assigns a scalar value to the outcome of any random experiment. In our case, this random process is image acquisition. This random value is added to the original image by some positive/negative values leading to the wrong pixel intensity level.
- **Noise is independent:** Noise on one pixel is independent of the noise level at any other pixel in the image. This is also an essential assumption for simpler mathematical modelling of the problem.

Figure 3. PDF/PMF for (a) Gaussian/normal, (b) Uniform, (c) Gamma and (d) Poisson distribution

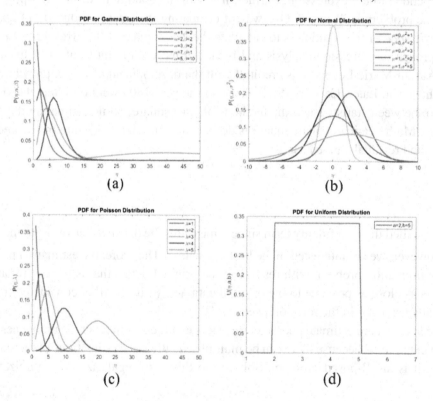

- **Noise follows a probability distribution:** Noise in an image can be approximated using a probability distribution. This helps in understanding the degradation process better and proposing the corresponding solution strategy.

Hence, in this section, different types of noise are described from the mathematical point of view by studying the suitable probability distributions which can model that scenario.

- **Additive Noise:** Replacing the operator $\odot$ in Equation (1) with an additive operator gives rise to the following additive noise model:

$$y = x + \eta \tag{4}$$

  - **Gaussian noise:** Gaussian noise follows normal distribution. Considering that η in Equation 4 is continuous normal random variable with known mean μ and variance σ_g^2, the probability density function (PDF) can be given by:

$$P\left(\eta ; \mu, \sigma_g^2\right) = \frac{1}{\sqrt{2\pi\sigma_g^2}} \exp\left(-\frac{(\eta-\mu)^2}{2\sigma_g^2}\right) \tag{5}$$

  - **Impulse noise:** Impulse noise can be of two different types: fixed-valued impulse noise (FVIN) and random-valued impulse noise (RVIN) (Q. Jin et al., 2017; López-Rubio, 2010; Rodriguez, 2013). Salt-and-pepper noise is an example of FVIN. Considering that the dynamic range of the image is $[g_{min} \ g_{max}]$; pixel values in FVIN are randomly replaced with values; either g_{min} or g_{max}. It can be mathematically represented in Equation 6 as follows:

$$y = \begin{cases} s = g_{min}, & \text{with probability } p/2 \\ s = g_{max}, & \text{with probability } p/2 \\ x, & \text{with probability } 1-p \end{cases} \tag{6}$$

because pixels corrupted by FVIN can have only two extreme random values $s = g_{min}$ or $s = g_{max}$; each with the same probability of occurrence $p/2$. Hence, it is equally probable for a pixel to be corrupted by either of these extreme values. As a result, in this case, the random variable s follows Bernoulli distribution.

On the other hand, in the case of random-valued impulse noise, a corrupted pixel can have any value uniformly distributed in the range $s \sim [g_{min}, g_{max}]$. Hence, for RVIN, image formation model can be represented as:

$$y = \begin{cases} s, & \text{with probability } p \\ x, & \text{with probability } 1-p \end{cases} \tag{7}$$

- **Atmospheric noise** (Mei et al., 2018): Atmospheric noise in remote sensing and underwater acoustic signals can be modelled using Cauchy distribution as given in Equation 8:

$$P\left(\eta ; \eta_0, \gamma\right) = \frac{1}{\pi} \frac{\gamma}{\gamma^2 + (\eta-\eta_0)^2} \tag{8}$$

where η_0 is the location parameter at the peak of the distribution and γ is the scale parameter specifying half width at half maximum (HWHM).

- **Uniform/quantization noise** (Zhang & Ng, 2019): When the outcome of a random process is restricted between the interval a and b in a continuous domain, its probability density function (PDF) is defined by uniform distribution $U(a,b)$. The lower a and upper b bound of the interval can be closed or open. It is defined in Equation 9 by:

$$U(\eta;a,b) = \begin{cases} \dfrac{1}{b-a}; & \text{for } a \leq \eta \leq b \\ 0; & \text{otherwise} \end{cases} \tag{9}$$

- **Speckle (multiplicative) noise:** Speckle occurs as a result of signal interference when the size of the particle is comparable to the wavelength. It commonly occurs in synthetic aperture radar (SAR) and ultrasound images. The image degradation model for data corrupted by multiplicative noise is given by:

$$y = x\eta \tag{10}$$

Speckle is usually modelled using Generalized Gaussian distribution (Cristea, 2015) or Gamma distribution (Aujol & Aubert, 2008; Dong & Zeng, 2013; Zhao et al., 2014). PDF for random variable η corrupted by Gamma distribution with mean 1 is given by:

$$P(\eta;\alpha,\beta) = \frac{\beta^{\alpha} x^{\alpha-1} \exp(-\beta x)}{"(\alpha)} \tag{11}$$

where α= shape parameter and $\beta=1/\theta$ is the inverse scale parameter; also called the rate parameter for scale parameter θ. Γ= gamma function.

- **Signal dependent photon noise:** Shot/photon noise is said to be signal-dependent as the intensity of noise level varies with the signal intensity. Usually found to approximate the photon counting process, it is modelled using Poisson distribution (Sarder & Nehorai, 2006; Willett & Nowak, 2004). The discrete nature of photon counting process and our interest in estimating not the absolute value but the average number of photons emitted and detected makes Poisson distribution an ideal candidate in this situation. It is given by:

$$P(\eta;\lambda) = \frac{e^{-\lambda}\lambda^{\eta}}{\eta!} \tag{12}$$

Intuitively speaking, considering that the rate of photons emitted is λ, the probability of obtaining η number of photons is given by P($\eta;\lambda$).

Plots of probability density/mass functions for noise approximated by different distributions are given in Figure 3.

MODEL DRIVEN APPROACHES

The Bayesian Framework for Estimation

Model-driven approaches derive solutions based on probabilistic assumptions of data corruption during forward transformation and the prior knowledge about data to be estimated. In this section, the Bayesian notion is brought up into the picture to bridge the correlation between Bayesian statistics and the resultant optimization problem. Furthermore, roles of probabilistic assumptions in deciding the form of data fidelity term/s under different categories of noise are discussed. To achieve this, in the next two sections, data fidelity terms (section on data fidelity term) and regularization schemes (section on regularization term) are discussed. This is followed by optimization approaches used to solve the criterion function (section on optimization techniques).

Data Fidelity Term

From an optimization point of view, it is the error between estimation and ground truth when ground-truth data is already available. Hence, given the set of feasible solutions as estimates, the best estimate is chosen to approximate the ground truth. This is very well presented in section: "*image denoising as an inverse problem*" where this error is formulated as the least square solution. However, after going through this section, it is realized that the formulation was based on Bayesian assumptions about data corruption. In the next paragraph, a numerical construction of data-fidelity terms from the Bayesian point of view is presented.

From the perspective of Bayesian statistical theory, Maximum a posteriori (MAP) is an estimator of unknown quantity based on some observable quantity and knowledge available as a prior belief of the data to be estimated. It is presented in terms of Bayes' Theorem as:

$$p(x \mid y) = \frac{p(y \mid x) \cdot p(x)}{p(y)} \tag{13}$$

where $p(x|y)$ is the posterior distribution of unknown quantity x after the observation y is available; conditioned on y. From the perspective of image restoration, it is the estimation of the parameters of the posterior distribution to obtain the clean data x from the available observation y. $p(y|x)$ is the maximum likelihood estimator (MLE) which is the method of estimating the parameters by maximizing the likelihood on observation y conditioned on x based on some probabilistic assumption under which obtaining the observation is most certain. It is measured as the statistical fitness of the observation as a function of unknown parameters. $p(x)$ is the prior distribution of the data to be estimated. From the perspective of learning theory, it is also known as regularization. As a result of non-uniqueness of solution under inverse problem domain, regularization schemes restrict the solution space to a narrow window. *Regularization schemes* is discussed in a separate subsection. $p(y)$ is the evidence; also called the normalization factor which is independent of x and does not have participate in optimizing the solution. Hence, it is dropped from further consideration. Elaborating Equation 13 and considering that variables $\{x,y\}$ is composed of n data points; the MAP estimator can be posed as an optimization problem as:

$$\hat{x} = \arg\max_{x} \left\{ p\left(x_1 | y_1\right) \cdot p\left(x_2 | y_2\right) \cdots p\left(x_n | y_n\right) \right\}$$
$$= \arg\max_{x} [p(y_1 \mid x_1)p\left(x_1\right) \cdot p(y_2 \mid x_2)p\left(x_2\right) \cdots p(y_n \mid x_n)p\left(x_n\right)] \tag{14}$$

$$\hat{x} = \arg\max_{x} \prod_{i=1}^{n} p(x_i \mid y_i) = \arg\max_{x} \prod_{i=1}^{n} [p(y_i \mid x_i) \cdot p\left(x_i\right)] \tag{15}$$

where $\arg\max_{x}$ returns that parameter x which increases the probability of obtaining the observation y based on statistical assumption on x. From the optimization point of view, maximizing the above expression is a cumbersome task given the multiplicative terms. Under the assumption that every data point i is independently distributed, the conditional probability distribution $p(x|y)$ is replaced by probabilities of individual data points. Hence, the joint probability distribution is represented as the product of individual probabilities. However, trying to optimize the Equation 15, complicates the optimization process because of n multiplicative terms. log is a monotonically increasing function that does not change the position of minima; it just pulls the function down or pushes it up. Similarly, when a negative sign is put in front, the function flips itself and the maximization problem gets changed into a minimization problem (again without changing the position of minima) as:

$$\hat{x} = \arg\min_{x} \sum_{i=1}^{n} -\log p(x_i \mid y_i) = \arg\min_{x} \sum_{i=1}^{n} [-\log p(y_i \mid x_i) - \log p\left(x_i\right)] \tag{16}$$

Without loss of generality, in all the future discussions, the individual data items are not referred to in their subscripted form unless required; to simplify further mathematical treatments.

Expression in Equation 16 is also known as the negative log probability using which the original optimization problem gets converted into the optimization of additive terms. When an image is corrupted by a different noise type approximated using a different probability distribution, the likelihood term is specified by different data fidelity terms; also called the energy term. This energy term is denoted by $E(x;y)$; written as:

$$p(y \mid x) \propto -\log\left[E\left(x;y\right) \right] \tag{17}$$

The energy term is also known as cost function, energy function, energy functional, data fidelity term, etc. However, to avoid confusion, consistency is maintained with the usage of *data-fidelity term*. Further, the data fidelity term defines the error between ground truth x and estimation $\hat{x}$. Since in the beginning, the estimation is initialized with the corrupted data, i.e. $x=y$, it is defined in the manner as in Equation 17. The resultant optimization problem is solved using any optimization technique.

To make the relationship between data-fidelity and likelihood term more concrete; $E(x;y)$ is expressed under different probabilistic assumptions.

- When the noise is additive in nature as $y=x+\eta$:

○   Considering that the underlying distribution is white Gaussian:

$$E(x;y) = \|y - x\|_2^2 \tag{18}$$

○   Under uniform/quantization noise where the underlying distribution is uniform, the data fidelity term is given by ℓ_∞ − norm as (Zhang & Ng, 2019):

$$E(x;y) = \|y - x\|_\infty \tag{19}$$

○   For modelling atmospheric noise which is specified using Cauchy distribution; its data fidelity term is given by (Mei et al., 2018):

$$E(x;y) = \int_{R^s} \log(\gamma^2 + (y - x)^2) dx \tag{20}$$

Here, the noise parameter γ need to be estimated before it can be used by the data-fidelity term.

•   When the image is corrupted by multiplicative noise, it can be approximated using Gamma distribution (Aujol & Aubert, 2008; Dong & Zeng, 2013; Zhao et al., 2014); which when used in data fidelity term; is given by:

$$E(x;y) = \int_{R^s} (\log x + \frac{x}{y}) dx \tag{21}$$

•   When data is corrupted by signal-dependent photon noise (Figueiredo & Bioucas-Dias, 2010), data-fidelity term in this case is given by:

$$E = \int_{R^s} (x - y \log x) dx \text{ with } x \geq 0 \text{ to maintain non-negativity constraint} \tag{22}$$

Regularization Term

The term $p(x)$ specified in Equation 16 is called the regularization term and is used to restrict the solution space to a narrower set by using some prior information on the data to be restored. According to Gibbs distribution (Levitan et al., 1995), it is specified by:

$$p(x) = e^{-\lambda R(x)} \tag{23}$$

where λ is the regularization hyperparameter which is used to adjust the relative contribution of the regularization term with respect to the data-fidelity term. Using negative -log probability according to the previous argument yields:

$$p(x) = \lambda R(x) \tag{24}$$

Tikhonov-Miller (van Kempen et al., 1997) and Total variation (Lellmann et al., 2009; Rudin et al., 1992; Shi et al., 2016) regularization are some of the common schemes for regularizing the solution obtained using an optimization technique. TM regularization is specified by:

$$R(x) = \|\nabla x\|_2^2 \tag{25}$$

where ∇ is the gradient of x in ∇x. The usage of TM is specially attractive in optimization problem since it leads to a quadratic solution as:

$$(y - x) + \lambda \Delta x \tag{26}$$

where Δ is the discrete Laplacian operator. However, they are limited by the fact that they do not possess feature selection capability. Further, due to the square term over the image gradient, it heavily penalises sharp changes in images like change in contrast and presence of edges.

Total variation is another type of regularization applied to ordinary least square techniques under two different assumptions. When sufficient number of observations are not available, then the value of parameters cannot be predicted with sufficient accuracy. This is called sparse sensing. The solution in this case will be piecewise-constant and smoothing will be approximated by stair-case function. Hence, additional information is needed to solve the problem exactly. Total variation can also be used under the condition that the system is over-determined owing to the presence of noise in the observation space. Hence, it needs to be solved under ℓ_1 norm. So, the formulation in this case is given by:

$$\|y - x\|_2^2 + \lambda \|\nabla x\|_1 \tag{27}$$

Solving the equation for total variation where $\tilde{N}=$ image gradient, requires us to find the divergence of the regularization term (Rudin et al., 1992), given by:

$$(y - x) + \lambda \, div \frac{\nabla x}{|x|} \tag{28}$$

Other commonly used priors are hyper-Laplacian prior (Shi et al., 2016) and wavelet-based priors (Blu & Luisier, 2007).

Regularization hyper-parameter λ: Since the very beginning, the parameter λ is carried forward without discussing its significance. In this section, its effect is empirically validated on denoising solution when TV is used as the regularization term in the objective function. Since TV is known for its denoising capability, increasing the value of λ decreases noise. However, for large values of λ, fine image features are not preserved as seen in Figure 4. Value of λ is checked between $\lambda=1e-5$ to $\lambda=1e-1$ where best peak signal-to-noise ratio (PSNR) is obtained for $\lambda=1e-2$ when image is corrupted by Gaussian noise level $\sigma 2=0.05$.

Figure 4. Effect of regularization parameter on image recovery. (a)Original, (b) noisy and image recovered by setting (c) λ=1e–5, (d) λ=le–2 and (e) λ=1e–5. (f) PSNR plot for different λ.

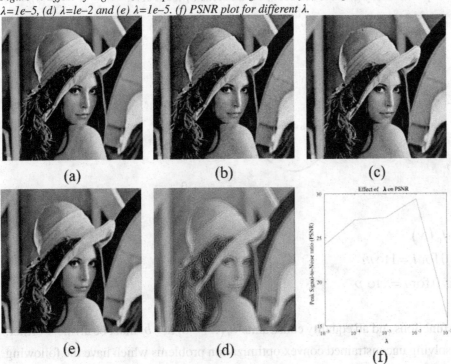

(a)   (b)   (c)

(e)   (d)   (f)

Optimization Techniques

In this section, theory related to optimization/minimization problems in general and convex optimization problems in particular is discussed. The section starts with the constrained optimization problem which consists of several inequality constraints specified by constraint functions defined over a convex objective function. Later, conversion from constrained to unconstrained optimizations problem and common algorithms are discussed for solving an unconstrained convex optimization problem.

Mathematically, an optimization problem has the following form(Boyd et al., 2004):

$$\begin{align} \min \quad & f_0(x) \\ \text{subject to} \quad & f_i(x) \le b_i \text{ for } i = 1 \text{ to } m \end{align}$$

(29)

The vector $x \in R^n$ is called the *optimization variable*, $f_0: R^n \to R$ is the *objective function*, $f_i: R^n \to R$ are the *constraint functions* and bi's are the constraints. A vector $\hat{x}$ is said to achieve the optimal value if it has the smallest objective among all the vectors to satisfy the constraint for all z such that $f_1(z) \le b_1 \dots$ $f_m(z) \le b_m$ and $f_0(z) \ge f_0(x^*)$. Since this work essentially focuses on convex optimization problem, Equation (29) is re-defined as:

Figure 5. Geometrical interpretation of gradient descent on a series of level sets.

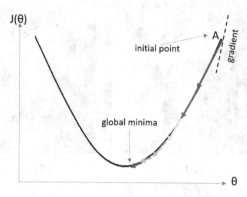

$$\begin{aligned}
&\min && f_0(x) \\
&\text{subject to} && f_i(x) \le 0 \text{ for } i = 1 \text{ to } m \\
&\text{subject to} && a_i^T x = b_i \le 0 \text{ for } i = 1 \text{ to } p
\end{aligned}$$

(30)

where $f_0 \dots f_m$ are convex functions and all equality constraints $h_i(x) = a_i^T x = b_i$ must be affine. Further, in this work, focus is on solving unconstrained convex optimization problems which have the following form:

$$\min f(x)$$

(31)

where $f: R^n \rightarrow R$ is convex in nature. Assuming that $f(x)$ is differentiable in nature, $\hat{x}$ is optimal when the following necessary and sufficient condition occurs:

$$\nabla f(\hat{x}) = 0$$

(32)

In this chapter, two different minimization techniques are discussed for solving convex optimization problem: *(gradient) descent method* and *primal-dual method*. Any algorithm that produces the minimizing sequence $\$ x^k, x^{\{k+1\}}, \cdots$ is called descent-based method:

$$x^{\{k+1\}} = x^k + t\Delta x$$

(33)

where $k=0,1, \dots$ is the iteration number and Δx is the search direction. For all descent-based methods, $f(x_{\{k+1\}}) \le f(x_k)$. The corresponding algorithm is given by Algorithm 1 (Boyd et al., 2004):

In the gradient-descent method, the search direction is negative gradient such that $\Delta x = -\tilde{N} f(x)$.

Given in Figure 5 is the geometrical interpretation of gradient descent on level sets (Boyd et al., 2004). Starting from the initial point x_0, the algorithm moves in the direction of gradient to achieve the local minima. For a convex function, the local minima is obtained from the series of steps defined by the step size. There is a trade-off between step-size, efficiency and accuracy of the algorithm. More is the

Algorithm 1: *General descent method*

1:	**Initialise:** initial point $x \in dom\, f$
2:	**repeat**
3:	Determine a descent direction Δx
4:	Choose step size $t > 0$
5:	Update: $x = x + t\Delta x$
6:	**until** stopping criteria is satisfied

step-size, faster is the line search towards local optima but convergence may not be optimal. For small step size, convergence is more accurate and optimal but efficiency has to suffer.

Stopping criteria: This is used to define when to stop the gradient step in the iterative formulation. In a common scenario, the iteration number is chosen as the stopping criteria. Other commonly used stopping criteria are as follows:

- $|f(x^k)| - f(x^*)$: number of iterations required to achieve the desired error ϵ where ϵ is the desired threshold x^* for the optimal value.
- Terminating when $\left| f\left(x^{\{k+1\}}\right) < f\left(x^k\right) \right|$ is small enough.
- Terminating when $|f(x^k)|$ is small enough.

Algorithm 1: *General descent method*

1:	**Initialise:** initial point $x \in dom\, f$
2:	**repeat**
3:	$\Delta x = -\nabla f(x)$
4:	Line search: choose step-size t
5:	Update: $x = x + t\Delta x$
6:	**until** stopping criteria is satisfied

In this work, the first methodology is chosen where the number of iterations is chosen as the stopping criteria.

In this paragraph, a class of convex optimizations problems known as proximal methods (Parikh & Boyd, 2014) is discussed. They are well-suited for solving large-scale, unconstrained and non-smooth convex problems. However, some extended versions are also used for solving unconstrained problems. On one hand, where basic operations in Newton's method are the calculation of gradient or hessian, in proximal techniques, the basic operation is finding proximal operator associated with different terms in the objective function. Considering a closed proper convex function $f : R^n \to R \cup \{\infty\}$, its proximal operator is denoted by:

Figure 6. Geometrical interpretation of proximal mapping at different points.

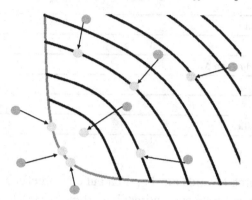

$$\mathrm{prox}\, f(v) = \arg\min_{x}\left(f(x) + \frac{1}{2}\|x - v\|_2^2 \right) \tag{34}$$

for every $v \in R^n$ even when $f \subset R^n$. The function on the righthand size is convex and has a unique minimizer for every v. The scaled version of the proximal operator is given by:

$$\mathrm{prox}_{\lambda}\, f(v) = \arg\min_{x}\left(f(x) + \frac{1}{2t}\|x - v\|_2^2 \right) \tag{35}$$

The geometrical interpretation of Equation 34 and 35 is given in Figure 6. Here, the light brown line is domain of f and dark brown lines are level sets of $f(x)$. Every point $v \in R^n$ (denoted in green colour) (but not necessarily within domain of f) is mapped to the corresponding yellow dot. Every point outside the domain of f is mapped towards the boundary of f and towards the minimum of f. For points inside, they are mapped toward the minima. The parameter t is a trade-off between the minimizer of f and being near to v. Parameter t has the same role as step-size in any gradient-based technique. Proximal operator can also be interpreted as a gradient step for the function f as:

$$\mathrm{prox}_{\lambda f}(v) = v - t\nabla f(v) \tag{36}$$

Finally, fixed point of the proximal operator of f acts as a minimizer for f. More precisely, $prox\, f(\hat{x}) = \hat{x}$ iff $\hat{x}$ is the minimizer for f.

Proximal minimization: Proximal minimization is available in different flavors in the form of different algorithms. They can be interpreted as the successive application of proximal operators to different terms in the objective function. Just like the application of negative gradient in each iteration k in a gradient-based method; for proximal minimization, it is defined by:

$$x^{k+1} = \mathrm{prox}_{\lambda}\, f(x^k) \tag{37}$$

If f has a minima, then x^k converges to a set of minimizers of f and $f(x^k)$ converges to its optimal value. Primal-dual proximal method (Chambolle & Pock, 2011; Condat, 2013) is one such proximal method used for solving convex optimization problems involving non-smooth terms.

LEARNING BASED APPROACHES

In computer science, learning theory is a subset of artificial intelligence (AI) with the intent of design and analysis of machine learning (ML) algorithms. Machine learning is a set of statistical techniques giving computers the ability to mimic the decision-making process by exposing a mathematical model over a vast amount of data. Further, deep learning (DL) is the extension and augmentation of ML theories by passing data through multilayer neural networks having thousands and millions of parameters just like neurons in the human brain (LeCun et al., 2015). Figure 7 puts the AI, ML and DL in the context of one another. It can be observed that DL is a subset of ML which itself is a subset of AI.

Figure 7. Comparison of artificial intelligence (AI), machine learning (ML) and deep learning (DL).

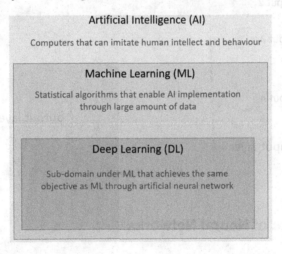

Just like a biological neuron whose action is determined by the combined effects of dendrites, soma and axon, an artificial neuron accepts n number of inputs and provides a single output based on weight matrices W, bias vectors b and non-linear activation functions φ like sigmoid, tanh, and ReLU activation functions. These non-linear functions show interaction effects among different weights and biases. The structure of an ideal neuron is given in Figure 8.

Mathematically, it is represented by $\varphi(Wx+b)$. All these neurons are connected among themselves from input to output in the form of a network. Basic neural network architecture is shown in Figure 9. It consists of an input and an output layer with several hidden layers in between. In a conventional NN architecture, all neurons are connected to every other neuron in the next layer and information flows in the forward direction only. This is called multi-layer perceptron (MLP) or more commonly, a fully connected network. However, in more recent variations, some of the connections are dropped to achieve the desired output (Srivastava et al., 2014).

Figure 8. Structure of an artificial neuron.

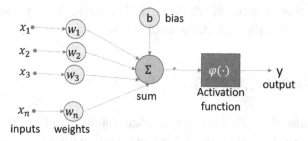

Figure 9. Basic neural network architecture.

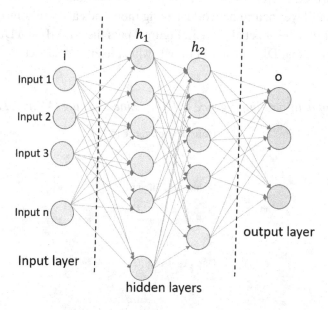

Basic Building Blocks of Neural Networks

The basic building blocks for neural networks include convolutional neural networks, recurrent neural networks, activation layers and normalization strategies and back-propagation.

- Back-propagation: Introduced in 1986, backpropagation is the most widely used algorithm for training feed-forward neural networks by updating weights calculated over loss function layer-wise from output to the input. Gradient of the loss function is calculated with respect to all layers; one layer at a time using chain rule. This makes it possible to use any gradient-based scheme for updation of weights. Mathematically, it is considered that training takes place between input/output pairs $\{y_i, x_i\}$. Weight matrix from node i in layer $l-1$ to node j in the next layer l is denoted by w_{jk}^{l} and the cost function is calculated between the estimated output $g(y)$ and target data (x) as follows:

$$g(y) = f^l\left(W^l\left(f^{l-1}W^{l-1}\cdots f^1\left(W^1 x\right)\right)\right) \tag{38}$$

To avoid re-computation of weights gradient, backpropagation computes the gradient values from back to front layer-wise, denoted by δl. If cost function is denoted by $C(xi, g(yi))$, then gradient is calculated as $\partial \dfrac{C}{\partial} W^l_{\{jk\}}$.

- **Convolutional neural network (CNN):** The inception of CNN completely revolutionized the field of deep learning. With its resemblance of multi-level and multi-scale feature detection capability, normal and dilated versions of CNN are used in a wide range of machine vision tasks. Parameters of a typical convolutional layer include the number and size of filters and regularization strategies for convolutional weights tuning. It works like a typical convolution operation encountered in digital image processing tasks with the difference that filters are dynamically learned for the desired feature that needs to be detected. The area to be convolved is known as the receptive field and the output of the filter is called the activation map. The operation is performed by computing the sum of the dot product between the filter and receptive field as shown in Fig. 10.

Figure 10. Filter operation on an image section (receptive field) producing output as the activation map.

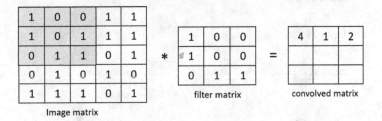

- **Recurrent neural network (RNN):** As an advancement of feed forward networks, RNN was developed to create a temporal relationship among data elements by storing intermediate states. It is due to this reason that it finds applications in natural language processing, speech recognition and video surveillance applications. Long-short term memory (Sherstinsky, 2020), bi-directional RNN (Schuster & Paliwal, 1997) and gated recurrent units (Chung et al., 2014) are some of the implementation strategies of RNN. As shown in Figure 11, the output is fed as feedback to the hidden layers.
- **Normalization strategies:** To simplify the training process by reducing internal co-variate shift, Batch normalization (Ioffe & Szegedy, 2015) was developed. Since the network needs to change it parameters across different epochs, it is feasible to feed normalized output to the next layer without being over-burdened.
- **Optimization techniques:** Although all the techniques in learning-based approaches are gradient-based. gradient descent cannot be used in its original form due to a large amount of data. Finding gradient on each data sample at one go is computationally intensive. On the contrary, random chunks of data can be taken in each attempt to minimize the cost function over entire training data. This chunk of data is called *batch* of data. Total samples in the dataset are covered

in "number of samples/ batch-size" iterations. All the iterations taken together to cover entire dataset constitute one epoch. When this minimization is carried out for a large number of epochs, it is empirically found to provide the same result as gradient descent but being less computationally intensive. Accommodating the calculation of previous gradient updates for the current estimation of gradient helps in making more oscillations in less sensitive direction and fewer oscillations in more sensitive direction. Exponential average of the previous gradient in stochastic gradient descent with momentum (SGDM) (Hinton et al., 2012) and the sum of squared gradients in AdaGrad (Duchi et al., 2011) are some of the approaches to help mitigate the sensitivity issue. To prevent the accumulation of gradients over the training period, squared gradients in the current estimate is multiplied with the decay rate. Adaptive moment estimation (ADAM) (Kingma & Ba, 2014) combines the calculation of both exponential average and sum of squared gradients to help achieve the best of both worlds.

Figure 11. Architecture of a basic RNN.

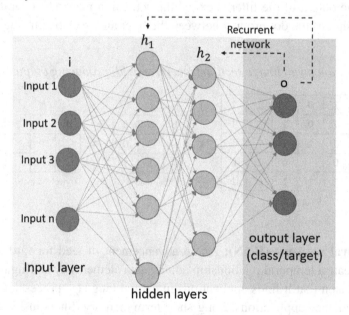

Learning-Based Approaches with Respect to Supervision Spectrum

With respect to the supervision spectrum, there are three main strategies: supervised, unsupervised and reinforcement learning.

- Supervised Learning: When training takes place over pairs $\{y_i, x_i\}_{i=1}^n$ where both input data y_i and labels x_i are available, it is called supervised learning. In the image restoration case, input data y is corrupted and output labels x are the ground truth data. Once the model is trained over noisy-clean image pairs, it is tested during inference time over unseen samples to check its generalizability. Commonly used techniques for supervised learning are linear and logistic regression, Naive Bayes and support vector machine (SVM).

- **Unsupervised Learning:** When the supervisory signal is not available, patterns are represented through a compact internal representation of the world. Principal component analysis (PCA) and clustering are two widely used strategies under unsupervised learning. Semi-supervised learning is a special class of unsupervised learning where small parts of labelled data are combined with large parts of unlabeled data. Self-supervised learning is yet another sub-domain under unsupervised setting where the supervisory signal is generated from unlabeled data and then used for training (Kolesnikov et al., 2019; Quan et al., 2020).
- **Reinforcement Learning:** RL is based on the notion of an award to intelligent agents in an environment to increase the cumulative award (François-Lavet et al., 2018).

Discriminative v/s Generative Learning

Both discriminative and generative learning models are described in the context of the image restoration scenario where y is the corrupted observation and x is the clean data to be estimated. According to Jebara-2004 (Jebara, 2012), discriminative and generative models can be defined as:

- Discriminative: Given the corrupted observation y, this is the conditional distribution of the clean target data x; denoted by $P(x|y)$.
- Generative: Given the corrupted observation y and clean target image x, it is the joint probability distribution between x and y; denoted by $P(x,y)=P(y|x) \cdot P(x)$.

This is pictorially represented in Figure 12. Discriminative and generative models are common types of graphical models. Logistic regression, support vector machine (SVM) and conditional random fields (CRF) can be discussed under discriminative modelling while naive Bayes, Bayesian networks and hidden Markov model (HMM), variational autoencoder (VAE) (Im Im et al., 2017; Kingma & Welling, 2013) and generative adversarial network (GAN) (Goodfellow et al., 2014) can be discussed under generative category. Both these models can be used for encoding probabilistic distributions over domains involving complex interactions of random variables like joint distribution over a large set of random variables.

Figure 12. Graphical representation of discriminative and generative models.

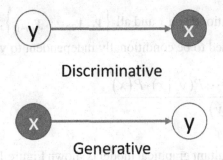

Discriminative

Generative

If y is the corrupted observation and x is the clean target data; both these models estimate the posterior distribution $P(x|y)$. Further, joint model over corrupted data $y=(y_1, y_2, ..., y_n)$ and clean counterpart x is given by:

$$\text{Joint distribution}(x,y) = P(x, y_1, y_2, ..., y_n) \tag{39}$$

To estimate $p(x|y)$, generative model estimates $p(y|x)$ and $p(x)$. However, discriminative model directly assumes functional form of $p(x|y)$ and estimate parameters directly from the training data. Graphically, the two models can be represented in Figure 13.

In the image restoration problem, y is the corrupted data and the unknown x is the clean data. Under the discriminative model, the arrow is pointing from $y \rightarrow x$ which means that $P(x|y)$ can be directly inferred from y. In the generative model, the arrow is pointing from $x \rightarrow y$ which means that the data generating process is used to estimate y from x. For this, $P(x)$ and $P(y|x)$ need to be estimated to obtain the posterior distribution $P(x|y)$.

Under discriminative learning, the corrupted observation y is treated as facts and x can be directly estimated from $P(x|y)$. However, the graphical model is hard to compute under the generative model if observations are dependent. This is represented by:

$$P(x \mid y) = P(x) \cdot P(y_i \mid x) \cdot P(y_2 \mid x, y_1) \cdots P(y_n \mid x, y_1, y_2, \cdots y_{n-1}) \tag{40}$$

Figure 13. Mathematical deductions of (a) discriminative and (b) generative models.

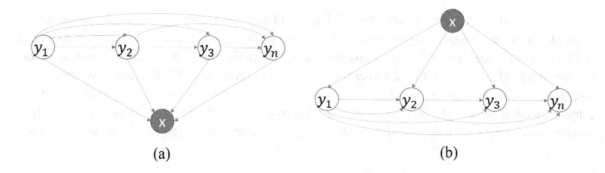

(a)   (b)

The probability of y_i is conditioned on x and all $\left\{ y_1, y_2, \cdots, y_{\{n-1\}} \right\}$. The solution can be simplified if all the observations are assumed to be conditionally independent to yield the following:

$$P(x \mid y) = \frac{P(y_1 \mid x), P(y_2 \mid x), \cdots, P(y_n \mid x) \cdot P(x)}{P(y)} \tag{41}$$

With this assumption, the resultant graphical model is shown Figure 12. Under discriminative modeling, the posterior probability can be directly estimated using training data. For example, using logistic regression, the posterior probability can be given by:

Figure 14. Change in graphical model under conditionally independent assumption.

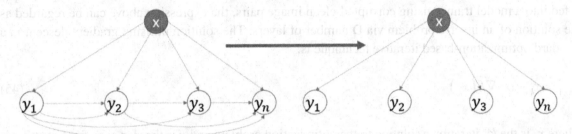

$$P(x \mid y) = \frac{1}{1 + exp\left(\alpha_0 + \sum_{i=1}^{n} \alpha_i y_i\right)} \tag{42}$$

BRIDGE BETWEEN MODEL AND DATA DRIVEN APPROACHES

Estimation of clean data $\hat{x} \simeq x$ can be obtained from a Bayesian perspective by solving the following risk minimization task using an optimization technique according to the Maximum a posteriori (MAP) criterion.

$$\hat{x} = \arg\min_{x} -\log\left[p(x \mid y)\right] = \arg\min_{x} -\log\left[p(y \mid x) \cdot p(x)\right] \tag{43}$$

where $p(y|x)$ is the likelihood term that takes the appropriate form based on the distribution used to model the degradation process, $p(x|y)$ is the posterior distribution and p(x) is the prior enforcing required properties to be fulfilled in the solution space. Choosing a suitable prior necessitates a thorough understanding of the working domain.

Researchers have been attempting to develop a link between model-driven optimization approaches and data-driven learning-based methods in recent years. Some representative efforts include sparse coding with feed-forward learners (Gregor & LeCun, 2010), sparse outliers removal using l_0-norm representations (Xin et al., 2016), and non-linear reactive diffusion models (Chen et al., 2015). Authors in (K. H. Jin et al., 2017) made an analogy between CNN and model-based techniques, claiming that image inversion problems can be solved via direct inversion of the forward model followed by a CNN. In a typical convolutional neural network (CNN), the output from the first layer is given as $x^1 = \varphi\left(W^{(1)} \otimes y + b^{(1)}\right) \in R^{\{w \times h \times c_1\}}$, while the output from the dth layer is given as:

$$x^{d+1} = \varphi\left(W^{(d+1)} \otimes x^d + b^{(d+1)}\right) \tag{44}$$

where $x^{d+1} \in R^{m \times n \times c_{d+1}}$. The number of filter outputs from the $(d+1)^{\text{th}}$ layer is represented by c_{d+1}. The weight matrices, biases, and convolution operation are represented by W, b, and $\otimes$ respectively. φ is a sigmoid or ReLU activation function, which is a non-linear activation function. When a corrupted input is fed into a model trained using corrupted-clean image pairs, the expression above can be regarded as the solution of an inverse problem via D number of layers. The solution utilising gradient descent in a standard optimization-based iterative technique is:

$$x_{k+1} = x_k - \alpha \cdot \nabla f\left(x_k\right) \tag{45}$$

where x_k is the kth iteration's solution to the optimization problem and α is the step size. f is a multivariate differentiable function whose solution descends to a local minima in successive steps. Equation 45's iterative technique can be considered as D layers of a neural network used to predict clean data from corrupted observations at inference time.

The loss between the estimation $\left(\hat{x}\right)$ and the ground truth (x) is minimised in a supervised discriminative learning environment by optimising a set of parameters through a learning process across N training pairs of noisy-clean data $\left\{y^{(i)}, x^{(i)}\right\}_{i=1}^{N}$. (K. Zhang et al., 2020; K. Zhang, Zuo, Gu, et al., 2017).

$$\begin{cases} \min_{\theta} L(\hat{x}, x) \\ \text{such that } \hat{x} = \arg\min_{x} \left\| y - x \right\|_p + \lambda R\left(x; \theta\right) \end{cases} \tag{46}$$

where $\|\bullet\|_p$ is the l_p-norm, the exact shape of which is determined by the forward observation model. $\mathcal{R}\left(x\right)$ is the penalty term with the hyperparameter λ. Equation 46's MAP guided learning process can be substituted by a non-linear function $\vartheta\theta_{(y)}$ parametrized by learning parameters (K. Zhang, Zuo, Gu, et al., 2017), where $\hat{x} = \vartheta_{\theta}\left(y\right)$ (K. Zhang, Zuo, Gu, et al., 2017).

Some more recent works are presented below which have tried to establish a link between model and data-driven approaches:

- **Deep Convolutional Neural Network for Inverse Problems in Imaging:** Authors in (K. H. Jin et al., 2017) proposed a U-Net architecture and established a link between the iterative reconstruction method and CNN. The intuition behind this is that the normal operator during inverse transformation in the iterative approach is the same as the convolutional filters in CNN. This is made possible by the combination of multi-resolution decomposition and residual learning. The basic difference between the conventional and learning-based approaches is that in the latter, the filters are learnable.
- **Training and Refining Deep Learning Based Denoisers without Ground Truth Data:** Stein's Unbiased Risk Estimator (SURE) used as a surrogate for mean square error loss in conventional approaches has been extended in the deep neural network for unsupervised training of neural network when the underlying distribution is Gaussian without the availability of ground truth data (Soltanayev & Chun, 2018). The authors empirically validated that under stochastic gradient-based optimizations in neural networks, the network produced the same results as if trained using the whole dataset.

- Blind Universal Bayesian Image Denoising with Gaussian Noise Level Learning: Based on Bayesian formulation of the problem for Gaussian image denoising, noise level estimation and denoiser network is combined using DnCNN architecture (el Helou & Susstrunk, 2020). Here, $p(y)$ in the MAP formulation is presented as the convolution between original image x and Gaussian noise level map with elements sampled from a zero-mean normal distribution with variance $\hat{A}_g^{l2}$.

- Learning Sparse Neural Networks through ℓ_0 Regularization: Just like in an iterative solution based on MAP estimates, where ℓ_0 norm is used for predicting sparse solutions, authors in (Louizos et al., 2017) proposed a solution for regularizing deep neural network to introduce sparsity by incorporating ℓ_0 regularization in the solution strategy. This is given by:

$$Q(\theta) = \frac{1}{N}\left(\sum_{i=1}^{n}\mathcal{L}\left(f\left(y_i;\theta\right),x_i\right)\right) + \|\theta\|_0 \tag{47a}$$

$$\theta^* = \arg\min_{\theta}\left\{Q(\theta)\right\} \tag{47b}$$

- **Deep Image prior:** As claimed by the authors in (Ulyanov et al., 2018), the structure of an untrained randomly initialized neural network acts as a prior just like a regularization term in iterative optimization-based solutions to inverse problems. In a typical optimization framework, objective function is given by:

$$\hat{x} = \arg\min_{x}\left\{E\left(x;x_0\right) + R\left(x\right)\right\} \tag{48}$$

where x_0 is the initial randomly sampled data, x is the estimation and $R(x)$ is the regularization term. $R(x)$ can be replaced by an implicit prior captured by randomly initialized neural network with a random vector z drawn from uniform distribution having the same size as that of x. This is given by:

$$\theta^* = \arg\min_{\theta} E\left(f_\theta\left(z\right),x_0\right)\text{ such that }\hat{x} = f_{\theta^*}\left(z\right) \tag{49}$$

where $f_\theta(z)$ is the randomly initialized neural network. In the learning-based approach, $x0$ is the target data which can be clean image, Gaussian noise corrupted or randomly perturbed pixel values. It is found that Gaussian corrupted pixels and clean target image yield the best results.

- **Learning Deep CNN Denoiser Prior for Image Restoration, Plug-and-Play Image Restoration with Deep Denoiser Prior:** In an attempt to integrate the flexibility of model-based optimization problems and efficiency of learning-based approaches, authors in (K. Zhang et al., 2020; K. Zhang, Zuo, Gu, et al., 2017) used a trained denoiser model with large modelling capacity as a prior under model-based approach. The resultant optimization problem was solved using a variable splitting approach like half-quadratic splitting or ADMM.

Figure 15. Visual results of denoising on BSD68 dataset for AWGN level σ=25.

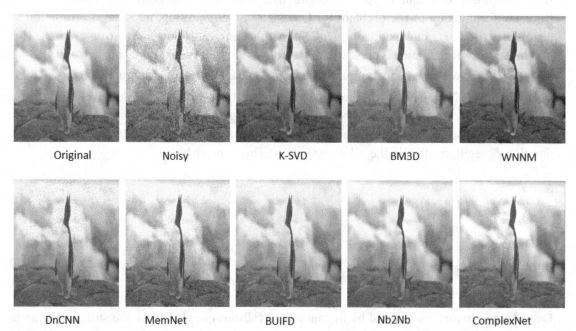

EXPERIMENTAL ANALYSIS

In this section, we conduct experiments on image denoising using different category of methods; namely, model-driven, data-driven and combination of these methods. The data used for experimentation are corrupted by additive white Gaussian noise (AWGN) with zero mean standard deviation specifying noise levels. Both grayscale images and colored images are used for the experiments. Eight comparing methods are used; as follows:

- **K-SVD** (Elad & Aharon, 2006): *Image Denoising Via Sparse and Redundant Representations Over Learned Dictionaries*. This is a dictionary learning approach for sparsely represented data. However, the dictionary is learned over a large dataset of high quality. The K-SVD algorithm is extended to accommodate global image prior that exploits sparsity over patches in every location of the image.
- **BM3D** (Dabov et al., 2007): *Image Denoising by Sparse 3-D Transform-Domain Collaborative Filtering*. Initially, blocks from the 2D image are obtained and arranged in 3D blocks. This is a filtering-based approach for denoising 2D data using a three-phase collaborative filtering strategy: transformation of 3D blocks, shrinkage in the transformed domain followed by the inverse transformation. The colored version of the method is referred to as CBM3D in the text.
- **WNNM**: *Weighted Nuclear Norm Minimization with Application to Image Denoising*. The authors in this paper exploit the non-local self-similarity in images. Further, low-rank matrix factorization is implemented by nuclear norm minimization (NNM). However, the solution to the NNM problem is tested under different weighting conditions of singular values.

Figure 16. Visual results of denoising on BSD68 dataset for AWGN level σ=45.

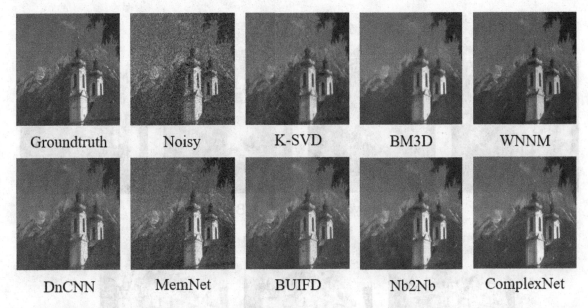

Figure17. Visual results of denoising color image from CBSD68 for AWGN level σ=25.

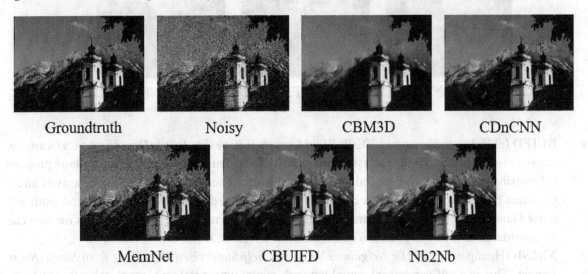

- **DnCNN** (K. Zhang, Zuo, Chen, et al., 2017): *Beyond a Gaussian Denoiser: Residual Learning of Deep CNN for Image Denoising.* This is an end-to-end learning-based approach for recover noisy data from corrupted observation by learning residual images.

- **MemNet** (Tai et al., 2017): *MemNet: A Persistent Memory Network for Image Restoration.* To imitate the persistent memory possessed by human beings, authors in this paper propose a deep neural network consisting of a recursive unit and gate unit. The recursive unit is used to map long-range dependencies often in deeper layers of the network. The gate unit is used to accommodate the output from several previous memory units for multi-level feature mapping to recover true data from corrupted inputs.

Figure 18. Visual results of denoising color image from CBSD68 for AWGN level σ=45.

| Groundtruth | Noisy | CBM3D | CDnCNN |

| MemNet | CBUIFD | Nb2Nb |

- **BUIFD** (el Helou & Süsstrunk, 2020): *Blind Universal Bayesian Image Denoising with Gaussian Noise Level Learning*. Under the assumption that data is Gaussian corrupted, the authors propose a denoising fusion function plugged into a deep network. The likelihood function is derived under Gaussian distribution and prior on corrupted data is assumed to be convolution ground-truth and noise Gaussian noise level in the maximum a posteriori formulation. Therefore, this method can be considered as the amalgamation of both model-driven and data-driven methods.
- **Nb2Nb** (Huang et al., 2021): *Neighbor2Neighbor: Self-Supervised Denoising from Single Noisy Images*. This is a self-supervised neural network model where training image pairs are sub-sampled from the same data. It exploits the fact the paired pixels obtained from paired images are neighbours and are similar in appearance to each other.
- **ComplexNet** (Quan et al., 2021): *Image Denoising Using Complex-Valued Deep CNN*. The complex cells present in the visual cortex of the human brain is responsible for interpreting visual data in terms of different orientations and frequency components. Further, two 1D complex filters simulate the same of ordinary non-separable filters. As mentioned in the paper, this also supports learning via activation function and residual learning; specifically dedicated to image restoration.

All the test experiments are conducted over datasets obtained from three sources: Berkeley Segmentation Dataset 68/Coloured BSD (CBSD) 68 (ROTH & BLACK, 2009), Set 5 (Bevilacqua et al., 2012) and set 14 (Zeyde et al., 2010) datasets. It is important

Table 1. PSNR and SSIM comparison for different methods at different levels of noise.

Dataset	Methods	PSNR				SSIM			
		AWGN Noise Level				AWGN Noise Level			
		25	35	45	60	25	35	45	60
BSD68	K-SVD	27.38	22.09	18.46	16.14	0.717	0.454	0.305	0.215
	BM3D	28.08	22.57	18.84	16.19	0.769	0.496	0.319	0.226
	WNNM	27.09	22.63	19.18	16.16	0.748	0.477	0.312	0.221
	DnCNN	27.46	25.79	24.28	23.23	0.763	0.682	0.624	0.547
	MemNet	27.71	25.99	24.99	23.37	0.775	0.710	0.651	0.610
	BUIFD	28.75	26.50	25.45	24.31	0.793	0.734	0.681	0.646
	Nb2Nb	27.74	26.02	26.01	25.29	0.721	0.707	0.672	0.643
	ComplexNet	28.35	26.89	26.05	25.93	0.791	0.737	0.698	0.672
Set5	K-SVD	28.29	22.34	18.96	17.11	0.742	0.457	0.298	0.213
	BM3D	29.60	24.00	19.66	16.94	0.801	0.511	0.328	0.224
	WNNM	28.45	22.54	19.06	16.43	0.774	0.481	0.311	0.222
	DnCNN	28.21	26.32	23.66	22.24	0.760	0.690	0.617	0.554
	MemNet	28.08	26.16	24.95	22.77	0.774	0.708	0.658	0.621
	BUIFD	29.61	27.78	26.00	24.26	0.817	0.770	0.720	0.680
	Nb2Nb	28.22	27.53	25.93	24.23	0.823	0.808	0.754	0.718
	ComplexNet	30.51	29.01	28.31	27.65	0.838	0.815	0.786	0.754
Set14	K-SVD	26.92	22.22	18.94	16.61	0.719	0.453	0.311	0.227
	BM3D	28.24	23.50	19.19	16.31	0.776	0.506	0.334	0.231
	WNNM	28.16	22.75	19.02	16.65	0.748	0.476	0.320	0.237
	DnCNN	27.88	26.10	24.41	22.61	0.759	0.691	0.626	0.556
	MemNet	28.38	26.02	24.52	23.18	0.771	0.703	0.650	0.609
	BUIFD	28.52	27.48	25.52	24.61	0.801	0.744	0.695	0.659
	Nb2Nb	27.82	27.08	25.40	24.33	0.778	0.732	0.686	0.628
	ComplexNet	28.17	26.73	25.49	25.52	0.788	0.756	0.707	0.682
CBSD68	BM3D	27.35	26.79	26.78	25.22	0.757	0.740	0.733	0.704
	DnCNN	29.85	28.89	27.22	25.53	0.859	0.818	0.766	0.735
	MemNet	30.37	28.87	27.18	25.39	0.864	0.810	0.778	0.737
	BUIFD	30.47	28.25	26.65	26.25	0.860	0.820	0.780	0.745
	Nb2Nb	29.67	28.77	27.42	25.50	0.855	0.814	0.779	0.744

to remember that in the captions of the visual results over coloured images, the methods BM3D, DnCNN and BUIFD are named as CBM3D, CDnCNN and CBUIFD respectively. Two image quality assessment metrics are used for the quantitative evaluation of the restored results; namely peak signal-to-noise ratio (PSNR) and structural similarity index.

Results on synthetic data from BSD68 dataset is visualized in Fig. 15 for AWGN noise level $\sigma=25$. Similarly, Figure 16 shows the results for noise level $\sigma=45$. The visual results can be divided into three different denoising techniques: model-driven, data-driven and combined approaches. As seen in Fig 15 and 16, K-SVD is unable to remove noise properly. This is also visible in the results obtained using WNNM. MemNet under learning-based strategy is unable to justify its claim of multiscale feature detection and representation. DnCNN is not able to remove noise properly when noise level is high (in Figure 16). Nb2Nb is not able to preserve details in the image but works quite good in noise removal. Among the learning-based approaches, ComplexNet produces the best visual results and BUIFD is the second-best performing method. However, some post-processing artefacts can be observed in the visual results of BUIFD. This is attributed to the underestimation of noise level in BUIFD.

Results on RGB is conducted on the same CBSD68 datasets. Figure 17 and 18 shows the results for AWGN $\sigma=25$ and level $\sigma=45$ respectively. However, since not all methods are developed for RGB data, only CBM3D, CDNCNN, MemNet, CBUIFD and Nb2Nb results are shown in Figure 17 and 18. CBUIFD delivers the best results when among all competing methods when the noise level is low ($\sigma=25$) but suffers from the post-processing artefacts under high noise level ($\sigma=45$). Blur is clearly discernible in the visual results of CBM3D and CDnCNN; but is more pronounced in CBM3D for both low and high levels of noise. Results generated by MemNet shows the similar trends with its insufficiency in handling noise.

To get a more comprehensive overview of the denoising performance of the competing of different methods, we have tabulated the metrics results in Table 1 for four different noise levels; namely $\sigma=25,35,45$ and 60 and four datasets; as mentioned previously. For both PSNR and SSIM, we observe that best values are achieved for ComplexNet and BUIFD. The excellent behavior of ComplexNet is attributed to its compressive representational ability of convolutional filters in the complex domain. Similarly, Bayesian approach incorporated in the fusion function in BUIFD is the reason for its effective performance for a wide range of noise levels.

CONCLUSION

This chapter started with the introduction of the inverse problem and its application in the image restoration domain. Since this work is dedicated to restoring images corrupted by noise only, the probabilistic models for approximating noise in different imaging contexts are discussed. Two different approaches under image denoising schemes are presented: mod*el-driven an*d da*ta-driven. O*ptimization strategies under the two different restoration methodologies are covered in the text. The authors paid special emphasis to the recent developments on the amalgamations of model and data-driven approaches. This is also experimentally validated under different levels of noise where different categories image denoising methods are tested for the noise removal performance.

REFERENCES

Aujol, J.-F., & Aubert, G. (2008). 'A Variational Approach to Remove Multiplicative Noise. *SIAM Journal on Applied Mathematics, 68*(4), 925–946. doi:10.1137/060671814

Blu, T., & Luisier, F. (2007). The SURE-LET approach to image denoising. *IEEE Transactions on Image Processing, 16*(11), 2778–2786. doi:10.1109/TIP.2007.906002 PMID:17990754

Boyd, S., Boyd, S. P., & Vandenberghe, L. (2004). *Convex optimization.* Cambridge University Press. doi:10.1017/CBO9780511804441

Chambolle, A., & Pock, T. (2011). A first-order primal-dual algorithm for convex problems with applications to imaging. *Journal of Mathematical Imaging and Vision, 40*(1), 120–145. doi:10.100710851-010-0251-1

Chen, Y., Yu, W., & Pock, T. (2015). On learning optimized reaction diffusion processes for effective image restoration. *Proceedings of the IEEE Conference on Computer Vision and Pattern Recognition*, 5261–5269. 10.1109/CVPR.2015.7299163

Chung, J., Gulcehre, C., Cho, K., & Bengio, Y. (2014). *Empirical evaluation of gated recurrent neural networks on sequence modeling.* ArXiv Preprint ArXiv:1412.3555.

Condat, L. (2013). A primal–dual splitting method for convex optimization involving Lipschitzian, proximable and linear composite terms. *Journal of Optimization Theory and Applications, 158*(2), 460–479. doi:10.100710957-012-0245-9

Cristea, A. (2015). *Ultrasound tissue characterization using speckle statistics.* Academic Press.

Dabov, K., Foi, A., Katkovnik, V., & Egiazarian, K. (2007). Image denoising by sparse 3-D transform-domain collaborative filtering. *IEEE Transactions on Image Processing, 16*(8), 2080–2095. doi:10.1109/TIP.2007.901238 PMID:17688213

Dong, Y., & Zeng, T. (2013). A convex variational model for restoring blurred images with multiplicative noise. *SIAM Journal on Imaging Sciences, 6*(3), 1598–1625. doi:10.1137/120870621

Duchi, J., Hazan, E., & Singer, Y. (2011). Adaptive subgradient methods for online learning and stochastic optimization. *Journal of Machine Learning Research, 12*(7).

el Helou, M., & Susstrunk, S. (2020). Blind universal Bayesian image denoising with Gaussian noise level learning. *IEEE Transactions on Image Processing, 29*, 4885–4897. doi:10.1109/TIP.2020.2976814 PMID:32149690

el Helou, M., & Süsstrunk, S. (2020). Blind universal Bayesian image denoising with Gaussian noise level learning. *IEEE Transactions on Image Processing, 29*, 4885–4897. doi:10.1109/TIP.2020.2976814 PMID:32149690

Elad, M., & Aharon, M. (2006). Image denoising via sparse and redundant representations over learned dictionaries. *IEEE Transactions on Image Processing, 15*(12), 3736–3745. doi:10.1109/TIP.2006.881969 PMID:17153947

Figueiredo, M. A. T., & Bioucas-Dias, J. M. (2010). Restoration of Poissonian images using alternating direction optimization. *IEEE Transactions on Image Processing, 19*(12), 3133–3145. doi:10.1109/TIP.2010.2053941 PMID:20833604

François-Lavet, V., Henderson, P., Islam, R., Bellemare, M. G., & Pineau, J. (2018). An Introduction to Deep Reinforcement Learning. *Foundations and Trends→ in Machine Learning, 11*(3–4), 219–354. doi:10.1561/2200000071

Goodfellow, I. J., Pouget-Abadie, J., Mirza, M., Xu, B., Warde-Farley, D., Ozair, S., Courville, A., & Bengio, Y. (2014). *Generative adversarial networks*. ArXiv Preprint ArXiv:1406.2661.

Gregor, K., & LeCun, Y. (2010). Learning fast approximations of sparse coding. *Proceedings of the 27th International Conference on International Conference on Machine Learning*, 399–406.

Hinton, G., Srivastava, N., & Swersky, K. (2012). Neural networks for machine learning lecture 6a overview of mini-batch gradient descent. *Cited On, 14*(8).

Huang, T., Li, S., Jia, X., Lu, H., & Liu, J. (2021). Neighbor2neighbor: Self-supervised denoising from single noisy images. *Proceedings of the IEEE/CVF Conference on Computer Vision and Pattern Recognition*, 14781–14790. 10.1109/CVPR46437.2021.01454

Im Im, D., Ahn, S., Memisevic, R., & Bengio, Y. (2017). Denoising criterion for variational auto-encoding framework. *Proceedings of the AAAI Conference on Artificial Intelligence, 31*(1).

Ioffe, S., & Szegedy, C. (2015). Batch normalization: Accelerating deep network training by reducing internal covariate shift. *International Conference on Machine Learning*, 448–456.

Jebara, T. (2012). *Machine learning: discriminative and generative* (Vol. 755). Springer Science & Business Media.

Jin, K. H., McCann, M. T., Froustey, E., & Unser, M. (2017). Deep convolutional neural network for inverse problems in imaging. *IEEE Transactions on Image Processing, 26*(9), 4509–4522. doi:10.1109/TIP.2017.2713099 PMID:28641250

Jin, Q., Grama, I., & Liu, Q. (2017). Optimal Weights Mixed Filter for removing mixture of Gaussian and impulse noises. *PLoS One, 12*(7), e0179051. doi:10.1371/journal.pone.0179051 PMID:28692667

Kingma, D. P., & Ba, J. (2014). *Adam: A method for stochastic optimization*. ArXiv Preprint ArXiv:1412.6980.

Kingma, D. P., & Welling, M. (2013). *Auto-encoding variational bayes*. ArXiv Preprint ArXiv:1312.6114.

Kolesnikov, A., Zhai, X., & Beyer, L. (2019). Revisiting self-supervised visual representation learning. *Proceedings of the IEEE/CVF Conference on Computer Vision and Pattern Recognition*, 1920–1929.

LeCun, Y., Bengio, Y., & Hinton, G. (2015). Deep learning. *Nature, 521*(7553), 436–444. doi:10.1038/nature14539 PMID:26017442

Lellmann, J., Becker, F., & Schnorr, C. (2009). Convex optimization for multi-class image labeling with a novel family of total variation based regularizers. *2009 IEEE 12th International Conference on Computer Vision*, 646–653.

Levitan, E., Chan, M., & Herman, G. T. (1995). Image-modeling Gibbs priors. *Graphical Models and Image Processing, 57*(2), 117–130. doi:10.1006/gmip.1995.1013

López-Rubio, E. (2010). Restoration of images corrupted by Gaussian and uniform impulsive noise. *Pattern Recognition, 43*(5), 1835–1846. doi:10.1016/j.patcog.2009.11.017

Louizos, C., Welling, M., & Kingma, D. P. (2017). *Learning Sparse Neural Networks through L_0 Regularization.* ArXiv Preprint ArXiv:1712.01312.

Mei, J.-J., Dong, Y., Huang, T.-Z., & Yin, W. (2018). Cauchy noise removal by nonconvex ADMM with convergence guarantees. *Journal of Scientific Computing, 74*(2), 743–766. doi:10.100710915-017-0460-5

Parikh, N., & Boyd, S. (2014). Proximal algorithms. *Foundations and Trends in Optimization, 1*(3), 127–239. doi:10.1561/2400000003

Quan, Y., Chen, M., Pang, T., & Ji, H. (2020). Self2self with dropout: Learning self-supervised denoising from single image. *Proceedings of the IEEE/CVF Conference on Computer Vision and Pattern Recognition*, 1890–1898. 10.1109/CVPR42600.2020.00196

Quan, Y., Chen, Y., Shao, Y., Teng, H., Xu, Y., & Ji, H. (2021). Image denoising using complex-valued deep CNN. *Pattern Recognition, 111*, 107639. doi:10.1016/j.patcog.2020.107639

Rodriguez, P. (2013). Total variation regularization algorithms for images corrupted with different noise models: A review. *Journal of Electrical and Computer Engineering, 2013*, 10. doi:10.1155/2013/217021

Rudin, L. I., Osher, S., & Fatemi, E. (1992). Nonlinear total variation based noise removal algorithms. *Physica D. Nonlinear Phenomena, 60*(1–4), 259–268. doi:10.1016/0167-2789(92)90242-F

Sarder, P., & Nehorai, A. (2006). Deconvolution methods for 3-D fluorescence microscopy images. *IEEE Signal Processing Magazine, 23*(3), 32–45. doi:10.1109/MSP.2006.1628876

Schuster, M., & Paliwal, K. K. (1997). Bidirectional recurrent neural networks. *IEEE Transactions on Signal Processing, 45*(11), 2673–2681. doi:10.1109/78.650093

Sherstinsky, A. (2020). Fundamentals of recurrent neural network (RNN) and long short-term memory (LSTM) network. *Physica D. Nonlinear Phenomena, 404*, 132306. doi:10.1016/j.physd.2019.132306

Shi, M., Han, T., & Liu, S. (2016). Total variation image restoration using hyper-Laplacian prior with overlapping group sparsity. *Signal Processing, 126*, 65–76. doi:10.1016/j.sigpro.2015.11.022

Soltanayev, S., & Chun, S. Y. (2018). *Training and Refining Deep Learning Based Denoisers without Ground Truth Data.* ArXiv Preprint ArXiv:1803.01314.

Srivastava, N., Hinton, G., Krizhevsky, A., Sutskever, I., & Salakhutdinov, R. (2014). Dropout: A simple way to prevent neural networks from overfitting. *Journal of Machine Learning Research, 15*(1), 1929–1958.

Tai, Y., Yang, J., Liu, X., & Xu, C. (2017). Memnet: A persistent memory network for image restoration. *Proceedings of the IEEE International Conference on Computer Vision*, 4539–4547. 10.1109/ICCV.2017.486

Ulyanov, D., Vedaldi, A., & Lempitsky, V. (2018). Deep image prior. *Proceedings of the IEEE Conference on Computer Vision and Pattern Recognition*, 9446–9454.

van Kempen, G. M. P., van Vliet, L. J., Verveer, P. J., & van der Voort, H. T. M. (1997). A quantitative comparison of image restoration methods for confocal microscopy. *Journal of Microscopy*, *185*(3), 354–365. doi:10.1046/j.1365-2818.1997.d01-629.x

Willett, R. M., & Nowak, R. D. (2004). Fast multiresolution photon-limited image reconstruction. *2004 2nd IEEE International Symposium on Biomedical Imaging: Nano to Macro (IEEE Cat No. 04EX821)*, 1192–1195.

Xin, B., Wang, Y., Gao, W., & Wipf, D. (2016). *Maximal sparsity with deep networks?* ArXiv Preprint ArXiv:1605.01636.

Zhang, K., Li, Y., Zuo, W., Zhang, L., van Gool, L., & Timofte, R. (2020). *Plug-and-play image restoration with deep denoiser prior.* ArXiv Preprint ArXiv:2008.13751.

Zhang, K., Zuo, W., Chen, Y., Meng, D., & Zhang, L. (2017). Beyond a gaussian denoiser: Residual learning of deep cnn for image denoising. *IEEE Transactions on Image Processing*, *26*(7), 3142–3155. doi:10.1109/TIP.2017.2662206 PMID:28166495

Zhang, K., Zuo, W., Gu, S., & Zhang, L. (2017). Learning deep CNN denoiser prior for image restoration. *Proceedings of the IEEE Conference on Computer Vision and Pattern Recognition*, 3929–3938. 10.1109/CVPR.2017.300

Zhang, X., & Ng, M. K. (2019). A Fast Algorithm for Solving Linear Inverse Problems with Uniform Noise Removal. *Journal of Scientific Computing*, *79*(2), 1214–1240. doi:10.100710915-018-0888-2

Zhao, X.-L., Wang, F., & Ng, M. K. (2014). A new convex optimization model for multiplicative noise and blur removal. *SIAM Journal on Imaging Sciences*, *7*(1), 456–475. doi:10.1137/13092472X

Chapter 12
Machine Learning and Image Processing Based Computer Vision in Industry 4.0

Ramya S.
SASTRA University (Deemed), India

Madhubala P.
SASTRA University (Deemed), India

Sushmitha E. C.
SASTRA University (Deemed), India

D. Manivannan
SASTRA University (Deemed), India

A. Al Firthous
CYRYX College, Maldives

ABSTRACT

Industry 4.0 reshapes the industrial landscape through new technologies such as robotics, data networking, machine learning (ML), and computer vision (CV). ML is a critical innovation in technology that enables enterprises and factory floors to embrace Industry 4.0. Systems and algorithms can learn from their failures using machine learning, a form of artificial intelligence (AI). A vision system becomes an essential component of sophisticated industrial systems for the quality control throughout the manufacturing process, and it allows robotic assembly to be provided with the necessary knowledge to create products from simple components. Predictive maintenance (PdM) is a form of digital transformation that services repairs as immediately as an issue emerges. The criterion above leads to a manufacturing environment that is intelligent and autonomous on recent breakthrough information and communication technologies. This chapter explores the challenges in Industry 4.0 with technologies such as cyber-physical systems (CPS), image processing, internet of things (IoT), computer vision, etc.

DOI: 10.4018/978-1-7998-8892-5.ch012

INTRODUCTION

Revolutions have always prompted economic and social reforms. In developed countries, urbanisation is accelerating. Industry 4.0 introduces the industries of the twenty-first century to constantly changing technologies. The German government established the word to define a sequence of technological advances in product development as well as the priorities of a framework for sustaining global standards across German industry (Villalba-Diez et al., 2019). The next industrial type, Industry 4.0, has been identified. It encompasses the digital modification of products, as well as the industries and value-creating activities that surround them.

The goal of Industry 4.0 is to create a 'smart factory,' a production facility that uses data from all types of sensors and all available sources to enhance processes. Computer Vision is a complicated method to smart manufacturing that enables computers and machines to "see" the real environment by extracting, processing, and analysing data from visual inputs. The computer vision market is on the edge of exploding; advantages of computer vision include time efficiency (it works around the clock), high precision, repeatability, and cost savings (cheaper than labour cost). Computer vision can be used in a variety of industries. Measurement inspections of machine parts, anomaly detection for any physical parts/components, defect identification, package inspection, product composition verification, and many more are just a few examples.

For the foreseeable future, image processing will play a critical role in both manufacturing and commercial activities. Image processing system applications are expected to result in self-organized production based on extensive data gathering, better and more efficient business models, and automated, visually identified information, as well as more efficient production through extensive networking of computer vision in operational processes. AI is the key to unlock understanding of industrial data captured from smart machines, IoT equipment, as well as customers and workforces. Machine learning and advanced analytics can automatically discover and contextualise trends in machine data to predict significant equipment breakdowns. Computer systems use precise data to interpret the physical world and communicate with one another in industrial sectors.

Industrial Revolution

Since the dawn of time, humans and machines have always had a hand-to-hand relationship. The Industrial Revolution caused a huge U-turn in world history, bringing enormous expansion in economic growth, social development, and population. As the Industrial Revolution developed, it is thought that the West's quality of life rose.

Britain was at the heart of the Industrial Revolution, architectural and technical innovations were developed there. By mid-eighteenth century, Britain had established a worldwide commerce empire with colonies in the Caribbean and North America, as well as considerable political and military power on India through East India Company's activities. The expansion of commerce as well as the emergence of business was two main factors for the Industrial Revolution.

Electricity and electrification entered a new era where development of hydro power generation in the Alps, which began in the 1890s, aided the rapid industrialization of coal-depleted northern Italy. By 1890s, these areas had become industrialised, and businesses like Bayer AG, Standard Oil, General Electric, and U.S. Steel had joined ship companies and railroad on the world's stock markets, creating the first large industrial conglomerates with increasing worldwide interests.

In 1970, Industry 3.0 began with partial automation, which was accomplished with the help of simple but large computers and Programmable Logic Controllers (PLC) (or memory-programmable controls). Many manufacturing processes have been automated through the introduction of Information Technology (IT) and electronics. Industry 4.0 first emerged in the 1990s as a result of technological improvements in the telecommunications and internet industries. The greatest changes in this era, however, began in 2011. The fourth industrial revolution has resulted in efficient system networking (or interconnection), often called as "cyber-physical production systems."

CHALLENGES AND TRENDS

When the Fourth Industrial Revolution takes shape, businesses will have a superabundance of opportunities, including better customer service, better data access, and enormous advances in enterprise. A major challenge for many companies wishing to embrace Industry 4.0 is a purchasing strategy that isn't always apparent. As a result, financial incentives for adoption are frequently ambiguous, and organisations are forced to spend more than necessary to implement new policy innovations.

Introducing together manufacturing technology and Smart Factories will bring record levels of speed and efficiency to a business, but the downside of this is that several more companies might see a workforce which will be unused to the new developments, and inadequately to adapt to them. Companies attempting to innovate are unsure of which standards will be adopted in next five years. The development of a common system that works for all parties, allows for both horizontal and vertical integration, and maximises the value of current and future investments will be a big task to overcome.

Industry 4.0 has an impact on research and innovation in industrial systems. One of the most important advantages of smart factories is their potential to be environmentally friendly. Industrial Internet of things and Cyber-Physical Systems, which monitor, evaluate, and control diverse industrial activities, are at the core of the fourth Industrial Revolution (Rai et al, 2021). Speed monitoring of conveyor, Fault Diagnosis, and Predictive Maintenance are major difficulties that must be overcome in order to ensure industrial safety and optimal functioning (Kang & Myeongsu, 2018).

FAULT DIAGNOSIS OF MACHINERY THROUGH ML ALGORITHMS

In terms of improving the business climate, IoT has become a fundamental foundation of Industry 4.0 in CPS in recent years. As a result, the use of CPS and IoT in applicable equipment and electrical systems has increased. However, the most difficult aspect of using IoT against cyber-attacks is cyber security. A dependable and safe online monitoring for the state of induction motors is to be provided.

An IoT platform is used to visualise the data processed through a graphical dashboard using machine learning algorithms. When a cyber-attack signal is identified, an IoT platform based on ML is instantly visualised as bogus data on the IoT platform's dashboard. The IoT architecture is based on ML can successfully display all motor status issues and network cyber-attacks (Tran et al, 2021).

Furthermore, fake data and all motor status defects caused by cyber-attacks are detected and visualised on display of an IoT platform with more clarified visualisation and high accuracy, assisting in improving motor status decision-making. Advanced ML techniques are employed to accurately detect motor

Figure 1. IoT framework for motor fault detection

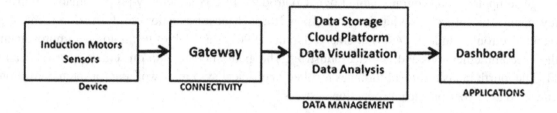

condition and cyber-attacks. IoT framework detecting motor problems and cyber-attacks and showing them on the IoT platform's primary dashboard is as shown in figure.1 provides low latency.

Because of their regular maintenance, inexpensive, and large working area, industrial equipment such as asynchronous motors play an important part in the industry. But, if a production process unexpectedly shuts down due to motor difficulties, it could cause significant damage over time. As a result, detecting and diagnosing induction motor failure has never been more important.

There are two types of motor failures: electrical and mechanical (Xiao et al, 2018). Mechanical weaknesses include misalignment faults, bearing faults, and air-gap eccentricity faults. Electrical failures include broken bar faults, stator short-circuits, and end ring faults, among others. Induction machines include a lot of moving parts, and bearings are one of them (Singh et al, 2020). Diagnosis of bearing defects and Early detection may help to avoid catastrophic failure. Vibration and current analysis (Ince et al, 2016) are two types of diagnosing methods.

On the basis of the observed vibration signal from the motor and a vibration damage threshold, its status can be monitored. A curve component analysis technique is used to examine vibration characteristics and establish nonlinear data. To detect early stages of a bearing fault, a bandwidth filter can be applied to the vibration signal to recover particular frequency bands for envelope spectrum analysis. The detected vibration energy was determined by statistical computations.

ML Techniques for Fault Diagnosis

Smart machines with various sensors, connectivity, data management, and application layer are all part of the industrial IoT concept. Sensor data analytics and large data management are both difficult IoT activities, especially for online IoT system state monitoring. IoT systems provide immediate feedback with appropriate adjustments and enable users to monitor status of machine at real time.

Intelligent signal analysis is the most commonly used in these procedures, and data gathering is essential for feature extraction and signal processing. Support Vector Machines (SVM), k-Nearest Neighbours (kNN),and Artificial Neural Networks (ANN) are the common classifiers used to fuse the vibration and current signal for multi-faults of asynchronous motors(Shao et al, 2017).The IoT architecture with the Random Forest (RF) technique detects motor failures induced by vibration in industrial settings with 99.03 percent accuracy, which is much better than conventional ML techniques.

The ML ensemble classifier using eXtreme Gradient Boosting (XGBoost) and RF method is a promising model for bearing defect diagnostic accuracy. However, because machine learning systems are judged on their ability to select acceptable fault features, understanding which features are also most sensitive to induction machine breakdown remains a challenge. In comparison to traditional feature extraction and selection methods, DL can effectively learn and extract the representative patterns from signals.

The main problems of rotary equipment are to improve the lifetime of induction device and efficiency of operation by effectively monitoring bearing failures (Wang et al, 2017). The emergence of IoT and ML approaches to smart industrial machines motivated this research. The system uses data collecting to diagnose induction motor issues using IoT and CPS ideas. An intelligence IoT system with an updated ML algorithm is being developed to identify induction motor bearing failure. Because of the model's great learning ability, it can effectively identify fake data that is deemed a cyber-attack.

Bearing diagnostics for induction machines are based on the outcomes of applying ML techniques to a variety of technical applications. These techniques maintain excellent classification accuracy and also save memory. When compared to linear models, it has several advantages. For multiclass classifications; there are various distinct machine learning algorithms.

The Random Forest algorithm is a tree-type classifier-based ensemble technique, well-known for its effectiveness in fault diagnosis. By employing bagging to suppress overfitting, this strategy can improve the model's performance. The votes of component predictors from each target are used to inform RF's decisions. RF algorithm combines a variety of decision trees. On the other hand, every decision tree in the forest is generated by a randomised small number of features then trained with a specific subset of training data set. The RF model's prediction is based on the average vote of every decision tree. As a result, the RF technique aids in the reduction of decision tree overfitting.

Random attribute vector is formed when random samples are collected from training instances of vibration signals. It is made up of a small number of attributes that are produced at random from the dataset that makes up the collection. The elements of the collection are used to build the decision tree. Every decision tree must have a unique outcome. Finally, the best classification result is determined by a majority vote procedure, with the highest-scoring prediction target chosen as the output. RF classifier model of figure.2 is coupled with IoT architecture after training and testing to identify online inputs of motor status and provide the information through an IoT display.

IoT architecture is built on effective ML algorithms for recognising various types of motor failure. In addition, cyber-attacks are taken into account, and IoT topology can identify and inhibit the attack. The data are readily visualised on an IoT platform, which helps with the decision-making process regarding motor statuses.

This enables the system to operate in a healthy state for an infinite length of time, so increasing the industry, which is a key objective of Industry 4.0.Furthermore, this IoT architecture offers a potential solution that may be applied to a variety of equipment in the future.

Process Flow for Fault Diagnosis

The process flow for detecting motor fault detection and depicting network status through IoT is mentioned in Figure.3.

Figure 2. RF Classifier model for fault diagnosis

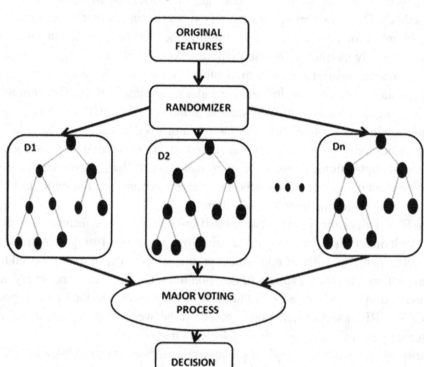

Figure 3. Process flow for diagnosing faults

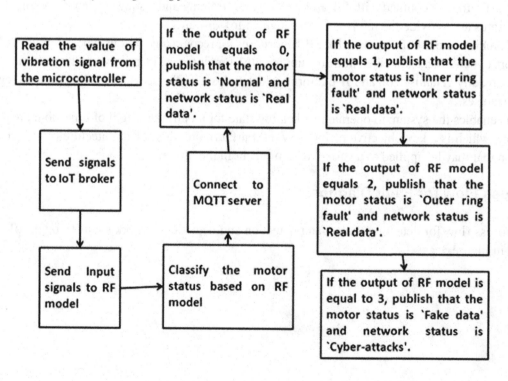

PREDICTIVE MAINTENANCE THROUGH VISION SYSTEM

Industrial IoT is a notion that has been examined in a variety of industries and is predicted to drive industry growth. Industry 4.0 and IoT have paved the path for more advanced predictive maintenance applications where the sensor's status is continuously monitored and recorded.

Operators, product managers, and data analysts have higher expectations for potentially helpful discoveries as the amount of data collected by combined with advances sensor-monitored industrial machinery grows. PdM is such major strategy that has resulted in the emergence of industry's ongoing digital revolution (Zenisek et al, 2019). Without the application of machine learning, computer vision can analyse and obtain information via audio and video, but ML adds the prediction performance of previously data input.

While corrective maintenance entails fixing something as soon as it breaks and preventive maintenance entails following empirically specified maintenance plans, PdM is based on the actual state of a system (Renwick et al, 1985). The utmost purpose of PdM is to calculate the exact Remaining Useful Lifetime (RUL) of a manufacturing machine. However, sets of data that allow for such aggressive longevity predictions are hard to come by. Because there are so many causes of poor automated machine behavior, many expensive run-to-failure tests on an entire fleet of machines would've been necessary, with no guarantee of a fruitful result. On a microscopic level, the importance of maintenance is highlighted. If there are any changes in system behaviour, such as concept drifts, that could indicate the start of problem. ML methods model robust systems in depth on a system level to find variations from the modeled state when examining continuous data streams (Kolokas et al, 2020).

ML Techniques for Predictive Analysis

The phrase predictive analytics is widely used in this context, and it refers to the application of statistical methodologies, like ML algorithms, to jobs like predictive maintenance. Linear Regression (LR), RF Regression, Boosted Trees, Bayesian Networks, Markov-Models, SVM, and ANN are some of the frequently used algorithms.

Modeling the state of a functioning machine that is assumed running "normally" and issuing a warning if indeed the notion begins to drift toward "unknown" or maybe "defective" using ML techniques. As a result, put together a small set of well-known ML algorithms based on Genetic Programming, such as LR, RF Regression, and Symbolic Regression (SR), to start creating two types of models: state detection models for verifying parameters of system and time series modeling techniques for predicting series of time in an n-step-ahead fashion (Samanta & Nataraj, 2008). Concept drift detection (Baena-Garcia et al, 2006) and concept drift prediction are two strategies that follow a brief introduction to data pre-processing and applied ML algorithms. The open source framework is used to implement the complete strategy.

The generalised least square technique is used to estimate the collection of multivariate LR coefficients. The RF Regression approach uses an ensemble with uncorrelated regression trees which are randomly generated using bagging as well as boosting to fit input data. Averaging tree estimations is used to estimate the target. This method was originally created for categorization purposes. Models take shape of a syntax tree consists of arbitrary mathematical symbols which is easily transformed into mathematical functions are referred to as SR. In the field of evolutionary algorithms, the stochastic genetic programming technique is used to create syntax trees. With so-called Offspring Selection, Genetic programming variant is used.

Figure 4. Process for predictive maintenance of a machine

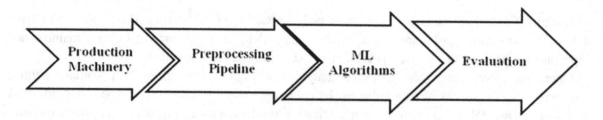

Figure.4 explains the entire working process of production machinery including pre-processing pipeline, ML algorithms used and its evaluation.

Splitting data for model training and testing is to be only configured because LR is deterministic and parameter-less. Grid search tunes the parameters of the stochastic algorithms: RF and SR. The use of regression model creating ML techniques aids the concept drift approach to detect by laying the framework. This is accomplished by employing a minimal number of well-known algorithms.

CONVEYOR SPEED MONITORING THROUGH IMAGE PROCESSING

Belt conveyor systems are frequently used to transfer dry bulk commodities across varied distances in a continuous manner (Liu et al, 2020). The belt conveyor speed control is at the heart of machine functioning. Measuring speed plays an important part in belt conveyor speed management during operation. There are various contact sensors and encoders that can reliably capture speed, but each has its own set of drawbacks.

To overcome the issues in the contact measurement speed system, the system integrates Region Of Interest (ROI) selection, picture boundary recognition, shape and texture definition, and the Polynomial LR ML technique (Gao et al, 2019)

In the discipline of measurement, machine vision has emerged as a prominent development trend. In the real-world measuring environment, the side of a belt is mounted on Couple-Charged Device (CCD) camera. The CCD camera's height is nicely matched with a belt, and it is actively taking photographs. The picture section of a belt side is chosen using ROI selection. To produce measurement findings, some software methods are utilised to process photos. From the other hand, image feature extraction (Caggiano et al, 2019) is in responsibility of identifying edge features. To achieve measuring speed, the entropy of the Grey-level Co-occurrence Matrix (GLCM) is determined. The ML algorithm is in charge of enhancing anti-interference performance.

The conveyor speed is captured and processed as in figure.5.

ML Based Approach for Speed Monitoring

ROI selection can help to save processing time by removing duplicate information. Image edge detection obtains picture edge information to aids to describe image textures. The speed of the conveyor can be calculated using entropy data based on the picture texture description. By developing a good fitting system based on an entropy data set, the Polynomial LR method can increase anti-interference performance.

Figure 5. Conveyor speed monitoring

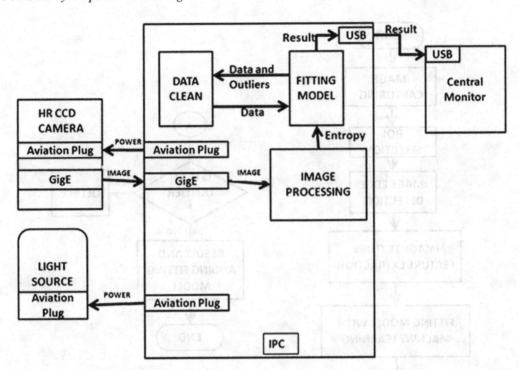

The belt as well as the backdrop makes up the majority of the original image. The side area and also the surface area are included in the belt component. Only the side piece of the belt should be included in the ROI. After that, ROI can be utilised to replace existing image to proceed to the next stage of image processing. Threshold segmentation is the most important aspect of ROI selection. The boundary of the side area is detected using the threshold segmentation approach (Zohra et al, 2021).

The conveyor's running speed can be changed at any moment during operation. The default arrangement uses a CCD camera to collect images (Zhang et al, 2021). When the conveyor operates at varying speeds, the conveyor sides' view may appear clear or fuzzy. The algorithm for speed monitoring is given in figure.6.

In the photograph of either a relatively slow speed, there are even more edges than in the picture of a fairly quick speed. Image edge detection strategies namely Bilateral high-pass filter and Canny edge detection technique extract picture's edge. The former preserves the edge by reducing low-frequency elements without sacrificing high-frequency data.

After detection of edges in the image, the difference in edge features between the photos taken from different speeds is instantly evident. An approach for describing the difference is to quantify the texture richness of the difference. It's important to remember while describing texture that the texture-analysis method takes into account the intensity distribution as well as the relative placements of pixels in a picture.

Image is translated to GLCM (Benčo & Hudec, 2007) to describe its structure and texture by looking at greyscale spatial correlation features. Thus, the measurement of texture regularity determines speed. The regularity of the images is represented by the randomization of GLCM elements.

Figure 6. Flowchart for speed monitoring

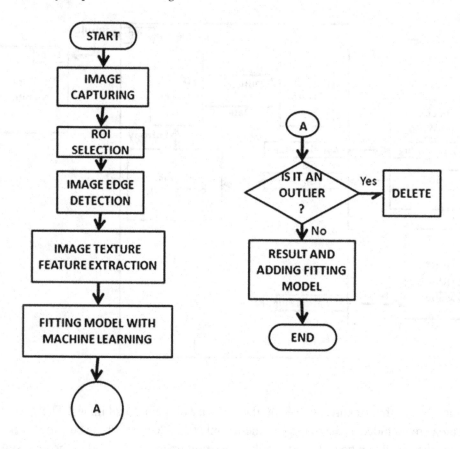

CONCLUSION

The introduction of Industry 4.0 was one of the most recent innovations in the industrial environment. There are countless opportunities for businesses in it, as well as numerous problems. IoT architecture's superiority in detecting motor defects and cyber-attacks with high precision were discussed. A method for detecting concept drift in streams of data as a possible indicator of poor system behaviour, presented a methodology for identifying error suggestion patterns in condition monitoring streams of data generated by complex systems of industry. In this chapter, Diagnosing of motor faults through assembling of RF and XGBoost algorithms are explained. PdM is performed by three algorithms:RF,SR and LR are dealt in detail. Speed monitoring of conveyors through ML techniques and GLCM convey the story of entire operation in an Industry.

REFERENCES

Baena-García, M., del Campo-Ávila, J., Fidalgo, R., Bifet, A., Gavalda, R., & Morales-Bueno, R. (2006, September). Early drift detection method. In *Fourth international workshop on knowledge discovery from data streams* (Vol. 6, pp. 77-86). Academic Press.

Benčo, M., & Hudec, R. (2007). Novel method for color textures features extraction based on GLCM. *Wuxiandian Gongcheng, 16*(4), 65.

Caggiano, A., Zhang, J., Alfieri, V., Caiazzo, F., Gao, R., & Teti, R. (2019). Machine learning-based image processing for on-line defect recognition in additive manufacturing. *CIRP Annals, 68*(1), 451–454. doi:10.1016/j.cirp.2019.03.021

Gao, Y., Qiao, T., Zhang, H., Yang, Y., Pang, Y., & Wei, H. (2019). A contactless measuring speed system of belt conveyor based on machine vision and machine learning. *Measurement, 139*, 127–133. doi:10.1016/j.measurement.2019.03.030

Ince, T., Kiranyaz, S., Eren, L., Askar, M., & Gabbouj, M. (2016). Real-time motor fault detection by 1-D convolutional neural networks. *IEEE Transactions on Industrial Electronics, 63*(11), 7067–7075. doi:10.1109/TIE.2016.2582729

Kang, M. (2018). Machine learning: Diagnostics and prognostics. *Prognostics and Health Management of Electronics: Fundamentals, Machine Learning, and the Internet of Things*, 163-191.

Kolokas, N., Vafeiadis, T., Ioannidis, D., & Tzovaras, D. (2020). A generic fault prognostics algorithm for manufacturing industries using unsupervised machine learning classifiers. *Simulation Modelling Practice and Theory, 103*, 102–109. doi:10.1016/j.simpat.2020.102109

Liu, X., Pei, D., Lodewijks, G., Zhao, Z., & Mei, J. (2020). Acoustic signal based fault detection on belt conveyor idlers using machine learning. *Advanced Powder Technology, 31*(7), 2689–2698. doi:10.1016/j.apt.2020.04.034

Rai, R., Tiwari, M. K., Ivanov, D., & Dolgui, A. (2021). Machine learning in manufacturing and industry 4.0 applications. *International Journal of Production Research, 59*(16), 4773–4778. doi:10.1080/0020 7543.2021.1956675

Renwick, J. T., & Babson, P. E. (1985). Vibration analysis---a proven technique as a predictive maintenance tool. *IEEE Transactions on Industry Applications, IA-21*(2), 324–332. doi:10.1109/TIA.1985.349652

Samanta, B., & Nataraj, C. (2008). Prognostics of machine condition using soft computing. *Robotics and Computer-integrated Manufacturing, 24*(6), 816–823. doi:10.1016/j.rcim.2008.03.011

Shao, S. Y., Sun, W. J., Yan, R. Q., Wang, P., & Gao, R. X. (2017). A deep learning approach for fault diagnosis of induction motors in manufacturing. *Chinese Journal of Mechanical Engineering, 30*(6), 1347–1356. doi:10.100710033-017-0189-y

Singh, J., Azamfar, M., Li, F., & Lee, J. (2020). A systematic review of machine learning algorithms for prognostics and health management of rolling element bearings: Fundamentals, concepts and applications. *Measurement Science & Technology, 32*(1), 012001. doi:10.1088/1361-6501/ab8df9

Tran, M. Q., Elsisi, M., Mahmoud, K., Liu, M. K., Lehtonen, M., & Darwish, M. M. (2021). Experimental setup for online fault diagnosis of induction machines via promising IoT and machine learning: Towards industry 4.0 empowerment. *IEEE Access: Practical Innovations, Open Solutions, 9*, 115429–115441. doi:10.1109/ACCESS.2021.3105297

Villalba-Diez, J., Schmidt, D., Gevers, R., Ordieres-Meré, J., Buchwitz, M., & Wellbrock, W. (2019). Deep learning for industrial computer vision quality control in the printing industry 4.0. *Sensors (Basel)*, *19*(18), 3987. doi:10.339019183987 PMID:31540187

Wang, X., Guo, J., Lu, S., Shen, C., & He, Q. (2017). A computer-vision-based rotating speed estimation method for motor bearing fault diagnosis. *Measurement Science & Technology*, *28*(6), 065012. doi:10.1088/1361-6501/aa650a PMID:28890607

Xiao, D., Huang, Y., Zhang, X., Shi, H., Liu, C., & Li, Y. (2018, October). Fault diagnosis of asynchronous motors based on LSTM neural network. In 2018 prognostics and system health management conference (PHM-Chongqing) (pp. 540-545). IEEE. doi:10.1109/PHM-Chongqing.2018.00098

Zenisek, J., Holzinger, F., & Affenzeller, M. (2019). Machine learning based concept drift detection for predictive maintenance. *Computers & Industrial Engineering*, *137*, 106031–106043. doi:10.1016/j.cie.2019.106031

Zhang, M., Chauhan, V., & Zhou, M. (2021, January). A machine vision based smart conveyor system. In *Thirteenth International Conference on Machine Vision* (Vol. 11605, pp. 84-92). SPIE. 10.1117/12.2586978

Zohra, F. T., Salim, O., Dey, S., Masoumi, H., & Karmakar, N. (2021, November). A Novel Machine Learning Based Conveyor Belt Health Monitoring Incorporating UHF RFID Backscattered Power. In *2021 IEEE 5th International Conference on Information Technology, Information Systems and Electrical Engineering (ICITISEE)* (pp. 230-234). IEEE. 10.1109/ICITISEE53823.2021.9655974

Chapter 13
Real–Time Torpidity Detection for Drivers in Machine Learning Environments

Sreedevi B.

ⓘ https://orcid.org/0000-0003-1225-4238

SASTRA University (Deemed), India

Durga Karthik

SASTRA University (Deemed), India

ABSTRACT

The World Health Organization (WHO) has conducted a survey on road accidents around the world. According to the survey, 13.5 lakh die each year due to road casualties and more concerning is that India accounts around 1.5 lakh road deaths every year. Major factors to blame on road accidents are driver carelessness, drowsiness, traffic discipline, vehicle faults, or even animal crossing. Different sensors, stability control systems, anti-breaking systems, navigation are added in the vehicles to make driving easier. Still, road accidents happen due to human mistakes. Drinking and driving and tiredness may cause a driver to go for torpidity. A machine learning system is developed to monitor the eye movements to detect if the driver is sleepy or not. If found, an alarm is issued to warn the driver to wake up or else to stop the vehicle and have a nap. In addition, if neither response is made, water sprinkling is automated on the driver's face.

INTRODUCTION

In the present scenario, advancement in technology has proved to be a great advantage as it has provided solutions for many complex issues in everyday life. This in turn has made work less exhaustive for employees, and it further enhances safety at work. Some of the popular applications uses vision based solution. Traffic monitoring, suspect detection, car parking camera are few such examples. These are complex systems. The vision based method is even used to detect vehicle operator (i.e. Driver), fatigue

DOI: 10.4018/978-1-7998-8892-5.ch013

(torpidity) or not. Torpidity causes human to lose concentration, as the person becomes tired, which leads to slow response time. Early signs of fatigue could pose a great threat, especially for the drivers.

Long-term concentration is essential in transport industry (pilots, steersmen, car driver, truck driver, etc.). These professionals should stay alert and act immediately to sudden events (Prakash Choudhary, 2016). Long hours of driving cause torpidity and leads to failed response. i). 30% of road accidents occur due to fatigue in drivers. ii). Studies reveal that a nap or poor concentration leads to road accidents. So, a technology is required to find driver's psychophysical status to reduce road accidents. The challenge lies in finding a technology, which should respond immediately.

Different sensors, stability control system, anti-breaking systems, navigation are added in the vehicles to make drivers effort easier. Still, road accidents happen due to human mistakes. Drunk and drive, tiredness may cause a driver to go for torpidity. Machine learning with vision based approach finds to be a good solution. A machine learning system is developed to monitor the eye movements to detect the driver is sleepy or not (Prakash Choudhary,2016; Cech, 2016; Yan, 2013; Marco Javier Flores,2009; Mohamed Hoseyn srigari, 2013; Fuletra, 2013; Tong, 2012). If found, an alarm is issued to warn the driver to wake up else to stop the vehicle and have a nap. In addition, if neither response is made, water sprinkling is automated on drivers face.

Background

At present, drowsiness or torpidity or fatigue for drivers is the main reason for road accidents which leads to rigorous wound or death added with considerable economic loss. Statistics reveals that a need for reliable detection system for driver's torpidity and alert mechanism before catastrophe. So, a machine learning technique is designed to detect and alert driver's torpidity (Yan, 2013; Marco Javier Flores, 2009; Mohamed Hoseyn srigari, 2013; Fuletra, 2013; Tong, 2012). Through this detection system, it is possible to avoid a number of road accidents by sending an alert to the driver with fatigue signs.

Driver drowsiness was detected using webcam (Chenyang Xu et al, 2013), eye pre-closure value calculation (Vaishnav Kshirsagar et al, 2019), IR LED sensors with microcontrollers (Manochitra, 2017), eye retina detection and pulse pattern detection (Chandrasena, 2018), Aurdino nano and eye blink sensors (Debasis Parida, 2021) . Alarming done using beagle board, hybrid approach, RF transmitter module (Chenyang Xu et al, 2013; Vaishnav Kshirsagar et al, 2019; Manochitra, 2017; Chandrasena, 2018; Debasis Parida, 2021) .The major objective of the literature survey focused to prevent accidents.

Existing System

The major reason for road accidents is due to driver's fatigue during driving. Hence, it has become vital to design an effective method to detect somnolence and alert driver.

Disadvantages

- Placing the system in a vehicle is inconvenient and one system for one vehicle is expensive.
- Only the drowsiness is detected and no method to alert.

Proposed System

Here in our system, driver's face is concentrated using a webcam connected to Raspberry Pi. The eye is taken as interest region as we make use of eye to calculate Eye Aspect Ratio (EAR) (Cech, 2016). Through EAR, the drowsiness of the driver is detected and buzzer is automatically induced (Rosebrock, 2017; Sullivan, 2014). In addition, sprinkling of water on driver's face is done if there is no response after alarming for a specific time period.

Advantages

- Raspberry Pi is easy to place in the vehicle and consumes less power comparatively.
- It is cost efficient, smaller in size and it is portable.

Objective

- To identify the torpidity of the driver.
- . To determine the allowable limit for blink of eyes.
- To develop a machine learning model using Raspberry Pi with USB camera to detect the movement of eyes and eye lids.

Hardware Requirements

- Raspberry pi
- Webcam
- IC 1293d
- 5v water pump
- 9v Battery
- Buzzer

Software Requirements

Operating system : Windows 8 +
Coding Language : PYTHON

FUNCTIONAL REQUIREMENTS

Purpose : Alerts when the driver is in torpidity state
Input : Real-time feeds of human face
Processing : Detecting facial landmarks using Dlib.
Output : Identifying driver's torpidity state.

Figure 1. Architecture Diagram

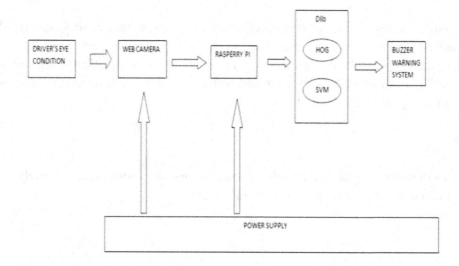

The functional requirements are shown in the figure1.0 as an architecture diagram.

Hardware Components

The hardware requirements are shown in the figure 2. The pin configuration is shown in the figure 3. The connections are shown in figure 4.

Figure 2. Webcam (left); Raspberri pi (center); 5v water pump motor (right)

Pin Configuration

Figure 3. Pin configuration (left); configuration (right)

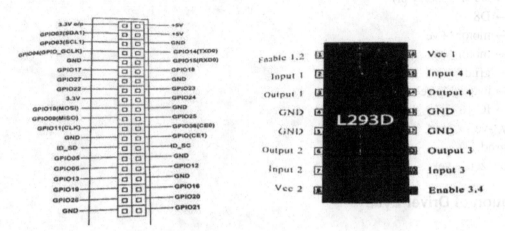

Connections

Figure 4. Connections

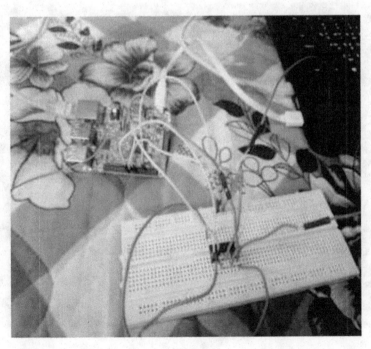

Pin Connections

IC 01 → D11 (raspberry pi)
IC 02 → D9 (raspberry pi)
IC 07 → D8
IC 03 → motor '+ve'
IC 06 → motor '-ve'
IC 04 → grnd
IC 08 → battery '+ve'
IC 08 → IC 16
Battery '-ve'→ grnd
T5 → grnd
T6 → buzzer '+ve'

Detection of Driver Eyes

The driver's face is identified in figure 5 and the movements of the eyes are constantly monitored in order to check the eyes of the driver as closed or not closed.

Figure 5. Driver's Eye Detection

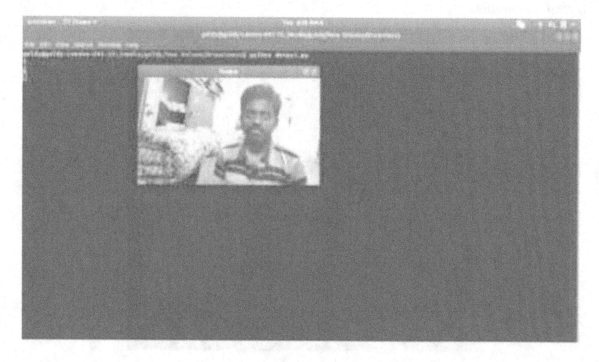

Identifying Eye Closure

When the driver's eyes are identified to be closed, as seen in figure 6, the counter starts incrementing. The counter is to zero when the drivers eye is found to be open within the period of time.

Figure 6. Detection of Eye Closure

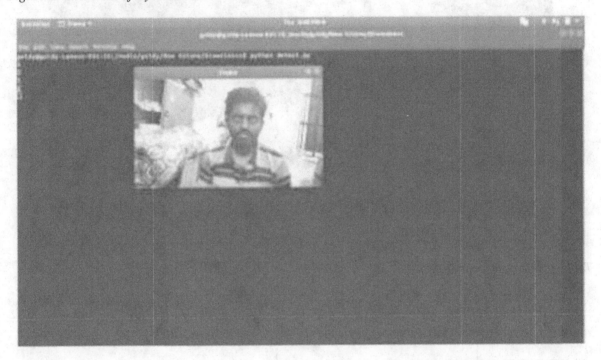

Induction of Alert

When the eyes of the driver are closed for more than 4 seconds, then a buzzer will automatically send an alarm as found in the figure 7. If the driver doesn't respond, water will be sprinkled after 7 seconds. The table 1 shows the different test phases and the responses, which proves that the system works properly.

Eye Monitoring

This process is done by making use of web camera. The webcam is kept in such a way that it continuously monitors the eye movements of the driver.

Pre-Processing

The processing is done on driver's eye to calculate the Eye Aspect Ratio. This ratio is similar to that of distance formula. If this ratio is smaller, then the driver is said to be in torpidity.

Figure 7. Driver Alert

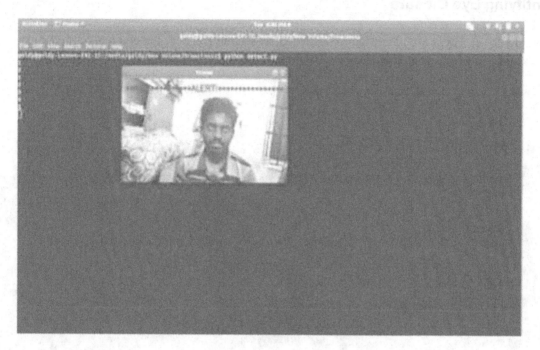

Table 1. Test cases and Results

S.NO	TEST ID	UTST02
1	Unit tested	Alert System
2	Purpose	To alert the driver
3	Pre-requirement	Real-time feeds of driver's eye movement, Buzzer and water sprinkling motor
4	Test data	Buzzer and water sprinkler
5	Test status	Pass
6	Test Result	Alerted

Buzzer Alert

If the torpidity of the driver remains in same state for 4 seconds continuously the buzzer alert is induced. It is stopped only when the driver opens the eyes.

Water Sprinkling

If the eyes of the driver are closed continuously for more than 7 seconds, water sprinkler is activated.

EXPECTED OUTPUT AND OUTCOME

The camera in smart phones is connected to a lap- top using python (Rosebrock, 2016) with Dlib. The eye movements are measured using facial landmark points (Tong, 2012). This model is tested with various faces. The model can be utilized in all vehicles especially for four wheelers. The model will help them to offer better safety apart from security privileges availed during manufacturing. The model not only ensures safety also help to create awareness for drivers by giving alert.

1. To identify whether the driver is in torpidity or not.
2. To determine the facial landmark parameters values using EAR (Eye Aspect Ratio).
3. To develop a model to ensure safety by identifying and calculating eye blinks.
4. To create awareness among people who knows driving but occasionally does it.

CONCLUSION

The study presents an analysis and pattern to detect the drowsiness of drivers. The proposed system is found to be effective in the avoidance of road accidents due to fatigue driving or drowsy driving. This study could further be extended to make a complete study on road safety. This could possibly be a tremendous advantage to the automobile industry, thereby avoiding the risk of accidents due to drowsy driving.

REFERENCES

Cech. (2016). *Real-Time Eye Blink Detection using Facial Landmarks*. Academic Press.

Chandrasena, H. M., & Wickramasinghe, D. M. J. (2018). Driver's Drowsiness Detecting and Alarming System. *International Journal of Information Technology and Computer Science*, 4(3), 127–139.

Flores. (2009). *Real-Time Warning System for Driver Drowsiness Using Visual Information*. Springer Science + Business Media.

Fuletra. (2013). A survey On Driver's Drowsiness Detection Techniques Presented. *IJRITCC*. doi:10.1109/ICCVW.2013.126

Kshirsagar, Bhole, Khobare, & Pujeri. (2019). Driver Drowsiness Detection And Alarming System. *Mythos Technology*, 3(1), 4980–4983.

Manochitra, V. (2017). Sleep Sensing And Alerting System For Drivers. SSRN *Electronic Journal*, 4(6), 1-5.

Parida. (2021). Arduino based Driver Drowsiness Detection & Alerting System. *Circuit Digest*.

Prakash Choudhary, R. S. S. D. (2016). *A Survey Paper on Drowsiness Detection & Alarm System for Drivers. International Research Journal of Engineering and Technology*.

RosebrockA. (2017). Error! Hyperlink reference not valid.Available: https://www.pyimagesearch.com/2017/05/08/drowsiness-detection-opencv/

Rosebrock, (2016). *Deep Learning For Computer Vision with Python*. Academic Press.

Sigari. (2013). A driver Face Monitoring System for Fatigue and Distraction Detection. *International Journal of Vehicular Technology*.

Sullivan. (2014). *Ensemble of Regression Trees*. Academic Press.

Tong. (2012). Semi-Supervised facial land mark annotation-Computational. *Vision Image Understanding*.

Xu, Chen, & Nie. (2013). *Driver Sleep Detection and Alarming System*. Project Report. University of Illinois at Urbana-Champaign.

Yan, Z. L. D. Y. J. (2013). Learn To combine Multiple Hypotheses for accurate face alignment. *Proceedings of IEEE International Conference on Computer Vision (ICCV-W)*.

Chapter 14
Potential Market–Predictive Features Based Bitcoin Price Prediction Using Machine Learning Algorithms

Umamaheswari P.

(iD) https://orcid.org/0000-0003-2007-697X

SASTRA University (Deemed), India

Abiramasundari S.

SASTRA University (Deemed), India

Kamaladevi M.

SASTRA University (Deemed), India

Dinesh P.

Anjalai Ammal Mahalingam Engineering College, India

ABSTRACT

Bitcoin is a type of digital currency or computerized money that is utilised for speculation around the world. Bitcoins are files that are saved in a digital wallet programme on a mobile phone or a PC. Every transaction and its timestamp data are recorded in a common list known as blockchain. In this research, the cost of bitcoin is estimated utilising data mining techniques and machine learning algorithms. The dataset is preprocessed with the use of data mining algorithms, which reduces data noise. Bitcoin's price fluctuates, and it is estimated using long short-term memory (LSTM), a type of neural networking, to extract acceptable patterns for modelling and prediction. Discovering recurring patterns in the bitcoin market is a necessary endeavour in order to achieve optimal bitcoin price functionality. The dataset consists of numerous regularly reported bitcoin price features every year. Linear regression (LR) technique is used to estimate the future cost of bitcoin. Daily price shift with the best possible precision by using the available data is also estimated.

DOI: 10.4018/978-1-7998-8892-5.ch014

INTRODUCTION

Bitcoin is a type of virtual currency that is commonly used in transactions and investments. Bitcoin is a decentralized money, which means that no single person or group owns it. Bitcoins are easy to use because they are not tied to any particular jurisdiction. The best approach to invest in bitcoins is to use a bitcoin exchange. Individuals can buy and sell bitcoins with a number of different currencies. Unlike traditional market assets, cryptocurrency markets are extremely volatile, and while they share many of the characteristics of traditional stock markets, they are extremely unstable. These marketplaces are indeed decentralized, unregulated, and prone to manipulation. Many entrepreneurs are now investing in block-chain, the well-known technology that underpins the most famous cryptocurrencies (Antonopoulos, A. M., 2017) including bitcoin, and this number is expected to rise as bitcoin's utility grows. Understanding how bitcoin works is crucial to comprehending why it would be so popular. Cryptocurrency, unlike conventional investments, is not linked to tangible assets or the US dollar. Its fundamental objective is to encourage two people in any location to directly exchange value. This indicates that the network is not controlled from a central location. There is no central bank or government that can stop down the system or arbitrarily boost or drop the value (Mehmet Balcilar et al, 2017) emphasized the modelling non linearity and accounting for tail behavior when exploring causal relationships between Bitcoin returns and tradingvolume, and that volume cannot help predict bitcoin price fluctuations at any point in the conditional distribution.The extent to which central banks begin to digitize their own currency will be intriguing to watch. Bitcoin is becoming more widespread as financial systems grow more computerized, but the digital currency's comeback is also linked to the state of global banking. (Rathan, K et al, 2019) Bitcoin-related technical considerations include the size of the blocks, confirmation time, amount of transaction, hash rate, profitability of mining, complexity, frequencies of transaction, and market capitalization. They calculate consumer interest through tweets and Google patterns. Bitcoin-related economic determinants are macroeconomic measures and foreign currency ratios.

The Long Short-Term Memory that uses the predictors has passed all the Model Confidence (MCS) tests. According to the technical viewpoint, the transaction fee's average is a good indicator of the exchange rate of bitcoin because it still surpassed 0.75. The LSTM using the predictors had higher mean maximum and minimum values. According to the analysis of sensitivity, the variables having a score of lower than 0.6 were excluded using the crossover approach and possible predictor's ranges are generated. According to (Ferdiansyah, F et al, 2019) a new predictive paradigm for cryptocurrency prediction models can overcome and enhance the challenge of input variable identification in LSTM without tight data assumptions. The findings highlighted its potential application in cryptocurrency prediction, as well as other industries like as healthcare data and financial time-series data. The remaining part of the paper is laid out as follows: The second section discusses relevant studies and methods for predicting bitcoin prices. The proposed system model for bitcoin price forecasts are shown in Section 3. The implementation of the prediction model is presented in Section 4. The suggested model's performance is evaluated in Section 5. Finally, Section 6 concludes the paper.

RELATED WORK

Many researchers have given their opinions about the bit coin prediction in terms of algorithm and framework. In this section, those topics were given in detail. To begin, (Mahar, K et al, 2021) have proposed that because the cryptocurrency is still relatively new. Working with data at greater frequencies (for example, every five minutes) and reducing the portfolio's holding period would be an adopt to this idea. Cryptocurrency market contains about 2000 kinds of coins for which the volume of transactions and circulation are huge but uneven. There were few miners on the network at the earlier time of crypto mining. The mining issue was therefore low. The few miners could extract enormous bitcoin quantities. (McNally, S et al, 2018) Another research used the data of bitcoin and concluded that Nakamoto has mined approximately ten lakhs of Bitcoin. It is however clear that once Nakamoto spends these Bitcoins, all of the users on the network will identify his identity since blockchain transactions can be tracked and their transfer to an individual can be tracked in the real world. Invented in 2009, Bitcoin is the first decentralized cryptocurrency and is not controlled by a centralized issue. To forecast the price of Bitcoin by using the price on the previous day and the turnover quantities, (Almeida et al, 2015) reviewed an ANN model. The biggest issue with their methodology is the need for a significant volume of a dataset for forecasting. (Shahbazi, Z., & Byun, Y. C., 2021) investigated the features of the blockchain's network dependent on the potential cost of the Bitcoin by ANN. The findings reported that the accuracy is 55%. The determinants of the Bitcoin rate were explored by (Georgoula et al, 2015), in addition to sentimental analysis by Support Vector Machine. The outcome revealed that the network's number of visits in Wikipedia and the number of hash rates had a favorable association with the price of Bitcoin. (Matta et al, 2015) planned for forecasting the exchange volumes of bitcoins. He investigated if the common feeling that aggregates could be used to estimate developments in the Bitcoin market in a series of Twitter messages. (McNally's et al, 2016) is concerned with forecasting Bitcoin values using machine learning. This was done with the use of multiple Recurrent Neural Networks, Auto-Regressive Integrated Moving Average, and Long Short-Term Memory patterns. The error rates for the Long Short-Term Memory, Recurrent Neural Network, and Auto-Regressive Integrated Moving Average version were 6.87%, 5.45%, and 53.47 percentage.

(Luisanna Cocco et al, 2016) developed a framework based on Bayesian Neural Networks, which has the best performance and the lowest order of magnitude of the mean absolute error computed on the anticipated price. This paradigm is consistent with what has been described in recent literature. The results show that the suggested system accurately predicts prices with good accuracy, indicating that the method can be used to anticipate the values of multiple cryptocurrencies. (Cristiano Garcia et al) and colleagues Experimented with bitcoin prediction and found it to be useful, accurate, fast, and robust to missing values. The outcomes were compared with the results using fuzzy and neuro-fuzzy emerging modelling techniques. (Mahar, K et al,2020) proposed using the LSTM algorithm to derive the accurate Bitcoin price in 2020. The collected findings demonstrate that LSTM can tackle this problem quickly and productively. (Jang, H., & Lee, J., 2017).) carried out an empirical study in which they compared the Bayesian neural network to various linear and non-linear benchmark models for estimating the Bitcoin process and that results shows that BNN is effective at predicting Bitcoin price time series and explaining the recent price volatility. (Karunya Rathan et al.) shown that their recommended learning technique suggests the optimum algorithm to choose and use for crypto currency prediction. The results of the experimental study reveal that linear regression outperforms the other in terms of price prediction accuracy. Although the computational overhead of the LSTM model is higher than that of brute force in nonlinear pattern recognition, deep learning was eventually proven to be highly efficient in anticipating the inherent chaotic dynamics of cryptocurrency markets, according to (Salim Lahmiri et al). suggested the LightGBM model outperforms the other techniques in terms of robustness, and the overall strength of the cryptocurrencies has an impact on forecasting performance. This can help investors build an adequate cryptocurrency strategy while also reducing risk. Limitations of the existing system can be summarized as follows

- The major flaw in traditional technique is the requirement for a large dataset for predicting.
- Previous studies have found that the price of bitcoin is affected by a variety of parameters such as trend, demand, movements, and seasonality.
- The literature gives an imperfect picture of the role of trading volume in forecasting bitcoin returns, because the bitcoin volume–return connection at the tails may differ from that around the mean of the return distribution.
- Furthermore, previous research has neglected the link between bitcoin returns at the second instant and trade volume.

PROPOSED SYSTEM MODEL

In this section, we discuss the proposed system model for bit coin prediction and data set used for this work. Primarily we focus on the basic functional unit of blockchain model. Each block consists of following elements.

Basic Block Chain Model

Based on the type of blockchain, the data have been stored into the block. Various information about the sender, receiver and the number of coins are stored in the bitcoin blockchain structure. A hash is like a fingerprint (long record consisting of some digits and letters). SHA 256 algorithm is used in order to produce hash value for each and every block. This hash value is then used to identify the blocks in blockchain structure. Once the block has been created, the hash value is attached to it automatically. Whenever a block is changed the associated hash value will also be changed. Hence, hash value is also used to identify the block which is changed.

Figure 1. Logical diagram of a block chain

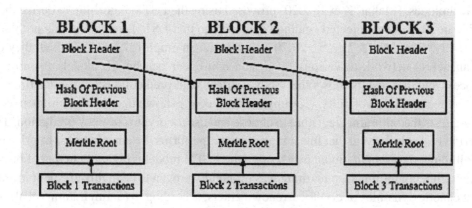

The chain of blocks has been created using the hash values of successive blocks. This chain is considered to be the main element in blockchain architecture's security. For example, the block 12 is pointed by block 11; block 22 is pointed by 21 etc. Each and every first block in the chain has been used to produce validated blocks too. <u>Merkle root</u> is one of the parts of a block in blockchain network. It is a hash of all hash values. Fig.1 depicts the structure of each block in the blockchain network.

Typically, data is often taken from various sources that are usually not too accurate, and more than half of our time is spent coping with data quality problems while operating on a machine learning problem. To assume that the data would be flawless is simply impractical. Owing to human error, shortcomings of measuring devices or defects in the method of data processing can be the reasons for flaws in data. With Adam optimizer and Mean Square Error(MSE), the model is developed and trained using LSTM. The price of bitcoin is expected as a consequence. From the dataset, aspects such as the date and closing price are extracted and Linear Regression is applied. As a result, the price of bitcoin is expected for the next 30 days. The technology used in this project and the reasoning for the use of these technologies are discussed here.

LSTM and Background Implementation

LSTM's Sequence Prediction functions as a supervised algorithm that is distinct from the edition of its autoencoder. As such, the entire data collection is broken down into inputs and outputs. LSTM is a good choice for handling input prediction problems simply as well as easily. LSTM yield better results compare to traditional predictive linear model. Hochreiter and Schmidhuber suggested the LSTM is the widely used recursive neural network (RNNs). The LSTM will achieve optimized predictions of the time series, then adapting Multivariate or multi-input in classical linear methods Problems prediction. The LSTM is in contrast to RNNs Characterized by incorporating information memory cells. LSTM has three main parts in its architecture as shown in fig.3. It gives the difference to it from other existing RNNs models. It has an input gate, the forget gate, and an output gate. Anaconda is a distribution of several programming languages that includes Python and R programming languages for scientific computation, such as data science, machine learning technologies, large-scale data mining, predictive analytics, etc., to simplify package management and implementation. Anaconda is suitable for use in Windows, Linux, and Mac Operating Systems. An open-source web-based framework, Jupiter notebook from that allows authoring and uploading of files that have live code with narrative text as well as calculations, visualizations. It facilitates cleaning and transform data and performing mathematical simulation, statistics, and machine learning models, etc.

Figure 2. Proposed system architecture

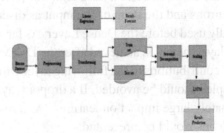

Tensor Flow makes it easy to acquire data, train models, serving predictions, and optimize future outcomes. Keras is an Application Programming Interface that helps users to create deep models and to take advantage of the full deployment capabilities of the Tensor Flow platform. It features numerous classification, regression and clustering algorithms. It is designed to work with NumPy and SciPy, the numeric and scientific Python libraries. Usually, such operations can be done more effectively with Python's built-in sequences.

Figure 3. LSTM Architecture

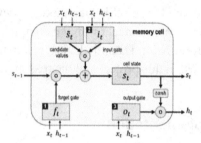

The LSTM layer adds some memory cells along with the number of time steps or epochs. The cell state is and is of interest horizontal line from St-1 to St long-term or short-term memory retaining. The LSTM output is state-modulated of these cells and when it arrives, that's key to foresee, rather than just the historical value of price entry. LSTM is remembered for networks Inputs by loop use. There is no such loop RNN model. When time goes on, on the other hand, the less probable the next iteration of the predicted value depends on the last value that got missed in forget gate. LSTM does this by learning how to recall the values via their forget-gates, we suggest that LSTM not be used as a black-box model. Normally, a time series is a set of numbers along time. The various modules of proposed system architecture is given in fig.2 In this research work, the data is separated into the train data and the test data to estimate the price of Bitcoin. After preprocessing, the values are scaled and reshaped to X train and Y train. Keras libraries and packages are imported for the implementation of RNN with LSTM. The initialization of RNN is performed first, then the input layer and the LSTM layer are added. The sigmoid activation function is used here and the units are allocated and the output layer was added. Then the recurrent neural network is compiled using Adam as the optimizer. The denote square error was used for evaluating the loss. Thus, the algorithm is utilized to estimate the price of Bitcoin. The result of this approach is explained in the next section.

LSTM Layer: The LSTM layer is the inner one, and all the gates described at the very beginning are already implemented by Keras, with the default hard-sigmoid [Keras2015] activation. The LSTM parameters are the number of neurons and the form of the input as discussed above.

Dropout Layer: This is usually used before the Dense Layer. As far as Keras is concerned, a dropout can be inserted after any hidden layer, here it is achieved after the LSTM. The Dropout layer is a barrier, which supersedes some neurons' contributions to the following layer while leaving all others unchanged. Overfitting on the training examples should be avoided. If a dropout layer is not there, the first group of training data has a disproportionately large impact on learning. As a result, learning of traits that occur only in following samples or batches would be prevented:

Thick Layer: this is the regularly connected layer.

Activation Layer: As we are solving the problem of regression, the last layer can provide a linear combination of the activations of the preceding layer with the weight vectors. This activation is also a linear one. Alternatively, it may be passed to the previous dense as a parameter.

IMPLEMENTATION RESULTS

Data Set and Preprocessing

The dataset is extracted from "Kaggle" which contains historical Bitcoin data from January 2012 to September 2020 with an interval of 1-minute. It consists of 1048576 rows and 8 columns. The preprocessing is achieved by applying the statistical mean procedure to minimize the noise of the data and to fill in the missing values. The timestamp value in the dataset is converted to the date month year format to guarantee readability. The dataset is separated into a train and a test collection after transformation. Underestimate the price of the bitcoin a seasonal decomposition is carried out. The Minmax scaler is used to scale the dataset, as LSTM is adaptive to scale. Preprocessing is the stage in which the data is converted, or encoded, in every machine learning process to get it to such a state that the machine can now quickly parse it. Preprocessing techniques have been used for converting the unprocessed data into standard format, which is then feed into the algorithms for getting effective results.

In fig.4 dataset with missing values is given .There will be columns value with "NAN. If we stick with the dataset as it is, then we begin to lose the outcome accuracy. The statistical mean method is used here to remove the missing value.

Figure 4. Dataset with Missing values

	Timestamp	Open	High	Low	Close	Volume_(BTC)	Volume_(Currency)	Weighted_Price
0	1325317920	4.39	4.39	4.39	4.39	0.455581	2.0	4.39
1	1325317980	NaN	NaN	NaN	NaN	NaN	NaN	NaN
2	1325318040	NaN	NaN	NaN	NaN	NaN	NaN	NaN
3	1325318100	NaN	NaN	NaN	NaN	NaN	NaN	NaN
4	1325318160	NaN	NaN	NaN	NaN	NaN	NaN	NaN
5	1325318220	NaN	NaN	NaN	NaN	NaN	NaN	NaN
6	1325318280	NaN	NaN	NaN	NaN	NaN	NaN	NaN
7	1325318340	NaN	NaN	NaN	NaN	NaN	NaN	NaN
8	1325318400	NaN	NaN	NaN	NaN	NaN	NaN	NaN
9	1325318460	NaN	NaN	NaN	NaN	NaN	NaN	NaN

Figure 5 illustrates that all NANs will be replaced by their mean values in a dataset. For example, in this dataset, the NAN values in the 'open' column are replaced by a mean value of 4056.08495. Similarly, all NAN values are also replaced with their respective mean values in other columns.

Figure 5. Preprocessed dataset

	Timestamp	Open	High	Low	Close	Volume_(BTC)	Volume_(Currency)	Weighted_Price
4572247	1600041060	10328.62	10328.62	10320.06	10320.06	0.701925	7247.408456	10325.040888
4572248	1600041120	10325.90	10325.90	10319.76	10320.63	5.946843	61391.782196	10323.424144
4572249	1600041180	10320.75	10320.78	10320.75	10320.78	0.020500	211.572844	10320.772555
4572250	1600041240	10320.86	10323.64	10320.86	10323.64	1.519091	15678.664557	10321.082832
4572251	1600041300	10324.60	10324.61	10321.93	10323.28	0.349238	3605.692837	10324.470065
4572252	1600041360	10324.35	10325.89	10324.35	10325.89	0.081143	837.754188	10324.419779
4572253	1600041420	10331.41	10331.97	10326.68	10331.97	0.572817	5918.026741	10331.444396
4572254	1600041480	10327.20	10331.47	10321.33	10331.47	2.489909	25711.238323	10326.175283
4572255	1600041540	10330.02	10334.78	10328.64	10334.78	4.572660	47253.747619	10333.972651
4572256	1600041600	10338.82	10338.82	10332.37	10332.37	1.292006	13349.565122	10332.429402

Figure 6 the new column named "date" is added to the dataset, which is transformed from the time-stamp value. Properly formatted and validated data increases data.

Figure 6. Transformed dataset

	Timestamp	Open	High	Low	Close	Volume_(BTC)	Volume_(Currency)	Weighted_Price	date
4572247	1600041060	10328.62	10328.62	10320.06	10320.06	0.701925	7247.408456	10325.040888	2020-09-13
4572248	1600041120	10325.90	10325.90	10319.76	10320.63	5.946843	61391.782196	10323.424144	2020-09-13
4572249	1600041180	10320.75	10320.78	10320.75	10320.78	0.020500	211.572844	10320.772555	2020-09-13
4572250	1600041240	10320.86	10323.64	10320.86	10323.64	1.519091	15678.664557	10321.082832	2020-09-13
4572251	1600041300	10324.60	10324.61	10321.93	10323.28	0.349238	3605.692837	10324.470065	2020-09-13
4572252	1600041360	10324.35	10325.89	10324.35	10325.89	0.081143	837.754188	10324.419779	2020-09-13
4572253	1600041420	10331.41	10331.97	10326.68	10331.97	0.572817	5918.026741	10331.444396	2020-09-13
4572254	1600041480	10327.20	10331.47	10321.33	10331.47	2.489909	25711.238323	10326.175283	2020-09-13
4572255	1600041540	10330.02	10334.78	10328.64	10334.78	4.572660	47253.747619	10333.972651	2020-09-13
4572256	1600041600	10338.82	10338.82	10332.37	10332.37	1.292006	13349.565122	10332.429402	2020-09-14

The graph in fig 7 shows the rise and fall of bitcoin price values in our dataset from 2012 to 2020. The graph has years on the x-axis and prices in USD on the y-axis. After the data is transformed, it is partitioned into two sets, the test set, and the train set. Separating data from research and trial sets is an essential aspect of evaluating data mining methods. Figure 5b shows that there is a positive autocorrelation for autocorrelation analysis. Positive autocorrelation happens when an error of a given sign tends to be preceded by an error in the same sign. Figure 8 shows a negative partial autocorrelation. Data for sequence prediction problems are likely to have scaled when training a neural network, such as a Long Short Term Memory.

From the experimental study, it is identified that there are more chances for overfitting if the size of training set is increased. Based on the results, it is concluded that LSTM produces accurate results since it works efficiently on bitcoin data. In this LSTM model, we have used Adam optimizer, which is better than other optimizers like Stochastic Gradient Descent that has a local minimum problem. Adam optimizer can also be applied in the Keras package in python.

Figure 7. Bitcoin price representation

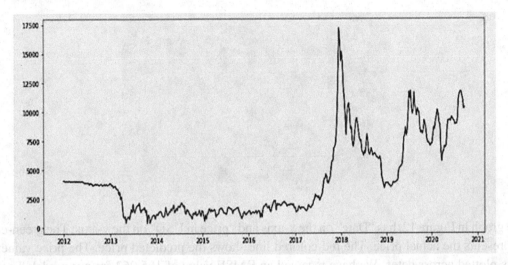

Figure 8. Autocorrelation

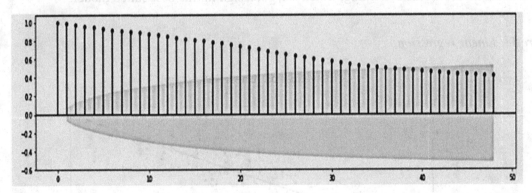

Figure 9. Partial Auto Correlation

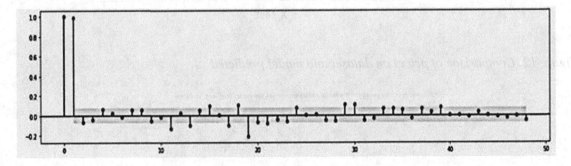

From above figure 10., it is evident that the lines train and test loss have almost the same values and reduces gradually.

Figure 10. Test and train loss of data after applying LSTM

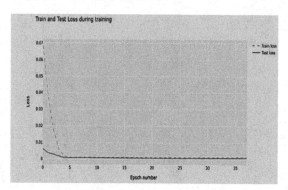

The graph in Figure 12. has "Date" on the x-axis and "price in USD" on the y-axis. The green-colored line represents the actual price. The red-colored line shows the predicted price. The price value in the graph is plotted across dates. We have received an RMSE value of 165.062 for our model. The above graph depicts that the Actual price on the dataset and the price predicted by our model are nearly the same and the model avoids overfitting, which is a good sign for the best-suited model.

Figure 11. Linear regression

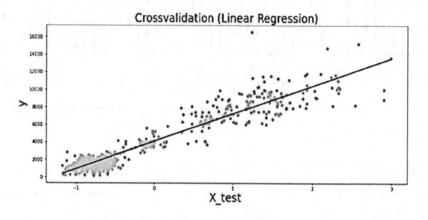

Figure 12. Comparison of prices on dataset and model predicted

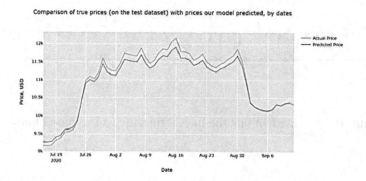

Based on our dataset, the last date in the dataset is September 14, 2020. Hence, the next 30 days' price values are forecasted in the above graph. The graph has time with month and year on the x-axis and Price in USD on the y-axis. The bitcoin historical dataset that we used has data till September 14 of 2020, hence we have forecasted the price values of the next 30 days i.e., till October 3 of 2020.

The graph in Figure .14 depicts the price values from the year 2012 to 2020 along with newly forecasted values. The green-colored line shows the price predicted for dates mentioned in the dataset along with newly forecasted price values. As a result, cryptographic enhancements need to be made for security purposes of the bitcoin transaction and exchange purposes.

Figure 13. Forecasting

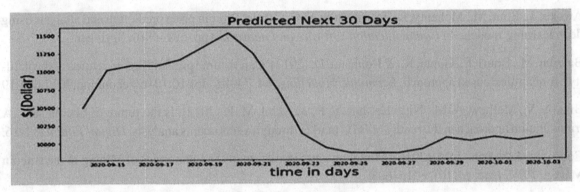

Figure 14. Forecasting price with the predicted price

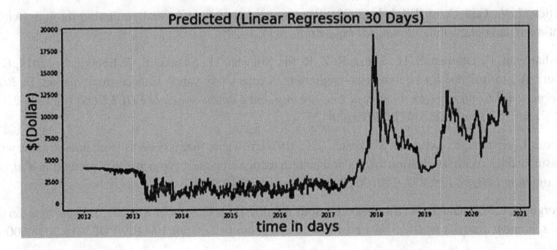

CONCLUSION

Bitcoin is a segregated cryptocurrency that works on a multiuser or client server systems. It is named as cryptocurrency since it applies various cryptographic techniques. The value of bitcoin gets affected based on the stock value. Bitcoins are very effective compared to traditional currencies. In stock market, various algorithms are used for estimating the price. But the conditions are different in predicting the value of Bitcoin. Bitcoin value is particularly used to make decision for investment. This proposed methodology has been implemented using three-layer LSTM model. Real dataset is used in this paper for predicting the future cost of Bitcoin in next 100 days from the present day. The proposed work yields better prediction rate with reduced error rate (<0.5). In future, the same concept can be incorporated with a dynamic framework for analyzing the real-time data which gives suggestion for investors in making decisions.

REFERENCES

Antonopoulos, A. M. (2017). *Mastering Bitcoin: Programming the open blockchain*. O'Reilly Media, Inc.

Awoke, T., Rout, M., Mohanty, L., & Satapathy, S. C. (2021). Bitcoin price prediction and analysis using deep learning models. In *Communication software and networks* (pp. 631–640). Springer.

Balcilar, M., Bouri, E., Gupta, R., & Roubaud, D. (2017). Can volume predict Bitcoin returns and volatility? A quantiles-based approach. *Economic Modelling*, *64*, 74–81. doi:10.1016/j.econmod.2017.03.019

Biju, A. V., Mathew, A. M., Nithi Krishna, P. P., & Akhil, M. P. (2022). Is the future of bitcoin safe? A triangulation approach in the reality of BTC market through a sentiments analysis. *Digital Finance*, 1-16.

Cocco, L., & Marchesi, M. (2016). Modeling and Simulation of the Economics of Mining in the Bitcoin Market. *PLoS One*, *11*(10), e0164603.

Cocco, L., Tonelli, R., & Marchesi, M. (2021). Predictions of bitcoin prices through machine learning based frameworks. *PeerJ. Computer Science*, *7*, e413.

Critien, J. V., Gatt, A., & Ellul, J. (2022). Bitcoin price change and trend prediction through twitter sentiment and data volume. *Financial Innovation*, *8*(1), 1–20.

Ferdiansyah, F., Othman, S. H., Radzi, R. Z. R. M., Stiawan, D., Sazaki, Y., & Ependi, U. (2019, October). A lstm-method for bitcoin price prediction: A case study yahoo finance stock market. In *2019 International Conference on Electrical Engineering and Computer Science (ICECOS)* (pp. 206-210). IEEE. doi:10.1109/ISEMANTIC.2019.8884257

Garcia, C., Esmin, A., Leite, D., & Škrjanc, I. (2019). Evolvable fuzzy systems from data streams with missing values: With application to temporal pattern recognition and cryptocurrency prediction. *Pattern Recognition Letters*, *128*, 278–282. doi:10.1016/j.patrec.2019.09.012

Georgoula, I., Pournarakis, D., Bilanakos, C., Sotiropoulos, D., & Giaglis, G. M. (2015). *Using time-series and sentiment analysis to detect the determinants of bitcoin prices*. doi:10.1109/PDP2018.2018.00060

Hansun, S., Wicaksana, A., & Khaliq, A. Q. (2022). Multivariate cryptocurrency prediction: Comparative analysis of three recurrent neural networks approaches. *Journal of Big Data*, *9*(1), 1–15.

Ho, A., Vatambeti, R., & Ravichandran, S. K. (2021). Bitcoin Price Prediction Using Machine Learning and Artificial Neural Network Model. *Indian Journal of Science and Technology*, *14*(27), 2300–2308.

Jang, H., & Lee, J. (2017). An empirical study on modeling and prediction of bitcoin prices with bayesian neural networks based on blockchain information. *IEEE Access: Practical Innovations, Open Solutions*, *6*, 5427–5437. doi:10.1109/ACCESS.2017.2779181

Li, Y., Jiang, S., Li, X., & Wang, S. (2022). Hybrid data decomposition-based deep learning for Bitcoin prediction and algorithm trading. *Financial Innovation*, *8*(1), 1–24.

Mahar, K., Narejo, S., & Zaki, M. A. (2020). *Bitcoin price prediction app using deep learning algorithm. In 2nd International Conference on Computational Sciences and Technologies.*, doi:10.1371/journal.pone.0164603.

Mahar, K., Narejo, S., & Zaki, M. A. (2020). Bitcoin price prediction app using deep learning algorithm. In *2nd International Conference on Computational Sciences and Technologies* (pp. 56-60).

McNally, S., Roche, J., & Caton, S. (2018, March). Predicting the price of bitcoin using machine learning. In *2018 26th euromicro international conference on parallel, distributed and network-based processing (PDP)* (pp. 339-343). IEEE.

Rathan, K., Sai, S. V., & Manikanta, T. S. (2019, April). Crypto-currency price prediction using decision tree and regression techniques. In *2019 3rd International Conference on Trends in Electronics and Informatics (ICOEI)* (pp. 190-194). IEEE. 10.1109/ICOEI.2019.8862585

Roy, S., Nanjiba, S., & Chakrabarty, A. (2018, December). Bitcoin price forecasting using time series analysis. In *2018 21st International Conference of Computer and Information Technology (ICCIT)* (pp. 1-5). IEEE. 10.1109/ICCITECHN.2018.8631923

Shahbazi, Z., & Byun, Y. C. (2021). Improving the cryptocurrency price prediction performance based on reinforcement learning. *IEEE Access: Practical Innovations, Open Solutions*, *9*, 162651–162659. doi:10.1109/ACCESS.2021.3133937

Wirawan, I. M., Widiyaningtyas, T., & Hasan, M. M. (2019, September). Short term prediction on bitcoin price using ARIMA method. In *2019 International Seminar on Application for Technology of Information and Communication (iSemantic)* (pp. 260-265). IEEE.

Yogeshwaran, S., Kaur, M. J., & Maheshwari, P. (2019, April). Project based learning: predicting bitcoin prices using deep learning. In *2019 IEEE Global Engineering Education Conference (EDUCON)* (pp. 1449-1454). IEEE. 10.1109/EDUCON.2019.8725091

Chapter 15
An Intelligent 8-Queen Placement Approach of Chess Game for Hiding 56-Bit Key of DES Algorithm Over Digital Color Images

Bala Krishnan Raghupathy

https://orcid.org/0000-0002-4752-6400

SASTRA University (Deemed), India

Rajesh Kumar N.

https://orcid.org/0000-0001-5394-218X

SASTRA University (Deemed), India

Priya Govindarajan

SASTRA University (Deemed), India

Manikandan G.

SASTRA University (Deemed), India

Senthilraj Swaminathan

University of Technology and Applied Sciences, Oman

ABSTRACT

Secured data transmission between the communication channels would be a challenging. Attainment of secured key transmission of cryptographic algorithms between communication channel partners is one of the most difficult tasks in data communication. Various cryptography and steganographic principles have been presented for this purpose. This chapter presents a new steganographic approach in which the 56-bit key of data encryption standard (DES) algorithm is safely conveyed between communicators by embedding it in a color digital image. The popular chess game-based 8 Queens placement scheme is used to identify pixel positions for the key embedding process. From observational consequences, it is accomplished that the nominated scheme would lead to achieving assured content contagion over the network.

DOI: 10.4018/978-1-7998-8892-5.ch015

INTRODUCTION

The rapid expansion of network communication and extension methods in the current period has increased the necessity for security in data repositioning and transmission of secret data, which is embedded in digital images and transferred over the network medium. Bulk data capabilities and efficient correlations among surrounding pixels are what distinguish digital images. Traditional encryption procedures based on the private and public key principles, such as Data Encryption Standard (DES), Advanced Encryption Standard (AES), and the international data encryption algorithm (IDEA), are not suitable for digital image encryption, especially for high-speed and real-time applications. Table 1 shows the comparative structure of various covert communication principles for the attainment of secret content sharing over the network or communication medium. Cryptography ensures secure communication by requiring a key to access the data. The term "steganography" refers to the logic of concealing a secret code in images that are not legible or understood. Both cryptography and steganography are employed to ensure data privacy. The fundamental difference between them, however, is that with cryptography, anyone can see that both sides are having a private conversation. The advantage of hidden writing over cryptography is that the designated hidden content does not appeal to itself as a topic of investigation. To put it another way, information hiding refers to the use of a document's secret content as a screen. All the traditional Electronic based transmissions may enable secret writing code within the transportation layer, such as text documents, videos, photos, protocol, or computer programmes, executable program files, in the digitized form of stego principles. To ensure the overall security of the confidential content, equally compacting requirements are introduced, because the steganographic arrangement is expensive and has a higher capability known as "payload." In general, a system is considered worthy of "content concealment" when it meets Friedrich's triangle requirements, namely, robustness, large capacity, and imperceptibility.

Table 1. Evolution of various Secret Content Sharing Principles

Communication Principle for Sharing the Secret Content	Obfuscation	Virtue	Unchangeable
Digital Signature Scheme (DSS)	No	Yes	No
Cryptography	Yes	No	Yes
Steganography	Yes / No	Yes / No	Yes

For the steganographic principles, all of the contents of a digitized file, with a high degree of redundancy, are known for their presence; redundant breaks refer to those sections adequate to change without any hypothesis to witness the change. This requirement is particularly well met by audio and image files. Transform and spatial domain steganography are two different types of steganography. In the spatial theme, the secret code is directly hidden via pixel manipulations, with Least Significant Bit (LSB) replacement being the most capable and popular way. However, in the transform domain, transformation techniques such as discrete wavelet transform (DWT) or discrete cosine transform (DCT) are used, and the coefficients are then tapped for the purpose of secret content concealment process. For algorithm compartmentalization, promoted steganography techniques have been divided into two categories. The first distinguishing algorithm is based on the file's kind. The next method is a more extensively used one, with categorization based on an imbedding technique, which is the focus of this proposed work. The following is a breakdown of how this document is structured. The Section II describes related efforts (Literature survey) on the content embedding method over the image and the constraints that have been observed. Section III introduces the proposed methodologies and its implementation, whereas Section IV describes the work's experimental outcome and metrics. Finally, Section V presents the significance of the proposed model and the Section VI depicts the conclusions.

Background

Many of the persisting covered writing techniques have been introduced in recent years to disguise secret data for secure data transmission. The private text or the confidential secret content is impelled in cover images in two ways in steganography: spatial domain and altered domain. Data is masked in the pixels in the spatial domain using algorithms like least significant bit replacement and pixel value differencing. All researchers of the content concealment and cryptographic domains frequently use these strategies to create stego objects with higher visual quality for the attainment of secured secret content transmission. Generic steganographic based secret content hiding and extraction process is presented in the Figure 1.

Figure 1. Evolution of the Basic Steganographic Scheme

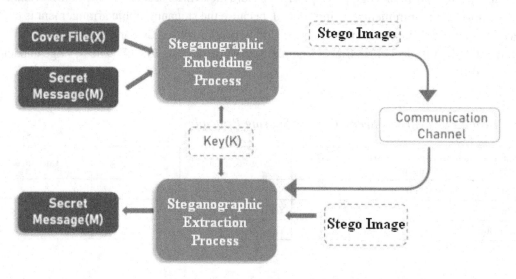

In the research work presented by the authors (L.C. Huang, 2013), a novel data hiding and its extraction process has been presented with the principle of reversible data hiding approach at lossless fashion. The above stated model offers high capacity of the secret content hiding on high quality digital images which focusing on sensitive medical data. Another model suggested by the authors (B. K. Raghupathy, 2014), for hiding the secret content on grayscale digital images by following the chess game based bishop tour traversal pattern for locating the pixel position for the embodiment process and the exact reverse at the receiver end is followed to extract the content without any loss. Another method for implementing RGB color image steganography and model proposed by the authors (Prasad. S, 2017), is based on the notion of overlapping block-based pixel-value differencing techniques. On the content concealing process, the authors (Shet K. S, 2017) proposed a competent model for the design and development of reconfigurable structures. The LSB and multi-bit based steganography principles were used in the above-mentioned research. A lossless steganography technique based on clustering and contouring principles on gray-scale images has been presented as an efficient steganography model (Manikandan. G, 2018). The authors (Naqvi. N, 2018), suggested a methodology for implementing steganography using the multilayer partiality homographic encryption concept. The work indicates that the model provides secure text content transmission with the cover image through communication channels.

The authors (Yang. C, 2018) proposed a methodology for secret content extraction from stego images based on the MLSB principle, and the scheme works well for content extraction due to the adoption of an ideal stego subset procedure. Another model proposed by the researchers (Margalikas. E, 2019) for safeguarding the secret content on color images is an image steganography strategy based on color palette transformation process in color space. Another scheme proposed by the authors (Kalita. M, 2019) for the implementation of adaptive color image steganography method for the achievement of confidential content embodiment process, and the model provides effective steganography deployment through adjacent pixel value differencing and LSB substitution procedures. To achieve privacy on medical imagery applications, the author (Lee H. Y, 2019) proposed an improved reversible data hiding process to improve the amount of privacy preservation value over the communication process at lossless fashion.

The authors (Eyssa. A, 2020) proposed a novel method for achieving secret content embodiment on all of the image's pixels, with the stego image being processed over a wireless communication system. The authors (Ayyappan. S, 2020) proposed a steganographic approach for secret content imbedding on medical images, which uses a reversible data concealment strategy as its foundation. It operates by embedding secret content in medical images using the EPR technique. The researchers (R. B. Krishnan, 2021) developed a novel approach for achieving concealed content embodiment on sensitive medical images at lossless fashion. The above-mentioned model works with Digital Imaging and Communications in Medicine (DICOM) images, and for pixel pattern identification, several chess-based approaches are used to navigate the pixel paths, with experimental results demonstrating the model's effectiveness. Another model proposed by the authors (Krishnan. R. B, 2022) for data concealing on images works by encrypting the image and then applying the secret information to the specified pixel channels, after which the image is descrambled to return to its original form. The model's chaotic level and uniqueness are demonstrated by the experimental results. It might be more powerful for detecting the places where content embodiment has been performed, and those regions must be correctly detected at the receiver end in order to achieve lossless content extraction.

PROPOSED MODEL

By combining the 8 Queens Placement Algorithm of the chess game with Least Significant Bit (LSB) substitution, the suggested method has been constructed to effectively transfer the 56 bit key of the DES algorithm. This combination, in conjunction with image traversal, strengthens the security of key exchange between users. Embedding and Extraction are the two phases of the operation. Both users are aware of the queen's location and traversal pattern. The following are the steps involved in the embedding and extraction phases.The proposed model works with the process of converting the secret content for transmission into binary stream for the embedding process. The conversion would be done by following the basic ASCII based stream generation process, the generated secret binary stream would then be embedded in pixel positions of the color image channels like Red, Green and Blue. The pixel positions for the embodiment process would be fixed on the basis of the 8 Queen placement process of the chess game. The following Figure 2 presents a single possible 8 Queen placement procedure along with the color channels on the image for embedding process. The workflow of the proposed model is presented in Figure 3.

Figure 2. Proposed 8-Queen Placement along with color channels for embedding process

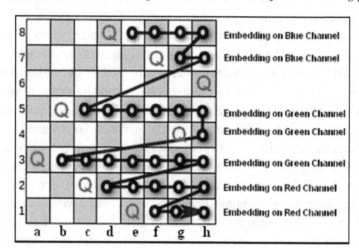

Figure 3. Work flow of the proposed model

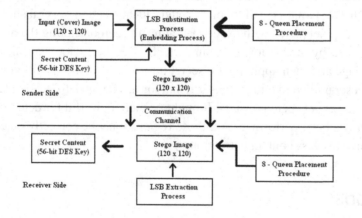

In order to execute the DES algorithm 56-bit key is required. The objective of the proposed model is to attain the secured transmission of the 56-bit key. In order to achieve the secured content embodiment process on color image the 56-bit key would be divided into three partitions as follows: Red channel Key value, Green channel Key value and Blue channel Key value. By static the key length (in bits) for the partitions have been fixed and are presented in the Table 2.

Table 2. Color channels with its fixed embedding capacity and locations

S. No	Color Channel	Bits (length)	Locations
1	Red	16	d2-e2-f2-g2-h2, f1-g1-h1
2	Green	28	c5-d5-e5-f5-g5-h5, h4, b3-c3-d3-e3-f3-g3-h3
3	Blue	12	e8-f8-g8-h8 g7-h7

The following are the steps involved in the secret content embedding and extraction phases.

Secret Content Embedding Process: (Sender- End)

Step 1: The sender decides the 56-bit key of DES algorithm to be transmitted

Step 2: A color image of dimension 120 x 120 is selected from the image repository between the sender and receiver

Step 3: A common pattern of 8-Queens placement procedure of chess game has been selected between the channel partners (sender and receiver)

Step 4: The 56-bit secret key of DES algorithm is embedded by following the LSB substitution procedure and the pixel positions (Stated in Table 2) and are located on the red, green and blue layers of the image (Step 3)

Step 5: Final Stego image is generated and is shared with the receiver in a secured channel

Secret Content Extraction Process: (Receiver- End)

Step 1: Receive the Stego image from the sender

Step 2: Apply the 8-Queens placement procedure of chess game to detect the locations and color channels for the extraction process.

Step 3: Apply LSB extraction process on the color channels on the image by following the pixel locations defined in the step 2.

Step 4: Cumulate the extracted bits from all the red, green and blue channels to obtain the 56-bit secret key of DES algorithm.

EXPERIMENTAL OBSERVATIONS

The proposed LSB-based embedding model for achieving 56-bit DES Key shielded transmission over the communication channel has been implemented in software MATLAB R2021a, and snapshots of outputs are shown below. The following four input colour images with the dimensions 120 x 120 are considered for processing in the experimental offshoot: (i) Cameraman (ii) Lena (iii) Baboon, and (iv) Bullet-Train. The proposed model's resilience has been tested using a variety of input color images, 56-bit key of DES and the outcome stego images are presented in the Table 3.The term "digital image processing" refers to a collection of metrics for evaluating different features of an image. PSNR (Peak Signal Noise Ratio) and MSE (Mean Squared Error) are two measures that are computed for the proposed model. Mean Squared Error is usually a collection of numerical values and is the metric used to detect the error level between two images are calculated as:

MSE (Color Image)

$$= \frac{1}{N^2} \sum_{i=1}^{N} \sum_{j=1}^{N} [\left(R(i,j) - R^*(i,j)\right)^2 + \left(G(i,j) - G^*(i,j)\right)^2 + \left(B(i,j) - B^*(i,j)\right)^2] \tag{a}$$

where R, G, and B indicate pixel values of color channels such as Red, Green, and Blue, and I and 'j' represent locations(i,j) of the original cover picture, R'(i,j), G'(i,j), and B'(i,j) represent color pixels of the generated stego image, and N x N specifies color image resolution. The figures: ratio of signal variation to reconstruction error variance is known as the peak signal to noise ratio. The following expressions are used to calculate it.

$$PSNR = 10\log_{10} \frac{255^2}{MSE} \tag{b}$$

The metrics like Mean Squared Error and Peak Signal Noise Ratio outcomes are computed by evaluating input images with stego images and the observations are presented in Table 4. Table 5 shows the histogram analysis of the cover and stego images. The experiment is conducted out on a number of cover images with a resolution of 120 by 120 pixels, each of which has a different pixel change rate value. According to the findings, the observed experimental values are close to the theoretical ideal values. The proposed embedding method effectively hides the hidden content from normal perception as a result.

SIGNIFICANCE OF THE PROPSOED MODEL

The chess game's 8-Queen Placement technique is used to locate the position for embedding the secret stream over the three-layered images in the nominated information concealing practice. All regular crypto and stego principles remain in place, but the encryption process and the pixels locating pattern for the embodiment process contain the secret key for secret content contegation. The nominated scheme, on the other hand, employs multiple locks to protect the confidentiality of the data to be shared: the first lock is based on the 8-Queen Placement principle, which locates pixels for LSB substitution embedding rather than the traditional embedding LSB execution on all pixels, and the second lock is based on secret stream embodiment on various layers. Based on the results of the experiments, it can be concluded that the suggested model provides an effective hybrid system of content concealing by combining the crypto and stego concepts.

Table 3. Input Images and its Corresponding Stego images with embedded secret content

S. No	Secret Text	Input Image (120 x 120)	Key for Embedding (56-bit)		Stego Image (120 x 120)
1	Welcome	Cameraman	01110111 01101100 01101111 01100101	01100101 01100011 01101101	Cameraman
2	Testing	Lena	01010100 01110011 01101001 01100111	01100101 01110100 01101110	Lena
3	College	Baboon	01100011 01101100 01100101 01100101	01101111 01101100 01100111	Baboon
4	maximum	Bullet-Train	01101101 01111000 01101101 01101101	01100001 01101001 01110101	Bullet-Train

Table 4. Observations of the proposed methodology in Color Images

Cover Images	MSE in dB			PSNR in dB		
	RED	GREEN	BLUE	RED	GREEN	BLUE
Cameraman	0.00036	0.00053	0.00067	82.56249	80.89918	79.85183
Lena	0.00012	0.00071	0.00018	87.39294	79.61143	85.63203
Baboon	0.00032	0.00071	0.00047	83.13325	79.61143	81.37234
Bullet-Train	0.00050	0.00107	0.00032	81.17623	77.83169	83.11443

Table 5. Histogram evolution of the Cover and Stego Images

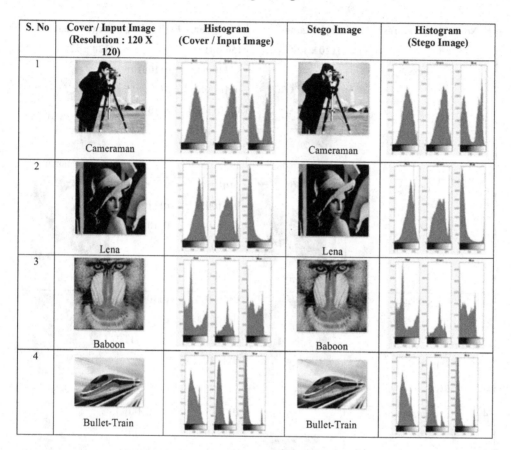

CONCLUSION

A lossless color image based steganography approach is described in the suggested study effort, which uses a chess game based 8-Queen placement principle based pixel locating process for LSB replacement. Our proposed method, along with accompanying probe remarks, demonstrates that the formed principle provides a meliorated scheme for executing secret content hiding on all levels of color images with dimensions 120 * 120.The model also provides no discernible trainings on the freshly created stego image, hence improving the scheme's quality via the metrics Mean Squared Error and Peak Signal Noise Ratio values. The proposed hidden content embedding strategy has been compared to certain democratic current principles, and the model's competency has been demonstrated through experimental results. To summarize, the proposed principle is very effective and ideal for information concealment applications.

REFERENCES

Ayyappan, S., Lakshmi, C., & Menon, V. (2020). A secure reversible data hiding and encryption system for embedding EPR in medical images. *Current Signal Transduction Therapy*, *15*(2), 124–135. doi:10.2174/1574362414666190304162411

Bala Krishnan, R., Rajesh Kumar, N., Raajan, N. R., Manikandan, G., Srinivasan, A., & Narasimhan, D. (2021). An approach for attaining content confidentiality on medical images through image encryption with steganography. *Wireless Personal Communications*, 1–17.

Eyssa, A. A., Abdelsamie, F. E., & Abdelnaiem, A. E. (2020). An efficient image steganography approach over wireless communication system. *Wireless Personal Communications*, *110*(1), 321–337. doi:10.100711277-019-06730-2

Huang, L. C., Hwang, M. S., & Tseng, L. Y. (2013). Reversible and high-capacity data hiding in high quality medical images. *Transactions on Internet and Information Systems (Seoul)*, *7*(1), 132–148. doi:10.3837/tiis.2013.01.009

Kalita, M., Tuithung, T., & Majumder, S. (2019). An adaptive color image steganography method using adjacent pixel value differencing and LSB substitution technique. *Cryptologia*, *43*(5), 414–437.

Krishnan, R. B., Raj, M. M., Kumar, N. R., Karthikeyan, B., Manikandan, G., & Raajan, N. R. (2022). Scrambling Based Riffle Shift on Stego-Image to Channelize the Ensured Data. *Intelligent Automation and Soft Computing*, *32*(1), 221–235. doi:10.32604/iasc.2022.021775

Lee, H. Y. (2019). Reversible Data Hiding for Medical Imagery Applications to Protect Privacy. *International Journal of Engineering Research & Technology (Ahmedabad)*, *12*(1), 42–49.

Manikandan, G., Bala Krishnan, R., Rajesh Kumar, N., Narasimhan, D., Srinivasan, A., & Raajan, N. R. (2018). Steganographic approach to enhancing secure data communication using contours and clustering. *Multimedia Tools and Applications*, *77*(24), 32257–32273.

Margalikas, E., & Ramanauskaitė, S. (2019). Image steganography based on color palette transformation in color space. *EURASIP Journal on Image and Video Processing*, *2019*(1), 1–13.

Naqvi, N., Abbasi, A. T., Hussain, R., Khan, M. A., & Ahmad, B. (2018). Multilayer partially homomorphic encryption text steganography (MLPHE-TS): A zero steganography approach. *Wireless Personal Communications*, *103*(2), 1563–1585.

Prasad, S., & Pal, A. K. (2017). An RGB colour image steganography scheme using overlapping block-based pixel-value differencing. *Royal Society Open Science*, *4*(4), 161066.

Raghupathy, B. K., Kumar, N. R., & Raajan, N. R. (2014). An enhanced bishop tour scheme for information hiding. *International Journal of Applied Engineering Research*, *9*(1), 145–151.

Sathish Shet, K., Aswath, A. R., Hanumantharaju, M. C., & Gao, X. Z. (2017). Design and development of new reconfigurable architectures for LSB/multi-bit image steganography system. *Multimedia Tools and Applications*, *76*(11), 13197–13219.

Yang, C., Luo, X., Lu, J., & Liu, F. (2018). Extracting hidden messages of MLSB steganography based on optimal stego subset. *Science China. Information Sciences*, *61*(11), 1–3.

Chapter 16
Deep Neural Network With Feature Optimization Technique for Classification of Coronary Artery Disease

Pratibha Verma
Dr. C.V. Raman University, India

Sanat Kumar Sahu
https://orcid.org/0000-0002-5686-7119
Govt. Kaktiya P.G. College Jagdalpur, India

Vineet Kumar Awasthi
Dr. C.V. Raman University, India

ABSTRACT

Coronary artery disease (CAD) is of significant concern among the population worldwide. The deep neural network (DNN) methods co-operate and play a crucial role in identifying diseases in CAD. The classification techniques like deep neural network (DNN) and enhanced deep neural network (EDNN) model are best suited for problem solving. A model is robust with the integration of feature selection technique (FST) like genetic algorithm (GA) and particle swarm optimization (PSO). This research proposes an integrated model of GA, PSO, and DNN for classification of CAD. The E-DNN model with a subset feature of CAD datasets gives enhanced results as compared to the DNN model. The E-DNN model gives a more correct and precise classification performance.

DOI: 10.4018/978-1-7998-8892-5.ch016

INTRODUCTION

Coronary Artery Disease (CAD) is the largest and most widespread form of the disease in the world, especially in developing countries and is the main cause of heart attacks. This harms mostly the common people because of its costly diagnosis. They often neglect the initial symptoms and signs of the CAD problem. This also affects the economic and psychological capacity of a person. The disease requires early and timely diagnosis for favorable treatment. Hence, it is important to establish a CAD screening system that can recognize the initial symptoms and reduce the financial burden. Computer science researchers working in the field of health sciences use DNN technique for the early identification and diagnosis of CAD (Alizadehsani et al., 2012). The DNN is based on the Traditional Artificial Neural Network (ANN). The ANN is based on the human brain working architecture and processing system. A new ANN based learning dimension, namely Deep Learning Network (DL) or Deep Neural Network (DNN), has also been developed and used. It is the same as the ANN learning system, but the internal architecture is changed with an increased number of the hidden layers. It has enhanced the computation speed of the learning algorithm (Sahu, S.K., & Verma P., 2022).

DNN and E-DNN have been proposed for the classification of CAD. Several physical and clinical tests are performed to identify the problem of CAD, but the number of tests can be decreased using the feature selection or feature optimization technique. The initial CAD dataset is chosen by the GA, which utilizes C4.5 as the learning classifiers, and PSO, which utilizes Ensemble learning of C4.5 and Random Forest as the learning classifiers or objective function, making CAD features more prominent (Verma, P., Awasthi, V.K., Shrivas, A.K., & Sahu, S.K. (2022).. The GA-J48 and PSO-EM (J48+RF) have reduced the unimportant features of CAD and also defined the vital features of CAD. All features of the CAD dataset have been used before feature selection to the classifier DNN and E-DNN for classification. Later, the selected features of CAD are used for the classification. The classifiers DNN and E-DNN have classified the CAD dataset with selected feature subsets. So, FST helps to reduce the time to identify CAD issues. So, less feature-subset enhances the operational efficiency of the proposed model.

RELATED WORK

A comprehensive literature review is necessary to understand the background of the problem. So, an in-depth literature study was carried out.

Verma et al.(2021) worekd Deep Belief Network (D.B.F.), H2OBinomial-Model-Deep Neural Network (H-DNN) to classify the Coronary Artery Disease (CAD) with selected components .Also used the PCA to reduce the components of CAD datasets.The Models gives the improved outcomes with select components of CAD.Amarbayasgalan, Park, Lee & Ryu (2019) used a reconstruction error (RE) based deep neural networks (DNNs) method and utilized the concept of the deep Autoencoder (AE) model for estimating RE. They used Coronary Heart Disease (CHD) benchmark dataset for the experiment and obtained 86.3371% accuracy. Verma & Mathur (2019) used the deep learning model and applied correlation-based feature subset selection with PSO search for detection of CHD and obtained 85.481% accuracy. Swain, Pani & Swain (2019) proposed a Dense Neural Network for the classification of Cleveland Heart disease data. They obtained a classification accuracy of 94.91% during testing, whereas83.67% accuracy was achieved by Miao & Miao (2018) by using the enhanced DNN learning with regularization and dropout model for heart disease diagnosis. Caliskan & Yuksel (2017) proposed the Deep Neural

Network classifier to classify coronary artery disease on benchmark datasets Cleveland, Hungarian, Long Beach, and Switzerland. The experimental outcome showed that the proposed DNN classifier better classifies the CAD datasets. The use and integration of bioinformatics tools to compare proteomics data in distinct conditions were implemented by Trindade et al. (2018). They made a case study using a systematic technique for finding the pathological similarities linking Aortic Valve Stenosis and CAD. Kim & Kang (2017) used machine learning techniques to predict CHD. In their finding, the NN-based prediction of CHD risk using feature correlation analysis (NN-FCA) has two stages. First is the feature selection stage, which ranked the important features of predicting CHD risk. Second, the analysis phase of the characteristic correlation determines the existence of correlations between the features and the data relationships of each output. They found NN-FCA to be better than FRS in predicting the risk of CHD. Bektas et al. (2017) found the useful features of the CAD dataset; t-test and Relief-f methods on Logistic Regression Analysis (LRA); Relief-f on Neural Network (NN) feature selection methods. The comparison of results shows that the accuracy was improved by 8.8% with improved specificity and sensitivity. Babič et al. (2017) analyzed three datasets and focused on two directions. Firstly, a predictive analysis based on Decision Trees, Naive Bayes, Support Vector Machines and Neural Networks. Secondly, the descriptive analysis is based on rules of association and decision. Their results were plausible compared to earlier studies. Dekamin & Shaibatalhamdi (2017) compared data mining methods in Coronary Heart Disease (CHD) prediction. They used Information Gain, Gini and SVM to select influential features, and variables with a greater weight were chosen for modeling purposes. The single classification algorithms and ensemble methods (hybrid model) were applied to develop a prediction with fewer errors. The result demonstrated that the hybrid model was better than the separate individual algorithms. The accuracy of the hybrid model is 95.83%, which cannot be obtained with other separate algorithms. Lohita et al. (2015) used classification techniques to predict CHD. The algorithms J48, Random Forest, Bagging, REP Tree, Naive Bayes, CART, and Decision Stump were used. The experimental analysis showed that the Bagging algorithm achieved maximum accuracy compared with other algorithms. El-bialy et al. (2015) worked on integrating the finding from the machine learning investigation on datasets targeting CAD disease. This technique avoids missing, incorrect, and inconsistent data issues that occur in the data collection. The Fast Decision Tree and prune C4.5 tree were applied to different datasets and the results were compared. The results showed that the classification accuracy of the collected datasets was 78.06% more than the average classification accuracy of all separate datasets, which was 75.48%. Alzahani et al. (2014) worked on diagnosing and predicting heart disease. The research approved using data mining techniques such as decision trees, classifiers of Naive Bayes, classification K-nearest neighbor (KNN), Support Vector Machine (SVM)) and Artificial Neural Network (ANN). The result showed that SVM and ANN have high performance in predicting the occurrence of Coronary Heart Disease (CHD). Alizadehsani et al. (2012) used three techniques to identify CAD. Algorithms C 4.5, Naive Bayes and the K-nearest neighbor (KNN) were used for the classification task. Ten folds s cross-validation measured the accuracy. The result showed that the highest accuracy obtained by the C4.5 was 74.20%.

PROPOSED FRAMEWORK

The overall implementation process of an efficient classifier as CAD with the least number of features is shown as the proposed system architecture in Figure 1. Two different categories of CAD datasets are applied in the classification model development; DNN and E-DNN classification algorithms with the combination of proposed GA and PSO are tested and evaluated with various performance measures.

Figure 1. The architecture of the proposed framework

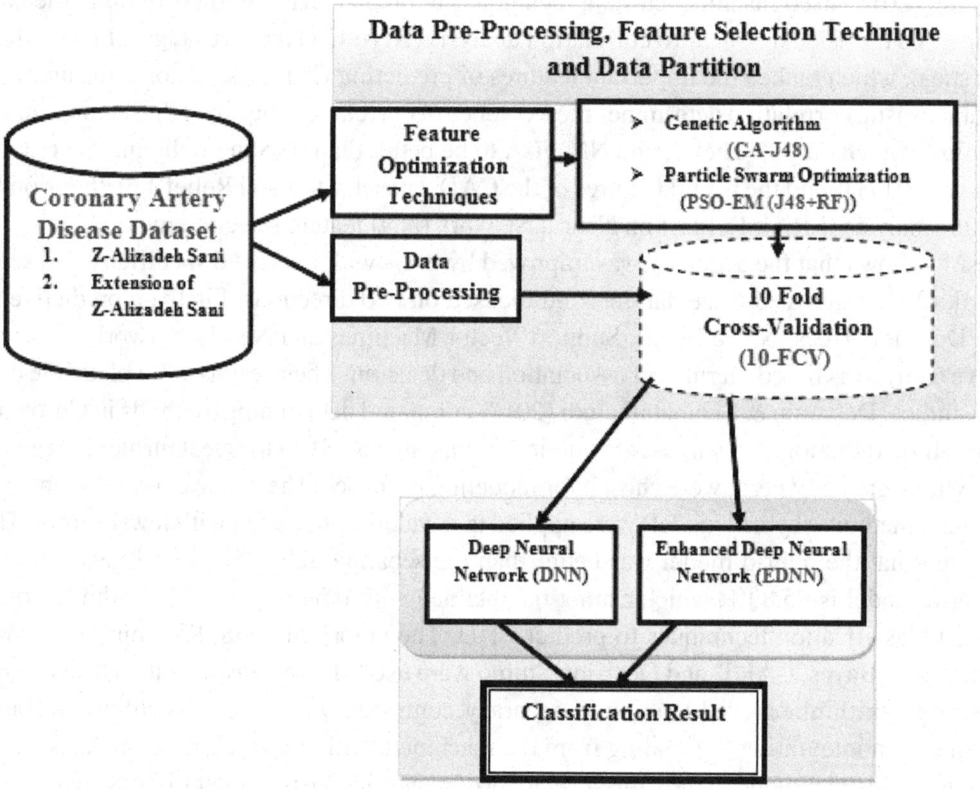

Now we explain the components of the proposed framework:

Datasets and Tools: The datasets used in this paper is available on the UC Irvine Machine Learning Repository. The datasets Z-Alizadeh Sani and extension Z-Alizadeh Sani hold the records of 303 CAD patients, each of which has 56 features and 59 features (Sani, Alizadehsani, & Roshanzami, 2017).

Feature Optimization Techniques: The wrapper based feature selection techniques evaluate and select attributes based on accuracy estimates by the target learning classifiers (Witten, Frank, & Hall, 2011; Witten & Frank, 2004).

Genetic Algorithm: Genetic algorithms (Goldberg, 1989) are often used to find solutions for optimization in research problems. A Genetic Algorithm (GA) is a branch of the broader class of evolutionary algorithms. GA mimics the same mechanisms found in nature, i.e., inheritance, mutation, selection, and crossing.

- We used the Wrapper Subset Evaluator (WSE) with an objective function J48 and the GA search method to select features for CAD datasets. We call this FST GA-J48 (Sahu & Shrivas, 2020).

Particle Swarm Optimization: Particle Swarm Optimization (PSO) is meta-heuristic that searches for very large locations of candidate solutions (Blum & Roli, 2001). The PSO is a population-based stochastic optimization technique developed by Dr. Eberhart and Dr. Kennedy in 1995 and inspired by bird flocking or fish schooling social behaviors"(Kennedy & Eberhart, 1995; Shi & Eberhart, 1998). These swarms conform to a cooperative way of finding food, and each member in the swarm continues shifting the search pattern according to the learning experiences of its own and other members (D. Wang, Tan, & Liu, 2018). In this, we have used the following ways for feature/attribute selection.

- We used the Wrapper Subset Evaluator (WSE) with an objective function (Ensemble J48+RF) and the PSO search method to select features for CAD datasets. We call this FST PSO-EM (J48+RF) (Verma, Awasthi, Sahu, & Shrivas, 2022).

Deep Neural Network: Deep learning is a sub-area of Machine Learning (ML) that produces a multi-layered representation of data, usually makes use of ANN and has enhanced the state-of-the-art in a variety of ML tasks (such as data classification, speech recognition, text classification and image classification) (Lang, 2019). It permits computational models composed of several processing layers to learn representations of data with more than one level of abstraction. It discovers complex configurations in massive information sets by the usage of the back-propagation algorithm to specify how a system should change its interior parameters, which are used to compute the representation in each layer from the illustration inside the preceding layer (Bengio, Courville, & Vincent, 2013; Lecun, Bengio, & Hinton, 2015; Schmidhuber, 2015). The number of epochs is the number of times a learning algorithm sees the complete dataset. In this work, we have used an epoch size equal to 10 epochs for DNN. After that, we increased the number of epochs and used an epoch size equal to 20. The DNN with a 20 epoch size is called the E-DNN (Tripathi, Goshisht, Sahu & Arora, 2021).

CLASSIFICATION RESULT

In this part, we calculate the performance of classifiers based on the confusion matrix:

Table 1. Confusion matrix

Actual Vs. Predicted	Positive	Negative
Positive	True Positive (TP)	False Negative (FN)
Negative	False Positive (FP)	True Negative (TN)

Where TP refers to the number of positive samples correctly classified by the classifier, TN is the number of negative samples classified correctly by the classifier; similarly, FP is the number of negative samples incorrectly classified, whereas FN is the number of positive samples incorrectly classified. The following performance indicators are commonly used to evaluate the classifier reliability:

Accuracy: is the percentage of correctly classified instances among all instances. The accuracy formula is shown in equation 1.

$$Accuracy = \frac{TP + TN}{TP + TN + FP + FN} \tag{1}$$

Sensitivity: analysis is the proportion of actual positives that are correctly identified or classified by the classifiers. It is also called True Positive Rate. The sensitivity formula is shown in equation 2.

$$Sensitivity = \frac{TP}{TP + FN} \tag{2}$$

Specificity: analysis is the proportion of actual negatives that are correctly identified or classified by the classifiers. It is also called the True Negative Rate. The specificity formula is shown in equation 3.

$$Specificity = \frac{TN}{TN + FP} \tag{3}$$

F1-Score: is the most intuitive performance estimation parameter. F-measure (F-score or F1-score) has been introduced to balance between sensitivity and specificity. The F1-score formula is shown in equation 4.

$$F1\text{-}Score = \frac{2TP}{\left(2TP + FP + FN\right)} \tag{4}$$

This work uses a data partition procedure, Cross-Validation (CV), with the most familiar 10 Fold Cross-Validation. 10 fold cross validation is a technique for data partition for training and testing. In this work, we have applied classification models, namely DNN and EDNN, to measure the performance of the classification result of CAD. Then the GA utilizes C4.5 as the learning classifiers and PSO utilizes Ensemble learning of C4.5 and Random Forest as the learning classifiers or objective function to select the relevant features (Verma, P., Awasthi, V. K., & Sahu, S. K., 2021). Then, we cut the factor of the dataset and received only selected features and the same instances (303) of the datasets and again calculated the performance of the classification results. A comparative study was also conducted to obtain the best classification models.

EXPERIMENTAL RESULT

Feature Selected by Feature Optimization Techniques

Table 2 shows the selected features by search method as Genetic Search, PSO Search and attributes evaluators as wrapper subset evaluator (WSE). In this result, we used J48 (C4.5) learning classifier under the GA. Similarly, we used ensemble J48 and RF learning classifier under the PSO search. The proposed GA-J48 and PSO-EM (J48+RF) are wrapper based FSTs that evaluate and select attributes based on accuracy estimates by the target learning with classifiers.

The outcome of FST like GA-J48 has identified 24 important features from both the CAD datasets. In the same way, the PSO-EM (J48+RF) has identified the 23 features of Z-Alizadeh Sani and 10 feature subsets of extension Z-Alizadeh Sani datasets.

Table 2. FSTs and their selected features.

FSTs	Dataset	Selected features	Name of features	Remarks
GA-J48	Z-Alizadeh Sani	24	f1,f2,f5,f7,f8,f9,f12,f14,f15,f17, f18, f22,f23,f24,f25,f29,f33, f34,f35,f49,f50,f52,f53,f54	GA with objective function J48 classifier
GA-J48	extension Z-Alizadeh Sani	24	f7,f10,f14,f18,f19,f21,f22,f25, f27, f28, f33,f35,f37,f41,f45, f46,f48,f49,f50,f53, f55,f56, f57,f58	GA with objective function J48 classifier
PSO-EM(J48+RF)	Z-Alizadeh Sani	23	f1,f4,f7,f8,f9,f11,f13,f15,f17,f22,f24,f 25,f29,f32,f33,f35,f38,f41, f45,f46,f49,f51,f54	PSO with objective function Ensemble J48 and RF classifier
PSO-EM(J48+RF)	extension Z-Alizadeh Sani	10	f1,f16,f26,f37,f45,f50,f52,f56, f57,f58	PSO with objective function Ensemble J48and RF classifier

Accuracy of Classification Models

In a comparative study of the classification models, the accuracy of the proposed classification models are shown in Table3.

As a result, note that the highest accuracy of the proposed E-DNN with FST GA-J48 model is only compared to the DNN and E-DNN classification with FSTs and without FST in Z-Alizadeh Sani dataset. In the case of extension, Z-Alizadeh Sani datasets the highest accuracy of the proposed E-DNN with both FSTs GA-J48 and PSO-EM(J48+RF) model when compared to the DNN and E-DNN classification with FSTs and without FST.

Table 3. Accuracy of classification models

Name of Classifiers	Z-Alizadeh Sani			extension Z-Alizadeh Sani			Remarks
	Without FST	FST (GA-J48)	FST (PSO-J48+RF)	Without FST	FST (GA-J48)	FST (PSO-J48+RF)	
DNN	85.48	84.82	86.47	88.78	91.75	92.08	Epoch-10
E-DNN	84.49	**86.80**	86.47	91.75	94.06	94.06	Epoch-20

The Sensitivity of Classification Models

The sensitivity test correctly identifies the CAD disease (True Positive Rate). Table 4 shows the sensitivity of the classification model.

Table 4. Sensitivity of classification models

Name of Classifiers	Z-Alizadeh Sani			extension Z-Alizadeh Sani			Remarks
	Without FST	FST (GA-J48)	FST (PSO-J48+RF)	Without FST	FST (GA-J48)	FST (PSO-J48+RF)	
DNN	84.72	85.65	86.11	84.72	88.89	89.35	Epoch-10
E-DNN	84.72	89.35	87.96	88.89	92.13	92.13	Epoch-20

The data shows that the maximum sensitivity obtained by the proposed E-DNN with FST GA-J48 model is only compared to the DNN and E-DNN classification with FSTs and without FST in Z-Alizadeh Sani dataset. In the case of extension, Z-Alizadeh Sani datasets have the highest sensitivity of the proposed E-DNN with both FSTs GA-J48 and PSO-EM(J48+RF) model compared to the DNN and E-DNN classification with FSTs and without FST.

The Specificity of Classification Models

Specificity relates to the classifier's skill to identify negative results. Table 5 shows the specificity of the classification model.

Table 5. Specificity of classification models

Name of Classifiers	Z-Alizadeh Sani			extension Z-Alizadeh Sani			Remarks
	Without FST	FST (GA-J48)	FST (PSO-J48+RF)	Without FST	FST (GA-J48)	FST (PSO-J48+RF)	
DNN	*87.36*	82.76	87.36	*98.85*	*98.85*	98.85	Epoch-10
E-DNN	83.90	80.46	82.76	98.84	98.85	98.85	Epoch-20

The data shows that the proposed DNN and E-DNN have the specificity of both datasets.

F1-Score of Classification Models

The classification performance measure in the F1-score is used when the False Negatives and False Positives are central. Table 6 shows the F1-Score of classification models.

The data shows that the proposed E-DNN model has the highest F1-Score of both datasets.

Table 6. F1-Score of classification models

Name of Classifiers	Z-Alizadeh Sani			extension Z-Alizadeh Sani			Remarks
	Without FST	FST (GA-J48)	FST (PSO-J48+RF)	Without FST	FST (GA-J48)	FST (PSO-J48+RF)	
DNN	89.27	88.94	90.07	91.50	93.89	94.15	Epoch-10
E-DNN	88.62	90.61	90.26	93.89	95.67	95.67	Epoch-20

Comparison of Performance Evaluation

Table 7 shows the comparative analysis of the proposed model and the existing model in terms of accuracy. The outcome demonstrates that the proposed model significantly improves CAD classification accuracy. The proposed ensemble model has obtained the highest accuracy in all cases.

Table 7. Accuracy of the proposed model compared with existing models

Name of author and year	Dataset	Algorithms	Accuracy %
Our Proposed model	Extension Z-Alizadeh Sani	DNN and E-DNN	E-DNN with GA-J48 and PSO-EM(J48+RF) Accuracy (**94.06%**)
Our Proposed model	Z-Alizadeh Sani	DNN and E-DNN	E-DNN with GA-J48 accuracy (**86.80%**)
Verma & Mathur (2019)	Coronary Heart Disease	Reconstruction Error (RE) based Deep Neural Networks (DNNs)	85.481% with correlation-based feature subset selection with PSO search
Swain et al. (2019)	Cleveland Heart Disease	Dense Neural Network type of deep learning network	**94.91%**
Miao & Miao (2018)	Heart Disease	Enhanced deep neural network (DNN) learning with regularization and dropout model	83.67%
Caliskan & Yuksel (2017)	Cleveland, Hungarian, Long Beach, and Switzerland datasets	Deep Neural Network (DNN)	Switzerland Accuracy Rate (**92.2%**) Cleveland Accuracy Rate (85.2%) Long Beach Accuracy Rate (84.00%) Hungarian Accuracy Rate (83.5%)
Amutha, Padmajavalli, & Prabhakar (2018)	Clinical records of 1000	Decision Tree algorithm, another adjusted variant of K-Nearest Neighbor (KNN) algorithm, K-Sorting and Searching (KSS)	The framework utilized six clinical attributes. AN mobile app "TMT Predict", enhanced to 84%.
Bektas, Ibrikci, & Ozcan (2017)	Cardiovascular dataset	Logistic regression RNA, NN, FST like Relief-F, independent t-test analysis,	84.1% NN with the oversampled dataset and the Relief-f feature selection method
Alizadehsani et al. (2013)	Z-Alizadeh Sani dataset	Bagging and C4.5 classification	79.54 (C4.5)
Alizadehsani et al. (2012)	Z-Alizadeh Sani dataset	SMO, Naïve Bayes, C4.5 and AdaBoost.	79.86 SMO

CONCLUSION

Deep Learning and feature selection/optimization methods can provide a great solution for identifying and classifying different diseases. The DNN and E-DNN methods co-operate to play a crucial role in identifying CAD. Several clinical tests are conducted to identify CAD problems, but these tests will decrease using FSTs. The FSTs, namely GA and PSO, have been proposed, which reduce the unimportant features of CAD and has a great role in quickly identifying important features of CAD.

The fewer features subset increased the efficiency and performance of the proposed model. The accuracy of the proposed E-DNN classification model is the highest compared to other models without FST in the Z-Alizadeh Sani dataset.

The proposed DNN and E-DNN with GA and PSO provided the highest accuracy in the experiment in both datasets. The proposed E-DNN has the highest sensitivity and fluctuated specificity of both datasets. The model also has the highest F1-Score of both datasets. The outcome of the comparative analysis of the proposed model and the existing model demonstrates that the proposed model significantly improves CAD classification accuracy. It is suggested that other classification and feature selection techniques can also be applied for better model performance.

REFERENCES

Alizadehsani, R., Habibi, J., Bahadorian, B., Mashayekhi, H., & Ghandeharioun, A. (2012). *Diagnosis of Coronary Arteries Stenosis Using Data Mining*. Academic Press.

Alizadehsani, R., Habibi, J., Sani, Z. A., Mashayekhi, H., Boghrati, B., Ghandeharioun, A., Alizadeh-Sani, F. (2013). Diagnosing Coronary Artery Disease via Data Mining Algorithms by Considering Laboratory and Echocardiography Features. *Journal of Rajaie Cardiovascular Medical and Research Center.* doi:10.5812/cardiovascmed.10888

Alizadehsani, R., Zangooei, M. H., Hosseini, M. J., Habibi, J., Khosravi, A., Roshanzamir, M., & Nahavandi, S. (2016). *Knowledge-Based Systems*. Advance online publication. doi:10.1016/j.knosys.2016.07.004

Alzahani, S. M., Althopity, A., Alghamdi, A., Alshehri, B., & Aljuaid, S. (2014). An Overview of Data Mining Techniques Applied for Heart Disease Diagnosis and Prediction. *Engineering and Technology Publishing*, 2(4), 310–315. doi:10.12720/lnit.2.4.310-315

Amarbayasgalan, T., Park, K. H., Lee, J. Y., & Ryu, H. K. (2019). Reconstruction error based deep neural networks for coronary heart disease risk prediction. *PLoS One*, 14(12), e0225991. Advance online publication. doi:10.1371/journal.pone.0225991 PMID:31805166

Amutha, A. J., Padmajavalli, R., & Prabhakar, D. (2018). A novel approach for the prediction of a treadmill test in cardiology using data mining algorithms implemented as a mobile application. *Indian Heart Journal*, 70(4), 511–518. doi:10.1016/j.ihj.2018.01.011 PMID:30170646

Babič, F., Olejár, J., Vantová, Z., & Paralič, J. (2017)... *Predictive and Descriptive Analysis for Heart Disease Diagnosis*, (September), 155–163. doi:10.15439/2017F219

Bektas, J., Ibrikci, T., & Ozcan, I. T. (2017). Classification of Real Imbalanced Cardiovascular Data Using Feature Selection and Sampling Methods: A Case Study with Neural Networks and Logistic Regression. *International Journal of Artificial Intelligence Tools*, 26(06), 1750019. doi:10.1142/S0218213017500191

Bengio, Y., Courville, A., & Vincent, P. (2013). *Representation Learning : A Review and New Perspectives*. Academic Press.

Blum, C., & Roli, A. (2001). Metaheuristics in Combinatorial Optimization : Overview and Conceptual Comparison Metaheuristics in Combinatorial Optimization : Overview and Conceptual Comparison. *ACM Computing Surveys*, 35(3), 268–308. Advance online publication. doi:10.1145/937503.937505

Broomhead, D. S., & Lowe, D. (1988). Radial Basis Functions, Multi-Variable Functional Interpolation and Adaptive Networks. *Royal Signals and Radar Establishment*, (4148).

Caliskan, A., & Yuksel, M. E. (2017). Classification of coronary artery disease datasets by using a deep neural network. *The EuroBiotech Journal*, 1(4), 271–277. doi:10.24190/ISSN2564-615X/2017/04.03

Dekamin, A., & Shaibatalhamdi, A. (2017). *Real-data comparison of data mining methods in the prediction of coronary artery disease in Iran*. Academic Press.

Dekamin, A., & Sheibatolhamdi, A. (2017). *Research Paper: A Data Mining Approach for Coronary Artery Disease Prediction in Iran*. Academic Press.

El-bialy, R., Salamay, M. A., Karam, O. H., & Khalifa, M. E. (2015). Feature Analysis of Coronary Artery Heart Disease Data Sets. *Procedia Computer Science, 65*(Iccmit), 459–468. doi:10.1016/j.procs.2015.09.132

Goldberg, D. E. (1989). Genetic Algorithms in Search Optimization &. *Machine Learning*. Advance online publication. doi:10.1007/3-540-44673-7

Haykin, S. (2008). *Neural Networks and Learning Machines*. Pearson Prentice Hall. doi:978-0131471399

Kennedy & Eberhart. (1995). *Particle Swarm Optimization*. Academic Press.

Kim, J. K., Kang, S., & Korea, S. (2017). *Neural Network-based Coronary Heart Disease Risk Predict i on using Feature Correlation Analysis*. Academic Press.

Lang, S., Bravo-marquez, F., Beckham, C., & Hall, M. (2019). *WekaDeeplearning4j : a Deep Learning Package for Weka based on DeepLearning4j*. doi:10.1016/j.knosys.2019.04.013

Lecun, Y., Bengio, Y., & Hinton, G. (2015). *Deep learning*. doi:10.1038/nature14539

Lohita, K., Sree, A. A., Poojitha, D., Renuga Devi, T., & Umamakeswari, A. (2015). Performance analysis of various data mining techniques in the prediction of heart disease. *Indian Journal of Science and Technology*, 8(35). Advance online publication. doi:10.17485/ijst/2015/v8i35/87458

Miao, K. H., & Miao, J. H. (2018). Coronary Heart Disease Diagnosis using Deep Neural Networks. (IJACSA). *International Journal of Advanced Computer Science and Applications*, 9(10), 1–8. doi:10.14569/IJACSA.2018.091001

Wang, Tan, & Liu. (2018). *Particle Swarm Optimization Algorithm : An Overview*. Advance online publication. doi:10.100700500-016-2474-6

Sahu, S. K., & Shrivas, A. K. (2020). Comparative study of classification models with genetic search based feature selection technique. In Cognitive Analytics: Concepts, Methodologies, Tools, and Applications (pp. 773-783). IGI Global. doi:10.4018/978-1-7998-2460-2.ch040

Sahu, S. K., & Verma, P. (2022). Stacked Auto Encoder Deep Neural Network with Principal Components Analysis for Identification of Chronic Kidney Disease. In Machine Learning and Deep Learning Techniques for Medical Science. CRC Press. doi:10.1201/9781003217497-19

Sani, Z. A., Alizadehsani, R., & Roshanzami, M. (2017). *Z-Alizadeh Sani Data Set*. UC Irvine Machine Learning Repository. Retrieved from https://archive.ics.uci.edu/ml/datasets/extention+of+Z-Alizadeh+sani+dataset

Schmidhuber, J. (2015). Deep learning in neural networks : An overview. *Neural Networks*, *61*, 85–117. doi:10.1016/j.neunet.2014.09.003 PMID:25462637

Shahzad, R. K., & Lavesson, N. (2012). *Comparative Analysis of Voting Schemes for Detection, Ensemble-based Malware*. Academic Press.

Shi & Eberhart. (1998). *A Modified Particle Swarm Optimizer*. Academic Press.

Swain, D., Pani, S. K., & Swain, D. (2019). An Efficient System for the Prediction of Coronary Artery Disease using Dense Neural Network with Hyper Parameter Tuning. *International Journal of Innovative Technology and Exploring Engineering*, *8*(6), 689–695.

Trindade, F., Ferreira, R., Magalhães, B., Leite-moreira, A., Falcão-pires, I., & Vitorino, R. (2018). How to use and integrate bioinformatics tools to compare proteomic data from distinct conditions? A tutorial using the pathological similarities between Aortic Valve Stenosis and Coronary Artery Disease as a case-study. *Journal of Proteomics*, *171*, 37–52. Advance online publication. doi:10.1016/j.jprot.2017.03.015 PMID:28336332

Tripathi, N., Goshisht, M. K., Sahu, S. K., & Arora, C. (2021). Applications of artificial intelligence to drug design and discovery in the big data era: A comprehensive review. *Molecular Diversity*, *25*(3), 1643–1664. doi:10.100711030-021-10237-z PMID:34110579

Verma, L., & Mathur, M. K. (2019). *Deep Learning based Model for Decision Support with Case Based Reasoning*. Academic Press.

Verma, P., Awasthi, V. K., & Sahu, S. K. (2021). Classification of Coronary Artery Disease Using Deep Neural Network with Dimension Reduction Technique. *2021 2nd International Conference for Emerging Technology (INCET)*, 1-5. 10.1109/INCET51464.2021.9456322

Verma, P., Awasthi, V. K., & Sahu, S. K. (2021). An Ensemble Model With Genetic Algorithm for Classification of Coronary Artery Disease. *International Journal of Computer Vision and Image Processing*, *11*(3), 70–83. doi:10.4018/IJCVIP.2021070105

Verma, P., Awasthi, V. K., Sahu, S. K., & Shrivas, A. K. (2022). Coronary Artery Disease Classification Using Deep Neural Network and Ensemble Models Optimized by Particle Swarm Optimization. *International Journal of Applied Metaheuristic Computing*, *13*(1), 1–25. doi:10.4018/IJAMC.292504

Verma, P., Awasthi, V. K., Shrivas, A. K., & Sahu, S. K. (2022). Stacked Generalization Based Ensemble Model for Classification of Coronary Artery Disease. In R. Misra, N. Kesswani, M. Rajarajan, B. Veeravalli, & A. Patel (Eds.), *Internet of Things and Connected Technologies. ICIoTCT 2021. Lecture Notes in Networks and Systems* (Vol. 340). Springer. doi:10.1007/978-3-030-94507-7_6

Witten, I. H., & Frank, E. (2004). *Datamining. Practical Machine Learning Tools and Technicals with Java Implementations* (2nd ed.). Elsevier.

Witten, I. H., Frank, E., & Hall, M. A. (2011a, May). Data Mining: Practical Machine Learning Tools and Techniques with Java Implementations. *ACM SIGMOD Record*.

Witten, I H, Frank, E., & Hall, M. A. (2011b). *Data mining*. doi:10.1002/1521-3773(20010316)40:6<9823::AID-ANIE9823>3.3.CO;2-C

Chapter 17
Detection and Classification of Diabetic Retinopathy Using Image Processing Algorithms, Convolutional Neural Network, and Signal Processing Techniques

Sudha S.
SASTRA University (Deemed), India

T. Gayathri Devi
SASTRA University (Deemed), India

Srinivasan A.
(iD) https://orcid.org/0000-0003-1171-5573
SASTRA University (Deemed), India

Mardeni Bin Roslee
Multimedia University, Malaysia

ABSTRACT

Diabetic retinopathy (DR) affects blood vessels in the retina and arises due to complications of diabetes. Diabetes is a serious health issue that must be considered and taken care of at the right time. Modern lifestyle, stress at workplaces, and unhealthy food habits affect the health conditions of our body. So the detection of lesions and treatment at an early stage is required. The detection and classification of early signs of diabetic retinopathy can be done by three different approaches. In Approach 1, an image processing algorithm is proposed. In Approach 2, convolutional neural network (CNN-VGG Net 16) is proposed for the classification of fundus images into normal and DR images. In Approach 3, a signal processing method is used for the detection of diabetic retinopathy using electro retinogram signal (ERG). Finally, the performance measures are calculated for all three approaches, and it is found that detection using CNN improves the accuracy.

DOI: 10.4018/978-1-7998-8892-5.ch017

INTRODUCTION

Diabetes is the main cause of unhealthy body conditions and it affects the regular activity of our body. The failure of absorption of glucose from food raises the level of blood sugar and it will lead to diabetes. Glucose is the main source of energy for each cell's functionality. High blood sugar arises due to a lack of insulin or the absence of production of enough insulin. Insulin, a hormone produced naturally by the pancreas and it helps to separate glucose from nutriment and also preserves glucose in the liver in the form of glycogen for later use. There are various causes of diabetes: unhealthy lifestyle, timely work, unbalanced diet, emotional stress, hereditary disease, etc. So as age progress, everyone has to undergo medical screening at least once a year. People do not find time to go for clinical testing as it is a time-consuming process. But the evolution of automated systems helps working and non-working age groups to take the self-test at home and it consumes only less time. Therefore it is necessary to propose automated eye testing & detection of signs at the early stage so that eye blindness can be prevented. The two stages of Diabetic Retinopathy include Non-Proliferative Diabetic Retinopathy (NPDR) and Proliferative Diabetic Retinopathy (PDR). Diabetic Retinopathy at the early stage is NPDR and the advanced stage is PDR. In the early stage, different visual lesions will appear in the fundus image which includes Microaneurysms, Hemorrhages, and Hard and Soft exudates. As the damage in the blood vessels proceeds new blood vessels will start to grow in the back part of the eye (retina) but the new blood vessels are very fragile so they can easily break and leak blood in the eye.

Microaneurysms-This is the preliminary sign of Diabetic Retinopathy. It occurs mostly with the appearance of small size red dots surrounded by bright yellowish areas. Since it is very small, its size is about 10-100 μm. It is appeared in the retina due to capillary widening or blood leakage in the back of the eye.

Hemorrhages –This is damage in the retina and it arises due to a considerable amount of blood leakage in the retina. It occurs with various shapes like circular shaped and flame-shaped hemorrhages and the size is larger than Microaneurysms. There are dot and blot hemorrhages that appear mainly in deep layers of the retina.

Exudates - The reaction of bio-chemical materials due to high blood sugar leaks yellowish like lipids and proteins in the retina. It is irregular in shape and the size is large. There are hard and soft exudates.

Cotton Wool Spots – It is otherwise called soft exudates. It appears either white-colored spongy-like circular or non-circular-shaped structures in the retina. This will also be created due to the reaction of biochemical materials in the retina. All the early-stage lesions are shown in Figure 1.

Diabetes affects almost all functions in our body. It affects the eyes and can lead to eye-blindness if the eyes are not properly treated. This eye disease is called Diabetic Retinopathy (DR). This chapter proposes three approaches to detect Diabetic Retinopathy: 1) Image Processing, 2) Deep convolutional neural network, and 3) signal processing. All approaches have their uniqueness and efficiency in detecting and classifying diabetic retinopathy. A fundus camera, either portable (hand-held) or non-portable, helps to take fundus images. Fundus images act as input for approaches 1 and 2, whereas the third approach utilizes recorded Electro Retinogram Signal (ERG). Image processing and Deep learning techniques do not consider the visual functionality of each retinal cell. In image processing, fundus images are pre-processed by green channel extraction and wiener filtering. Wiener filtering is used to deblur the fundus images. After pre-processing, lesions are segmented using k-means segmentation. Then features like texture and Scale-Invariant Feature Transform (SIFT) are extracted. These features are used to train and test cascaded rotation forest classifier. The deep convolutional neural network (approach 2) extracts

Figure 1. Early signs of Diabetic Retinopathy

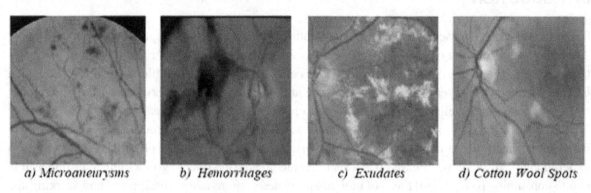

a) *Microaneurysms*   b) *Hemorrhages*   c) *Exudates*   d) *Cotton Wool Spots*

features through various layers such as the convolutional layer, max-pooling layer, fully connected layer, and soft max layer. Subsequently, it tests the fundus images to determine whether the fundus image is normal or DR. The third approach uses an Electroretinogram signal (ERG) and signal processing algorithm to classify ERG signals into normal or diabetic retinopathy.

LITERATURE REVIEW

Sugeno et al. (2021) proposed Efficient Net-B3 and image processing algorithms to grade the severity of DR and to extract red and white lesions of DR. This combined approach achieved specificity and sensitivity values of approximately 0.98 for the detection of DR. The CNN architecture is proposed by Samanta et al. (2020) for the detection of four classes of DR. It utilizes small dataset consist of 3050 images used for training and 419 images used for validation. The detection process consumes limited power and speed of operation. Kappa score is recorded as 0.88 for validation and 0.98 for training.

The five class labels convolutional neural network is described by Harry Pratt et al. (2016) to classify DR and non-DR images. The proposed deep learning approach classifies both non-proliferative and proliferative stages of diabetic retinopathy and got an accuracy of 75% on the Kaggle dataset. An integrated approach of Deep learning and smart-phone based DR detection is proposed by Hacisoftaoglu et al.(2020). It has been stated that ResNet50 outperformed well when compared to other architectures. The integrated approach achieved an accuracy of 98.6%.

Sharath Kumar et al. (2019) proposed an image processing algorithm to classify retinal images as Diabetic Retinopathy images [DR] and non-DR with two field mydriatic fundus images. Optic disk is extracted by applying wavelets at multi level and region growing algorithms. Using histogram method, blood vessels are extracted. Lesions are identified by multistage intensity transformations and histograms. The sensitivity is measured as 80% and specificity is 50%. The improved DR detection approach is proposed [6] and seven reliable features are extracted from microaneurysms and hemorrhages. These features are used to train RBF classifier. Morphological operation and watershed transform is used for blood vessel detection and segmenting optic disc. The algorithm achieved sensitivity of 87% and specificity of 93%.

Sudha and Srinivasan (2017) reviewed all the image processing, neural network and fuzzy logic approaches to notice and classify various lesions of diabetic retinopathy and the comparison of all the detection results have been made by measuring the sensitivity, specificity and accuracy. Shu-I et al.

(2020) introduced entropy image for DR detection. Input image is pre-processed by unsharp masking. The entropy image is acquired from the green component of fundus image. Finally, the features are pulled out from both of the entropy image and the pre-processed image. The Bichannel CNN utilize these features for detecting DR and non-DR.

Jebaseeli et al. (2019) proposed a method for segmenting blood vessels using Tandem Pulse Coupled neural network (TPCNN). Feature vectors are generated from TPCNN model and classification is done using n-SVM classifiers in the deep learning approach. This method of segmentation of blood vessels achieved 74.45% sensitivity and 99.40% specificity. Kamble et al. (2020) proposed an experiment to extract various features based on A-IFS histon segmentation. These features are used to train Radial Basis Function Neural Network classifier to classify Non DR and DR fundus images. This experiment has got an accuracy of 89.4%.

PROPOSED METHODOLOGY

Image Processing

In this approach, fundus images are collected from the database. It may be blur and rotational. So pre-processing is done to become understandable and the methods such as green channel extraction and median filtering are used for pre-processing. In the processing stage, segmentation of lesions is done by k-means segmentation and in post-processing, features such as Gray level dependency matrix (GLDM) and Scale-invariant feature transform (SIFT) are extracted. Texture features are extracted from the difference image and GLDM computes features by considering four different directions. SIFT utilizes five steps to extract features and the resultant features are invariant to illumination, scaling, and rotation. The Cascaded Rotation forest classifier (CRF) classifies the fundus image into normal and DR images.CRF classifier combines the predictions of multiple base classifiers. Therefore the classification is accurate and it reduces variance and bias. This image processing algorithm is suitable for finding all the lesions such as Microaneurysms, Haemorrhages, Exudates, and cotton white spots. In this approach, 500 images are taken for training and 400 images are applied for testing the classifier. Hybrid features help to achieve maximum accuracy of 95%.

As already mentioned, three different approaches are proposed to detect diabetic retinopathy. In approach 1, Image processing algorithms are used. The steps involved in fundus Image processing include 1) Pre-processing 2) Processing-Segmentation and feature extraction and 3) classification. Pre-processing – Sometimes fundus images captured may be blurred and rotational with irregular size. Therefore, it is essential to pre-process the fundus image before it is processed for detecting diabetic retinopathy. This includes green channel extraction and median filtering. The Green channel is most sensitive to eyes and contains bright or light information and it is less sensitive to noise. The Green channel has a high signal-to-noise ratio and de-noises the signal very well.

Median filtering

It is a non-linear filter and used to eliminate random noises. Sometimes in fundus images, blood vessels may not be clear or broken. Therefore by applying median filter fundus images can be smoothened and all vessel edges can be preserved. In this filtering, a window slides over the fundus image and captures

Figure 2. Output of pre-processing

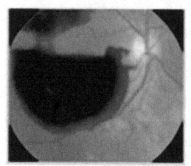
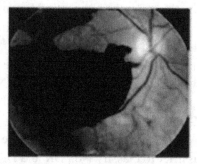
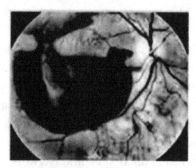

a)Input fundus Image   *b)Green channel extraction*   *c)Median filtering Image*

the median value of the pixels. A median value of pixels within the window is the output of the pixel being considered. The steps involved in median filtering are 1) Taking input fundus image 2) Applying 1D median filter along horizontal direction 3) Taking the result and filter again in the vertical direction to get denoised output.

Processing

After the image is pre-processed, lesions are segmented using k-means segmentation. The steps involved in segmentation process include 1) Get the pre-processed image 2) Assign the number of clusters 3) Assign the centroid to each cluster 4) Fix each pixel to the nearest centroid 5) Form the clusters 6) Determine new centroid for each cluster 7) Re-distribute each pixel to the nearest new centroid.8) Continue until there is no change in centroid.

Figure 3. Results of K-means segmentation

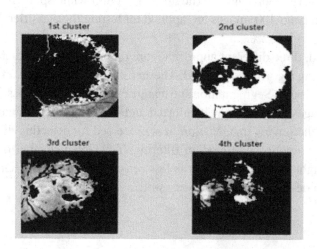

As a result of this segmentation, lesions or affected portions in the retinal image form the cluster and normal or unaffected portions come to another cluster.

Feature Extraction

Output from segmentation is the input for the feature extraction step. In this feature extraction, the Gray level dependency matrix (GLDM) and Scale-invariant feature transform (SIFT) are extracted. The steps involved in GLDM includes 1) Get the segmented image (I) 2) Evaluate difference image $D(p,q) = I(p, q) - I(p + \Delta p, q + \Delta q)$. Here, I is the segmented image, and Δp and Δq are the progressive positions in the image. 3) Compute probability density function of $D(p,q)$ 4) Extract texture features at four directions 5) combine all extracted features to create feature vector.

Scale Invariant Feature Transforms (SIFT)

The steps involved in SIFT feature extraction include 1) Characterize scale-space 2) Apply difference of Gaussians and find key-points 3) Discard unrelated key-points with the help of laplacian function 4) Assign attitudes to the key-points from the gradients and create histograms 5)Form and normalize the feature vector. The features that are obtained from SIFT are scaling, rotation, and illumination invariant.

Classification

The ensemble classifiers are Bagging, Boosting, Random Forest, and Cascaded Rotation Forest (CRF) classifiers. Here, for the identification of diabetic retinopathy, the CRF classifier is proposed because diversity and individual accuracy of base classifiers promote to get a high degree of accuracy of classification. The collection of features forms the feature set and it is divided into M subsets to train each base classifier and Cascaded Rotation Forest (CRF) classifier combines the votes of all base classifiers. Forest indicates decision trees that compute posterior probabilities for each class. There are two phases: the training phase and the classification phase. The steps involved in the training phase are: Create Rotation matrix R_i, where i= 1....M and M is the number of base classifiers and build the number of base classifiers. In the classification phase: 1) Base classifiers compute posterior probabilities for the data x that belong to class C_j. 2)Base classifiers compute the confidence of each class 3)Based on the largest confidence using the averaging approach, x will be assigned to the particular class.

In this Image processing approach, 500 images are taken for training and 400 images are applied for testing the classifier. Hybrid features help to achieve maximum accuracy of 94.5%. The performance measures are accuracy, sensitivity, and specificity. These are calculated using True positives (TP), True Negatives (TN), False positives (FP), and False Negatives (FN). True positive is the correctly classified DR images. False Negative is DR images misclassified as normal. True Negative is correctly detected normal images and False positive is the number of normal images classified as DR. Therefore,

$$\text{Sensitivity} = TP/ (TP + FN) \tag{1}$$

$$\text{Specificity} = TN/ (TN + FP) \tag{2}$$

Accuracy = Total correct outputs /Total test inputs ×100   (3)

CONVOLUTIONAL NEURAL NETWORKS

It involves convolution layer, ReLu layer, Max pooling, Fully connected, and Softmax layers. There are five class labels: Normal, Mild, Moderate, Severe, and PDR. In this approach, 600 images are taken for training, and 500 fundus images are applied for testing. The sensitivity and specificity obtained by this CNN approach are 96.5% and 96.7% respectively.

In approach 2, Deep Convolutional Neural Network (DCNN) is used to detect various lesions of diabetic retinopathy. The architecture of DCNN is shown in Figure 4. The work flow consists of 8 stages and it is shown in Figure 5. The Convolution operation is done between the fundus image and the filter. The resultant output is fed to the ReLu layer. It converts negative value pixels to zeros and stores only positive value pixels. The Max pooling layer reduces the size of pixels by considering only the max value pixels and the pixels with minimum values are discarded. The softmax layer is the classification layer and it classifies the image based on a probability function. CNN involves complex operations but it extracts more reliable features. This approach does not utilize any segmentation algorithm. It classifies the fundus image only based on features. There are five class labels: Normal, Mild, Moderate, Severe, and PDR.

In this approach, 600 images are taken for training, and 500 fundus images are applied for testing. The sensitivity and specificity obtained by this CNN approach are 96.6% and 96.8% respectively.

SIGNAL PROCESSING ALGORITHM

In approach 3, a signal processing algorithm is proposed to notice and classify diabetic retinopathy using Electro Retinogram signal (ERG). ERG signal is taken from patients using sensors. There are various types of retinal sensors that collect eye responses to the stimulation. Various retinal cells such as photoreceptors (rods and cones activity), bipolar cells are recorded. Diabetes also affects the activity of the cells of the retina. So, the proposed algorithm detects diabetic retinopathy in the frequency domain. Detection in the frequency domain is more accurate than in the time domain. Mel Frequency Cepstral coefficients (MFCC) are extracted and they are required to train and test the SVM classifier. There are five steps involved in MFCC feature extraction and it is shown in Figure 6. 1) creation of short frames 2)

Figure 4. Architecture of Deep Convolutional Neural Network

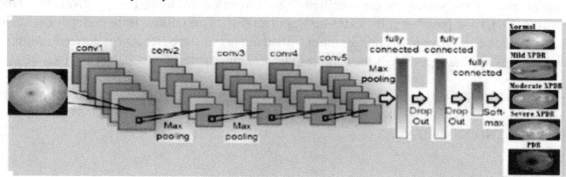

Figure 5. Stages of DCNN to detect Diabetic Retinopathy

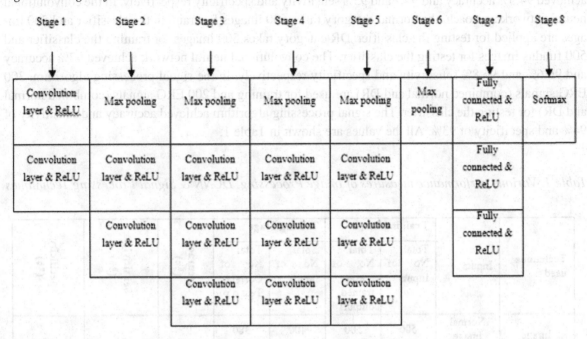

computation of power spectrum 3) Summing up energy after Mel filter banks are employed 4) Applying Discrete Cosine Transform (DCT) 5) Extraction of DCT coefficients.

MFCC features are applied to train support vector machine classifier. SVM fits the right hyper plane with maximum margin and it classifies the ERG signals into healthy and Diabetic Retinopathy.

In this approach, 300 ERG signals are collected from the nearby hospitals to train the classifier and 200 signals are used for testing the classifier. The sensitivity and specificity obtained by this signal processing approach is 94% and 93% respectively.

Figure 6. Block diagram of MFCC feature extraction

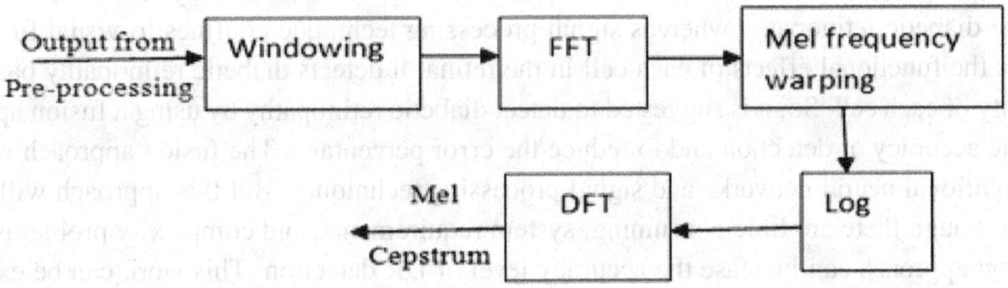

RESULTS AND DISCUSSIONS

In the Image processing approach, for each category (normal & DR) 500 fundus images are taken for training the classifier and 400 fundus images are taken for testing. The image processing algorithm achieved 94.5% accuracy and 94% and 95% sensitivity and specificity respectively. In the convolutional neural network approach, the normal category takes 600 images for training the classifier and 500 images are applied for testing the classifier. DR category takes 500 images for training the classifier and 500 fundus images for testing the classifier. The convolutional neural network achieved 97% accuracy and 96.6% and 96.8% sensitivity and specificity respectively. In the signal processing algorithm, 300 ERG signals (combined normal and DR) are used for training and 200 ERG signals (combined normal and DR) for testing the classifier. The signal processing algorithm achieved accuracy and sensitivity of 94% and specificity of 93%. All the values are shown in Table 1.

Table 1. Various performance measures of Image Processing, DCNN & Signal Processing Techniques

Technique used	Inputs	Training Stage		Testing Stage		Accuracy (%)	Sensitivity (%)	Specificity (%)
		Total No of Inputs	Total No of correct trained outputs	Total No of inputs	Total No of Correct Test o/p			
Image Processing	Normal Image	500	500	400	380	95	94	95
	DR Image	500	500	400	376	94		
Deap Learning	Normal Image	600	600	500	484	97	96.6	96.8
	DR Image	500	500	500	483	97		
Signal Processing Technique	ERG signals	300	300	200	188	94	94	93

CONCLUSION AND FUTURE SCOPE

Image processing algorithm and convolutional neural network concentrate only on lesions structures to identify the diabetic retinopathy whereas signal processing technique confines to visual functionality and studies the functional effects of each cell in the retina. It detects diabetic retinopathy based on the functionality of each cell. So, it is suggested to detect diabetic retinopathy by using a fusion approach to upgrade the accuracy of detection and to reduce the error percentage. The fusion approach will utilize both convolutional neural networks and signal processing techniques. But this approach will consume time. Even though there are time-consuming, system requirements, and complexity problems, the proposed fusion approach can increase the accuracy level of DR detection. This work can be extended in the future by incorporating the internet of things and cloud computing. The user can upload a fundus image through login credentials, which will be processed in the cloud, and the detection result will be sent directly through the user's mobile or mail. This way, periodic checking, early diagnosis, and timely treatment are enhanced. The present system can be improvised to detect other eye diseases like glaucoma and macular edema.

ACKNOWLEDGMENT

We want to thank M/s. Sudarshan Eye Clinic, Sankara Nethralaya, Chennai, M/s. IntuVision Labs Pvt Ltd., and M/s.Akbar eye hospital, Ananthapur, for their kind support in terms of providing clinical images & diagnostic datasets.

Compliance with Ethical Standards:

Funding: Any agency did not fund this work.

Conflict of Interest: The authors declare that no conflict of interest in getting and processing the various fundus images from multiple hospitals and available databases.

Ethical approval: The authors declare that this study does not involve human participants or animals.

REFERENCES

Hacisoftaoglu, R. E., Karakaya, M., & Sallam, A. B. (2020). Deep learning frameworks for diabetic retinopathy detection with smartphone-based retinal imaging systems. *Pattern Recognition Letters, 135,* 409–417. doi:10.1016/j.patrec.2020.04.009 PMID:32704196

Jemima Jebaseeli, T., Anand Deva Durai, C., & Dinesh Peter, J. (2019). Segmentation of retinal blood vessels from ophthalmologic Diabetic Retinopathy images. *Computers & Electrical Engineering, 73,* 245–258. doi:10.1016/j.compeleceng.2018.11.024

Kamble, V. V., & Kokate, R. D. (2020). Automated diabetic retinopathy detection using radial basis function. *Procedia Computer Science, 167,* 799–808. doi:10.1016/j.procs.2020.03.429

Kumar, S., Adarsh, A., Kumar, B., & Singh, A. K. (2020). An automated early diabetic retinopathy detection through improved blood vessel and optic disc segmentation. *Optics & Laser Technology, 121,* 105815. doi:10.1016/j.optlastec.2019.105815

Pratt, H., Coenen, F., Broadbent, D. M., Harding, S. P., & Zheng, Y. (2016). Convolutional Neural Networks for Diabetic Retinopathy. *Procedia Computer Science, 90,* 200–205. doi:10.1016/j.procs.2016.07.014

Samanta, A., Saha, A., Satapathy, S. C., Fernandes, S. L., & Zhang, Y. (2020). Automated detection of diabetic retinopathy using convolutional neural networks on a small dataset. *Pattern Recognition Letters, 135,* 293–298. doi:10.1016/j.patrec.2020.04.026

Sharath Kumar, P. N., & Deepak, R. U. (2019). Automated Detection System for Diabetic Retinopathy Using Two Field Fundus Photography. *Procedia Computer Science, 93,* 486–494. doi:10.1016/j.procs.2016.07.237

Shu-I, P., Hong-Zin, L., Ke-Hung, C., Ming-Cheng, T., Jiann-Torng, C., & Gen-Min, L. (2020). Detection of Diabetic Retinopathy Using Bichannel Convolutional Neural Network. *Journal of Ophthalmology, 2020,* 9139713. PMID:32655944

Sudha, S., & Srinivasan, A. (2017). Unravelling Diabetic Retinopathy through Image Processing, Neural Networks, And Fuzzy Logic: A Review. *Asian Journal of Pharmaceutical and Clinical Research*, *10*(4), 32–37. doi:10.22159/ajpcr.2017.v10i4.17023

Sugeno, A., Ishikawa, Y., Ohshima, T., & Muramatsu, R. (2021). Simple methods for the lesion detection and severity grading of diabetic retinopathy by image processing and transfer learning. *Computers in Biology and Medicine*, *137*, 104795. doi:10.1016/j.compbiomed.2021.104795 PMID:34488028

Chapter 18
Image Security Using Visual Cryptography

Bala Krishnan R.

iD https://orcid.org/0000-0002-4752-6400

SASTRA University (Deemed), India

Manikandan G.

SASTRA University (Deemed), India

Rajesh Kumar N.

iD https://orcid.org/0000-0001-5394-218X

SASTRA University (Deemed), India

N. Rajesh

Bule Hora University, Ethiopia

ABSTRACT

The use of digital image in a variety of disciplines has skyrocketed, particularly in multimedia, medicine, and social media. The integrity and confidentiality of digital images communicated over the internet can be jeopardized by a variety of security threats. As a result, the content of these digital images must be preserved at all costs for a variety of domain-specific applications. Visual cryptography scheme (VCs) is an image-based approach to encrypt the secret image in such a way, and human visual system (HVS) can be used to decrypt the image. The core concepts of visual cryptography and applications of several visual cryptography schemes are covered in this chapter. The authors describe a unique reversible data hiding method for protecting secret shares using a covering subset and recovering the secret image using an overlaying technique. This chapter also covers a comparative analysis of 2-out-of-n and 3-out-of-n visual cryptography schemes.

DOI: 10.4018/978-1-7998-8892-5.ch018

INTRODUCTION

A secret is piece of information or collection of data which is kept from the knowledge of any but the initiated or privileged. Secret contents are used in various fields such as, education, entertainment, manufacturing, logistics, healthcare and medicine. So the protection of secret content is very crucial in the modern internet communication. Secret sharing is an extra special method as compared to conventional scheme. Secret sharing is a process which a secret can be distributed between groups of participants, whereby each participant is allocated a piece of the secret. This piece of the secret is known as a share. The secret can only be reconstructed when a sufficient number of shares are combined together. While these shares are separate, no information about the secret can be accessed. That is, the shares are completely useless while they are separated. Within a secret sharing scheme, the secret is divided into a number of shares and distributed among n persons. When any k or more of these persons (where $k \leq n$) bring their shares together, the secret can be recovered. However, if k - 1persons attempt to reconstruct the secret, they will fail. Secret sharing involves four major steps, which is shown in Table 1.

Table 1. Major steps in secret sharing

Steps	Description
Secret shares	Non-overlapped piece of information from the secret image
Image Splitter	The process is responsible for the division of secret image
Coalition	A sub collection of shares that need to satisfy the required condition
Stacker	A process responsible for reconstructing the secret image

Principle of Secret Splitting

Secret sharing is introduced by Israeli cryptographer Adi Shamir and American Cryptographer George Blakely in 1979. The main theme of this algorithm is to split the secret into multiple parts and distribute the secret shares among group of participants. Each part contains a small amount of original information in the form of invisible mode and they don't reveal any information. The secret is reconstructed by sufficient number of qualified shares. A simple secret sharing divides a message between two participants. Consider the following scenario:

A sender named as 'Danie' has a secret message M, represented as an integer that he would like to share the secret between two receivers Alice and Bob. There will be other way to reconstruct the secret without the participation of both receivers. The following is the solution of the above statement.

Let 'r' be a random number. Then r and '$M - r$' are independently random. Daniel gives '$M - r$' to the first recipient and r to the second recipient as their shares. Each share reveals no information about the number, he message M. To recover the message, Alice and Bob have to simply add their shares together.

An alternative method is used by Daniel to split a message between Alice and Bob:

1. Daniel creates a random-bit string R, of the same length as the message M.
2. He XORs the message (M) with random-bit string (R) to create S. i.e., $M \oplus R = S$.

3.   Then, Sender distributes the random-bit string *R* to Alice and *S* to Bob.
4.   Later, both recipients combined together and perform XOR operation to reconstruct the message. i.e., $R \oplus S = M$.

This method is ideally secure and fast to implement as, the secret message is encrypted with one time pad and providing the cipher text to one person and the pad to other person. Here, individual piece is absolutely worthless. Secret sharing is classified into two types such as Cryptography and Visual Cryptography. Cryptography is the process of converting plaintext into ciphertext using different techniques. This conventional scheme is mostly used to protect numeric and text based information. In this scheme encryption strength mostly relies on the strength of key and single ciphertext is transmitted over the communication channel. The reverse of the encryption approach can be used to decrypt the ciphertext into plain text.

In contrast, Visual Cryptography is a sub discipline of secret sharing. It is an extended version secret sharing also knows as Visual Secret Sharing. Visual Cryptography or Visual Secret Sharing is a special type of cryptography technique which describes a secret image is divided into 'n' number of pieces using any cryptography techniques and the secret image is recovered by stacking process.

Visual Cryptography

Visual Cryptography is a subset of secret sharing. It is first invented by Israeli computer scientist Moni Naor and Adi Shamir in 1994 at the "EUROCRYPT" conference. It is a special type of cryptography technique which allows visual information that could be encrypted through special encoding style and the decryption needs a human visual system. A plain image is split into 'n' share images and distribute among a group of participants. Plain image can be retrieved by stacking the allowed subset of shares together. Stack less than shares reveal no clue about the secret. Visual Cryptography technique is illustrated in Figure 1.

Figure 1. Traditional visual cryptography scheme

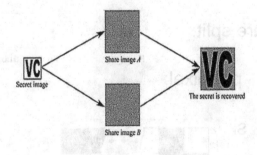

Visual Cryptography Model

At first Naor and Shamir proposed a binary visual cryptography that contains only black and white pixels. In this scheme, the secret image is split into a set of black and white pixels. For example, Consider a secret binary image with size of m × n, where m = width, n = height, Boolean values are used to split the secret image into set of black and white pixels. Visual Cryptography set the value 'zero' for white and 'one' for black to generate the secret shares.

Secret image is restored from the set of black and white pixels based on the fixed threshold parameter d, where $1 \leq d \leq m$. $H(V) \geq d$, then the sub pixels are interpreted as black, $H(V) \leq d - \alpha .m$, then the sub pixels are interpreted as white, Where $H(V)$ represents the Hamming weight of the 'OR' ed m-vector V.

The threshold parameter (d) is an integer value for the point at which dark pixels are different from white pixels. The m denotes the pixel expansion. This pixel expansion scheme leads to quality degradation in the restored image. The parameter $\alpha > 0$ is the relative contrast difference of the scheme. It is used to decrease the loss of contrast in the recovered image.

Definition 1.0: A result of the *k-out-of-n* visual cryptography approach composed of two collections of $n \times m$ matrices C_0 and C_1. To share a white pixel, the sender should randomly select one of the matrices in C_0 and in order to share a black pixel, the dealer should randomly choose any matrix in C_1. The chosen matrix defines the color of the m sub pixels in each n transparency.

It is considered valid if the following three cases are fulfilled:

1. For any $S \in C_0$, the OR m-vector V of any k of the n rows in S satisfies $\omega_H(V) \leq d - \alpha m$.
2. For any $S \in C1$, the OR m-vector V of any k of the n rows in S satisfies $\omega_H(V) \geq d$.
3. For any subset $\{r_1, r_2, .., r_t\} \subseteq \{1,2,...,n\}$ with $t<k$, the two collections of $t \times m$ matrices accessed by restricting each $n \times m$ matrices in C_0 and C_1 to rows r_1, r_2,...,r_t, are indistinguishable. Hence, they contain the same matrices with the same frequencies.

The schematic diagram of visual cryptography splitting and stacking is shown in the Figure 2 and Figure 3.

Figure 2. Visual cryptography splitting

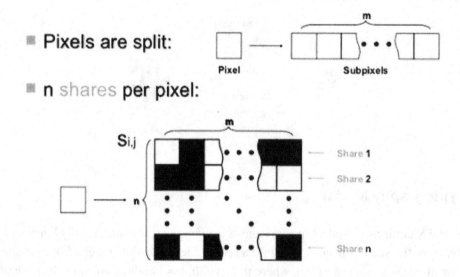

Figure 3. Visual cryptography stacking

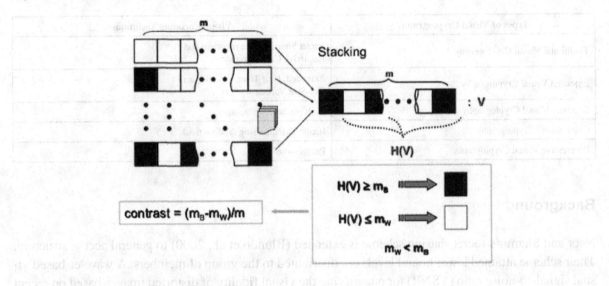

In Visual Cryptography, secret shares are generated based on either pixel expansion or non-pixel expansion methods. Israeli cryptographer's invented a 2 out of 2 a pixel expansion based visual cryptography scheme with 4 sub pels. In this scheme, a binary secret image is extending into share images based on the code table. The black and white pixels are processed individually with the help of code book and shown in Figure 4.

Figure 4. Codebook 2 out of 2

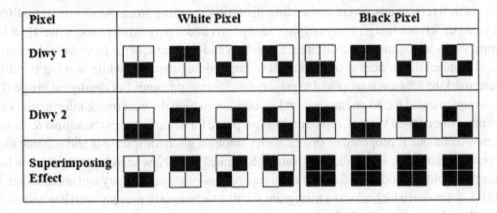

Types of Visual Cryptography

Visual cryptography is a special technique because, secret contents are encoded in the form of secret shares and decoding process requires collection of all qualified shares. Visual Cryptography is classified into five major categories based on the encoding style and shown in Table 2.

Table 2. Types of visual cryptography

Types of Visual Cryptography	Visual Encoding Technique
Traditional Visual Cryptography	Secret Sharing, Size invariant and Recursive Cryptography
Extended Visual Cryptography	Extended, Half-Tone, Cheating and Dot-Size Variant
Dynamic Visual Cryptography	Multiple Secret Sharing
Color Visual Cryptography	Image Sharing using random mask
Progressive Visual Cryptography	Progressive

Background

Naor and Shamir's secret sharing scheme is extended (Blundo et al., 2000) to general access structure. Their scheme attained lower bound levels are distributed to the group of members. A wavelet-based visual signal-to-noise ratio (VSNR) for quantifying the visual fidelity of distorted images based on recent psychophysical findings reported by the authors involving both near-threshold and supra threshold distortions (Chandler & Hemami, 2002). A relationship between Secret Sharing and Visual Cryptography was analyzed (Bonis & Santis, 2004). The scheme focused to achieve more randomness on secret sharing. Reversible data embedding theory has marked a new epoch for data hiding and information security. Performance of the proposed scheme is shown to be better than the original difference expansion scheme by Tian and its improved version was also presented (Kamstra & Heijmans, 2005). Tian's difference expansion transform, the correction bits do not contribute to the embedding capacity at all. Of course, the correction bits may slightly degrade the image quality. A dynamical expandable difference search and selection mechanism is used to balance the use of differences in two embedding directions. This mechanism effectively avoids severe embedding distortion resulting from the use of large differences in the previous difference image. It also exploit zero points and a payload-dependent overflow location map to improve the histogram-based difference selection and shifting scheme proposed (Hu et al.,2009). Distribution of pixel differences is used to achieve large hiding capacity while keeping the distortion low. A watermarking scheme is proposed to preserve the copyright control of the digital image (Hwang, 2000). It is implemented based on the random key number to hide the watermark information in Visual Cryptography. An extended Visual Cryptography is proposed for natural images (Nakajima & Yamaguchi, 2002). A new technique is proposed to share a secret among a group of scientists and suitable for where group of people involved in secret sharing (Naor & Shamir, 1994). New secret sharing scheme based on the Shamir threshold method invented with extra capabilities of steganography and authentication (Tsai & Lin, 2004). A scheme which adopts a histogram shifting technique to prevent overflow and underflow is proposed (Wei-Liang et al., 2009). Performance comparisons with other existing schemes are provided to demonstrate the superiority of the proposed scheme.

VISUAL CRYPTOGRAPHY SCHEME

A visual cryptography strategy (VCS) is a method of secret splitting strategy which converts a secret image into n portions of dual form. VCS is a highly-effective method because the secret information is transmitted in the form of secret shares. The secret image can be recovered simply by stacking the shares together without any complex computations at the receiver side. The shares are very safe because individual shares reveal nothing about the secret image. The shares of VC printed on transparencies are very difficult to be overlapped with proper alignment even if we ignore the printing errors. An overview of different visual cryptography approaches are depicted in Figure 5. An overview of visual secret share computation process is demonstrated in Figure 6.

Figure 5. Different types of visual cryptography

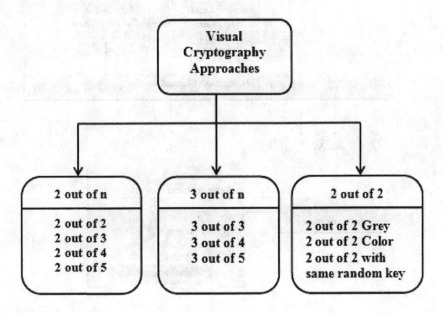

Visual Security Index

Using VSI first extract the edge information from the plain and encrypted images using an efficient edge detector applied over multiple thresholds and obtains a carefully designed weighted similarity measure. The texture features of the plain and encrypted images are extracted using the concurrence matrix and estimate the texture similarity. Visual Security Index (VSI) are used to propose to measuring the visual security of encrypted images of low quality.VSI on different types of distortion and in different quality ranges as well as to check the performance of other metrics developed for visual quality assessment on encrypted images.

Figure 6. Visual cryptography architecture

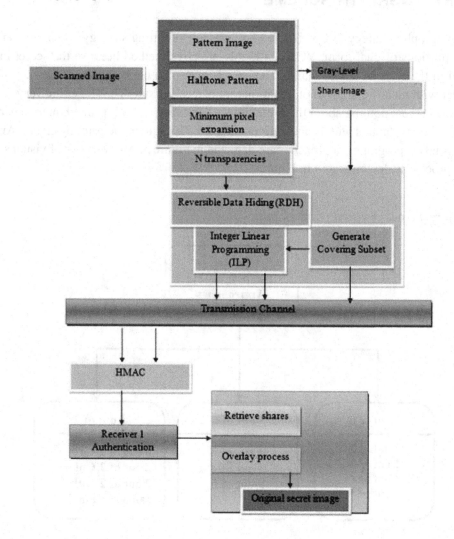

Halftone

Halftone is the reprographic technique that simulates continuous tone imagery through the use of dots, varying either in size, in shape or in spacing. Where continuous tone imagery contains an infinite range of colors or grays, the halftone process reduces visual reproductions to a binary image that is printed with only one color of ink. Halftone contact screens can be MAGENTA or GRAY in color.

Tint Screen: It is used in the plate making process to create the uniform tone pattern and contains a hard dot structure that is specified by a dot percentage.

- Highlight = 5-10% in size
- Midtone = 30-70% in size
- Shadow = 90-95% in size
- Highlights: the whitest tonal value

- Midtones: the gray tonal values
- Shadows: the darkest black tonal value

Implementation

Each pixel of secret image 'I' is represented by 'm' (m = 2) sub pixels in each of the 'n' (n=2) shared images. The resulting structure of each shared image is described by Boolean matrix 'S', where $S=[S_{i,j}]$ an [n x m] [2 X 2] matrix.

If $S_{i,j} = 1$ if the jth sub pixel in the ith share is black, If $S_{i,j} = 0$ if the jth sub pixel in the ith share is white, when the shares are stacked together secret image can be seen but the size is increased by 'm' times. The black pixel matrix is represented by C0 and white pixel matrix is represented by C1. To encrypt a black pixel, randomly select one of the matrices from C0 and to encrypt a white pixel randomly select one of the matrices from C1.

Where, C0 = {all the matrices obtained by permuting the columns of [1 0; 1 0]}

C1 = {all the matrices obtained by permuting the columns of [1 0; 0 1]}

Image Encoding and Decoding

In Visual Cryptography, a secret binary image has taken as a input image to encode the secret. In case of color image, binaries it to get a binary image. A black pixel is represented by 1 and a white pixel by 0. For a better result in case of text images make use of larger size fonts. Encode the text image, encoding each black and white pixel. For each black pixel (1) in the secret image replace it by two sub pixels, for black pixel the sub pixels distribution will be different in one shares different in other i.e. either [1 0] in share1 and [0 1] in share2 or by randomly permuting it i.e. [0 1] for share1 and [1 0] for share2. For each white pixel (0) in the secret image pixel the sub pixels distribution will be same in both the shares i.e. either [1 0] in share1 and [1 0] in share2 or by randomly permuting it to [0 1] for share1 and [0 1] for share 2. The white pixel in the secret image is replaced by a half white and a half black sub pixels making a 100% pure white pixel a 50% white pixel i.e. half black and half white. Thus a white pixel in the secret image becomes a gray pixel in the final overlapped image. This is the reason the reconstructed image loses its contrast as compare to the original image. To decode the image, stack both the shares and the secret message will be reconstructed. The code book of 2 out of 2 schemes is shown in Figure 7.

Prepare matrix based on black or white

$S_0 = [1\ 0;\ 0\ 1];$
$S_{00} = [0\ 1;\ 1\ 0];$
$S_1 = [1\ 0;\ 1\ 0];$
$S_{11} = [0\ 1;\ 0\ 1];$

Major Steps Involved in Visual Cryptography Scheme

Step 1: Start
Step 2: Take any secret message (text, picture etc.) in image format
Step 3: Apply Visual Cryptography technique
Step 4: Perform Pixel expansion

Step 5: Generate visual secret shares
Step 6: Save all the generated secret shares
Step 7: Collect all sufficient secret shares
Step 8: Stack all or the defined number of shares
Step 9: Stop

Figure 7. Encoding results of binary image

Pixel	Probability	Share1	Share2	Share1 × Share2
	50%			
	50%			
	50%			
	50%			

APPLICATIONS OF VISUAL CRYPTOGRAPHY

Visual Cryptography technique can be used for various security applications including access control, image protection, copyright content and intellectual property protection, identification and visual authentication. A 2 out of 2 Visual cryptography share generation and stacking process is shown in Figure 8.

Figure 8. Application of visual cryptography

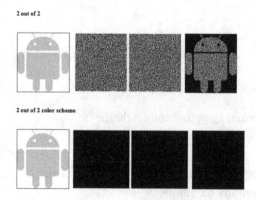

CONCLUSION

In this chapter, the researcher presented an efficient construction of VSI using the skill of linear programming. This scheme minimizes the pixel expansion subject to the constraints satisfying the region incrementing requirements. Unit matrices are introduced as the building blocks and the numbers of the unit matrices chosen to form the basis matrices of VSI are set as the decision variables. A solution to these decision variables by our linear program delivers a feasible set of basis matrices of the required VSI with the minimum pixel expansion. The pixel expansions and contrasts derived from our VSI are better than the previous results. Since no construction method has ever been reported in the literature survey, a minimum pixel expansion method based on linear programming approach is a better approach in this context. VSI is novel and innovative from both the theoretical and practical point of view. The experimental results show that the proposed scheme achieves high level contrast on different secret regions of secret image. It enhances the adaptability and flexibility of our VSI in practical applications.

REFERENCES

Blundo, C., De Santis, A., & Naor, M. (2000). Visual Cryptography for grey level images. *Information Processing Letters*, 75(6), 255–259. doi:10.1016/S0020-0190(00)00108-3

Chandler, D. M., & Hemami, S. S. (2002). Additivity models for suprathreshold distortion in quantized wavelet-coded images. In *Human Vision and Electronic Imaging VII* (Vol. 4662, pp. 105–118). SPIE. doi:10.1117/12.469507

De Bonis, A., & De Santis, A. (2004). Randomness in secret sharing and visual cryptography schemes. *Theoretical Computer Science*, 314(3), 351–374. doi:10.1016/j.tcs.2003.12.018

Hu, Y., Lee, H.-K., & Li, J. (2009). DE-based reversible data hiding with improved overflow location map. *IEEE Transactions on Circuits and Systems for Video Technology*, 19(2), 250–260. doi:10.1109/TCSVT.2008.2009252

Hwang, R. J. (2000). A digital image copyright protection scheme based on visual cryptography. *Tamkang Journal of Science and Engineering*, 3, 97–106.

Kamstra, L., & Heijmans, H. (2005). Reversible data embedding into images using wavelet techniques and sorting. *IEEE Transactions on Image Processing*, 14(12), 2082–2090. doi:10.1109/TIP.2005.859373 PMID:16370461

Nakajima, M., & Yamaguchi, Y. (2002). Extended visual cryptography for natural images. *Journal of WSCG*, 303–310.

Naor, M., & Shamir, A. (1994). Visual Cryptography. *Proc. International Conference on the Theory and Application of Cryptographic Techniques*, 1-12.

Tai, Yeh, & Chang. (2009). Reversible Data Hiding Based on Histogram Modification of Pixel Differences. *IEEE Transactions on Circuits and Systems for Video Technology*, *19*(6), 906–910. doi:10.1109/TCSVT.2009.2017409

Tsai, W.-H., & Lin, C.-C. (2004). Secret image sharing with steganography and authentication. *Journal of Systems and Software*, *73*(3), 405–414. doi:10.1016/S0164-1212(03)00239-5

Chapter 19
Multipath Convolutional Neural Network for Brain Tumor Detection (CNN)

Mukesh Kumar Chandrakar
Bhilai Institute of Technology, Durg, India

Anup Mishra
Bhilai Institute of Technology, Durg, India

Arun Kumar
Bhilai Institute of Technology, Durg, India

ABSTRACT

Brain tumor segmentation is a new automated medical image diagnosis application. A robust strategy to brain tumor segmentation and detection is an ongoing research problem, and the performance metrics of present tumor detection systems are little understood. Deep neural networks employing convolution neural networks (CNN) are being investigated in this regard; however, no generic architecture that can be employed as a robust technique for brain tumor diagnosis has been discovered. The authors have suggested a multipath CNN architecture for brain tumor segmentation and identification that outperforms existing approaches. The proposed work has been tested for datasets BRATS2013, BRTAS2015, and BRATS2017 with significant improvement in dice index and timing values by utilizing the capability of multipath CNN architecture, which combines both local and global paths. It was the objective to provide a simple and reliable method to determine segmentation and detection of brain tumor using brain tumor interface techniques (BCI).

DOI: 10.4018/978-1-7998-8892-5.ch019

INTRODUCTION AND BACKGROUND RESEARCH

Medical image processing covers wide research scope in the field of computer-aided diagnosis (CAD) for diagnosing various diseases. The analysis of the diagnosis deals with several medical imaging modalities such as MRI, X-ray, radiographic image, CT, mammograms etc. (Sinha, 2014). Image segmentation plays a very important role in the diagnosis and detection of abnormalities in medical images like tumors. There are numerous segmentation methods which are classified on the basis of pixel, region and threshold, referred as pixel-based method, region based and object-based methods. Segmentation plays very important role in CAD based tumor detection and used just before post-processing. The post-processing determines cancer stage or size and dimension of tumor (Sinha, 2014). Therefore, appropriate soft computing method is necessary to produce most efficient segmentation results. Currently, deep learning methods are used in such applications of medical imaging (Sinha, 2018). Assessment of human brain and its ability is also investigated with the help of medical imaging data and deep learning (Sinha, 2018) and so as the tumor detection. The cognitive brain tumor computing is associated with the model using cognition concept for training data. The mixing of training data of different types of tumor images is applied to the model that ensures effective training. The feature space and training model improve the performance (M. K. Chandrakar, 2022)

The human brain is the most interesting and complicated structure in the human body, which is made up of hundreds of billions of neurons and has stimulated a great deal of organ research. The regulation of muscles and the integration of body behavior, sensory perceptions, memory, cognition, speech, feeling, intelligence and consciousness are some of the central functions of the human brain (Cornish, 2017). The forebrain, midbrain, and hindbrain are three major components of the brain. There are four major brain regions: left and right brain, diencephalon, brain stem (midbrain, pons, and medulla oblongata) and cerebellum. All the methods that has been researched upon have been extensively studied and found that deep learning has tremendous scope of obtaining improved segmentation results that could help getting better diagnosis results for different medical images(M.K. Chandrakar, 2018)

The authors provided a classification model of mental tasks using electroencephalogram (EEG) on the concept of transfer learning, resolving data scarcity difficulties. CNN and SVM were used to validate the work. The accuracy of the results was the greatest, at 86.45 percent, using a typical benchmark of many other people's works for the same dataset as mentioned in(D. Singh and S. Singh, 2020.) there are many machine learning classification algorithms are available in machine learning like SVM, bagging, random forest in(S. S. Kshatri, 2021).

Suppose we live in rural areas far from health facilities or do not have enough money to pay our medical bills, or do not have time to leave our jobs sickly. In such a case it can be extremely useful to detect diseases using advanced devices. Many algorithms of AI were put forward and created to identify and diagnose diseases such as cancer, lung diseases, RA, DIR, Alzheimer's, hepatitis, Dengue fever, Liver and Parkenson's disease by computer scientists.(Bhardwaj, 2017).Deep learning involves using large neural networks of interconnected neurons and the ability to alter their hyperparameters as new data are obtained. (LeCun, 2015).as show in fig. 1

In adults, tumors develop in the cerebral cortex. In memory, thought, and other rational roles, the brain has a part to play. Tumors often develop in infants in the brain stem and cerebellum. The brain stem is near the cerebellum and regulates movement and coordination. Cancers, strokes and infections can affect the brain (Tarver, 2012). In July 2012, cancer and stroke were listed as the third and fourth leading cause of death in Malaysia, respectively. According to the World Health Organization, cancer and stroke has been the second and third leading cause of death after (WHO)(Smith, 2014).

Figure 1. Major Parts of Human Brain

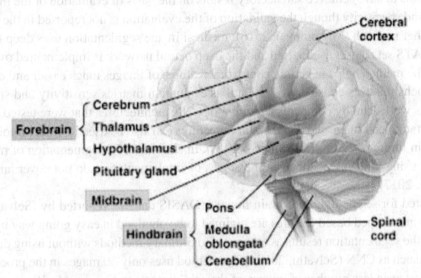

Magnetic resonance imaging (MRI) is the most common imaging method for the identification of abnormal brain tumors. Traditionally, MRI images are analyzed manually by radiologists for the purpose of detecting abnormal brain disorders. It takes time and is difficult to interpret large amounts of images manually. Computer-enabled recognition also helps to diagnose it correctly and easily. (Mohmand Shahjahan Majib, 2021)A brain tumor is a life-threatening neurological condition caused by the unregulated development of cells inside the brain or skull. The death rate of people with this condition is steadily increasing. If a brain tumor cannot be identified in an early stage, it can surely lead to death. A brain tumor is a clump of irregular cells in the brain that forms a mass . The human brain is enclosed by a rigid skull. Any expansion in such a small area will trigger severe issues. Brain tumors can be cancerous and non-cancerous. Although MRI and Computer Tomography (CT) are the two modalities widely used for marking the abnormalities in terms of shape, size, or location of brain tissues which in turn help in detecting the tumors, MRI is preferred more by the doctors.ML algorithms are popularly being used in the field of health-informatics.

Other necessary components of medical image processing employing optimization and deep learning based soft computing methods is de-noising of images because the noisy images if subjected to segmentation then the result and diagnosis analysis would not be appropriate (Bhonsle, 2018 & Sinha, 2017). The k-means method is considered as descent method in segmentation of medical images especially brain tumor images (Patel, 2014 & Patel, 2010) but these methods are also optimized using fuzzy based approaches such as fuzzy based clustering (Sinha, 2015). In (Patel, 2010 & Sinha, 2015), mammograms were well tested with fuzzy method of clustering used for breast cancer detection. Content based medical image retrieval (Singh, 2010), quality assessment of medical images subjected to compression (Kumar,

2011) and application of an appropriate method of optimization in medical image segmentation (Sinha, 2020) are few of important applications of medical imaging and interpretation of images.

In (Neethu, 2017), convolutional neural network (CNN) was implemented for brain tumor detection in which the classification stage employed the CNN based deep leaning method for brain tumor detection. This paper claims to have achieved satisfactory results on the basis of evaluation of the method in terms of sensitivity and specificity though the validation of the evaluation is not reported in the work (Neethu, 2017). In another research (Mohammad, 2016), medical image segmentation uses deep learning tested over 2013 BRATS set dataset as reported and the deep neural network is implemented over MR images of the brain. The method helps in getting contextual features of images much easier and efficiently. The number of epochs that was considered is 10 and as evaluation metrics sensitivity and specificity were presented. This work actually compares a number of CNN architectures that were tested in the medical image segmentation and suggested that these architectures can also be used in brain tumor segmentation and detection in future research (Mohammad, 2016). In (Kazi, 2017), segmentation of medical images was presented using k-means method but the stages of implementation do not cover any role of deep learning (Kazi, 2017).

CNN is tested for segmentation of brain images (OASIS dataset, reported by (Selvathi, 2018) and connectedness and shaped based features are claimed to be obtained in easy going way using CNN and that enhanced the segmentation results as compared to ordinary methods without using deep neural network methods such as CNN (Selvathi, 2018). The method uses only 30 mages in the process of training and test included even less number of images of the said datasets, which is only 10 images. The region segmentation is achieved and the metrics include sensitivity and accuracy in addition to PSNR also. This research tested well with brain images and regions are well segmented but the major limitations include very less number of images tested and the metrics by which the method is evaluated do not show much satisfactory values (Selvathi, 2018). The work is also not compared with any existing method although the CNN architecture suggested by (Mohammad, 2016) is discussed in related research.

Zahra (2018) in their medical image segmentation using deep learning (Sobhaninia, 2018) and (Kebir, 2018) in their work on detection of abnormalities using CNN (Sobhaninia, 2018) have studied and attempted implementation of CNN in the segmentation and subsequently in the detection of abnormalities in medical images since abnormality detection only helps in tumor or any other cancer diagnosis. LinkNet architecture of CNN with the use of dice score were the salient features of (Sobhaninia, 2018) which is considered as the metric for overlap measurement. The dice score was obtained as 0.72 which is considered satisfactory. However, the method could not only focus on brain tumor but general abnormalities in medical images. The k-means and CNN are used in (Kebir, 2018) and measured accuracy of the segmentation. The comparison with any existing research and lack of validation are major issues with this research. In (Ren, 2019), Ren et al. (2019) presented segmentation of 3D MR images of brain which results 0.84 of dice score that is around 84%. The paper highlights about two important modules, adversarial and task reorganization and uses MRBrainS18 dataset was used for validation of the work. The authors claim that this method is very useful in multiclass segmentation based application of brain tumor detection.

In (Ramirez, 2018) and (Madhupriya, 2019) it was studied how the brain segmentation results could be improved and optimized that were tested using deep learning based methods. Dice similarity index was measured as 85% and tested on MRI images of brain (Remirez, 2018) but the segmentation results were not appropriate in boundaries of the MRI images. In (Selvraj, 2013) a review of segmentation of brain tumor images was studied using various types of methods and recommended deep learning as a robust method (Selvaraj, 2013 & Madhupriya, 2019). In (Alpana, 2019), it was discussed the role of CNN in brain tumor segmentation as an example of deep learning method (Alpana, 2019). All these methods and researches were either studies or reviews.

In (Wang, 2019), brain tumor segmentation based research was studied which was tested over the BRATS2015 databases and implemented deep learning (Wang, 2019). Dice index was evaluated in addition to the total time taken in the segmentation process which could be slightly improved. This work compared deep learning and SVM method and found deep learning outperforming in terms of match indices using true positive and true negative terms (Xiao, 2016). In (Malathi, 2019), CNN for brain tumor segmentation was implemented over BRATS2015 databases and obtained dice indices and sensitivity but the results were obtained for limited number of the images only (Malathi, 2019).

We have studied the literature on brain tumor segmentation using deep learning and few other methods tested over BRATS2015 databases and others also. The major findings of the study of literature suggests that:

§   No robust quality measures are used to evaluate the performance
§   No robust set of databases over which the methods were tested, however few deep learning based methods were tested over a common brain tumor dataset.
§   The improvement in tumor area and tumor stage determination are not observed in most of the research.

In this section, you will want to describe the general perspective of your paper. Toward the end of the introduction, you should specifically state your paper's objectives.

BRAIN TUMOR DETECTION METHOD USING CONVOLUTION NEURAL NETWORK (CNN)

We used all three datasets of MRI images from open datasets - BRATS 2013, BRATS 2015, BRATS 2017 (Wang, 2019 & Xiao, 2016). When programming a CNN, each convolution layer within a neural network has following attributes:

- Input is a tensor with shape (number of images) x (image width) x (image height) x (image depth).
- Convolutional kernels whose width and height are hyper-parameters, and whose depth must be equal to that of the image. Convolutional layers convolve the input and pass its result to the next layer. This is similar to the response of a neuron in the visual cortex to a specific stimulus

Now, we performed the segmentation slice by slice from the axial view and accordingly the model is processed sequentially over each 2D axial image. Pixel is associated with different image modalities namely; T1, T2, T1C and FLAIR. Like most CNN-based segmentation models, the method predicts the class of a pixel by processing the M×M patch centered on that pixel. The input X of CNN model is thus an M × M 2D patch with several modalities.

Each feature map can be thought of as a topologically arranged map of responses of spatially local nonlinear feature extractor (the parameters of which are learned), applied identically to each spatial neighborhood of the input planes in a sliding window fashion. In first convolution layer, the individual input planes correspond to different MRI modalities (in typical computer vision applications, the individual input planes correspond to the red, green and blue color channels). In subsequent layers, the input planes typically consist of the feature maps of the previous layer1. Performed for each feature map is the sum of the application of R different 2-dimensional N × N convolution filters (one per input channel/modality), plus a bias term which is added pixel-wise to each resulting spatial position.

Though the input to this operation is a M × M × R 3-dimensional tensor, the spatial topology being considered is 2-dimensional in the X-Y axial plane of the original brain volume. Special attention was given to the treatment of border pixels by the convolution operation. Throughout the proposed architecture, we employed the so-called valid-mode convolution, meaning that the filter response is not computed for pixel positions that are less than N/2 pixels away from the image border.

PROPOSED METHODOLOGY

We propose to use Deep Learning in Feature Extraction process of Medical Image Analysis. This work will be completed in following important stages:

- **Medical image database:** A database of real time medical images (MRI, CT and X-rays) of more than 100 persons will be developed. This will include persons of different age groups and sex. Few open-source databases will also be studied and subjected to the proposed work for comparing with the results of real time images.
- **Pre-processing:** This stage provides image pre-processing and denoising methods that are to be used for denoising medical images. Methods for speckle reduction and other additive noise signals will be studied and almost robust approach will be used for de-noising the medical images. The results will be compared in terms of peak signal to noise ratio (PSNR) and optimal method and its result will be subjected to further stages of implementation.
- **Segmentation and Feature Extraction:** Images after noise removal will be segmented using appropriate segmentation methods such as k-means and fuzzy k-means techniques. The segmented medical images will be subjected to feature extraction that includes size and shape-based features also few other statistical parameters.
- **Deep Learning for Feature Extraction:** Now, the important stage that we propose to implement in novel manner is use of Deep Learning for feature extraction and Training. The Deep learning aims using Convolutional neural network to give better results of accuracy of medical image analysis. Convolutional Neural Network (CNN) is a model of deep learning as classic example of deep learning. Convolutional neural networks (CNN) are both fully and locally connected to hidden layers unlike traditional neural network because for all fully connected networks, the operation becomes computationally intensive. **CNNs use parameter sharing, pooling and dropout also which reduce the number of common features to large extent and hence addressing the computational issues.** When CNNs are tested for large data set which is actually the requirement in classification-based applications the more computation is required. Fig. 1.2 shows a typical architecture of the deep neural network.

Figure 2. Transfer learning setting

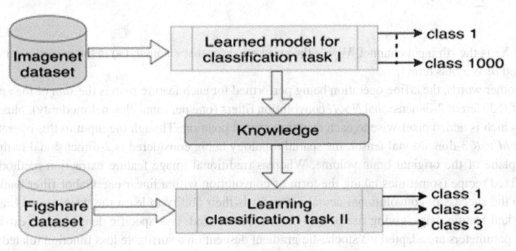

IMPLEMENTATION

An N×N filter convolved with an M× M input patch will result in a Q × Q output, where Q = M − N + 1. In Figure 1, M = 7, N = 3 and thus Q = 5. Note that the size (spatial width and height) of the kernels are hyper parameters that must be specified by the user. The steps of implementation are:

- A fully automatic method is proposed tested on BRATS 2013, 2015, 2018 scoreboard.
- To segment a brain, our method takes between 25 seconds and 3 minutes, which is one order of magnitude faster than most state-of-the-art methods.
- The CNN implements a novel two-pathway architecture that learns about the local details of the brain as well as the larger context. We also propose a two-phase training procedure which we have found is critical to deal with imbalanced label distributions.
- We employed a novel architecture as an efficient and conceptually clean alternative to popular structured output methods.

Novelty of the architecture lies in the way we consider the outputs of local paths as well as larger context (global paths). Also, the timing has been significantly improved. Moreover, the two stage training is generally not implemented as combined to evaluate the performance of the tumor detection unlike what we have attempted.

Computing a feature map in a convolutional layer as shown in Fig. 1 that consists of the following three steps:

Convolution of Kernels (Filters)

Each feature map **O**s is associated with one kernel (or several, in the case of Maxout). The feature map **O**s is computed as follows:

$$O_s = b_s + \sum_r W_{sr} * X_r$$

where $\mathbf{X}r$ is the rth input channel, $\mathbf{W}sr$ is the sub-kernel for that channel, $(*)$ is the convolution operation and bs is a bias term4.

In other words, the affine operation being performed for each feature map is the *sum* of the application of R different 2-dimensional $N \times N$ convolution filters (one per input channel/modality), plus a bias term which is added pixel-wise to each resulting spatial position. Though the input to this operation is a $M \times M \times R$ 3-dimensional tensor, the spatial topology being considered is 2-dimensional in the X-Y axial plane of the original brain volume. Whereas traditional image feature extraction methods rely on a fixed recipe (sometimes taking the form of convolution with a linear e.g. Gabor filter bank), the key to the success of convolutional neural networks is their ability to learn the weights and biases of individual feature maps, giving rise to data-driven, customized, task-specific dense feature extractors. These parameters are adapted via stochastic gradient descent on a surrogate loss function related to the misclassification error, with gradients computed efficiently via the backpropagation algorithm

Special attention is paid to the treatment of border pixels by the convolution operation. Throughout the proposed multipath architecture, we employed the so-called *valid-mode* convolution, meaning that the filter response is not computed for pixel positions that are less than bN=2c pixels away from the image border. An NxN filter convolved with an MxM input patch will result in a $Q \times Q$ output, where $Q = M - N + 1$. In Fig. 1, $M = 7$, $N = 3$ and thus $Q = 5$. Note that the size (spatial width and height) of the kernels are hyper parameters that must be specified by the user.

Non-Linear Activation Function

To obtain features that are non-linear transformations of the input, an element-wise non-linearity is applied to the result of the kernel convolution. There are multiple choices for this non-linearity, such as the sigmoid, hyperbolic tangent and rectified linear functions. Maxout nonlinearity is shown to be particularly effective at modeling useful features (Remirez, 2018; Wang, 2019 & Xiao, 2016). Maxout features are associated with multiple kernels $\mathbf{W}s$. This implies each Maxout map $\mathbf{Z}s$ is associated with K feature maps: f$\mathbf{O}s$; $\mathbf{O}s$+1;::::; $\mathbf{O}s$+K-1g. Note that in Fig. 1, the Maxout maps are associated with $K = 2$ feature maps. Maxout features correspond to taking the max over the feature maps $\mathbf{O}$, individually for each spatial position:

$$Z_{s,i,j} = \max\{O_{s,i,j}, O_{s+1,i,j}, ..., O_{s+k-1,i,j}\}$$

where i; j are spatial positions. Maxout features are thus equivalent to using a convex activation function, but whose shape is adaptive and depends on the values taken by the kernels.

Max Pooling (Output Pool)

This operation consists of taking the maximum feature (neuron) value over sub-windows within each feature map. This can be formalized as follows: where p determines the max pooling window size. The sub-windows can be overlapping or not (Fig. 1 shows an overlapping configuration). The max-pooling operation shrinks the size of the feature map. This is controlled by the pooling size p and the stride hyperparameter, which corresponds to the horizontal and vertical increments at which pooling sub-windows are positioned. Let S be the stride value and $Q \times Q$ be the shape of the feature map before max-pooling. The figure depicts that the MRI images are subjected for feature extraction after selecting ROC (region of convergence) and then tumor region is identified.

The output of the max-pooling operation would be of size $D \times D$, where $D = (Q - p) = S + 1$.

Figure 3. Output of the max pooling operation

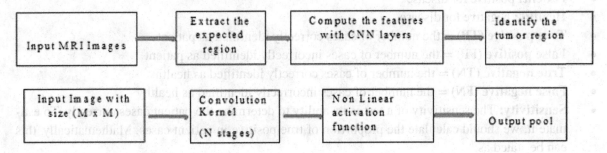

TRAINING OF THE METHOD

Now the training is discussed in this section.

Gradient Descent: By interpreting the output of the convolutional network as a model for the distribution over segmentation labels, a natural training criterion is to maximize the probability of all labels in our training set or, equivalently, to minimize the negative log-probability:

$$\log p(\mathbf{Y}\mathbf{j}\mathbf{X}) = \mathrm{P}i\,j - \log p(Yi\,jj\mathbf{X}) \text{ for each labeled brain.}$$

Two-phase training: The training isdone by:

- The *complete* tumor region (including all four tumor structures).
- The *core* tumor region (including all tumor structures except "edema").
- The *enhancing* tumor region (including the "enhanced tumor" structure).

For each tumor region, *Dice* (identical to F measure), *Sensitivity* and *Specificity* are computed as follows:

$$\text{Dice } (P,\ T) = \frac{|\mathrm{P1} \cdot \mathrm{T1}|}{(|\mathrm{P1}| + |\mathrm{T1}|)/2}$$

$$\text{Sensitivity } (P,\ T) = \frac{|\mathrm{P1} \cdot \mathrm{T1}|}{|\mathrm{T1}|}$$

$$\text{Specificity } (P,\ T) = \frac{|P0 \cdot T0|}{|T0|}$$

where P represents the model predictions and T represents the ground truth labels. We also note as T_1 and T_0 the subset of voxels predicted as positives and negatives for the tumor region in question. Similarly, for P_1 and P_0.

- **Patient:** positive for disease
- **Healthy:** negative for disease
- **True positive (TP)** = the number of cases correctly identified as patient
- **False positive (FP)** = the number of cases incorrectly identified as patient
- **True negative (TN)** = the number of cases correctly identified as healthy
- **False negative (FN)** = the number of cases incorrectly identified as healthy
- **Sensitivity:** The sensitivity of a test is its ability to determine the patient cases correctly. To estimate it, we should calculate the proportion of true positive in patient cases. Mathematically, this can be stated as:
- Sensitivity= TP/ (TP+FN)
- **Specificity:** The specificity of a test is its ability to determine the healthy cases correctly. To estimate it, we should calculate the proportion of true negative in healthy cases. Mathematically, this can be stated as:
- Specificity=TN/(TN+FP)

EXPECTED OUTCOME OF PROPOSED WORK

- A thorough medical image review for CT, MRI and X-ray Images will be carried out if the proposed task were implemented.
- A larger range of medical image modalities will also result, but for CT, MRI and X-rays, both findings will surely be discussed.
- Methods used in traditional machine learning methods are contrasted with current. Deep learning can help to improve the outcomes of traditional learning approaches in a core focus of our study.
- The comparison will be conducted in terms of both quantitative and quality statistical parameters such as medical image diagnosis precision, PSNR and computational time.
- A set of metrics of performance measurement such as accuracy of CAD based medical image analysis will be suggested so that the same can be used for wide range of applications of medical image analysis. Since the research work on medical image processing using deep learning is limited in current research and therefore the proposed research work would give future prospects of Deep Learning based implementations in the field of medical image processing, analysis and diagnosis of diseases.

MULTIPATH CNN

In Multipath-CNN concept, we considered two path CNN architecture which has two pathways: a "local" path focusing on details and a "global" path more focused on the context. This can be seen in Fig. 2. In any conventional CNN, the input image is given to the CNN network as can be seen in Fig. 2 that the images are subjected to local and global path of CNN and after down sampling the tumor region is finally detected. The results of global as well as local path CNN are combined so that we can get the reduced size of features and identification of tumor is made more efficient and less time consuming.

The specifications of different parameters are:

Input- 6 X 40 x 40
Local path – 84 x 34 x 34, 84 x 30 x 30, 84 x 25 x 25
Global path – 180 x 25 x 25
concatenation layer - 264 x 25 x 25

Figure 4. Multipath CNN

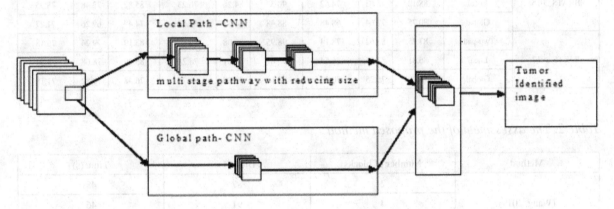

The training and testing are done with combination of HGG, LGG brain images. A comparison of our method for all three datasets is shown in Fig. 3. The images in left side are input images from three different datasets and the results are highlighted in right side after detection of tumor region in the input images. In the results, we can see that red, green, blue and yellow colors represent necrosis (label 1), edema (label 2), non-enhancing (label 3) and enhancing (label 4) tumors respectively.

The performance of the datasets was evaluated and compared in terms of sensitivity, specificity and Dice index as shown in *Table 1*. One of the promising method of deep learning (Wang, 2019) has been also compared with the proposed method and found that both time and Dice index are much better than (Wang, 2019). The comparison was done for BRATS2015 databases only since the method (Wang, 2019) tested this database only. If the improvement is resulted in terms of time as well Dice index for this databases which means that our results for BRATS2013 and BRATS2017 also outperform (Wang, 2019). In single path either as global or local, we can see that the performance measures are less as compared to two path system of implementation. This can be seen for all databases though in few cases, the improvement is not much. In other cases, the improvement in performance metrics Dice index,

Specificity and Sensitivity are better than the values of single path systems. There are other measures like accuracy and some region based statistics used for evaluation of performance but research studies (Sinha, 2004; Sinha, 2018 & Bhonsle, 2018) suggest that the measures used in this paper cover the scope of other metrics also which means that the metrics used are very effective and significant in case of brain tumor detection. In the applications related to breast cancer detection (Bonsle, 2018; Sinha, 2017; Patel, 2014; Patel, 2010 & Sinha, 2015), the region based features or measures are also useful for analysis of performance for the work.

Table 1. Performance of all datasets using multipath CNN

Data Set	Method Name	Dice (%)			Specificity (%)			Sensitivity(%)		
		Complete	Core	Enhancing	Complete	Core	Enhancing	Complete	Core	Enhancing
BRATS 2013	Two-path	87.22	81.14	79.68	94.01	83.45	75.38	84.72	79.18	76.37
	Local	86.72	79.48	77.72	91.58	80.05	72.51	84.15	78.85	74.22
	Global	81.61	77.85	74.29	93.15	84.16	71.08	78.18	71.34	72.47
BRATS 2015	Two-path	88.79	76.82	73.25	92.63	91.36	78.92	86.62	73.62	81.62
	Local	88.12	75.63	74.62	90.32	84.26	76.23	85.82	72.48	78.95
	Global	80.75	72.64	68.48	88.48	86.43	69.17	74.49	69.26	71.27
BATTS 2017	Two-path	87.25	83.62	78.14	98.95	89.08	79.87	83.19	79.24	76.18
	Local	86.81	82.05	76.54	98.81	89.81	78.28	83.29	78.68	73.54
	Global	78.09	75.25	70.48	97.18	90.28	81.71	76.48	70.82	71.18

Table 2. The assessment of the proposed method

Method	Number of blocks	Dice (%)	Time (s)
(Wang, 2019)	2	87	48
	4	91	46
	6	86	43
Proposed method of multipath CNN	2	88	29
	4	93	27
	6	89	26

Table 2 clearly shows improvement of the proposed work in comparison with a most important research in the field in terms of time as well as Dice percentage for all values of blocks.

CONCLUSION

With the aid of this proposed work, it is possible to infer that the image processing technique may be used to determine the growth and efficiency of brain tumours.Two new methods have been introduced in this paper to identify brain tumours. These modern methods are focused on both image recognition and

Figure 5. Multipath CNN result- Red, green, blue and yellow colors represent necrosis (label 1), edema (label 2), non-enhancing (label 3) and enhancing (label 4) tumors respectively.

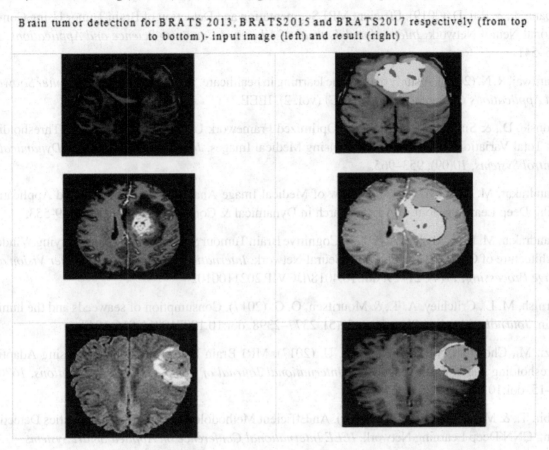

Brain tumor detection for BRATS 2013, BRATS2015 and BRATS2017 respectively (from top to bottom)- input image (left) and result (right)

neural networks. The techniques for image processing used in medicine, for example the MRI machine, are extremely useful and important. The robustness of the established system is the encouragement of human visual inspection, which normally directly underlines or notes the existence of abnormalities in the brain.

As a deep neural network-based strategy for brain tumor identification, we suggested a multipath CNN algorithm. The unique implementation of the architecture makes use of both local and global pathways. The improvement in performance is measured in terms of Dice index and time, and a considerable improvement was reported. The three datasets, BRTAS2013, BRATS2015, and BRATS2017, were examined for implementation, and the performance measures were determined to be better than those of a very promising method in the existing literature. The installation of two pathways, encompassing both local and global paths, considerably improved performance metrics, particularly time.Future scope of the paper includes developing a dataset for brain tumor images and testing with the use of CN based deep learning. The datasets are already available but developing it for real-time samples would probably help to get more robust outcome. The number of performance metrics and sample size can be extended to generalize the result and findings in more robust way. The tumor area and other dimensional parameters can also be included in the future work of this contribution.

REFERENCES

Alpana, J., & Rai, D. (2019). Efficient MRI Segmentation and Detection of Brain Tumor Using Convolutional Neural Network. *International Journal of Advanced Computer Science and Applications*, *10*, 536–541.

Bhardwaj, R. N. (2017). A study of machine learning in healthcare. *IEEE 41st Annual Computer Software and Applications Conference (COMPSAC)* (vol. 2). IEEE.

Bhonsle, D., & Sinha, G. R. (2018). An Optimized Framework Using Adaptive Wavelet Thresholding and Total Variation Technique for De-Noising Medical Images. *Jour of Adv Research in Dynamical & Control Systems*, *10*(09), 953–965.

Chandrakar, M. K. A. M. (2018). Review of Medical Image Analysis, Segmentation and Application Using Deep Learning. Jour of Adv Research in Dynamical & Control Systems, 10(1), 549-553.

Chandrakar, M. K., & Mishra, A. (2022). Cognitive Brain Tumour Segmentation Using Varying Window Architecture of Cascade Convolutional Neural Network. *International Journal of Computer Vision and Image Processing*, *11*(4), 21–29. doi:10.4018/IJCVIP.2021100102

Cornish, M. L., Critchley, A. T., & Mouritsen, O. G. (2017). Consumption of seaweeds and the human brain. *Journal of Applied Phycology*, *29*(5), 2377–2398. doi:10.100710811-016-1049-3

Kazi, M., Chowhan, S., & Kulkarni, V. U. (2017). MRI Brain Image Segmentation Using Adaptive Thresholding and K-means Algorithm. *International Journal of Computers and Applications*, *167*(8), 11–15. doi:10.5120/ijca2017914330

Kebir, T., & Mekaoui. (2018, November). An Efficient Methodology of Brain Abnormalities Detection using CNN Deep Learning Network. *IEEE International Conference on Applied Smart Systems.*

Kshatri, S. S., Singh, D., Narain, B., Bhatia, S., Quasim, M. T., & Sinha, G. R. (2021). An Empirical Analysis of Machine Learning Algorithms for Crime Prediction Using Stacked Generalization: An Ensemble Approach. *IEEE Access: Practical Innovations, Open Solutions*, *9*, 67488–67500. doi:10.1109/ACCESS.2021.3075140

Kshatri, S. S., Singh, D., Narain, B., Bhatia, S., Quasim, M. T., & Sinha, G. R. (2021). An Empirical Analysis of Machine Learning Algorithms for Crime Prediction Using Stacked Generalization: An Ensemble Approach. *IEEE Access: Practical Innovations, Open Solutions*, *9*, 67488–67500. doi:10.1109/ACCESS.2021.3075140

Kumar, B., Sinha, G. R., & Thakur, K. (2011). Quality assessment of compressed MR medical images using general regression neural network. *International Journal of Pure and Applied Sciences and Technology*, *7*(2), 158–169.

LeCun, Y. B., Bengio, Y., & Hinton, G. (2015). Deep learning. *Nature*, *521*(7553), 436–444. doi:10.1038/nature14539 PMID:26017442

LeCun, Y. B., Bengio, Y., & Hinton, G. (2015). Deep learning. *Nature*, *521*(7553), 436–444. doi:10.1038/nature14539 PMID:26017442

Madhupriya, G., Narayanan, M. G., Praveen, S., & Nivetha, B. (2019, October). Brain Tumor Segmentation with Deep Learning Technique. *IEEE 3rd International Conference on Trends in Electronics*, 758-763. 10.1109/ICOEI.2019.8862575

Malathi, M., & Sinthia, P. (2019). Brain Tumour Segmentation Using Convolutional Neural Network with Tensor Flow. *Asian Pacific Journal of Cancer Prevention*, 20(7), 2095–2101. doi:10.31557/APJCP.2019.20.7.2095 PMID:31350971

Mohammad, H., Axel, D., Antoine, B., Aaron, C., Pierre, M. Larochelle, H. (2016). Brain Tumor Segmentation with Deep Neural Networks. *Elsevier Medical Image Analysis*, 35, 18-31.

Mohmand Shahjahan Majib, M. M. (2021). VGG-SCNet: A VGG Net-Based Deep Learning Framework for Brain Tumor Detection on MRI Images. *IEEE Access: Practical Innovations, Open Solutions*, 9, 116942–116952. doi:10.1109/ACCESS.2021.3105874

Neethu, O., & Shruti. (2017). A Reliable Method for Brain Tumor Detection Using CNN Technique. *IOSR Journal of Electrical and Electronics Engineering*, 1, 64-68.

Patel, B., & Sinha, G. R. (2010). An adaptive K-means clustering algorithm for breast image segmentation. *International Journal of Computers and Applications*, 10(4), 35–38. doi:10.5120/1467-1982

Patel, B., & Sinha, G. R. (2014). Abnormality Detection and Classification in Computer-aided Diagnosis (CAD) of Breast Cancer Images. *Journal of Medical Imaging and Health Informatics*, 4(6), 881–885. doi:10.1166/jmihi.2014.1349

Remirez, I., Martin, A., & Schiavi, E. (2018, April). Optimization of A Variational Model Using Deep Learning: An Application to Brain Tumor Segmentation. *IEEE 15th International Symposium on Biomedical Imaging*, 631-635. 10.1109/ISBI.2018.8363654

Ren, X., Zhang, L., & Wang, Q. (2019, October). Brain MR Image Segmentation in Small Dataset with Adversarial Defense and Task Reorganization. *International Workshop on Machine learning in medical imaging*, 11861, 1-8. 10.1007/978-3-030-32692-0_1

Selvaraj, D., & Dhanasekaran, R. (2013). MRI Brain Image Segmentation Technique – A Review. *Indian Journal of Computer Science and Engineering*, 4, 264–281.

Selvathi, D., & Vanmathi, T. (2018, May). Brain Region Segmentation Using Convolutional Neural Network. *IEEE International Conferences on Electrical Energy System*, 661-666. 10.1109/ICEES.2018.8442394

Singh, B., Sinha, G. R., & Kar, M. (2010, March). Content Based Retrieval of MRI Images Using Integration of Color, Texture & Shape Features. In *IEEE International Conference on Advances in Communication, Network, and Computing*. IEEE Computer Society.

Singh, D., & Singh, S. (2020). Realising transfer learning through convolutional neural network and support vector machine for mental task classification. *Electronics Letters*, 56(25), 1375–1378. doi:10.1049/el.2020.2632

Sinha, G. R. (2015). Fuzzy based Medical Image Processing. In Advances in Medical Technologies and Clinical Practice (AMTCP) Book Series (pp. 45-61). IGI Global Publishers.

Sinha, G. R. (2017). Study of Assessment of Cognitive Ability of Human Brain using Deep Learning. *International Journal of Information Technology (Springer)*, *1*(1), 1–6. doi:10.100741870-017-0025-8

Sinha, G. R. (2020). Introduction and background to optimization theory. In Modern Optimization Methods for Science, Engineering and Technology. IOP Publishing.

Sinha, G. R., & Patel, B. (2014). *Medical Image Processing: Concepts and Application.* Prentice Hall of India.

Sinha, G. R., Raju, S., Patra, R., Aye, D. W., & Khin, D. T. (2018). Research Studies on Human Cognitive Ability. *International Journal of Intelligent Defense Support Systems*, *5*(4), 298–304. doi:10.1504/IJIDSS.2018.099891

Smith, R. A.-B., Manassaram-Baptiste, D., Brooks, D., Cokkinides, V., Doroshenk, M., Saslow, D., Wender, R. C., & Brawley, O. W. (2014). Cancer screening in the United States, 2014: A review of current American Cancer Society guidelines and current issues in cancer screening. *CA: a Cancer Journal for Clinicians*, *64*(1), 30–51. doi:10.3322/caac.21212 PMID:24408568

Smith, R. A.-B., Manassaram-Baptiste, D., Brooks, D., Cokkinides, V., Doroshenk, M., Saslow, D., Wender, R. C., & Brawley, O. W. (2014). Cancer screening in the United States, 2014: A review of current American Cancer Society guidelines and current issues in cancer screening. *CA: a Cancer Journal for Clinicians*, *64*(1), 30–51. doi:10.3322/caac.21212 PMID:24408568

Sobhaninia, Z. (2018, September). Brain Tumor Segmentation Using Deep Learning by Type Specific Sorting of Images. In *International Conference on Computer Vision and Pattern Recognition*. Cornell University.

Tarver, T. (2012). *Cancer Facts & Figures 2012.* American Cancer Society.

Tarver, T. (2012). *Cancer Facts & Figures 2012. American Cancer Society (ACS).* American Cancer Society. doi:10.1080/15398285.2012.701177

Wang, Y., Changsheng, L., Zhu, T., & Chongchong, Y. (2019, July). A Deep Learning Algorithm for Fully Automatic Brain Tumor Segmentation. *IEEE International Joint Conference on Neural Networks*, 1-5. 10.1109/IJCNN.2019.8852210

Xiao, Z., Huang, R., Ding, Y., Tian, L., Rongfeng, D., & Qin, Z. (2016, September). A Deep Learning-Based Segmentation Method for Brain Tumor in MR Images. *IEEE International Conference on Computational Advances in Bio and Medical Sciences.*

Chapter 20
Image Enhancement Under Gaussian Impulse Noise for Satellite and Medical Applications

Hazique Aetesam
Indian Institute of Technology, Patna, India

Suman Kumar Maji
Indian Institute of Technology, Patna, India

Jerome Boulanger
MRC Laboratory of Molecular Biology, Cambridge, UK

ABSTRACT

Remote sensing technologies such as hyperspectral imaging (HSI) and medical imaging techniques such as magnetic resonance imaging (MRI) form the pillars of human advancement. However, external factors like noise pose limitations on the accurate functioning of these imaging systems. Image enhancement techniques like denoising therefore form a crucial part in the proper functioning of these technologies. Noise in HSI and MRI are primarily a mixture of Gaussian and impulse noise. Image denoising techniques designed to handle mixed Gaussian-impulse (G-I) noise are thus an area of core research under the field of image restoration and enhancement. Therefore, this chapter discusses the mathematical preliminaries of G-I noise followed by an elaborate literature survey that covers the evolution of image denoising techniques for G-I noise from filtering-based to learning-based. An experimental analysis section is also provided that illustrates the performance of several denoising approaches under HSI and MRI, followed by a conclusion.

DOI: 10.4018/978-1-7998-8892-5.ch020

Figure 1. Difference between HSI and MSI

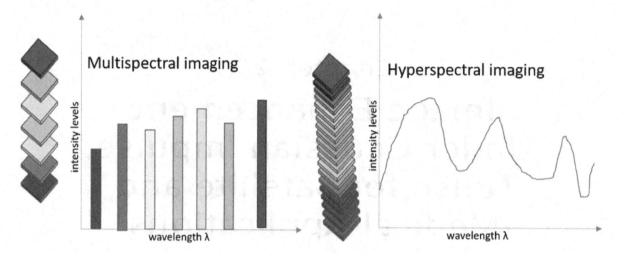

INTRODUCTION

Gaussian noise is the most common type of noise present in the image acquisitions systems. Since modelling Gaussian noise is simple and convenient, most of the optimization methods design the criterion function under this noise assumption. However, errors due to transmission errors, malfunctioning detector elements and faulty memory locations replace the underlying pixel intensity levels with random values. Since the intensity levels of these corrupted pixels are very different from the neighboring ones, they do not possess any information about the original pixel intensity or Gaussian corrupted pixels. Applying an algorithm designed for Gaussian noise to these kinds of images results in sub-optimal results. Since this is the result of impulse noise which heavily corrupt a limited number of pixels randomly, this random error cannot be properly modelled using Gaussian distribution. Since image denoising is a low-level computer vision task, its successful application helps in the accurate delivery of high-level vision-tasks like image classification, object detection, target tracking and semantic segmentation.

This chapter starts with the discussion on two different imaging domains corrupted by mixed Gaussian-impulse noise; namely hyperspectral imaging (HSI) and magnetic resonance imaging (MRI). Since Gaussian-impulse noise is the dominant character of noise in these imaging domains, image formation model under this noise assumption is imperative to appreciate the advantages obtained by applying denoising schemes specific to Gaussian-impulse noise. The next section talks about the image denoising schemes under four different solution strategies with emphasis on the types of Gaussian-impulse noise (i.e., fixed-valued or random-valued) and their limitations. In the last section, rigorous experimental evaluation on the two imaging domains; namely HSI and MRI are performed; followed by a conclusion.

Hyperspectral Imaging

Hyperspectral Imaging (HSI) is a notable development in the spectral imaging technology where images are captured using spectrometers over a wide range of electromagnetic spectrum; even beyond the visible parts. This helps in the visualization of those regions which are not captured using conventional RGB cameras. The typical range of EM spectrum used is **400*nm*** to **2500*nm***.

Figure 2. Basic image acquisition setup in hyperspectral imaging.

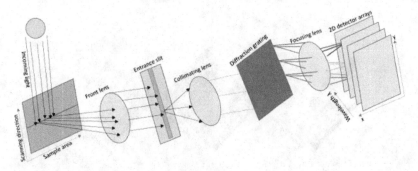

The spectrum of each pixel is defined by its reflectance from a range of wavelengths. On the other hand, a 2D image in the spatial plane is defined by its (*x,y*) coordinates. An entire cube is defined by (*x,y,λ*); where *λ* = wavelength of light at which image is captured. An HSI datacube is differentiated from multi-spectral imaging (MSI) based on their mode of acquisition; "discrete and narrow". In MSI, each spatial band is separated by discrete wavelengths while in HSI, it is contiguous. Moreover, in HSI each spatial image plane is captured over very narrow range of wavelengths; however, in MSI, this range is somewhat broader. This distinction is very well visualized in Figure 1, where x-*ax*is represents the wavelength range where a particular pixel is captured and y-*ax*is represents the reflectance captured at different wavelengths over that pixel. This representation of a pixel is also called the spectral signature of a pixel. We can see from the figure that in HSI pixel is recorded for a continuous stretch but in MSI, there are periodic breaks. Along with the spatial resolution over a 2D plane in conventional imaging systems, in HSI, there is a related resolution type, called spectral resolution. More is the spectral resolution; more is the number of narrow bands over which entire image is captured. However, there is a trade-off between spectral resolution and signal-to-noise ratio which we shall discuss in a later section. Also, based on the argument of spectral resolution, we can conclude that HSI has better spectral resolution than MSI.

Basic Imaging Setup

The basic setup of hyperspectral imaging is shown in Figure 2. It consists of a focusing lens which focuses the parallel incoming light into a narrow beam to be projected onto a narrow slit. The most important part of the setup is a diffraction grating which is an optical equipment that splits incoming light into different wavelengths just like a prism and project them into different spatial locations at the imaging sensor. However, the diffraction grating is restricted by its limited wavelength range of operation. Based on how pixels are recorded at the imaging sensor; there are three different modes of acquisition (shown in Figure 3):

- **Spatial Scanners:** They can be of two different types: pushbroom and wiskbroom scanners. In the former, data is collected using moving platform over one spatial dimension of the scene under investigation. In the latter; which is also called point scanning method; point-like aperture is utilized and sensors are 1-dimensional rather than 2D.
- **Spectral Scanners:** These scanners record a mono-chromatic data (2D image) at different wavelengths and club them together to obtain a 3D data.

Figure 3. HSI scanning technologies.

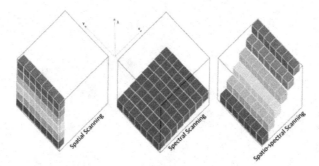

- **Non-Scanning Method:** Also called the snapshot imaging technique, the whole datacube is captured at once using this method. However, it is computationally more intensive.
- **Spatio-Spectral Scanners:** Developed quite recently in 2014 with the introduction of more advanced sensor technologies, spatio-spectral scanners acquire a colour coded representation for each spatial location (*x,y*).

Drawbacks/Limitations due to Noise

Image degradation in hyperspectral imaging is the contribution of multiple factors:

- **Factors responsible for Gaussian noise:**

There are two different factors responsible for Gaussian noise in HSI. Dark current denotes the emission of thermal energy from the charged coupled devices (CCD). This leads to statistical variation in the number of electrons that go to a high energy state; thus contributing to more intensity levels in the output image than what is present in the actual remotely sensed scene (Manea & Calin, 2015). When the spectral resolution is high; more number of bands need to be recorded with closely separated energy levels; contributing to limited radiance energy (Y. Chen et al., 2017). Higher spectral resolution means finer divisions in wavelength binning and limited capture of radiance energy. This results in low-intensity levels which means low signal-to-noise ratio (SNR).

- **Factors Responsible for Impulse Noise:**

Due to errors in the sensor elements or faulty memory locations during quantization of pixel values; dead pixels are recorded at sensor locations; rather than true intensity levels (Aggarwal & Majumdar, 2016). In a real-time application of remote sensing using HSI, data needs to be continuously transmitted to ground-based stations using wireless media. Over-/under-estimation of digitized values leads to errors that are random in nature (Arab et al., 2019). Radiometric resolution is the number of bits used to specify the intensity levels of a pixel. High radiometric resolution means a greater number of bits used to specify the pixel values. Usually, to mitigate the communication burden while transmitting data to ground-based stations, images are normalized to a lesser number of pixels. This is rendered as horizontal/vertical stripes in the remotely sensed images (Z. Wang et al., 2020) (see Fig. 4).

Figure 4. Noisy Indian pines (left), Salinas dataset obtained from Airborne Visible/Infrared Imaging Spectrometer (AVIRIS) sensor (center) and Horizontal stripe noise in Urban hyperspectral data (right).

As discussed in the preceding paragraphs, noise is HSI data is modelled using mixed Gaussian-impulse noise (Aetesam et al., 2019; Aetesam, Maji, et al., 2020; Aetesam, Poonam, et al., 2020; Aetesam & Maji, 2022b; He et al., 2015a, 2018; H. Zhang et al., 2013). Fig. 4 shows some real examples of HSI data acquired from different spectrometers.

Magnetic Resonance Imaging

Magnetic Resonance Imaging (MRI) was invented independently by two physicists named Felix Bloch and Edward Mills Purcell in 1947. It was initially used at the clinical level in 1977 by three clinicians: Paul Lauterbur, Peter Mansfield and Raymond Damadian. MRI makes use of magnetic field and radio frequencies rather than ionizing radiation used in x-rays and CT scans. Hence, it is a safer imaging modality but is limited by its noisy and slow operation. The strength of the field is measured in Tesla (T). The majority of MRI machines used in clinical practice operate at 1.5T to 3T magnetic field strength which is 50 thousand times more than that of the earth's magnetic field.

Working Principle and Imaging Setup

Angular momentum and spin of magnetic materials are changed when placed in an external magnetic field. These properties at the sub-atomic level are interpreted by quantum electrodynamics. Every sub-atomic particle is rotating at its position giving rise to an electromagnetic field in its environment just like a current-carrying particle according to Faraday's Law of magnetic induction. Nuclear spin is denoted by $\mathcal{I}$ and its value varies between 0 and 8 in increments of ½. Electron also has its spin of $\frac{1}{2}$. Even/even isotope has spin $\mathcal{I} = 0$. Odd/odd isotope also has spin $\mathcal{I} = 0$. Only for even/odd isotope, $\mathcal{I} = \frac{1}{2}$. Only such isotopes are suitable for nuclear magnetic resonance (NMR) when placed in an external field. The human body is composed of 70% water content which is made up of hydrogen and oxygen atoms. Owing to its abundance with $\mathcal{I} = \frac{1}{2}$, MRI relies on the magnetic properties of hydrogen atoms to produce images. The hydrogen atom is composed of a single proton with no neutron. As a spinning charged particle, it produces a magnetic field called magnetic dipole moment (MDM); de-

Figure 5. Block diagram for an MRI system.

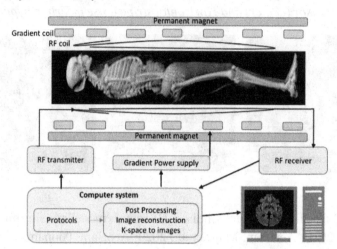

noted by μ. For protons, it is $\mu = \gamma\mathcal{I}$; where $\gamma=$ gyromagnetic ratio. Normally, protons are oriented randomly so there is no overall magnetic field.

The MRI system is composed of a primary magnet, the gradient magnets, radio-frequency coils and a computer system. A typical MRI setup is shown in Figure 5. MRI differs from CT scan as it uses magnetic field and radio frequency rather than ionizing radiation. The primary magnetic field B_0 refers to the strength of the static permanent field. This magnetic field is directed carefully to enable hydrogen atom spin and precession, as is shown in Figure 6.

The radiofrequency or RF coils are used to receive signals to create images as protons resume their state in primary magnetic field after the application of RF pulse. This is called relaxation as shown in Figure 7. Relaxation in the longitudinal axis is $T1$ relaxation. Relaxation in the transverse axis is $T2$ relaxation. M is a net magnetization vector that rotates in space that can be resolved in three components: $M_x(t)$ and $M_y(t)$ called the longitudinal components and $M_z(t)$ being the transverse component; as a function of time. After the RF pulse, several protons flip to their low energy state parallel to the magnetic field i.e., z-axis; giving energy to the surrounding medium. Hence, M does not precess around B_0 indefinitely but returns to its initial alignment parallel to B_0 to its equilibrium magnitude M_0. This results in changes in the longitudinal relaxation, known as $T1$ relaxation or spin-lattice relaxation. The longitudinal magnetization $T1$ relaxation is not instantaneous. We owe this to Felix Bloch.

Figure 6. Precession of H protons after application of B_0.

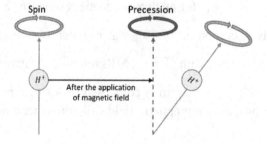

Figure 7. T-1 Relaxation (left) and T-2 Relaxation (right).

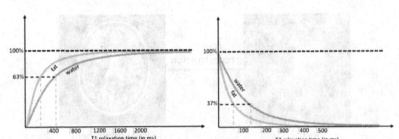

$$M_{z,t} = M_0\left(1 - e^{-t/T_1}\right)$$

On a plot of magnetization over time, magnetization increases in time in the $T1$ curve. The longitudinal relaxation time $T1$ denotes the time required for M_z to grow from 0 to $(1-1/e)$ or about 63% of its final value. The $T1$ relaxation time varies depending on the tissue composition and structure. For example, water molecules move rapidly and do not move to a low energy state quickly. So $T1$ relaxation takes longer. After the RF pulse, protons that are in phase begin to de-phase to the transverse x–y axis. This is known as spin-spin relaxation. Although M_0 (net magnetization due to the application of primary magnetic field) is very small with respect to the external magnetic field B_0, the entire MR acquisition is based on the manipulation of M_0. Since M_0 is so tiny and it is pointing in the same direction as B_0, it cannot be measured directly. We can measure it in the transverse plane. We make use of radiofrequency pulse at Larmor frequency. So, for H_2 protons, it is 63 Mhz. This generates a new magnetic field called B_1. The protons tend to precess around B_1. So, if B_1 is applied along the z-axis, the photons start to precess around the x–y plane, giving rise to $M_{x,y}$. If there is no dephasing, the protons continue to precess with constant amplitude. But the signal dissipates. The reason for this is that it turns out that $M_{x,y}$ is not a single dipole but it is the sum of multiple individual dipoles. So, it is the vector dipole. These individual dipoles start to get out of phase once radio-frequency is stopped. This exponential decay is given by Felix plot:

$$M_{xy,t} = M_0\left(1 - e^{-t/T_2}\right)$$

This results in a reduction in transverse magnetization with T2 as the transverse relaxation time denoting the time required for M_x or M_y to decay to $1/e$ from the initial maximum value. Plotting transverse magnetization in the x-y plane versus time shows a decrease in magnetization over time (Figure 7 (**right**)). In reality, spins dephase more quickly than T2 due to inhomogeneity in the magnetic field B_0. The combination of T2 relaxation and field inhomogeneity is called T2*. T2 relaxation time varies between tissues. For example, water molecules move quickly and as a result, there is less inhomogeneity. Therefore, T2 relaxation takes longer. The net magnetic vector is the sum of longitudinal and transverse magnetization.

The computer system receives the RF signal and performs analog to digital conversion. The digital signal representing the imaged body parts are stored in temporary image space or k-space as shown in Figure 8.

Figure 8. Fourier Transform of the K-space signal.

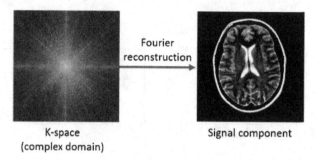

Limitations/ Drawbacks due to Noise

To appreciate the need of recovering image details from a corrupted MR image, we need to look at the physical significance of the image acquisition process in generating noise and artefacts in the image. The original image obtained from RF coils are in the frequency domain; present in temporary storage; called k-space. It consists of real and imaginary components of signal and noise. The noise component present is complex and Gaussian in nature (Henkelman, 1985). To convert it into imaging space, inverse discrete Fourier transform (IDFT) is computed. The resultant image is composed of complex-valued signals in real and imaginary planes (Nowak, 1999). Signal in the resultant image is still corrupted by additive Gaussian noise; due to the orthogonality of Fourier transform. In the following two paragraphs, we separately discuss factors contributing to Gaussian and impulse noise in MR images.

- **Factors Leading to Gaussian Noise**

Gaussian noise is created due to thermal agitation generated from the patient's body in the receivers' coils elements. This, thermal/ Nyquist/Johnson noise, leads to thermal agitation in charge carriers within the electrical equipment (McGraw et al., 2004). Static field intensity, tissue inhomogeneity and bandwidth of the receiver's elements are among the other factors leading to noise in MR images (Luisier et al., 2012). Greater is the amount of the static magnetic field; more is the precession frequency and more is the amount of RF energy received by RF coils during the relaxation phase. Hence, lower levels of static field intensity produce low contrast images; hence low signal-to-noise ratio (SNR). Low bandwidth of the receiver elements causes less RF energy from protons returning to the relaxation state. Hence, low SNR images. Stochastic variation in signal intensity, also known as magnetic susceptibility, is denoted by $\chi=J/B$, where B= external magnetic field and J= internal polarization. This internal polarization J is the function of tissue composition. Most biological tissues are diamagnetic which oppose the external magnetic field; lowering the overall magnetization vector and leading to a decreased contrast in the acquired images. On the other hand, there are low contributing para-, superpara- and ferromagnetic materials (in blood cells) (Ibrahim et al., 2009) as well. In pulsed nuclear magnetic resonance imaging (T1- and T2-weighted images), when RF coils generate signals at Larmor frequency, all protons precess together. As a result, the magnetic field of one proton is affected by the magnetic field of neighboring protons. This leads to free induction decay or overall dampening of the signal strength. This results in low RF energy detected by coils (Veraart et al., 2016).

- **Factors Leading to Impulse Noise**

In general, impulse noise is generated during analog-to-digital conversion of signal and error in bit transmission (HosseinKhani et al., 2019; Sheela & Suganthi, 2020). The RF energy generated by protons and detected by RF coils need to be converted to discrete pixel values. Due to sampling, quantization errors and faulty memory locations, random noise is augmented to the original pixel values. It also occurs due to an error in the transmission of RF signal in the free space to the coils (Halefoğlu, 2018; HosseinKhani et al., 2016; Mafi et al., 2017). Sometimes, the alignment of the RF coils is improper; leading to random errors.

Noise in MRI is, therefore, more complex due to the coexistence of different types of noise (Liu et al., 2018), and with the developments in modern MRI systems, the previous stationary noise model (Gudbjartsson & Patz, 1995) in MRI is being replaced with more complex mixed noise patterns (Aja-Fernández & Vegas-Sánchez-Ferrero, 2016; Liu et al., 2018). Following the above discussions, one can apprehend that Gaussian noise due to thermal agitation (Aetesam & Maji, 2022a; Bermudez et al., 2018; Moreno López et al., 2021; Tasdizen, 2009; Y. Wang & Zhou, 2006; Y. Zhu et al., 2020) as well as impulse noise due to transmission errors (Halefoğlu, 2018; Isa et al., 2015a; Shlykov et al., 2020; Toprak & Güler, 2007a, 2007b) contribute heavily to MR image degradation. Therefore, in this chapter, we have considered a Gaussian-impulse mixed noise model for MRI denoising (Aetesam & Maji, 2020, 2021; Halefoğlu, 2018; Isa et al., 2015b; Shlykov et al., 2020).

Image Formation Model

For an image corrupted by Gaussian noise, image formation model is given by:

$$y = x + g \tag{1}$$

where g is additive Gaussian noise following normal distribution $N\left(0, \sigma_n^2\right)$ with mean 0 and standard deviation σg. Gaussian noise affects all pixels in the similar manner with same intensity. On the other hand, for an image corrupted by impulse noise, the pixel value is replaced with a random value, mainly because of bit transmission error or faulty memory locations in the camera sensors. Impulse noise can be of two different types: fixed-valued impulse noise (FVIN) and random-valued impulse noise (RVIN) (Q. Jin et al., 2017; López-Rubio, 2010a; Rodriguez, 2013). Salt-and-pepper noise is an example of FVIN. With the assumption that the dynamic range of the image is [gm_{in} gm_{ax}], in FVIN, pixel values are randomly replaced with values; either gm_{in} or gm_{ax}. It can be mathematically represented in Equation 2 as follows:

$$y = \begin{cases} s = g_{\min}, & \text{with probability } p/2 \\ s = g_{\max}, & \text{with probability } p/2 \\ x, & \text{with probability } 1-p \end{cases} \tag{2}$$

considering that pixels corrupted by FVIN can have only two extreme random values $s=g_{\min}$ or $s=g_{\max}$; each with the same probability of occurrence $p/2$. Hence, it is equally probable for a pixel to be corrupted by either of these extreme values. As a result, in this case, the random variable s follows Bernoulli distribution. On the other hand, in the case of random-valued impulse noise, a corrupted pixel can have any value uniformly distributed in the range $s=[g_{min}, g_{max}]$. Hence, for RVIN, image formation model can be represented as:

$$y = \begin{cases} s, \text{with probability } p \\ x, \text{with probability } 1-p \end{cases} \tag{3}$$

Further, for an image corrupted by a combination of Gaussian noise and RVIN, image formation model can be modified as:

$$y = \begin{cases} s, \text{with probability } p \\ x+g, \text{with probability } 1-p \end{cases} \tag{4}$$

It can be inferred from Equation 4 that a pixel is corrupted by either Gaussian noise or RVIN. The intuition behind this is that every pixel is initially corrupted by Gaussian noise. If a pixel is further corrupted by impulse pixel with probability p; it does not possess any information about the original pixel or the Gaussian corrupted pixel. Therefore, a pixel is either corrupted by impulse noise or Gaussian noise (López-Rubio, 2010a). Under such a scenario, if a pixel is corrupted by Gaussian noise, it is corrupted with probability $1-p$. Additionally, RVIN can be considered as a more general case of salt-and-pepper noise; as RVIN considers any random value uniformly from the range $[g_{min}, g_{max}]$. This includes the extreme values g_{min} and g_{max} as well. Thus, FVIN is a limiting case of RVIN. Conclusively, for an image corrupted by mixed noise, the image formation model can be simplified as (T. Huang et al., 2017) (Equation 5):

$$y_i = x_i + g_i + s_i \tag{5}$$

So, for a pixel corrupted by Gaussian noise, $s_i=0$ and a pixel corrupted by impulse noise which was earlier corrupted by Gaussian noise, $s=y-x-g$. For a general scenario, the subscript can be dropped to obtain the final image formation model in Equation 6:

$$y = x + g + s \tag{6}$$

Further, it is important to notice that due to pixel value range clipping (in our case $g_{min}=0$ and $g_{max}=1$), the distribution does not remain uniform or multi-modal but follows Laplace distribution (T. Huang et al., 2017; Jiang et al., 2014; Yuan & Ghanem, 2017; Zeng et al., 2019); denoted as $\mathcal{L}(0,\sigma_s)$, with 0 as the location parameter and σs as the scale parameter. More is the intensity level of noise; more is the value of this parameter σs. To validate the argument made here, an empirical study is conducted on data corrupted by Gaussian/impulse noise. In Figure 9, clean le*na i*mage (Figure. 9a) is corrupted by Gaussian (Figure 9b) and impulse (Figure 9c) noise. Figure 9d and Figure 9e show the histogram of noise for Gaussian and impulse noise respectively. Further, Figure 9f shows the histogram of a 1-D signal corrupted by theoretical Laplacian distribution. It can be observed that the histogram of impulse noise in Figure 9e resembles more to that of the theoretical Laplace distribution than to the Gaussian distribution.

Figure 9. (a) Original image corrupted by (b) Gaussian noise (σ2=0.04) and (c) impulse noise (10%), empirical distribution of (d) Gaussian and (e) impulse noise, (f) signal corrupted by ideal Laplace distribution.

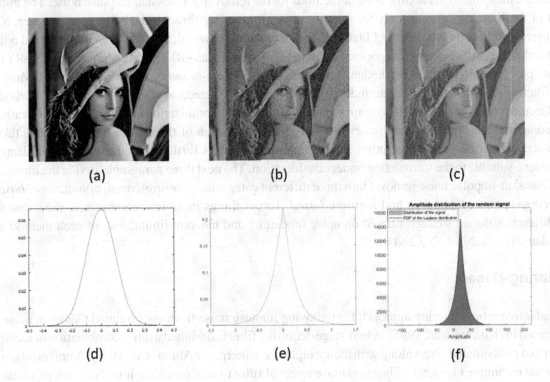

Hence, the following conclusion can be made here: *Laplace distribution is used to approximate impulse noise.*

Heavy-tailed distribution: It is a category of distribution that has many values away from the central mean value (Foss et al., 2011). In other words, it has heavier tails than exponential distribution. This has applications in micro-finance and marketing domains. However, the scope of this chapter is limited to the imaging domain. Laplace distribution belongs to the family of heavy-tailed distributions because it decays slower than that of Gaussian distribution (can also be seen in Figure 9f). Impulse noise is also called sparse noise because it affects only a limited number of pixels, but whichever pixel it affects; it affects them heavily. Another way of interpreting Laplace distribution is: the probability that a pixel is Laplace distributed is quite low but if it; the random value associated with that pixel is quite high. Since this is in direct correspondence with the plot of theoretical Laplace distribution, this is one more motivation to approximate impulse noise with Laplace distribution.

Note: A word of caution before ending this section: *The term impulse noise, sparse noise or Laplacian noise is used synonymously in this chapter. They mean the same irrespective of the terminology used.*

PREVIOUS WORK ON GAUSSIAN IMPULSE NOISE

There are many bases of classification of methods for the removal of Gaussian-impulse noise. The initial part of the literature account only for impulse noise. Proceeding through the subsequent paragraph, it is observed that there is a dearth of literature for mixed noise removal. Further, even under mixed noise removal, there are three major categories: Gaussian+FVIN, Gaussian+RVIN and Gaussian+FVIN+RVIN. Other basis of classification is whether the technique is *filtering-based* or *optimization-based*. Most of the filtering-based methods operate under a two-phase strategy: detection of impulse corrupted pixels and replacement of erroneous pixels with appropriate values. Under optimization and filtering+optimization-based approaches, probabilistic framework and prior information of the data to be recovered is taken into account for designing the optimization framework which is further solved using an optimization technique suitable to the formulation under consideration. The next three paragraphs divide the literature on Gaussian-impulse noise removal into three different categories: *filtering-based*, *optimization-based*, *filtering+optimization-based* and *learning-based*. To put things more into comparison, the summary of different solution strategies based on noise modelling and inherent limitation/s of each method are tabulated (see Table 1, 2, 3 and 4).

Filtering-Based

An adaptive robust filtering approach for removing impulse noise from uncorrelated Gaussian noise is proposed in (Kim & Efron, 1995). A two-stage denoising filter is designed using a combination of identity filter and rank ordered filters along with their weighted counterparts(Abreu et al., 1996). A universal noise removal technique to extend a Gaussian noise removal filter to accommodate impulse noise and further extended to remove any combination of Gaussian-impulse noise is explored in (Garnett et al., 2005). Here, Rank ordered absolute difference (ROAD) statistic is utilized to differentiate the edge pixels from impulse corrupted pixels. The resultant ROAD measure is incorporated into the bilateral filter to create a new non-linear filter: trilateral filter. A modification of ROAD statistic called optimal weights mixed filter is proposed in (Q. Jin et al., 2017) with special emphasis on the removal of Gaussian-impulse noise. Here, ROAD statistic is combined with weights optimization. However, the method works only for low noise levels. In (Srinivasan & Ebenezer, 2007), the noisy pixels are replaced either with median value/neighbourhood pixel within the filtering window. To reduce the computational complexity, the window size is reduced to 3×3. The authors claim that this method of salt-and-pepper noise removal also works for high noise cases up to 90% and detail preserving edges up to 80% noise level. As an extension to the Srinivasan et al. method (Srinivasan & Ebenezer, 2007), authors in (Gupta et al., 2015) proposed a simple median filter for the detection of random-valued impulse corrupted pixels using dual-threshold values and different filtering window sizes. For an image corrupted by Gaussian and uniform impulse noise, a two-step process for the estimation of noise parameters followed by kernel regression scheme is followed in (López-Rubio, 2010a). Noise parameters are estimated with the assumption of Gaussian and triangular distribution for modelling data corrupted by Gaussian and impulse noise types respectively. The rationale behind this formulation of impulse noise is that a pixel corrupted by impulse noise does not carry any information about the original data or data previously corrupted by Gaussian noise. However, the method fails for a sufficiently high level of impulse noise. To mitigate the blurring effect in adaptive median filter and streaking artefact in Decision-based Algorithm, Modified Decision-based Unsymmetric Trimmed Median Filter (MBDUTMF) is proposed in (Esakkirajan et al., 2011) for the removal of Salt-and-Pepper noise. However, the choice of a small filtering window does not accommodate contextual information from a large section of neighbouring pixels. In a paper by (Xiong & Yin, 2011), authors divide each pixel into four distinct clusters and rule-based decisions are made to classify a pixel as noisy or noiseless. Region outlyingness ratio (ROR) detects impulse corrupted pixels based on absolute deviation to the median in each cluster. The detection phase is combined with non-local means for data filtering. An improved version of adaptive center weighted median filter (ACWMF); called improved ACWMF is combined with detail preserving variational method to recover impulse corrupted data. In IACWMF, fast iterative strategy is used to give different marks to noise candidates (Zhou et al., 2012). A quaternion vector filter is used in (L. Jin et al., 2012) to remove impulse noise from video sequences where directional colour distance in chromaticity and luminosity channels are calculated along horizontal, vertical and diagonal directions between the current and adjacent frames. A two-stage filtering approach for image corrupted by impulse noise is proposed in (Ramadan, 2012) where noisy pixels detected in the first phase are chosen as potential candidates for filtering in the second phase. Based on the self-similarity of image patches, a patch-based method towards the restoration of images corrupted by Gaussian- and random valued impulse noise is proposed in (Delon & Desolneux, 2013). The method works in two steps: first, identification of corresponding patches and estimating the underlying true uncorrupted patch amongst different corrupted versions. A decision-based impulse noise detector and an edge-preserving filter are proposed in (Lien et al., 2012). Directional absolute relative difference (DARD) statistic is introduced in (S. Chen et al., 2013) to remove impulse noise whereas spatial gradient filtering is used for filtering Gaussian noise from images. Noise model: G+FVIN, G+RVIN. Further, a VLSI architecture is designed for hardware implementation. The authors in (Smolka & Kusnik, 2015) claims to use a novel approach for measuring local pixel similarity based on the sum of distances in a given colour space between pixel of a block and samples taken from the neighbourhood of the central pixel. In order to remove spatial bias towards the center of uncorrupted pixels, author in (Kandemir et al., 2015) propose a three-phase approach for the removal of impulse noise. This includes detection, recalibration of weights and new intensity value replaced using unbiased weighted mean filter (UWMF). A patch-based weighted means filter is designed in (Hu et al., 2016) for the removal of mixed noise. Here, the concept of trilateral filter and non-local means filter is amalgamated to remove both Gaussian and impulse. In a paper by (L. Jin et al., 2016) et. Al, an effective distance measure obtained from quaternion representation of pixels, pixels are classified as noisy or noiseless based on four directional samples. Further, the modified peer group concept is utilized to detect impulse corrupted pixels and weighted vector median filter to used to recover those pixels. An adaptive non-local means approach is proposed in (X. Wang et al., 2016) for salt and pepper noise removal in an iterative fashion where the similarity weights are updatable across different iterations. Adaptive Riesz Mean Filter (ARmF) is used in [] for removing salt and pepper noise (Enginoğlu et al., 2019).

Fuzzy logic gained approaches have been explored in many denoising works pertaining to Gaussian-impulse noise. Therefore, in this paragraph, we explicitly describe such approaches. Authors in (Morillas et al., 2009) combined the concept of peer group with fuzzy logic to find the similarity of a peer group based on the pixel under consideration. Further, fuzzy switching noise filter is cascaded with fuzzy-based averaging filter. A two-step fuzzy detector and filtering process in designed for removal of impulse noise from coloured images inspired from ordered difference statistic(Camarena et al., 2010). A fuzzy logic approach for the removal of Gaussian-impulse noise from coloured images is proposed in (Camarena et al., 2012). An adaptive fuzzy filter is used in (Ahmed & Das, 2013) for the detection and filtering of impulse noise from corrupted data for noise level as high as 97%. A combination of fuzzy logic and

Table 1. Image Denoising using filtering-based approaches under impulse/Gaussian+impulse noise.

Paper	Noise-model	Limitations
(Kim & Efron, 1995)	G+FVIN	
(Abreu et al., 1996)	G+RVIN, G+FVIN	Computationally intensive.
(Garnett et al., 2005)	G+FVIN	Small window size produces blue at high noise levels
(Srinivasan & Ebenezer, 2007)	FVIN	Only works for salt-and-pepper noise
(Morillas et al., 2009)	G+RVIN	Rule-based fuzzy logic does not consider diverse noise patterns.
(López-Rubio, 2010a)	G+RVIN	Fails to work at sufficiently high levels of noise
(Camarena et al., 2010)	FVIN, RVIN	
(Esakkirajan et al., 2011)	FVIN	Does not accommodate contextual information from large section of neighbouring pixels
(Xiong & Yin, 2011)	FVIN, RVIN, G+RVIN, G+FVIN	
(Camarena et al., 2012)	G+FVIN, G+RVIN	
(Zhou et al., 2012)	RVIN	
(Ramadan, 2012)	FVIN	
(L. Jin et al., 2012)	RVIN	
(Lien et al., 2012)	FVIN	Does not work under mixed noise scenario
(Delon & Desolneux, 2013)	G+RVIN	creates blocking artefacts as a result of patch-based restoration
(Ahmed & Das, 2013)	FVIN	Works for only salt and pepper noise.
(S. Chen et al., 2013)	G+FVIN, G+RVIN	
(Gupta et al., 2015)	RVIN	Not able to differentiate noisy from edge pixels at high noise levels
(Smolka & Kusnik, 2015)	G+ RVIN	Image gradient sensitive to noise.
(Kandemir et al., 2015)	FVIN	
(Roy et al., 2016)	RVIN, FVIN	
(Hu et al., 2016)	RVIN, G+RVIN	Computationally intensive
(L. Jin et al., 2016)	RVIN	
(X. Wang et al., 2016)	FVIN	Iterative NLM is computationally demanding where the original implementation of NLM is already time consuming.
(Q. Jin et al., 2017)	G+FVIN	Works only for low noise levels
(Arora et al., 2018)	FVIN	Introduces blur due to small window size
(Roy et al., 2018)	RVIN	
(Gonzalez-Hidalgo et al., 2018)	FVIN	Handles only salt-and-pepper noise.
(Enginoğlu et al., 2019)	FVIN	
(González-Hidalgo et al., 2021)	FVIN	

SVM classification is used in (Roy et al., 2016) for the detection of noisy pixels from uncorrupted ones. An ANN is used for training the classification network. Similarly, an adaptive fuzzy filter is designed in (Roy et al., 2018) for removing RVIN from coloured images where correlation among noisy channels are considered and window size changes with local noise intensity. The information sets concepts from fuzzy logic and noise adaptive information set based switched median filter is used for the removal of impulse noise from medical images in (Arora et al., 2018). However, it focuses only on the removal of salt-and-pepper noise and introduces blur into the image due to the small window size. Authors in (Gonzalez-Hidalgo et al., 2018) design a fuzzy mathematical morphology-based filter to remove the consideration of noisy pixels in the computation of clean data. The authors claim to filter 5% to 98% of salt-and-pepper noise from images. Same set of authors propose a combination of fuzzy mathematical morphology and weighted arithmetic mean aggregation function to reduce wide range of salt-and-pepper noise(González-Hidalgo et al., 2021). Authors in (Mafi et al., 2019) provide an extensive overview of different kinds of filtering methods under Gaussian and impulse noise. Bases of classification include: spatial domain, transform domain, fuzzy-based, image morphology and neural network based. Table 1 provides a comparative analysis of the filtering-based methods in terms of the noise models and limitations of these approaches.

Optimization-Based

The optimization problem suggested in (Fu et al., 2006) compared the solution of two different optimization frameworks with additive Gaussian and non-Gaussian assumptions respectively along with forward observation operator. This is accomplished using ℓ-2 (Least-mixed norm (LMN)) and ℓ-1 (Least absolute deviation (LAD)) terms as the fidelity terms with ℓ-1 regularization term. The solution is obtained using interior point method where the problem is projected as linear/quadratic programming. In (López-Rubio, 2010a), error in the noisy sample is predicted using iterative reweighted norm and local image gradient covariance matrix is approximated using kernel regression. Using the low-rank assumption of image data and sparsity assumption of impulse corrupted pixels, an annihilating low-rank Hankel matrix (ALOHA) is proposed in (K. H. Jin & Ye, 2015) for data corrupted by Salt-and-pepper noise and random-valued impulse noise. The resultant optimization approach is extended to multi-channel images and ADMM is utilized as the optimization strategy. Authors in (Meng et al., 2014) modelled the mixed noise removal problem as the matrix completion problem from corrupted samplings using a combination of nuclear and L1 norm. solved using ALM method. A weighted least square approach is proposed in (Rodriguez et al., 2012) for the removal for mixed noise for greyscale and color images. A variational approach is formulated in (J. Zhang et al., 2012) to model the local and non-local consistency in images corrupted by mixed Gaussian impulse noise. Here local image smoothness is modelled using hyper-Laplacian prior while non-local sparse features are modelled using self-similar prior. The resultant optimization problem is solved using Split-Bregman. By framing the problem of impulse and mixed Gaussian-impulse noise removal, authors in (Yan, 2013) proposed a combination of blind inpainting and constrained ℓ_0- minimization for the recovery of clean data. The method is also extended to the image deconvolution case. A higher-order total variation as the regularization strategy for the removal of mixed Gaussian-impulse noise for data corrupted by noise and linear blurring operator is proposed in (S. Wang et al., 2013). The numerical problem is solved using a modified version of ADMM. Similarly, authors in (Wu, 2016) proposed a variable-splitting approach for the removal of Gaussian+salt and pepper noise and Gaussian+random-valued impulse noise. The classical ADMM is used for solving the optimization

Table 2. Image Denoising using optimization-based approaches under impulse/Gaussian+impulse noise.

Paper	Noise-model	Limitations
(Fu et al., 2006)	RVIN	Computationally intensive, especially under variable splitting optimization methods. Performance dependent on manual selection of hyperparameter selection.
(K. H. Jin & Ye, 2015)	FVIN+RVIN	
(Yan, 2013)	RVIN, G+RVIN	
(S. Wang et al., 2013)	G+RVIN	
(Wu, 2016)	G+RVIN, G+FVIN	
(Jiang et al., 2016)	G+RVIN, G+FVIN	
(López-Rubio, 2010b)	G+RVIN	
(Rodr\'\iguez et al., 2012)	G+FVIN, G+RVIN	Due to re-weighted norm, it provides only approximate results.
(J. Zhang et al., 2012)	G+RVIN, G+FVIN	
(Ma, Ng, et al., 2013)	FVIN, RVIN	ℓ_1-norm problems are difficult to optimize.
(Yuan & Ghanem, 2017)	FVIN, RVIN	Mathematically intractable due to non-convex problem
(Zeng et al., 2019)	FVIN, RVIN	
(Yuan & Ghanem, 2015)	FVIN, RVIN	
(Jung et al., 2017)	FVIN, RVIN	
(Wen et al., 2016)	FVIN	
(Jiang et al., 2014)	G+RVIN, G+FVIN	Limited by the underlying prior assumption on data and noise modelling.
(Meng et al., 2014)	G+FVIN	
(T. Huang et al., 2017)	G+RVIN, G+FVIN	
(Langer, 2017)	G+RVIN, G+FVIN	Parameter estimation can be expensive.
(Langer, 2019)	G+RVIN, G+FVIN	
(H. Zhu & Ng, 2020)	FVIN, RVIN, G+RVIN.	Requires data to be sparse in some domain.

problem. An automated parameter selection approach under L_1/L_2-TV is proposed in (Langer, 2017) which does not require initial estimation of outlier pixels. The resultant minimization is solved using ADM. The same author uses L_1/L_2-TV along with locally adaptive spatially variant regularization parameter (Langer, 2019). A box constraint minimization of L_1-TV is proposed in (Ma, Ng, et al., 2013) to remove impulse noise data. As claimed by the authors, the exact derivation of TV and its non-local version along with their proximal operators is the novelty of this work. In a variation to the one-phase approach (which does not require prior detection of impulse pixels), impulse corrupted pixels are first detected before being filtered. A patch-based representation model is used in (Jiang et al., 2016) along with sparsity constrained ℓ_1- norm as regularization term and data fidelity terms for the removal of Gaussian and both fixed-valued and random-valued impulse corrupted data. Authors in (Yuan & Ghanem, 2017) proposed an optimization-based solution for the removal of FVIN and RVIP using ℓ_0- norm minimization. To handle the resulting non-convex problem, the problem is reformulated as a biconvex mathematical program with equilibrium constraints which is further solved using proximal ADMM (PADMM). Based on non-Lipschitzian theories of ℓ_1 non-convex and non-convex TV variational models for the solution of data corrupted by impulse noise, authors in (Zeng et al., 2019) dealt the underlying problem by iteratively adding constraints to the supports of non-Lipschitzian terms. It is used for FVIN and RVIN. In the paper by (Yuan & Ghanem, 2015) et al, authors propose a non-convex approach for recovering data

Table 3. Image Denoising using filtering+optimization-based approaches under impulse/Gaussian+impulse noise.

Paper	Noise-model	Limitations
(Cai et al., 2007)	FVIN	Since the first step is detection of impulse corrupted pixels, the second step of optimization strategy is dependent on the successful application of first step; which in most of the cases fails for high impulse noise levels
(Y.-M. Huang et al., 2009)	G, FVIN, RVIN	Does not work for heavilty corrupted pixels
(Chan et al., 2010)	FVIN, RVIN	
(Xiao et al., 2011)	G+FVIN, G+RVIN	The resulting ℓ_0 - ℓ_1 is hard to optimize.
(Ma, Yu, et al., 2013)	FVIN	
(Lan & Zuo, 2014)	RVIN	
(Tofighi et al., 2015)	G+FVIN	
(Kimiaei & Rostami, 2016)	FVIN	
(J. Wang et al., 2020)	G+RVIN	Simulated annealing is a slow optimization technique.

corrupted by Gaussian and impulse noise using L_0-TV. The resultant optimization problem is solved using proximal alternating direction method of multipliers (PADMM). A non-smooth and non-convex TV-regularised L_q functional is used in (Jung et al., 2017) to remove impulse noise. The objective function is minimized using linearized ADMM. A compressed sensing based spare recovery of impulse corrupted data in proposed in (Wen et al., 2016) where the non-convex nature of general L_p norm residual error is handled using proximal projection of lp norm. This is solved using alternating direction method. Mixed noise removal for data corrupted by Gaussian+FVIN and Gaussian+RVIN is discussed in (Jiang et al., 2014) by Weighted Encoding with Sparse Non-Local Regularization (WESNR). Here, the sparsity and non-local prior is integrated into the regularization term for mixed-noise removal. A non-local low-rank regulariser is combined with the Laplacian scale mixture for the representation of impulse corrupted data in (Huang et al., 2017). In contrast with ℓ_p norm-based methods which require selection of proper thresholds, in this work, thresholds are adaptively learned from the observed noisy data. A structured dictionary learning approach is proposed in (H. Zhu & Ng, 2020) where two model-based approaches are proposed using L_p norm data fidelity (for noise reduction) and L_q norm regularization terms (for structural sparse model selection). Table 2 provides a comparative analysis of the filtering-based methods in terms of the noise models and limitations of these approaches.

Filtering+Optimization Based

The authors in (Cai et al., 2007) used a two-phase approach for the removal of impulse noise. In the first phase, impulse corrupted pixels are detected using an adaptive median filter and in the second phase, a variant of l_1- fidelity term is used. The global convergence of the resulting optimization problem is studied using two different optimization approaches: conjugate-gradient method and quasi-Newton method; even for high levels of noise. However, the method is only applicable for salt-and-pepper impulse noise. An alternating minimization approach is proposed in (Y.-M. Huang et al., 2009) to restore images corrupted by blur and Gaussian-impulse noise. After the detection of impulse corrupted pixels

Table 4. Learning-based approaches under Gaussian-impulse noise.

Paper	Noise-model	Limitations
(Islam et al., 2018)	G+FVIN, G+RVIN	
(Abiko & Ikehara, 2019)	G+FVIN, G+RVIN	Computationally intensive during training process.
(L. Jin et al., 2019)	RVIN	
(Noor et al., 2020)	G+FVIN	

in the first phase, l_1-data fidelity in the presence of TV regularization is explored in (Chan et al., 2010). The resulting variational approach is solved using a superlinearly convergent algorithm based upon Fenchel-duality and inexact semismooth Newton techniques. Authors in (Xiao et al., 2011) proposed a three-stage denoising approach: detection of outlier pixels using median filter, dictionary learning to reconstruct outlier-free pixels followed by $L_1 - L_0$ minimization of the resultant optimization problem. An impulse noise removal approach for FVIN under Gaussian/uniform blur is proposed in (Ma, Yu, et al., 2013) using a variational approach comprising three terms: data fidelity term, sparse representation prior and TV regularization term. However, the initial step is the pre-detection phase for impulse corrupted pixels. A combination of variational edge-preserving regularization method and adaptive switching median filter/adaptive non-local switching median filter is proposed in (Lan & Zuo, 2014) for detection of noisy pixels for the recovery of uncorrupted data from random-valued impulse corrupted pixels. In another work(Tofighi et al., 2015), to utilize local variations among pixels, the epigraphical projection of TV function is appended to Weiner filter. Weiner filter helps to exploit global correlations in the image. A two-phase impulse noise denoising approach is proposed in (Kimiaei & Rostami, 2016). Here, candidate salt-and-pepper corrupted pixels are identified using an adaptive median filter followed by a regularization functional in the second phase. A hybrid approach of conjugate gradient descent is employed for the global convergence of the algorithm. Authors in (J. Wang et al., 2020) proposed an underwater acoustic channel noise reduction using a combination of normal and symmetric alpha stable distribution. Here, the impulse noise is reduced using adaptive window median filter and Gaussian noise is suppressed using an enhanced wavelet threshold scheme (estimated using simulated annealing). However, simulated annealing used for global optimization is slow. Table 3 provides a comparative analysis of the filtering+optimization-based methods in terms of the noise models and limitations of these approaches.

Learning-Based

In recent times, it is observed that there is an emergence of learning-based methods designed specifically for the removal of Gaussian-impulse noise. Authors in (Islam et al., 2018) devised a rank- ordered filter (ROF) like median filter followed by bicubic interpolation as the preprocessing steps to feed the resultant data into a four stage convolutional network for learning clean data from noisy input. A two-stage training process is used in (Abiko & Ikehara, 2019) for the recovery of data corrupted by Gaussian and impulse noise. A two-stage noise elimination process is introduced in (Noor et al., 2020) using median filter for removing impulse noise and residual convolutional network for removing Gaussian noise. A two-stage learning approach is presented in (L. Jin et al., 2019) to recover the mixed nature of corrupted images. Here, the output of the classifier network is fed along with the noisy input data to a convolutional network to reconstruct the original data. The classifier identifies the noise-free pixels from the data. Table 4 provides a comparative analysis of the learning-based methods in terms of the noise models and limitations of these approaches.

EXPERIMENTAL ANALYSIS

The performance of all three classes of image denoising techniques (described in the previous section) under remote sensing and medical imaging is investigated in this section. It will be divided into two sections:

Analysis on Remote Sensing

In this section, experiments on synthetically corrupted hyperspectral data (HSI) and real data obtained from hyperspectral sensors are conducted. An HSI data consists of 3D data acquired from a wide range of electromagnetic spectrum. This facilitates visualization and analysis of those target areas which are not visible through conventional RGB cameras. The experimental evaluation is performed over nine different comparing methods; as follows:

- **LRMR**: Hyperspectral Image Restoration Using Low-Rank Matrix Recovery (H. Zhang et al., 2013).
- **LRTV**: Total-variation-regularized low-rank matrix factorization for hyperspectral image restoration (He et al., 2015b).
- **NMoG-RPCA:** Denoising hyperspectral image with non-iid noise structure (Y. Chen et al., 2017)
- **LRTDTV:** Hyperspectral image restoration via total variation regularized low-rank tensor decomposition(Y. Wang et al., 2017).
- **LRTDGS:** Hyperspectral image restoration using weighted group sparsity-regularized low-rank tensor decomposition (Y. Chen et al., 2019).
- **NAILRMA:** Hyperspectral image denoising via noise-adjusted iterative low-rank matrix approximation (He et al., 2015a).
- L1HyMixDe: Hyperspectral Mixed Noise Removal By ℓ_1-Norm-Based Subspace Representation (Zhuang & Ng, 2020).
- **HSI Prior:** Deep Hyperspectral Prior: Single-Image Denoising, Inpainting, Super-Resolution **(Sidorov & Yngve Hardeberg, 2019)**.
- **Bayesian-HSI:** Bayesian approach in a learning-based hyperspectral image denoising framework (Aetesam et al., 2021).

Two set of experiments are conducted. First one is for synthetic multi-spectral data synthetically corrupted by mixed Gaussian-impulse noise. The data is obtained from CAVE datasets in the wavelength range 400-700 nm producing 31 spectral bands. There are in total 32 images. One of them is chosen for our experimentation purpose by synthetically corrupting them with different levels of Gaussian-impulse noise. The visual results are depicted in Figure 10 for noise level **(G,I)= (10db, 15%)**.

Table 5. Mean PSNR and mean SSIM

Noise Levels		Methods	Datasets					
Gaussian (dB)	Impulse (%)		WDC		CAVE		ICVL	
			PSNR	SSIM	PSNR	SSIM	PSNR	SSIM
20	5	Noisy	33.81	0.825	30.45	0.81	30.79	0.78
		LRMR	35.41	0.899	32.69	0.86	36.05	0.883
		LLRGTV	36.86	0.854	31.11	0.829	37.79	0.903
		LRTDGS	43.49	0.944	34.71	0.9	38.07	0.914
		NAILRMA	37.72	0.91	34.96	0.877	38.41	0.929
		HSI Prior	40.12	0.912	36.87	0.95	40.77	0.94
		Bayesian-HSI	43.86	0.935	37.23	0.961	41.33	0.951
15	10	Noisy	28.86	0.706	29.7	0.746	29.44	0.766
		LRMR	34.04	0.866	33.77	0.866	34.41	0.854
		LLRGTV	33.77	0.85	33.5	0.849	34.75	0.862
		LRTDGS	34.42	0.863	36.08	0.873	35.09	0.862
		NAILRMA	33.89	0.832	34.08	0.753	34.1	0.785
		HSI Prior	34.92	0.855	37.63	0.891	35.6	0.86
		Bayesian-HSI	36.34	0.89	38.7	0.919	37.96	0.88
12	15	Noisy	27.69	0.687	28.51	0.616	28.27	0.615
		LRMR	30.81	0.707	32.04	0.816	31.03	0.778
		LLRGTV	30.72	0.69	31.84	0.806	31.42	0.794
		LRTDGS	31.41	0.711	32.44	0.828	32.21	0.818
		NAILRMA	33.89	0.732	31.17	0.714	31.68	0.747
		HSI Prior	31.53	0.679	33.28	0.831	32.25	0.829
		Bayesian-HSI	32.47	0.743	34.95	0.872	33.22	0.723
10	20	Noisy	24.53	0.507	25.33	0.514	26.1	0.507
		LRMR	29.01	0.669	28.84	0.746	28.57	0.706
		LLRGTV	28.97	0.651	26.98	0.746	28.99	0.732
		LRTDGS	29.3	0.673	30.51	0.787	30.14	0.778
		NAILRMA	29.11	0.642	29.57	0.673	29.83	0.714
		HSI Prior	29.24	0.624	31.01	0.781	30.03	0.739
		Bayesian-HSI	30.85	0.692	32.26	0.796	30.23	0.784
5	25	Noisy	23.6	0.436	23.86	0.478	23.81	0.487
		LRMR	27.51	0.532	28.37	0.676	27.42	0.625
		LLRGTV	27.48	0.514	28.67	0.702	27.95	0.681
		LRTDGS	27.54	0.54	28.73	0.736	28.37	0.736
		NAILRMA	27.38	0.508	28.07	0.633	28.14	0.677
		HSI Prior	27.31	0.51	28.97	0.747	28.2	0.733
		Bayesian-HSI	31.35	0.677	30.01	0.764	30.12	0.769

Figure 10. Experimental results on synthetically corrupted multispectral data obtained from the CAVE dataset for noise level (G, I)= (10 dB, 15%)

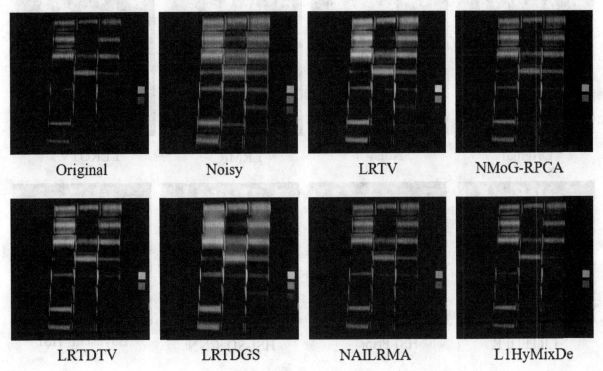

Original	Noisy	LRTV	NMoG-RPCA
LRTDTV	LRTDGS	NAILRMA	L1HyMixDe

Our second set of experiments are conducted on Washington DC dataset which is a popular benchmark for testing the restoration performance of different methods. The dataset is obtained from Hyperspectral Digital Imaging Collection Experiment (HYDICE) in the wavelength range **400nm** to **2500nm**. The size of the original data is **1280×307×191** where 191 is the total number of bands. To show the restoration performance over this dataset, a layerwise PSNR and SSIM comparison is shown in Figure 11. As we can observe, there are intermittent drop in the plot for both PSNR and SSIM for a few layers. This is more prominent in the layerwise SSIM results. A pseudo-color representation of visual results is depicted in Figure 12. As we can observe, the image restored by LLRGTV most closely represent the original data. On the other hand, artefacts can be observed in the results obtained by HSI Prior. However, ignoring the colour reproducibility of the respective methods, the visual produced by Bayesian-HSI is most detail preserving.

To provide an overall metric performance averaged over all layers of WDC data, we represent the PSNR and SSIM results in Table 5 for five different levels of Gaussian-impulse noise, namely, **(G,I)=(20dB,5%), (G;I)=(15dB,10%), (12dB,15%), (10dB, 20%)** and **(5dB,25%)**. For both PSNR and SSIM, Bayesian-HSI provides the best metric results.

Figure 13 shows the experimental results on real *Indian Pines* hyperspectral data obtained from Airborne Visible/Infrared Imaging Spectrometer (AVIRIS). The dimension of the 3D datacube is **145×145×224** obtained in the wavelength range **0.4–2.5μm**. The results are visualized in Figure 13.

Figure 11. PSNR and SSIM for WDC dataset for homogeneous ((G; I) = (10 dB, 20%)) noise.

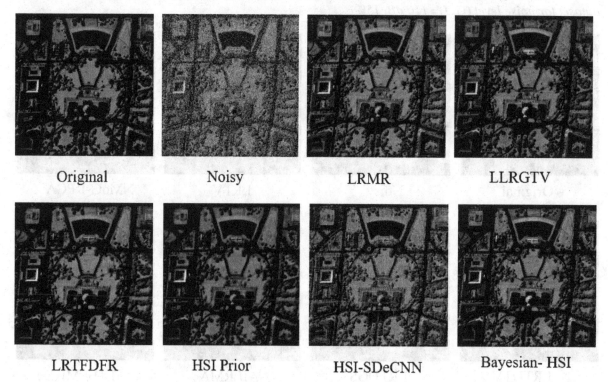

Analysis on Medical Imaging

In this section, experiments are conducted on one synthetically corrupted data obtained from Brainweb database and another from Open Access Series of Imaging Studies (OASIS); which is a real MR database. Each Brainweb dataset is synthesized to simulate three common imaging modalities under MRI:

Figure 12. Denoising results for Washington DC datasets for noise levels (G, I) = (10 dB, 20%).

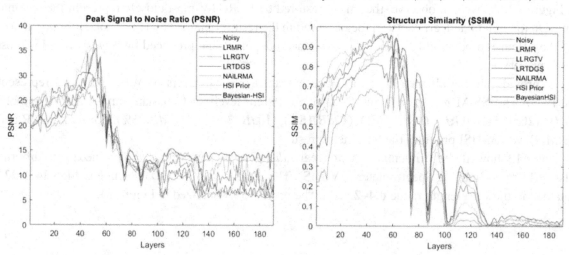

Figure13. Denoising results over real HSI data

T1, T2 and proton-density (PD)-weighted images. Depending on sampling interval along z-axis, images with variable number of slices can be obtained. However, to fully explore the potential of competing methods, the MR data of size **181×217×181** is used; where 181 is the number of slices along the depth axis. The image is synthetically corrupted with varying levels of Gaussian-impulse noise. The visual results are shown in Figure 14 for six different comparing methods:

- **ONLM:** An optimized blockwise nonlocal means denoising filter for 3-D magnetic resonance images (Coupé et al., 2008).
- **AONLM:** Adaptive non-local means denoising of MR images with spatially varying noise levels (Manjón et al., 2010).
- **PRINLM:** New methods for MRI denoising based on sparseness and self-similarity (Manjón et al., 2012).
- **MRNLM:** Adaptive multiresolution non-local means filter for three-dimensional magnetic resonance image denoising (Coupé et al., 2012).
- **Cure-Let:** A CURE for noisy magnetic resonance images: Chi-square unbiased risk estimation. (Luisier et al., 2012)
- **Rice-VST:** Noise estimation and removal in MR imaging: The variance-stabilization approach (Foi, 2011).

In the above set of methods, ONLM, AONLM, PRINLM and MRNLM are the filtering-based approaches, CURE-Let is the optimization-based approach proposing an unbiased estimator of true data;

Figure 14. Simulated MR data obtained from Brainweb dataset; synthetically corrupted by Gaussian-impulse noise (G,I)=(10dB,12%).

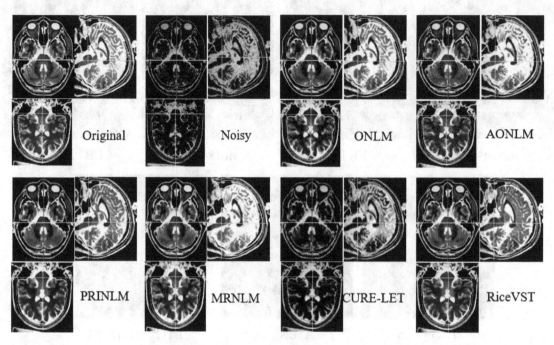

while Rive-VST performs variance stabilization and inverse variance stabilization using optimization-based strategy and image denoising step using BM4D.

Experiments on real data have been conducted on the image obtained from Open Access Series on Imaging Studies (OASIS). The dimensions of the data is **512×512×6**. The visual results are shown in Figure 15. As it can be observed, diagnostic image quality is not retained in the visual result of ONLM while residual noise can be observed in the results of Rice-VST.

CONCLUSION

The aim of this chapter was to provide a comprehensive overview of image denoising methods under the assumption of Gaussian-impulse noise. This chapter opened with the image formation model under Gaussian-impulse noise. We observed that Gaussian noise is modelled using normal distribution with zero mean and variance σ^2 providing the noise level parameter. Impulse noise is modelled using Laplace distribution as normal distribution is not able to capture the heavy-tailed nature of impulse corrupted data. Since the characteristic nature of noise in hyperspectral imaging and magnetic resonance imaging is a combination of Gaussian and impulse noise, we provide a brief introduction to these imaging domains; emphasizing the factors leading to Gaussian-impulse noise in them. This was a necessary motivation to create a background for our subsequent experimental discussions pertaining to these imaging domains. Further, an extensive literature for images corrupted by Gaussian+impulse noise is presented. This was divided into four different categories: filtering-based, optimization-based, filtering+optimization based and learning-based. Since no method is universal in its ability to handle noise, we categorized these

Figure 15. Images obtained along all three anatomical planes for the real dataset obtained from OASIS dataset using Magnetization Prepared RApid Gradient Echo (MPRAGE) sequence.

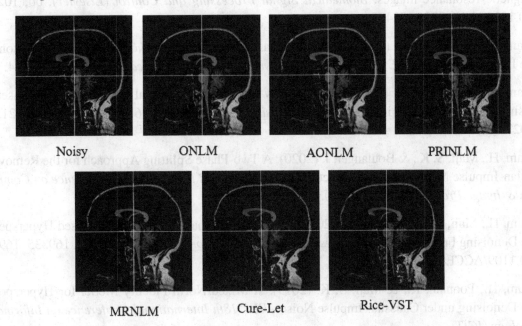

methods based on Gaussian, fixed-valued impulse noise and random-valued impulse noise. We also mentioned the limitations associated with each technique. In the last section, experimental analysis on the stated imaging domains were carried out under the assumption of Gaussian-impulse noise; using state-of-the-art methods.

In a subsequent work, it will be interesting to explore image restoration literature for other types of noise models as well. This includes the Cauchy distribution for modelling atmospheric noise, the Gamma distribution for speckle patterns in synthetic aperture radar (SAR) images and ultrasonography, and the Poisson distribution for modelling signal dependent shot noise. It will also be relevant to investigate other image enhancement problems such as image deconvolution, super-resolution, and image inpainting.

REFERENCES

Abiko, R., & Ikehara, M. (2019). Blind denoising of mixed Gaussian-impulse noise by single CNN. *ICASSP 2019-2019 IEEE International Conference on Acoustics, Speech and Signal Processing (ICASSP)*, 1717–1721.

Abreu, E., Lightstone, M., Mitra, S. K., & Arakawa, K. (1996). A new efficient approach for the removal of impulse noise from highly corrupted images. *IEEE Transactions on Image Processing*, 5(6), 1012–1025. doi:10.1109/83.503916 PMID:18285188

Aetesam, H., & Maji, S. K. (2020). L2- L1 Fidelity based Elastic Net Regularisation for Magnetic Resonance Image Denoising. *2020 International Conference on Contemporary Computing and Applications (IC3A)*, 137–142. 10.1109/IC3A48958.2020.233285

Aetesam, H., & Maji, S. K. (2021). Noise dependent training for deep parallel ensemble denoising in magnetic resonance images. *Biomedical Signal Processing and Control (Elsevier), 66*, 102405. doi:10.1016/j.bspc.2020.102405

Aetesam, H., & Maji, S. K. (2022a). Attention-Based Noise Prior Network for Magnetic Resonance Image Denoising. *2022 IEEE 19th International Symposium on Biomedical Imaging (ISBI)*, 1–4.

Aetesam, H., & Maji, S. K. (2022b). Perceptually-motivated adversarial training for deep ensemble denoising of hyperspectral images. *Remote Sensing Letters, 13*(8), 767–777. doi:10.1080/215070 4X.2022.2077152

Aetesam, H., Maji, S. K., & Boulanger, J. (2020). A Two-Phase Splitting Approach for the Removal of Gaussian-Impulse Noise from Hyperspectral Images. *5th IAPR International Conference on Computer Vision & Image Processing (CVIP 2020)*.

Aetesam, H., Maji, S. K., & Yahia, H. (2021). Bayesian Approach in a Learning-Based Hyperspectral Image Denoising Framework. *IEEE Access: Practical Innovations, Open Solutions, 9*, 169335–169347. doi:10.1109/ACCESS.2021.3137656

Aetesam, H., Poonam, K., & Maji, S. K. (2019). A Mixed-Norm Fidelity Model for Hyperspectral Image Denoising under Gaussian-Impulse Noise. *IEEE 18th International Conference on Information Technology (ICIT)*.

Aetesam, H., Poonam, K., & Maji, S. K. (2020). Proximal approach to denoising hyperspectral images under mixed-noise model. *IET Image Processing, 14*(14), 3366–3372. doi:10.1049/iet-ipr.2019.1763

Aggarwal, H. K., & Majumdar, A. (2016). Hyperspectral image denoising using spatio-spectral total variation. *IEEE Geoscience and Remote Sensing Letters, 13*(3), 442–446. doi:10.1109/LGRS.2016.2518218

Ahmed, F., & Das, S. (2013). Removal of high-density salt-and-pepper noise in images with an iterative adaptive fuzzy filter using alpha-trimmed mean. *IEEE Transactions on Fuzzy Systems, 22*(5), 1352–1358. doi:10.1109/TFUZZ.2013.2286634

Aja-Fernández, S., & Vegas-Sánchez-Ferrero, G. (2016). *Statistical analysis of noise in MRI*. Springer International Publishing. doi:10.1007/978-3-319-39934-8

Arab, M. A., Calagari, K., & Hefeeda, M. (2019). Band and quality selection for efficient transmission of hyperspectral images. *Proceedings of the 27th ACM International Conference on Multimedia*, 2423–2430. 10.1145/3343031.3351047

Arora, S., Hanmandlu, M., & Gupta, G. (2018). Filtering impulse noise in medical images using information sets. *Pattern Recognition Letters*.

Bermudez, C., Plassard, A. J., Davis, L. T., Newton, A. T., Resnick, S. M., & Landman, B. A. (2018). Learning implicit brain MRI manifolds with deep learning. *Medical Imaging 2018. Image Processing, 10574*, 105741L. PMID:29887659

Cai, J.-F., Chan, R. H., & di Fiore, C. (2007). Minimization of a detail-preserving regularization functional for impulse noise removal. *Journal of Mathematical Imaging and Vision, 29*(1), 79–91. doi:10.100710851-007-0027-4

Camarena, J.-G., Gregori, V., Morillas, S., & Sapena, A. (2010). Two-step fuzzy logic-based method for impulse noise detection in colour images. *Pattern Recognition Letters, 31*(13), 1842–1849. doi:10.1016/j.patrec.2010.01.008

Camarena, J.-G., Gregori, V., Morillas, S., & Sapena, A. (2012). A simple fuzzy method to remove mixed Gaussian-impulsive noise from color images. *IEEE Transactions on Fuzzy Systems, 21*(5), 971–978. doi:10.1109/TFUZZ.2012.2234754

Chan, R. H., Dong, Y., & Hintermüller, M. (2010). An Efficient Two-Phase {\rm L}^{1} -TV Method for Restoring Blurred Images with Impulse Noise. *IEEE Transactions on Image Processing, 19*(7), 1731–1739. doi:10.1109/TIP.2010.2045148 PMID:20227978

Chen, S., Shi, W., & Zhang, W. (2013). An efficient universal noise removal algorithm combining spatial gradient and impulse statistic. *Mathematical Problems in Engineering, 2013,* 2013. doi:10.1155/2013/480274

Chen, Y., Cao, X., Zhao, Q., Meng, D., & Xu, Z. (2017). Denoising hyperspectral image with non-iid noise structure. *IEEE Transactions on Cybernetics, 48*(3), 1054–1066. doi:10.1109/TCYB.2017.2677944 PMID:28767377

Chen, Y., He, W., Yokoya, N., & Huang, T.-Z. (2019). Hyperspectral image restoration using weighted group sparsity-regularized low-rank tensor decomposition. *IEEE Transactions on Cybernetics, 50*(8), 3556–3570. doi:10.1109/TCYB.2019.2936042 PMID:31484156

Coupé, P., Manjón, J., Robles, M., & Collins, D. L. (2012). Adaptive multiresolution non-local means filter for three-dimensional magnetic resonance image denoising. *IET Image Processing, 6*(5), 558–568. doi:10.1049/iet-ipr.2011.0161

Coupé, P., Yger, P., Prima, S., Hellier, P., Kervrann, C., & Barillot, C. (2008). An optimized blockwise nonlocal means denoising filter for 3-D magnetic resonance images. *IEEE Transactions on Medical Imaging, 27*(4), 425–441. doi:10.1109/TMI.2007.906087 PMID:18390341

Delon, J., & Desolneux, A. (2013). A patch-based approach for removing impulse or mixed gaussian-impulse noise. *SIAM Journal on Imaging Sciences, 6*(2), 1140–1174. doi:10.1137/120885000

Enginoğlu, S., Erkan, U., & Memiş, S. (2019). Pixel similarity-based adaptive Riesz mean filter for salt-and-pepper noise removal. *Multimedia Tools and Applications, 78*(24), 35401–35418. doi:10.100711042-019-08110-1

Esakkirajan, S., Veerakumar, T., Subramanyam, A. N., & PremChand, C. H. (2011). Removal of high density salt and pepper noise through modified decision based unsymmetric trimmed median filter. *IEEE Signal Processing Letters, 18*(5), 287–290. doi:10.1109/LSP.2011.2122333

Foi, A. (2011). Noise estimation and removal in MR imaging: The variance-stabilization approach. *2011 IEEE International Symposium on Biomedical Imaging: From Nano to Macro,* 1809–1814. 10.1109/ISBI.2011.5872758

Foss, S., Korshunov, D., Zachary, S., & ... (2011). *An introduction to heavy-tailed and subexponential distributions* (Vol. 6). Springer. doi:10.1007/978-1-4419-9473-8

Fu, H., Ng, M. K., Nikolova, M., & Barlow, J. L. (2006). Efficient minimization methods of mixed l2-l1 and l1-l1 norms for image restoration. *SIAM Journal on Scientific Computing*, *27*(6), 1881–1902. doi:10.1137/040615079

Garnett, R., Huegerich, T., Chui, C., & He, W. (2005). A universal noise removal algorithm with an impulse detector. *IEEE Transactions on Image Processing*, *14*(11), 1747–1754. doi:10.1109/TIP.2005.857261 PMID:16279175

Gonzalez-Hidalgo, M., Massanet, S., Mir, A., & Ruiz-Aguilera, D. (2018). Improving salt and pepper noise removal using a fuzzy mathematical morphology-based filter. *Applied Soft Computing*, *63*, 167–180. doi:10.1016/j.asoc.2017.11.030

González-Hidalgo, M., Massanet, S., Mir, A., & Ruiz-Aguilera, D. (2021). Impulsive Noise Removal with an Adaptive Weighted Arithmetic Mean Operator for Any Noise Density. *Applied Sciences (Basel, Switzerland)*, *11*(2), 560. doi:10.3390/app11020560

Gudbjartsson, H., & Patz, S. (1995). The Rician distribution of noisy MRI data. *Magnetic Resonance in Medicine*, *34*(6), 910–914. doi:10.1002/mrm.1910340618 PMID:8598820

Gupta, V., Chaurasia, V., & Shandilya, M. (2015). Random-valued impulse noise removal using adaptive dual threshold median filter. *Journal of Visual Communication and Image Representation*, *26*, 296–304. doi:10.1016/j.jvcir.2014.10.004

Halefoğlu, A. M. (2018). *High-Resolution Neuroimaging: Basic Physical Principles and Clinical Applications*. BoD–Books on Demand. doi:10.5772/intechopen.68268

He, W., Zhang, H., Shen, H., & Zhang, L. (2018). Hyperspectral image denoising using local low-rank matrix recovery and global spatial–spectral total variation. *IEEE Journal of Selected Topics in Applied Earth Observations and Remote Sensing*, *11*(3), 713–729. doi:10.1109/JSTARS.2018.2800701

He, W., Zhang, H., Zhang, L., & Shen, H. (2015a). Hyperspectral image denoising via noise-adjusted iterative low-rank matrix approximation. *IEEE Journal of Selected Topics in Applied Earth Observations and Remote Sensing*, *8*(6), 3050–3061. doi:10.1109/JSTARS.2015.2398433

He, W., Zhang, H., Zhang, L., & Shen, H. (2015b). Total-variation-regularized low-rank matrix factorization for hyperspectral image restoration. *IEEE Transactions on Geoscience and Remote Sensing*, *54*(1), 178–188. doi:10.1109/TGRS.2015.2452812

Henkelman, R. M. (1985). Measurement of signal intensities in the presence of noise in MR images. *Medical Physics*, *12*(2), 232–233. doi:10.1118/1.595711 PMID:4000083

HosseinKhani, Z., Karimi, N., Soroushmehr, S. M. R., Hajabdollahi, M., Samavi, S., Ward, K., & Najarian, K. (2016). Real-time removal of random value impulse noise in medical images. *2016 23rd International Conference on Pattern Recognition (ICPR)*, 3916–3921.

HosseinKhani, Z., Hajabdollahi, M., Karimi, N., Najarian, K., Emami, A., Shirani, S., Samavi, S., & Soroushmehr, S. M. R. (2019). Real-time removal of impulse noise from MR images for radiosurgery applications. *International Journal of Circuit Theory and Applications*, *47*(3), 406–426. doi:10.1002/cta.2591

Hu, H., Li, B., & Liu, Q. (2016). Removing mixture of gaussian and impulse noise by patch-based weighted means. *Journal of Scientific Computing*, 67(1), 103–129. doi:10.100710915-015-0073-9

Huang, T., Dong, W., Xie, X., Shi, G., & Bai, X. (2017). Mixed noise removal via Laplacian scale mixture modeling and nonlocal low-rank approximation. *IEEE Transactions on Image Processing*, 26(7), 3171–3186. doi:10.1109/TIP.2017.2676466 PMID:28278467

Huang, Y.-M., Ng, M. K., & Wen, Y.-W. (2009). Fast image restoration methods for impulse and Gaussian noises removal. *IEEE Signal Processing Letters*, 16(6), 457–460. doi:10.1109/LSP.2009.2016835

Ibrahim, T. S., Hue, Y.-K., & Tang, L. (2009). Understanding and manipulating the RF fields at high field MRI. *NMR in Biomedicine: An International Journal Devoted to the Development and Application of Magnetic Resonance In Vivo*, 22(9), 927–936. doi:10.1002/nbm.1406 PMID:19621335

Isa, I. S., Sulaiman, S. N., Mustapha, M., & Darus, S. (2015a). Evaluating denoising performances of fundamental filters for T2-weighted MRI images. *Procedia Computer Science*, 60, 760–768. doi:10.1016/j.procs.2015.08.231

Isa, I. S., Sulaiman, S. N., Mustapha, M., & Darus, S. (2015b). Evaluating denoising performances of fundamental filters for T2-weighted MRI images. *Procedia Computer Science*, 60, 760–768. doi:10.1016/j.procs.2015.08.231

Islam, M. T., Rahman, S. M. M., Ahmad, M. O., & Swamy, M. N. S. (2018). Mixed Gaussian-impulse noise reduction from images using convolutional neural network. *Signal Processing Image Communication*, 68, 26–41. doi:10.1016/j.image.2018.06.016

Jiang, J., Wang, Z., Chen, C., & Lu, T. (2016). L1-l1 norms for face super-resolution with mixed gaussian-impulse noise. *2016 IEEE International Conference on Acoustics, Speech and Signal Processing (ICASSP)*, 2089–2093. 10.1109/ICASSP.2016.7472045

Jiang, J., Zhang, L., & Yang, J. (2014). Mixed noise removal by weighted encoding with sparse nonlocal regularization. *IEEE Transactions on Image Processing*, 23(6), 2651–2662. doi:10.1109/TIP.2014.2317985 PMID:24760906

Jin, K. H., & Ye, J. C. (2015). *Sparse+ low rank decomposition of annihilating filter-based Hankel matrix for impulse noise removal*. ArXiv Preprint ArXiv:1510.05559.

Jin, L., Liu, H., Xu, X., & Song, E. (2012). Quaternion-based impulse noise removal from color video sequences. *IEEE Transactions on Circuits and Systems for Video Technology*, 23(5), 741–755. doi:10.1109/TCSVT.2012.2207272

Jin, L., Zhang, W., Ma, G., & Song, E. (2019). Learning deep CNNs for impulse noise removal in images. *Journal of Visual Communication and Image Representation*, 62, 193–205. doi:10.1016/j.jvcir.2019.05.005

Jin, L., Zhu, Z., Xu, X., & Li, X. (2016). Two-stage quaternion switching vector filter for color impulse noise removal. *Signal Processing*, 128, 171–185. doi:10.1016/j.sigpro.2016.03.025

Jin, Q., Grama, I., & Liu, Q. (2017). Optimal Weights Mixed Filter for removing mixture of Gaussian and impulse noises. *PLoS One*, 12(7), e0179051. doi:10.1371/journal.pone.0179051 PMID:28692667

Jung, Y. M., Jeong, T., & Yun, S. (2017). Non-convex TV denoising corrupted by impulse noise. *Inverse Problems and Imaging (Springfield, Mo.)*, *11*(4), 689–702. doi:10.3934/ipi.2017032

Kandemir, C., Kalyoncu, C., & Toygar, Ö. (2015). A weighted mean filter with spatial-bias elimination for impulse noise removal. *Digital Signal Processing*, *46*, 164–174. doi:10.1016/j.dsp.2015.08.012

Kim, S. R., & Efron, A. (1995). Adaptive robust impulse noise filtering. *IEEE Transactions on Signal Processing*, *43*(8), 1855–1866. doi:10.1109/78.403344

Kimiaei, M., & Rostami, M. (2016). Impulse noise removal based on new hybrid conjugate gradient approach. *Kybernetika*, *52*(5), 791–823. doi:10.14736/kyb-2016-5-0791

Lan, X., & Zuo, Z. (2014). Random-valued impulse noise removal by the adaptive switching median detectors and detail-preserving regularization. *Optik (Stuttgart)*, *125*(3), 1101–1105. doi:10.1016/j.ijleo.2013.07.114

Langer, A. (2017). Automated parameter selection in the-TV model for removing Gaussian plus impulse noise. *Inverse Problems*, *33*(7), 74002. doi:10.1088/1361-6420/33/7/074002

Langer, A. (2019). Locally adaptive total variation for removing mixed Gaussian–impulse noise. *International Journal of Computer Mathematics*, *96*(2), 298–316. doi:10.1080/00207160.2018.1438603

Lien, C.-Y., Huang, C.-C., Chen, P.-Y., & Lin, Y.-F. (2012). An efficient denoising architecture for removal of impulse noise in images. *IEEE Transactions on Computers*, *62*(4), 631–643. doi:10.1109/TC.2011.256

Liu, X., Liu, Q., Wu, Z., Wang, X., Sole, J. P., & Frangi, A. (2018). Mixed-Model Noise Removal in 3D MRI via Rotation-and-Scale Invariant Non-Local Means. *Sipaim–Miccai Biomedical Workshop*, 33–41.

López-Rubio, E. (2010a). Restoration of images corrupted by Gaussian and uniform impulsive noise. *Pattern Recognition*, *43*(5), 1835–1846. doi:10.1016/j.patcog.2009.11.017

López-Rubio, E. (2010b). Restoration of images corrupted by Gaussian and uniform impulsive noise. *Pattern Recognition*, *43*(5), 1835–1846. doi:10.1016/j.patcog.2009.11.017

Luisier, F., Blu, T., & Wolfe, P. J. (2012). A CURE for noisy magnetic resonance images: Chi-square unbiased risk estimation. *IEEE Transactions on Image Processing*, *21*(8), 3454–3466. doi:10.1109/TIP.2012.2191565 PMID:22491082

Ma, L., Ng, M. K., Yu, J., & Zeng, T. (2013). Efficient box-constrained tv-type-l^1 algorithms for restoring images with impulse noise. *Journal of Computational Mathematics*, *31*(3), 249–270. doi:10.4208/jcm.1301-m4143

Ma, L., Yu, J., & Zeng, T. (2013). Sparse Representation Prior and Total Variation–Based Image Deblurring under Impulse Noise. *SIAM Journal on Imaging Sciences*, *6*(4), 2258–2284. doi:10.1137/120866452

Mafi, M., Martin, H., & Adjouadi, M. (2017). High impulse noise intensity removal in MRI images. *2017 IEEE Signal Processing in Medicine and Biology Symposium (SPMB)*, 1–6.

Mafi, M., Martin, H., Cabrerizo, M., Andrian, J., Barreto, A., & Adjouadi, M. (2019). A comprehensive survey on impulse and Gaussian denoising filters for digital images. *Signal Processing*, *157*, 236–260. doi:10.1016/j.sigpro.2018.12.006

Manea, D., & Calin, M. A. (2015). Hyperspectral imaging in different light conditions. *Imaging Science Journal*, *63*(4), 214–219. doi:10.1179/1743131X15Y.0000000001

Manjón, J., Coupé, P., Buades, A., Louis Collins, D., & Robles, M. (2012). New methods for MRI denoising based on sparseness and self-similarity. *Medical Image Analysis*, *16*(1), 18–27. doi:10.1016/j.media.2011.04.003 PMID:21570894

Manjón, J., Coupé, P., Martí-Bonmatí, L., Collins, D. L., & Robles, M. (2010). Adaptive non-local means denoising of MR images with spatially varying noise levels. *Journal of Magnetic Resonance Imaging*, *31*(1), 192–203. doi:10.1002/jmri.22003 PMID:20027588

McGraw, T., Vemuri, B. C., Chen, Y., Rao, M., & Mareci, T. (2004). DT-MRI denoising and neuronal fiber tracking. *Medical Image Analysis*, *8*(2), 95–111. doi:10.1016/j.media.2003.12.001 PMID:15063860

Meng, F., Yang, X., & Zhou, C. (2014). The augmented lagrange multipliers method for matrix completion from corrupted samplings with application to mixed Gaussian-impulse noise removal. *PLoS One*, *9*(9), e108125. doi:10.1371/journal.pone.0108125 PMID:25248103

Moreno López, M., Frederick, J. M., & Ventura, J. (2021). Evaluation of MRI Denoising Methods Using Unsupervised Learning. *Frontiers in Artificial Intelligence*, *4*, 75. doi:10.3389/frai.2021.642731 PMID:34151253

Morillas, S., Gregori, V., & Hervás, A. (2009). Fuzzy peer groups for reducing mixed Gaussian-impulse noise from color images. *IEEE Transactions on Image Processing*, *18*(7), 1452–1466. doi:10.1109/TIP.2009.2019305 PMID:19447709

Noor, A., Zhao, Y., Khan, R., Wu, L., & Abdalla, F. Y. O. (2020). Median filters combined with denoising convolutional neural network for Gaussian and impulse noises. *Multimedia Tools and Applications*, *79*(25), 18553–18568. doi:10.100711042-020-08657-4

Nowak, R. D. (1999). Wavelet-based Rician noise removal for magnetic resonance imaging. *IEEE Transactions on Image Processing*, *8*(10), 1408–1419. doi:10.1109/83.791966 PMID:18267412

Ramadan, Z. M. (2012). Efficient restoration method for images corrupted with impulse noise. *Circuits, Systems, and Signal Processing*, *31*(4), 1397–1406. doi:10.100700034-011-9380-z

Rodriguez, P. (2013). Total variation regularization algorithms for images corrupted with different noise models: A review. *Journal of Electrical and Computer Engineering*, *2013*, 10.

Rodriguez, P., Rojas, R., & Wohlberg, B. (2012). Mixed Gaussian-impulse noise image restoration via total variation. *2012 IEEE International Conference on Acoustics, Speech and Signal Processing (ICASSP)*, 1077–1080.

Roy, A., Manam, L., & Laskar, R. H. (2018). Region adaptive fuzzy filter: An approach for removal of random-valued impulse noise. *IEEE Transactions on Industrial Electronics*, *65*(9), 7268–7278. doi:10.1109/TIE.2018.2793225

Roy, A., Singha, J., Devi, S. S., & Laskar, R. H. (2016). Impulse noise removal using SVM classification based fuzzy filter from gray scale images. *Signal Processing*, *128*, 262–273. doi:10.1016/j.sigpro.2016.04.007

Sheela, C. J. J., & Suganthi, G. (2020). An efficient denoising of impulse noise from MRI using adaptive switching modified decision based unsymmetric trimmed median filter. *Biomedical Signal Processing and Control, 55,* 101657. doi:10.1016/j.bspc.2019.101657

Shlykov, V., Kotovskyi, V., Višniakov, N., & Šešok, A. (2020). Model for Elimination of Mixed Noise from MRI Heart Images. *Applied Sciences (Basel, Switzerland), 10*(14), 4747. doi:10.3390/app10144747

Sidorov, O., & Yngve Hardeberg, J. (2019). Deep Hyperspectral Prior: Single-Image Denoising, Inpainting, Super-Resolution. *Proceedings of the IEEE International Conference on Computer Vision Workshops.* 10.1109/ICCVW.2019.00477

Smolka, B., & Kusnik, D. (2015). Robust local similarity filter for the reduction of mixed Gaussian and impulsive noise in color digital images. *Signal, Image and Video Processing, 9*(1), 49–56. doi:10.100711760-015-0830-0

Srinivasan, K. S., & Ebenezer, D. (2007). A new fast and efficient decision-based algorithm for removal of high-density impulse noises. *IEEE Signal Processing Letters, 14*(3), 189–192. doi:10.1109/LSP.2006.884018

Tasdizen, T. (2009). Principal neighborhood dictionaries for nonlocal means image denoising. *IEEE Transactions on Image Processing, 18*(12), 2649–2660. doi:10.1109/TIP.2009.2028259 PMID:19635697

Tofighi, M., Kose, K., & Cetin, A. E. (2015). Denoising images corrupted by impulsive noise using projections onto the epigraph set of the total variation function (PES-TV). *Signal, Image and Video Processing, 9*(1), 41–48. doi:10.100711760-015-0827-8

Toprak, A., & Güler, I. (2007a). Impulse noise reduction in medical images with the use of switch mode fuzzy adaptive median filter. *Digital Signal Processing, 17*(4), 711–723. doi:10.1016/j.dsp.2006.11.008

Toprak, A., & Güler, I. (2007b). Impulse noise reduction in medical images with the use of switch mode fuzzy adaptive median filter. *Digital Signal Processing, 17*(4), 711–723. doi:10.1016/j.dsp.2006.11.008

Veraart, J., Novikov, D. S., Christiaens, D., Ades-Aron, B., Sijbers, J., & Fieremans, E. (2016). Denoising of diffusion MRI using random matrix theory. *NeuroImage, 142,* 394–406. doi:10.1016/j.neuroimage.2016.08.016 PMID:27523449

Wang, J., Li, J., Yan, S., Shi, W., Yang, X., Guo, Y., & Gulliver, T. A. (2020). A novel underwater acoustic signal denoising algorithm for Gaussian/non-Gaussian impulsive noise. *IEEE Transactions on Vehicular Technology, 70*(1), 429–445. doi:10.1109/TVT.2020.3044994

Wang, S., Huang, T.-Z., Zhao, X., & Liu, J. (2013). An alternating direction method for mixed Gaussian plus impulse noise removal. *Abstract and Applied Analysis, 2013,* 2013. doi:10.1155/2013/850360

Wang, X., Shen, S., Shi, G., Xu, Y., & Zhang, P. (2016). Iterative non-local means filter for salt and pepper noise removal. *Journal of Visual Communication and Image Representation, 38,* 440–450. doi:10.1016/j.jvcir.2016.03.024

Wang, Y., Peng, J., Zhao, Q., Leung, Y., Zhao, X.-L., & Meng, D. (2017). Hyperspectral image restoration via total variation regularized low-rank tensor decomposition. *IEEE Journal of Selected Topics in Applied Earth Observations and Remote Sensing, 11*(4), 1227–1243. doi:10.1109/JSTARS.2017.2779539

Wang, Y., & Zhou, H. (2006). Total variation wavelet-based medical image denoising. *International Journal of Biomedical Imaging*, ●●●, 2006. PMID:23165057

Wang, Z., Wang, G., Pan, Z., Zhang, J., & Zhai, G. (2020). Fast stripe noise removal from hyperspectral image via multi-scale dilated unidirectional convolution. *Multimedia Tools and Applications*, *79*(31-32), 23007–23022. doi:10.100711042-020-09065-4

Wen, F., Liu, P., Liu, Y., Qiu, R. C., & Yu, W. (2016). Robust Sparse Recovery in Impulsive Noise via \ell _p -\ell _1 Optimization. *IEEE Transactions on Signal Processing*, *65*(1), 105–118. doi:10.1109/TSP.2016.2598316

Wu, T. (2016). Variable splitting based method for image restoration with impulse plus Gaussian noise. *Mathematical Problems in Engineering*, *2016*, 2016. doi:10.1155/2016/3151303

Xiao, Y., Zeng, T., Yu, J., & Ng, M. K. (2011). Restoration of images corrupted by mixed Gaussian-impulse noise via l1–l0 minimization. *Pattern Recognition*, *44*(8), 1708–1720. doi:10.1016/j.patcog.2011.02.002

Xiong, B., & Yin, Z. (2011). A universal denoising framework with a new impulse detector and nonlocal means. *IEEE Transactions on Image Processing*, *21*(4), 1663–1675. doi:10.1109/TIP.2011.2172804 PMID:22020688

Yan, M. (2013). Restoration of images corrupted by impulse noise and mixed Gaussian impulse noise using blind inpainting. *SIAM Journal on Imaging Sciences*, *6*(3), 1227–1245. doi:10.1137/12087178X

Yuan, G., & Ghanem, B. (2015). l0tv: A new method for image restoration in the presence of impulse noise. *Proceedings of the IEEE Conference on Computer Vision and Pattern Recognition*, 5369–5377.

Yuan, G., & Ghanem, B. (2017). L0 TV: A Sparse Optimization Method for Impulse Noise Image Restoration. *IEEE Transactions on Pattern Analysis and Machine Intelligence*, *41*(2), 352–364. doi:10.1109/TPAMI.2017.2783936 PMID:29990015

Zeng, C., Wu, C., & Jia, R. (2019). Non-Lipschitz models for image restoration with impulse noise removal. *SIAM Journal on Imaging Sciences*, *12*(1), 420–458. doi:10.1137/18M117769X

Zhang, H., He, W., Zhang, L., Shen, H., & Yuan, Q. (2013). Hyperspectral image restoration using low-rank matrix recovery. *IEEE Transactions on Geoscience and Remote Sensing*, *52*(8), 4729–4743. doi:10.1109/TGRS.2013.2284280

Zhang, J., Xiong, R., Zhao, C., Ma, S., & Zhao, D. (2012). Exploiting image local and nonlocal consistency for mixed Gaussian-impulse noise removal. *2012 IEEE International Conference on Multimedia and Expo*, 592–597. 10.1109/ICME.2012.109

Zhou, Y. Y., Ye, Z. F., & Huang, J. J. (2012). Improved decision-based detail-preserving variational method for removal of random-valued impulse noise. *IET Image Processing*, *6*(7), 976–985. doi:10.1049/iet-ipr.2011.0312

Zhu, H., & Ng, M. K. (2020). Structured dictionary learning for image denoising under mixed gaussian and impulse noise. *IEEE Transactions on Image Processing*, *29*, 6680–6693. doi:10.1109/TIP.2020.2992895 PMID:32406836

Zhu, Y., Shen, W., Cheng, F., Jin, C., & Cao, G. (2020). Removal of high density Gaussian noise in compressed sensing MRI reconstruction through modified total variation image denoising method. *Heliyon*, *6*(3), e03680. doi:10.1016/j.heliyon.2020.e03680 PMID:32258499

Zhuang, L., & Ng, M. K. (2020). Hyperspectral Mixed Noise Removal By \ell _1 -Norm-Based Subspace Representation. *IEEE Journal of Selected Topics in Applied Earth Observations and Remote Sensing*, *13*, 1143–1157. doi:10.1109/JSTARS.2020.2979801

Chapter 21
Algorithmic Approach for Spatial Entity and Mining

Priya Govindarajan
SASTRA University (Deemed), India

Balakrishnan R.
https://orcid.org/0000-0002-4752-6400
SASTRA University (Deemed), India

Rajesh Kumar N.
https://orcid.org/0000-0001-5394-218X
SASTRA University (Deemed), India

ABSTRACT

Mining has gained its momentum in almost every arena of research. The mining can be either spatial or non-spatial based on the search query. For classifying or for grouping the spatial data, algorithms with extended perspectives are projected in this chapter. Besides framing algorithms, one can also provide mass points based on the required attributes as well as indexing techniques. The extended algorithms can also be manipulated for efficient and robust solution with respect to different parameters.

MOTIVATION

Many databases contain both spatial and non-spatial information, for which algorithms are being devised with prolonged comparative study and also keeping in perspective of different parameters for analyzing spatial information (Zhang et.al., 2022, Medad et.al., 2020). The wide spread knowledge (Germanaite et.al., 2021, Govindarajan & K.S., 2014) indicates there is no such system which drastically reduces the fault cost and time during the search.

We have ventured an extended technique, which efficiently reduces the privilege for accessing the featured dataset (Cheng & junli.,2013) and the searched object. The indexed objects higher score values

DOI: 10.4018/978-1-7998-8892-5.ch021

are pruned while accessing the spatial dataset. The extended versions of algorithms are being proposed for efficient outcome.

For accessing and retrieving data in different applications, objects are being ranked. (Isaj et.al., 2019) Until the identification of summed up value, the no. of times an object are being accessed should be minimized or brought down. The algorithms are being devised, keeping an eye on the above constraints.

ALGORITHMIC SCHEMA

Trouble-Free Probing (TP)

Trouble-free Probing (TP), computes the mass of every object (*Algorithm 1*). It uses two globalized term (assuming) X_k for manipulating the top-k results and Y calculates the value of top-k. Algorithm invokes at root node of the tree. The algorithm works recursively on the nodes of the tree, until it encounters (Sivakami & G.M.K, 2011) a terminating node. Once the non-terminating node is reached the mass M is calculated through the execution of a range of search on the tree T. The point b is ignored if its upper bound mass $M_+(b)$ can't be greater than best-k mass Y. The term X_k and Y are overwritten when the mass M(b) is greater than Y.

Algorithm TP (node N) (Algorithm 1)
    1 For all entries in B (belongs to) N do
    2 If N is terminating node Then
    3 Take the subsidiary node N'-B
    4 SP (N')
    5 Else
    6 A = 1 to m do
    7 If $M_+(b) > Y$ Then
    8 Calculate M using tree T; Update $M_+(b)$
    9 If M>Y Then
    10 Overwrite X_k (and Y) by B

Extended Branch and Bound (EBB)

While computing, Trouble-free algorithm seems to be inefficient for huge data sets. Hence a version of Extended Branch and Bound (EBB) is proposed (*Algorithm 2*) for accessing huge data sets. Let N be the root node of T, If N comes under the terminating category f, and then mass M(f) is manipulated. With the aid of mass for the component $M_c(f)$ one can drive the $M_+(f)$, an upper bound of M(f). If $M_+(f)<=Y$, (Thakoor N. et.al., 2008) then one cannot fetch best result with the sub-tree of f than those in X_k and removed from Z(subset of T).To fetch high mass, M(f) is sorted in descending order then the nodes of the subsidiary are called recursively by the entries in Z. X_k of top-k results (You wan, et.al., 2008) are updated by manipulating the mass of all N simultaneously. Whenever EBB is called recursively the globalised variables X_k and Y are updated then and there.

The vital design is to manipulate the terminating entries f in the tree T (Man Lung Yiu, et.al., 2011). If the higher bound M(f) <= Y, then there is no need to access the sub-tree T, by which the numerous mass computations can be saved.

Extended Branch and Bound (EBB) Algorithm. (Algorithm 2)

X_k = k size of Min-Stack (Empty at the beginning)
Y = 0

Algorithm EBB (Node N)
1. Z = {f/f (belongs to) N};
2. If N is terminating then
3. For i = 1 to m do
4. Manipulating M_c(f) for all f (belongs to) Z simultaneously ;
5. Entries f in Z are removed, such that M_+(f)<=Y;
6. f(belongs to)Z; Sort it in descending order of M(f);
7. For all entries of f(belongs)Z such that -> M(f)>Y do
8. subsidiary node N' by f is read;
9. EBB(N');
10. Else
11. For i=1 to m do
12. Manipulate M_c(f) for all f(belongs to)Z simultaneously;
13. Entries f in Z are removed such that M_+(f) <= Y;
14. Finally X_k (And Y) are updated by the value (entries) in Z.

TP is inept for large dataset and it verifies all objects in T and their mass. Whereas EBB marginally decline the number of objects to be scrutinized, this is considered to be the huge advantage than TP. EBB is not expensive when compared with TP, since EBB lessens the number of objects to be scrutinized.

Extended Feature-Join (EFJ)

To execute a multi-way spatial for the evaluation of top-k spatial query on the tree t1, t2,…,tn., to project the feature points with their combinations(including neighborhood objects).By which high score spatial regions are predicted (Raymond T.Ng & Jiawei Han, 2002). Primarily the combination, followed by the constraints for a permutation to be trimmed and finally project the combination based on the query results.Tuple(t1,t2,…,tn) for any c (belongs to) (1,n), t_c(entry) -> feature tree T_c. The mass is defined by, åw(t_c) where c= 1 to n.

EFJ *(Algorithm 3)* denotes J as a max-heap, which is projected in descending order with perspective to their mass. The combined mass of the combination {t1,t2,..,tn} are projected (in the algorithm) as an higher bound of the mass for the entire combinations as (s1,s2,..,sn) such that s_c is the sub-tree of t_c for each c (belongs to) (1,n).

Primarily the tree is en-stacked and then the reverse operation is being carried off with the aid of the mass which is largest. The Projected_mass (No fault tolerance cost) is called, if all the entries are non-terminating node. To find the predicted result, all the nodes are loaded i.e.., {P1,P2,…,Pn}If all are de-stacked, (Koudas N. & Sevcik K.C. 1998) then the subsidiary-node which is at the highest level is accessed, for a new combinations. The new permutation is put into J for its subsequent processing. The query is succeeded if it has highest mass than Y. Loop continues until J becomes empty.

Extended Feature Join (EFJ) Algorithm (Algorithm 3)

X_k = k size of Min-Stack (Empty at the beginning)
Y = 0

Algorithm EFJ (Tree T, Trees t1,t2,..,tn)
1. J = Max-Stack (mass – combined);
2. Put (t1.root, t2.root,…,tn.root) into J;
3. While J (not empty) do
4. De-stack (t1,t2,…,tn) from J;
5. If c (belongs to) (1,n), t_c -> Non-terminating node
6. For c = 1 to n do
7. Take subsidiary-node P_c -> t_c;
8. Projected_mass(T.root , P1,…,Pn);
9. Else
10. t_c = Taking the entry which is high from (t1,t2,..,tn);
11. Take the subsidiary-node N_c -> t_c;
12. For each entry do
13. Add (t1,t2,..,tn) into J, if mass>Y and its taken into account as the succeeded query.

Algorithm Projected_mass (Node N, Nodes P1,…,Pn)
1. For Each entry e (belong to) N do
2. If N = terminating node Then
3. Calculate M(f) for P1,…,Pn;
4. If M(f)>Y Then
5. Take the subsidiary-node N' -> e;
6. Projected_mass(N',P1,…,Pn);
7. Else
8. Calculate M(f) by P1,…,Pn;
9. Finally overwrite X_k (And Y) by e.

AMALGAMATION OF ALGORITHMIC APPROACH OF SPATIAL ENTITY AND IMAGE PROCESSING

In the era of heterogenous datasets, where one does have the privilege of extracting data from various sources for usage and there by which one can improvise the utilization of data. The universe includes many domains with different perspectives of spatial data. Different sources of data may have variety of details with perspective to location, area, and semantics. These layers of information would aggravate the inconsistency of data, which indirectly decreases the quality of data.

To overcome these loopholes, one can impose this algorithmic approach to process and to mine image-based datasets. These algorithmic approach increases the quality of data extraction and imposes an extraction of consistent data for further processing. (Khodizadeh-Nahari et.al., 2021)

RESULT DISCUSSION

The efficiency of the algorithm was scrutinized using different data sets. We implemented the algorithms using PC with 1GB-RAM, with memory buffer (LRU) which was spotted to 0.5 percent of the sum of tree size. We tabled (table 1) the total Execution Time (ET) (in seconds) and fault Tolerance Cost (TC) (number of page fault).

Table1. Summarization of TC and ET for all the Algorithms.

Parameter	TP	EBB	EFJ
Tolerance Cost (TC)	18012	2013	484
Execution Time(ET) (in secs)	582.0	5.0	1.3

Three real spatial data sets were scrutinized. One set of data is used as object data and others as feature data sets. Object sets of data contains 12,422 residential (flat) locations, where as the primary sets of feature data had 200 schools, another sets of feature data sets contains 3,424 Wal-mart stores. The query search is for a residential place, which is very close to a school (with expected educational quality) which is indirectly close to a Wal-Mart. The execution time and tolerance cost were recorded (Graph 1) for all the above cited algorithms.

Figure 1. Depicts the summarization of TC and ET for the algorithms

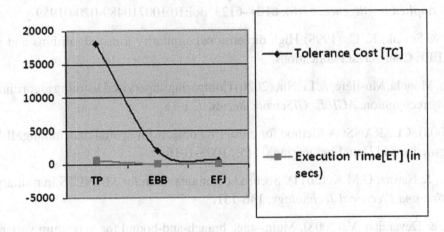

CONCLUSION

This paper, projects different extended as well as novel types of algorithms for top-k spatial queries. The objects were ranked based on their attribute value/quality with respective to their neighborhood object. The basis of TP, was to scrutinize all objects on the data sets, which increases the time and cost indirectly. Therefore, EBB came into frame, which prunes the object that cannot fetch the better result by the upper bound mass for terminating entries in the tree. The EBB algorithm, Execution time and Tolerance cost was much better than TP. The algorithm EFJ, obtains succeeded combinations of mass through a multiway join schema on feature tree/data sets and then the search for relevant object is made.

The experimental outcome projects that BB is adaptable and robust towards huge data sets with perspective to wide range of parameters. When number and each individual feature data set are small, then EFJ is best all the way. By which one can extract quality and consistent data through mining with perspective to data and images.

REFERENCES

Cheng, Y., & Zhang, T. (2013). *A maximal Clique Enumeration based on ordered star neighborhood for co-location patterns.* IEEE Conference Publications.

Germanaite, I. E. (2021). General Spatial Pattern and Meta-Pattern Model for Problems That Need Analytical Approach in Complex Spatial Systems. *Applied Sciences, 12*(1), 302.

Govindarajan, P., & Ravichandran, K. S. (2014). Data mining- an evolutionary arena. *Research Journal of Applied Sciences, Engineering and Technology, 7*(22), 4749–4753. doi:10.19026/rjaset.7.861

Isaj, S., Zimányi, E., & Pedersen, T. B. (2019). Multi-source spatial entity linkage. *Proceedings of the 16th International Symposium on Spatial and Temporal Databases*, 1-10.

Khodizadeh-Nahari, M., Ghadiri, N., Baraani-Dastjerdi, A., & Sack, J.-R. (2021). A novel similarity measure for spatial entity resolution based on data granularity model: Managing inconsistencies in place descriptions. *Applied Intelligence, 51*(8), 6104–6123. doi:10.100710489-020-01959-y

Koudas, N., & Sevcik, K. C. (1998) High dimensional similarity joins: algorithms and performance evaluation. IEEE Conference Publications.

Medad, Gaio, Moncla, Mustière, & Le Nir. (2020) Comparing supervised learning algorithms for spatial nominal entity recognition. *AGILE: GIScience Series, 1*, 1-18.

Ng, R. T. (2002). CLARANS: A Method for clustering objects for spatial data mining. IEEE Transactions on Knowledge and Data Engineering, 15(5), 1003-1016.

Sivakami, R., & Nawaz, G.M.K. (2011). Secured communication for MANETS in military. *Computer Communication and Electrical Technology*, 146-151.

Thakoor, N., & Devarajan, V. (2008). Multi-stage branch-and-bound for maximum variance disparity clustering. IEEE Conference Publications.

Wan, Zhou, & Bian. (2008). *CODEM: A novel spatial co-location and de-location patterns mining algorithm.* IEEE Conference Publications.

Yiu, M. L., & Lu, H. (2011). Ranking spatial data by quality preferences. IEEE Transactions on Knowledge and Data Engineering, 23(3).

Zhang & Lan. (2022). Detect Megaregional Communities Using Network Science Analytics. *Urban Science, 6*(1), 12.

Chapter 22
A Combined Feature Selection Technique for Improving Classification Accuracy

S. Meganathan

(iD) https://orcid.org/0000-0003-4570-8259
SASTRA University (Deemed), India

A. Sumathi
SASTRA University (Deemed), India

Ahamed Lebbe Hanees
South Eastern University of Sri Lanka, Sri Lanka

ABSTRACT

Feature selection has become revenue to many research regions that manage machine learning and data mining since it allows the classifiers to be cost-efficient, time-saving, and more precise. In this chapter, the feature selection strategy is consolidating by utilizing the combined feature selection technique, specifically recursive feature elimination, chi-square, info-gain, and principal component analysis. Machine learning algorithms like logistic regression, random support vector machine, and decision trees are applied in three different datasets that are pre-processed with combined feature selection technique. Then these algorithms are ensembled using voting classifier. The improvement in accuracy of the classifiers is observed by the impact of the combined feature selection.

INTRODUCTION

Dimensionality reduction is the way toward eliminating repetitive or insignificant highlights from the first informational index. So the execution season of the classifier that measures the information decreases, likewise precision increments on the grounds that unessential highlights can incorporate noisy

DOI: 10.4018/978-1-7998-8892-5.ch022

data influencing the order exactness adversely. With include determination the umderstandability can be improved and cost of information dealing with decreases.

Feature selection, as a dimensionality decrease strategy, expects to pick a little subset of the significant highlights from the original features by eliminating unimportant, excess or noisy highlights. Feature selection, normally can prompt better learning execution, i.e., higher learning precision, lesser computational expense, and better model interpretability.

This work utilizes combined feature selection technique and Machine learning strategies for forecast with higher exactness rate. The proposed strategy has used with the machine learning method. The component determination system shows the significance of choice procedure. It gives the better precision for calculations with the diminished dataset.

We utilize three particular dataset namely, skin ailment dataset (1st dataset). The UCI facility provided the dataset. The dataset includes 22 Histopathological features and 12 clinical attributes. The target variable contains the characteristics from 1 to 6. 2nd dataset-> was acquired from UCI which is a diabetic dataset called Pima Diabetes dataset .3rd dataset->Diabetes dataset was acquired from kaggle. It contains 50 segments and 1 lakh records. Diabetes dataset maintains portrayal in an exceedingly twofold association that involves 0 and 1 which represents diabetes non-affected and diabetes affected independently.

The CFS is employed to select the rule credits. Four component assurance methods namely Principal component analysis, Recursive feature elimination, Chi-square and Info-gain are joined for performing the endeavour. This system performs diversely on the datasets. Joining the methodologies which are performing particularly would pass highest outcomes. So, selecting the customary features which are looked over all the four component assurance strategy records. Diabetes dataset maintains request during a twofold arrangement that contains 0 and 1 which represents diabetes non-affected and diabetes affected independently.

LITERATURE SURVEY

Xie and Wang (2011) introduced a new strategy called half breed highlight determination, it improves F-score value along with Sequential Forward Search (IFSFS). The research got the main F-score by separating courses of real numbers assessment and isolation among extra genuine number arrangement. The better F-score and Sequential Forward Search are merged as ideal segment during time spent component assurance, be that as it may, that improved F-score as channel methodology evaluation model, and, SFS as appraisal system covering procedure.

Aruna et al (2012) came out with a hybrid feature decision procedure explicitly IGSBFS (Information Gain and Sequential Backward Floating Search), which solidifies potential gains channels just as covers pick ideal part beginning with first rundown of abilities reliant upon a characteristic model of NB. Information Gain variable evaluator are used in the opposite assurance progressively or otherwise called as straight forward decision along with skimming forward decision (IGSBFS) (FS2). In IGSBFS, IG functions as channels to dispose of abundance features. The course of action precision of the offered, method put forward is 98.9% with 10 features.

Xie et al (2013) developed an alternate hybrid FS computation across F-score where critical attributes as per a disorder dataset. Incorporate subset age pertinent features, glancing through techniques, for instance, SBFS, ESFS, and SFFS and summarized F-score to survey meaning of every segment. These techniques merge the advantages of channels and covers to pick the absolute component subset from the principal rundown of abilities to bring together the consistent and profitable classifiers.

Maryam et al (2017) put forth a hybrid procedure incorporate assurance methodology, Chi GA (Chi-Square and Genetic Algorithm), uses great conditions with channel, covering procedures picking the ideal component determining out remarkable component. Chi-square used as channel method to wipe out abundance features, GA picks ideal part SVM used a divider and the preliminary yield proposes model-based multiclass SVM with Chi-Square.

Verma and Pal (2019) came out with a new hybrid strategy by joining the channel-based segment assurance methodologies that are of Feature importance, Univariate (chi-square) what's more, Correlation coefficient. In order to endorse the profitability of the suggested incorporate assurance methodologies, the researchers used five request estimations to be explicit: choice tree (DT), SVM, Random Forest (RF), and Naive Bayes (NB)

Polat and Gunes (2007) utilized Principal Component Analysis for highlight determination and Adaptive NeuroFuzzy Inference System for order. The strategy got 89.47% exactness with 10-overlay approval

Christobel and Sivaprakasam (2013) identified a hybrid model utilized SVM and outspread premise bit work. By eliminating the sections with 0, another dataset shaped with 460 cases. The cross breed order model showed 78% exactness by applying irregular traintest.

Alharbi and Alghahtani (2019) built up a crossover model that includes hereditary calculation and Extreme learning machine calculation to determine diabetes of type 2 have an accuracy of 97.5%.

Ahmed (2016) utilized J48, Logistic Regression and Naïve Bayes calculation for grouping. With 80–20% train test split J48, Logistic Regression and Naïve Bayes accomplished 73.5%, 74.4% and 74.2% individually.

Farahmandian et al. (2015) applied diverse order algorithms like KNN, ID3, NB, C5.0, CART and SVM. From those model, SVM showed a precision of 81.77%, that has higher exactness than other model.

METHODOLOGY

Based on the literature study, feature selection techniques gives better results and models with reduced dataset conveyed more powerful and worthy outcomes. It is a strategy that utilizes combined feature selection technique and machine learning concepts for prediction with higher precision rate. The proposed strategy has used the machine learning method before and after the feature selection for categorization system and shows the significance of feature selection procedure as it gives the highest accuracy for algorithms with the reduced dataset which contains the only features that are selected using combined feature selection technique.

Feature Selection

It is a method where we include related features that can make use of expected outcomes and reduces an unnecessary factor which impact the performance. The purposes for this is to decrease the pre-processing time, overfitting and intricacy of classification algorithms. At that point in addition, that calculates the factors that improve prediction performance.

PCA

Principal Component Analysis is that the strategy in dimensionality decline method that are performed by picking the elemental credits that passes on all essential data within the dataset. Best features are taken for the change that it accomplishes the target variable. It's completely utilized by showing each credits onto the central few head parts to induce lower-dimensional data while noticing the foremost limit activity of the data's collection as potential. The essential head segment will comparably be fanned out as a course that develop the qualification of the projected information. The ith head section are going to be taken as a course even to the crucial I-1 fundamental parts that develop the excellence within the projected information.

CHI-SQUARE

Chi-square technique primarily assists in dimensionality decrease methodology by detecting the association linking non-target variables to the objective components. It is employed to discover the autonomy of two occasions. It examines that the occurrence of a feature and the occurrence of an objective worth are reliant or not. Chi-square is indicated by

$$x^2 = (O_i - E_i)^2 / e_i$$

INFO-GAIN

It is mostly employed in feature selection strategies. It supports with finding the gain value of the every factor in regards to the objective variable. It is determined by contrasting the entropy esteems when change happened to get necessary features for expectation. The feature which has the best gain values is chosen for reduced dataset. Large information gain acquire demonstrates that it has a small entropy esteem.

RFE

Recursive feature elimination is a valued component determination strategy since it is not difficult to utilize and organize, this is productive in lessening the amount of features that are highly applicable in anticipation. This method had a superiority of opting the number of features and abstains from the most fragile component repeatedly up to the predetermined quantity of attributes to construct the model.

Combined Feature Selection

Every principal attributes are collected from this method. The leading dimensionality reduction methods namely Principal component analysis, Information gain, Chi-square and also Recursive feature elimination are get together to carry out the work. These four strategies performs variously on the datasets. Uniting the approaches which are functioning diversely will convey greater results. So, selecting the basic highlights which are chosen from all the four feature selection method.

Proposed CFS:
Input: Dataset (Including N features)

Output: Selected features

Step 1: Individual FS methods are applied to the Dataset

Step 2: Selects important features based on threshold values

Step 3: CFS selects the first level features f1i to f1n, threshold value is assigned to number of FS methods. Selects the second level features f2i to f2m, threshold value is assigned to number of FS methods-1.

Step 4: Selected important features are assigned for classification

Machine Learning Classifiers

Here, various classifiers like Logistic Regression, Random Forest, Decision Tree and SVM are used and also ensemble using voting classifier to check the efficiency of CFS technique.

Logistic Regression

It is a quantifiable examination method accustomed expect information esteem that are pertinent on prior impression of an information assortment. it's a critical calculation within the control of AI. The strategy allows an estimation being employed in an AI application to portray information reliant upon real data. As more appropriate data comes in, the estimation improves at expecting portrayals inside datasets. It predicts a dependent data characteristic by examining the connection between this free attributes.

$$f(x) = \frac{L}{1 + e^{-k(x-x_0)}}$$

f(x) yield of the task

L greatest gain of the curve

k the curle logistic development

x0 the value of x of the crooked midpoint

x cardinal number

Decision Tree

It is a Supervised ML system being employed for both categorization and regression problems, hence all things considered this is essentially liked for categorization problems. Decision Tree is a tree-composed classification algorithm, in that the inside nodes thinks about to the peak of a dataset, the trees branch set up to the option's rule then the leaf nodes include the outcome and this characteristics is dictated from the formula,

$$fi_i = \frac{\sum_{j:node\_j\_splits\_on\_feature\_i} ni_j}{\sum_{k \in all\_nodes} ni_k}$$

fi sub(i)= the value of feature i

ni sub(j)= the value of node j

Support Vector Machin

It is unequivocal method which relies upon the edge support rule. It executes fundamental risk deprecia-tion, which enhances the complicacy of the classifier determined to accomplish astonishing speculation execution. It discovers the hyperplane that constructs the border connecting the classes. The way that depicts the hyperplane are called look after vectors. In such circumstances, Support vector machine appraisal makes a hyperplane which perfectly disengages the path to the non-covering classes. Since it could, a greater time, this is preposterous, thus SVM can discover hyperplanes that help edges also.

$$f(x) = \text{sgn}\left[\sum_{i=1}^{N} a_i y_i K(x_i \bullet x_j) + b\right]$$

Random Forest

It is a classifier which is utilized in gathering and relapse and has a diverse possible trees on various subsets of the dataset and grasps the customary to enhance the discerning exactness of that dataset. It is essentially make use of classification issues. It is high-handed to a solitary decision tree, since it reduces the misdiagnozation by normalizing the results. It is dictated by,

$$norm\_fi_i = \frac{fi_i}{\sum_{j \in all\_features} fi_j}$$

$$RFfi_i = \frac{\sum_{j \in all\_trees} norm\_fi_{ij}}{T}$$

RFfi sub(i) = value of variables i found from the trees in Random Forest model
normfi sub(ij) = the normalized attribute value for i in tree j
T = total number of trees

Voting Ensemble

It is a method that combines group of distinct models and predicts a category considering the chance of selected class as the output. It averages the revelations of all the classification algorithm into Voting Classifier and anticipates the class based on the most significant predominant piece of casting a vote. The contemplation is rather than producing distinct submitted technique and discovering the exactness for all of the classifiers, we build a single design which instructs by these models and predicts yield according to their consolidated larger piece of favour of all yield class.

Workflow

Figure 1. Proposed Work

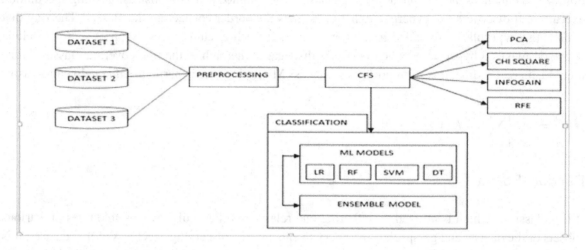

EXPERIMENTAL RESULTS

Four feature selection techniques are combined to form a combined feature selection which is utilized to choose features prior to passing the data to the classifiers. Classification accuracies are observed before and after the feature selection are shown below:

Accuracy of the Classifiers without Combined Feature Selection Technique

In this section, The Accuracy of the classifiers of the three datasets before Combined Feature Selection Technique are shown.

The Figure 2 displays the accuracies of the classifiers for the 1st dataset (skin disease) before applying combined feature selection technique.

The Figure 3 displays the accuracies of the classifiers for the 2nd dataset (PIMA diabetes) before applying combined feature selection technique

The Figure 4 displays the accuracies of the classifiers for the 3rd dataset (diabetes) before applying combined feature selection technique

IMPORTANT FEATURES

In this section, the important features selected from combined feature selection technique for all the three datasets are shown.

The Figure 5 shows the features selected from the combined feature selection for the skin disease dataset.

Figure 2. Accuracy of the 1ˢᵗ Dataset

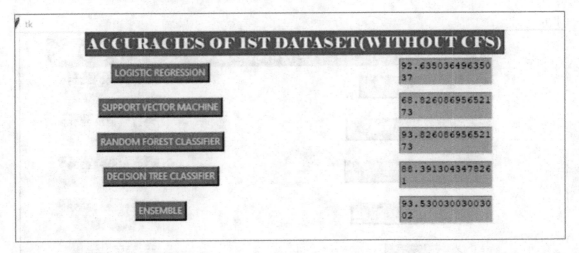

Figure 3. Accuracies of the 2ⁿᵈ Dataset

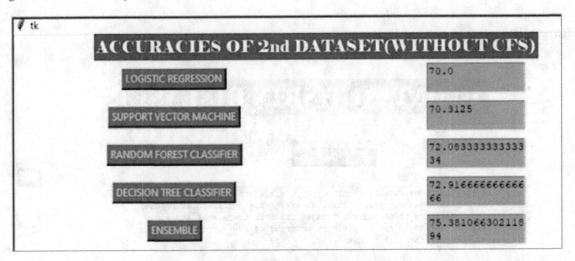

The Figure 6 shows the features selected from the combined feature selection for the Pima diabetes dataset.

The Figure 7 shows the features selected from the combined feature selection for the diabetes dataset.

ACCURACY OF THE CLASSIFIERS WITH COMBINED FEATURE SELECTION TECHNIQUE:

In this section, The Accuracy of the classifiers of the three datasets after Combined Feature Selection Technique are shown

The Figure 8 displays the classifier's accuracy for the 1ˢᵗ dataset (skin disease) using reduced dataset obtained from applying combined feature selection technique.

Figure 4. Accuracies of the 3ʳᵈ Dataset

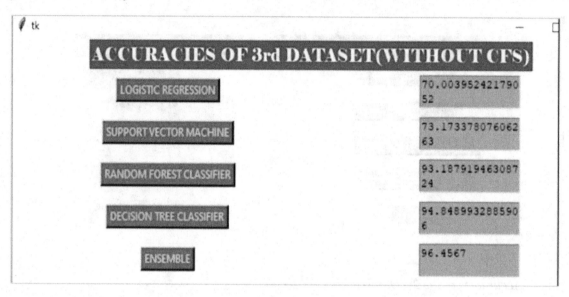

Figure 5. Important features of 1ˢᵗ dataset

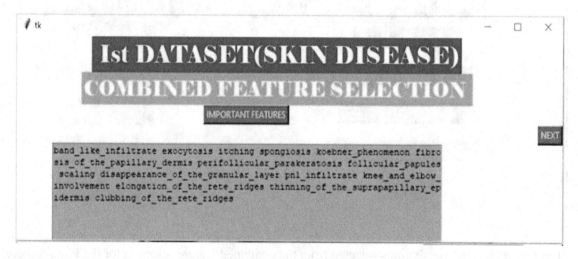

The Figure 9 displays the classifier's accuracy for the 2ⁿᵈ dataset (PIMA diabetes) using reduced dataset obtained from applying combined feature selection technique.

The Figure 10 displays the classifier's accuracy for the 3ʳᵈ dataset (diabetes dataset) using reduced dataset obtained from applying combined feature selection technique.

The Table 1 shows the accuracy of all the classifiers before and after combined feature selection technique for all the three dataset.

Figure 6. Important features of 2nd dataset

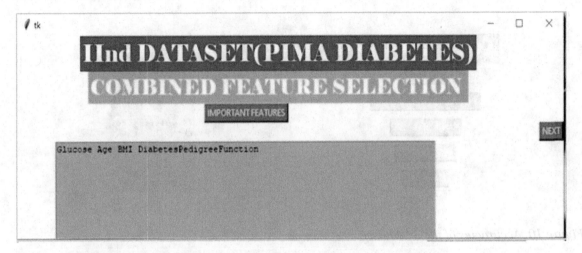

Figure 7. Important features of 3rd dataset

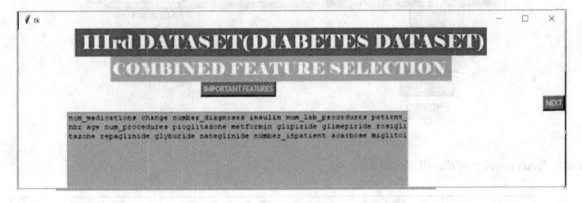

Figure 8. Accuracies of the 1st Dataset

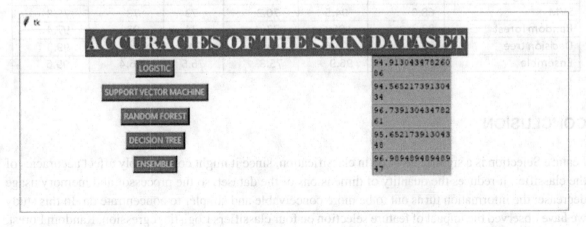

Figure 9. Accuracies of the 2ⁿᵈDataset

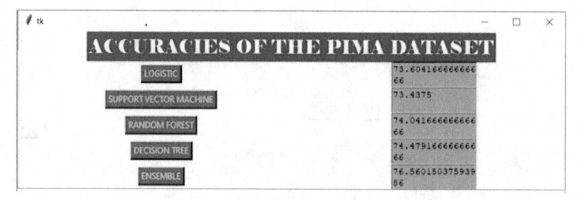

Figure 10. Accuracies of the 3ʳᵈDataset

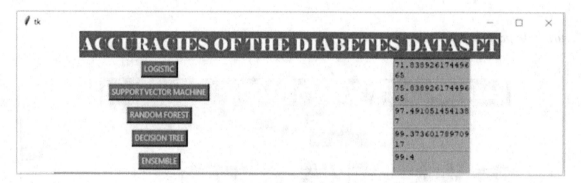

Table 1. Accuracies of the all classifiers

	1ˢᵗ dataset		2ⁿᵈ dataset		3ʳᵈ dataset	
	Without CFS	With CFS	Without CFS	With CFS	Without CFS	with CFS
Logistic regression	92.6	94.9	70	73.6	70	71.8
SVM	68.0	94.5	70.3	73	73	75.8
Random forest	93.7	96	72	74	93	97.4
Decision tree	88.4	95.6	64	74.4	94	99.3
Ensemble	93	96.9	75.3	76.5	96.4	99.6

CONCLUSION

Feature Selection is a significant issue in classification, since it might considerably affect accuracies of the classifier. It reduces the quantity of dimensions of the dataset, so the processor and memory usage decrease; the information turns out to be more conceivable and simpler to concentrate on. In this study we have observed the impact of feature selection on four classifiers Logistic regression, Random Forest, Decision Tree and Support Vector Machine. A consolidated component determination (CFS) is employed to select the rule credits. The segment affirmation method like Chi-square, RFE, Info-gain and PCA are joined to perform out the undertaking. These frameworks task differently on the dataset. Classification accuracy is improved in Post-usable dataset for all the classifiers. The Classifiers are then combined using an ensemble Voting Classifier. The CFS with ensemble classifier are employed with three different datasets, which provides the best accuracy when compared with the other classifiers.

REFERENCES

Ahmed, T. M. (2016). Using data mining to develop models for classifying diabetic patient controllevel based on historical medical records. *Journal of Theoretical and Applied Information Technology*, 316–323.

Alharbi, A., & Alghahtani, M. (2019). Using genetic algorithm and elm neural network for feature extraction and classification of type-2 diabetic mellitus. *Applied Artificial Intelligence*, *33*(4), 311–328. doi:10.1080/08839514.2018.1560545

Aruna, S., Nandakishore, L. V., & Rajagopalan, S. P. (2012). A hybrid feature selection method based on IGSBFS and naive bayes for the diagnosis of erythemato-squamous diseases. *International Journal of Computers and Applications*, *41*(7), 13–18. doi:10.5120/5552-7623

Christobel, Y. A., & Sivaprakasam, P. (2013). A new Classwise k Nearest Neighbors(CKNN) method for classificationof diabetes disease. *International Journal of Engineering and Advanced Technology*, 396–400.

Farahamandian, M., Lotfi, Y., & Maleki, I. (2015). Data mining algorithms application in diabetes disease diagnosis. *MAGNT Reaserch Report*, 989-997.

Maryam, N. A. (1867). A hybrid feature selection method using multiclass SVM for diagnosis of erythemato-squamous disease. *AIP Conference Proceedings*.

Polat, K., & Gunes, S. (2007). An expert system approach based on principal component analysis and adaptive neuro-fuzzy inference system to diagnosis of diabetic disease. *Digital Signal Processing*, *17*(4), 702–710. doi:10.1016/j.dsp.2006.09.005

Verma, A. K., & Pal, S. (2019). Prediction of skin disease with three different feature selection techniques using stacking ensemble method. *Applied Biochemistry and Biotechnology*. PMID:31845194

Xie, J., Lei, J., Xie, W., Shi, Y., & Liu, X. (2013). Two-stage hybrid feature selection algorithms for diagnosing erythemato-squamous diseases. *Health Information Science and Systems*, *1*(1), 1–14. doi:10.1186/2047-2501-1-10 PMID:26042184

Xie, X., & Wang, C. (2011). Using support vector machines with a novel hybrid feature selection method for diagnosis of erythemato-squamous. *Expert Systems with Applications*, *38*(5), 5809–5815. doi:10.1016/j.eswa.2010.10.050

Chapter 23
Generalization and Efficiency on Finger Print Presentation Attack Anomaly Detection

Hemalatha J.

Department of Computer Science and Engineering, AAA College of Engineering and Technology, India

Vivek V.

AAA College of Engineering and Technology, India

Kavitha Devi M. K.

Thiagarajar College of Engineering, India

Sekar Mohan

AAA College of Engineering and Technology, India

ABSTRACT

Biometric identification systems are highly used for verification and identification like fingerprint recognition, voice recognition, face recognition, etc. The very famous biometric technique is fingerprint recognition. A fingerprint is the pattern of ridges and valleys on the surface of a fingertip. The endpoints and crossing points of ridges are called minutiae. The basic assumption is that the minutiae pattern of every finger is unique and does not change during one's life. In the present era, fingerprint-based biometric authentication system gets popularized, but still, this biometric system is vulnerable to various attacks, particularly presentation attacks. This chapter explains how the knowledge-driven neural networks work on fingerprint anomaly detection. In addition, the various features available to detect the anomaly in biometric are also discussed.

DOI: 10.4018/978-1-7998-8892-5.ch023

INTRODUCTION

In the recent days due to the advancements in science and technology we are finding biometric recognition systems in huge places especially in confidential places. The biometric recognition application system emerges with high security control based on the users requirements and their convenience level. Examples of some biometric recognition application systems are: i) fingerprint lock and eyerish recognition in smart phones, mobile payments fingerprint recognition in voters system, palm print recognition, crossing in international borders, computerized patient records, cryptographic key generation credit cards and etc. Among all the biometric recognition systems fingerprint recognition systems are widely using system (Antonelli, 2006; Baldisserra, 2006). Even though the fingerprint biometric system communities have developed huge significant advancements, it has highly affected by more external attacks and thereby we are in need of further advancements then and there. The biological morphological structure of friction ridge skin is given below.

Figure 1. Biological morphological structure of friction ridge skin

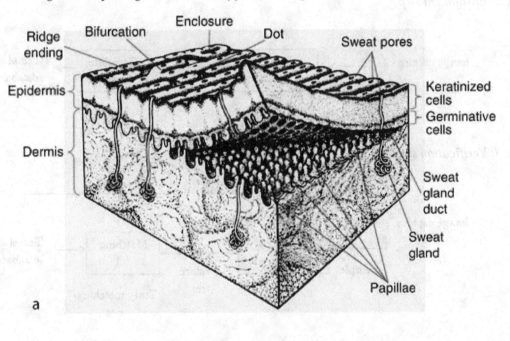

At the time of primary friction ridge growth, parallel nervous and cardiovascular systems also will grow. The character of capillary nerves under the dermis portion yields the vascular fingerprint with unique features to every human fingerprint. This unique feature will helps to not changing the fingerprint patterns even on any cuts or bruises on the fingers.

Fundamental parameters of recognizing the individuals: There are two fundamental parameters are there to recognizing the individual fingerprints: i) uniqueness- Humans having the same DNA (monozygatic twins) have unique fingerprint features and so every human have the unique fingerprint features. ii) Permanence - the accuracy of fingerprint recognition for a human will not be changed throughout his life rather there is some cuts or bruises on the fingers.

Due to the emergence of fingerprint sensing technology, many recognition algorithms are emerged among them ten print recognition algorithm is more accurate. The basic recognition system has two step processes: i) enrollment- a human fingerprint is acquired then features are extracted from it and then template will be generating, later template will be matched with unique user identifier the resultant will be stored in the database. ii) Recognition – based on the context individual recognition will be validated.

Figure 2. Enrollment step

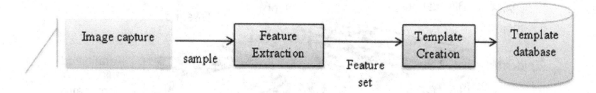

Figure 3. Verification step

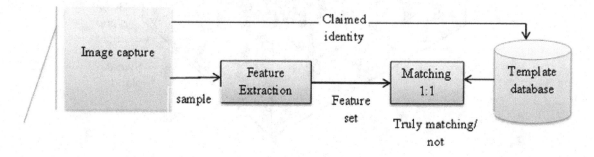

Figure 4. Identification step

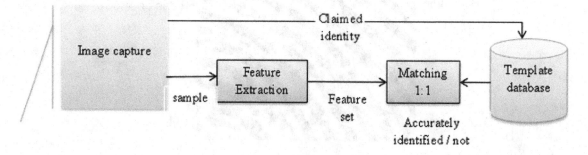

Fingerprint acquisition – The method of catching the friction ridge for fingerprint recognition is called fingerprint acquisition.

Fingerprint Extraction Systems

Feature extraction is the key role phase to accurately recognize the fingerprints. Among all the characteristics of a fingerprint the most important characteristics are interleaved dark ridges, bright valleys. The features of fingerprint recognition are basically classified into level 1, level 2 and level 3 features.

Level 1 features: It consists of global features such as whorl, arch, loop, singular point features such as deltas, cores, ridge spacing and orientation. All the above features can be extracted by some image processing techniques such as ridge detection with maximum curvature and some machine learning techniques.

Level 2 features: It consists of local features; it presents the idea of ridges shows the discontinuity like bifurcations, minutiae points and etc. These minutiae can be changed from one individual fingerprint to the other. For example in a curved fingerprint it can have more than 100 minutiae. /the details of both spatial and angular concurrence with nearly 15 minutiae will produce high confidence of fingerprints matching. The technique used for these feature extractions are gabor filter (image processing technique) or some machine learning algorithm(Howard, 2017; Marcel, 2014, Rowe, 2006; Smith,2011).

Level 3 features: It consists of feature characteristics such as scars, dots creases, sweat pores etc. It may vary from human to human so it provides some additional unique feature to the extractors.

Fingerprint Recognition

Fingerprint recognition is a technique or an algorithm which can compare two fingerprint samples based on the similarity score and to recognize whether the given samples are similar or not. If the similarity score is nearly 0 then there is vast difference among the samples otherwise the given two samples or similar. In the other case if the similarity score is above some threshold t then the samples are highly matched. This fingerprint matching algorithm can be approached by three categories.

i) Correlation based fingerprint matching algorithm - when provides the two samples of fingerprint images, it finds the correlation among the pixels for rotations, displacements.
ii) Minutiae based fingerprint matching algorithm – This algorithm calculates the association among the given sample minutiae and testing minutiae. The outcome of this algorithm will be the paired minutiae.
iii) Non minutiae fingerprint matching algorithm – This algorithm properly use the pattern of ridge characteristics such as finger texture information, local ridge orientation and etc.

Fingerprint Recognition System (FPRS)

Before seeing the fingerprint biometric attacks we will discuss about where this recognition system is not working and its influence factors. Due to some influence factors, there exist many cases where this fingerprint recognition system is not used. Those are environmental impacts, dust on fingerprint sensor, some disease and electromagnetic radiation.

The fingerprint recognition system consists of five basic steps to follow:

i)   Fingerprint acquires system – human fingerprint attribute is scanned using some physical sensor and it will transfer to the digitalized computer.

ii)   Image Enhancement – Quality of the fingerprints caught by the sensors will be checked and enhanced on this session. Various image processing methods are there to enhance the sensed fingerprint such as edge filter, frequency spectrum; both discrete cosine and fast fourier transform Gabor filter, curvlet denosing and etc.

iii) Thresholding – Basically in image processing process, the images are acquired and resized into 256*256 gray levels then later it will be represented in binary formats. Various thresholding schemes such as adaptive thresholding, region based binary formatted images will be separated into papillary lines called ridges and background images called valleys.

iv)   Thinning or skeletization – The output from the papillary lines are having high variations in thickness. In this thinning step all the papillary lines will be stripped into exactly one pixel.

v)   Minutiae Extraction – In this step the thinning pixels will be detected and extracted all the minutiae pixels on the images.

Not all the times but fingerprint recognition system may attacked by some vulnerabilities or some attacks. The below figure depicts basic flow that the possibility of fingerprint system get vulnerable.

Figure 5. Vulnerabilities in Fingerprint recognition system

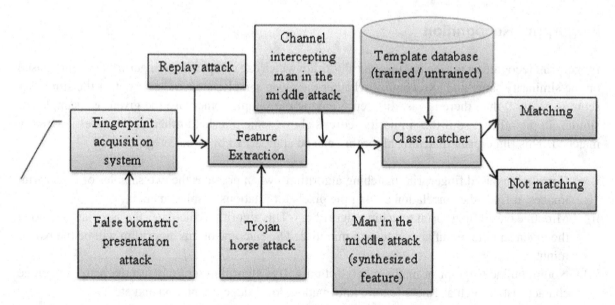

WHAT IS ANOMALY IN FPRS?

In the view of sharing data easily in digital world, data is a matter in the present days. We cannot share the data blindly without adding any security because data has a value. It is not enough to simply collect the data, process the data, store the data and sharing the data many violence's are taking place while sharing the data. In that place we can place over Anomaly detection. Anomaly detection is an application of data science through that we can recognize the modifications, nonconformities, and exemptions from the norm in a dataset. Often it is called outlier detection where we have looks at the dataset for finding the outlying data points from the usual data points or from any usual activity

For example: Credit card companies used to gather records on the whole thing we purchase, accounting with money we spend, spending place, spending reasons, purchasing frequency and etc. finally they will chase our account details and automatically fraudulent starts. Here, Anomaly detection starts work to investigate entirely the data overhead to recognize fraudulent credit card action in a fraction of seconds of a transaction enchanting place.

There are many applications of Anomaly detection such as fraud detection, fingerprint recognition, social media watching, Forensics and etc.

Various Attacks in FPRS

As we discussed in the above, the fingerprint recognition system is used in many real time application such as smart phones, online banking's, national ID, and etc. In the parallel side the vulnerabilities of the security to presentation attack is also increasing. The methods to find about the presentation attacks are as follows:

a) Gummy fingers- Gummy fingers is a fabricated one which can looks and make like an accurate original finger to trace the or steal the identity.
b) 2dim/3dim printed fingerprint
c) Fingerprint altered – In order to avoid identification the original fingerprints will be purposefully or intentionally tampered.
d) Finger cadaver – Is a form of presentation attack where it will fabricate the fingers with multitude ranges from molding to casting to use advanced printing techniques.

Due to the widespread use of fingerprint recognition such as smartphone unlocking, financial transaction authentication presentation attack is the most common and state-of –the-art now. International Organization for Standard IEC301071:2016 (ISO, 1988) gives the definition for the presentation attack as "as "presentation to a biometric data collection subsystem aimed at interfering with the operation of a biometric authentication system". The best and famous method to perform presentation attack is to use fingerprint spoofing that is using the rubber finger (Matsumoto, 2012). Rubber finger is a spoofing method which can be made by gelatin, latex, and wood glue. It accurately imitates the friction rib pattern. These can be created using a variety of manufacturing processes, from simple moulding and casting to the use of advanced 2D and 3D printing techniques (Tarang Chugh, 2019; Ghiani, 2017; Cao, 2016; Engelsma, 2018).

These fingerprint spoofing attack (Biggio, 2012) were described to evade fingerprint system security with tepe positive rate of more than 70 percentage.

For example in the real world incident happened in Sept. 2013, Germany countries Chaos Computer Clu has lacerated the capacitive sensor of emerged Apple iPhone 5s with inbuilt Touch ID fingerprint technology. This was happened by using the high resolution photograph of the registered user`s fingerprint to produce a spoof fingerprint by wood glue. In the another incident, in July 2016, Michigan State University researchers helped police department in a murder case by exposing a fingerprint secure smartphone via two dimensional fingerprint spoof.

Figure 6. PA fabrication materials for the study

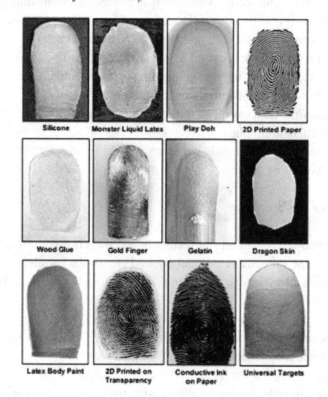

METHODS USED FOR DETECTING ANOMALIES IN FPRS

General Methods

As the likelihood of fingerprint PA attacks increases, the detection of presentation attacks is an urgent need to be the forefront of ensuring the safekeeping of fingerprint credit systems. In answer, a sequence of live fingerprint detection races happend since 2009 to advance cutting-edge technology, evaluate proposed PAD solutions, and the final version was held in 2017 (Mura, 2018, Pankanti, 2002). In general, presentation attacks are either (i) a hardware-based approach, that is, a sensor augmented fingerprint reader to collect evidence of subject survival, or (ii) a software-based approach, that is, a presented fingerprint image. It can be detected by extracting features from (or a series of frames) (Mura, 2018; Marasco, 2015). A hardware-based approach proposes special types of sensors, such as) (Hogan, 2015), to detect vitality characteristics. The open source fingerprint reader, which can be built using off-the-shelf hardware, uses a dual camera design that provides two complementary streams of information for spoofing detection (Engelsma, 2018).

Figure 7. The Fingerprint Spoof Buster (Chugh, 2018)

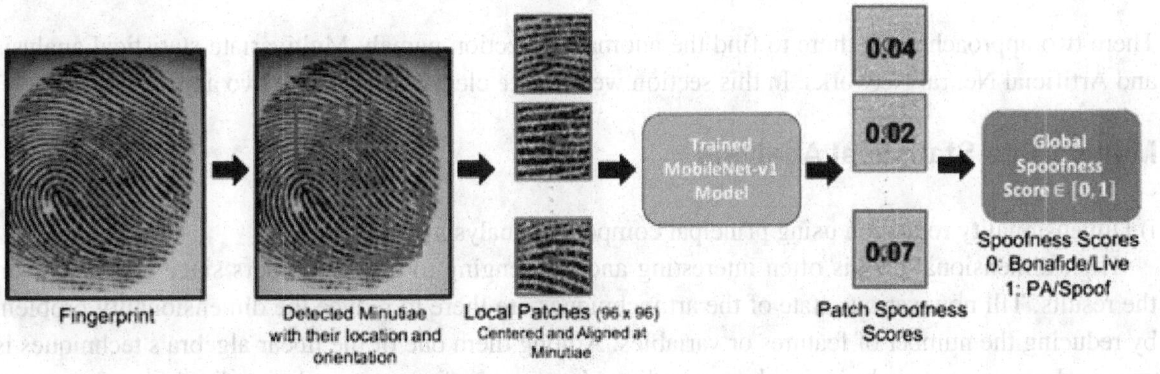

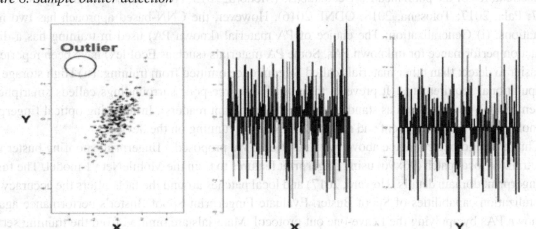

Methods using Machine Learning

In contrast to hardware-based solutions, software-based solutions work with all fingerprint readers on the market. While examining the literature art there are various techniques are there with handcrafter features such as a) features with anatomical distribution and pore location (Marcialis, 2010), b) sweat from physiological features (Marasco, 2012), c) texture-based features (eg BSIF (Ghiani, 2013), WLD (Gragnaniello, 2013) and LCPD (Gragnaniello, 2015). The major drawback on the above said PAD approach is poor performance of generalization for new PA materials (Rattani, 2015). Few researchers said about the PAD model has an open set detection problem. One of the detection in a PA made of a new material using a Weibull calibration SVM, which is a variant of the SVM based on extreme statistical properties. Ding and Ross (Ding, 2016; Jain,1988) used texture features extracted only from the actual fingerprint image. Train an ensemble of multiple single-class SVMs.

Anomaly detection can be done by plotting the data points in two dimensional data representations x and y. It helps to find visually the data points located outside are detected and suspected as anomalies. From the above figure it is quite difficult to find the outliers from the one variable at a time. Whereas by the combination of X and Y variable it ends to identify anomaly or not easily.

Figure 8. Sample outlier detection

APPROACHES IN ANOMALY DETECTION

There two approaches are there to find the anomaly detection namely Multivariate statistical analysis and Artificial Neural Networks. In this section we will see clearly about these two approaches.

Multivariate Statistical Analysis

i) Dimensionality reduction using principal component analysis (PCA)

High dimensional data is often interesting and challenging to the researchers since its impacts on the results. Till now various state of the art techniques are there to reduce the dimensionality problem by reducing the number of features or variables. Among them one of the linear algebra's techniques is principal component analysis. It achieves by linearly maps the features into lower dimensional space so that the feature variances in low dimensional representation can be maximized. In Principal Component Analysis, covariance matrix is constructed for the given sample data and then from the resultant covariance matrix Eigen vectors will be calculated. The largest eigen value from the eigen vectors is directly used to reconstruct the variance of original data. As a result the reconstructed data has reduced with few spanned feature vectors by eliminated some unimportant variance.

ii)   Multivariate anomaly detection

Identifying the anomaly with one or two variables then it is easy to be done by data visualization. When we have high dimensional data then multivariate statistics provides the best result. When we deal with collection of data points, it may have Gaussian distribution. So for the given data points we have to calculate probability distribution p(x) and it may considered as training data. Then when a new sample given named x, it should exactly compared with $p(x)$ with some threshold say r. During the comparison if $p(x)<r$ then it will conclude as anomaly. The reason behind is normal examples tends larger $p(x)$ and anomalous examples tends to small $p(x)$.

Methods using Deep Learning

The novel Convolutional Neural Network -based fingerprint PAD solution shown to outstrip the hand-crafted features of the published LivDet database (Menotti, 2015; Nogueira, 2016; Jang, 2017; Chugh, 2017; Pala, 2017; Tolosana, 2018; ODNI, 2016). However, the CNN-based approach has two main limitations. (i) Generalization: The choice of PA material (known PA) used in training has a direct impact on performance for unknown PAs. Some PA materials (such as EcoFlex) have been reported to be easier to detect than other materials called Silgum once omitted from training. (ii) High storage and computational requirements: It prevents the use of resource-poor surroundings calleds smartphones and embedded devices (such as stand-alone smart fingerprint readers). Introducing optical fingerprint technology requires an efficient and robust PAD solution running on the device.

Chugh et al to overcome the above two limitations. We proposed a fingerprint spoofing buster with a centralized local patch (96x96) using fingerprint features to train the MobileNet v1 model. The fusion of fingerprint domain details (Howard, 2017) and local patches around the facts offers the accuracy and generalization capabilities of Spoof Buster. Evaluate Fingerprint Spoof Buster's performance against unknown PAs by applying the Leave-one out protocol. Materials are omitted from the training set and are used to assess the performance of cross-materials or generalizations. From the Convolutional Neural Network- PA samples of both 3DtDNE, Bonafide can be utilized to learning the associations among various PA materials. The grouping of PA materials can be done by the material properties and its performance among the materials. Later we can include them in the training and to find the corresponding materials set. It can enhance the generalization performance. And parallel Fingerprint Spoof Buster can be optimized for smartphone application and real-time implication.

Auto Encoder Networks

In the concept of auto encoder neural networks, data coding's will be trained in an unsupervised form. The concept of auto encoders is used to learn the encoding from some data set for reducing the dimensionality. In the continuation of reduction, auto encoder tires to produce from the reduced encoding which is so close to the original inputs. The architecture of autoencoder is a feed forward non-recurrent neural network which has an input layer, an output layer and one or more hidden layers connecting them. The number output is layer is almost equals the input layer. The autoencoder networks are trained on input datum and then it compress by reconstructing the input variables. At the time of dimensionality reduction the reconstructed data is again back as original variables.

Figure 9. Autoencoder network

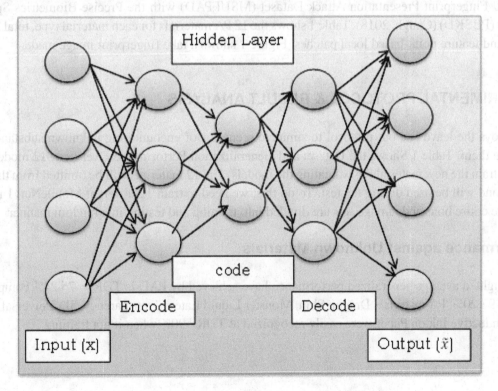

Proposed FPRS for Fingerprint Presentation Attack Anomaly Detection

Main contribution of this chapter is as follows.

1. To assess the performance of generalization in Fingerprint Spoof Buster with CNN based PAD approach with the help of PA materials.
2. To use 3D t-SN characteristics for finding the characterization set of PAD materials may cover the entire PA feature space.
3. To study about the optimization of Fingerprint Spoof Buster (Chugh, 2018)

i) Fingerprint Spoof Buster

Fingerprint Spoof Buster, a popular CNN-based PAD model (Howard, 2017), uses a local patch (96x96) centered on the fingerprint feature (see Figure 2). Achieved the latest performance (Chugh, 2018) in the public LivDet database [11] and surpassed the IARPA Odin project [28] True Detection Rate = 97 .0% at False Detection Rate = 0 .2%

ii) Presentation Attack Database

The database iamges with a collection of 5,740 Bonafide, 4,910 Presentation attacks are taken. It consists of MSU Fingerprint Presentation Attack Dataset (MSUFPAD) with the Precise Biometrics SpoofKit Dataset (PBSKD) (Chugh, 2018). Table 1 shows the 12 PA materials for each material type, total impressions, and feature point-based local patches. Figure 1 shows a fake fingerprint image made.

EXPERIMENTAL PROTOCOL & RESULT ANALYSIS

It employs the leave one out protocol to simulate scenarios of encountering unknown substances and evaluate them. Table 1 Shows the Dataset and Generalization Performance Overview. 12 models have used to train the new material for evaluating the models. The 12 materials will be omitted from the training set and will be used during the test. To do this, we need to train 12 different MobileNetv1 models. Here the entire bonafinde image sets are divided into training and testing in a random manner.

Performance against Unknown Materials

The weighted average generalized performance have achieved by PAD is TDR = 75.24% compared to TDR = 97.20%. PA materials Dragon Skin, Monster Liquid Latex, Transparency, 3D Universal Target, and Conductive Ink on Paper were easily recognized at TDR [3] 90% when it not training.

Table 1. The performance of Fingerprint SpoofBuster on unknown PA's

Fingerprint PA Material	Images	Patches	Generalization Performance
2D Printed Paper	481	7381	55.44%
3D Universal Targets	40	1085	95.00%
Play Doh	715	17602	58.42%
Dragon Skin	285	7700	97.48%
Transparency	137	3846	95.83%
Gold Fingers	295	9402	88.22%
Gelatin	294	10508	54.95%
Latex Body Paint	176	6366	76.35%
Monster Liquid Latex	882	27458	94.77%
Conductive ink on paper	50	2205	90.00%
Silicone	1160	38145	67.62%
Wood glue	397	12681	86.38%
PA's Totally	**4912**	**144379**	Average:
Bonafide Totally	**5743**	**228143**	**75.24%**

PA Material Characteristics

While comparing the PA materials it is easier to detect even it is not showing in the training. The following material properties were measured for a particular dataset of fingerprint images taken with a CrossMatch Guardian 200 optical reader. These material properties were selected in consultation with materials science experts.

Figure 10. Light absorbance attributes of 12 PA materials

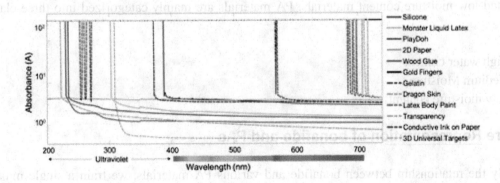

Figure 11. FT Infrared Spectroscopy of 12 PA materials

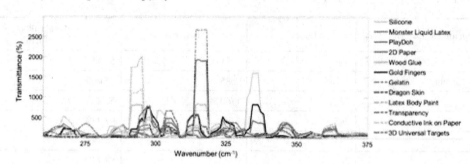

Ultraviolet-visible (UVVis) spectroscopy: The Ultraviolet-visible is retort to a specific material signifies the fascination of monochromatic radiation at different wavelengths. The peak UVVis response indicates that the material has a high absorption of light at a given level. Wavelength (Perkampus, 2013). Absorbance was measured using a Perkin Elmar Lambda 900 UV / Vis / NIR spectrometer. Material properties shown in Figure 3. Fourier Transform Infrared (FT / IR) Spectroscopy: It is characteristic of its molecular structure. The frequency of the absorbed radiation matches the vibration frequency (Smith, 2011). Figure 4 shows the FT / IR response of 12 PA materials measured

Material elasticity: Spoofing made of elastic material is more deformed than less elastic material, and when the spoofing is pressed against the glass plate of the fingerprint reader, the friction ribs are greatly deformed. Twelve different PA materials are classified into three classes based on the observed elasticity.

- High elasticity
- Medium elasticity
- Low elasticity

Moisture content: Moisture content is a significant material which perform the fingerprint image as more contrast and more differently.

PA materials with great dampness content can yield high contrast images with the Cross Match reader associated low moisture content materials. PA materials are mainly categorized into three classes of moisture.

- High water content
- Medium Moisture
- Low moisture content

Feature Representation of bonafide and PAs

To study the relationship between bonafide and various PA materials, we train a single multi-class MobileNetv1 model to distinguish between 13 classes. bonafide and 12 PA materials. The training split contains a randomly selected set of 100 frames, or half the total number of frames from each bonafide and PA material (whichever is less), for a total of 1,102 frames. Similarly, the testing set can built from the remaining set of images. This protocol has been embraced to diminish bias because of the imbalanced training datasets. A 1024-dimensional feature vector is extracted from the congestion layer of the

MobileNetv1 network (Howard, 2017) and projected into 3D using the tSNE approach (Maaten, 2008). Figures 5 (a) and 5 (f) show the demonstration of various subgroups of Bonafide and PA materials in the 3DtSNE feature space from various perspectives chosen to offer a broad vision. Bonafide and silicone is included in all charts for perspective. 3D charts are generated and accessible in the Plotly library.

Figure 12. The bonafide and different subsets of PA materials

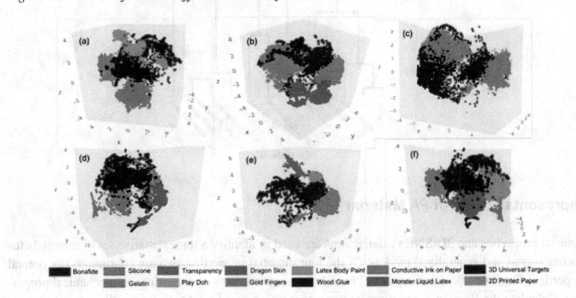

Figure 13. Average Pearson correlation values on twelve PA materials based on its characteristics.

	Silicone	Monster Liquid Latex	Play Doh	2D Paper	Wood Glue	Gold Fingers	Gelatin	Dragon Skin	Latex Body Paint	Transparency	Conductive Ink on Paper	3D Targets
Silicone	1	0.43	0.37	0.03	0.48	0.16	0.31	0.73	0.03	0.17	0.1	0.04
Monster Liquid Latex	0.43	1	0.24	0.04	0.66	0.31	0.82	0.48	0.14	0.32	0.16	0.27
Play Doh	0.37	0.24	1	0.09	0.15	0.13	0.19	0.48	0.37	0.34	0.3	0.39
2D Paper	0.03	0.04	0.09	1	0.04	0.26	0	0.06	0.27	0.64	0.59	-0.01
Wood Glue	0.48	0.66	0.15	0.04	1	0.33	0.57	0.5	0.23	0.16	0.29	0.32
Gold Fingers	0.16	0.31	0.13	0.26	0.33	1	0.31	0.15	0.11	0.35	0.34	0.37
Gelatin	0.31	0.82	0.19	0	0.57	0.31	1	0.4	0.23	0.15	0.09	0.35
Dragon Skin	0.73	0.48	0.48	0.06	0.5	0.15	0.4	1	0.12	0.28	0.16	0.15
Latex Body Paint	0.03	0.14	0.37	0.27	0.23	0.11	0.23	0.12	1	0.34	0.52	0.53
Transparency	0.17	0.32	0.34	0.64	0.16	0.35	0.15	0.28	0.34	1	0.72	0.14
Conductive Ink on Paper	0.1	0.16	0.3	0.59	0.29	0.34	0.09	0.16	0.52	0.72	1	0.18
3D Targets	0.04	0.27	0.39	-0.01	0.32	0.37	0.35	0.15	0.53	0.14	0.18	1

Figure 14. Representation of the hierarchical clustering of available PAs

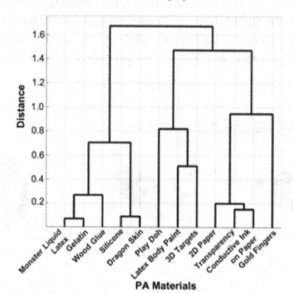

Representative set of PA Material

Material properties and 3DtSNE visualizations are used to identify a representative set of materials for training robust and generalized models. Of the four material properties, two are continuous (ie, optical properties) Then we calculate four 12x12 correlation matrices in two categories (ie, mechanical properties). Calculate the Pearson correlation for two consecutive variables 14. Between all material pairs to generate two correlation matrices C^{uvvis} and C^{ftir}. For two PA materials, for two categorical variables m_i and m_j belong to the same category, we assign $C_{i,j} = 1$, else $C_{i,j} = 0$, to generate $C^{elastic}$ and $C^{moisture}$.

- The PA materials Silicone, Play-Doh, Gelatin, and 2D printed paper are the closest to genuine fingerprints in the 3DtSNE functional area when compared to other materials. This explains why excluding one of them results in poor generalization performance when tested against them.
- These PA materials appear in the various clusters of the dendrogram (see Figures 5 (a) and 7). Since silicone is between Bonafide and Dragon Skin,
- The PA material Dragon Skin is easy to find if silicone is included in the training (see Figures 5 (b) and (d)). These materials are also in the same cluster and show common material properties. PA material Transparency is easily distinguishable when 2D Printed Paper is included in training. In the tSNE visualization, we observe that 2D Printed Paper forms two clusters, where one of the clusters is collocated with transparency (see Figures 5 (a) and (e)).
- PA materials Wood Glue and Gelatin are collocated in feature space assisting each other if included in training (see Figure 5 (c)), but Gelatin is closer to Bonafide which explains its worse performance compared to Wood Glue. These materials also form a second level cluster in the dendrogram.
- PA material latex body paint is between paper conductive ink and paper conductive ink, PA material monster liquid latex is between Bonafide and 3D universal target with 3D tSNE visualization, paper conductive ink and 3D reflects the high detection rate of universal targets. Though, the

above said materials will not group till final aggregation step, suggesting the alternatives in material properties which may investigate in future.

From the inventions it may conclude that six PA materials shield practically the whole space of Bonafide. To achieve these 6 PA materials the model can trained with Bonafide. From this we can strongly believe that for any new materials PAD performance can be estimated via investigating the material properties and envisioning a few samples in tSNE space, rather than collecting a large data set for each new material. To address the second limitation of the high resource requirements of the CNN-based PAD approach, the next section proposes fingerprint spoofing buster optimization.

CONCLUSION

The state-of-the-art CNN-based PAD approach has two major limitations. (I) generalization to materials has not been grasped at the training time (ii) computational cost is very high and memory requirements are very high comparatively for execution. In this discussion, 12 different PA materials were used to evaluate the generalized performance of a state-of-the-art PAD approach, the fingerprint spoofing buster. To illustrate the performance of cross-material experiments, we investigate PA material clustering by using 4 properties of optical and mechanical later by 3DtSNE visualization. This may raise a conclusion that PA subset materials are very essential to do PAD training more robustly. In addition, two optimizations for state-of-the-art PADs are discussed and employed the Android app which can runs on standard smartphones and performs real-time PA detection without significant performance degradation. Future work will evaluate and compare several PAD solutions and include new PA materials.

REFERENCES

Antonelli, R. (2006). Fake Finger Detection by Skin Distortion Analysis. *IEEE TIFS, 1*(3), 360–373.

Baldisserra, D., Franco, A., Maio, D., & Maltoni, D. (2006). Fake Fingerprint Detection by Odor Analysis. In *Proc. ICB*. Springer.

Biggio, Z., Akhtar, Z., Fumera, G., Marcialis, G. L., & Roli, F. (2012). Security Evaluation of Biometric Authentication Systems under Real Spoofing Attacks. *IET Biometrics, 1*(1), 11–24. doi:10.1049/iet-bmt.2011.0012

Cao & Jain. (2016). *Hacking mobile phones using 2D Printed Fingerprints*. MSU Tech. report, MSU-CSE-16-2.

Chugh, T., Cao, K., & Jain, A. K. (2018). Fingerprint Spoof Buster: Use of Minutiae-centered Patches. *IEEE TIFS, 13*(9), 2190–2202. doi:10.1109/TIFS.2018.2812193

Chugh, T., Cao, K., & Jain, A. K. (2017). Fingerprint Spoof Detection Using Minutiae-based Local Patches. *Proc. IEEE IJCB*. 10.1109/BTAS.2017.8272745

Chugh & Jain. (2019). *Fingerprint Presentation Attack Detection: Generalization and Efficiency*. IEEE.

Ding, Y., & Ross, A. (2016). An ensemble of one-class SVMs for fingerprint spoof detection across different fabrication materials. *Proc. IEEEWIFS*, 1–6. 10.1109/WIFS.2016.7823572

Engelsma, J. J., Arora, S. S., Jain, A. K., & Paulter, N. G. (2018). Universal 3D Wearable Fingerprint Targets: Advancing Fingerprint Reader Evaluations. *IEEE TIFS*, *13*(6), 1564–1578. doi:10.1109/TIFS.2018.2797000

Engelsma, J. J., Cao, K., & Jain, A. K. (2018). *Raspireader: Open source fingerprint reader*. IEEE TPAMI.

Ghiani, L., Hadid, A., Marcialis, G. L., & Roli, F. (2013). Fingerprint liveness detection using Binarized Statistical Image Features. *Proc. IEEE BTAS*, 1–6. 10.1109/BTAS.2013.6712708

Ghiani, L., Yambay, D. A., Mura, V., Marcialis, G. L., Roli, F., & Schuckers, S. A. (2017). Review of the Fingerprint Liveness Detection (LivDet) competition series: 2009 to 2015. *Image and Vision Computing*, *58*, 110–128. doi:10.1016/j.imavis.2016.07.002

Gragnaniello, Poggi, Sansone, & Verdoliva. (2013). Fingerprint liveness detection based on Weber Local Image Descriptor. *Proc. IEEE Workshop on Biometric Meas. Syst. Secur. Med. Appl.*, 46–50.

Gragnaniello, G., Poggi, G., Sansone, C., & Verdoliva, L. (2015). Local contrast phase descriptor for fingerprint liveness detection. *Pattern Recognition*, *48*(4), 1050–1058. doi:10.1016/j.patcog.2014.05.021

Hogan. (2015). *Multiple reference OCT system*. US Patent 9,113,782.

Howard, A. G., Zhu, M., Chen, B., Kalenichenko, D., Wang, W., Weyand, T., Andreetto, M., & Adam, H. (2017). *Mobilenets: Efficient convolutional neural networks for mobile vision applications*. arXiv preprint arXiv:1704.04861.

International Standards Organization. (2016). *ISO/IEC 30107-1:2016, Information Technology—Biometric Presentation Attack Detection—Part 1: Framework*. https://www.iso.org/standard/53227.html

Jain, A. K., & Dubes, R. C. (1988). *Algorithms for Clustering Data*. Prentice-Hall, Inc.

Jang, H.-U., Choi, H.-Y., Kim, D., Son, J., & Lee, H.-K. (2017). Fingerprint spoof detection using contrast enhancement and convolutional neural networks. In *ICISA* (pp. 331–338). Springer. doi:10.1007/978-981-10-4154-9_39

Maaten, L. V. D., & Hinton, G. (2008). Visualizing Data using t-SNE. *JMLR*, *9*(Nov), 2579–2605.

Marasco & Ross. (2015). A Survey on Antispoofing Schemes for Fingerprint Recognition Systems. *ACM Computing Surveys*.

Marasco & Sansone. (2012). Combining perspiration-and morphology-based static features for fingerprint liveness detection. *PR Letters*, *33*(9), 1148–1156.

Marcel, S., Nixon, M. S., & Li, S. Z. (2014). *Handbook of Biometric AntiSpoofing*. Springer.

Marcialis, L., Roli, F., & Tidu, A. (2010). Analysis of fingerprint pores for vitality detection. *Proc. 20th ICPR*, 1289–1292. 10.1109/ICPR.2010.321

Matsumoto, T., Matsumoto, H., Yamada, K., & Hoshino, S. (2012). Impact of artificial gummy fingers on fingerprint systems. *Proceedings of the Society for Photo-Instrumentation Engineers*, *4677*, 275–289. doi:10.1117/12.462719

Menotti, D., Chiachia, G., Pinto, A., Schwartz, W. R., Pedrini, H., Falcao, A. X., & Rocha, A. (2015). Deep representations for iris, face, and fingerprint spoofing detection. *IEEE TIFS*, *10*(4), 864–879. doi:10.1109/TIFS.2015.2398817

Mura, V., Orru, G., Casula, R., Sibiriu, A., Loi, G., Tuveri, P., Ghiani, L., & Marcialis, G. L. (2018). LivDet 2017 Fingerprint Liveness Detection Competition 2017. *Proc. ICB*, 297–302. 10.1109/ICB2018.2018.00052

Nogueira, R. F., de Alencar Lotufo, R., & Machado, R. C. (2016). Fingerprint Liveness Detection Using Convolutional Neural Networks. *IEEE TIFS*, *11*(6), 1206–1213. doi:10.1109/TIFS.2016.2520880

ODNI. (2016). *IARPA. IARPA-BAA-16-04 (Thor)*. https://www.iarpa.gov/index.php/research-programs/odin/odinbaa

Pala, F., & Bhanu, B. (2017). Deep Triplet Embedding Representations for Liveness Detection. In Deep Learning for Biometrics (pp. 287–307). Springer.

Pankanti, S., Prabhakar, S., & Jain, A. K. (2002). On the Individuality of Fingerprints. *IEEE TPAMI*, *24*(8), 1010–1025.

Perkampus, H.-H. (2013). *UV-VIS Spectroscopy and its Applications*. Springer Science & Business Media.

Rattani, A., Scheirer, W. J., & Ross, A. (2015). Open Set Fingerprint Spoof Detection Across Novel Fabrication Materials. *IEEE TIFS*, *10*(11), 2447–2460.

Rowe, R. K., & Sidlauskas, D. P. (2006). *Multispectral biometric sensor*. US Patent 7,147,153.

Smith, B. C. (2011). *Fundamentals of Fourier Transform Infrared spectroscopy*. CRC press.

Tolosana, R., Gomez-Barrero, M., Kolberg, J., Morales, A., Busch, C., & Ortega-Garcia, J. (2018). Towards Fingerprint Presentation Attack Detection Based on Convolutional Neural Networks and Short WaveInfrared Imaging. *Proc. BIOSIG*, 1–5.

Chapter 24
Predictive Analytics on Female Infertility Using Ensemble Methods

Simi M. S.
Adi Shankara Institute of Engineering and Technology, India

Manish T. I.
https://orcid.org/0000-0002-1347-5510
SCMS School of Engineering and Technology, India

ABSTRACT

With the accessibility of healthcare data for a significant proportion of patients in hospitals, using predictive analytics to detect diseases earlier has become more feasible. Identifying and recording key variables that contribute to a specific medical condition is one of the most difficult challenges for early detection and timely treatment of diseases. Conditions such as infertility that are difficult to detect or diagnose can now be diagnosed with greater accuracy with the help of predictive modeling. Infertility detection, particularly in females, has recently gained attention. In this work, the researchers proposed an intelligent prediction for female infertility (PreFI). The researchers use 26 variables for the early diagnosis and determine a subset of these 26 variables as biomarkers. These biomarkers contribute significantly to a better prediction of the problem. The researchers designed PreFI using ensemble methods with biomarkers and improved the performance of the predictive system.

INTRODUCTION

The amount of data in our medical systems has steadily increased with the advent of electronic medical records and increased computing power (IHTT, 2013). The number of patients and the amount of data stored per patient have both increased, resulting in an increase in data. As a result, in the health-care industry, implementing a solid data analytics platform has become critical (Raghupathi, 2010). The process of generating actionable insights by defining problems and applying statistical models and analysis to

DOI: 10.4018/978-1-7998-8892-5.ch024

existing data is referred to as data analytics (Cooper, 2012). The analysis of this large dataset can be used to generate data that will help doctors diagnose diseases earlier and more accurately (Raghupathi, 2014).

Electronic Health Records (EHR) have been incorporated to provide more coordinated and patient-centered care. The use of an Electronic Health Records (EHR) in the ICU significantly reduces central line-associated bloodstream infections and surgical intensive care unit mortality rates (Flatow, 2015). Electronic Health Records (EHR) provide secure access to patient data, which improves care quality and productivity (Tharmalingam, 2016). Electronic Health Records (EHR) systems have been used to manage chronic diseases such as diabetes, and it has been discovered that if providers participate in health information exchanges, regular use of the Electronic Health Records (EHR) can reduce data fragmentation and increase provider continuity of care (Rinner, 2016). Using patient data, specialized AI systems assist specialists in their clinical workflow by recognizing and diagnosing various diseases (Simi, 2017). In the emergency department (ED), using a decision tree with Electronic Health Records (EHR) improves medical decision making, increases patient quality of life, and is cost-effective (Ben-Assuli, 2016). Another cost-benefit analysis of using Electronic Health Records (EHR) to collect data yielded encouraging results (Beresniak, 2016).

One of the most common diseases affecting humans is infertility. In accordance with World Health Organization (WHO), this issue affects 60 to 80 million people (WHO, 2004), with infertility affecting 17% of females between the ages of 20 and 24. More than 186 million people worldwide are infertile, with the majority living in developing countries (Bittles, 2010). Female infertility can occur for a variety of reasons. In some cases, the disease could be caused by physiological factors. Sometimes there is no obvious cause for the disease. Ovulation disorders, endometriosis, tube damage, uterine disorders, and even lifestyle and environmental elements can all contribute to infertility (Amoako, 2015).

The excessive time it takes to detect the true reason of infertility is one of the most typical trends. A test to confirm a condition can take up to six months, however this delay in diagnosis can alter the likelihood of total cure or the pace with which the disease is cured. Our research focuses on the early detection of unexplained infertility issues. Because clinicians are often unable to diagnose the causes of unexplained infertility, the couple must undergo a battery of costly tests to determine the cause of infertility. Clinicians can easily predict unexplained infertility using our proposed system, and the couple can opt for assisted reproductive technology (ART). As there is no time lag between detection and treatment, the success rate of ART can be significantly improved.

Predictive modelling for infertility diagnosis is still in its initial phases of development. The majority of articles only predict infertility as certain or uncertain (Idowu, 2016). They don't look into the data's causes or conclusions. The majority of this research was done in hospitals with limited population data sets. In this work, the authors classify a broader range of inferences and identify likely, unlikely, and other probable (but not imminent) cases of infertility. For five types of ensemble learners, the authors predict with greater than 90% accuracy. The researchers expanded the number of variables in our work to include twenty-six variables in total, thirteen of which the researchers used for the first time. Our work also made significant contributions to prediction by adapting random forest (RF) (T.K. Ho, 1995) and J48 (Quinlan, 1993).

In this work, the researchers explored various available predictive techniques for early diagnosis of female infertility problems and proposed an intelligent prediction for female infertility (PreFI). The major contributions of our work are (a) the identification of key variables that contribute to female infertility and (b) expanding the prediction system from binary classification to a problem of prediction among 9 classes, including unexplained infertility. The researchers used 26 variables for the early diagnosis. The researchers determined a subset of these 26 variables as biomarkers.

These biomarkers contribute significantly to better prediction of our problem. Apart from base classifiers, the researchers also explored ensembles of those algorithms. Ensemble methods are learning algorithms that combine a number of base classifiers and then use a weighted average of their predictions to label new data. In this ensemble, classification is performed using the simple average voting based ensemble of RF, J48, and LDA. The researchers determined that the use of 26 variables improves the prediction of female infertility. By using base classifiers, the researchers demonstrated early diagnosis of nine classes. The researchers designed a new predictive system using ensemble methods with biomarkers and improved the performance of the predictive system. The researchers performed comparative analysis for predicting female infertility using base classifiers and our new ensemble techniques and observed that the mispredictions were substantially reduced.

BACKGROUND

In the current study, the accuracy rates of the developed models were greater than 90%. Predicting female infertility has been the subject of considerable research. Simi (2017) compared the accuracy of two different classification algorithms—J48 and RF—to assess women's infertility. The results showed that RF (96.6%) had a higher accuracy rate than J48 (86.5%). Overall, the accuracy rates of the two algorithms were high. According to Liao S (2019), female-related factors (female cause of infertility, female age, and ovarian response) paired with antral follicle count (AFC) can be used to determine the likelihood of clinical pregnancy. The antral stage follicle biomarkers are also significant predictors of ovarian response in fertility treatments.

Despite the development of advanced ART for the management of various types of subfertile women, such as tubal factor, unexplained infertility, and so on, the ageing process of the ovary and poor ovarian reserve remain a major challenge for clinicians in achieving a successful pregnancy (Coskun, 2018). In a case series by Zhang (2018) on the prediction of the endometriosis fertility index in patients with endometriosis-associated infertility after laparoscopic treatment, 72.38 percent of patients had infertility for less than three years, while 27.62 percent had infertility for more than three years. Primary infertility affected 48.95% of patients, while secondary infertility affected 51.5%. In the same study, 90.1 percent of patients were under the age of 35, 7.93 percent were between the ages of 36 and 39, and 1.91 percent were over the age of 40.

Many studies have been carried out in order to predict the causes of infertility in couples. According to the findings of this study, the support vector machine with a polynomial kernel function predicted with a 76.7% accuracy (Dormahammadi, 2014). Women with PCOS are more likely to become infertile. Infertility is caused by infrequent ovulation, in which the ovary is unable to release a mature egg. This infertility has an impact on a woman's ability to conceive. A study found that 18% of East Indian females have PCOS-related infertility (Palvi Soni, 2018). Cristiana Neto (2021) compares the performance of multiple algorithms, namely, Support Vector Machines, Multilayer Perceptron Neural Network, RF, Logistic Regression, and Gaussian Naïve Bayes. Finally, it was discovered that RF provides the best classification and that using data sampling techniques improves the results, resulting in an accuracy of 0.95 and a precision of 0.96.

Unexplained infertility is currently diagnosed after five to ten years of medical procedures. Women over the age of 40 have lower fertility potential than younger women. They also have significantly lower success rates with fertility treatments such as IVF (IVF). If the treatment was started later, the success rate would be significantly lower. Women over the age of 40 have an IVF success rate of 10-15%. PreFI will assist those patients in starting treatment as soon as they are diagnosed with unexplained infertility. As a result, the treatment outcome can be improved to a significant degree. There is, however, limited infertility dataset may quietly restrict the researchers from doing this kind of studies.

PROPOSED TECHNIQUE

Bagging (Leo Breiman, 1994) predictors is a technique for producing multiple versions of a predictor and combining them to produce an aggregated predictor. When predicting a numerical outcome, the aggregation takes an average of the versions and a plurality vote when predicting a class. Making bootstrap replicas of the learning set and using these as new learning sets results in multiple versions. Bagging can provide significant accuracy gains in tests on real and simulated data sets using classification and regression trees, as well as subset selection in linear regression. The instability of the prediction method is critical. Bagging can improve accuracy if perturbing the learning set causes significant changes in the predictor constructed. Bagging generates bootstrap samples of objects 2 and trains a classifier on each one. Majority voting is used to combine the classifier votes. Classifiers in some implementations generate estimates of the posterior probabilities for the classes.

Boosting (Freund, 1997) is a method family. The goal is to improve the performance of a weak classifier by incorporating it into an ensemble structure. The ensemble classifiers are added one at a time, so that each subsequent classifier is trained on data that was "hard" for the previous ensemble members. Increasing the ability to convert weak learners into strong learners. A weak learner appears to be slightly better than a random guess, whereas a strong learner is very close to perfect performance. It works by sequentially training a group of learners and combining them for prediction, with the later learners focusing more on the mistakes of the earlier learners.

Some base classifier predictions as features learn to produce a metamodel that combines their predictions. Stacking is the process of learning a linear metamodel. It is also possible to combine different base models into a heterogeneous ensemble in order to achieve base model diversity, such that base models are trained by different learning algorithms using the same training set. As a result, model ensembles are made up of a set of base models and a metamodel that has been trained to determine how base model predictions should be combined (Subasi, 2020).

Ensemble methods are learning algorithms that build a set of classifiers and then use a (weighted) vote of their predictions to classify new data (Hansen, 1990). Bayesian averaging is the original ensemble method, but more recent algorithms include error-correcting output coding, Bagging, and boosting (Dieterich, 2000). An ensemble of classifiers is a group of classifiers whose individual decisions are combined in some way to classify new examples (typically through weighted or unweighted voting). The accuracy and diversity of the classifiers is a necessary and sufficient condition for an ensemble of classifiers to be more accurate than any of its individual members (Hansen, 1990).

Learning multiple classifier systems is another name for ensemble learning (Zhou, 2012). Most ensemble methods employ a single base learning algorithm to produce homogeneous learners, i.e., learners of the same kind, resulting in homogeneous ensembles; however, some methods employ multiple learning algorithms to produce heterogeneous learners, i.e., learners of distinct kinds, resulting in heterogeneous ensembles.

In this study, the authors use an Ensemble Learner to forecast the cause of infertility in females who are trying to have a baby, decreasing the course of treatment and effectively assisting physicians in planning the course of their treatment. The data was obtained from a fertility clinic by the authors. This has 1678 entries and 26 features. It includes data from patients who were diagnosed between January 2014 and October 2016. The research looked at those under the age of 50. (In layman's terms, premenopausal women.) The authors used mean decrease accuracy (MDA), a variable important in R (Cooper, 2012), as well as clinical doctor recommendations to select features. Features with a high mean decrease in accuracy are more useful in data classification (Louppe, 2013).

The researchers adopted model stacking for developing the Female Infertility Predictor. In fact, the authors also make use of bagging and boosting by applying RF and gradient boosting models, i.e., all three techniques are applied together. The pseudo code for the ensemble is given below, and the working model is also seen in Figure 1.

PreFI is the ensemble for the prediction of female infertility. Which incorporates the benefits of important variables chosen with the help of MeanDecreaseAccuracy (MDA) variable selection. This ensemble reasonably reduces the time to find the actual cause of infertility, and thus the expenses are also reduced. With infertility, all patients are in the risk zone, whereas 30% of infertility causes are unknown. Patients with unexplained infertility can be easily identified by clinical doctors using this new system, PreFI, and treatment can begin immediately.

Unexplained infertility is currently diagnosed after five to ten years of medical procedures. Since women over the age of 40 have a lower fertility potential than younger women, they are less fertile. In addition, they have significantly lower success rates with fertility treatments such as in vitro fertilization (IVF). If the treatment is started later, the success rate will drop significantly. The success rate of IVF in women over the age of 40 is 10-15%. PreFI will assist those patients who have been diagnosed with unexplained infertility in starting treatment as soon as possible.

RESULTS AND DISCUSSION

The researchers developed a total of four ensembles for female infertility prediction. The E1 integrates the prediction results of J48 and LDA. For E2, J48 and RF are combined. E3 is the combination of RF and LDA, and E4 was obtained as the result of integrating the three base learners. Tumer Ghosh (1996) shows how correlation among individual classifiers can affect the performance of an ensemble. So we selected three classifiers with appropriate correlation. Ensemble E1 combines prediction of base learner J48 and LDA. The correlation between them is 0.05. The accuracy of the E1 predictor is 89.9%, with a correctly classified instance of 448 (89.95%) and incorrectly classified instances of 50 (10.04%). The Ensemble E2 integrates the prediction of individual classifiers RF and J48. The accuracy of prediction is 92.8%. The number of correctly classified instances is 462 (92.77%) out of 498, and there are 36 (7.23%) misclassifications. The correlation between RF and J48 is 0.13. The ensemble E3 combined RF and LDA of correlation 0.57. The predictive accuracy is 91.9%. The number of correctly classified instances is 458 (91.97%) and the number of incorrectly classified instances is 40 (8.03%).

When comparing these three ensembles, it can be seen that Ensemble E2 is the best among the three, with the highest predictive accuracy of 92.8%. So, as the second part implementation, the authors devel-

Figure 1. Working model

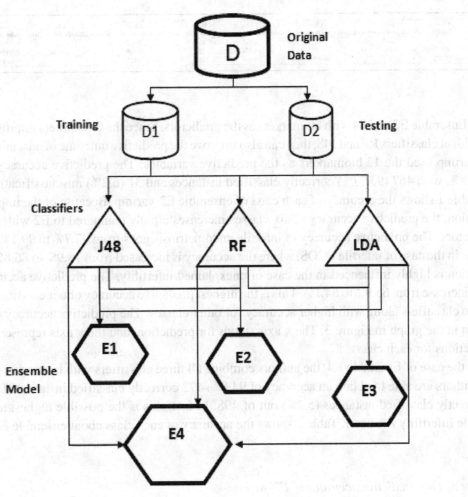

Figure 2. Algorithm 1. PreFI

Algorithm 1 Pseudo-code of PreFI

C-: number of classifiers

1. **foreach** $c=1,......,C$ **do**
   select predictive variables A
   build classifier model c_A with the selected variables A
   obtain prediction p_1 from classifier

end

2. apply integration method over predictions $p_1,.......,p_c$
3. obtain prediction P

Table 1. Class Accuracy of Ensembles E2-varimp

	Class: fertility	Class: infertile_endometriosis	Class: infertile_multiple_iui_failure	Class: infertile_oats	Class: infertile_pcos	Class: infertile_poor_overian_reserve	Class: infertile_tubal_factor	Class: infertility	Class: unexplained_infertility
RF	0.991	0.943	0.733	0.935	0.816	0.968	1	0.841	0.841
J48	0.972	0.914	0.8	0.774	0.789	0.839	0.906	0.818	0.75
StackModel	0.991	0.971	0.733	0.935	0.868	0.968	1	0.886	0.841

oped Ensemble E2 and E4 with biomarkers as the predictors. Since the biomarkers improve the results of individual classifiers RF and J48, they can also improve the predictive outcome of ensembles. Ensembles E2-varimp used the 12 biomarkers as the predictive variables. The predictive accuracy of E2-varimp is 93.8%, with 467 (93.77%) correctly classified instances and 31 (6.2%) misclassifications out of 498.

Table 1 shows the accuracy of each class of ensemble E2-varimp. Because of the important variable selection, the predictive accuracy of six classes increases rapidly compared to E2 with all variables as predictors. The predictive accuracy of infertile endometriosis goes from 97.7% to 99.1%. Another huge hike is in the case of infertile PCOS, where the accuracy is increased from 78.9% to 86.8%. The variable selection is highly influenced in the case of unexplained infertility. The predictive accuracy attained a huge increase from 65.9% to 84.1%. This is the highest predictive accuracy obtained using a combination of two classifiers along with higher accuracy for other classes. The predictive accuracy of each class is shown in the graph in Figure 3. The x axis stands for prediction, and the y axis represents the count of predictions for each class.

In the case of Ensemble E4, the authors combine all three classifiers with biomarker predictors, and the authors are able to obtain an accuracy of 94.8%. 472 correctly classified instances (94.77%) and 26 incorrectly classified instances (5.2%) out of 498. In fact, this is the possible highest accuracy of our Female Infertility Predictor. Table 2 shows the accuracy of each class about ensemble E4.

Figure 3. The Predictive accuracy of E2-varimp

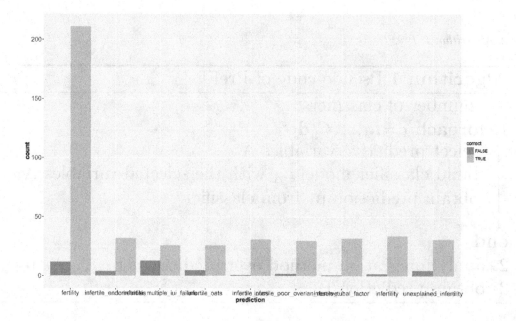

Table 2. Class Accuracy of Ensembles E4

	Class: fertility	Class: infertile_endometriosis	Class: infertile_multiple_iui_failure	Class: infertile_oats	Class: infertile_pcos	Class: infertile_poor_overian_reserve	Class: infertile_tubal_factor	Class: infertility	Class: unexplained_infertility
RF	0.991	1	0.733	0.968	0.816	0.935	1	0.841	0.841
J48	0.972	0.914	0.8	0.774	0.789	0.839	0.906	0.818	0.75
LDA	0.977	0.886	0.467	0.581	0.737	0.806	0.719	0.636	0.545
StackModel	0.991	1	0.8	0.968	0.868	0.935	1	0.864	0.909

The predictive accuracy of each class is shown in the graph in Figure 4. The x axis stands for prediction, and the y axis represents the count of predictions for each class. Detailed accuracy of ensemble E4 with sensitivity, specificity, positively predicted value, negatively predicted value, prevalence, and detection rate of nine classes were described in Table 3.

From Table 2, it is clear that for the combination of ensemble rules RF, J48, and LDA, prediction is better than the other combinations. Furthermore, our ultimate aim is to reduce the time lag in the case of unexplained infertility. The causes of unexplained infertility are different from person to person, and the clinical doctors are unable to point out the causes most of the time. Here the E4 shows a significant improvement of more than 90% predictive accuracy in the case of unexplained infertility classes. The authors compared the results of four ensembles. The combination of three rules (E4) performs better, with a predictive accuracy of 94.8%. And finally, the unexplained infertility class is able to predict with an accuracy of 91%.

From Table 2 and Figure 4, the authors observe that for seven classes, there is an improvement in the predictive accuracy and this is the highest among all other combinations. This means that the E4 performs much better than the base learners and the other combinations. And our proposed method could improve the performance of prediction. Which indicates that our method could be used to deal with female infertility detection in an effective manner with no time lag. The combinations have no change in the accuracy of the two classes.

In summary, the authors could conclude as follows: the ensemble with the combination of three base learners with biomarkers as predictors could be able to obtain the highest predictive accuracy and the highest class-wise accuracy, especially in the case of unexplained accuracy. This means that the combi-

Table 3. Detailed Accuracy of Ensembles E4

Class Type	Sensitivity	Specificity	Pos. Pred. Value	Neg. Pred. Value	Prevalence	Detection Rate
fertility	0.9906	0.9930	0.9906	0.9930	0.4277	0.4237
Infertile_endometriosis	1.0000	1.0000	1.0000	1.0000	0.0702	0.0702
Infertile_multiple_iui_failure	0.8000	1.0000	1.0000	0.9873	0.0602	0.0481
Infertile_oats	0.9677	0.9850	0.8108	0.9978	0.0622	0.0602
Infertile_pcos	0.8684	0.9913	0.8918	0.9891	0.0763	0.0662
Infertile_poor_overian_reserve	0.9354	0.9978	0.9666	0.9957	0.0622	0.0582
Infertile_tubal_factor	1.0000	0.9978	0.9697	1.0000	0.0642	0.0642
infertility	0.8636	0.9933	0.9268	0.9268	0.0883	0.0763
Unexplained_infertility	0.9090	0.9823	0.8333	0.9911	0.0883	0.0803

Figure 4. The Predictive accuracy of E4

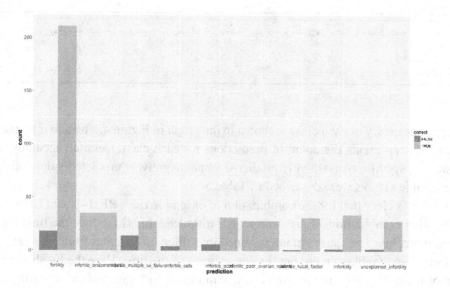

nations perform significantly better than the base learners. And our proposed method could improve the performance of prediction. Which indicates that our method could be used to deal with female infertility detection in an effective manner with no time lag.

CONCLUSION

In this paper, the authors have presented an ensemble method for dealing with an early female infertility diagnosis. In a variety of applications, combining or integrating the predictions of several classifiers

Figure 5. Summary of all learners

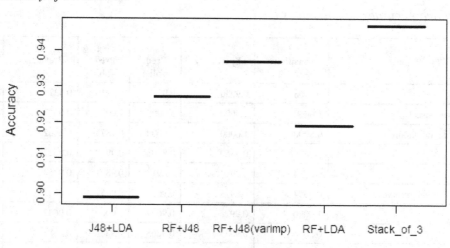

has improved performance. This paper provides an analytical framework for evaluating the benefits of combining classification results. The researchers discovered that combining individual classifiers improved female fertility prediction accuracy. The results of this study make it easier to understand the relationships between variables, classifiers, and combinations in output space. The results show that the proposed ensembles are adequate, as they outperform the results of the individual classifier. This means that with three classifier algorithms as base classifiers, the proposed method could deal with female infertility prediction with a predictive accuracy of 94.8%, which is also better than the conventional method of diagnosis. The future enhancement of this study is that we can redesign this with more data to improve the reliability and authenticity of the results.

ACKNOWLEDGMENT

This research received no specific grant from any funding agency in the public, commercial, or not-for-profit sectors.

REFERENCE

Akande, V. A., Hunt, L. P., Cahill, D. J., Caul, E. O., Ford, W. C. L., & Jenkins, J. M. (2003). Tubal damage in infertile women: Prediction using chlamydia serology. *Human Reproduction (Oxford, England)*, *18*(9), 1841–1847. doi:10.1093/humrep/deg347 PMID:12923136

Amadi, L., Onwudiegwu, U., Adeyemi, A., Nwachukwu, C., & Abiodun, A. (2019). Usefulness of Chlamydia serology in prediction of tubal factor infertility among infertile patients at Federal Medical Centre, Bida, North Central Nigeria. *International Journal of Reproduction, Contraception, Obstetrics and Gynecology*, *8*(2), 412–419. doi:10.18203/2320-1770.ijrcog20190261

Amoako, A. A., & Balen, A. H. (2015). *Female Infertility: Diagnosis and Management*. Endocrinology and Diabetes.

Ben-Assuli, O., Ziv, A., Sagi, D., Ironi, A., & Leshno, M. (2016). Cost-effectiveness evaluation of EHR: Simulation of an abdominal aortic aneurysm in the emergency department. *Journal of Medical Systems*, *40*(6), 141. doi:10.100710916-016-0502-9 PMID:27114352

Beresniak, A., Schmidt, A., Proeve, J., Bolanos, E., Patel, N., Ammour, N., Sundgren, M., Ericson, M., Karakoyun, T., Coorevits, P., Kalra, D., De Moor, G., & Dupont, D. (2016). Cost-benefit assessment of using electronic health records data for clinical research versus current practices: Contribution of the Electronic Health Records for Clinical Research (EHR4CR) European Project. *Contemporary Clinical Trials*, *46*, 85–91. doi:10.1016/j.cct.2015.11.011 PMID:26600286

Bittles, A. H., & Black, M. L. (2010). The impact of consanguinity on neonatal and infant health. *Early Human Development*, *86*(11), 737–741. doi:10.1016/j.earlhumdev.2010.08.003 PMID:20832202

Breiman. (1994). *Bagging predictors*. Technical Report 421, Department of Statistics, University of California at Berkeley.

Cooper, A. (2012). What is analytics? Definitions and essential characteristics. *JISC CETIS Analytics Series, 1*(5).

Coskun, B., Dilbaz, B., Karadag, B., Coskun, B., Tohma, Y. A., Dur, R., & Akkurt, M. O. (2018). The role of anti-Mullerian hormone in predicting the response to clomiphene citrate in unexplained infertility. *Taiwanese Journal of Obstetrics & Gynecology, 57*(5), 713–717. doi:10.1016/j.tjog.2018.08.018 PMID:30342657

Dietterich, T. (2000). An experimental comparison of three methods for constructing ensembles of decision trees: Bagging, boosting and randomization. *Machine Learning, 40*(2), 139–157. doi:10.1023/A:1007607513941

Dormahammadi, S., Alizadeh, S., Asghari, M. & Shami, M. (2014). Proposing a prediction model for diagnosing causes of infertility by data mining algorithms. *Journal of Health Administration, 57*(17), 46–57.

Flatow, V. H., Ibragimova, N., Divino, C. M., Eshak, D. S., Twohig, B. C., Bassily-Marcus, A. M., & Kohli-Seth, R. (2015). Quality outcomes in the surgical intensive care unit after electronic health record implementation. *Applied Clinical Informatics, 6*(04), 611–618. doi:10.4338/ACI-2015-04-RA-0044 PMID:26767058

Freund, Y., & Schapire, R. E. (1997). A Decision-Theoretic Generalization of On-Line Learning and an Application to Boosting. *Journal of Computer and System Sciences, 55*(1), 119–139. doi:10.1006/jcss.1997.1504

Hansen, L. K., & Salamon, P. (1990). Neural Network Ensembles. *IEEE Transactions on Pattern Analysis and Machine Intelligence, 12*(10), 993–1001. doi:10.1109/34.58871

Ho, T. K. (1995). Random Decision Forests. *Proceedings of the 3rd International Conference on Document Analysis and Recognition, 1416,* 278-282.

Idowu, P. A., Balogun, J. A., & Alaba, O. B. (2016). Data Mining Approach for Predicting the Likelihood of Infertility in Nigerian Women. Handbook of Research on Healthcare Administration and Management, 76-104.

IHTT. (2013). *Transforming Health Care through Big Data Strategies for leveraging big data in the health care industry.* IHTT.

Infecundity, infertility, and childlessness in developing countries. (2004). Macro and the World Health Organization, World Health Organization, DHS Comparative Reports No 9.

Liao, S., Xiong, J., Tu, H., Hu, C., Pan, W., Geng, Y., Pan, W., Lu, T., & Jin, L. (2019). Prediction of in vitro fertilization outcome at different antral follicle count thresholds combined with female age, female cause of infertility, and ovarian response in a prospective cohort of 8269 women. *Medicine, 98*(41), e17470–e17470. doi:10.1097/MD.0000000000017470 PMID:31593108

Louppe, G., Louis, W., Antonio, S., & Pierre, G. (2013). Understanding variable importance in forests of randomized trees. *Advances in Neural Information Processing Systems*, 431–439.

Neto, C., Silva, M., Fernandes, M., Ferreira, D., & Machado, J. (2021). Prediction models for Polycystic Ovary Syndrome using data mining. In T. Antipova (Ed.), *Advances in Digital Science. ICADS 2021. Adv Intell Syst Comput., 1352.* doi:10.1007/978-3-030-71782-7_19

Quinlan, J. R. (1993). *C4.5: Programs for Machine Learning.* Morgan Kaufmann Publishers.

Raghupathi, W., & Raghupathi, V. (2010). Data Mining in Health Care. In S. Kudyba (Ed.), *Healthcare Informatics: Improving Efficiency and Productivity* (pp. 211–223). Taylor & Francis. doi:10.1201/9781439809792-c11

Raghupathi, W., & Raghupathi, V. (2014). Big data analytics in healthcare: Promise and potential. *Health Information Science and Systems, 2*(1), 3. doi:10.1186/2047-2501-2-3 PMID:25825667

Rinner, C., Sauter, S. K., Endel, G., Heinze, G., Thurner, S., Klimek, P., & Duftschmid, G. (2016). Improving the informational continuity of care in diabetes mellitus treatment with a nationwide Shared EHR system: Estimates from Austrian claims data. *International Journal of Medical Informatics, 92,* 44–53. doi:10.1016/j.ijmedinf.2016.05.001 PMID:27318070

Simi, M. S., & Nayaki, K. S. (2017, April). *Data analytics in medical data: A review.* Paper presented at the IEEE International Conference on Circuit, Power and Computing Technologies (ICCPCT). 10.1109/ICCPCT.2017.8074337

Simi, M. S., Nayaki, K. S., Parameswaran, M., & Sivadasan, S. (2017). *Exploring female infertility using predictive analytic.* Paper presented at the IEEE Global Humanitarian Technology Conference (GHTC).

Soni, P., & Vashisht, S. (2018). Exploration on Polycystic Ovarian Syndrome and Data Mining Techniques. *2018 3rd International Conference on Communication and Electronics Systems (ICCES),* 816-820. 10.1109/CESYS.2018.8724087

Subasi, A. (2020). *Practical Machine Learning for Data Analysis Using Python.* Elsevier.

Tharmalingam, S., Hagens, S., & Zelmer, J. (2016). The value of connected health information: Perceptions of electronic health record users in Canada. *BMC Medical Informatics and Decision Making, 16*(1), 93. doi:10.118612911-016-0330-3 PMID:27422571

Tumer, K., & Ghosh, J. (1996). Analysis of decision boundaries in linearly combined neural classifiers. *Pattern Recognition, 29*(2), 341–348. doi:10.1016/0031-3203(95)00085-2

Zhang, X., Liu, D., Huang, W., Wang, Q., Feng, X., & Tan, J. (2018). Prediction of endometriosis fertility index in patients with endometriosis-associated infertility after laparoscopic treatment. *Reproductive Biomedicine Online, 37*(1), 53–59. doi:10.1016/j.rbmo.2018.03.012 PMID:29628331

Zhou, Z.-H. (2012). *Ensemble Methods: Foundations and Algorithms.* Chapman & Hall/CRC. doi:10.1201/b12207

Compilation of References

Abadi, M., Barham, P., Chen, J., Chen, Z., Davis, A., Dean, J., Devin, M., Ghemawat, S., Irving, G., Isard, M., Kudlur, M., Levenberg, J., Monga, R., Moore, S., Murray, D. G., Steiner, B., Tucker, P., Vasudevan, V., Warden, P., … Zheng, X. (n.d.). *TensorFlow: A system for large-scale machine learning*. Academic Press.

Abeer, A. A., Mohammed, Z., Prashant, K. S., Aseel, A., Wesam, A. H., Hussam, T., Sureshbabu, R., Rajnish, R., (2022). Human-Computer Interaction for Recognizing Speech Emotions Using Multilayer Perceptron Classifier. *Journal of Healthcare Engineering*. doi:10.1155/2022/600544

Abhishek, B., Krishi, K., Meghana, M., Daaniyaal, M., & Anupama, H. S. (2020). Hand gesture recognition using machine learning algorithms. *Computer Science and Information Technology*, *1*(3), 116–120.

Abiko, R., & Ikehara, M. (2019). Blind denoising of mixed Gaussian-impulse noise by single CNN. *ICASSP 2019-2019 IEEE International Conference on Acoustics, Speech and Signal Processing (ICASSP)*, 1717–1721.

Abreu, E., Lightstone, M., Mitra, S. K., & Arakawa, K. (1996). A new efficient approach for the removal of impulse noise from highly corrupted images. *IEEE Transactions on Image Processing*, *5*(6), 1012–1025. doi:10.1109/83.503916 PMID:18285188

Abrishambaf, R., Demirel, H., & Kale, I. (2008). A Fully CNN Based Fingerprint Recognition System. *IEEE International Workshop on Cellular Neural Networks and Their Applications*. 10.1109/CNNA.2008.4588667

Adek, R. T., & Ula, M. (2020). A Survey on The Accuracy of Machine Learning Techniques for Intrusion and Anomaly Detection on Public Data Sets. *2020 International Conference on Data Science, Artificial Intelligence, and Business Analytics (DATABIA)*. 10.1109/DATABIA50434.2020.9190436

Aetesam, H., & Maji, S. K. (2022a). Attention-Based Noise Prior Network for Magnetic Resonance Image Denoising. *2022 IEEE 19th International Symposium on Biomedical Imaging (ISBI)*, 1–4.

Aetesam, H., Poonam, K., & Maji, S. K. (2019). A Mixed-Norm Fidelity Model for Hyperspectral Image Denoising under Gaussian-Impulse Noise. *IEEE 18th International Conference on Information Technology (ICIT)*.

Aetesam, H., & Maji, S. K. (2020). L2- L1 Fidelity based Elastic Net Regularisation for Magnetic Resonance Image Denoising. *2020 International Conference on Contemporary Computing and Applications (IC3A)*, 137–142. 10.1109/IC3A48958.2020.233285

Aetesam, H., & Maji, S. K. (2021). Noise dependent training for deep parallel ensemble denoising in magnetic resonance images. *Biomedical Signal Processing and Control (Elsevier)*, *66*, 102405. doi:10.1016/j.bspc.2020.102405

Aetesam, H., & Maji, S. K. (2022b). Perceptually-motivated adversarial training for deep ensemble denoising of hyperspectral images. *Remote Sensing Letters*, *13*(8), 767–777. doi:10.1080/2150704X.2022.2077152

Aetesam, H., Maji, S. K., & Boulanger, J. (2020). A Two-Phase Splitting Approach for the Removal of Gaussian-Impulse Noise from Hyperspectral Images. *5th IAPR International Conference on Computer Vision & Image Processing (CVIP 2020)*.

Aetesam, H., Maji, S. K., & Yahia, H. (2021). Bayesian Approach in a Learning-Based Hyperspectral Image Denoising Framework. *IEEE Access: Practical Innovations, Open Solutions, 9*, 169335–169347. doi:10.1109/ACCESS.2021.3137656

Aetesam, H., Poonam, K., & Maji, S. K. (2020). Proximal approach to denoising hyperspectral images under mixed-noise model. *IET Image Processing, 14*(14), 3366–3372. doi:10.1049/iet-ipr.2019.1763

Affix, M., Indah, S., & Oyas, W. (2018). Herbal Leaf Classification Using Images in Natural Background. *International Conference on Information and Communications Technology (ICOIACT)*, 612-616.

Agarwal, D. D. (2020). Posture and activity analysis for patients in rehabilitation. *IJARIIT, 6*, 148–153.

Aggarwal, H. K., & Majumdar, A. (2016). Hyperspectral image denoising using spatio-spectral total variation. *IEEE Geoscience and Remote Sensing Letters, 13*(3), 442–446. doi:10.1109/LGRS.2016.2518218

Ahmed, F., & Das, S. (2013). Removal of high-density salt-and-pepper noise in images with an iterative adaptive fuzzy filter using alpha-trimmed mean. *IEEE Transactions on Fuzzy Systems, 22*(5), 1352–1358. doi:10.1109/TFUZZ.2013.2286634

Ahmed, H. M., & Essa, H. S. (2021). Survey of intelligent surveillance system for monitoring international border security. *Materials Today: Proceedings*.

Ahmed, T. M. (2016). Using data mining to develop models for classifying diabetic patient controllevel based on historical medical records. *Journal of Theoretical and Applied Information Technology*, 316–323.

Ahuja, R., Chug, A., Kohli, S., Gupta, S., & Ahuja, P. (2019). The impact of features extraction on sentiment analysis. *Procedia Computer Science, 152*, 341–348. doi:10.1016/j.procs.2019.05.008

Aja-Fernández, S., & Vegas-Sánchez-Ferrero, G. (2016). *Statistical analysis of noise in MRI*. Springer International Publishing. doi:10.1007/978-3-319-39934-8

Akande, V. A., Hunt, L. P., Cahill, D. J., Caul, E. O., Ford, W. C. L., & Jenkins, J. M. (2003). Tubal damage in infertile women: Prediction using chlamydia serology. *Human Reproduction (Oxford, England), 18*(9), 1841–1847. doi:10.1093/humrep/deg347 PMID:12923136

Alharbi, A., & Alghahtani, M. (2019). Using genetic algorithm and elm neural network for feature extraction and classification of type-2 diabetic mellitus. *Applied Artificial Intelligence, 33*(4), 311–328. doi:10.1080/08839514.2018.1560545

Alizadehsani, R., Habibi, J., Sani, Z. A., Mashayekhi, H., Boghrati, B., Ghandeharioun, A., Alizadeh-Sani, F. (2013). Diagnosing Coronary Artery Disease via Data Mining Algorithms by Considering Laboratory and Echocardiography Features. *Journal of Rajaie Cardiovascular Medical and Research Center*. doi:10.5812/cardiovascmed.10888

Alizadehsani, R., Habibi, J., Bahadorian, B., Mashayekhi, H., & Ghandeharioun, A. (2012). *Diagnosis of Coronary Arteries Stenosis Using Data Mining*. Academic Press.

Alizadehsani, R., Zangooei, M. H., Hosseini, M. J., Habibi, J., Khosravi, A., Roshanzamir, M., & Nahavandi, S. (2016). *Knowledge-Based Systems*. Advance online publication. doi:10.1016/j.knosys.2016.07.004

Allam, J. P., Samantray, S., Behara, C., Kurkute, K. K., & Sinha, V. K. (2022). A customized deep learning algorithm for drowsiness detection using single-channel EEG signal. In *Artificial Intelligence-Based Brain-Computer Interface* (pp. 189–201). Academic Press.

Al-Masawabe, M. M., Samhan, L. F., Alfarra, A. H., Aslem, Y. E., & Abu-Naser, S. S. (2022). Papaya maturity Classification Using Deep Convolutional. *Neural Networks.*

Al-Mutib, K., Mattar, E., & Alsulaiman, M. (2015). Implementation of fuzzy decision based mobile robot navigation using stereo vision. *Procedia Computer Science, 62,* 143–150. doi:10.1016/j.procs.2015.08.427

Alnaim, N. (2020). *Hand gesture recognition using deep learning neural networks* [Doctoral dissertation]. Brunel University London.

Alpana, J., & Rai, D. (2019). Efficient MRI Segmentation and Detection of Brain Tumor Using Convolutional Neural Network. *International Journal of Advanced Computer Science and Applications, 10,* 536–541.

Al-sudani, A. R. (2020). Yawn based driver fatigue level prediction. *Proceedings of 35th International Confer, 69,* 372-382.

Alzahani, S. M., Althopity, A., Alghamdi, A., Alshehri, B., & Aljuaid, S. (2014). An Overview of Data Mining Techniques Applied for Heart Disease Diagnosis and Prediction. *Engineering and Technology Publishing, 2*(4), 310–315. doi:10.12720/lnit.2.4.310-315

Amadi, L., Onwudiegwu, U., Adeyemi, A., Nwachukwu, C., & Abiodun, A. (2019). Usefulness of Chlamydia serology in prediction of tubal factor infertility among infertile patients at Federal Medical Centre, Bida, North Central Nigeria. *International Journal of Reproduction, Contraception, Obstetrics and Gynecology, 8*(2), 412–419. doi:10.18203/2320-1770.ijrcog20190261

Amarbayasgalan, T., Park, K. H., Lee, J. Y., & Ryu, H. K. (2019). Reconstruction error based deep neural networks for coronary heart disease risk prediction. *PLoS One, 14*(12), e0225991. Advance online publication. doi:10.1371/journal.pone.0225991 PMID:31805166

Amoako, A. A., & Balen, A. H. (2015). *Female Infertility: Diagnosis and Management.* Endocrinology and Diabetes.

Amutha, A. J., Padmajavalli, R., & Prabhakar, D. (2018). A novel approach for the prediction of a treadmill test in cardiology using data mining algorithms implemented as a mobile application. *Indian Heart Journal, 70*(4), 511–518. doi:10.1016/j.ihj.2018.01.011 PMID:30170646

Andrianakos, G., Dimitropoulos, N., Michalos, G., & Makris, S. (2019). An approach for monitoring the execution of human based assembly operations using machine learning. *Procedia CIRP, 86,* 198–203. doi:10.1016/j.procir.2020.01.040

Antonelli, R. (2006). Fake Finger Detection by Skin Distortion Analysis. *IEEE TIFS, 1*(3), 360–373.

Antonopoulos, A. M. (2017). *Mastering Bitcoin: Programming the open blockchain.* O'Reilly Media, Inc.

Apeksha, A., Akshat, S., Ajay, A., Nidhi, C., Dilbag, S., Abeer, A. A., Aseel, A., & Heung-No, L.,(2022). *Two-Way Feature Extraction for Speech Emotion Recognition Using Deep Learning.* doi:10.3390/s22062378

Arab, M. A., Calagari, K., & Hefeeda, M. (2019). Band and quality selection for efficient transmission of hyperspectral images. *Proceedings of the 27th ACM International Conference on Multimedia,* 2423–2430. 10.1145/3343031.3351047

Arora, S., Hanmandlu, M., & Gupta, G. (2018). Filtering impulse noise in medical images using information sets. *Pattern Recognition Letters.*

Arowolo, O. F., Arogunjo, E. O., Owolabi, D. G., & Markus, E. D. (2021). Development of a Human Posture Recognition System for Surveillance Application. *International Journal of Computing and Digital Systems, 10.*

Arun & Viknesh. (2022). Leaf Classification for Plant Recognition Using EfficientNet Architecture. In *2022 IEEE Fourth International Conference on Advances in Electronics, Computers and Communications (ICAECC).* IEEE.

Aruna, S., Nandakishore, L. V., & Rajagopalan, S. P. (2012). A hybrid feature selection method based on IGSBFS and naive bayes for the diagnosis of erythemato-squamous diseases. *International Journal of Computers and Applications, 41*(7), 13–18. doi:10.5120/5552-7623

Aubry, M., Paris, S., Hasinoff, S. W., Kautz, J., & Durand, F. (2014). Fast Local Laplacian Filters: Theory and Applications. *ACM Transactions on Graphics, 33*(5), 167:1-167:14. doi:10.1145/2629645

Aujol, J.-F., & Aubert, G. (2008). 'A Variational Approach to Remove Multiplicative Noise. *SIAM Journal on Applied Mathematics, 68*(4), 925–946. doi:10.1137/060671814

Awoke, T., Rout, M., Mohanty, L., & Satapathy, S. C. (2021). Bitcoin price prediction and analysis using deep learning models. In *Communication software and networks* (pp. 631–640). Springer.

Ayyappan, S., Lakshmi, C., & Menon, V. (2020). A secure reversible data hiding and encryption system for embedding EPR in medical images. *Current Signal Transduction Therapy, 15*(2), 124–135. doi:10.2174/1574362414666190304162411

Babenko, A., & Lempitsky, V. (2015). Aggregating deep convolutional features for image retrieval. *Proc. IEEE International Conference on Computer Vision*, 1269–1277.

Babič, F., Olejár, J., Vantová, Z., & Paralič, J. (2017)... *Predictive and Descriptive Analysis for Heart Disease Diagnosis*, (September), 155–163. doi:10.15439/2017F219

Baena-García, M., del Campo-Ávila, J., Fidalgo, R., Bifet, A., Gavalda, R., & Morales-Bueno, R. (2006, September). Early drift detection method. In *Fourth international workshop on knowledge discovery from data streams* (Vol. 6, pp. 77-86). Academic Press.

Bala Krishnan, R., Rajesh Kumar, N., Raajan, N. R., Manikandan, G., Srinivasan, A., & Narasimhan, D. (2021). An approach for attaining content confidentiality on medical images through image encryption with steganography. *Wireless Personal Communications*, 1–17.

Balcilar, M., Bouri, E., Gupta, R., & Roubaud, D. (2017). Can volume predict Bitcoin returns and volatility? A quantiles-based approach. *Economic Modelling, 64*, 74–81. doi:10.1016/j.econmod.2017.03.019

Baldisserra, D., Franco, A., Maio, D., & Maltoni, D. (2006). Fake Fingerprint Detection by Odor Analysis. In *Proc. ICB*. Springer.

Bao, Kiet, Dinh, & Hie. (2020). Plant species identification from leaf patterns using histogram of oriented gradients feature space and convolution neural networks. *Journal of Information and Telecommunication, 4*(2), 140-150.

Barrett, L. F., Adolphs, R., Marsella, S., Martinez, A. M., & Pollak, S. D. (2019). Emotional Expressions Reconsidered: Challenges to Inferring Emotion From Human Facial Movements. *Psychological Science in the Public Interest, 20*(1), 1–68. doi:10.1177/1529100619832930 PMID:31313636

Barron, J. T., & Poole, B. (2016). *The Fast Bilateral Solver*. doi:10.1007/978-3-319-46487-9_38

Barua, S., Ahmed, M. U., Ahlström, C., & Begum, S. (2019). Automatic driver sleepiness detection using EEG, EOG and contextual information. *Expert Systems with Applications, 115*, 121–135. doi:10.1016/j.eswa.2018.07.054

Bektas, J., Ibrikci, T., & Ozcan, I. T. (2017). Classification of Real Imbalanced Cardiovascular Data Using Feature Selection and Sampling Methods: A Case Study with Neural Networks and Logistic Regression. *International Journal of Artificial Intelligence Tools, 26*(06), 1750019. doi:10.1142/S0218213017500191

Ben-Assuli, O., Ziv, A., Sagi, D., Ironi, A., & Leshno, M. (2016). Cost-effectiveness evaluation of EHR: Simulation of an abdominal aortic aneurysm in the emergency department. *Journal of Medical Systems*, *40*(6), 141. doi:10.100710916-016-0502-9 PMID:27114352

Benčo, M., & Hudec, R. (2007). Novel method for color textures features extraction based on GLCM. *Wuxiandian Gongcheng*, *16*(4), 65.

Bengio, Y., Courville, A., & Vincent, P. (2013). *Representation Learning : A Review and New Perspectives*. Academic Press.

Benitez-Quiroz, C. F., Srinivasan, R., & Martinez, A. M. (2016). Emotionet: An accurate, real-time algorithm for the automatic annotation of a million facial expressions in the wild. *Proceedings of IEEE International Conference on Computer Vision & Pattern Recognition (CVPR)*. 10.1109/CVPR.2016.600

Beresniak, A., Schmidt, A., Proeve, J., Bolanos, E., Patel, N., Ammour, N., Sundgren, M., Ericson, M., Karakoyun, T., Coorevits, P., Kalra, D., De Moor, G., & Dupont, D. (2016). Cost-benefit assessment of using electronic health records data for clinical research versus current practices: Contribution of the Electronic Health Records for Clinical Research (EHR4CR) European Project. *Contemporary Clinical Trials*, *46*, 85–91. doi:10.1016/j.cct.2015.11.011 PMID:26600286

Bermudez, C., Plassard, A. J., Davis, L. T., Newton, A. T., Resnick, S. M., & Landman, B. A. (2018). Learning implicit brain MRI manifolds with deep learning. *Medical Imaging 2018. Image Processing*, *10574*, 105741L. PMID:29887659

Bhardwaj, R. N. (2017). A study of machine learning in healthcare. *IEEE 41st Annual Computer Software and Applications Conference (COMPSAC)* (vol. 2). IEEE.

Bhattacharyya, A., Chatterjee, S., Sen, S., Sinitca, A., Kaplun, D., & Sarkar, R. (2021). A deep learning model for classifying human facial expressions from infrared thermal images. *Scientific Reports*, *11*(1), 20696. doi:10.103841598-021-99998-z PMID:34667253

Bhonsle, D., & Sinha, G. R. (2018). An Optimized Framework Using Adaptive Wavelet Thresholding and Total Variation Technique for De-Noising Medical Images. *Jour of Adv Research in Dynamical & Control Systems*, *10*(09), 953–965.

Biggio, Z., Akhtar, Z., Fumera, G., Marcialis, G. L., & Roli, F. (2012). Security Evaluation of Biometric Authentication Systems under Real Spoofing Attacks. *IET Biometrics*, *1*(1), 11–24. doi:10.1049/iet-bmt.2011.0012

Biju, A. V., Mathew, A. M., Nithi Krishna, P. P., & Akhil, M. P. (2022). Is the future of bitcoin safe? A triangulation approach in the reality of BTC market through a sentiments analysis. *Digital Finance*, 1-16.

Biswal. (2022). *Top 10 Deep Learning Algorithms You Should Know in 2022*. https://www.simplilearn.com/tutorials/deep-learning-tutorial/deep-learning-algorithm

Bittles, A. H., & Black, M. L. (2010). The impact of consanguinity on neonatal and infant health. *Early Human Development*, *86*(11), 737–741. doi:10.1016/j.earlhumdev.2010.08.003 PMID:20832202

Blum, C., & Roli, A. (2001). Metaheuristics in Combinatorial Optimization : Overview and Conceptual Comparison Metaheuristics in Combinatorial Optimization : Overview and Conceptual Comparison. *ACM Computing Surveys*, *35*(3), 268–308. Advance online publication. doi:10.1145/937503.937505

Blundo, C., De Santis, A., & Naor, M. (2000). Visual Cryptography for grey level images. *Information Processing Letters*, *75*(6), 255–259. doi:10.1016/S0020-0190(00)00108-3

Blu, T., & Luisier, F. (2007). The SURE-LET approach to image denoising. *IEEE Transactions on Image Processing*, *16*(11), 2778–2786. doi:10.1109/TIP.2007.906002 PMID:17990754

Bouwmans, T., Javed, S., Sultana, M., & Jung, S. K. (2019). Deep neural network concepts for background subtraction: A systematic review and comparative evaluation. *Neural Networks*, *117*, 8–66. doi:10.1016/j.neunet.2019.04.024 PMID:31129491

Boyd, S., Boyd, S. P., & Vandenberghe, L. (2004). *Convex optimization.* Cambridge University Press. doi:10.1017/CBO9780511804441

Breiman. (1994). *Bagging predictors.* Technical Report 421, Department of Statistics, University of California at Berkeley.

Broomhead, D. S., & Lowe, D. (1988). Radial Basis Functions, Multi-Variable Functional Interpolation and Adaptive Networks. *Royal Signals and Radar Establishment*, (4148).

Brunetti, A., Buongiorno, D., Trotta, G. F., & Bevilacqua, V. (2018). Computer vision and deep learning techniques for pedestrian detection and tracking: A survey. *Neurocomputing*, *300*, 17–33. doi:10.1016/j.neucom.2018.01.092

Bulat & Tzimiropoulos, G. (2016). Human pose estimation via convolutional part heatmap regression. *Proc. Eur. Conf. Comput. Vis.,* 717–732.

Byeon, Y. H., Lee, J. Y., Kim, D. H., & Kwak, K. C. (2020). Posture recognition using ensemble deep models under various home environments. *Applied Sciences (Basel, Switzerland)*, *10*(4), 1287. doi:10.3390/app10041287

Cach, N. (2021). *Hybrid Deep Learning Models for Sentiment Analysis.* doi:10.1155/2021/9986920

Caggiano, A., Zhang, J., Alfieri, V., Caiazzo, F., Gao, R., & Teti, R. (2019). Machine learning-based image processing for on-line defect recognition in additive manufacturing. *CIRP Annals*, *68*(1), 451–454. doi:10.1016/j.cirp.2019.03.021

Cai, J.-F., Chan, R. H., & di Fiore, C. (2007). Minimization of a detail-preserving regularization functional for impulse noise removal. *Journal of Mathematical Imaging and Vision*, *29*(1), 79–91. doi:10.100710851-007-0027-4

Caliskan, A., & Yuksel, M. E. (2017). Classification of coronary artery disease datasets by using a deep neural network. *The EuroBiotech Journal*, *1*(4), 271–277. doi:10.24190/ISSN2564-615X/2017/04.03

Camarena, J.-G., Gregori, V., Morillas, S., & Sapena, A. (2010). Two-step fuzzy logic-based method for impulse noise detection in colour images. *Pattern Recognition Letters*, *31*(13), 1842–1849. doi:10.1016/j.patrec.2010.01.008

Camarena, J.-G., Gregori, V., Morillas, S., & Sapena, A. (2012). A simple fuzzy method to remove mixed Gaussian-impulsive noise from color images. *IEEE Transactions on Fuzzy Systems*, *21*(5), 971–978. doi:10.1109/TFUZZ.2012.2234754

Cao & Jain. (2016). *Hacking mobile phones using 2D Printed Fingerprints.* MSU Tech. report, MSU-CSE-16-2.

Cao, Y., Long, M., Wang, J., & Liu, S. (2017). Collective deep quantization for efficient cross-modal retrieval. *Proc. Thirty-First AAAI Conference on Artificial Intelligence*, 3974–3980. 10.1609/aaai.v31i1.11218

Cech. (2016). *Real-Time Eye Blink Detection using Facial Landmarks.* Academic Press.

Chaabene, S., Bouaziz, B., Boudaya, A., Hökelmann, A., Ammar, A., & Chaari, L. (2021). Convolutional neural network for drowsiness detection using EEG signals. *Sensors (Basel)*, *21*(5), 1734. doi:10.339021051734 PMID:33802357

Chambolle, A., & Pock, T. (2011). A first-order primal-dual algorithm for convex problems with applications to imaging. *Journal of Mathematical Imaging and Vision*, *40*(1), 120–145. doi:10.100710851-010-0251-1

Chandler, D. M., & Hemami, S. S. (2002). Additivity models for suprathreshold distortion in quantized wavelet-coded images. In *Human Vision and Electronic Imaging VII* (Vol. 4662, pp. 105–118). SPIE. doi:10.1117/12.469507

Chandrakar, M. K. A. M. (2018). Review of Medical Image Analysis, Segmentation and Application Using Deep Learning. *Jour of Adv Research in Dynamical & Control Systems*, *10*(1), 549-553.

Chandrakar, M. K., & Mishra, A. (2022). Cognitive Brain Tumour Segmentation Using Varying Window Architecture of Cascade Convolutional Neural Network. *International Journal of Computer Vision and Image Processing*, *11*(4), 21–29. doi:10.4018/IJCVIP.2021100102

Chandrasena, H. M., & Wickramasinghe, D. M. J. (2018). Driver's Drowsiness Detecting and Alarming System. *International Journal of Information Technology and Computer Science*, *4*(3), 127–139.

Chan, R. H., Dong, Y., & Hintermüller, M. (2010). An Efficient Two-Phase $\{\rm L\}^{1}$ -TV Method for Restoring Blurred Images with Impulse Noise. *IEEE Transactions on Image Processing*, *19*(7), 1731–1739. doi:10.1109/TIP.2010.2045148 PMID:20227978

Chao, W.-L., Liu, J.-Z., & Ding, J.-J. (2013). Facial age estimation based on label-sensitive learning and age-oriented regression. *Pattern Recognition*, *46*(3), 628–641. doi:10.1016/j.patcog.2012.09.011

Chen, J., Adams, A., Wadhwa, N., & Hasinoff, S. W. (2016). Bilateral guided upsampling. *ACM Transactions on Graphics*, *35*(6), 203:1-203:8. doi:10.1145/2980179.2982423

Chen, Y., Yu, W., & Pock, T. (2015). *On learning optimized reaction diffusion processes for effective image restoration*. doi:10.1109/CVPR.2015.7299163

Chen, C., & Shah, M. (2018). Real-World Anomaly Detection in Surveillance Videos. IEEE.

Cheng, Y., & Zhang, T. (2013). *A maximal Clique Enumeration based on ordered star neighborhood for co-location patterns*. IEEE Conference Publications.

Chen, S., Shi, W., & Zhang, W. (2013). An efficient universal noise removal algorithm combining spatial gradient and impulse statistic. *Mathematical Problems in Engineering*, *2013*, 2013. doi:10.1155/2013/480274

Chen, Y., Cao, X., Zhao, Q., Meng, D., & Xu, Z. (2017). Denoising hyperspectral image with non-iid noise structure. *IEEE Transactions on Cybernetics*, *48*(3), 1054–1066. doi:10.1109/TCYB.2017.2677944 PMID:28767377

Chen, Y., He, W., Yokoya, N., & Huang, T.-Z. (2019). Hyperspectral image restoration using weighted group sparsity-regularized low-rank tensor decomposition. *IEEE Transactions on Cybernetics*, *50*(8), 3556–3570. doi:10.1109/TCYB.2019.2936042 PMID:31484156

Chi-Man, P., & Moon-Chuen, L. (2003). Log-Polar Wavelet Energy Signatures for Rotation and Scale Invariant Texture Classification. *IEEE Trans. on Pattern Analysis and Machine Intelligence*, *25*(5), 590-603.

Chithra, P. L., & Janes, P. S. (2018). A Survey on Various Leaf Identification Techniques for Medicinal Plants. *Proc. International Conference on Advancements in Computing Technologies*, 38-42.

Chollet, F. (2017). Xception: deep learning with depthwise separable convolutions. *The IEEE Conference on Computer Vision and Pattern Recognition (CVPR)*. 10.1109/CVPR.2017.195

Chou, Y., Roy, S., Chang, C., Butman, J. A., & Pham, D. L. (2018, April). Deep learning of resting state networks from independent component analysis. In *2018 IEEE 15th International Symposium on Biomedical Imaging (ISBI 2018)* (pp. 747-751). IEEE. 10.1109/ISBI.2018.8363681

Christobel, Y. A., & Sivaprakasam, P. (2013). A new Classwise k Nearest Neighbors(CKNN) method for classificationof diabetes disease. *International Journal of Engineering and Advanced Technology*, 396–400.

Chugh & Jain. (2019). *Fingerprint Presentation Attack Detection: Generalization and Efficiency*. IEEE.

Chugh, T., Cao, K., & Jain, A. K. (2017). Fingerprint Spoof Detection Using Minutiae-based Local Patches. *Proc. IEEE IJCB*. 10.1109/BTAS.2017.8272745

Chugh, T., Cao, K., & Jain, A. K. (2018). Fingerprint Spoof Buster: Use of Minutiae-centered Patches. *IEEE TIFS, 13*(9), 2190–2202. doi:10.1109/TIFS.2018.2812193

Chung, J., Gulcehre, C., Cho, K., & Bengio, Y. (2014). *Empirical evaluation of gated recurrent neural networks on sequence modeling.* ArXiv Preprint ArXiv:1412.3555.

Cocco, L., & Marchesi, M. (2016). Modeling and Simulation of the Economics of Mining in the Bitcoin Market. *PLoS One, 11*(10), e0164603.

Cocco, L., Tonelli, R., & Marchesi, M. (2021). Predictions of bitcoin prices through machine learning based frameworks. *PeerJ. Computer Science, 7*, e413.

Coldewey. (2019). *This hand-tracking algorithm could lead to sign language recognition, techcrunch.* https://techcrunch.com/2019/08/19/this-hand-tracking-algorithm-could-lead-to-sign-language-recognition/

Condat, L. (2013). A primal–dual splitting method for convex optimization involving Lipschitzian, proximable and linear composite terms. *Journal of Optimization Theory and Applications, 158*(2), 460–479. doi:10.100710957-012-0245-9

Cooper, A. (2012). What is analytics? Definitions and essential characteristics. *JISC CETIS Analytics Series, 1*(5).

Cornish, M. L., Critchley, A. T., & Mouritsen, O. G. (2017). Consumption of seaweeds and the human brain. *Journal of Applied Phycology, 29*(5), 2377–2398. doi:10.100710811-016-1049-3

Cosentino, S., Randria, E. I. S., Lin, J., Pellegrini, T., Sessa, S., & Takanishi, A., (2018). Group emotion recognition strategies for entertainment robots. *2018 IEEE/RSJ International Conference on Intelligent Robots and Systems (IROS)*, 813-818. 10.1109/IROS.2018.8593503

Coskun, B., Dilbaz, B., Karadag, B., Coskun, B., Tohma, Y. A., Dur, R., & Akkurt, M. O. (2018). The role of anti-Mullerian hormone in predicting the response to clomiphene citrate in unexplained infertility. *Taiwanese Journal of Obstetrics & Gynecology, 57*(5), 713–717. doi:10.1016/j.tjog.2018.08.018 PMID:30342657

Coupé, P., Manjón, J., Robles, M., & Collins, D. L. (2012). Adaptive multiresolution non-local means filter for three-dimensional magnetic resonance image denoising. *IET Image Processing, 6*(5), 558–568. doi:10.1049/iet-ipr.2011.0161

Coupé, P., Yger, P., Prima, S., Hellier, P., Kervrann, C., & Barillot, C. (2008). An optimized blockwise nonlocal means denoising filter for 3-D magnetic resonance images. *IEEE Transactions on Medical Imaging, 27*(4), 425–441. doi:10.1109/TMI.2007.906087 PMID:18390341

Cowie, R., Douglas-Cowie, E., Tsapatsoulis, N., Votsis, G., Kollias, S., Fellenz, W., & Taylor, J. G. (2001). Emotion recognition in human-computer interaction. *IEEE Signal Processing Magazine, 18*(1), 32–80. doi:10.1109/79.911197

Cristea, A. (2015). *Ultrasound tissue characterization using speckle statistics.* Academic Press.

Critien, J. V., Gatt, A., & Ellul, J. (2022). Bitcoin price change and trend prediction through twitter sentiment and data volume. *Financial Innovation, 8*(1), 1–20.

Cui, H., Liu, A., Zhang, X., Chen, X., Wang, K., & Chen, X. (2020). EEG-based emotion recognition using an end-to-end regional-asymmetric convolutional neural network. *Knowledge-Based Systems, 205*, 106243. doi:10.1016/j.knosys.2020.106243

Cui, J., Lan, Z., Liu, Y., Li, R., Li, F., Sourina, O., & Müller-Wittig, W. (2022). A compact and interpretable convolutional neural network for cross-subject driver drowsiness detection from single-channel EEG. *Methods (San Diego, Calif.), 202*, 173–184. doi:10.1016/j.ymeth.2021.04.017 PMID:33901644

Dabov, K., Foi, A., Katkovnik, V., & Egiazarian, K. (2007). Image denoising by sparse 3-D transform-domain collaborative filtering. *IEEE Transactions on Image Processing*, *16*(8), 2080–2095. doi:10.1109/TIP.2007.901238 PMID:17688213

Daniel, C., & António, J. R. (2019). Facial Expression Recognition Using Computer Vision: *A Systematic Review*. *Applied Sciences (Basel, Switzerland)*, *9*(21), 4678. doi:10.3390/app9214678

De Bonis, A., & De Santis, A. (2004). Randomness in secret sharing and visual cryptography schemes. *Theoretical Computer Science*, *314*(3), 351–374. doi:10.1016/j.tcs.2003.12.018

Deepa, R., & Sandhya, M. K. (2019, June). An efficient hand gesture recognition system using deep learning. In *International Conference on Intelligent Computing, Information and Control Systems* (pp. 514-521). Springer.

Defferrard, M., & Bresson, X. V. P. (2016). Convolutional neural networks on graphs with fast localized spectral filtering. Advances in Neural Information Processing Systems, 3844–3852.

Dekamin, A., & Shaibatalhamdi, A. (2017). *Real-data comparison of data mining methods in the prediction of coronary artery disease in Iran*. Academic Press.

Dekamin, A., & Sheibatolhamdi, A. (2017). *Research Paper: A Data Mining Approach for Coronary Artery Disease Prediction in Iran*. Academic Press.

Delon, J., & Desolneux, A. (2013). A patch-based approach for removing impulse or mixed gaussian-impulse noise. *SIAM Journal on Imaging Sciences*, *6*(2), 1140–1174. doi:10.1137/120885000

Dhall, A., Goecke, R., Lucey, S., & Gedeon, T. (2011). Static facial expression analysis in tough conditions: Data, evaluation protocol and benchmark. *IEEE International Conference on Computer Vision Workshops (ICCV Workshops)*, 2106-2112. 10.1109/ICCVW.2011.6130508

Dhall, A., Goecke, R., Lucey, S., & Gedeon, T. (2012). Collecting large, richly annotated facial-expression databases from movies. *IEEE MultiMedia*, *19*(3), 34–41. doi:10.1109/MMUL.2012.26

Dietterich, T. (2000). An experimental comparison of three methods for constructing ensembles of decision trees: Bagging, boosting and randomization. *Machine Learning*, *40*(2), 139–157. doi:10.1023/A:1007607513941

Dinama, D. M., A'yun, Q., Syahroni, A. D., Sulistijono, I. A., & Risnumawan, A. (2019). Human Detection and Tracking on Surveillance Video Footage Using Convolutional Neural Networks. *International Electronics Symposium (IES)*, 534-538. 10.1109/ELECSYM.2019.8901603

Ding, W., Hu, B., Liu, H., Wang, X., & Huang, X. (2020). Human posture recognition based on multiple features and rule learning. *International Journal of Machine Learning and Cybernetics*, *11*(11), 2529–2540. doi:10.100713042-020-01138-y

Ding, Y., & Ross, A. (2016). An ensemble of one-class SVMs for fingerprint spoof detection across different fabrication materials. *Proc. IEEEWIFS*, 1–6. 10.1109/WIFS.2016.7823572

Dong, Y., & Zeng, T. (2013). A convex variational model for restoring blurred images with multiplicative noise. *SIAM Journal on Imaging Sciences*, *6*(3), 1598–1625. doi:10.1137/120870621

Dormahammadi, S., Alizadeh, S., Asghari, M. & Shami, M. (2014). Proposing a prediction model for diagnosing causes of infertility by data mining algorithms. *Journal of Health Administration*, *57*(17), 46–57.

Duchi, J., Hazan, E., & Singer, Y. (2011). Adaptive subgradient methods for online learning and stochastic optimization. *Journal of Machine Learning Research*, *12*(7).

el Helou, M., & Susstrunk, S. (2020). Blind universal Bayesian image denoising with Gaussian noise level learning. *IEEE Transactions on Image Processing*, *29*, 4885–4897. doi:10.1109/TIP.2020.2976814 PMID:32149690

Elad, M., & Aharon, M. (2006). Image denoising via sparse and redundant representations over learned dictionaries. *IEEE Transactions on Image Processing, 15*(12), 3736–3745. doi:10.1109/TIP.2006.881969 PMID:17153947

El-bialy, R., Salamay, M. A., Karam, O. H., & Khalifa, M. E. (2015). Feature Analysis of Coronary Artery Heart Disease Data Sets. *Procedia Computer Science, 65*(Iccmit), 459–468. doi:10.1016/j.procs.2015.09.132

Elharrouss, O., Almaadeed, N., & Al-Maadeed, S. (2021). A review of video surveillance systems. *Journal of Visual Communication and Image Representation, 77*, 103116. doi:10.1016/j.jvcir.2021.103116

Engelsma, J. J., Arora, S. S., Jain, A. K., & Paulter, N. G. (2018). Universal 3D Wearable Fingerprint Targets: Advancing Fingerprint Reader Evaluations. *IEEE TIFS, 13*(6), 1564–1578. doi:10.1109/TIFS.2018.2797000

Engelsma, J. J., Cao, K., & Jain, A. K. (2018). *Raspireader: Open source fingerprint reader*. IEEE TPAMI.

Enginoğlu, S., Erkan, U., & Memiş, S. (2019). Pixel similarity-based adaptive Riesz mean filter for salt-and-pepper noise removal. *Multimedia Tools and Applications, 78*(24), 35401–35418. doi:10.100711042-019-08110-1

Erick, M., & Jose, C. (2016). Automated Plant Species Identification: Challenges and Opportunities. *Proc. ICT for Promoting Human Development and Protecting the Environment*, 26-36.

Esakkirajan, S., Veerakumar, T., Subramanyam, A. N., & PremChand, C. H. (2011). Removal of high density salt and pepper noise through modified decision based unsymmetric trimmed median filter. *IEEE Signal Processing Letters, 18*(5), 287–290. doi:10.1109/LSP.2011.2122333

Eyssa, A. A., Abdelsamie, F. E., & Abdelnaiem, A. E. (2020). An efficient image steganography approach over wireless communication system. *Wireless Personal Communications, 110*(1), 321–337. doi:10.100711277-019-06730-2

Farahamandian, M., Lotfi, Y., & Maleki, I. (2015). Data mining algorithms application in diabetes disease diagnosis. *MAGNT Reaserch Report*, 989-997.

Farbman, Z., Fattal, R., & Lischinski, D. (2011). Convolution Pyramids. *ACM Transactions on Graphics, 30*(6), 175. doi:10.1145/2070781.2024209

Fatemeh, N., Ciprian, A. C., Dorota, K., Tomasz, S., Sergio, E., & Gholamreza, A. (2021). Survey on Emotional Body Gesture Recognition. IEEE Transactions on Affective Computing, 12(2).

Feng, N., & Bin, W. (2018). Integral Contour Angle: An Invariant Shape Descriptor for Classification and Retrieval of Leaf Images. *25th IEEE International Conference on Image Processing (ICIP)*, 1223-1227.

Ferdiansyah, F., Othman, S. H., Radzi, R. Z. R. M., Stiawan, D., Sazaki, Y., & Ependi, U. (2019, October). A lstm-method for bitcoin price prediction: A case study yahoo finance stock market. In *2019 International Conference on Electrical Engineering and Computer Science (ICECOS)* (pp. 206-210). IEEE. doi:10.1109/ISEMANTIC.2019.8884257

Figueiredo, M. A. T., & Bioucas-Dias, J. M. (2010). Restoration of Poissonian images using alternating direction optimization. *IEEE Transactions on Image Processing, 19*(12), 3133–3145. doi:10.1109/TIP.2010.2053941 PMID:20833604

Flatow, V. H., Ibragimova, N., Divino, C. M., Eshak, D. S., Twohig, B. C., Bassily-Marcus, A. M., & Kohli-Seth, R. (2015). Quality outcomes in the surgical intensive care unit after electronic health record implementation. *Applied Clinical Informatics, 6*(04), 611–618. doi:10.4338/ACI-2015-04-RA-0044 PMID:26767058

Flores. (2009). *Real-Time Warning System for Driver Drowsiness Using Visual Information*. Springer Science + Business Media.

Foi, A. (2011). Noise estimation and removal in MR imaging: The variance-stabilization approach. *2011 IEEE International Symposium on Biomedical Imaging: From Nano to Macro*, 1809–1814. 10.1109/ISBI.2011.5872758

Foss, S., Korshunov, D., Zachary, S., & ... (2011). *An introduction to heavy-tailed and subexponential distributions* (Vol. 6). Springer. doi:10.1007/978-1-4419-9473-8

François-Lavet, V., Henderson, P., Islam, R., Bellemare, M. G., & Pineau, J. (2018). An Introduction to Deep Reinforcement Learning. *Foundations and Trends→ in Machine Learning, 11*(3–4), 219–354. doi:10.1561/2200000071

Freund, Y., & Schapire, R. E. (1997). A Decision-Theoretic Generalization of On-Line Learning and an Application to Boosting. *Journal of Computer and System Sciences, 55*(1), 119–139. doi:10.1006/jcss.1997.1504

Fu, H., Ng, M. K., Nikolova, M., & Barlow, J. L. (2006). Efficient minimization methods of mixed l2-l1 and l1-l1 norms for image restoration. *SIAM Journal on Scientific Computing, 27*(6), 1881–1902. doi:10.1137/040615079

Fukushima, K. (1980). Neocognitron: A self-organizing neural network model for a mechanism of pattern recognition unaffected by shift in position. *Biological Cybernetics, 36*(4), 193–202. doi:10.1007/BF00344251 PMID:7370364

Fuletra. (2013). A survey On Driver's Drowsiness Detection Techniques Presented. *IJRITCC.* doi:10.1109/ICCVW.2013.126

Galanopoulos, A., Ayala-Romero, J. A., Leith, D. J., & Iosifidis, G. (2021). AutoML for Video Analytics with Edge Computing. *IEEE INFOCOM 2021 - IEEE Conference on Computer Communications*, 1-10. 10.1109/INFOCOM42981.2021.9488704

Ganesh, B., & Kumar, C. (2018). Deep learning Techniques in Image processing. *National Conference On Emerging Trends in Computing Technologies (NCETCT-18).*

Gangadharan, S., & Vinod, A. P. (2022). Drowsiness detection using portable wireless EEG. *Computer Methods and Programs in Biomedicine, 214*, 106535.

Gao, Y., Qiao, T., Zhang, H., Yang, Y., Pang, Y., & Wei, H. (2019). A contactless measuring speed system of belt conveyor based on machine vision and machine learning. *Measurement, 139*, 127–133. doi:10.1016/j.measurement.2019.03.030

Gao, Z., Wang, X., Yang, Y., Li, Y., Ma, K., & Chen, G. (2020). A Channel-fused Dense Convolutional Network for EEG-based Emotion Recognition. *IEEE Transactions on Cognitive and Developmental Systems*, 1–1. doi:10.1109/TCDS.2020.2976112

Garcia, C., Esmin, A., Leite, D., & Škrjanc, I. (2019). Evolvable fuzzy systems from data streams with missing values: With application to temporal pattern recognition and cryptocurrency prediction. *Pattern Recognition Letters, 128*, 278–282. doi:10.1016/j.patrec.2019.09.012

Garnett, R., Huegerich, T., Chui, C., & He, W. (2005). A universal noise removal algorithm with an impulse detector. *IEEE Transactions on Image Processing, 14*(11), 1747–1754. doi:10.1109/TIP.2005.857261 PMID:16279175

Gastal, E. S. L., & Oliveira, M. M. (2012). Adaptive manifolds for real-time high-dimensional filtering. *ACM Transactions on Graphics, 31*(4), 1–13. doi:10.1145/2185520.2185529

Georgoula, I., Pournarakis, D., Bilanakos, C., Sotiropoulos, D., & Giaglis, G. M. (2015). *Using time-series and sentiment analysis to detect the determinants of bitcoin prices.* doi:10.1109/PDP2018.2018.00060

Germanaite, I. E. (2021). General Spatial Pattern and Meta-Pattern Model for Problems That Need Analytical Approach in Complex Spatial Systems. *Applied Sciences, 12*(1), 302.

Gharbi, M., Shih, Y., Chaurasia, G., Ragan-Kelley, J., Paris, S., & Durand, F. (2015). Transform recipes for efficient cloud photo enhancement. *ACM Transactions on Graphics, 34*(6), 228:1-228:12. doi:10.1145/2816795.2818127

Gharbi, M., Chen, J., Barron, J. T., Hasinoff, S. W., & Durand, F. (2017). Deep bilateral learning for real-time image enhancement. *ACM Transactions on Graphics, 36*(4), 1–12. doi:10.1145/3072959.3073592

Ghiani, L., Hadid, A., Marcialis, G. L., & Roli, F. (2013). Fingerprint liveness detection using Binarized Statistical Image Features. *Proc. IEEE BTAS*, 1–6. 10.1109/BTAS.2013.6712708

Ghiani, L., Yambay, D. A., Mura, V., Marcialis, G. L., Roli, F., & Schuckers, S. A. (2017). Review of the Fingerprint Liveness Detection (LivDet) competition series: 2009 to 2015. *Image and Vision Computing*, *58*, 110–128. doi:10.1016/j.imavis.2016.07.002

Goldberg, D. E. (1989). Genetic Algorithms in Search Optimization &. *Machine Learning*. Advance online publication. doi:10.1007/3-540-44673-7

Gomez-Donoso, F., Escalona, F., Pérez-Esteve, F., & Cazorla, M. (2021). Accurate multilevel classification for wildlife images. *Computational Intelligence and Neuroscience*. PMID:33868399

Gong, M., & Shu, Y. (2020). Real-time detection and motion recognition of human moving objects based on deep learning and multi-scale feature fusion in video. *IEEE Access: Practical Innovations, Open Solutions*, *8*, 25811–25822. doi:10.1109/ACCESS.2020.2971283

Gonzalez-Hidalgo, M., Massanet, S., Mir, A., & Ruiz-Aguilera, D. (2018). Improving salt and pepper noise removal using a fuzzy mathematical morphology-based filter. *Applied Soft Computing*, *63*, 167–180. doi:10.1016/j.asoc.2017.11.030

González-Hidalgo, M., Massanet, S., Mir, A., & Ruiz-Aguilera, D. (2021). Impulsive Noise Removal with an Adaptive Weighted Arithmetic Mean Operator for Any Noise Density. *Applied Sciences (Basel, Switzerland)*, *11*(2), 560. doi:10.3390/app11020560

Goodfellow, I. J., Pouget-Abadie, J., Mirza, M., Xu, B., Warde-Farley, D., Ozair, S., Courville, A., & Bengio, Y. (2014). *Generative adversarial networks*. ArXiv Preprint ArXiv:1406.2661.

Goodfellow, I. J., Erhan, D., Carrier, P. L., Courville, A., Mirza, M., Hamner, B., Cukierski, W., Tang, Y., Thaler, D., & Lee, D. H. (2013). Challenges in representation learning: A report on three machine learning contests. *International Conference on Neural Information Processing*, 117–124. 10.1007/978-3-642-42051-1_16

Gopal, S. P. N. (2021). *Image Processing Techniques That You Can Use in Machine Learning Projects*. neptune.ai/blog/image-processing-techniques-you-can-use-in-machine-learning

Gordo, A., Almaz'an, J., Revaud, J., & Larlus, D. (2016). Deep image retrieval: Learning global representations for image search. *Proc. European Conference on Computer Vision*, 241–257. 10.1007/978-3-319-46466-4_15

Govindarajan, P., & Ravichandran, K. S. (2014). Data mining- an evolutionary arena. *Research Journal of Applied Sciences, Engineering and Technology*, *7*(22), 4749–4753. doi:10.19026/rjaset.7.861

Gragnaniello, Poggi, Sansone, & Verdoliva. (2013). Fingerprint liveness detection based on Weber Local Image Descriptor. *Proc. IEEE Workshop on Biometric Meas. Syst. Secur. Med. Appl.*, 46–50.

Gragnaniello, G., Poggi, G., Sansone, C., & Verdoliva, L. (2015). Local contrast phase descriptor for fingerprint liveness detection. *Pattern Recognition*, *48*(4), 1050–1058. doi:10.1016/j.patcog.2014.05.021

Gregor, K., & LeCun, Y. (2010). Learning fast approximations of sparse coding. *Proceedings of the 27th International Conference on International Conference on Machine Learning*, 399–406.

Gromer, M., Salb, D., Walzer, T., Madrid, N. M., & Seepold, R. (2019). ECG sensor for detection of driver's drowsiness. *Procedia Computer Science*, *159*, 1938–1946. doi:10.1016/j.procs.2019.09.366

Gross, R., Matthews, I., Cohn, J., Kanade, T., & Baker, S. (2010). Multi-pie. *Image and Vision Computing*, *28*(5), 807–813. doi:10.1016/j.imavis.2009.08.002 PMID:20490373

Guarda, L., Tapia, J., Droguett, E. L., & Ramos, M. (2022). A novel Capsule Neural Network based model for drowsiness detection using electroencephalography signals. *Expert Systems with Applications*, *201*, 116977. doi:10.1016/j.eswa.2022.116977

Guclu, O., & Can, A. B. (2019). k-SLAM: A fast RGB-D SLAM approach for large indoor environments. *Computer Vision and Image Understanding*, *184*, 31–44. doi:10.1016/j.cviu.2019.04.005

Gudbjartsson, H., & Patz, S. (1995). The Rician distribution of noisy MRI data. *Magnetic Resonance in Medicine*, *34*(6), 910–914. doi:10.1002/mrm.1910340618 PMID:8598820

Guoqing, X., Chen, L., & Qi, W. (2019). Unified multi-scale method for fast leaf classification and retrieval using geometric information. *IET Image Processing*, *13*(12), 2328–2334. doi:10.1049/iet-ipr.2018.6551

Guo, Y., Zhang, J., Yin, C., Hu, X., Zou, Y., Xue, Z., & Wang, W. (2020). Plant Disease Identification Based on Deep Learning Algorithm in Smart Farming. *Discrete Dynamics in Nature and Society*, 1–11. doi:10.1155/2020/2479172

Gupta, S. (2021). Deep learning based human activity recognition (HAR) using wearable sensor data. *International Journal of Information Management Data Insights*, *1*(2), 100046. doi:10.1016/j.jjimei.2021.100046

Gupta, V., Chaurasia, V., & Shandilya, M. (2015). Random-valued impulse noise removal using adaptive dual threshold median filter. *Journal of Visual Communication and Image Representation*, *26*, 296–304. doi:10.1016/j.jvcir.2014.10.004

Hacisoftaoglu, R. E., Karakaya, M., & Sallam, A. B. (2020). Deep learning frameworks for diabetic retinopathy detection with smartphone-based retinal imaging systems. *Pattern Recognition Letters*, *135*, 409–417. doi:10.1016/j.patrec.2020.04.009 PMID:32704196

Hadhami, A., & Yassine, B. A. (2021). *Speech Emotion Recognition with deep learning.*. doi:10.1016/j.procs.2020.08.027

Halefoğlu, A. M. (2018). *High-Resolution Neuroimaging: Basic Physical Principles and Clinical Applications*. BoD–Books on Demand. doi:10.5772/intechopen.68268

Hall, E. L. (1993, August). Fundamental principles of robot vision. In Intelligent Robots and Computer Vision XII: Active Vision and 3D Methods (Vol. 2056, pp. 321-333). SPIE.

Hanane, E., El-Habib, N., (2021). *Combining Context-Aware Embeddings and an Attentional Deep Learning Model for Arabic Affect Analysis on Twitter.*. doi:10.1109/ACCESS.2021.3102087

Hansen, L. K., & Salamon, P. (1990). Neural Network Ensembles. *IEEE Transactions on Pattern Analysis and Machine Intelligence*, *12*(10), 993–1001. doi:10.1109/34.58871

Hansun, S., Wicaksana, A., & Khaliq, A. Q. (2022). Multivariate cryptocurrency prediction: Comparative analysis of three recurrent neural networks approaches. *Journal of Big Data*, *9*(1), 1–15.

Haykin, S. (2008). *Neural Networks and Learning Machines*. Pearson Prentice Hall. doi:978-0131471399

He, K., & Sun, J. (2015). *Fast Guided Filter*. https://arxiv.org/abs/1505.00996

Healey, J. A., & Picard, R. W. (2005). Detecting stress during real-world driving tasks using physiological sensors. *IEEE Transactions on Intelligent Transportation Systems*, *6*(2), 156–166. doi:10.1109/TITS.2005.848368

Hegarty, J., Daly, R., DeVito, Z., Ragan-Kelley, J., Horowitz, M., & Hanrahan, P. (2016). Rigel: Flexible multi-rate image processing hardware. *ACM Transactions on Graphics*, *35*(4), 1–11. doi:10.1145/2897824.2925892

Henkelman, R. M. (1985). Measurement of signal intensities in the presence of noise in MR images. *Medical Physics*, *12*(2), 232–233. doi:10.1118/1.595711 PMID:4000083

He, W., Zhang, H., Shen, H., & Zhang, L. (2018). Hyperspectral image denoising using local low-rank matrix recovery and global spatial–spectral total variation. *IEEE Journal of Selected Topics in Applied Earth Observations and Remote Sensing, 11*(3), 713–729. doi:10.1109/JSTARS.2018.2800701

He, W., Zhang, H., Zhang, L., & Shen, H. (2015a). Hyperspectral image denoising via noise-adjusted iterative low-rank matrix approximation. *IEEE Journal of Selected Topics in Applied Earth Observations and Remote Sensing, 8*(6), 3050–3061. doi:10.1109/JSTARS.2015.2398433

He, W., Zhang, H., Zhang, L., & Shen, H. (2015b). Total-variation-regularized low-rank matrix factorization for hyperspectral image restoration. *IEEE Transactions on Geoscience and Remote Sensing, 54*(1), 178–188. doi:10.1109/TGRS.2015.2452812

Hinton, G., Srivastava, N., & Swersky, K. (2012). Neural networks for machine learning lecture 6a overview of mini-batch gradient descent. *Cited On, 14*(8).

Ho, A., Vatambeti, R., & Ravichandran, S. K. (2021). Bitcoin Price Prediction Using Machine Learning and Artificial Neural Network Model. *Indian Journal of Science and Technology, 14*(27), 2300–2308.

Hogan. (2015). *Multiple reference OCT system*. US Patent 9,113,782.

Hossein, S., Mir, M. P., & Mohammad, T., (2019). *A Robust Sentiment Analysis Method Based on Sequential Combination of Convolutional and Recursive Neural Networks*. . doi:10.1007/s11063-019-10049-1

HosseinKhani, Z., Karimi, N., Soroushmehr, S. M. R., Hajabdollahi, M., Samavi, S., Ward, K., & Najarian, K. (2016). Real-time removal of random value impulse noise in medical images. *2016 23rd International Conference on Pattern Recognition (ICPR)*, 3916–3921.

HosseinKhani, Z., Hajabdollahi, M., Karimi, N., Najarian, K., Emami, A., Shirani, S., Samavi, S., & Soroushmehr, S. M. R. (2019). Real-time removal of impulse noise from MR images for radiosurgery applications. *International Journal of Circuit Theory and Applications, 47*(3), 406–426. doi:10.1002/cta.2591

Ho, T. K. (1995). Random Decision Forests. *Proceedings of the 3rd International Conference on Document Analysis and Recognition, 1416*, 278-282.

Howard, A. G., Zhu, M., Chen, B., Kalenichenko, D., Wang, W., Weyand, T., Andreetto, M., & Adam, H. (2017). *Mobilenets: Efficient convolutional neural networks for mobile vision applications*. arXiv preprint arXiv:1704.04861.

Huahu, X., Jue, G., & Jian, Y. (2010). Application of speech emotion recognition in intelligent household robot. *International Conference on Artificial Intelligence and Computational Intelligence, 1*, 537-541. 10.1109/AICI.2010.118

Huang, L. C., Hwang, M. S., & Tseng, L. Y. (2013). Reversible and high-capacity data hiding in high quality medical images. *Transactions on Internet and Information Systems (Seoul), 7*(1), 132–148. doi:10.3837/tiis.2013.01.009

Huang, T., Dong, W., Xie, X., Shi, G., & Bai, X. (2017). Mixed noise removal via Laplacian scale mixture modeling and nonlocal low-rank approximation. *IEEE Transactions on Image Processing, 26*(7), 3171–3186. doi:10.1109/TIP.2017.2676466 PMID:28278467

Huang, T., Li, S., Jia, X., Lu, H., & Liu, J. (2021). Neighbor2neighbor: Self-supervised denoising from single noisy images. *Proceedings of the IEEE/CVF Conference on Computer Vision and Pattern Recognition*, 14781–14790. 10.1109/CVPR46437.2021.01454

Huang, Y.-M., Ng, M. K., & Wen, Y.-W. (2009). Fast image restoration methods for impulse and Gaussian noises removal. *IEEE Signal Processing Letters, 16*(6), 457–460. doi:10.1109/LSP.2009.2016835

Hubel, D. H., & Wiesel, T. N. (1962). Receptive fields, binocular interaction and functional architecture in the cat's visual cortex. *The Journal of Physiology, 160*(1), 106-154.2.

Hugo Proenc, A. (2018). Deep-Prwis: Periocular Recognition without The Iris And Sclera Using Deep Learning Frameworks. *IEEE Transactions on Information Forensics and Security, 13*(4), 888–896. doi:10.1109/TIFS.2017.2771230

Hu, H., Li, B., & Liu, Q. (2016). Removing mixture of gaussian and impulse noise by patch-based weighted means. *Journal of Scientific Computing, 67*(1), 103–129. doi:10.100710915-015-0073-9

Hui, L., & Song, Y. (2018). Research on face recognition algorithm based on improved convolution neural network, *IEEE Conference on Industrial Electronics and Applications (ICIEA)*. 10.1109/ICIEA.2018.8398186

Huo, Z., Gu, B., Yang, Q., & Huang, H. (2018). *Decoupled Parallel Backpropagation with Convergence Guarantee.* https://arxiv.org/abs/1804.10574

Hussain, M., Bird, J. J., & Faria, D. R. (2018). A Study on CNN Transfer Learning for Image Classification. *UK Workshop on computational Intelligence*, 191-202.

Hu, Y., Lee, H.-K., & Li, J. (2009). DE-based reversible data hiding with improved overflow location map. *IEEE Transactions on Circuits and Systems for Video Technology, 19*(2), 250–260. doi:10.1109/TCSVT.2008.2009252

Huynh, T. V. (2022). FPGA-based Acceleration for ConvolutionalNeural Networks on PYNQ-Z2. *International Journal of Computing and Digital Systems, 11*(1), 441–449. doi:10.12785/ijcds/110136

Hwang, R. J. (2000). A digital image copyright protection scheme based on visual cryptography. *Tamkang Journal of Science and Engineering, 3*, 97–106.

Ibrahim, T. S., Hue, Y.-K., & Tang, L. (2009). Understanding and manipulating the RF fields at high field MRI. *NMR in Biomedicine: An International Journal Devoted to the Development and Application of Magnetic Resonance In Vivo, 22*(9), 927–936. doi:10.1002/nbm.1406 PMID:19621335

Idowu, P. A., Balogun, J. A., & Alaba, O. B. (2016). Data Mining Approach for Predicting the Likelihood of Infertility in Nigerian Women. Handbook of Research on Healthcare Administration and Management, 76-104.

IHTT. (2013). *Transforming Health Care through Big Data Strategies for leveraging big data in the health care industry.* IHTT.

Im Im, D., Ahn, S., Memisevic, R., & Bengio, Y. (2017). Denoising criterion for variational auto-encoding framework. *Proceedings of the AAAI Conference on Artificial Intelligence, 31*(1).

Ince, T., Kiranyaz, S., Eren, L., Askar, M., & Gabbouj, M. (2016). Real-time motor fault detection by 1-D convolutional neural networks. *IEEE Transactions on Industrial Electronics, 63*(11), 7067–7075. doi:10.1109/TIE.2016.2582729

Infecundity, infertility, and childlessness in developing countries. (2004). Macro and the World Health Organization, World Health Organization, DHS Comparative Reports No 9.

Inoue, K., Kaizu, Y., Igarashi, S., & Imou, K. (2019). The development of autonomous navigation and obstacle avoidance for a robotic mower using machine vision technique. *IFAC-PapersOnLine, 52*(30), 173–177. doi:10.1016/j.ifacol.2019.12.517

Insafutdinov, E., Andriluka, M., Pishchulin, L., Tang, S., Levinkov, E., Andres, B., & Schiele, B. (2017). ArtTrack: Articulated multi-person tracking in the wild. *Proc. IEEE Conf. Comput. Vis. Pattern Recognit.*, 1293–1301.

International Standards Organization. (2016). *ISO/IEC 30107-1:2016, Information Technology—Biometric Presentation Attack Detection—Part 1: Framework.* https://www.iso.org/standard/53227.html

Ioffe, S., & Szegedy, C. (2015). Batch normalization: Accelerating deep network training by reducing internal covariate shift. *International Conference on Machine Learning*, 448–456.

Iqbal, M. J., Iqbal, M. M., Ahmad, I., Alassafi, M. O., Alfakeeh, A. S., & Alhomoud, A. (2021). Real-Time Surveillance Using Deep Learning. *Security and Communication Networks*.

Isa, I. S., Sulaiman, S. N., Mustapha, M., & Darus, S. (2015a). Evaluating denoising performances of fundamental filters for T2-weighted MRI images. *Procedia Computer Science*, *60*, 760–768. doi:10.1016/j.procs.2015.08.231

Isaj, S., Zimányi, E., & Pedersen, T. B. (2019). Multi-source spatial entity linkage. *Proceedings of the 16th International Symposium on Spatial and Temporal Databases*, 1-10.

Islam, M. Z., Hossain, M. S., ul Islam, R., & Andersson, K. (2019, May). Static hand gesture recognition using convolutional neural network with data augmentation. In *2019 Joint 8th International Conference on Informatics, Electronics & Vision (ICIEV) and 2019 3rd International Conference on Imaging, Vision & Pattern Recognition (icIVPR)* (pp. 324-329). IEEE.

Islam, M. T., Rahman, S. M. M., Ahmad, M. O., & Swamy, M. N. S. (2018). Mixed Gaussian-impulse noise reduction from images using convolutional neural network. *Signal Processing Image Communication*, *68*, 26–41. doi:10.1016/j. image.2018.06.016

Jabbar, R., Shinoy, M., Kharbeche, M., Al-Khalifa, K., Krichen, M., & Barkaoui, K. (2020, February). Driver drowsiness detection model using convolutional neural networks techniques for android application. In *2020 IEEE International Conference on Informatics, IoT, and Enabling Technologies (ICIoT)* (pp. 237-242). IEEE.

Jain, A. K., & Dubes, R. C. (1988). *Algorithms for Clustering Data*. Prentice-Hall, Inc.

Jain, A., & Sharma, N. (2022). Accelerated AI Inference at CNN-Based Machine Vision in ASICs: A Design Approach. *ECS Transactions*, *107*(1), 5165–5174. doi:10.1149/10701.5165ecst

Jang, H., & Lee, J. (2017). An empirical study on modeling and prediction of bitcoin prices with bayesian neural networks based on blockchain information. *IEEE Access: Practical Innovations, Open Solutions*, *6*, 5427–5437. doi:10.1109/ACCESS.2017.2779181

Jang, H.-U., Choi, H.-Y., Kim, D., Son, J., & Lee, H.-K. (2017). Fingerprint spoof detection using contrast enhancement and convolutional neural networks. In *ICISA* (pp. 331–338). Springer. doi:10.1007/978-981-10-4154-9_39

Jebara, T. (2012). *Machine learning: discriminative and generative* (Vol. 755). Springer Science & Business Media.

Jemima Jebaseeli, T., Anand Deva Durai, C., & Dinesh Peter, J. (2019). Segmentation of retinal blood vessels from ophthalmologic Diabetic Retinopathy images. *Computers & Electrical Engineering*, *73*, 245–258. doi:10.1016/j.compeleceng.2018.11.024

Jiang, H. (2020). The Analysis of Plants Image Recognition Based on Deep Learning and Artificial Neural Network. *IEEE Access. Special Section on Data Mining For Internet of Things*, (8), 68828–68841.

Jiang, J., Wang, Z., Chen, C., & Lu, T. (2016). L1-l1 norms for face super-resolution with mixed gaussian-impulse noise. *2016 IEEE International Conference on Acoustics, Speech and Signal Processing (ICASSP)*, 2089–2093. 10.1109/ICASSP.2016.7472045

Jiang, J., Zhang, L., & Yang, J. (2014). Mixed noise removal by weighted encoding with sparse nonlocal regularization. *IEEE Transactions on Image Processing*, *23*(6), 2651–2662. doi:10.1109/TIP.2014.2317985 PMID:24760906

Jibi, G. T., Ashwani, K. D., & Thomas, M. T. (2018). Advanced Plant Leaf Classification Through Image Enhancement and Canny Edge Detection. *7th International Conference on Reliability, Infocom Technologies and Optimization (ICRITO)*, 518-522.

Jin, K. H., & Ye, J. C. (2015). *Sparse+ low rank decomposition of annihilating filter-based Hankel matrix for impulse noise removal.* ArXiv Preprint ArXiv:1510.05559.

Jin, K. H., McCann, M. T., Froustey, E., & Unser, M. (2017). Deep convolutional neural network for inverse problems in imaging. *IEEE Transactions on Image Processing, 26*(9), 4509–4522. doi:10.1109/TIP.2017.2713099 PMID:28641250

Jin, L., Liu, H., Xu, X., & Song, E. (2012). Quaternion-based impulse noise removal from color video sequences. *IEEE Transactions on Circuits and Systems for Video Technology, 23*(5), 741–755. doi:10.1109/TCSVT.2012.2207272

Jin, L., Zhang, W., Ma, G., & Song, E. (2019). Learning deep CNNs for impulse noise removal in images. *Journal of Visual Communication and Image Representation, 62*, 193–205. doi:10.1016/j.jvcir.2019.05.005

Jin, L., Zhu, Z., Xu, X., & Li, X. (2016). Two-stage quaternion switching vector filter for color impulse noise removal. *Signal Processing, 128*, 171–185. doi:10.1016/j.sigpro.2016.03.025

Jin, Q., Grama, I., & Liu, Q. (2017). Optimal Weights Mixed Filter for removing mixture of Gaussian and impulse noises. *PLoS One, 12*(7), e0179051. doi:10.1371/journal.pone.0179051 PMID:28692667

Ji, S., Xu, W., Yang, M., & Yu, K. (2013). 3D Convolutional Neural Networks for Human Action Recognition. *IEEE TPAMI, 35*(1), 221–231. doi:10.1109/TPAMI.2012.59 PMID:22392705

Jolly, S. (2000). Understanding body language: Birdwhistell's theory of kinesics. *Corporate Communications, 5*(3), 133–139. doi:10.1108/13563280010377518

Jonathan, A. P., Paoline, G. P. K., & Amalia, Z. (2018). Facial Emotion Recognition Using Computer Vision. *IEEE The 1st 2018 INAPR International Conference.*10.1109/INAPR.2018.8626999

Jufeng, Y., Jie, L., Hui, S., Kai, W., Paul, L. R., & Ming-Hsuan, Y. (2018). Dynamic Match Kernel with Deep Convolutional Features for Image Retrieval. *IEEE Transactions on Image Processing*, (99), 1–15. PMID:29994213

Junfeng, W., & Yitong, W. (2016). A novel image retrieval approach with Bag-of-Word model and Gabor feature. *Proc. IEEE TrustComBigData SEISPA,* 1706-1711.

Jung, Y. M., Jeong, T., & Yun, S. (2017). Non-convex TV denoising corrupted by impulse noise. *Inverse Problems and Imaging (Springfield, Mo.), 11*(4), 689–702. doi:10.3934/ipi.2017032

Kalita, M., Tuithung, T., & Majumder, S. (2019). An adaptive color image steganography method using adjacent pixel value differencing and LSB substitution technique. *Cryptologia, 43*(5), 414–437.

Kamble, V. V., & Kokate, R. D. (2020). Automated diabetic retinopathy detection using radial basis function. *Procedia Computer Science, 167*, 799–808. doi:10.1016/j.procs.2020.03.429

Kamstra, L., & Heijmans, H. (2005). Reversible data embedding into images using wavelet techniques and sorting. *IEEE Transactions on Image Processing, 14*(12), 2082–2090. doi:10.1109/TIP.2005.859373 PMID:16370461

Kandemir, C., Kalyoncu, C., & Toygar, Ö. (2015). A weighted mean filter with spatial-bias elimination for impulse noise removal. *Digital Signal Processing, 46*, 164–174. doi:10.1016/j.dsp.2015.08.012

Kang, M. (2018). Machine learning: Diagnostics and prognostics. *Prognostics and Health Management of Electronics: Fundamentals, Machine Learning, and the Internet of Things*, 163-191.

Kapil & Nitin. (2018). Plant Species Identification using Leaf Image Retrieval: A Study. *International Conference on Computing, Power and Communication Technologies (GUCON),* 405-411.

Kazi, M., Chowhan, S., & Kulkarni, V. U. (2017). MRI Brain Image Segmentation Using Adaptive Thresholding and K-means Algorithm. *International Journal of Computers and Applications, 167*(8), 11–15. doi:10.5120/ijca2017914330

Kebir, T., & Mekaoui. (2018, November). An Efficient Methodology of Brain Abnormalities Detection using CNN Deep Learning Network. *IEEE International Conference on Applied Smart Systems.*

Kennedy & Eberhart. (1995). *Particle Swarm Optimization.* Academic Press.

Khdier, Jasim, & Aliesawi, (2020). Deep Learning Algorithms Based Voiceprint Recognition System In Noisy Environment, *Journal of Physics, International Conference of Modern Applications on Information and Communication Technology,* 1804.

Khodizadeh-Nahari, M., Ghadiri, N., Baraani-Dastjerdi, A., & Sack, J.-R. (2021). A novel similarity measure for spatial entity resolution based on data granularity model: Managing inconsistencies in place descriptions. *Applied Intelligence, 51*(8), 6104–6123. doi:10.100710489-020-01959-y

Kim, J. K., Kang, S., & Korea, S. (2017). *Neural Network-based Coronary Heart Disease Risk Predict i on using Feature Correlation Analysis.* Academic Press.

Kimiaei, M., & Rostami, M. (2016). Impulse noise removal based on new hybrid conjugate gradient approach. *Kybernetika, 52*(5), 791–823. doi:10.14736/kyb-2016-5-0791

Kim, J. H., Hong, H. G., & Park, K. R. (2017). Convolutional Neural Network-Based Human Detection in Nighttime Images Using Visible Light Camera Sensors. *Sensors (Basel), 5*(5), 1065. doi:10.339017051065 PMID:28481301

Kim, J. H., Matson, E. T., Myung, H., Xu, P., & Karray, F. (Eds.). (2014). *Robot Intelligence Technology and Applications 2.* Springer. doi:10.1007/978-3-319-05582-4

Kim, S. R., & Efron, A. (1995). Adaptive robust impulse noise filtering. *IEEE Transactions on Signal Processing, 43*(8), 1855–1866. doi:10.1109/78.403344

Kingma, D. P., & Ba, J. (2014). *Adam: A method for stochastic optimization.* ArXiv Preprint ArXiv:1412.6980.

Kingma, D. P., & Welling, M. (2013). *Auto-encoding variational bayes.* ArXiv Preprint ArXiv:1312.6114.

Ko, B. (2018, January 30). A Brief Review of Facial Emotion Recognition Based on Visual Information. *Sensors (Basel), 18*(2), 401. doi:10.339018020401 PMID:29385749

Koelstra, S., Muhl, C., Soleymani, M., Lee, J.-S., Yazdani, A., Ebrahimi, T., Pun, T., Nijholt, A., & Patras, I. (2012). DEAP: A Database for Emotion Analysis;Using Physiological Signals. *IEEE Transactions on Affective Computing, 3*(1), 18–31. doi:10.1109/T-AFFC.2011.15

Ko, K.-E., & Sim, K.-B. (2018). Deep convolutional framework for abnormal behavior detection in a smart surveillance system. *Engineering Applications of Artificial Intelligence, 67,* 226–234. doi:10.1016/j.engappai.2017.10.001

Kolesnikov, A., Zhai, X., & Beyer, L. (2019). Revisiting self-supervised visual representation learning. *Proceedings of the IEEE/CVF Conference on Computer Vision and Pattern Recognition,* 1920–1929.

Kolokas, N., Vafeiadis, T., Ioannidis, D., & Tzovaras, D. (2020). A generic fault prognostics algorithm for manufacturing industries using unsupervised machine learning classifiers. *Simulation Modelling Practice and Theory, 103,* 102–109. doi:10.1016/j.simpat.2020.102109

Kopaczka, M., Kolk, R., & Merhof, D. (2018). A fully annotated thermal face database and its application for thermal facial expression recognition. *IEEE International Instrumentation and Measurement Technology Conference (I2MTC)*, *1–6*. 10.1109/I2MTC.2018.8409768

Koudas, N., & Sevcik, K. C. (1998) High dimensional similarity joins: algorithms and performance evaluation. IEEE Conference Publications.

Krishnan, D., Fattal, R., & Szeliski, R. (2013). Efficient preconditioning of laplacian matrices for computer graphics. *ACM Transactions on Graphics, 32*(4), 142:1-142:15. doi:10.1145/2461912.2461992

Krishnan, R. B., Raj, M. M., Kumar, N. R., Karthikeyan, B., Manikandan, G., & Raajan, N. R. (2022). Scrambling Based Riffle Shift on Stego-Image to Channelize the Ensured Data. *Intelligent Automation and Soft Computing, 32*(1), 221–235. doi:10.32604/iasc.2022.021775

Krizhevsky, A., Sutskever, I., & Hinton, G. E. (2012). ImageNet Classification with Deep Convolutional Neural Networks. *Advances in Neural Information Processing Systems, 25*. https://papers.nips.cc/paper/2012/hash/c399862d3b-9d6b76c8436e924a68c45b-Abstract.html

Krizhevsky, A., Sutskever, I., & Hinton, G. E. (2012). ImageNet Classification with Deep Convolutional Neural Networks. *Advances in Neural Information Processing Systems.*

Kshatri, S. S., Singh, D., Narain, B., Bhatia, S., Quasim, M. T., & Sinha, G. R. (2021). An Empirical Analysis of Machine Learning Algorithms for Crime Prediction Using Stacked Generalization: An Ensemble Approach. *IEEE Access: Practical Innovations, Open Solutions*, 9, 67488–67500. doi:10.1109/ACCESS.2021.3075140

Kshirsagar, Bhole, Khobare, & Pujeri. (2019). Driver Drowsiness Detection And Alarming System. *Mythos Technology, 3*(1), 4980–4983.

Kumar, B., Sinha, G. R., & Thakur, K. (2011). Quality assessment of compressed MR medical images using general regression neural network. *International Journal of Pure and Applied Sciences and Technology*, 7(2), 158–169.

Kumar, S., Adarsh, A., Kumar, B., & Singh, A. K. (2020). An automated early diabetic retinopathy detection through improved blood vessel and optic disc segmentation. *Optics & Laser Technology, 121*, 105815. doi:10.1016/j.optlastec.2019.105815

Lang, S., Bravo-marquez, F., Beckham, C., & Hall, M. (2019). *WekaDeeplearning4j : a Deep Learning Package for Weka based on DeepLearning4j.* doi:10.1016/j.knosys.2019.04.013

Langer, A. (2017). Automated parameter selection in the-TV model for removing Gaussian plus impulse noise. *Inverse Problems, 33*(7), 74002. doi:10.1088/1361-6420/33/7/074002

Langer, A. (2019). Locally adaptive total variation for removing mixed Gaussian–impulse noise. *International Journal of Computer Mathematics, 96*(2), 298–316. doi:10.1080/00207160.2018.1438603

Langner, O., Dotsch, R., Bijlstra, G., Wigboldus, D. H., Hawk, S. T., & van Knippenberg, A. (2010). Presentation and validation of the radboud faces database. *Cognition and Emotion, 24*(8), 1377–1388. doi:10.1080/02699930903485076

Lan, X., & Zuo, Z. (2014). Random-valued impulse noise removal by the adaptive switching median detectors and detail-preserving regularization. *Optik (Stuttgart), 125*(3), 1101–1105. doi:10.1016/j.ijleo.2013.07.114

Lan, Z., Sourina, O., Wang, L., Scherer, R., & Muller-Putz, G. R. (2018). Domain adaptation techniques for EEG-based emotion recognition: A comparative study on two public datasets. *IEEE Transactions on Cognitive and Developmental Systems, 11*(1), 85–94. doi:10.1109/TCDS.2018.2826840

LeCun, Y., Bengio, Y., & Hinton, G. (2015). Deep learning. *Nature, 521*(7553), 436–444. doi:10.1038/nature14539 PMID:26017442

Lee & Kim. (2019). Development of Specific Area Intrusion Detection System using YOLO. *International Journal of Innovative Technology and Exploring Engineering, 8*(2), 852-856.

Lee, H. Y. (2019). Reversible Data Hiding for Medical Imagery Applications to Protect Privacy. *International Journal of Engineering Research & Technology (Ahmedabad), 12*(1), 42–49.

Lellmann, J., Becker, F., & Schnorr, C. (2009). Convex optimization for multi-class image labeling with a novel family of total variation based regularizers. *2009 IEEE 12th International Conference on Computer Vision*, 646–653.

Levitan, E., Chan, M., & Herman, G. T. (1995). Image-modeling Gibbs priors. *Graphical Models and Image Processing, 57*(2), 117–130. doi:10.1006/gmip.1995.1013

Li, Liu, Yang, Sun, & Wang. (2021). *Speech emotion recognition using recurrent neural networks with directional self-attention*. . doi:10.1016/j.eswa.2021.114683

Li, S., & Deng, W. (2020). Deep Facial Expression Recognition: A Survey. *IEEE Transactions on Affective Computing*. doi:10.1109/TAFFC.2020.2981446

Liao, S., Xiong, J., Tu, H., Hu, C., Pan, W., Geng, Y., Pan, W., Lu, T., & Jin, L. (2019). Prediction of in vitro fertilization outcome at different antral follicle count thresholds combined with female age, female cause of infertility, and ovarian response in a prospective cohort of 8269 women. *Medicine, 98*(41), e17470–e17470. doi:10.1097/MD.0000000000017470 PMID:31593108

Li, C., Guo, C., Han, L. H., Jiang, J., Cheng, M. M., Gu, J., & Loy, C. C. (2021). Low-light image and video enhancement using deep learning: A survey. *IEEE Transactions on Pattern Analysis and Machine Intelligence*, (01), 1–1. doi:10.1109/TPAMI.2007.250595 PMID:34752382

Li, C., Guo, J., Porikli, F., & Pang, Y. (2018). LightenNet: A convolutional neural network for weakly illuminated image enhancement. *Pattern Recognition Letters, 104*, 15–22. doi:10.1016/j.patrec.2018.01.010

Lien, C.-Y., Huang, C.-C., Chen, P.-Y., & Lin, Y.-F. (2012). An efficient denoising architecture for removal of impulse noise in images. *IEEE Transactions on Computers, 62*(4), 631–643. doi:10.1109/TC.2011.256

Lin. (2000). An Introduction to Face Recognition Technology. *Informing Science Special Issue on Multimedia Informing Technologies Part 2, 3*(1).

Lin, C. W., Hong, S., Lin, M., Huang, X., & Liu, J. (2022). Bird posture recognition based on target keypoints estimation in dual-task convolutional neural networks. *Ecological Indicators, 135*, 108506. doi:10.1016/j.ecolind.2021.108506

Li, P., Meziane, R., Otis, M. J. D., Ezzaidi, H., & Cardou, P. (2014, October). A Smart Safety Helmet using IMU and EEG sensors for worker fatigue detection. In *2014 IEEE International Symposium on Robotic and Sensors Environments (ROSE) Proceedings* (pp. 55-60). IEEE.

Liu, X., Guo, B., & Meng, C. (2016, November). A method of simultaneous location and mapping based on RGB-D cameras. In *2016 14th International Conference on Control, Automation, Robotics and Vision (ICARCV)* (pp. 1-5). IEEE. 10.1109/ICARCV.2016.7838786

Liu, X., Liu, Q., Wu, Z., Wang, X., Sole, J. P., & Frangi, A. (2018). Mixed-Model Noise Removal in 3D MRI via Rotation-and-Scale Invariant Non-Local Means. *Sipaim–Miccai Biomedical Workshop*, 33–41.

Liu, X., Pei, D., Lodewijks, G., Zhao, Z., & Mei, J. (2020). Acoustic signal based fault detection on belt conveyor idlers using machine learning. *Advanced Powder Technology*, *31*(7), 2689–2698. doi:10.1016/j.apt.2020.04.034

Liu, Y., Chen, X., Wang, Z., Wang, Z. J., Ward, R. K., & Wang, X. (2018). Deep learning for pixel-level image fusion: Recent advances and future prospects. *Information Fusion*, *42*, 158–173. doi:10.1016/j.inffus.2017.10.007

Liu, Y., Yu, H., Gong, C., & Chen, Y. (2020). A real time expert system for anomaly detection of aerators based on computer vision and surveillance cameras. *Journal of Visual Communication and Image Representation*, *68*, 102767. doi:10.1016/j.jvcir.2020.102767

Liu, Z., Li, H., Zhou, W., Hong, R., & Tian, Q. (2015). Uniting keypoints: Local visual information fusion for large-scale image search. *IEEE Transactions on Multimedia*, *17*(4), 538–548. doi:10.1109/TMM.2015.2399851

Li, Y., Jiang, S., Li, X., & Wang, S. (2022). Hybrid data decomposition-based deep learning for Bitcoin prediction and algorithm trading. *Financial Innovation*, *8*(1), 1–24.

Li, Y., Zheng, W., Cui, Z., Zong, Y., & Ge, S. (2018c). EEG emotion recognition based on graph regularized sparse linear regression. *Neural Processing Letters*, 1–17. doi:10.100711063-017-9609-3

Li, Y., Zheng, W., Wang, L., Zong, Y., & Cui, Z. (2019). From regional to global brain: A novel hierarchical spatial-temporal neural network model for EEG emotion recognition. *IEEE Transactions on Affective Computing*.

Li, Y., Zheng, W., Zong, Y., Cui, Z., Zhang, T., & Zhou, X. (2018b). A bi-hemisphere domain adversarial neural network model for EEG emotion recognition. *IEEE Transactions on Affective Computing*.

Lohita, K., Sree, A. A., Poojitha, D., Renuga Devi, T., & Umamakeswari, A. (2015). Performance analysis of various data mining techniques in the prediction of heart disease. *Indian Journal of Science and Technology*, *8*(35). Advance online publication. doi:10.17485/ijst/2015/v8i35/87458

López-Rubio, E. (2010). Restoration of images corrupted by Gaussian and uniform impulsive noise. *Pattern Recognition*, *43*(5), 1835–1846. doi:10.1016/j.patcog.2009.11.017

Louizos, C., Welling, M., & Kingma, D. P. (2017). *Learning Sparse Neural Networks through L_0 Regularization*. ArXiv Preprint ArXiv:1712.01312.

Louppe, G., Louis, W., Antonio, S., & Pierre, G. (2013). Understanding variable importance in forests of randomized trees. *Advances in Neural Information Processing Systems*, 431–439.

Lowe, D. G. (2004). Distinctive Image Features from Scale-Invariant Keypoints. *International Journal of Computer Vision*, *60*(2), 91–110. doi:10.1023/B:VISI.0000029664.99615.94

Lucey, P., Cohn, J. F., Kanade, T., Saragih, J., Ambadar, Z., & Matthews, I. (2010). The Extended Cohn-Kanade Dataset (CK+): A complete dataset for action unit and emotion-specified expression. *IEEE Computer Society Conference on Computer Vision and Pattern Recognition - Workshops*, 94-101. 10.1109/CVPRW.2010.5543262

Luisier, F., Blu, T., & Wolfe, P. J. (2012). A CURE for noisy magnetic resonance images: Chi-square unbiased risk estimation. *IEEE Transactions on Image Processing*, *21*(8), 3454–3466. doi:10.1109/TIP.2012.2191565 PMID:22491082

Lundqvist, D., Flykt, A., & Ohman, A. (1998). *The Karolinska Directed Emotional Faces – KDEF, CD ROM from Department of Clinical Neuroscience, Psychology section, Karolinska Institutet*. KDEF. Available online https://www.emotionlab.se/resources/kdef

Lyons, M. J., Akamatsu, S., Kamachi, M., & Gyoba, J. (1998). Coding facial expressions with Gabor wave. *Proceedings of the IEEE International Conference on Automatic Face and Gesture Recognition*, 200–205. 10.1109/AFGR.1998.670949

Maaten, L. V. D., & Hinton, G. (2008). Visualizing Data using t-SNE. *JMLR, 9*(Nov), 2579–2605.

Madhupriya, G., Narayanan, M. G., Praveen, S., & Nivetha, B. (2019, October). Brain Tumor Segmentation with Deep Learning Technique. *IEEE 3rd International Conference on Trends in Electronics*, 758-763. 10.1109/ICOEI.2019.8862575

Mafi, M., Martin, H., & Adjouadi, M. (2017). High impulse noise intensity removal in MRI images. *2017 IEEE Signal Processing in Medicine and Biology Symposium (SPMB)*, 1–6.

Mafi, M., Martin, H., Cabrerizo, M., Andrian, J., Barreto, A., & Adjouadi, M. (2019). A comprehensive survey on impulse and Gaussian denoising filters for digital images. *Signal Processing, 157*, 236–260. doi:10.1016/j.sigpro.2018.12.006

Mahar, K., Narejo, S., & Zaki, M. A. (2020). Bitcoin price prediction app using deep learning algorithm. In *2nd International Conference on Computational Sciences and Technologies* (pp. 56-60).

Mahar, K., Narejo, S., & Zaki, M. A. (2020). *Bitcoin price prediction app using deep learning algorithm. In 2nd International Conference on Computational Sciences and Technologies.*, doi:10.1371/journal.pone.0164603.

Mahmudul Hassan, S. K., & Kumar Maji, A. (2021). Identification of Plant Species using Deep Learning. In *Proceedings of International Conference on Frontiers in Computing and Systems. Advances in Intelligent Systems and Computing*, (1255), 115-125. 10.1007/978-981-15-7834-2_11

Mairal, J., Koniusz, P., Harchaoui, Z., & Schmid, C. (2014). Convolutional kernel networks. Proc. Advances in Neural Information Processing Systems, 2627–2635.

Ma, L., Ng, M. K., Yu, J., & Zeng, T. (2013). Efficient box-constrained tv-type-l^1 algorithms for restoring images with impulse noise. *Journal of Computational Mathematics, 31*(3), 249–270. doi:10.4208/jcm.1301-m4143

Ma, L., Yu, J., & Zeng, T. (2013). Sparse Representation Prior and Total Variation–Based Image Deblurring under Impulse Noise. *SIAM Journal on Imaging Sciences, 6*(4), 2258–2284. doi:10.1137/120866452

Malathi, M., & Sinthia, P. (2019). Brain Tumour Segmentation Using Convolutional Neural Network with Tensor Flow. *Asian Pacific Journal of Cancer Prevention, 20*(7), 2095–2101. doi:10.31557/APJCP.2019.20.7.2095 PMID:31350971

Manea, D., & Calin, M. A. (2015). Hyperspectral imaging in different light conditions. *Imaging Science Journal, 63*(4), 214–219. doi:10.1179/1743131X15Y.0000000001

Manikandan, G., Bala Krishnan, R., Rajesh Kumar, N., Narasimhan, D., Srinivasan, A., & Raajan, N. R. (2018). Steganographic approach to enhancing secure data communication using contours and clustering. *Multimedia Tools and Applications, 77*(24), 32257–32273.

Manikandan, V. P., & Rahamathunnisa, U. (2022). A neural network aided attuned scheme for gun detection in video surveillance images. *Image and Vision Computing, 120*, 104406. doi:10.1016/j.imavis.2022.104406

Manjón, J., Coupé, P., Buades, A., Louis Collins, D., & Robles, M. (2012). New methods for MRI denoising based on sparseness and self-similarity. *Medical Image Analysis, 16*(1), 18–27. doi:10.1016/j.media.2011.04.003 PMID:21570894

Manjón, J., Coupé, P., Martí-Bonmatí, L., Collins, D. L., & Robles, M. (2010). Adaptive non-local means denoising of MR images with spatially varying noise levels. *Journal of Magnetic Resonance Imaging, 31*(1), 192–203. doi:10.1002/jmri.22003 PMID:20027588

Manochitra, V. (2017). Sleep Sensing And Alerting System For Drivers. SSRN *Electronic Journal, 4*(6), 1-5.

Maragret, L. M., Christopher, B., & Robert, B. (2020). Real-Time Speech Emotion Recognition Using a Pre-trained Image Classification Network. *Effects of Bandwidth Reduction and Companding, 2020*, 14. Advance online publication. doi:10.3389/fcomp.2020.00014

Marasco & Ross. (2015). A Survey on Antispoofing Schemes for Fingerprint Recognition Systems. *ACM Computing Surveys*.

Marasco & Sansone. (2012). Combining perspiration-and morphology-based static features for fingerprint liveness detection. *PR Letters*, *33*(9), 1148–1156.

Marcel, S., Nixon, M. S., & Li, S. Z. (2014). *Handbook of Biometric AntiSpoofing*. Springer.

Marcialis, L., Roli, F., & Tidu, A. (2010). Analysis of fingerprint pores for vitality detection. *Proc. 20th ICPR*, 1289–1292. 10.1109/ICPR.2010.321

Margalikas, E., & Ramanauskaitė, S. (2019). Image steganography based on color palette transformation in color space. *EURASIP Journal on Image and Video Processing*, *2019*(1), 1–13.

Maryam, N. A. (1867). A hybrid feature selection method using multiclass SVM for diagnosis of erythemato-squamous disease. *AIP Conference Proceedings*.

Matsumoto, T., Matsumoto, H., Yamada, K., & Hoshino, S. (2012). Impact of artificial gummy fingers on fingerprint systems. *Proceedings of the Society for Photo-Instrumentation Engineers*, *4677*, 275–289. doi:10.1117/12.462719

McGraw, T., Vemuri, B. C., Chen, Y., Rao, M., & Mareci, T. (2004). DT-MRI denoising and neuronal fiber tracking. *Medical Image Analysis*, *8*(2), 95–111. doi:10.1016/j.media.2003.12.001 PMID:15063860

McNally, S., Roche, J., & Caton, S. (2018, March). Predicting the price of bitcoin using machine learning. In *2018 26th euromicro international conference on parallel, distributed and network-based processing (PDP)* (pp. 339-343). IEEE.

Medad, Gaio, Moncla, Mustière, & Le Nir. (2020) Comparing supervised learning algorithms for spatial nominal entity recognition. *AGILE: GIScience Series, 1*, 1-18.

Mei, J.-J., Dong, Y., Huang, T.-Z., & Yin, W. (2018). Cauchy noise removal by nonconvex ADMM with convergence guarantees. *Journal of Scientific Computing*, *74*(2), 743–766. doi:10.100710915-017-0460-5

Melinte, D. O., & Vladareanu, L. (2020, April 23). Facial Expressions Recognition for Human-Robot Interaction Using Deep Convolutional Neural Networks with Rectified Adam Optimizer. *Sensors (Basel)*, *20*(8), 2393. doi:10.339020082393 PMID:32340140

Melissa, N., Stolar, M. L., Robert, S. B., & Michael, S., (2017). *Real Time Speech Emotion Recognition Using RGB Image Classification and Transfer Learning*. doi:10.1109/ICSPCS.2017.8270472

Meng, F., Yang, X., & Zhou, C. (2014). The augmented lagrange multipliers method for matrix completion from corrupted samplings with application to mixed Gaussian-impulse noise removal. *PLoS One*, *9*(9), e108125. doi:10.1371/journal.pone.0108125 PMID:25248103

Menotti, D., Chiachia, G., Pinto, A., Schwartz, W. R., Pedrini, H., Falcao, A. X., & Rocha, A. (2015). Deep representations for iris, face, and fingerprint spoofing detection. *IEEE TIFS*, *10*(4), 864–879. doi:10.1109/TIFS.2015.2398817

Miao, K. H., & Miao, J. H. (2018). Coronary Heart Disease Diagnosis using Deep Neural Networks. (IJACSA). *International Journal of Advanced Computer Science and Applications*, *9*(10), 1–8. doi:10.14569/IJACSA.2018.091001

Michel, F., & Valstar, M. P. (2010). Induced Disgust, Happiness and Surprise: an Addition to the MMI Facial Expression Database. In *Proceedings of lREC*. MMI. Available online: https://mmifacedb.eu/

Minaee, S., Mehdi, M., & Amirali, A. (2021). Deep-Emotion: Facial Expression Recognition Using Attentional Convolutional Network. *Sensors, 21*(9). . doi:10.3390/s21093046

Miranda Correa, J. A., Abadi, M. K., Sebe, N., & Patras, I. (2018). AMIGOS: A Dataset for Affect, Personality and Mood Research on Individuals and Groups. *IEEE Transactions on Affective Computing*, 1–1. doi:10.1109/TAFFC.2018.2884461

Mohammad, H., Axel, D., Antoine, B., Aaron, C., Pierre, M. Larochelle, H. (2016). Brain Tumor Segmentation with Deep Neural Networks. *Elsevier Medical Image Analysis*, *35*, 18-31.

Mohana, B., & Rani, S. (2019). CM Drowsiness Detection Based on Eye Closure and Yawning Detection. *Int. J. Recent Technol. Eng*, *8*, 1–13.

Mohedano, E., McGuinness, K., O'Connor, N. E., Salvador, A., & Marqu'es, F. (2016). Bags of local convolutional features for scalable instance search. *Proc. International Conference on Multimedia Retrieval*, 327–331.

Mohmand Shahjahan Majib, M. M. (2021). VGG-SCNet: A VGG Net-Based Deep Learning Framework for Brain Tumor Detection on MRI Images. *IEEE Access: Practical Innovations, Open Solutions*, *9*, 116942–116952. doi:10.1109/ACCESS.2021.3105874

Moreno López, M., Frederick, J. M., & Ventura, J. (2021). Evaluation of MRI Denoising Methods Using Unsupervised Learning. *Frontiers in Artificial Intelligence*, *4*, 75. doi:10.3389/frai.2021.642731 PMID:34151253

Morillas, S., Gregori, V., & Hervás, A. (2009). Fuzzy peer groups for reducing mixed Gaussian-impulse noise from color images. *IEEE Transactions on Image Processing*, *18*(7), 1452–1466. doi:10.1109/TIP.2009.2019305 PMID:19447709

Moujahid, A., Dornaika, F., Arganda-Carreras, I., & Reta, J. (2021). Efficient and compact face descriptor for driver drowsiness detection. *Expert Systems with Applications*, *168*, 114334. doi:10.1016/j.eswa.2020.114334

Muhammad, U. S. L., & Junaid, Q. (2018). *Using Deep Autoencoders for Facial Expression Recognition.* arXiv:1801.08329v1

Muhammad, K. N., Thomas, M. D., Daniel, H., & Stephan, J. (2016). Feature description with SIFT, SURF, BRIEF, BRISK, or FREAK? A general question answered for bone age assessment. *Computers in Biology and Medicine*, *68*, 67–75. doi:10.1016/j.compbiomed.2015.11.006 PMID:26623943

Mura, V., Orru, G., Casula, R., Sibiriu, A., Loi, G., Tuveri, P., Ghiani, L., & Marcialis, G. L. (2018). LivDet 2017 Fingerprint Liveness Detection Competition 2017. *Proc. ICB*, 297–302. 10.1109/ICB2018.2018.00052

Murugeswari, M., & Veluchamy, S. (2014, May). Hand gesture recognition system for real-time application. In *2014 IEEE International Conference on Advanced Communications, Control and Computing Technologies* (pp. 1220-1225). IEEE. 10.1109/ICACCCT.2014.7019293

Nakajima, M., & Yamaguchi, Y. (2002). Extended visual cryptography for natural images. *Journal of WSCG*, 303–310.

Naor, M., & Shamir, A. (1994). Visual Cryptography. *Proc. International Conference on the Theory and Application of Cryptographic Techniques*, 1-12.

Naqvi, N., Abbasi, A. T., Hussain, R., Khan, M. A., & Ahmad, B. (2018). Multilayer partially homomorphic encryption text steganography (MLPHE-TS): A zero steganography approach. *Wireless Personal Communications*, *103*(2), 1563–1585.

Neethu, O., & Shruti. (2017). A Reliable Method for Brain Tumor Detection Using CNN Technique. *IOSR Journal of Electrical and Electronics Engineering*, *1*, 64-68.

Neto, C., Silva, M., Fernandes, M., Ferreira, D., & Machado, J. (2021). Prediction models for Polycystic Ovary Syndrome using data mining. In T. Antipova (Ed.), *Advances in Digital Science. ICADS 2021. Adv Intell Syst Comput., 1352.* doi:10.1007/978-3-030-71782-7_19

Ng, R. T. (2002). CLARANS: A Method for clustering objects for spatial data mining. IEEE Transactions on Knowledge and Data Engineering, 15(5), 1003-1016.

Ngugi, Abelwahab, & Abo-Zahhad. (2021). Recent advances in image processing techniques for automated leaf pest and disease recognition – A review. *Information Processing in Agriculture, 8*(1), 27-51.

Nikitha, J., Keerthana, S., Balakrishnan, S., & Sathya, S. P. (2022, April). Comparative Analysis on Datasets for Sign Language Detection System. In *2022 International Conference on Sustainable Computing and Data Communication Systems (ICSCDS)* (pp. 1652-1657). IEEE. 10.1109/ICSCDS53736.2022.9761026

Nogueira, R. F., de Alencar Lotufo, R., & Machado, R. C. (2016). Fingerprint Liveness Detection Using Convolutional Neural Networks. *IEEE TIFS, 11*(6), 1206–1213. doi:10.1109/TIFS.2016.2520880

Nojiri, N., Kong, X., Meng, L., & Shimakawa, H. (2019). Discussion on machine learning and deep learning based makeup considered eye status recognition for driver drowsiness. *Procedia Computer Science, 147*, 264–270. doi:10.1016/j.procs.2019.01.252

Noor, A., Zhao, Y., Khan, R., Wu, L., & Abdalla, F. Y. O. (2020). Median filters combined with denoising convolutional neural network for Gaussian and impulse noises. *Multimedia Tools and Applications, 79*(25), 18553–18568. doi:10.100711042-020-08657-4

Nowak, R. D. (1999). Wavelet-based Rician noise removal for magnetic resonance imaging. *IEEE Transactions on Image Processing, 8*(10), 1408–1419. doi:10.1109/83.791966 PMID:18267412

Nur-A-Alam, A.M., Based, M.A., Haider, J., & Kowalski, M. (2021). An intelligent system for automatic fingerprint identification using feature fusion by Gabor filter and deep learning. *Computers & Electrical Engineering, 95*(107387).

ODNI. (2016). *IARPA. IARPA-BAA-16-04 (Thor)*. https://www.iarpa.gov/index.php/research-programs/odin/odinbaa

Pala, F., & Bhanu, B. (2017). Deep Triplet Embedding Representations for Liveness Detection. In Deep Learning for Biometrics (pp. 287–307). Springer.

Pandey, B., Pandey, D. K., Mishra, B. P., & Rhmann, W. (2021). A comprehensive survey of deep learning in the field of medical imaging and medical natural language processing: Challenges and research directions. *Journal of King Saud University-Computer and Information Sciences*.

Pankaja, K., & Thippeswamy, G. (2017). Survey on Leaf Recognization and Classification. *International Conference on Innovative Mechanisms for Industry Applications*, 442-450. 10.1109/ICIMIA.2017.7975654

Pankanti, S., Prabhakar, S., & Jain, A. K. (2002). On the Individuality of Fingerprints. *IEEE TPAMI, 24*(8), 1010–1025.

Parida. (2021). Arduino based Driver Drowsiness Detection & Alerting System. *Circuit Digest*.

Parikh, N., & Boyd, S. (2014). Proximal algorithms. *Foundations and Trends in Optimization, 1*(3), 127–239. doi:10.1561/2400000003

Paris, S., & Durand, F. (n.d.). *A Fast Approximation of the Bilateral Filter using a Signal Processing Approach*. Academic Press.

Patel, B., & Sinha, G. R. (2010). An adaptive K-means clustering algorithm for breast image segmentation. *International Journal of Computers and Applications, 10*(4), 35–38. doi:10.5120/1467-1982

Patel, B., & Sinha, G. R. (2014). Abnormality Detection and Classification in Computer-aided Diagnosis (CAD) of Breast Cancer Images. *Journal of Medical Imaging and Health Informatics, 4*(6), 881–885. doi:10.1166/jmihi.2014.1349

Patel, K. K., Kar, A., Jha, S. N., & Khan, M. A. (2012). Machine vision system: A tool for quality inspection of food and agricultural products. *Journal of Food Science and Technology, 49*(2), 123–141. doi:10.100713197-011-0321-4 PMID:23572836

Perkampus, H.-H. (2013). *UV-VIS Spectroscopy and its Applications.* Springer Science & Business Media.

Pock, T., Unger, M., Cremers, D., & Bischof, H. (n.d.). 2008. Fast and Exact Solution of Total Variation Models on the GPU. *CVPR Workshop on Visual Computer Vision on GPUs. Cited On,* 101–124.

Polat, K., & Gunes, S. (2007). An expert system approach based on principal component analysis and adaptive neuro-fuzzy inference system to diagnosis of diabetic disease. *Digital Signal Processing, 17*(4), 702–710. doi:10.1016/j.dsp.2006.09.005

Pornntiwa, P., Emmanuel, O., Lambert, S., & Marco, W. (2017). Data Augmentation for Plant Classiðcation. *Proc. International Conference, ACIVS,* 615-626.

Poursadeghiyan, M., Mazloumi, A., Saraji, G. N., Baneshi, M. M., Khammar, A., & Ebrahimi, M. H. (2018). Using image processing in the proposed drowsiness detection system design. *Iranian Journal of Public Health, 47*(9), 1371. PMID:30320012

Prakash Choudhary, R. S. S. D. (2016). *A Survey Paper on Drowsiness Detection & Alarm System for Drivers.* International Research Journal of Engineering and Technology.

Prakash, A., & Walambe, R. (2018). *Military surveillance robot implementation using robot operating system. In 2018 IEEE Punecon.* IEEE.

Prasad, S., & Pal, A. K. (2017). An RGB colour image steganography scheme using overlapping block-based pixel-value differencing. *Royal Society Open Science, 4*(4), 161066.

Pratt, H., Coenen, F., Broadbent, D. M., Harding, S. P., & Zheng, Y. (2016). Convolutional Neural Networks for Diabetic Retinopathy. *Procedia Computer Science, 90,* 200–205. doi:10.1016/j.procs.2016.07.014

Praveen, K. S., & Shreya, S. (2015). Evolution of hand gesture recognition: A review. *International Journal of Engineering and Computer Science, 4,* 9962–9965.

Preetha, S., & Sheela, S. V. (2010). *Analysis of Fingerprint Biometric Authentication Using CNN, Social Science Research Network.* Elsevier.

Pugh, A. (1983). Second generation robotics. In *Robot Vision* (pp. 3–10). Springer. doi:10.1007/978-3-662-09771-7_1

Quan, Y., Chen, M., Pang, T., & Ji, H. (2020). Self2self with dropout: Learning self-supervised denoising from single image. *Proceedings of the IEEE/CVF Conference on Computer Vision and Pattern Recognition,* 1890–1898. 10.1109/CVPR42600.2020.00196

Quan, Y., Chen, Y., Shao, Y., Teng, H., Xu, Y., & Ji, H. (2021). Image denoising using complex-valued deep CNN. *Pattern Recognition, 111,* 107639. doi:10.1016/j.patcog.2020.107639

Qu, C., Calyam, P., Yu, J., Vandanapu, A., Opeoluwa, O., Gao, K., Wang, S., Chastain, R., & Palaniappan, K. (2021). DroneCOCoNet: Learning-based edge computation offloading and control networking for drone video analytics. *Future Generation Computer Systems, 125,* 247–262. doi:10.1016/j.future.2021.06.040

Quinlan, J. R. (1993). *C4.5: Programs for Machine Learning.* Morgan Kaufmann Publishers.

Raghupathi, W., & Raghupathi, V. (2010). Data Mining in Health Care. In S. Kudyba (Ed.), *Healthcare Informatics: Improving Efficiency and Productivity* (pp. 211–223). Taylor & Francis. doi:10.1201/9781439809792-c11

Raghupathi, W., & Raghupathi, V. (2014). Big data analytics in healthcare: Promise and potential. *Health Information Science and Systems, 2*(1), 3. doi:10.1186/2047-2501-2-3 PMID:25825667

Raghupathy, B. K., Kumar, N. R., & Raajan, N. R. (2014). An enhanced bishop tour scheme for information hiding. *International Journal of Applied Engineering Research*, *9*(1), 145–151.

Rai, P., & Rehman, M. (2019). ESP32 Based Smart Surveillance System. *2nd International Conference on Computing, Mathematics and Engineering Technologies (iCoMET)*, 1-3. 10.1109/ICOMET.2019.8673463

Rai, R., Tiwari, M. K., Ivanov, D., & Dolgui, A. (2021). Machine learning in manufacturing and industry 4.0 applications. *International Journal of Production Research*, *59*(16), 4773–4778. doi:10.1080/00207543.2021.1956675

Rajamohana, S. P., Radhika, E. G., Priya, S., & Sangeetha, S. (2021). Driver drowsiness detection system usina g hybrid approach of convolutional neural network and bidirectional long short term memory (CNN_BILSTM). *Materials Today: Proceedings*, *45*, 2897–2901. doi:10.1016/j.matpr.2020.11.898

Rajavel, R., Ravichandran, S. K., Harimoorthy, K., Nagappan, P., & Gobichettipalayam, K. R. (2022). IoT-based smart healthcare video surveillance system using edge computing. *Journal of Ambient Intelligence and Humanized Computing*, *13*(6), 3195–3207. doi:10.100712652-021-03157-1

Ramadan, Z. M. (2012). Efficient restoration method for images corrupted with impulse noise. *Circuits, Systems, and Signal Processing*, *31*(4), 1397–1406. doi:10.100700034-011-9380-z

Ranganathan, H., Chakraborty, S., & Panchanathan, S. (2016). Multimodal Emotion Recognition using Deep Learning Architectures. *IEEE Winter Conference on Applications of Computer Vision*. 10.1109/WACV.2016.7477679

Rathan, K., Sai, S. V., & Manikanta, T. S. (2019, April). Crypto-currency price prediction using decision tree and regression techniques. In *2019 3rd International Conference on Trends in Electronics and Informatics (ICOEI)* (pp. 190-194). IEEE. 10.1109/ICOEI.2019.8862585

Rattani, A., Scheirer, W. J., & Ross, A. (2015). Open Set Fingerprint Spoof Detection Across Novel Fabrication Materials. *IEEE TIFS*, *10*(11), 2447–2460.

Ravi, C., & Basavaraj, V. (2021). Sentiment Analysis using Deep Belief Network for User Rating Classification. *International Journal of Innovative Technology and Exploring Engineering*, *10*(8).

Ravikumar, A. (2021). Non-relational multi-level caching for mitigation of staleness & stragglers in distributed deep learning. *Proceedings of the 22nd International Middleware Conference: Doctoral Symposium*, 15–16. 10.1145/3491087.3493678

Ravikumar, A., & Sriraman, H. (2021). Staleness and Stagglers in Distibuted Deep Image Analytics. *2021 International Conference on Artificial Intelligence and Smart Systems (ICAIS)*, 848–852. 10.1109/ICAIS50930.2021.9395782

Ravikumar, A., Sriraman, H., Sai Saketh, P. M., Lokesh, S., & Karanam, A. (2022). Effect of neural network structure in accelerating performance and accuracy of a convolutional neural network with GPU/TPU for image analytics. *PeerJ. Computer Science*, *8*, e909. doi:10.7717/peerj-cs.909 PMID:35494877

Remazeilles, A., & Chaumette, F. (2007). Image-based robot navigation from an image memory. *Robotics and Autonomous Systems*, *55*(4), 345–356. doi:10.1016/j.robot.2006.10.002

Remirez, I., Martin, A., & Schiavi, E. (2018, April). Optimization of A Variational Model Using Deep Learning: An Application to Brain Tumor Segmentation. *IEEE 15th International Symposium on Biomedical Imaging*, 631-635. 10.1109/ISBI.2018.8363654

Renwick, J. T., & Babson, P. E. (1985). Vibration analysis---a proven technique as a predictive maintenance tool. *IEEE Transactions on Industry Applications*, *IA-21*(2), 324–332. doi:10.1109/TIA.1985.349652

Ren, X., Zhang, L., & Wang, Q. (2019, October). Brain MR Image Segmentation in Small Dataset with Adversarial Defense and Task Reorganization. *International Workshop on Machine learning in medical imaging, 11861*, 1-8. 10.1007/978-3-030-32692-0_1

Rinner, C., Sauter, S. K., Endel, G., Heinze, G., Thurner, S., Klimek, P., & Duftschmid, G. (2016). Improving the informational continuity of care in diabetes mellitus treatment with a nationwide Shared EHR system: Estimates from Austrian claims data. *International Journal of Medical Informatics, 92*, 44–53. doi:10.1016/j.ijmedinf.2016.05.001 PMID:27318070

Rodriguez, P. (2013). Total variation regularization algorithms for images corrupted with different noise models: A review. *Journal of Electrical and Computer Engineering, 2013*, 10. doi:10.1155/2013/217021

Rodriguez, P., Rojas, R., & Wohlberg, B. (2012). Mixed Gaussian-impulse noise image restoration via total variation. *2012 IEEE International Conference on Acoustics, Speech and Signal Processing (ICASSP)*, 1077–1080.

Rosebrock, (2016). *Deep Learning For Computer Vision with Python*. Academic Press.

RosebrockA. (2017). Error! Hyperlink reference not valid.Available: https://www.pyimagesearch.com/2017/05/08/drowsiness-detection-opencv/

Rowe, R. K., & Sidlauskas, D. P. (2006). *Multispectral biometric sensor*. US Patent 7,147,153.

Roy, S., Nanjiba, S., & Chakrabarty, A. (2018, December). Bitcoin price forecasting using time series analysis. In *2018 21st International Conference of Computer and Information Technology (ICCIT)* (pp. 1-5). IEEE. 10.1109/ICCITECHN.2018.8631923

Roy, A., Manam, L., & Laskar, R. H. (2018). Region adaptive fuzzy filter: An approach for removal of random-valued impulse noise. *IEEE Transactions on Industrial Electronics, 65*(9), 7268–7278. doi:10.1109/TIE.2018.2793225

Roy, A., Singha, J., Devi, S. S., & Laskar, R. H. (2016). Impulse noise removal using SVM classification based fuzzy filter from gray scale images. *Signal Processing, 128*, 262–273. doi:10.1016/j.sigpro.2016.04.007

Rudin, L. I., Osher, S., & Fatemi, E. (1992). Nonlinear total variation based noise removal algorithms. *Physica D. Nonlinear Phenomena, 60*(1–4), 259–268. doi:10.1016/0167-2789(92)90242-F

Ryfial, A., Desmin, T., & Dasrit, K. (2015). Image Classification Using SIFT Feature Extraction, Bag of Features and Support Vector Machine. *Procedia Computer Science, 72*, 24–30. doi:10.1016/j.procs.2015.12.101

Saha, S., Pal, M., Konar, A., & Janarthanan, R. (2013, December). Neural network based gesture recognition for elderly health care using kinect sensor. In *International Conference on Swarm, Evolutionary, and Memetic Computing* (pp. 376-386). Springer. 10.1007/978-3-319-03756-1_34

Sahu, S. K., & Shrivas, A. K. (2020). Comparative study of classification models with genetic search based feature selection technique. In Cognitive Analytics: Concepts, Methodologies, Tools, and Applications (pp. 773-783). IGI Global. doi:10.4018/978-1-7998-2460-2.ch040

Sahu, S. K., & Verma, P. (2022). Stacked Auto Encoder Deep Neural Network with Principal Components Analysis for Identification of Chronic Kidney Disease. In Machine Learning and Deep Learning Techniques for Medical Science. CRC Press. doi:10.1201/9781003217497-19

Salman, F. M., & Abu-Naser, S. S. (2022). Classification of Real and Fake Human Faces Using Deep Learning. *International Journal of Academic Engineering Research, 6*(3).

Samanta, A., Saha, A., Satapathy, S. C., Fernandes, S. L., & Zhang, Y. (2020). Automated detection of diabetic retinopathy using convolutional neural networks on a small dataset. *Pattern Recognition Letters*, *135*, 293–298. doi:10.1016/j.patrec.2020.04.026

Samanta, B., & Nataraj, C. (2008). Prognostics of machine condition using soft computing. *Robotics and Computer-integrated Manufacturing*, *24*(6), 816–823. doi:10.1016/j.rcim.2008.03.011

Sani, Z. A., Alizadehsani, R., & Roshanzami, M. (2017). *Z-Alizadeh Sani Data Set*. UC Irvine Machine Learning Repository. Retrieved from https://archive.ics.uci.edu/ml/datasets/extention+of+Z-Alizadeh+sani+dataset

San, P. P., Kakar, P., Li, X. L., Krishnaswamy, S., Yang, J. B., & Nguyen, M. N. (2017). Deep learning for human activity recognition. In *Big data analytics for sensor-network collected intelligence* (pp. 186–204). Academic Press. doi:10.1016/B978-0-12-809393-1.00009-X

Sarder, P., & Nehorai, A. (2006). Deconvolution methods for 3-D fluorescence microscopy images. *IEEE Signal Processing Magazine*, *23*(3), 32–45. doi:10.1109/MSP.2006.1628876

Sarkar, P., & Etemad, A. (2020). Self-Supervised Learning for ECG-Based Emotion Recognition. *ICASSP 2020 - 2020 IEEE Int. Conf. Acoust. Speech Signal Process,* 3217–3221. 10.1109/ICASSP40776.2020.9053985

Sathish Shet, K., Aswath, A. R., Hanumantharaju, M. C., & Gao, X. Z. (2017). Design and development of new reconfigurable architectures for LSB/multi-bit image steganography system. *Multimedia Tools and Applications*, *76*(11), 13197–13219.

Sathya, B. S., Mohana, V. S., Raju, S., & Abhai, K. V. (2011). Content based leaf image retrieval (CBLIR) using shape, color and texture features. *Indian Journal of Computer Science and Engineering*, *2*(2), 202–211.

Sayed, A. S., Ammar, H. H., & Shalaby, R. (2020, October). Centralized multi-agent mobile robots SLAM and navigation for COVID-19 field hospitals. In *2020 2nd Novel Intelligent and Leading Emerging Sciences Conference (NILES)* (pp. 444-449). IEEE. 10.1109/NILES50944.2020.9257919

Schmidhuber, J. (2015). Deep learning in neural networks : An overview. *Neural Networks*, *61*, 85–117. doi:10.1016/j.neunet.2014.09.003 PMID:25462637

Schmidhuber, J., & Hochreiter, S. (1997). Long short-term memory. *Neural Computation*, *9*(8), 1735–1780. doi:10.1162/neco.1997.9.8.1735 PMID:9377276

Schmidt, P., Reiss, A., Duerichen, R., Marberger, C., & Van Laerhoven, K. (2018). Introducing WESAD, a Multimodal Dataset for Wearable Stress and Affect Detection. *Proc. 20th ACM Int. Conf. Multimodal Interact.,* 400–408. 10.1145/3242969.3242985

Schuller, B. W. (2018). Speech emotion recognition: Two decades in a nutshell, benchmarks, and ongoing trends. *Communications of the ACM*, *61*(5), 90–99. doi:10.1145/3129340

Schuster, M., & Paliwal, K. K. (1997). Bidirectional recurrent neural networks. *IEEE Transactions on Signal Processing*, *45*(11), 2673–2681. doi:10.1109/78.650093

Schwarz, C., Gaspar, J., Miller, T., & Yousefian, R. (2019). The detection of drowsiness using a driver monitoring system. *Traffic Injury Prevention, 20*(sup1), S157-S161.

Selvaraj, D., & Dhanasekaran, R. (2013). MRI Brain Image Segmentation Technique – A Review. *Indian Journal of Computer Science and Engineering*, *4*, 264–281.

Selvathi, D., & Vanmathi, T. (2018, May). Brain Region Segmentation Using Convolutional Neural Network. *IEEE International Conferences on Electrical Energy System*, 661-666. 10.1109/ICEES.2018.8442394

Sethuramasamyraja, B., Ghaffari, M., & Hall, E. L. (2003, September). Automatic calibration and neural networks for robot guidance. In Intelligent Robots and Computer Vision XXI: Algorithms, Techniques, and Active Vision (Vol. 5267, pp. 137-144). SPIE. doi:10.1117/12.515036

Shafiul Azam, M. (2020). Iris Recognition Using Convolutional Neural Network. *International Journal of Computers and Applications*, *175*(12), 24–28. doi:10.5120/ijca2020920602

Shahbazi, Z., & Byun, Y. C. (2021). Improving the cryptocurrency price prediction performance based on reinforcement learning. *IEEE Access: Practical Innovations, Open Solutions*, *9*, 162651–162659. doi:10.1109/ACCESS.2021.3133937

Shahzad, R. K., & Lavesson, N. (2012). *Comparative Analysis of Voting Schemes for Detection, Ensemble-based Malware*. Academic Press.

Shana, L., & Christopher, C. S. (2019, March). Video Surveillance using Deep Learning-A Review. In *2019 International Conference on Recent Advances in Energy-efficient Computing and Communication (ICRAECC)* (pp. 1-5). IEEE.

Shao, S. Y., Sun, W. J., Yan, R. Q., Wang, P., & Gao, R. X. (2017). A deep learning approach for fault diagnosis of induction motors in manufacturing. *Chinese Journal of Mechanical Engineering*, *30*(6), 1347–1356. doi:10.100710033-017-0189-y

Sharath Kumar, P. N., & Deepak, R. U. (2019). Automated Detection System for Diabetic Retinopathy Using Two Field Fundus Photography. *Procedia Computer Science*, *93*, 486–494. doi:10.1016/j.procs.2016.07.237

Sharma, S., Khare, S. K., Bajaj, V., & Ansari, I. A. (2021). Improving the separability of drowsiness and alert EEG signals using analytic form of wavelet transform. *Applied Acoustics*, *181*, 108164.

Sharma, S., & Singh, S. (2021). Vision-based hand gesture recognition using deep learning for the interpretation of sign language. *Expert Systems with Applications*, *182*, 115657. doi:10.1016/j.eswa.2021.115657

Sharma, V., Gupta, M., Kumar, A., & Mishra, D. (2021). Video Processing Using Deep Learning Techniques: A Systematic Literature Review. *IEEE Access: Practical Innovations, Open Solutions*, *9*, 139489–139507. doi:10.1109/ACCESS.2021.3118541

Sheela, C. J. J., & Suganthi, G. (2020). An efficient denoising of impulse noise from MRI using adaptive switching modified decision based unsymmetric trimmed median filter. *Biomedical Signal Processing and Control*, *55*, 101657. doi:10.1016/j.bspc.2019.101657

Shehzed, A., Jalal, A., & Kim, K. (2019). Multi-Person Tracking in Smart Surveillance System for Crowd Counting and Normal/Abnormal Events Detection. *2019 International Conference on Applied and Engineering Mathematics (ICAEM)*, 163-168. 10.1109/ICAEM.2019.8853756

Shen, M., Zou, B., Li, X., Zheng, Y., Li, L., & Zhang, L. (2021). Multi-source signal alignment and efficient multi-dimensional feature classification in the application of EEG-based subject-independent drowsiness detection. *Biomedical Signal Processing and Control*, *70*, 103023.

Sherstinsky, A. (2020). Fundamentals of recurrent neural network (RNN) and long short-term memory (LSTM) network. *Physica D. Nonlinear Phenomena*, *404*, 132306. doi:10.1016/j.physd.2019.132306

Shi & Eberhart. (1998). *A Modified Particle Swarm Optimizer*. Academic Press.

Shilpa, P. C., Rissa, S., Susmi, J., Vinod, P., (2021). *Sentiment Analysis Using Deep Learning*. doi:10.1109/ICICV50876.2021.9388382

Shi, M., Han, T., & Liu, S. (2016). Total variation image restoration using hyper-Laplacian prior with overlapping group sparsity. *Signal Processing*, *126*, 65–76. doi:10.1016/j.sigpro.2015.11.022

Shlykov, V., Kotovskyi, V., Višniakov, N., & Šešok, A. (2020). Model for Elimination of Mixed Noise from MRI Heart Images. *Applied Sciences (Basel, Switzerland)*, *10*(14), 4747. doi:10.3390/app10144747

Shorfuzzaman, M., Hossain, M. S., & Alhamid, M. F. (2021). Towards the sustainable development of smart cities through mass video surveillance: A response to the COVID-19 pandemic. *Sustainable Cities and Society*, *64*, 102582. doi:10.1016/j.scs.2020.102582 PMID:33178557

Shu-I, P., Hong-Zin, L., Ke-Hung, C., Ming-Cheng, T., Jiann-Torng, C., & Gen-Min, L. (2020). Detection of Diabetic Retinopathy Using Bichannel Convolutional Neural Network. *Journal of Ophthalmology*, *2020*, 9139713. PMID:32655944

Sidorov, O., & Yngve Hardeberg, J. (2019). Deep Hyperspectral Prior: Single-Image Denoising, Inpainting, Super-Resolution. *Proceedings of the IEEE International Conference on Computer Vision Workshops*. 10.1109/ICCVW.2019.00477

Sigari. (2013). A driver Face Monitoring System for Fatigue and Distraction Detection. *International Journal of Vehicular Technology*.

Simi, M. S., & Nayaki, K. S. (2017, April). *Data analytics in medical data: A review*. Paper presented at the IEEE International Conference on Circuit, Power and Computing Technologies (ICCPCT). 10.1109/ICCPCT.2017.8074337

Simi, M. S., Nayaki, K. S., Parameswaran, M., & Sivadasan, S. (2017). *Exploring female infertility using predictive analytic*. Paper presented at the IEEE Global Humanitarian Technology Conference (GHTC).

Singh, B., Sinha, G. R., & Kar, M. (2010, March). Content Based Retrieval of MRI Images Using Integration of Color, Texture & Shape Features. In *IEEE International Conference on Advances in Communication, Network, and Computing*. IEEE Computer Society.

Singh, D., & Singh, S. (2020). Realising transfer learning through convolutional neural network and support vector machine for mental task classification. *Electronics Letters*, *56*(25), 1375–1378. doi:10.1049/el.2020.2632

Singh, J., Azamfar, M., Li, F., & Lee, J. (2020). A systematic review of machine learning algorithms for prognostics and health management of rolling element bearings: Fundamentals, concepts and applications. *Measurement Science & Technology*, *32*(1), 012001. doi:10.1088/1361-6501/ab8df9

Sinha, G. R. (2015). Fuzzy based Medical Image Processing. In Advances in Medical Technologies and Clinical Practice (AMTCP) Book Series (pp. 45-61). IGI Global Publishers.

Sinha, G. R. (2020). Introduction and background to optimization theory. In Modern Optimization Methods for Science, Engineering and Technology. IOP Publishing.

Sinha, G. R. (2017). Study of Assessment of Cognitive Ability of Human Brain using Deep Learning. *International Journal of Information Technology (Springer)*, *1*(1), 1–6. doi:10.100741870-017-0025-8

Sinha, G. R., & Patel, B. (2014). *Medical Image Processing: Concepts and Application*. Prentice Hall of India.

Sinha, G. R., Raju, S., Patra, R., Aye, D. W., & Khin, D. T. (2018). Research Studies on Human Cognitive Ability. *International Journal of Intelligent Defense Support Systems*, *5*(4), 298–304. doi:10.1504/IJIDSS.2018.099891

Sivakami, R., & Nawaz, G.M.K. (2011). Secured communication for MANETS in military. *Computer Communication and Electrical Technology*, 146-151.

Smith, B. C. (2011). *Fundamentals of Fourier Transform Infrared spectroscopy*. CRC press.

Smith, R. A.-B., Manassaram-Baptiste, D., Brooks, D., Cokkinides, V., Doroshenk, M., Saslow, D., Wender, R. C., & Brawley, O. W. (2014). Cancer screening in the United States, 2014: A review of current American Cancer Society guidelines and current issues in cancer screening. *CA: a Cancer Journal for Clinicians, 64*(1), 30–51. doi:10.3322/caac.21212 PMID:24408568

Smolka, B., & Kusnik, D. (2015). Robust local similarity filter for the reduction of mixed Gaussian and impulsive noise in color digital images. *Signal, Image and Video Processing, 9*(1), 49–56. doi:10.100711760-015-0830-0

Sobhaninia, Z. (2018, September). Brain Tumor Segmentation Using Deep Learning by Type Specific Sorting of Images. In *International Conference on Computer Vision and Pattern Recognition.* Cornell University.

Soltanayev, S., & Chun, S. Y. (2018). *Training and Refining Deep Learning Based Denoisers without Ground Truth Data.* ArXiv Preprint ArXiv:1803.01314.

Son, T. L., Guee-Sang, L., Soo-Hyung, K., & Hyung-Jeong, Y. (2018). Emotion Recognition via Body Gesture:Deep Learning Model Coupled with Keyframe Selection. MLMI. doi:10.1145/3278312.3278313

Song, T., Liu, S., Zheng, W., Zong, Y., & Cui, Z. (2020). Instance-Adaptive Graph for EEG Emotion Recognition. *Proc. AAAI Conf. Artif. Intell., 34*, 2701–2708. 10.1609/aaai.v34i03.5656

Song, T., Zheng, W., Lu, C., Zong, Y., Zhang, X., & Cui, Z. (2019). MPED: A multi-modal physiological emotion database for discrete emotion recognition. *IEEE Access: Practical Innovations, Open Solutions, 7*, 12177–12191. doi:10.1109/ACCESS.2019.2891579

Song, T., Zheng, W., Song, P., & Cui, Z. (2018). EEG emotion recognition using dynamical graph convolutional neural networks. *IEEE Transactions on Affective Computing.*

Soni, P., & Vashisht, S. (2018). Exploration on Polycystic Ovarian Syndrome and Data Mining Techniques. *2018 3rd International Conference on Communication and Electronics Systems (ICCES)*, 816-820. 10.1109/CESYS.2018.8724087

Sreenu, G., & Durai, S. (2019). Intelligent video surveillance: A review through deep learning techniques for crowd analysis. *Journal of Big Data, 6*(1), 1–27. doi:10.118640537-019-0212-5

Srinivasan, K. S., & Ebenezer, D. (2007). A new fast and efficient decision-based algorithm for removal of high-density impulse noises. *IEEE Signal Processing Letters, 14*(3), 189–192. doi:10.1109/LSP.2006.884018

Srivastava, N., Hinton, G., Krizhevsky, A., Sutskever, I., & Salakhutdinov, R. (2014). Dropout: A simple way to prevent neural networks from overfitting. *Journal of Machine Learning Research, 15*(1), 1929–1958.

Subasi, A. (2020). *Practical Machine Learning for Data Analysis Using Python.* Elsevier.

Sudha, S., & Srinivasan, A. (2017). Unravelling Diabetic Retinopathy through Image Processing, Neural Networks, And Fuzzy Logic: A Review. *Asian Journal of Pharmaceutical and Clinical Research, 10*(4), 32–37. doi:10.22159/ajpcr.2017.v10i4.17023

Sugeno, A., Ishikawa, Y., Ohshima, T., & Muramatsu, R. (2021). Simple methods for the lesion detection and severity grading of diabetic retinopathy by image processing and transfer learning. *Computers in Biology and Medicine, 137*, 104795. doi:10.1016/j.compbiomed.2021.104795 PMID:34488028

Sujith, B. (2014). Jyothiprakash. Pedestrian Detection-A Comparative Study Using HOG and COHOG. *IJIRCCE, 2*(5), 358–364.

Šuligoj, F., Šekoranja, B., Švaco, M., & Jerbić, B. (2014). Object tracking with a multiagent robot system and a stereo vision camera. *Procedia Engineering, 69*, 968–973. doi:10.1016/j.proeng.2014.03.077

Sullivan. (2014). *Ensemble of Regression Trees*. Academic Press.

Susskind, J. M., Anderson, A. K., & Hinton, G. E. (2010). *The Toronto face database. Department of Computer Science, University of Toronto* Tech. Rep.

Swain, D., Pani, S. K., & Swain, D. (2019). An Efficient System for the Prediction of Coronary Artery Disease using Dense Neural Network with Hyper Parameter Tuning. *International Journal of Innovative Technology and Exploring Engineering, 8*(6), 689–695.

Tai, Y., Yang, J., Liu, X., & Xu, C. (2017). Memnet: A persistent memory network for image restoration. *Proceedings of the IEEE International Conference on Computer Vision*, 4539–4547. 10.1109/ICCV.2017.486

Tai, Yeh, & Chang. (2009). Reversible Data Hiding Based on Histogram Modification of Pixel Differences. *IEEE Transactions on Circuits and Systems for Video Technology, 19*(6), 906–910. doi:10.1109/TCSVT.2009.2017409

Tan, M., & Le Quoc, V. (2020). EfficientNet: Rethinking Model Scaling for Convolutional Neural Networks. *International conference on machine learning*, 6105-6114.

Tao, Y., Zongyang, Z., Jun, Z., Xinghua, C., & Fuqiang, Z. (2021). Low-altitude small-sized object detection using lightweight feature-enhanced convolutional neural network. *Journal of Systems Engineering and Electronics, 32*(4), 841–853. doi:10.23919/JSEE.2021.000073

Tarver, T. (2012). *Cancer Facts & Figures 2012. American Cancer Society (ACS)*. American Cancer Society. doi:10.1080/15398285.2012.701177

Tarver, T. (2012). *Cancer Facts & Figures 2012*. American Cancer Society.

Tasdizen, T. (2009). Principal neighborhood dictionaries for nonlocal means image denoising. *IEEE Transactions on Image Processing, 18*(12), 2649–2660. doi:10.1109/TIP.2009.2028259 PMID:19635697

Thakoor, N., & Devarajan, V. (2008). Multi-stage branch-and-bound for maximum variance disparity clustering. IEEE Conference Publications.

Tharmalingam, S., Hagens, S., & Zelmer, J. (2016). The value of connected health information: Perceptions of electronic health record users in Canada. *BMC Medical Informatics and Decision Making, 16*(1), 93. doi:10.118612911-016-0330-3 PMID:27422571

Tofighi, M., Kose, K., & Cetin, A. E. (2015). Denoising images corrupted by impulsive noise using projections onto the epigraph set of the total variation function (PES-TV). *Signal, Image and Video Processing, 9*(1), 41–48. doi:10.100711760-015-0827-8

Tolias, G., Avrithis, Y., & J'egou, H. (2013). To aggregate or not to aggregate: Selective match kernels for image search. *Proc. IEEE International Conference on Computer Vision*, 1401–1408. 10.1109/ICCV.2013.177

Tolias, G., & Chum, O. (2017). Asymmetric feature maps with application to sketch based retrieval. *Proc. IEEE conference on computer vision and pattern recognition*, 6185–6193. 10.1109/CVPR.2017.655

Tolosana, R., Gomez-Barrero, M., Kolberg, J., Morales, A., Busch, C., & Ortega-Garcia, J. (2018). Towards Fingerprint Presentation Attack Detection Based on Convolutional Neural Networks and Short WaveInfrared Imaging. *Proc. BIOSIG*, 1–5.

Tong. (2012). Semi-Supervised facial land mark annotation-Computational. *Vision Image Understanding*.

Toprak, A., & Güler, I. (2007a). Impulse noise reduction in medical images with the use of switch mode fuzzy adaptive median filter. *Digital Signal Processing, 17*(4), 711–723. doi:10.1016/j.dsp.2006.11.008

Tran, M. Q., Elsisi, M., Mahmoud, K., Liu, M. K., Lehtonen, M., & Darwish, M. M. (2021). Experimental setup for online fault diagnosis of induction machines via promising IoT and machine learning: Towards industry 4.0 empowerment. *IEEE Access: Practical Innovations, Open Solutions*, 9, 115429–115441. doi:10.1109/ACCESS.2021.3105297

Trindade, F., Ferreira, R., Magalhães, B., Leite-moreira, A., Falcão-pires, I., & Vitorino, R. (2018). How to use and integrate bioinformatics tools to compare proteomic data from distinct conditions? A tutorial using the pathological similarities between Aortic Valve Stenosis and Coronary Artery Disease as a case-study. *Journal of Proteomics*, 171, 37–52. Advance online publication. doi:10.1016/j.jprot.2017.03.015 PMID:28336332

Tripathi, N., Goshisht, M. K., Sahu, S. K., & Arora, C. (2021). Applications of artificial intelligence to drug design and discovery in the big data era: A comprehensive review. *Molecular Diversity*, 25(3), 1643–1664. doi:10.100711030-021-10237-z PMID:34110579

Tsai, W.-H., & Lin, C.-C. (2004). Secret image sharing with steganography and authentication. *Journal of Systems and Software*, 73(3), 405–414. doi:10.1016/S0164-1212(03)00239-5

Tuia, D., Kellenberger, B., Beery, S., Costelloe, B. R., Zuffi, S., Risse, B., Mathis, A., Mathis, M. W., van Langevelde, F., Burghardt, T., Kays, R., Klinck, H., Wikelski, M., Couzin, I. D., van Horn, G., Crofoot, M. C., Stewart, C. V., & Berger-Wolf, T. (2022). Perspectives in machine learning for wildlife conservation. *Nature Communications*, 13(1), 1–15. doi:10.103841467-022-27980-y PMID:35140206

Tumer, K., & Ghosh, J. (1996). Analysis of decision boundaries in linearly combined neural classifiers. *Pattern Recognition*, 29(2), 341–348. doi:10.1016/0031-3203(95)00085-2

Turkoglu, M., Alcin, O. F., Aslan, M., Al-Zebari, A., & Sengur, A. (2021). Deep rhythm and long short term memory-based drowsiness detection. *Biomedical Signal Processing and Control*, 65, 102364. doi:10.1016/j.bspc.2020.102364

Ulyanov, D., Vedaldi, A., & Lempitsky, V. (2018). Deep image prior. *Proceedings of the IEEE Conference on Computer Vision and Pattern Recognition*, 9446–9454.

van Kempen, G. M. P., van Vliet, L. J., Verveer, P. J., & van der Voort, H. T. M. (1997). A quantitative comparison of image restoration methods for confocal microscopy. *Journal of Microscopy*, 185(3), 354–365. doi:10.1046/j.1365-2818.1997.d01-629.x

Vasudevan, N., & Karthick, T. (2022). Analysis of Plant Leaf Diseases Recognition using Image Processing with Machine Learning Techniques. *2022 International Conference on Advances in Computing, Communication and Applied Informatics (ACCAI)*. 10.1109/ACCAI53970.2022.9752577

Veraart, J., Novikov, D. S., Christiaens, D., Ades-Aron, B., Sijbers, J., & Fieremans, E. (2016). Denoising of diffusion MRI using random matrix theory. *NeuroImage*, 142, 394–406. doi:10.1016/j.neuroimage.2016.08.016 PMID:27523449

Verma, L., & Mathur, M. K. (2019). *Deep Learning based Model for Decision Support with Case Based Reasoning*. Academic Press.

Verma, P., Awasthi, V. K., & Sahu, S. K. (2021). Classification of Coronary Artery Disease Using Deep Neural Network with Dimension Reduction Technique. *2021 2nd International Conference for Emerging Technology (INCET)*, 1-5. 10.1109/INCET51464.2021.9456322

Verma, A. K., & Pal, S. (2019). Prediction of skin disease with three different feature selection techniques using stacking ensemble method. *Applied Biochemistry and Biotechnology*. PMID:31845194

Verma, P., Awasthi, V. K., & Sahu, S. K. (2021). An Ensemble Model With Genetic Algorithm for Classification of Coronary Artery Disease. *International Journal of Computer Vision and Image Processing*, *11*(3), 70–83. doi:10.4018/IJCVIP.2021070105

Verma, P., Awasthi, V. K., Sahu, S. K., & Shrivas, A. K. (2022). Coronary Artery Disease Classification Using Deep Neural Network and Ensemble Models Optimized by Particle Swarm Optimization. *International Journal of Applied Metaheuristic Computing*, *13*(1), 1–25. doi:10.4018/IJAMC.292504

Verma, P., Awasthi, V. K., Shrivas, A. K., & Sahu, S. K. (2022). Stacked Generalization Based Ensemble Model for Classification of Coronary Artery Disease. In R. Misra, N. Kesswani, M. Rajarajan, B. Veeravalli, & A. Patel (Eds.), *Internet of Things and Connected Technologies. ICIoTCT 2021. Lecture Notes in Networks and Systems* (Vol. 340). Springer. doi:10.1007/978-3-030-94507-7_6

Vijayan, V., & Pushpalatha, K. P. (2020). A comparative analysis of RootSIFT and SIFT methods for drowsy features extraction. *Procedia Computer Science*, *171*, 436–445. doi:10.1016/j.procs.2020.04.046

Villalba-Diez, J., Schmidt, D., Gevers, R., Ordieres-Meré, J., Buchwitz, M., & Wellbrock, W. (2019). Deep learning for industrial computer vision quality control in the printing industry 4.0. *Sensors (Basel)*, *19*(18), 3987. doi:10.339019183987 PMID:31540187

Wan, Zhou, & Bian. (2008). *CODEM: A novel spatial co-location and de-location patterns mining algorithm.* IEEE Conference Publications.

Wang, Tan, & Liu. (2018). *Particle Swarm Optimization Algorithm : An Overview.* Advance online publication. doi:10.100700500-016-2474-6

Wang, Y., Changsheng, L., Zhu, T., & Chongchong, Y. (2019, July). A Deep Learning Algorithm for Fully Automatic Brain Tumor Segmentation. *IEEE International Joint Conference on Neural Networks*, 1-5. 10.1109/IJCNN.2019.8852210

Wang, Y., Wang, W., Liu, D., Jin, X., Jiang, J., & Chen, K. (2022). Enabling Edge-Cloud Video Analytics for Robotics Applications. IEEE Transactions on Cloud Computing. doi:10.1109/TCC.2022.3142066

Wang, H., Zhang, L., & Yao, L. (2021). Application of genetic algorithm based support vector machine in selection of new EEG rhythms for drowsiness detection. *Expert Systems with Applications*, *171*, 114634.

Wang, J., Li, J., Yan, S., Shi, W., Yang, X., Guo, Y., & Gulliver, T. A. (2020). A novel underwater acoustic signal denoising algorithm for Gaussian/non-Gaussian impulsive noise. *IEEE Transactions on Vehicular Technology*, *70*(1), 429–445. doi:10.1109/TVT.2020.3044994

Wang, S., Huang, T.-Z., Zhao, X., & Liu, J. (2013). An alternating direction method for mixed Gaussian plus impulse noise removal. *Abstract and Applied Analysis*, *2013*, 2013. doi:10.1155/2013/850360

Wang, S., Wang, A., Ran, M., Liu, L., Peng, Y., Liu, M., Su, G., Alhudhaif, A., Alenezi, F., & Alnaim, N. (2022). Hand Gesture Recognition Framework Using a Lie Group Based Spatio-Temporal Recurrent Network with Multiple Hand-Worn Motion Sensors. *Information Sciences*, *606*, 722–741. doi:10.1016/j.ins.2022.05.085

Wang, X. (2013). Intelligent multi-camera video surveillance: A review. *Pattern Recognition Letters*, *34*(1), 3–19. doi:10.1016/j.patrec.2012.07.005

Wang, X., Guo, J., Lu, S., Shen, C., & He, Q. (2017). A computer-vision-based rotating speed estimation method for motor bearing fault diagnosis. *Measurement Science & Technology*, *28*(6), 065012. doi:10.1088/1361-6501/aa650a PMID:28890607

Wang, X., Shen, S., Shi, G., Xu, Y., & Zhang, P. (2016). Iterative non-local means filter for salt and pepper noise removal. *Journal of Visual Communication and Image Representation*, *38*, 440–450. doi:10.1016/j.jvcir.2016.03.024

Wang, Y., Peng, J., Zhao, Q., Leung, Y., Zhao, X.-L., & Meng, D. (2017). Hyperspectral image restoration via total variation regularized low-rank tensor decomposition. *IEEE Journal of Selected Topics in Applied Earth Observations and Remote Sensing*, *11*(4), 1227–1243. doi:10.1109/JSTARS.2017.2779539

Wang, Y., & Zhou, H. (2006). Total variation wavelet-based medical image denoising. *International Journal of Biomedical Imaging*, ●●●, 2006. PMID:23165057

Wang, Z., Wang, G., Pan, Z., Zhang, J., & Zhai, G. (2020). Fast stripe noise removal from hyperspectral image via multi-scale dilated unidirectional convolution. *Multimedia Tools and Applications*, *79*(31-32), 23007–23022. doi:10.100711042-020-09065-4

Wen, F., Liu, P., Liu, Y., Qiu, R. C., & Yu, W. (2016). Robust Sparse Recovery in Impulsive Noise via \ell _p -\ell _1 Optimization. *IEEE Transactions on Signal Processing*, *65*(1), 105–118. doi:10.1109/TSP.2016.2598316

Willett, R. M., & Nowak, R. D. (2004). Fast multiresolution photon-limited image reconstruction. *2004 2nd IEEE International Symposium on Biomedical Imaging: Nano to Macro (IEEE Cat No. 04EX821)*, 1192–1195.

Wirawan, I. M., Widiyaningtyas, T., & Hasan, M. M. (2019, September). Short term prediction on bitcoin price using ARIMA method. In *2019 International Seminar on Application for Technology of Information and Communication (iSemantic)* (pp. 260-265). IEEE.

Witten, I H, Frank, E., & Hall, M. A. (2011b). *Data mining.* doi:10.1002/1521-3773(20010316)40:6<9823::AID-ANIE9823>3.3.CO;2-C

Witten, I. H., & Frank, E. (2004). *Datamining. Practical Machine Learning Tools and Technicals with Java Implementations* (2nd ed.). Elsevier.

Witten, I. H., Frank, E., & Hall, M. A. (2011a, May). Data Mining: Practical Machine Learning Tools and Techniques with Java Implementations. *ACM SIGMOD Record*.

Wu, T. (2016). Variable splitting based method for image restoration with impulse plus Gaussian noise. *Mathematical Problems in Engineering*, *2016*, 2016. doi:10.1155/2016/3151303

Xiao, D., Huang, Y., Zhang, X., Shi, H., Liu, C., & Li, Y. (2018, October). Fault diagnosis of asynchronous motors based on LSTM neural network. In 2018 prognostics and system health management conference (PHM-Chongqing) (pp. 540-545). IEEE. doi:10.1109/PHM-Chongqing.2018.00098

Xiaohan, Y., Shengwu, X., & Yongsheng, G. (2015). Leaf Image Retrieval Using Combined Feature of Vein and Contour. *Proc. International conference image and vision computing New Zealand (IVCNZ)*, 1-6.

Xiao, Y., Zeng, T., Yu, J., & Ng, M. K. (2011). Restoration of images corrupted by mixed Gaussian-impulse noise via l1–l0 minimization. *Pattern Recognition*, *44*(8), 1708–1720. doi:10.1016/j.patcog.2011.02.002

Xiao, Z., Huang, R., Ding, Y., Tian, L., Rongfeng, D., & Qin, Z. (2016, September). A Deep Learning-Based Segmentation Method for Brain Tumor in MR Images. *IEEE International Conference on Computational Advances in Bio and Medical Sciences*.

Xie, J., Lei, J., Xie, W., Shi, Y., & Liu, X. (2013). Two-stage hybrid feature selection algorithms for diagnosing erythemato-squamous diseases. *Health Information Science and Systems*, *1*(1), 1–14. doi:10.1186/2047-2501-1-10 PMID:26042184

Xie, X., & Wang, C. (2011). Using support vector machines with a novel hybrid feature selection method for diagnosis of erythemato-squamous. *Expert Systems with Applications, 38*(5), 5809–5815. doi:10.1016/j.eswa.2010.10.050

Xin, B., Wang, Y., Gao, W., & Wipf, D. (2016). *Maximal sparsity with deep networks?* ArXiv Preprint ArXiv:1605.01636.

Xiong, B., & Yin, Z. (2011). A universal denoising framework with a new impulse detector and nonlocal means. *IEEE Transactions on Image Processing, 21*(4), 1663–1675. doi:10.1109/TIP.2011.2172804 PMID:22020688

Xu, Chen, & Nie. (2013). *Driver Sleep Detection and Alarming System.* Project Report. University of Illinois at Urbana-Champaign.

Xu, L., Yan, Q., Xia, Y., & Jia, J. (2012). Structure extraction from texture via relative total variation. *ACM Transactions on Graphics, 31*(6), 139:1-139:10. doi:10.1145/2366145.2366158

Yang, C., Lai, X., Hu, Z., Liu, Y., & Shen, P. (2019). Depression tendency screening use text based emotional analysis technique. *J. Phys. Conf., 1237*(3), 1–10. doi:10.1088/1742-6596/1237/3/032035

Yang, C., Luo, X., Lu, J., & Liu, F. (2018). Extracting hidden messages of MLSB steganography based on optimal stego subset. *Science China. Information Sciences, 61*(11), 1–3.

Yan, M. (2013). Restoration of images corrupted by impulse noise and mixed Gaussian impulse noise using blind in-painting. *SIAM Journal on Imaging Sciences, 6*(3), 1227–1245. doi:10.1137/12087178X

Yan, W., Wei, S., Wei, T., Antonio, L., Dawei, Y., Xinlei, L., Shuyong, G., Yixuan, S., Weifeng, G., Wei, Z., & Wenqiang, Z. (2022). *A Systematic Review on Affective Computing: Emotion Models.* Databases, and Recent Advances.

Yan, Z. L. D. Y. J. (2013). Learn To combine Multiple Hypotheses for accurate face alignment. *Proceedings of IEEE International Conference on Computer Vision (ICCV-W).*

Ye, F., & Yang, J. (2021). A Deep Neural Network Model for Speaker Identification. *Applied Sciences (Basel, Switzerland), 11*(3603), 1–18. doi:10.3390/app11083603

Yeşim, Ü. S., & Asaf, V. (2020). *A Speech Emotion Recognition Model Based on Multi-Level Local Binary and Local Ternary Patterns.* doi:10.1109/ACCESS.2020.3031763

Yin, L., Wei, X., Sun, Y., Wang, J., & Rosato, M. J. A. (2006). 3D facial Expression database for facial behavior research. *Proceedings of the International Conference on Automatic Face and Gesture Recognition,* 211–216.

Yiu, M. L., & Lu, H. (2011). Ranking spatial data by quality preferences. IEEE Transactions on Knowledge and Data Engineering, 23(3).

Yogeshwaran, S., Kaur, M. J., & Maheshwari, P. (2019, April). Project based learning: predicting bitcoin prices using deep learning. In *2019 IEEE Global Engineering Education Conference (EDUCON)* (pp. 1449-1454). IEEE. 10.1109/EDUCON.2019.8725091

Yuan, G., & Ghanem, B. (2015). l0tv: A new method for image restoration in the presence of impulse noise. *Proceedings of the IEEE Conference on Computer Vision and Pattern Recognition,* 5369–5377.

Yuan, G., & Ghanem, B. (2017). L0 TV: A Sparse Optimization Method for Impulse Noise Image Restoration. *IEEE Transactions on Pattern Analysis and Machine Intelligence, 41*(2), 352–364. doi:10.1109/TPAMI.2017.2783936 PMID:29990015

Yu, C., Wang, J., Peng, C., Gao, C., Yu, G., & Sang, N. (2018). Bisenet: Bilateral segmentation network for real-time semantic segmentation. In *Proceedings of the European conference on computer vision (ECCV)* (pp. 325-341). 10.1007/978-3-030-01261-8_20

Zeng, C., Wu, C., & Jia, R. (2019). Non-Lipschitz models for image restoration with impulse noise removal. *SIAM Journal on Imaging Sciences, 12*(1), 420–458. doi:10.1137/18M117769X

Zenisek, J., Holzinger, F., & Affenzeller, M. (2019). Machine learning based concept drift detection for predictive maintenance. *Computers & Industrial Engineering, 137*, 106031–106043. doi:10.1016/j.cie.2019.106031

Zhang & Lan. (2022). Detect Megaregional Communities Using Network Science Analytics. *Urban Science, 6*(1), 12.

Zhang, K., Li, Y., Zuo, W., Zhang, L., van Gool, L., & Timofte, R. (2020). *Plug-and-play image restoration with deep denoiser prior.* ArXiv Preprint ArXiv:2008.13751.

Zhang, Q., Shen, X., Xu, L., & Jia, J. (2014). Rolling Guidance Filter. In D. Fleet, T. Pajdla, B. Schiele, & T. Tuytelaars (Eds.), Computer Vision – ECCV 2014 (pp. 815–830). Springer International Publishing. doi:10.1007/978-3-319-10578-9_53

Zhang, T., Cui, Z., Xu, C., Zheng, W. J., & Yang. (2020). Variational Pathway Reasoning for EEG Emotion Recognition. *Proc. AAAI Conf. Artif. Intell., 34*, 2709–2716. . doi:10.1609/aaai.v34i03.5657

Zhang, H., He, W., Zhang, L., Shen, H., & Yuan, Q. (2013). Hyperspectral image restoration using low-rank matrix recovery. *IEEE Transactions on Geoscience and Remote Sensing, 52*(8), 4729–4743. doi:10.1109/TGRS.2013.2284280

Zhang, J., Xiong, R., Zhao, C., Ma, S., & Zhao, D. (2012). Exploiting image local and nonlocal consistency for mixed Gaussian-impulse noise removal. *2012 IEEE International Conference on Multimedia and Expo*, 592–597. 10.1109/ICME.2012.109

Zhang, K., Zuo, W., Chen, Y., Meng, D., & Zhang, L. (2017). Beyond a gaussian denoiser: Residual learning of deep cnn for image denoising. *IEEE Transactions on Image Processing, 26*(7), 3142–3155. doi:10.1109/TIP.2017.2662206 PMID:28166495

Zhang, K., Zuo, W., Gu, S., & Zhang, L. (2017). Learning deep CNN denoiser prior for image restoration. *Proceedings of the IEEE Conference on Computer Vision and Pattern Recognition*, 3929–3938. 10.1109/CVPR.2017.300

Zhang, L., Wang, L., & Lin, W. (2012). Generalized biased discriminant analysis for content-based image retrieval. { *Cybernetics, 42*(1), 282–290. PMID:21968743

Zhang, M., Chauhan, V., & Zhou, M. (2021, January). A machine vision based smart conveyor system. In *Thirteenth International Conference on Machine Vision* (Vol. 11605, pp. 84-92). SPIE. 10.1117/12.2586978

Zhang, T., Zheng, W., Cui, Z., Zong, Y., & Li, Y. (2017). Spatial-temporal recurrent neural network for emotion recognition. *IEEE Transactions on Cybernetics PP*, (99), 1–9.

Zhang, X., Liu, D., Huang, W., Wang, Q., Feng, X., & Tan, J. (2018). Prediction of endometriosis fertility index in patients with endometriosis-associated infertility after laparoscopic treatment. *Reproductive Biomedicine Online, 37*(1), 53–59. doi:10.1016/j.rbmo.2018.03.012 PMID:29628331

Zhang, X., & Ng, M. K. (2019). A Fast Algorithm for Solving Linear Inverse Problems with Uniform Noise Removal. *Journal of Scientific Computing, 79*(2), 1214–1240. doi:10.100710915-018-0888-2

Zhang, X., Wang, X., Yang, X., Xu, C., Zhu, X., & Wei, J. (2020). Driver drowsiness detection using mixed-effect ordered logit model considering time cumulative effect. *Analytic Methods in Accident Research, 26*, 100114. doi:10.1016/j.amar.2020.100114

Zhang, Y., Zhu, T., Ning, H., & Liu, Z. (2021). Classroom student posture recognition based on an improved high-resolution network. *EURASIP Journal on Wireless Communications and Networking, 2021*(1), 1–15. doi:10.118613638-021-02015-0

Zhao, Y., Chen, Z., Gao, X., Song, W., Xiong, Q., Hu, J., & Zhang, Z. (2022). Plant Disease Detection Using Generated Leaves Based on DoubleGAN. IEEE/ACM Transactions on Computational Biology and Bioinformatics, 19(3).

Zhao, X.-L., Wang, F., & Ng, M. K. (2014). A new convex optimization model for multiplicative noise and blur removal. *SIAM Journal on Imaging Sciences*, 7(1), 456–475. doi:10.1137/13092472X

Zhao, Y., Gong, L., Huang, Y., & Liu, C. (2016). A review of key techniques of vision-based control for harvesting robot. *Computers and Electronics in Agriculture*, 127, 311–323. doi:10.1016/j.compag.2016.06.022

Zhao, Z., Zhou, N., Zhang, L., Yan, H., Xu, Y., & Zhang, Z. (2020). Driver fatigue detection based on convolutional neural networks using EM-CNN. *Computational Intelligence and Neuroscience*.

Zheng, L., Yang, Y., & Tian, Q. (2018). SIFT meets CNN: A decade survey of instance retrieval. *IEEE Trans. Pattern Anal.*, 40(5), 1224–1244. doi:10.1109/TPAMI.2017.2709749 PMID:29610107

Zheng, W. L., & Lu, B. L. (2015). Investigating critical frequency bands and channels for EEG-based emotion recognition with deep neural networks. *IEEE Transactions on Autonomous Mental Development*, 7(3), 162–175. doi:10.1109/TAMD.2015.2431497

Zhong, P., Wang, D., & Miao, C. (2020). EEG-Based Emotion Recognition Using Regularized Graph Neural Networks. *IEEE Transactions on Affective Computing*, 1–1. doi:10.1109/TAFFC.2020.2994159

Zhou, W., Yang, M., Wang, X., Li, H., Lin, Y., & Tian, Q. (2016). Scalable feature matching by dual cascaded scalar quantization for image retrieval. *Proc. IEEE conference on computer vision and pattern recognition*, 38(1), 159–171. 10.1109/TPAMI.2015.2430329

Zhou, Y. Y., Ye, Z. F., & Huang, J. J. (2012). Improved decision-based detail-preserving variational method for removal of random-valued impulse noise. *IET Image Processing*, 6(7), 976–985. doi:10.1049/iet-ipr.2011.0312

Zhou, Z.-H. (2012). *Ensemble Methods: Foundations and Algorithms*. Chapman & Hall/CRC. doi:10.1201/b12207

Zhuang, L., & Ng, M. K. (2020). Hyperspectral Mixed Noise Removal By \ell _1 -Norm-Based Subspace Representation. *IEEE Journal of Selected Topics in Applied Earth Observations and Remote Sensing*, 13, 1143–1157. doi:10.1109/JSTARS.2020.2979801

Zhu, H., & Ng, M. K. (2020). Structured dictionary learning for image denoising under mixed gaussian and impulse noise. *IEEE Transactions on Image Processing*, 29, 6680–6693. doi:10.1109/TIP.2020.2992895 PMID:32406836

Zhu, Y., Shen, W., Cheng, F., Jin, C., & Cao, G. (2020). Removal of high density Gaussian noise in compressed sensing MRI reconstruction through modified total variation image denoising method. *Heliyon*, 6(3), e03680. doi:10.1016/j.heliyon.2020.e03680 PMID:32258499

Zohra, F. T., Salim, O., Dey, S., Masoumi, H., & Karmakar, N. (2021, November). A Novel Machine Learning Based Conveyor Belt Health Monitoring Incorporating UHF RFID Backscattered Power. In *2021 IEEE 5th International Conference on Information Technology, Information Systems and Electrical Engineering (ICITISEE)* (pp. 230-234). IEEE. 10.1109/ICITISEE53823.2021.9655974

About the Contributors

A. Srinivasan is working as Associate Professor in the Department of Electronics and Communication Engineering, Srinivasa Ramanujan Centre, SASTRA Deemed University, Kumbakonam, Thanjavur, Tamil Nadu, India and has teaching experience of more than 20 years. He obtained his Ph.D at SASTRA Deemed University. He has published 5 Indian patents and more than 40 articles in National and International peer reviewed journals and two in book chapters. Acted as a guest editor for the SCOPUS indexed Far East Journal of Electronics and Communications. Organized workshops, National and International conferences. He is having membership in IET, Institution of Engineers (India), Broadcasting society of India, Indian Society of Systems for Science & Engineering and got Amateur radio license from the Indian Ministry of Communications and Information Technology. Currently he is supervising 3 research scholars and two scholars awarded Ph.D. His research areas are Image Processing, Signal Processing, Optical Communication, Internet of Things, Deep Learning and Machine Learning.

* * *

Hazique Aetesam received the B. Tech. degree in information technology from Jamia Hamdard, New Delhi, India, in 2013, and the M.Tech. degree in computer science and engineering from the Birla Institute of Technology, Ranchi, India, in 2016. He completed his Ph.D. degree in computer science and engineering from Indian Institute of Technology Patna, India, 2022. He is working on the low-level computer vision problems pertaining to hyperspectral imaging and magnetic resonance imaging domains. His current research interests include the amalgamation of model and data-driven methods in low-level vision problems.

S. Miruna Joe Amali completed her B.E. (Computer Science and Engineering) degree in 2001 from P.S.N.A College of Engineering and Technology and the M.E. (Computer Science and Engineering) degree in 2005 from Thiagarajar College of Engineering, Madurai. She has industry experience and has worked in HCL Technologies, Chennai as Lead Engineer. She pursued her Ph.D. full-time research in the Thiagarajar College of Engineering, Madurai, under Anna University, Chennai from 2009 to 2012. She is currently working as Professor in Computer Science and Engineering Department of K.L.N. College of Engineering, Sivagangai. Her research interests are Soft Computing, Evolutionary algorithms specifically Differential Evolution, surrogate model integration and their applications to Engineering Optimization problems.

K. S. Arun received his B.E (ECE) degree. Currently, he is working as Security Delivery Associate Manager in Accenture Security, Australia.

Vineet Kumar Awasthi is working as assistant professor in Dept of IT & CS, Dr C V Raman University, Kota, Bilaspur (CG). He has completed his Ph.D. on portfolio optimization at 2019. He has published different research papers in reputed journals list in SCI, SCOPUS and UGC. He has also participated and presented different research articles in national and international conferences.

Sreedevi B. got her doctorate in 2014 in the area of Ad Hoc Networks at SASTRA University. Her area of interest includes Wireless Networks, Neural Networks, Fuzzy Logic and Machine Learning. She holds life membership in IETE and ISTE.

Sucithra B. is a post graduate student of the Department of Computer Science and Engineering, Anna University, Chennai. Her research interests include Image processing, and data mining.

Jérôme Boulanger graduated in 2003 from École Nationale Supérieure de Physique, Marseille and received in 2007 the Ph.D. degree in signal processing and telecommunication from the University of Rennes 1, France. From 2007 to 2008, he was with the Institut Curie in Paris and till 2010 with the Radon Institute from Applied Mathematics in Linz, Austria. In 2011, he joined the CNRS at Institut Curie in Paris. His research is focused on image processing for microscopy image analysis.

Manjula Devi C. received B.E. (CSE) and M.Tech.(IT) from Anna University, Chennai in 2006 and 2013 respectively and received her M.B.A (HRM) from Anna University. Since 2009, she is in teaching profession and her main research interest is in Data mining, IoT and Deep Learning. Currently, she is working as Assistant Professor in Velammal College of Engineering and Technology, Madurai. She has published 7 research papers in International Journals 8 research papers in International and National Conferences. She is a member in ISTE.

Mukesh Chandrakar is working as Assistant Professor in Bhilai Institute of Technology Durg, India. He has been pursuing his Doctoral Research in the area of Medical Image Diagnosis. He hold M.Tech. degree from Chhattisgarh Swami Vivekaknand Technical University Bhilai, India.

Yathishan D. is pursuing M.Tech in (IoT and Automation) at Sastra Deemed to be University, Thanjavur. He graduated B.Tech in Electrical and Electronics Engineering at Nehru College of Engineering and Research Centre, Thrissur.

C. Deisy is working as professor in Dept.of Information Technology, Thiagarajar College of Engineering, Madurai, Tamilnadu. Area of Interest is AI and Machine Learning.

Manivannan Doraipandian received his B.E in Electrical and Electronics Engineering from Bharathidasan University, Tiruchy, Tamilnadu, India (1996), M.Tech in Computer science and Engineering (2002) from the SASTRA University, Tamilnadu, India. Currently he is working as Senior Assistant Professor of Computer Science Department, School of Computing at SASTRA University, Tamilnadu, India. His area of interest in academic research is cryptography, security in Embedded Systems, Wireless Sensor

Networks using ARM processors and embedded communication systems. In the past few years, his research interests have been focused on platforms capable of handling low power processor for Wireless Sensor Node and applications in distributed embedded platform, as well as information security related topics in the embedded systems domain.

Sushmitha E. C. is studying M.Tech, IoT, and Automation in SASTRA Deemed University, Thanjavur, Tamil Nadu.

Rajapackiyam Ezhilarasie received her B.Tech in CSE from P.M.C.T.W, Thanjavur in 2003 and M.Tech in CSE from SASTRA University, Thanjavur in 2011. She has more than five years of teaching experience. Her main areas of research interests are operating systems, embedded systems, wireless sensor networks and virtualisation. She is currently working as an Assistant Professor in the Department of Computer Science and Engineering, School of Computing, SASTRA University, Thanjavur.

A. Firthous is a Lecturer in Information Technology, Department of Information Technology CYRYX College G. Light Sky, Bodurasgefaanu Magu #5 Maldives.

Manikandan G. is a Senior assistant professor at SASTRA Deemed to be University. He received his M.Tech., and Ph.D., degree in Computer Science from SASTRA Deemed to be University in 2009 and 2018 respectively. He is the author of more than 50 journal papers. His current research interests include Steganography, Privacy Preservation in Data Mining and Machine Learning. He is a member of ISSE.

Senbagavalli G. is working as a Associate Professor in the Department of Electronics and Communication Engineering, AMC Engineering College, Bengaluru. She completed her Ph.D in the Faculty of Electronics and Communication Engineering, VTU,Belagavi, India in the year 2021. She received her M.Tech. degree in VLSI system design from JNTU, Andhra Pradesh India in the year 2008. B.E. in Electronics and Communication Engineering from Madras University, India in the year 2001. She has 18 years of experience in Teaching and Research from Reputed Engineering Colleges. She has published 15 papers in National/International Conferences, journals and two in book chapters. She is a Lifetime Member of ISTE and IETE. Her field of interests includes Image and video processing, Computer vision and VLSI Design.

Angelin Gladston is working as an Associate Professor at the Department of Computer Science and Engineering, Anna University, Chennai. Her research interests include software engineering, software testing, social network analysis and data mining.

Priya Govindarajan is working as an Assistant Professor in the department of Computer Science and Engineering at SASTRA Deemed to be University, Kumbakonam, India. She received her Master degree in Computer Applications and Ph.D., degree in Computer Science from SASTRA Deemed to be University in 2010 and 2019 respectively. Her current research interests include Data Mining, Machine Learning, Deep Learning and Content Mining. She has published many papers in a wide range of highly recognized international & high impact journals and conferences.

Hemalatha J. received the B.E and ME degree in Computer Science and Engineering under Anna University Chennai in 2007 and 2013. She completed her ph.d in Computer Science and Engineering, under Anna University Chennai in 2019. In July 2013, she joined the Department of Computer Science and Engineering at P.S.R Engineering College, Sivakasi. India She joined as Assistant professor in Kalasalingam Academy of research and Education in the year of 2018. And later she worked as Associate Professor and Academic coordinator in Sri Vidya College of Engineering and Technology. Currently she is working as Assistant Professor and Research Coordinator in AAA College of Engineering and Technology. She has published more than 15 papers in reputed International Journals. She is an author of many scopus indexed book chapters. Her research interests include Digital steganography, Steganalysis, Machine Learning and Image Processing.

Sriram J. is currently pursuing Master's degree in SASTRA Deemed to be University, Thanjavur. He received his B.Tech in Mechatronics Engineering from SASTRA Deemed to be University, Thanjavur, Tamilnadu, India (2021). His area of interest in academic research is Wireless Sensor Networks and Internet Of Things.

Hanees Lebbe received the B. Sc. Special degree in Computer Science with upper class honors from South Eastern University of Sri Lanka, Sri Lanka in 2002, and M.Tech with First Class distinction with D+ from Bharathidasan University, India in 2011. Now he is a Senior Lecturer in Computer Science since 2003 and serving as Head of the Department at Department of Mathematical Sciences, South Eastern University of Sri Lanka, Sri Lanka. His research interests include network security and wireless sensor networks and data mining.

Kavitha Devi M. K. received her Under Graduate and Graduate Degree in Computer Science and Engineering, and her Ph.D. Degree in Information and Communication Engineering in 1994, 2004 and 2011 respectively. Her research focuses on Recommender Systems, Information Security & Hiding, Cloud Computing, and Big Data. She has published more than 40 refereed Journal and International Conference papers in these areas. She is the reviewer in referred Journals including IEEE Intelligent Systems and Springer - Journal of The Institution of Engineers (India): Series B. She organized Faculty Development Programs, Workshops and Conference. Under her guidance, 8 Ph.D. scholars completed and 2 Ph.D scholars pursuing from Anna University, Chennai are working in her area. Currently, she is an Professor at the Department of Computer Science and Engineering, Thiagarajar College of Engineering, Madurai, India.

Suman Kumar Maji (Member, IEEE) received the B.Tech. degree in electronics and communication engineering from the West Bengal University of Technology, India, in 2006, the Postgraduate degree in telecommunication networks from the Indian Institute of Technology Kharagpur, India, in 2008, and the Ph.D. degree in computer science from INRIA Bordeaux, France, in 2013. From 2014 to 2015, he worked as a Research Engineer with the Institute of Hematology, University Paris 7, and INSERM. He is currently working as an Assistant Professor with the Department of Computer Science and Engineering, Indian Institute of Technology Patna, India. His research interests include medical imaging, bioinformatics, machine learning, and image processing. Dr. Maji has authored several conferences and journal papers and is the recipient of various research fellowships and awards such as the European CORDIS Doctoral

Fellowship, in 2010, the Region Aquitaine OPTAD Research Fellowship, in 2010, the FRM Research Fellowship, in 2014, and the SERB Early Career Research Award from DST, Govt of India, in 2017.

S. Meganathan received B.Sc and M.Sc degrees in Computer Science from Bharathidasan University, Tiruchirappalli, Tamilnadu in 1994 and 1996 respectively and Ph.D. in Computer Science from SASTRA University 2013. He is currently working as a Senior Assistant Professor at the Department of Computer Science and Engineering of Srinivasa Ramanujan Centre in SASTRA University, Tamilnadu, India. He has published 26 research articles in peer-reviewed journals and 12 conference papers so far. He is currently supervising 4 Ph.D. scholars in the data mining area. His research interest is weather forecasting models, machine learning algorithms and data analytics using machine learning tools.

Anup Mishra is currently Professor and Head in Electrical and Electronics Engineering in Bhilai Institute of Technology Durg, India. He has published many articles in Biomedical image processing and analysis Biomedical signal processing.

Aishwarya N. is pursuing MTech in IoT and automation at SASTRA University.

Rajesh Kumar N. is an Assistant Professor in the Department of Computer Science and Engineering, Srinivasa Ramanujan Centre, SASTRA Deemed to be University, Kumbakonam. He received his Master degree in Computer Applications from Alagappa University, Karaikudi in 2009, and his PhD degree in Computer Science from SASTRA Deemed to be University in 2021. His current research interests include information hiding, image processing and cryptography. He has published over 21 research papers in journals and conferences of repute.

Umamaheswari P. received M.Tech in Computer Science from SASTRA Deemed University, Thanjavur, Tamil Nadu, and India in the year 2011 and M.B.A from Alagappa University, Karaikudi, Tamil Nadu, and India in the year 2006. She is pursuing Doctoral degree in Computer Science and Engineering from SASTRA Deemed University. She has 17 years of teaching experience for UG and PG courses in Computer Science and presently working as Assistant Professor in the department of computer science and engineering at SASTRA University, SRC Campus, and Kumbakonam. Her research interest in Data Mining, Machine Learning and Deep learning. She published research papers in International Conferences and Scopus Indexed Journals.

Bala Krishnan Raghupathy is an Assistant Professor in the Department of Computer Science and Engineering, Srinivasa Ramanujan Centre, SASTRA Deemed to be University, Kumbakonam. He received his M.Tech., and Ph.D., degree in Computer Science from SASTRA Deemed to be University in 2012 and 2021 respectively. His current research interests include Intrusion Detection and Prevention Systems, Information hiding, Image processing and cryptography. He has published over 30 research papers in journals and conferences of repute.

Alageswaran Ramaiah received B.E. (CSE) from M.K. University and M.E. (CS) from Bharthidasan University in 1993 and 2003 respectively and received his M.B.A (Systems) from M.K. University. He received his doctoral degree in the field of Wireless Sensor Networks from School of Computing, SASTRA University, Thanjavur in 2013. Since 1994, he is in teaching profession and his main research interest is in Wireless Sensor Networks, IoT and Light Weight Cryptography. His other research interests include Embedded System Design, Real Time Operating Systems, Embedded Networking and RFID based system design. Currently, he is working as Associate Professor in School of Computing, SASTRA Deemed University, Thanjavur. He has published 11 research papers in International Journals 12 research papers in International and National Conferences. He has authored a book titled "Database Management Systems". He also published online Chapter on Evolution of Fog computing and Its Role in IoT Applications in IGI Global and COViD-19: Implications for Commerce & Management, Economics and Information Technology in Weser Publications.

Mardeni Roslee is Deputy Director, Research Management Centre (RMC) & Chairman, Centre for Wireless Technology, Faculty of Engineering, Multimedia University. Advisor / Previous Past Chair, IEEE Malaysia, Communication Society and Vehicular Technology Society.

Malini S. did BTech in Electronics and Communication from Kerala University Did ME in Anna University in Communication Systems. Did PhD in Kerala University in Image Processing Interested Research. Topics are in image processing, machine learning, deep learning, Python.

Palanivel S. is working as an Assistant Professor in School of Computing SASTRA Deemed Universitym

Sudha S. received M.Tech degree from SASTRA Deemed university, Thanjavur in 2010. She is an Assistant Professor in the Department of Electronics and communication Engineering, Srinivasa Ramanujan centre, SASTRA Deemed university, Kumbakonam from July 2006 to now. And she is now a research scholar at SASTRA, Thanjavur. Areas of interests are Image processing & Signal processing. She has published over 10 research papers in journals and conferences of repute.

Sanat Kumar Sahu is working as an Assistant Professor in the Department of Computer Science, Govt. Kaktiya PG College, Jagdalpur (Bastar) Chhattisgarh, India. He obtained his master's degree in Computer Application from Guru Ghasidas Vishwavidyalaya, Bilaspur, India and MPhil,Ph.D. in Computer Science from Dr. C.V. Raman University, Bilaspur, India. He has more than 9 years teaching and 4 years of research experience. He has published more than 14 research papers in reputed journals and attended workshop and conference at national and international level. His area of interest includes soft computing, machine learning, and data mining.

Harini Sriraman is an Associate Professor with Vellore Institute of Technology. She has more than 13 years of teaching experience. Her research interest includes Distributed and Parallel computing, Accelerating Deep Learning performance using HPC environment, Hardware based Domain Specific Acceleration and Energy efficient and sustainable computing. OrCID: https://orcid.org/0000-0002-2192-8153.

A. Sumathi received M.Sc degree in Computer Science from Bharathidasan University, Tamilnadu, India, in 2005 and her M.Phil., Degree in Computer science from Periyar University, Tamilnadu, India in 2007. M.Tech Degree in CSE from SASTRA University, Tamilnadu, India in 2011. She is currently working as Assistant Professor at the Department of Computer Science and Engineering of Srinivasa Ramanujan Centre in SASTRA University, Tamilnadu, India. She has published more than 20 research articles in peer-reviewed journals. Her research interests include DataMining and its applications and Computational Biology.

Senthilra Swaminathan completed his Ph.D. in 2008 with specialization of Graph Theory in Mathematical Sciences. Currently working as a Head of General Requirement Department (Mathematics), University of Technology and Applied Sciences-Sur, Sultanate of Oman. He is a Course Coordinator of Mathematics for Applied Bio-Technology and also a General Coordinator for Mathematics courses in UTAS(CAS), He has published many research papers in National and International level reputed Journals and presented many research articles in various Conferences. He is also acting as a senior life member in many national and international journals and society.

Gayathri Devi T. is currently working as an Assistant Professor in the department of ECE in SASTRA deemed to be university, Kumbakonam. She received the M.Sc., degree in Electronics Science from the Bharthidasan University, Trichy in 1999, the M.Phil., degree in Electronics, the M.Tech., degree in Advanced Communication Systems from the SASTRA University, Thanjavur in 2009 and completed the Ph.D in School of Computing in SASTRA deemed to be university Thanjavur in 2021. Her research areas are Image Processing. Embedded Systems and optical communication.

Kavitha T. is working as a Professor in the Department of Computer Engineering, New Horizon College of Engineering. She completed her Ph.D in the Faculty of Information and Communication Engineering, Anna University Chennai, India in the year 2014. She received her M.E. degree in Systems Engineering and Operations Research from Anna University, Chennai India in the year 2006. B.E. in Electronics and Communication Engineering from Bharathidasan University, India in the year 2000. She has 21+ years of experience in Teaching and Research from Reputed Engineering Colleges. She is Anna University and VTU recognized supervisor for guiding Ph.D and M.S(by Research) Programme. Under her guidance, a scholar had completed Ph.D at Anna University. She has received Funds from different agencies like ISTE-SRM, VTU-TEQIP, IE, VTU, AICTE-ISTE, and AICTE to organize FDP, Workshop, Training, and Conference. She is also a Mentor for the projects who got funds from VTU and KSCKT. Presently she is guiding three scholars under VTU. She has filed Five Indian Patents into her credit. She has published 33 papers in National/International Conferences, Three in book chapters, and 16 in International Journals. She is a Lifetime Member of ISTE, IETE and IE. Her field of interests includes Wireless Networks, Wireless Sensor Networks, information security, Internet of Things, Deep Learning, and Machine Learning.

A. Umamakeswari is working as the Dean, School of Computing, SASTRA Deemed University. Research Area of Interest includes, Embedded Systems, IoT, BlockChain, and Machine Learning.

Subramani V. is pursuing Masters of Technology (IoT and Automation) from SASTRA Deemed to be university. He graduated Bachelor of Technology (Electronics and communication engineering) from Kalasalingam academy of research and education in 2021.

Pratibha Verma is Research Scholar at Computer Science in Department of IT, Dr. C.V. Raman University, Kota, Bilaspur.

438

Index

Ensure Quality Research is Introduced to the Academic Community

Become an Evaluator for IGI Global Authored Book Projects

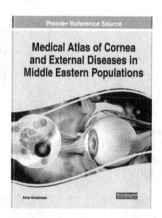

The overall success of an authored book project is dependent on quality and timely manuscript evaluations.

Applications and Inquiries may be sent to:
development@igi-global.com

Applicants must have a doctorate (or equivalent degree) as well as publishing, research, and reviewing experience. Authored Book Evaluators are appointed for one-year terms and are expected to complete at least three evaluations per term. Upon successful completion of this term, evaluators can be considered for an additional term.

If you have a colleague that may be interested in this opportunity, we encourage you to share this information with them.

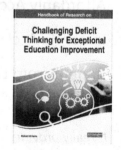

Printed in the United States
by Baker & Taylor Publisher Services